ALSO BY IAN FRAZIER

TRAVELS IN SIBERIA

TRAVELS IN

SIBERIA

Ian Frazier

Farrar, Straus and Giroux   New York

Farrar, Straus and Giroux
18 West 18th Street, New York 10011

Distributed in Canada by D&M Publishers, Inc.
Printed in the United States of America
First edition, 2010

Portions of this book originally appeared, in somewhat different form, in *The New Yorker*.

Grateful acknowledgment is made to Katya Arnold for permission to print the sketch on page 42. All other illustrations are by the author.

Library of Congress Cataloging-in-Publication Data
Frazier, Ian.
    Travels in Siberia / Ian Frazier.— 1st ed.
      p.   cm.
    Includes bibliographical references and index.
    ISBN 978-0-374-27872-4 (hardcover : alk. paper)
    1. Frazier, Ian—Travel—Russia (Federation)—Siberia.   2. Siberia (Russia)—
Description and travel.   3. Siberia (Russia)—History.   4. Siberia (Russia)—Social
life and customs.   5. Siberia (Russia)—History, Local.   I. Title.

DK756.2 .F73 2010
957—dc22

                                  2010005784

Designed by Jonathan D. Lippincott

www.fsgbooks.com

10 9 8 7 6 5 4 3 2 1

The author has omitted some names and identifying characteristics.

To Jay, again,
with love

Contents

NORWAY

SWEDEN

Arctic Ocean

Baltic Sea

FINLAND

•Murmansk

Barents Sea

Kara Sea

POLAND

•St. Petersburg

BELARUS

Arkhangelsk

Severnaya Dvina R.

Pestovo
Cherepovets   •Vologda

Moscow

•Velikii Ustyug

•Kiev

Kirov

Ural Mountains

UKRAINE

S   I   B

Kazan•

Kama River

•Perm

Khanty-Mansiisk•

Ob River

•Volga River

Ekaterinburg•

R   U   S

Tyumen•

Tobol River

•Tobolsk

Berezovyi Yar•

Irtysh River

GEORGIA

Caspian Sea

TRANS-SIBERIAN
RAILWAY

Omsk•

Yashkino

ARMENIA

Tomsk•

Novosibirsk•

AZERBAIJAN

Akademgorodok•

Kemerovo•

Aral Sea

KAZAKHSTAN

TURKMENISTAN

0 Miles   200   400

0 Kilometers   400

IRAN

CHINA

UZBEKISTAN

© 2010 Jeffrey L. Ward

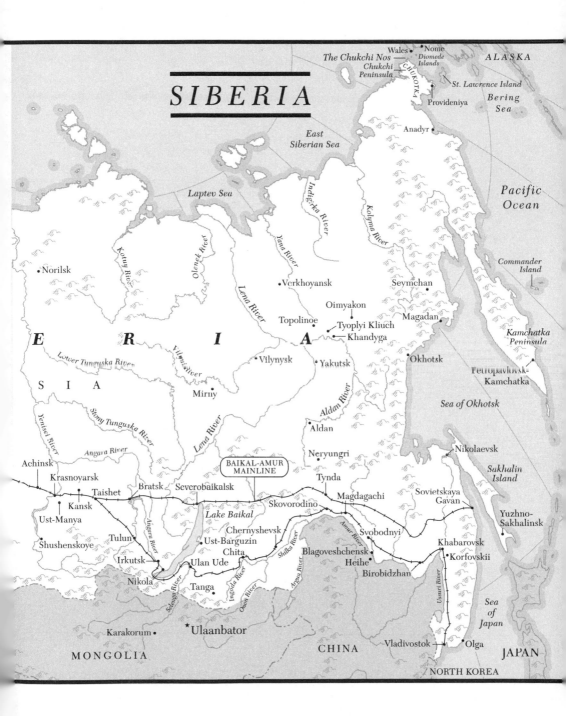

SIBERIA

ALASKA

Wales — Nome
The Chukchi Nos — Diomede Islands
Chukchi Peninsula
CHUKOTKA
Provideniya
St. Lawrence Island

Bering Sea

East Siberian Sea

Anadyr

Laptev Sea

Pacific Ocean

Norilsk

Kotuy River
Olenek River
Indigirka River
Yana River
Kolyma River

Verkhoyansk
Seymchan

Commander Island

Lena River
Oimyakon
Topolinoe
Tyoplyi Kliuch
Khandyga
Magadan

E R I A

Vilyui River

Vilynysk
Yakutsk
Okhotsk

Petropavlovsk-Kamchatka

Kamchatka Peninsula

S I A

Lower Tunguska River
Mirny

Aldan River

Stony Tunguska River

Sea of Okhotsk

Yenisei River
Angara River

Aldan

Achinsk
Krasnoyarsk
Neryungri
Nikolaevsk

Kansk
Taishet
Bratsk
Severobaikalsk
BAIKAL-AMUR MAINLINE
Tynda
Magdagachi
Sovietskaya Gavan

Sakhalin Island

Ust-Manya
Skovorodino

Shushenskoye
Tulun
Chernyshevsk
Lake Baikal
Svobodnyi
Yuzhno-Sakhalinsk

Irkutsk
Ust-Barguzin
Chita
Amur River
Khabarovsk

Nikola
Ulan Ude
Shilka River
Blagoveshchensk
Heihe
Korfovskii

Tanga
Ingoda River
Argun River
Birobidzhan

Selenga River
Onon River
Ussuri River

Karakorum
★Ulaanbator
CHINA
Vladivostok
Olga

Sea of Japan

MONGOLIA
NORTH KOREA
JAPAN

PART I

Chapter 1

Officially, there is no such place as Siberia. No political or territorial entity has Siberia as its name. In atlases, the word "Siberia" hovers across the northern third of Asia unconnected to any place in particular, as if designating a zone or a condition; it seems to show through like a watermark on the page. During Soviet times, revised maps erased the name entirely, in order to discourage Siberian regionalism. Despite this invisibility, one can assume that Siberia's traditional status as a threat did not improve.

A tiny fraction of the world's population lives in Siberia. About thirty-nine million Russians and native peoples inhabit that northern third of Asia. By contrast, the state of New Jersey, where I live, has about a fifth as many people on about .0015 as much land. For most people, Siberia is not the place itself but a figure of speech. In fashionable restaurants in New York and Los Angeles, Siberia is the section of less-desirable tables given to customers whom the maître d' does not especially like. In one of the most important places to be seen having lunch in midtown Manhattan, Siberia is the tables next to the ketchup room, where the condiments are stored.

Newspaper gossip columns take the word even more metaphorically. When an author writes a book about a Park Avenue apartment building, and the book offends some of the residents, and a neighbor who happens to be a friend of the author offers to throw him a book party in her apartment, and the people in the Park Avenue building hear about this plan, the party giver is risking "social Siberia," one of them warns.

In this respect (as in many others) Siberia and America are alike. Apart from their actual, physical selves, both exist as constructs, expressions of the mind. Once when I was in western Russia, a bottler of mineral water was showing my two Russian companions and me around his new dacha outside the city of Vologda. The time was late evening; darkness had fallen. The mineral-water bottler led us from room to room, throwing on all the lights and pointing out the amenities. When we got to the kitchen, he flipped the switch but the light did not go on. This seemed to upset him. He fooled with the switch, then hurried off and came back with a stepladder. Mounting it, he removed the glass globe from the overhead light and unscrewed the bulb. He climbed down, put globe and bulb on the counter, took a fresh bulb, and ascended again. He reached up and screwed the new bulb into the socket. After a few twists, the light came on. He turned to us and spread his arms wide, indicating the beams brightly filling the room. "*Ahhh*," he said triumphantly, "*Amerika!*"

Nobody has ever formally laid out the boundaries of the actual, physical Siberia. Rather, they were established by custom and accepted by general agreement. Siberia is, of course, huge. Three-fourths of Russia today is Siberia. Siberia takes up one-twelfth of all the land on earth. The United States from Maine to California stretches across four time zones; in Siberia there are eight. The contiguous United States plus most of Europe could fit inside it. Across the middle of Siberia, latitudinally for thirty-six hundred miles, runs the Russian taiga, the largest forest in the world.

The Ural Mountains, which cross Russia from the Arctic Ocean to Kazakhstan, are the western edge of Siberia. The Urals also separate Europe from Asia. As a mountain range with the big job of dividing two continents, the Urals aren't much. It is possible to drive over them, as I have done, and not know. In central Russia, the summits of the Urals average between one thousand and two thousand feet. But after you cross the Urals, the land opens out, the villages are farther apart, the concrete bus shelters along the highway become fewer, and suddenly you realize you're in Siberia.

To the east, about three thousand miles beyond the Urals, Siberia ends at the Pacific Ocean, in the form of the Sea of Japan, the Sea of Okhotsk, and the Bering Sea. Since Soviet times, Russians have called this part of Siberia the Russian Far East.

The Arctic Ocean borders Siberia on the north. West to east, its seas are the Kara Sea, the Laptev Sea, and the East Siberian Sea. For most of the year (though less consistently than before) this line is obscured under ice. The land here for as much as 250 miles in from the sea is tundra—a treeless, mossy bog for a couple of months of summer, a white near-wasteland otherwise.

In the south, Siberia technically ends at the border between Russia and Kazakhstan, Mongolia, and China, although Siberian watersheds and landforms continue on into them. This region is mostly steppe. The steppes of Siberia are part of the great Eurasian steppe, which extends from almost the Pacific westward as far as the Danube. For more than two thousand years, the Eurasian steppe produced nomadic barbarians who descended upon and destroyed cultivated places beyond the steppe's margins. The steppes were why China built the Great Wall. Out of the steppes in the thirteenth century came Genghis Khan and the Mongol hordes, civilization's then worst nightmare, the wicked stepfathers of the Russian state and of its tsars and commissars.

Sakhalin Island, which almost touches the Russian coast north of Japan, is considered part of Siberia. The island was a prison colony during tsarist times. Six hundred miles northeast of Sakhalin, the peninsula of Kamchatka descends from the Siberian mainland, dividing the Sea of Okhotsk from the Bering Sea. Kamchatka lies within the Pacific Rim's Ring of Fire and has active volcanoes. Kamchatka's Klyuchevskaya volcano, at 15,580 feet, is the highest point in Siberia. Among Russians, Kamchatka has served as a shorthand term for remoteness. Boris Pasternak's memoir, *Safe Conduct*, says that for Russian schoolchildren the far back of the class where the worst students sat was called Kamchatka. When the teacher had not yet heard the correct answer, he would cry to the back bench, as a last resort, "To the rescue, Kamchatka!"

Coincidentally, Kamchatka was the first geographic fact that many people my age in America knew about Siberia. I am of the baby-boom generation, who grew up during the Cold War. In our childhood, a new board game came out called Risk, which was played on a map representing the world. The object of Risk was to multiply your own armies, move them from one global region to the next while eliminating the armies of your opponents, and eventually take over the world. This required luck, ruthlessness, and intercontinental strategizing, Cold War–style. The armies were little plastic counters colored red, blue, yellow, brown, black, and green. Of the major global powers, you basically understood which color was supposed to stand for whom. The Kamchatka Peninsula controlled the only crossing of the game board's narrow sea between Asia and North America, so gaining Kamchatka was key.

Risk didn't openly mention the world politics of the day—the Soviet Union's name wasn't even on the board, just regions called Yakutsk, Ural, Ukraine, etc.—so the struggle with the dark forces was only implied. But that mysteriousness was very James Bond–like and thrilling, too. Among my friends in my hometown of Hudson, Ohio, Risk had a period of great popularity, completely eclipsing the previous favorite, Monopoly, and its old capitalist-against-capitalist theme.

Some of our Risk games went on for days. A favorite story among us was of an all-day game one September just before school started for the year. One of the players had not reenrolled in college for the fall and thus had become eligible for the military draft. A few weeks before, he had received his draft notice, and in fact he was supposed to show up for his induction physical that very day. Our friend played along with the rest of us, conquering countries and drinking beer without a care. In those years, being drafted meant you were going to Vietnam, almost for sure, and not showing up for your induction physical, it went without saying, was a crime. We kept suggesting to our friend that maybe he should get busy—call the draft board, at least, do something about the situation. Late in the afternoon a call came from his father, a prominent lawyer in Akron, with the news that our friend's draft deferment had been approved. To cheering and amazement he hung up the phone, opened another beer, and returned to the game.

On the Risk game board, the lines between regions and around continents were angular and schematic, after the manner of familiar Cold War maps having to do with nuclear war. On the walls at think-tank strategy sessions and as illustrations for sobering magazine articles, these maps showed the arcs of nuclear missiles spanning the globe—theirs heading for us, ours heading for them. Almost all the missile arcs went over Siberia. In the Cold War, Siberia provided the "cold"; Siberia was the blankness in between, the space through which apocalypse flew.

In the best and funniest of all Cold War movies, *Doctor Strangelove*, the arc of the nuclear bomber sent to attack Russia by the deranged General Jack D. Ripper crosses the war map at the Pentagon slowly, inch by inch, while frantic officials argue what to do. Then we see the plane's pilot, Slim Pickens, in a cowboy hat, and his brave crew. Then there's an exterior shot of the B-52 flying low to elude the Russian radar. Below the plane, practically at its wing tips, rise the tops of skinny pine trees. Then clearings open up, all covered with snow. Then more pines. This can only be Siberia. Suspensefully, the sound track plays "When Johnny Comes Marching Home." As a kid I knew the scenery was probably just stock footage, not really Siberia. Still, it seemed romantic to me—so far away and white and pure. I watched the scenery more closely than the plane.

Cold War movies with happy endings showed the bomber or missile flight paths on the Big Board making U-turns and heading back home or out to sea. Doom had been averted, as the generals threw their caps in the air and shouted for joy. In a sense, that ending actually did occur. The United States and Russia are no longer aiming so many missiles at each other, and you almost never see those maps with dozens of missile arcs on them anymore. The apocalyptic tracks in the sky over Siberia have gone from being hypothetical to being practically nonexistent. Today, Siberia is an old battlefield in which the battle it is known for never took place; the big worries have moved elsewhere.

As a landmass, Siberia got some bad breaks geographically. The main rivers of Siberia are (west to east) the Ob, the Yenisei, the Lena, and the Amur. I have seen each of these, and though the Mississippi may be mighty, they can make it look small. The fact that these rivers' tributary systems interlock allowed adventurers in the seventeenth century to go by river from the Ural Mountains to the Pacific Ocean with only five portages. Seeking furs, these men had crossed all Siberia in less than a hundred years, and built fortresses and founded cities along the way. In western Siberia, there are cities more than four hundred years old. Siberia's rivers still serve as important north–south avenues for barge traffic, and in the winter as ice highways for trucks.

The problem with Siberia's big rivers is the direction they flow. Most of Siberia's rivers go north or join others that do, and their waters end up in the Arctic Ocean. Even the Amur, whose general inclination is to the northeast and whose destination is the Pacific, empties into the stormy Sea of Okhotsk. In the spring, north-flowing rivers thaw upstream while they're still frozen at their mouths. This causes them to back up. This creates swamps. Western Siberia has the largest swamps in the world. In much of Siberia, the land doesn't do much of anything besides gradually sag northward to the Arctic. The rivers of western Siberia flow so slowly that they hardly seem to move at all. There, the rivers run muddy; in eastern Siberia, with its real mountains and sharper drop to the Pacific, many of the rivers run clear.

In general, then, much of Siberia drains poorly and is quite swampy. Of the mosquitoes, flies, and invisible biting insects I will say more later. They are a whole other story.

Another bad geographic break is Siberia's continentality. The land simply stretches on and on; eventually you feel you're in the farthest, extra, out-of-sight section of the parking lot, where no one in the history of civilization has ever bothered to go. Only on the sea can you travel as far and still be in apparently the same place. The deeper into Siberia, the farther from the mitigating effect of temperate oceans, the harsher the climate's extremes become. Summers in the middle of Siberia are hot, sometimes dry and dusty, sometimes hazy with smoke from taiga fires. In the winters, temperatures drop to the lowest on the planet outside Antarctica. In the city of Verkhoyansk, in northeast-central Siberia, the cold reaches about −90°. When I mentioned this frequently noted Siberian fact to my friends and guides in St. Petersburg, they scoffed, as Russians tend to do. Then they said they knew of someplace in Siberia even colder.

Because of the cold, a lot of central Siberia and most of the east lie under permafrost—ground permanently frozen, sometimes to more than three thousand feet down. Permafrost also covers all the tundra region. Agriculture on any large scale is impossible in the permafrost zone, though in more forgiving parts of it people have kitchen gardens, and greenhouse farming occasionally succeeds. Much of Siberia's taiga rests on permafrost, implying a shaky future for the forest if the permafrost melts, and a shakier one, scientists say, for the earth's atmospheric chemistry. Huge amounts of climate-changing methane would be released into the air.

Cities and villages in the permafrost zone must have basic necessities brought in. Fuel comes in steel barrels that are about three feet high and hold fifty-three gallons. Around settled places these empty barrels are everywhere, sometimes littering the bare tundra surreally as far as you can see. In 1997, the *Los Angeles Times* estimated that in Chukotka, the part of farthest Siberia just across from Alaska, the Soviets had left behind about two million barrels, or about sixteen barrels for each person living there. Fewer people, and probably more barrels, are in Chukotka today.

What, then, is good about Siberia?

Its natural resources, though hard to get at, are amazing. Its coal reserves, centered in the Kuznetsk Basin mining region in south-central Siberia, are some of the largest in the world. The Kuznetsk Basin is also rich in iron ore, a combination that made this region Russia's armory. Siberia has minerals like cobalt, zinc, copper, lead, tin, and mercury in great abundance; in Norilsk, the second-largest city in the world above the Arctic Circle, the Soviets dug the world's largest nickel mine. The diamond mines at Mirny, near the Vilyui River, are second only to South Africa's. Siberia has supplied the Russian treasury with silver and gold since tsarist times; during the 1930s, the Kolyma region of eastern Siberia produced, by means of the cruelest mines in history, about half the gold then being mined in the world. Russia has some of the world's largest reserves of petroleum and natural gas. A lot of those reserves are in Siberia.

Along the route of the Trans-Siberian Railway, trains of oil tank cars extend across the landscape for miles. Each tank car, black and tarry-looking, with faded white markings, resembles the one that follows it; slowly rolling past a grade crossing of the Trans-Siberian Railway, a trainload of these cars defines monotony. The Trans-Siberian Railway covers 9,288 kilometers between Moscow and the Pacific port of Vladivostok, or 5,771 miles. In other words, if it were twenty-one miles longer, it would be exactly twice as long as Interstate 80 from New Jersey to California. Lying awake near the tracks in some remote spot, you hear trains going by all through the night with scarcely a pause. Sitting beside the tracks and observing the point in the distance where they and the cables above them merge—the Trans-Siberian Railway is all-electric, with overhead cables like a streetcar line—you find that the tracks are empty of traffic only for five or ten minutes at a time.

Besides oil, the railway carries coal, machinery parts, giant tires, scrap iron, and endless containers saying HANJIN or SEA-LAND or MAERSK on their sides, just like the containers stacked five stories high around the Port of Newark, New Jersey, and probably every other port in the world. Now and then a passenger train goes by, and if the time is summer and the weather, as usual, hot, many shirtless passengers are hanging from the open windows with the curtains flapping beside them. Not even the most luxurious car on the Trans-Siberian Railway offers air-conditioning. Then more freight comes along, sometimes timber by the trainload. Siberian timber can be three or four feet in diameter, a size only rarely seen on logging trucks in America today. Some of these trees are called *korabel'nie sosni*—literally, "caravel pines," trees from which ships' masts were made.

American companies have tried to put together deals to harvest Siberian timber, but as a rule the deals go wrong. Executives of these companies eventually give up in disgust at Russian business practices, particularly the corruption and bribery. In one story—hearsay, only—a major timber company of the American Northwest withdrew from negotiations after its representative in Siberia was taken up in a helicopter, ostensibly to look at some trees, and then was dangled from the door until he agreed to a contract disadvantageous to his company. He agreed, landed safely, and advised his company to get out of Siberia. Some environmentalists say that Russian corruption is the Siberian forests' true preserver and best friend.

Geologists have always liked Siberia, especially its eastern part, where a lot is going on with the earth. Well into eastern Siberia—to a north–south range of mountains roughly paralleling the Lena River Valley—you are still in North America, tectonically speaking. The North American Plate, sliding westward, meets the Eurasian Plate there, while to the south, the Amursky and the Okhotsky plates complicate the collision by inserting themselves from that direction. All this plate motion causes seismic activity and an influx of seismologists. Eastern Siberia is among the most important places for seismic studies in the world. Farther west, Siberia offers other remarkable geology, in a formation called the Siberian Traps. These are outpourings of volcanic rock that covered a huge portion of present central Siberia 245 million years ago, in an event that is believed to have caused the massive die-off of predinosaur species known as the Permian extinction.

Paleontologists come to Siberia not for dinosaur fossils, which are not found nearly as often as in the Mongolian steppes to the south, but for more recent fossils of prehistoric bison, mammoths, rhinos, and other species that lived ten thousand to fifteen thousand years ago. The Siberian mammoth finds alone have been a bonanza, some of them not fossils but the actual creatures themselves, still frozen and almost intact, or mummified in frozen sediments. A museum in Yakutsk displays the fossilized contents of a fossilized mammoth stomach, in cross section, beside a whole preserved mammoth leg with its long, druidical hair still hanging down. In the eighteenth and nineteenth centuries, discoveries of mammoth remains were so common that for a while mammoth ivory became a major export of Siberia.

To astronomers, Siberia provides the advantage of skies largely untroubled by light pollution and, in some places, cloud-free for more than two hundred days a year. Looking up at the clarity of the night in Siberia, you feel that you are in the sky yourself. Never in my life have I seen so many satellites and shooting stars. Because of the big target Siberia presents to space, it gets hit by a lot of objects from there. In the early morning of June 30, 1908, something came out of the heavens and struck the taiga near the Stony Tunguska River in south-central Siberia, a region traveled only by reindeer herders. The impact created a blast that felled trees outward from it in a radial pattern covering an area about twenty-eight miles across.

Even today scientists aren't completely sure what the thing was. Speculation has included plasma from the sun, an antimatter explosion, a black hole (probably not, because a black hole would have made a corresponding exit explosion on the other side of the earth, in the North Atlantic), a meteorite, an asteroid, or a comet. Today the comet theory has the most support. The relative lack of mineral residue points to a comet, because meteorites and asteroids are made of iron or silicates, while comets are mostly dirt and ice. Whatever caused the explosion, the impact on the planet was the biggest that humans know about in historic times.

Travelers who crossed Siberia in the early eighteenth century noted the remarkable animals they saw—elk "of monstrous size," fierce aurochs, wild boars, wild horses and asses, flying squirrels in great numbers, foxes, hares, beavers, bears. Of the swans, cranes, pelicans, geese, ducks, bitterns, and other birds, one traveler wrote, "After sundown these manifold armies of winged creatures made such a terrific clamour that we could not even hear our own words." Philipp Johann von Strahlenberg, a Swede captured by Peter the Great's army at the Battle of Poltava in 1709 and sent with other Swedish prisoners to Siberia, wrote that the region had six species of deer, including the roe deer, the musk deer, the reindeer, and the great stag. He also noted a special kind of bird whose nests were so soft that they were used for socks. About

290 years later in Siberia I saw few or none of these marvels, except in museums, where some of the specimens are facing a second extinction from moths and general disintegration.

The main four-legged animal I encountered in Siberia was the cow. Little herds appear all the time, especially in western Siberia, grazing along the road or moving at twilight from the woods or the swamp into a glade. Siberian cows are skinnier than the ones in America, and longer legged, often with muddy shins, and ribs showing. Some wear bells. Herders, usually not on horseback, follow them unhurriedly. The boys have motormen's caps and sweaters with holes; the women, usually older, wear rubber boots, long trousers under their skirts, and scarves around their heads against the insects. Beef in Siberian stores is gristly, tough, and expensive. Siberian dairy products, however, are cheap and good. The butter and ice cream of Siberia are the best I've tasted anywhere.

At times Siberia has supplied a lot of western Russia's butter, and some of England's and Western Europe's, too. Just before the First World War, 16 percent of the world's exports of butter came from Siberia. N. S. Korzhanskii, a revolutionary who knew the father of the Russian Revolution, V. I. Lenin, when Lenin was living in England in 1903, recalled a meal in Lenin's London apartment at which "I was amazed at the wonderful, beautiful-smelling creamy butter, and was just about to burst out with some remark about the wealth of the British, when Vladimir Ilyich said, 'Yes. That must be ours. From Siberia.'" Lenin spoke to his landlady, and then informed his guests that the butter had come from the Barabinsk Steppe. "I passed through it twice," Lenin added. "On my way into exile and back again. A marvellous place. With a great future. The Englishwoman told me that they all know Barabinsk butter and Chulym cheese."

Lenin went to Siberia on two separate occasions. The exile he was referring to followed his arrest for revolutionary activities in St. Petersburg in December 1895. Lenin was twenty-five then, and still using his original name, Vladimir Ilyich Ulyanov. Sentenced to three years' exile, Lenin was sent to Shushenskoye, a village on the Yenisei River in central Siberia. Exile under the tsars could be a rather mild proposition, especially compared to what the Soviets would later devise; during his exile Lenin received a government stipend of twelve rubles a month, which covered room and board as well as extras like books. He was able to get a lot of reading done. On the way to Shushenskoye, he stopped for a couple of months in Krasnoyarsk and read in the library of a rich distiller named Iudin. The research he did there later helped in the writing of his *Development of Capitalism in Russia*. In Shushenskoye, he translated a book by the English Socialists Beatrice and Sidney Webb, hunted, skated on the Yenisei, and entertained his girlfriend, Nadezhda Konstantinovna Krupskaya, who came to Shushenskoye to visit. They later married and honeymooned there. All in all, Siberia seems to have agreed with Lenin splendidly and seasoned him as a political thinker. His revolutionary name, which he assumed in 1901, may have been inspired by the great Siberian river, the Lena (the name of his native river, the Volga, having already been taken by the father of Russian socialism, Georgi Plekhanov, known as Volgin).

The second time Lenin was sent to Siberia he had been dead for seventeen years. After the 1917 revolution, which succeeded in no small measure because of his vision and practicality, Lenin guided the Bolshevik putsch through civil war and consolidation of national power. Then in 1923 he suffered a series of strokes; a convalescence did not restore his health, and he died of another stroke in January 1924. Because of Lenin's importance to the revolution and the saintlike status the Communists gave him, the Soviet government decided to have his body preserved. Embalmers and other technicians did such a skillful job that when they were done he looked better than he had in the months before he died. To house him, the government built a temporary and then a permanent tomb on Red Square in Moscow, where his body went on display for the crowds who filed reverently by.

In 1941, with the Germans approaching, an icon as important as Lenin could not be left at risk of destruction or capture, so the body was packed into a railroad car and shipped to the western Siberian city of Tyumen for safekeeping. There, far from the front, it waited out the war. In 1945, after the Allied victory, Lenin again returned from Siberia and went back to his Red Square tomb. Russians who had seen him both before and after his stay in Tyumen reported that when he went on display again he looked "much the worse for wear," his second Siberian sojourn having had a less salutary effect, apparently, than his first. The experts in charge of such details soon got him back into shape again.

Like Lenin, many of the objects in museums and churches in the Kremlin and elsewhere in western Russia have spent some time in Siberia.

During the Second World War, state treasures and works of art and historic archives were put in crates and shipped east. A lot of western Russia's heavy industry also moved to temporary factories beyond the Urals. The instinct to withdraw, to disappear far into the interior, figures often in Russian history. During invasions from the West, Russia's strategic option of nearly unlimited retreat made it, in a sense, unkillable. After Napoleon began his invasion of Russia in 1812, an adviser told Tsar Alexander I, "I am not afraid of military reverses . . . Your empire has two powerful defenders in its vastness and its climate. The emperor of Russia will always be formidable in Moscow, terrible in Kazan, and invincible in Tobolsk." Tobolsk, at the junction of the Irtysh and Tobol rivers, was at the time the administrative capital and ecclesiastical seat of western Siberia.

On the question of whether Russia's vast size has benefited or hurt it overall, historians and others disagree. Those who take the negative side say that Russia has been too big and spread out ever to function properly, that it has been "crippled by its expanse," that much of its land is not worth the trouble, and that Siberia is a road leading nowhere. A few years ago, two public-policy experts at a Washington think tank wrote a book advising Russia to close down its remote and hard-to-supply Siberian cities and villages and concentrate the population in locations more practical for transportation and the global market. The far places should be left to a few skeleton-crew outposts, and the difficult environment allowed to revert to wilderness, the experts maintained.

Those on the positive side of the argument (a larger number, in total, than the nays) say, basically, that Russia was not really Russia before it began to move into Asia. Before, it was a loose collection of principalities centered on trading cities like Novgorod and Vladimir and Moscow. The pro-Siberians say that other nations became empires by crossing oceans, while Russia did the same by expanding across the land it was already on. At weak moments in Russia's history, it could have been partitioned between hostile countries that then were more powerful—Lithuania, Poland, Sweden, the Ottoman Empire, Germany—had not the resources and hard-to-subdue vastness of Siberia kept it alive. Possessed of Siberia, Russia became a continental country and not only an ethnic entity on the map of Eastern Europe. Or as Joseph Stalin once told a Japanese interviewer, "Russia is an Asiatic land, and I myself am an Asiatic."

(Stalin, by the way, was exiled to Siberia repeatedly during his years as a young revolutionary, and he claimed that he had escaped from Siberia six times. He was, of course, alive during the Second World War and so did not make a posthumous visit via cold storage.)

The first Russian ruler to style himself officially as tsar, Ivan IV (*Ivan Grozny*, Ivan the Fear-inspiring, "the Terrible"), was also the first to add "Lord of All the Siberian Land" to his titles. He was able to do this because he had conquered the Tatar city of Kazan, a Muslim stronghold on the Volga River that had long blocked Russian moves eastward. In 1552, Ivan led a large army against Kazan, besieged the city, mined the walls, overcame the defenders, killed many of the men, enslaved men and women and children, and then had his clergy sprinkle the streets, walls, and houses with holy water to bring the benediction of the Almighty to this formerly infidel place. The conquest destroyed the Tatar khanate of Kazan. Farther to the east, the khan of Sibir, taking note of the event, became Ivan's tribute-paying vassal, thus making Ivan his titular lord.

With Kazan out of the way, Russian adventurers could go beyond the frontiers to previously unexplored lands across the Urals. In 1581 and 1582, a band of Cossacks led by a Volga River pirate named Yermak Timofeyevich followed rivers into the country of the khan of Sibir, fought several battles with the khan's forces, defeated him, captured his leading general, and occupied his fortress town, Isker, on the Tobol River. The khan, Kutzum by name, later regrouped and killed many of the Cossacks, including (in 1585) Yermak himself. But by then Yermak had sent envoys to Ivan with news of his victory and a rich tribute of sable furs, black fox furs, and noble captives. This impressed Ivan favorably with Siberia's possibilities, and the state then secured Yermak's foothold with contingents of troops. By 1587, the Russians had begun to build the city of Tobolsk a short distance downstream from Isker, the former stronghold of the Siberian khan.

Such an enlargement of Ivan's territories gave added plausibility to the grandeur of the name "Tsar." Ivan had reinforced it in other ways, too, primarily by announcing the many royal lines he was descended from. His mother, Ivan said, was a descendant of Mamai, khan of the Golden Horde, whose rulers traditionally came from the line of Genghis Khan. Ivan also claimed direct descent from the Caesars of Rome, through a progenitor named Pruss, supposedly Caesar Augustus's brother.

Ivan's paternal grandfather, Ivan III ("the Great"), had counted among his wives Sophia Paleologue, niece of the last Byzantine emperor, another important relation.

That emperor had disappeared forever, along with the Orthodox church in Constantinople, when the Ottoman Turks captured that city and desecrated and destroyed its churches in 1453. Then only Russia, nominally Orthodox since the tenth century, remained as the seat of the true faith. Soon after Ivan IV's reign, Moscow became by tsar's decree "the Third Rome," Rome itself having been lost to the heresy and corruption of the Catholic church, and Constantinople, the Second Rome, now engulfed by Islam. Moscow would be the Third Rome, with no other to follow; there the true and orthodox faith would be preserved.

After Russia had acquired Siberia, tsars of the seventeenth century sometimes were told by Westerners that their dominion exceeded the size of the surface of the full moon. This information pleased the tsars, who probably did not look too closely into the math of the statement. The surface area of the moon is about 14,646,000 square miles. (Although the tsars would've measured in desyatin, or square versts, or something else.) When the moon is full, the part that's visible is of course half the entire moon, or 7,323,000 square miles. Whether Russia in the seventeenth century could honestly claim to be larger than that is not certain. It had not yet taken over the Baltic territories, the Crimea, Ukraine, or the Caucasus, and most of its Siberian territory was unknown in size. Mapmakers then had little information about Siberia's eastern regions and were not even sure whether it joined North America. Those details weren't important, however. To say that Russia was larger than the full moon sounded impressive, and had an echo of poetry, and poetry creates empires.

Chapter 2

When I was in my early forties, I became infected with a love of Russia. By then I had left Ohio, moved to New York City, become a writer. On the street in New York one day I saw my first actual from-Russia Russian. My then landlord, a Romanian named Zvi, pointed him out to me. This Russian was stocky, broad, with big hands and wide fingers. He wore a light gray shirt, open at the neck. His pallid, unshaven face was almost the same colorless color as his eyes, and his thick, straight gray hair was combed up off his forehead. I nodded to him, and he nodded back. I considered this a very satisfactory first sighting. My landlord said that this man had been allowed to leave the Soviet Union because of the diplomacy of the great President Jimmy Carter and added with admiration that already the man had become a much-feared landlord himself in Brooklyn.

At about the same time, I saw a notice for a lecture to be given by two recently arrived Russian émigré artists, Vitaly Komar and Alex Melamid. The notice advertised them as conceptual artists and said that in Moscow before they emigrated they had been unable to find work because they were dissidents. Everybody had heard of and sympathized with Russian dissidents. The term came nowhere near to describing how contrary and daft Komar and Melamid really were. At the lecture, only Melamid spoke English. Komar interjected comments in Russian that Melamid attempted to translate. First they showed slides of themselves buying the soul of Andy Warhol. There in the photo stood Warhol himself, a bit addled-looking but game, handing over the deed to his soul to these Russians, who were giving him a dollar bill in return. Melamid also announced they had recently gone to Crete and discovered the skeleton of the famous Minotaur, providing as proof a slide of a human skeleton with a bull's skull for a head. They then showed portraits of people's ancestors, which they said they were available to paint on commission; all the portraits were carefully rendered paintings of dinosaurs. A series of slides showed the pair at an altar they had built in the Negev Desert in Israel, a stop on their way to the United States. Upon this altar they had made a pile of their Russian suitcases and then set them ablaze, symbolizing the finality of their leaving home.

Later I wrote a long magazine profile of Komar and Melamid. After it appeared, Melamid and his wife, Katya Arnold, invited my wife and me to go drinking with them. We did, and had a great time, and the four of us became friends.

Meanwhile in the Soviet Union events were occurring that don't need to be retold. One big change followed the next, people sloughed off communism like an old skin, and the Soviet Union disappeared. Nobody knew where Russia was going, but for the moment, anyway, it seemed to be free. The exile that our Russian friends had chosen, and the separation from friends and family that all had assumed would be forever, no longer had to be that. With American citizenship and passports, Alex and Katya could now travel to Russia like anybody. When they had lived in Moscow, Alex, and Komar, had been kicked out of the Union of Soviet Artists; now a gallery in Moscow was mounting a show of their work, and they would go back to superintend. Katya, who would accompany them, would be seeing Moscow and her friends and family for the first time since she had left in '78—fifteen years. She asked my wife and me if we'd like to come on the trip. In my family, I'm more usually the traveler, and we had a four-year-old daughter besides. I said I'd come along.

The time of year was late July. Alex and his partner went over first and Katya and I followed a day or two after. We flew Finnair, on an evening flight that took seven hours to get to Helsinki, and we talked or read all the way. In Helsinki we ghosted around in that strange airport's boreal no-time-zone, then boarded a smaller plane for Moscow. It's hard, now that such journeys have become commonplace, to reconstruct how exciting the approach to Moscow was. From the looks of it, Russia was all trees. Sheremetyevo Airport, Moscow's venue for international flights, appeared from the window to be in the middle of an endless, deeply green forest. The plane landed and sat on the runway for a while. Finally it came up to the terminal and the door opened. The mobile ramp that extended out to the plane door met it about a foot too high. We had to duck our heads and step up to get off the plane.

From the ramp we went into a short hall. At its end was a sign saying *Vykhod* (Exit) with an arrow pointing to the left. We turned to the left, and after a few steps met a uniformed army officer in greatcoat and cap who wordlessly pointed us back the opposite way. Why they hadn't simply used a sign pointing the exit to the right to begin with, thus obviating the need for the soldier, I could not grasp. We came down some stairs into a hall leading to Passport Control. On the floor at the foot of the stairs was a large, vividly red spill of liquid—possibly raspberry syrup, possibly transmission fluid. I tried without success to pick up its smell. Instead I was hit by the smell of Russia, one I've encountered often since, all over that country. The components of the smell are still a mystery. There's a lot of diesel fuel in it, and cucumber peels, and old tea bags, and sour milk, and a sweetness—currant jam, or mulberries crushed into the waffle treads of heavy boots—and fresh wet mud, and a lot of wet cement. Every once in a while, in just the right damp basement in America, I find a cousin of the Russia-smell unexpectedly there.

We got into one of the lines for the passport booths. Katya is a compact, forceful woman unruffled in most situations, with a wide smile made wider and sunnier by the gap between her two front teeth. Now she looked pale, and the skin stretched tight around her eyes as she muttered to herself, "I should never have come back here. This was a stupid idea." The light above the passport booth flashed green, and Katya went in. Some minutes passed, the light flashed again, and it was my turn.

Again, I had never seen anything like this before. The bright, harsh lighting, the thick glass between me and the young passport officer, the lonely singularity of myself in the booth, the atmosphere of real-life no-fooling—all this rattled me. The passport officer gestured for me to take off my baseball cap. Later I would learn of the remarkable ability possessed by all Russians, even the sweetest and gentlest, to make their faces rock hard instantly when they want them to be. The young officer used the rock face on me, and it had its effect. When he looked down to examine my passport and visa, I noticed my reflection in the glass between us. My face had an expression of deep seriousness and fear that the moment did not, in reality, call for. When he looked up again to give me back my documents, he saw that I had relaxed, and he let a sly smile show through the rock. It was a kid's grin, suggesting that we had only been playing a game, and I was now a point down.

Beyond the booths, Katya found our luggage, and she asked me to stay with it while she went to the ladies' room. In a few minutes she returned, shaking her head. "Why did I come back here?" she repeated. "This place is insane. The women's bathroom is totally insane."

"Why is the women's bathroom insane?"

"In the women's bathroom there is a woman doing her dishes. Where could she have come from? I have no idea. There are dishes and pots all over. She is scrubbing away. There are chicken bones on the edge of the sink."

We found a cart and put our bags on it and pushed it past a final set of officers, and then through heavy windowless doors, and suddenly we were outside in the muggy afternoon. A few feet from the doors, a crowd waiting to meet the arrivals strained against a low barricade. At the front of the press stood Katya's older brother, Mitya Arnold, a physicist with dark, mournful eyes and a salt-and-pepper beard longer and fuller than Tolstoy's. He leaped at Katya and took her in a hug. Next to Mitya was the driver he had hired, a man named Stas, as big and slope-shouldered and patient and jowly and put-upon as any Russian coachman I'd ever read about, differing from them only in the light-green Teenage Mutant Ninja Turtles T-shirt he had on.

We drove from Sheremetyevo into the city. I remember all the details of our arrival in slow motion, because the whole event was a kind of epiphany. Even today Katya says she feels guilty for having exposed me to this contagion, the love of Russia that infected me. The shoulders of the road had been mowed incompletely or not at all. In places the weeds grew six and seven feet high beside the pavement. In other places they were lower; evidently the cows roaming the roadside had grazed them down. Openings in the greenery revealed sunlit trunks of birches, spotted like dalmatians, black on white. A woman in a babushka strolled the ditch carrying a basket of peeled woven twigs—looking for mushrooms, Katya said.

Closer to the city the traffic thickened. On the sides of buses and streetcars there were no ads, another new one on me. Those vehicles, and the trucks, and some of the cars were covered in a coating of road dust so matte and so thorough that they could have been made of adobe. Traffic cops with batons gestured one vehicle or another to the side—soliciting bribes, Stas said. Heavy, unfiltered exhaust hung in the air. Then suburban high-rises ascended around us, and then the buildings and onion domes of Moscow itself. We drove down streets, then lanes, then alleys barely wider than the car, until we stopped in the courtyard of the apartment building of Chuda, Katya's best friend. Chuda and her husband, Kolya, were there to meet us, with more hugs and tears; from then all the conversation was in Russian, and I became a cat or a dog, understanding nothing except once in a while my own name.

The staircase to Chuda's apartment looked like a stone ramp into which feet had gradually worn steps over the course of a thousand years. The entry was so dark you couldn't see, but there was more light as you went up. The lower half of the wall along the staircase had just been painted a bright policeman blue and the paint had an eye-watering smell like something junkies would sniff deliberately. Chuda opened the embossed, padded door to her apartment and we went into the front hall, my suitcase now streaked blue where it had bumped against the fresh paint. I did not understand that I was to take off my shoes. Chuda demonstrated for me by pantomime and gave me a backless pair of house slippers to put on. I stood around not knowing what to do, unable to make small talk, or any talk at all.

In the kitchen, we sat down to a big meal Chuda had prepared. I ate delicious fried fish and drank icy-cold vodka, trying to project mute goodwill and gratitude. Her son Kolya had been among the people who had stood with Yeltsin when he defied the generals' putsch in August, just a year before. She said Kolya's photo had been in the news—he was standing on a barricade in his white shirt like a hero of the War of 1812, she said. Katya translated fragments of the story for me. Neither she nor I had slept for at least a day, so after a while Chuda showed me a bed in her son's room where I could take a nap. I lay down but didn't sleep, or read, or even think. I stared at the ceiling, where a paper airplane hung from the chandelier. This paper airplane had sharp angles, and fins, and a strange projectile sleekness, like the elegant arrowhead-shaped MiG fighter jet. No one in America would have made such a paper airplane. It swayed in the breeze from the tall, narrow windows.

I was thoroughly stunned. Love, with an assist from novelty, had blindsided me. I had been overcome, lost permanently. This kind of thing happens to people in middle age, I realize. It's embarrassing. The feeling began the minute I stepped off the plane, with the absurd business of the exit sign and the correcting soldier.

In the days that followed I went all over Moscow with Alex and Katya and Chuda's younger son, Tisha, a high school kid then, who speaks good English. I saw the Kremlin, Katya's elementary school, St. Basil's Cathedral, Lenin's tomb, Lenin himself (after viewing him I was able to read several books about him I would not have read before, because now I considered him a personal acquaintance). I visited churches on whose grounds people were cutting the lawn with scythes. I rode the metro, absorbed in the details of the subway cars, reminiscent of an American electric train set of the 1950s. I joined a tour of the Novodevichy Monastery and its cemetery and saw the graves of Chekhov, Khrushchev and his wife, Ilf and Petrov, Mikoyan (designer of the MiG), and Gogol. I spent longer than other people wanted to spend looking at the Rublev icons in the Tretyakov Gallery; and so on.

One evening at Chuda's apartment, she and her husband and Katya and Mitya and Mitya's wife, Irina, and their daughter, and some other people and I were sitting around the large dining room table drinking vodka, and the moment came when the foreigner must account for himself. Through Katya they asked me questions about myself, my family, my work. Then they asked how I liked Moscow. I said that Moscow was the greatest place I'd ever been, and Russia the greatest country I'd ever seen.

On one of my later visits to Moscow I was standing at Sheremetyevo Airport in a line at the ticket counter at Aeroflot Airlines waiting to buy a ticket to New York. The guy in front of me was speaking Russian, and after a minute I could tell by his accent that he must be an American. We began a conversation. He said he was a journalist originally from New

York who had been living in Moscow for many years. Still in the grip of my infatuation, and wanting to hear it confirmed in someone else, I ventured that he must really like Russia to have lived here so long.

"*Like* it?" he said. "I hate it! I hate this fucking country. Russia is the worst fucking country in the world!"

I asked why he thought that.

"My God! What are you talking about? This country is a total disaster! Nothing fucking works. The people treat each other horribly—oh, how they love to abuse each other! They're schemers, liars, bribe takers. If you don't know how to bribe people you won't ever get anywhere here. Everybody's working some stupid fucking angle. The place is filthy, trash all over . . ." He went on and on.

When he finally paused, I asked, "Well, if you hate Russia so much, why are you flying Aeroflot?"

He looked away, toward the floor. "Because they let you smoke," he said.

And indeed, he was certainly right about that. The woman who sold me my ticket was smoking, as was the flight attendant who took the ticket at the gate. So were most of the passengers. Through the airport window I saw two Aeroflot pilots squatting on their haunches in that way Russian men do, each enjoying a smoke on the tarmac not far from the planes. When I stepped into the cabin, the density of the fumes in there would have been sufficient to smoke meat. (Sometime after that I learned that Aeroflot had changed its policy; now, like other airlines, it does not allow smoking on its flights.)

Eventually, of course, I came to understand that the guy had a point, and not just about the smoking. Trying to reconcile the passion I felt for Russia with the way Russia actually is took some doing. I employed various strategies. We all know of famous authors who gave the world great works of literature yet were not such good people themselves. I supposed maybe Russia was an entire country like that. Certainly, it had the great books to show. That explanation proving unsatisfactory, I tried a simpler formula: Russia as both great and horrible, or as the greatest horrible country in the world. I had other formulas and explanations after that one. More recently I have given up trying to reconcile or explain.

As I read books about Russia, I took comfort in the discovery that Russia-love is an independent force out there in the ether of ideas, and that it had afflicted other vulnerable people before me. For example, John Reed, author of perhaps the best book ever written about Russia by an American, *Ten Days That Shook the World*. I feel a connection to Reed even closer than I do to Lenin, because Reed and I were on the same organization in college, a humor magazine called the *Harvard Lampoon*. Reed graduated in 1910, and I graduated sixty-three years later. Soon after college, Reed had a great success as a war correspondent following Pancho Villa's armies in Mexico. When the First World War started, Reed went to France, sent back a number of dispatches from there, and then managed to get himself banned from the Western front. While doing some reporting, he wangled his way over to the German lines, where, for unknown reasons, he accepted the offer of a German officer to take a couple of shots at the French. Reed had returned to New York by the time word of this exploit reached the papers, and the French, understandably, afterward refused to allow him reentry into France.

For his next war-reporting journey, Reed therefore had no choice but to explore the Eastern front instead. Entering via the Caucasus, Reed continued north through the war zone into Russia. He had not been there long before the infatuation struck. In a dispatch published in *Metropolitan* magazine in 1916 (and in Reed's subsequent book, *The War in Eastern Europe*), he wrote:

> Russia's is an original civilization that spreads by its own power. Loose and easy and strong, it invades the life of the far-flung savage tribes of Asia; it crosses the frontiers into Rumania, Galicia, East Prussia—in spite of organized efforts to stop it . . . And it takes hold of the minds of men because it is the most comfortable, the most liberal way of life. Russian ideas are the most exhilarating, Russian thought the freest, Russian art the most exuberant; Russian food and drink are to me the best, and Russians themselves are, perhaps, the most interesting human beings that exist.

Later, other American intellectuals of Reed's generation would get even more worked up ("The whole beautiful land is even more glorious than I thought, and no one should stay away from here a minute"), but by then the encomia were directly political, and all leftist. I think Russia-infatuation may be like the messianic and other religious exaltations that sometimes seize visitors to Jerusalem. The contributing factors seem to be text (Bible, Koran; Tolstoy, Marx) plus the actual earthly location where the text was fulfilled, or is to be. The combination of holy writ and earthly realization may act as a kind of psychic force-multiplier to unhinge the mind.

In Reed's case, his malady turned out to be fatal. The following year he returned to Russia and witnessed the October Revolution; back in America he holed up for two months in a rented room in Greenwich Village and produced *Ten Days That Shook the World*. After it was published to wide acclaim (Lenin himself admired it), Reed became a figure of the revolution in his own right and went to the new USSR to participate in the conferences and torturous political machinations of the day. While attending the Congress of the Peoples of the East, in Baku, he caught typhus. Trying to return to America, he ended up in prison in Finland, where his health deteriorated more. Returning finally to Moscow, he died there in 1920. He was not quite thirty-three. The Soviets buried him with honors in the Kremlin Wall. He is one of only two Americans buried there. His politics may have been crazy, and he may have gone overboard about Russia, but there never was a braver writer than John Reed.

On that first trip, after about ten days in Moscow, Alex and Katya and I continued on to Siberia. The story of how that came about is long. A few months earlier, Alex had received a letter from a friend he'd known in college named Sasha Khamarkhanov. Sasha was a poet, and a Buryat. The Buryat are an indigenous people of Siberia with their own republic east of Lake Baikal. The Buryat Autonomous Republic is part of the Russian Federation and its capital is Ulan-Ude (pronounced oo-LAHN oo-DAY). In his letter, Sasha said that he was now an official in the Ministry of Culture of the Buryat Republic, and that he was inviting Alex to come to Ulan-Ude, and bring any other American artists or writers who wanted to join him, for the purpose of cultural exchange. Alex wrote back saying he would certainly come. Afterward he asked me if I would like to go to Siberia with him, and I said yes. That plan, tentative and theoretical as it was, had existed before the later details about the gallery show and the trip to Moscow.

I half doubted the Siberia trip would really happen. In Moscow, trying to set it up, Katya made many phone calls at odd hours to find out
when and from where flights left for Ulan-Ude. Such Western conveniences as reserving airline tickets over the phone had not yet become
routine in Russia. Finally she found a flight, and one afternoon Stas
drove us and our luggage out to Domodedovo Airport, Moscow's main
airport for domestic travel. When we arrived, the place was in near chaos,
packed with people in the steamy heat, most of the passengers not standing in lines but mobbing the counters in throngs. We tried to work our
way through them and onto a plane but gave up not very near the departure gate. Stas took us back to Chuda's, where it turned out we could not
stay because other houseguests had just shown up. Stas then drove us to
Alex's mother's apartment. Alex's mother, Lyudmila Borisovna, let us in,
and when she heard we had just been at Domodedovo, she made us take
showers immediately. "The last thing we need around here is cholera,"
she said.

A couple of days later Katya and I (Alex would be taking a later flight)
went back to Domodedovo and by pushing and persistence jammed ourselves into a Siberian-bound plane. The seats were like lawn chairs with
a single piece of canvas for the back; one's knees supported the spine of
the passenger in front while one leaned on the passenger behind. For
the first time I heard that characteristic sound of Russian departures, the
clink of vodka bottles in plastic shopping bags. The plane waited for a
while on the runway and the cabin became stuffy, so some of the male
passengers removed their shirts and undershirts. Finally the plane took
off and flew through the night, and the passengers slept all jumbled up
with one another. An eight- or nine-year-old girl on my right slept on my
right side while I sprawled on the uniformed man on my left. Just before
dawn, the uniformed man woke up and looked out the window. As the
plane descended to land at Omsk, he turned to me, gestured at the view,
and said, "*Sibir'!*"

In Russian, the word—*Sibir'*—is pure onomatopoeia. A shiver begins
with the first letter and concludes with the palatalized *r* at the end,
which, combined with the *bi* preceding it, amounts to *brrr*. Only a cosmic Dickens of place-naming would have chosen a name with such a
chilly and mysterious sound. And yet *Sibir'*, so resonant in Russian, is not
of Russian provenance, but whispers of deepest Asia. In all geography,

no name has the same magic: Siberia; Siberia; Siberia. After I got interested in it I wondered what the name meant and where it had come from. Farley Mowat, the Canadian author, says in *The Siberians* that "Siberia" means "the sleeping land." That derivation has a ring to it, but I found no other source saying the same. Valentin Rasputin, the Siberian short-story writer and essayist, proposes that the word comes from the Russian *sebe beri* (take for yourself), contracted to *se' beri*, which he translates as "take what you can, take it all." Rasputin's etymology is ironic; he is an environmentalist who writes often about the plundering of Siberia. Elsewhere he suggests, more seriously, that *Sibir'* was originally the name of a town and that the word meant a center or meeting place.

Among scholars who have studied the question, there is a consensus that *Sibir'* referred to a town on the Irtysh River where the khanate defeated by Yermak and his Cossacks in 1581 had its capital. The town, or fortress, was also known as Isker, or Ibis-Sibir, or Abir-i-Sibir. As Russia enlarged itself across Asia, the original name of *Sibir'* kept being reapplied to larger areas until it came to mean not just a locality but the whole place.

Etymologists say that the word *Sibir'* consists of two Turkic words that have close equivalents in Mongolian. The first word, *su* or *si*, meant "water," and the second, *berr* or *birr*, meant "a wild, unpopulated land." The naming pattern follows a common one of simple geographic description used by native peoples, whereby, for example, Baikal derives from the Turkic *bey*, big, and *kul*, lake. *Sibir'*, therefore, meant a wilderness with water. "Marshy wilderness" would come close to describing parts of western Siberia today.

The first appearance of the word *Sibir'* in a written text was in *The Secret History of the Mongols*, composed in Central Asia probably in the year 1228. This epic, written in the vertical script adopted from the Uighurs by the previously illiterate Mongols during the time of Genghis Khan, describes Genghis's mythic origins, birth, conquests, and the victories of his generals and armies. No original of *The Secret History* survives—document conservation not being a Mongol strong point—but several near-contemporary Chinese translations made their way into Chinese archives. Part of *The Secret History* tells of the campaign of Genghis's son Jochi in 1207 against the People of the Forest. The campaign succeeded, and the People of the Forest submitted to Jochi, bringing him "white gerfalcons, white geldings and black sables." The chronicler continues:

> After Joci had subjugated the People of the Forest from the Sibir, Kesdim, Bayit, Tugas, Tenlek, To'eles, Tas and Bajigit up to this side, he came back bringing with him the commanders of ten thousand and of thousands of the Kirgisut to pay homage to Cinggis Qa'an . . . Cinggis Qa'an favored Joci, saying, "You, the eldest of my sons, who only now for the first time have left home, you have been lucky. Without wounding or causing suffering to man or gelding in the lands where you went, you came back having subjugated the fortunate People of the Forest. I shall give this people to you." So he ordered.

In this context, *Sibir'* seems to mean both the place and the tribe in it. The other names listed are of tribes to the west of the Mongols' territory; "up to this side" means to where Mongol lands began. Jochi would be the first ruler of the expanded western part of the Mongol empire, an area that in the reign of his son Batu would include Kiev and Novgorod and other Russian principalities. (Jochi's line, by the way, founded the Golden Horde, later ruled by Khan Mamai, from whom Ivan the Terrible traced his Tatar descent.)

In about 1305, the Persian traveler and historian Rashid ad-Din, discussing the territory of the Khirgiz people, wrote of a land he called *Aber Sibir*. And in the Russian chronicles of 1406, mention is made of the killing of a famous and dangerous khan, Tokhtamysh, "in the land of Sibir, near the town of Changa." (The Russian chronicles were church annals that recorded, in official and formulaic language, the important happenings of the year.) Those two mentions of Siberia are perhaps the earliest ones to be found in any text after *The Secret History*.

The first known reference to Siberia in a book published in Europe appeared in a narrative called *The Bondage and Travels of Johann Schiltberger, a Native of Bavaria, in Europe, Asia, and Africa*, which was written (probably dictated) in about 1443 and published in 1473. Schiltberger led a tumultuous life of long journeys, narrow escapes, and face-to-face encounters with historical figures of the age. He was born in 1381, and at about age thirteen entered the service of a lord named

Leinhart Richtaringen. When his lord joined other Bavarian Knights on the Crusade of King Sigismund of Hungary to the Holy Land, Schiltberger went along. King Sigismund quickly led his army into one of the great disasters of the Crusades. At the Battle of Nicopolis on the Danube River in present-day Bulgaria, an Ottoman Turk army led by Bajazet, the sultan, routed the crusaders, caused Sigismund to flee, killed Leinhart Richtaringen, and captured ten thousand prisoners, whom Bajazet ordered to be beheaded on the spot. The three men Schiltberger was roped to had their heads cut off, but Schiltberger, then only fifteen, was spared. He became the sultan's slave.

Bajazet afterward returned to besieging Constantinople, a favorite occupation of the Ottomans. Schiltberger first saw that city from the attackers' side. Bajazet, however, soon had to lift the siege and go to war against a more deadly enemy, Tamerlane. This former Turkic tribal chief who rose to become the leader of a great Tatar army was the worst scourge of civilization since Genghis Khan. In 1402, Tamerlane met Bajazet at the Battle of Ankara in Asia Minor, defeated him, put him in a cage, and took plunder, including slaves. As a slave of Tamerlane for several years, Schiltberger was able to report on some of the notable atrocities of his master, such as his burning alive of thirty thousand people in a temple in Damascus, his constructing of pyramids of human heads, and his trampling of children prisoners younger than seven beneath the hooves of his cavalry. Once when Tamerlane was besieging the city of Hispahan, he made peace on the condition that it lend him its archers; after twelve thousand archers were sent, he ordered his soldiers to round them all up and cut off their thumbs. He then entered the city unopposed and killed almost everyone.

Dying in a manner befitting his nature, Tamerlane fell into an incurable rage when he could not revenge himself enough on some people who had betrayed him. He went out howling, and after his burial was heard to howl every night for a year. Schiltberger then became the property of a series of Tamerlane's sons and grandsons; just who owned him in this period is hard to keep track of. On a journey with one of his later masters, a khan named Tchekre, Schiltberger went north into what he calls "Great Tartaria." There they met another khan who was planning an expedition "into a country called Ibissibur," by geographic context clearly Siberia. Schiltberger's master accompanied this khan, and

Schiltberger devotes about a page to the journey, with a surprisingly accurate piece of ethnological data: "There are also in the above-named country, dogs, that go in carts and sledges; they are also made to carry luggage, and are as large as donkeys."

Schiltberger's subsequent travels eventually brought him to the shores of the Black Sea, where, with five other slaves of the Muslims, he escaped and hailed a passing ship from Europe. The sailors asked the escapees to prove their identity as Christians by reciting the Ave Maria, the Paternoster, and the Credo. The memories of Schiltberger and his companions not failing them, the sailors then took them to Constantinople, where Schiltberger told his story to the Byzantine emperor, John VIII Paleologue, who cared for them and helped them on their way. After more plot twists, Schiltberger finally found himself back in Bavaria. He had been gone for thirty-one years. A Bavarian duke gave him a position in his retinue, and there, presumably, the much-journeyed Schiltberger stayed put for the rest of his life.

Over the centuries to come, thousands of travelers, willing and otherwise, would see Siberia and write books about it. By his brief mention and description of Ibissibur, Johann Schiltberger became the first in a long literary line. If plot (as we are told) equals character, and vice versa, then maybe a similar equivalence exists between setting and genre. That is, perhaps the two presuppose each other, as in the sea story, the American Western, the English parlor mystery, etc. Schiltberger's example leads us to expect that Siberia's genre will be the travel story, not surprisingly, because one can't begin to know a place that big without moving around. Sometimes the Siberian genre will also be the slave narrative, a personal account of bondage and suffering, also as per Schiltberger. His precedent also points to another, lighter Siberian genre, just as inseparable from geographic vastness—the picaresque.

Our plane had touched down at Omsk and taxied to a stop on the runway. Through the windows nothing was visible but a distant, nondescript horizon in gray morning light. From my vantage, no buildings could be seen. Following the custom of Russian commercial aviation, the plane then sat, with nothing at all happening, for an indefinite amount of time. Eventually from the outer vagueness a motorized boarding ladder emerged and drove slowly to the plane, its door finally opened, and the passengers disembarked. With pointing arm fully extended, an airline employee indicated a group of tiny buildings just barely within sight. These were the terminal. In a mass with some stragglers, the passengers began to walk in that direction. Katya and I found each other and joined the trek.

Chapter 3

What I have to say next concerns the Omsk airport men's room. I regret this. I've noticed that in books by Siberian travelers of the past they don't talk about bathrooms, and that's probably good. I reluctantly break with this tradition for two reasons. First, I am an American, and Americans pay attention to and care about bathrooms. The habit may show childishness and weak-mindedness, but there it is. Second, if the world really is going to become a global community, then some of our trading partners (I'm talking to you, too, China) need to know how far apart we are on the subject of bathrooms.

The men's room at the Omsk airport was unbelievably disgusting. Stepping through the door, or even near the door, was like receiving a blow to the face from the flat of a hand. No surface inside the men's room, including the ceiling, was clean. There were troughs and stools, but no partitions, stalls, or doors. Everything done was done in full view. The floor was strewn with filth of a wide and eye-catching variety. At the urinal raised cement footprints offered the possibility of keeping your feet out of the flooding mire, but as the footprints themselves were hardly filth-free, the intention failed. Certain of this place's images that I won't describe remain inexpugnable from my mind. I got out of there as fast as was practical and reeled away into the terminal's dim lobby.

Soon Katya appeared, also reeling, from her trip to the ladies'. The force of revulsion propelled us clear out of the terminal and into its cracked and weed-surrounded parking lot, where we finally risked taking deep breaths again. First we washed with packaged detergent hand wipes. Then on our hands and the soles of our shoes we poured rubbing alcohol that Katya had brought along. Readers may think us squeamish. (And, in fairness to the Omsk airport, later we did discover the public bathrooms reserved for foreigners, which were upstairs in the terminal, and not as bad; also, for all I know, in the new Russian economy the Omsk airport has upgraded its facilities by now.)

But as I would find out, though the Omsk men's room was especially awful, that kind of bathroom experience is more the rule than not in Siberia. Winter temperatures there often fall so low that in the outhouses, liquids freeze very quickly, and over the months a sort of stalagmite effect is created, growing up through the hole in the floor. As for the holes themselves, only in the nicer outhouses are they made with a jigsaw that cuts them into the conventional oval shape; more generally they are hacked with an ax into fractured parallelograms. In indoor bathrooms within the permafrost zone, the fragility of the plumbing means that toilet paper cannot be flushed away, and so it is disposed of separately, usually in its own plastic bucket beside the john . . . Again, I apologize.

Now that I've brought up a few of these details, however, and gotten the subject out of the way, I won't have to refer to it again. In future descriptions of Siberian sanitary arrangements, a more than occasional bathroom along the lines of the Omsk airport men's room may be inferred.

After a couple of hours and a second collection of tickets, the passengers bound for Ulan-Ude set out on another group hike across the runway, this time to a new plane. The day had become sunny and breezy, and I enjoyed the stroll. Seeing the plane parked by itself off in the distance and watching it grow in size as we approached it restored some of its miraculousness, a quality ordinary air travel takes away. You forget that a machine's ability to fly is really an act of sorcery, until you observe the thing just sitting there before takeoff, gleaming in the sun. A common Russian word for airplane, *samolyot* (literally, "flies itself"), is not a coinage made to describe a new invention but has been around since the Arabian Nights, when *kovyor samolyot* meant "flying carpet." As we came to the boarding stairs, the two pilots, neither much more than a teenager, stood talking casually by the plane as if they'd just finished building it in their backyard.

On this flight, unfortunately, we sat in the same section as a bunch of mafia guys. I use the term for sake of convenience. I don't know if they were really mafia. They wore dramatically tailored suits, they emitted strong fragrances of cologne, their women had on skimpy clothes and furs, and Katya said they were mafia guys. A small man accompanying them carried bags of expensive provisions, mostly alcoholic, like cognac and champagne, and foods that sent off odors to fill the plane. The group occupied many seats together, putting their belongings on empty ones and ignoring any passengers who showed up complaining that the seats were theirs. They also ignored everything they were instructed to do for takeoff, made no use of seat belts, did not remain seated, walked around the plane, drank and laughed and yelled, and (remarkably) did not pass out, frustrating passengers who were hoping they would. They kept the party rolling all the way to Ulan-Ude.

Movies and TV shows about gangsters expect you always to identify with those characters, and it's fun to do that, and I try to. Sometimes, though, the fantasy falters, and I find myself identifying not with Tony Soprano and his friends but with anyone unlucky enough to be next to him in an enclosed environment like a plane.

The airport at Ulan-Ude lay in the middle of an immense flat space covered with low tufts of grass. Sasha Khamarkhanov and his brother Kolya met us at the gate. Sasha was a thin, shy, bespectacled man with the attentive manner of someone who always expects to hear something great. Kolya was of a comic-foil rotundity, almost oval, and wore a blue suit and shades. The luggage took about an hour to appear, and as we waited, Katya and Kolya and Sasha discussed our flight and the weather. Katya mentioned the heat, and Kolya said, "Yesterday was even hotter, and that was difficult for me, because I'm fat." Finally the luggage came and we put it into Kolya's English-made car and drove into Ulan-Ude.

The impressions of first-time visitors to that city often rise to and descend from their first glimpse of the sculpture of the head of Lenin overlooking Ulan-Ude's central square. For me these impressions were: sooty, yellow-gray air, reminiscent of Akron, Ohio, in the 1950s; extensive industrial plants, with a silver aircraft or a monstrous black locomotive with a red star on it poised on a platform by the plant gates; tiers of gray buildings, some connected to one another by aerial walkways; apartment-building roofs thick with antennae in every possible style, some like flowers, some like hot-dog grills, some like spirals, or asterisks, or radiators, or Afro combs; then a huge open square; and then, The Head.

It is said to be the largest head of Lenin in the world. Indeed, without even bothering to check, I'll assert it's the largest head of anybody in the world. (I'm talking whole head, now, and not just the face, as on Mount Rushmore.) The Head is gunmetal blue-gray, almost Mayan in its strong features and its upcurled top lip. Including its pedestal, The Head, with just a hint of neck, and no shoulders or body, rises about thirty-five feet above the ground. An open parade-type area spreads in front of it, and it's flanked by rectangular, hedge-enclosed lawns. Government buildings of four and five stories, in predictable Soviet-era architectural styles, face the square on all sides. The first time I saw The Head I thought it creepy, like a sci-fi symbol that ranks of drone soldiers would goose-step before. On later trips to Ulan-Ude I noticed The Head only in passing, writing it off as just another odd thing that people in the long-gone past had built and left behind.

If I had been stunned in Moscow, I was even more so in Ulan-Ude. New data came at me like rapidly served tennis balls I could not hope to return. Mostly I sort of stumbled around in a daze and did a very indifferent job as a cultural representative of American literature. First we went to Sasha's apartment and had a big meal prepared by his wife, Tania. We also met their teenage daughter, Arjenna, and their eight-year-old son, Tioshi. The meal involved several courses and featured *omul'*, the signature fish of Lake Baikal, and a traditional Buryat dish called *pozhe*, which are dumplings stuffed with ground lamb and chopped wild onions. We drank vodka, naturally, which Sasha put to his lips only after dipping the fourth finger of his right hand into his shot glass and sprinkling drops in four directions. Sasha's colleagues from the Ministry of Culture, Zoya and Alyosha, showed up and joined us. Zoya was a short, competent-looking woman with big spectacles. Alyosha was not a Buryat but a very pale Russian-Russian, with three gold teeth and short red hair. During the meal he turned to me and asked me what style I wrote in and blushed violently. I said I wrote in a factual style.

Some of us then got in a boxy tan microbus with large tires and no springs and rode for hours on dusty roads to Lake Baikal. Alyosha drove, and Sasha, Zoya, Katya, Tioshi, a cousin of Tioshi's, and I sat in the back. The ride went over such troublesome roads, and the seats were so hard, that I was reduced eventually to exhausted, brute irritability. At one point we switchbacked up a road only to find it blocked near the top by a piece of unoccupied earthmoving equipment; we then had to bounce all the way back down. Finally, late in the afternoon, we arrived at a four-story log *dom otdykha* (house of rest), a resort on Baikal's western shore. Sasha installed us in small, bare rooms without locks on the doors. I undressed and lay down on the bed and tried to nap. Very soon a young woman, possibly a maid, pushed the door open and searched the room for some cigarettes she'd left there. After she closed the door, I dressed again and went out to sit by the lake.

Seeing how droopy I had become, Katya assumed the protective attitude of a fierce older sister. At dinner she found the food suspect and would let me eat nothing but tea and bread. She gave the rest of our dinners to Tioshi and his cousin, who quickly finished them. Sasha asked me questions about the similarity between writers' unions in Russia and the National Endowment for the Arts in America, and I made such a hash of an answer, even in English, that Katya stopped translating. Sasha pressed vodka on us but I begged off. He said, "If you were in the company of only Buryats, you would be *forced* to drink," but his tone was mild, and I did not take offense. He told us that most Buryats knew the list of their ancestors by heart to far back in the past, and that he could recite his father and his father and so on back to a brother of Genghis Khan. He said that Buryats became ill if they did not eat enough horse meat, and that some families in Ulan-Ude kept a side of horse frozen on the balconies of their apartments in the winter. He added that you could buy canned pony year-round in Ulan-Ude.

The next morning all had been prepared for me to take a *banya*—a Russian steam bath. The bathhouse I was directed to had once been the hull of a wooden fishing boat. Soon after I went in and sat down and started sweating, it caught fire. I wondered if the heavy smoke coming through the wood paneling on the ceiling was part of the program. Then I heard shouts, grabbed a towel, stepped outside, and saw flames leaping up and a workman in overalls prying at the roof boards with a long crowbar. Katya appeared and told me to run and jump in the lake, as one traditionally does after a *banya*. I ran, jumped, and nearly seized up from the shock. Baikal is quite cold.

After breakfast, when our plates had just been cleared, the cook came out of the kitchen and asked Katya what was the matter with the two of us that morning. Katya said that we were not feeling well. The cook looked at us, puzzled. "But last night you ate *very* well," she said.

For that day's excursion, Sasha piled us back into the microbus and we set out on another long haul, to the village of Barguzin, on a large river of the same name that enters Baikal from the northeast. Barguzin is more than 350 years old and has been almost *the* classic village of Siberian exile since tsarist times. All kinds of people have been exiled there, from Decembrist revolutionaries in the 1830s to Katarina Breshkovskaya, the "little grandmother of the Russian Revolution." There is even a Russian folk song about exile called "Barguzin Wind."

All I knew then about Barguzin was how lonesome it looked at the first view, sitting on a plateau above a broad green floodplain extending to distant mountain ranges. Somehow that encircling open space seemed to imply judgment, as if at any moment a huge finger might point down at the village out of the sky. Almost nowhere in America anymore do you see a village like that, with no outlying development, just landscape all around. To reach the village, the road crossed a high bridge over the Barguzin River, where Alyosha had to stop the microbus and honk the horn and race the engine and make feints, attempting to induce a large herd of cattle standing on the bridge to move. They had chosen that spot, no doubt, because of the river breeze, for relief from Barguzin's plentiful flies. Siberian cows are hard to scare; these looked as if they'd just as soon be run over as not.

Along Barguzin's bumpy streets of dirt and sand stood many dark brown log houses with elaborate wood trim on the eaves and around the windows, and several big brick-and-plaster houses with columns and gates and yards. The village had once been among the fanciest places in Siberia, Zoya said, back when its merchants traded furs and gold by caravan between China and western Russia. In the village square, a Lenin statue, silver from head to foot, strode forward into space. We stopped first at the old cemetery, where Zoya had been doing historical work with the eventual goal of restoration. Again, cows disinclined to move loitered here and there. The village had once had a large Jewish merchant population, Zoya told us. Many of the inscriptions on the headstones in the cemetery were in Yiddish. Almost every headstone had been knocked sideways or down.

Zoya led us to a grave in the cemetery's corner and said it was that of a famous Decembrist named Mikhail Karlovich Küchelbecker, a man famous, actually, at one or two removes. Mikhail Küchelbecker's older brother, Wilhelm Küchelbecker, was a poet and a friend of Pushkin's who turns up often in stories of that poet's action-filled life. Kukhla, as the elder Küchelbecker was called, even fought a duel with Pushkin, after Pushkin wrote some verses that said that reading Küchelbecker's verses brought on a malady called "küchelbeckorrhea." Kukhla challenged Pushkin, Pushkin accepted, Kukhla shot at Pushkin and missed. Declining to return fire, Pushkin threw his gun down in the snow and went to embrace his friend. Kukhla angrily insisted that Pushkin fire. Pushkin protested that his gun was now jammed with snow, and nothing came of the duel in the end.

Barguzin's Küchelbecker, Mikhail Karlovich, was exiled here after serving an eight-year sentence of solitary confinement for his part in the uprising of young officers against the tsar on December 14, 1825. In Barguzin, Mikhail Küchelbecker married the postmaster's daughter, an ugly woman who mistreated him, and he eventually lost his mind and died. Zoya said that recent study had positively identified the skeleton in the grave as his from scoliosis of the spine, a lame leg, and the iron ring on his finger. Many Decembrists when finally released from their shackles had finger rings made from the links of their chains, she said; later, Decembrist shackle rings and bracelets became highly fashionable accessories in salons in St. Petersburg.

We walked around the village, took photographs, picnicked on a bluff over the river. Then we visited Barguzin's museum and historical society, an old building consisting mainly of one big gallery with tall, curtain-draped windows and pictures made of fur on the walls. The museum's curators, a couple named Lizaveta and Vladimir, showed us around. Lizaveta wore her hair up, nineteenth-century-style, above a long dress of dark red velvet with white lace at the hem and collar. Vladimir, a sturdy man with blue eyes and a forward-thrusting, chestnut-colored beard, had made the pictures, mostly landscapes, which he had assembled by cutting and stitching various Siberian animals' pelts. Some of the pelts he had obtained himself in the wild. Lizaveta led us around the gallery from picture to picture and explained how different kinds of fur represented different landscape shades; the deep blue-gray of the fur of the Baikal seal, for example, duplicated the color of Lake Baikal in a storm.

I had brought along my fishing rod, and Sasha had arranged for Vladimir and me to fish together in the river. After more admiring of the pictures, we drove by Vladimir's house so he could get his stuff. He went in and in a few minutes came out; he wore hip boots, jeans, a white shirt with blousy sleeves such as one might wear in America to portray a pirate in a school play, a white mesh cap with a blue insignia, and a big hunting knife in a handsome cedar scabbard he had carved himself. I wore a long-sleeved flannel shirt, bathing trunks (which I'd had on under my trousers), and sneakers. My fishing rod was a light four-piece graphite travel model to which I had attached a little open-face Shakespeare spinning reel. Vladimir looked at my rig and said, "Looks like American weapon." His rod and reel looked like a Russian one, or maybe Czech—a telescoping metal pole as thick as a broomstick, a flat reel that called to mind an old reel-to-reel tape recorder, and thick, milky-colored monofilament line. I showed him the lures I'd brought, mostly copper spinners shaped like poplar leaves, and treble-hooked steel spoons painted red and white or inset with fake garnets for eyes. He showed me his spoons, some of which were actual soup spoons with a hole drilled at the end for the line and a large single hook welded where the handle used to be.

Everyone in Barguzin apparently had gone to the river that day. Little brush and few trees grew along the river's banks, so you could see the people along it both near and far. Some people swam, some washed pots, some did laundry. Suds from the laundering trailed on the brown water far downstream. Other fishermen had distributed themselves along the banks. One group brought their equipment and refreshments in a two-wheel cart with automobile tires drawn by a shaggy pony. Vladimir put me at what he said was a good spot, but I was afraid I might hook the young men swimming in their undershorts nearby, and so I waded far out, mud squishing up into my sneakers and the lukewarm muddy water rising to my armpits. I cast and cast, using a spinner called an Abu-Reflex Shyster, which has brought me luck all over the United States and Canada, and eventually I caught a pike about sixteen inches long. I held it up and shouted to Vladimir, who looked back at me and smiled. Soon after that I saw him lift out of the water a pike longer than his arm. In the next half hour he caught another of about the same size.

Back at his house, he expertly butchered out the fish to filets, rubbed them with handfuls of coarse salt, and skewered them on sharp, thin pieces of wet cedar. He left the scales on and said cooking would burn them away. While he built a fire in a pit in his yard, Lizaveta gave us a tour of the house and garden. The house was a combination of wood-frame and logs, and it had nooks, lofts, and additions. A broad window above a desk in the study looked out on a wild panorama of river and sky. The study's built-in bookshelves held an extensive library; Lizaveta said she had a degree in geography from Irkutsk University. I noticed a many-volume set of Herman Melville in Russian, and *Never Cry Wolf* (*Ne Kri Volki*) by Farley Mowat. By my own unscientific reckoning, in Russia Farley Mowat is the most widely read recent English-language author. Everybody there seems to know *Ne Kri Volki*.

The family's garden was a wonder—raised beds, little wooden irriga-tion troughs, staked plants, trellises, sanded paths. All the fruits and veg-etables were small, because of the short growing season. The carrots and red raspberries and currants Lizaveta gave us to try had the explosive flavor of their intense, brief summer. Branches of a small tree hung heavy with just-ripened Siberian cherries. The Siberian cherry is about the size and color of a cough drop and has a small stone. At the gallery we'd vis-ited earlier in the day there had been a bowl of these cherries, and I had eaten them almost excessively.

For dinner we had Vladimir's fish, and tomatoes and carrots and cu-cumbers from the garden, and boiled *omul'* with scallions, and pieces of chocolate we'd brought, and a Chinese white wine served in glasses with leaves painted on them. I tried to look engaged as unknown subjects were discussed around me. Lizaveta brought tea and homemade straw-berry jam, which was tastier, if possible, than the cherries. We sat out-side, ignoring the flies. The sun began to go down and the endless scenery before us came right up to our toes. In the near distance a cou-ple of guys on the riverbank horsed around. First they fished but didn't catch anything. Then they undressed to their shorts and swam, splashing and diving. Then one of them retrieved a bar of soap from his piled-up clothes and both had a thorough wash. Vladimir said the stouter of the two was the local Orthodox priest.

Vladimir and Lizaveta wanted me to sign a guest book, but they did not have it handy, and so brought me an invitation to the opening of a show of Vladimir's fur pictures, and I signed that. I wrote how much I had admired the pictures, and the Siberian cherries as well, and I added something self-congratulatory about how far away I was from home that they did not understand when Katya translated it.

On the drive back to the place where we were staying, the microbus quit after an hour or so and rolled to a stop. We got out in the northern twilight on a straight road of gray-brown gravel built up and graded through a dense, swampy forest of birch. I walked back and forth along the road for a while, and made a short detour down into the woods, just to see what it was like. There I had my first taste of Siberian mosquitoes, or vice versa. Alyosha took out a vehicle manual and pored over it. At one end of the road, a pale full moon rose. Then he removed the engine cover, laid his tools on the car seat, and went to work. The rest of us sat in the vehicle or on the road and talked. As the twilight imperceptibly darkened, the ratcheting of his wrenches and the murmur of our conversations were the only sounds.

Later that evening, everybody who had come with Sasha, except for Katya and me, had to go back to Ulan-Ude. Sasha left us some Chinese beer, and instructions about who would bring us back to the city. We had moved to a new resort, one that offered more privacy in the form of individual cabins and locks the size of stage props to secure their doors. This resort had a sand beach on Baikal and its own private spring of supposedly medicinal water that smelled of sulfur and iron. I was made a bit nervous, however, by the resort's manager, a large, blunt-featured man in a thigh-length sport shirt, and especially by his habit of carrying a Kalashnikov assault rifle everywhere he went. He carried it any old way, however he happened to have last picked it up—by the barrel, by the butt, by the strap—as if it were some miscellaneous object he was bringing in from the car. Once passing by the dining hall I saw him clearing tables after breakfast as his Kalashnikov leaned muzzle-down against the wall nearby. Also, several horses roamed the resort grounds, and they loved to knock their heads against the cabins. You'd be taking a nap and—*thunk*—the head of a horse just outside would hit the wall.

Alex arrived from Moscow, at last. He had gotten a ride from the Ulan-Ude airport with a young couple, friends of Sasha's. His exhibition had gone well, he had drunk cognac and slept on the plane, and he appeared in a remarkably untroubled mood. For a few days we walked on the beach, built fires there, took hikes in the woods. I had never seen a forest of such variety, with sky-high larches, rank on rank of birches, poplars four feet around, and an understory full of blueberry, currant, and red raspberry bushes, along with ferns of many kinds and mushrooms soggy with rainwater and shot through with worms. The food in the resort's dining room was neither good nor plentiful, so we added to it with fish Katya and I caught in a nearby river, the Maksimikha, using grasshoppers for bait. The fish were small, but wrapped in wet paper from Katya's sketchbook and baked in the coals of our beach fire, they tasted fine. While improvising a fishing pole for Katya from a willow sapling, I cut deep into the ball of my thumb with my barlow pocketknife, and I made a fuss about that.

(Considering the knife unlucky from then on, I wanted no more to do with it and gave it to Katya to keep permanently. For years she carried it with her. Then when she was on vacation in Barcelona, a thief grabbed her backpack and ran off with it, and the knife was inside. I had found the knife originally on the shore of Rock Creek, in western Montana. One of its blades had been stuck about half an inch into a log, and evidently it had been there for a good while, because the wood left a deep rust stain on the steel. I'd be curious to know where that peripatetic knife is now.)

Some nights Alex and Katya and I sat on the beach until late and talked about weighty questions. Alex expatiated on what a con job the art world was and said all of American modernism was the result of artists in the thirties and forties sleeping with Peggy Guggenheim. He proved, by arguments I can't reproduce, that Picasso was the worst artist of the twentieth century. Katya said it had been strange to see Russian friends again. She remembered when it became fashionable among her friends to take up religion in the waning days of communism, sort of as a defiant alternative; now she believed that religion had ruined the lives of some of them and had caused them to have too many children and do other constraining things. She said she feared religion and looked on its continuing revival in Russia with dread. She had decided, she said, that she didn't believe in God, but in a basic goodness in people. I said maybe that was the same thing.

In the middle of the discussion, a drunk came out of the darkness holding a big fish he wanted to trade for vodka. But we had only Chinese beer, and he didn't want beer.

I never did figure out what was up with that resort. Someone who worked at it told Katya many mafia came there. The oddness of the owner seemed to bear that out, as did some crude wooden mannequins dressed in shirts and trousers that we found in the forest; they had been thoroughly blasted with double-aught buckshot at close range. This made me think my nervousness was justified, and the place lacked any redeeming higher qualities. But one afternoon I came into the dining hall to get some boiled water for drinking, and the VCR was playing *V. I. Warshawski*, a detective movie starring Kathleen Turner, on the extra-large-screen TV. The movie had just ended and the credits were scrolling on a background of bright blue. As the movie's theme music

rose, a girl of about ten who was standing in front of the screen and staring at it began to dance to the theme music. The few people in the dining room drinking tea paid no attention, but I watched as she stepped
and pirouetted in the blue light of the TV screen. The smells from the
kitchen, the Russian voices, the American music, all hung suspended for
a moment around the dancing of the girl. Another perhaps overgeneral-
ized fact about Russians is this: Russians can really dance.

The whole time at that resort and at the one before it, I barely noticed Lake Baikal. I had heard that it was beautiful; I looked at it once or
twice and said, "Yes, beautiful," and that was it. Luckily I would see Baikal again. But now, as it happened, I was due to teach a workshop in
Montana in a few days, so I had to go. One morning I left a lot of my
fishing stuff with Katya, said goodbye and many thanks to her and to
Alex, and rode back to Ulan-Ude with the same young couple who had
brought Alex from there. For some reason the drive down to the city
was no problem compared to the bumpy and dusty journey the other
way. My plane would leave the next evening. I spent my final night in
Ulan-Ude at Sasha's apartment. For dinner, his wife, Tania, again made
pozhe, and this time, eating without the distractions of cultural confusion
and jet lag, I understood that it is one of the great dishes of the world.

Before and after dinner, Sasha and I had a conversation about literature that went surprisingly far, considering my complete lack of Russian
and the limitations of his spoken English. Like many educated Russians,
he had read most of his country's literature and a lot of ours. One by one,
he showed me his collection of American writers, taking the volumes
down carefully from his shelves: Frost, Kerouac, Hemingway, Melville,
Thomas Wolfe. He said Wolfe was his favorite because he gave much
more the flavor of being American. Sasha had translated many poems of
Frost's. He said that his favorite writer in any language was an early
twentieth-century poet named Velimir Khlebnikov. When I admitted
I had never heard of Khlebnikov, he fell into sadness and almost began
to grieve, shaking his head and saying what a pity that was.

I could see that Sasha would have been a good friend to have in
school; he understood what was going on even without words, he laughed
to himself about the ridiculousness of life, and he had no desire to push
anybody around. The only time I saw him in a coercive frame of mind
was for a few minutes the next day, before he took me to the airport,

when we stopped at the post office to buy postcards. I found one I liked—it showed a red bus and a yellow bus going by Ulan-Ude's central square—because it reminded me exactly of Cleveland, Ohio, when I was a boy. I tried to buy every copy the post office had, and Sasha, perhaps thinking my interest in the card campy and ironical (as I guess it sort of was), hustled me from the post office before I'd bought more than a dozen or so.

My ignorance of Khlebnikov seemed to shake his view of the world. How could such a great Russian poet be unknown in the United States? After our first conversation about Khlebnikov, he mentioned his disappointment and puzzlement a few times more. I felt bad about this, so when I returned I looked up the works of Khlebnikov in the New York Public Library. Most of its books by him were in Russian, and I sat down with a small volume of his verse from the early 1900s to see what I could make of it using a Russian-English dictionary. The success of my attempt can be imagined. Today I can tell you Khlebnikov's years of birth and death (1885–1922) but not much more. Russian friends have said he often uses obscure language and colloquialisms, and is hard to translate even for someone who knows how. I still remain convinced that there must be something great about Khlebnikov, based on the passion that Sasha had.

My trip back to Moscow went off without complications, luckily. When the ticket taker at the Omsk airport briefly questioned the Omsk–Moscow leg of my ticket, I glimpsed the complete nowhere in which I would have found myself had any explanation been required of me. In Moscow, Stas picked me up at the airport and took me again to the apartment of the ever-kind Chuda and Kolya, who must've had about fifty houseguests that summer. Being now mostly without translators among all-Russian speakers threw me even farther into shock. Chuda later told Katya I had looked panicked and pale. At my departure for New York, Stas drove me to Sheremetyevo Airport and explained (I think) in careful detail what I should do at the customs inspection if they asked about silver jewelry I'd bought in Ulan-Ude. When I didn't understand, he explained more slowly and carefully than before.

On the flight from Helsinki to New York, I sat next to a Swedish building contractor. Previously I had heard Swedish accents only in movies or comedy routines, and had half doubted that such an accent could

be real. This contractor was big and curly haired, with a single uninterrupted eyebrow. He told me stories of the building trade, and when descriptions of distance were required he tried to be as accurate as possible.
He would stop, think, and then say that so-and-so had been about as far
as from us to the cabin's movie screen, or to a particular seat three rows
away. A Haitian taxi driver brought me from Kennedy Airport to Brooklyn and home. Because of stomach trouble, I had been eating nothing
but black bread and tea for the last few days. When I told the Haitian
this and described my many meals of only bread and tea, he shook his
head repeatedly and expressed his sympathy. While we were stopped at
a cash machine so I could get the money to pay him, the driver went
across the street to a Baskin-Robbins and bought himself the largest ice
cream sundae they had.

In my adult life, no trip had ever made such a change in me. I couldn't
get over where I'd been and what I'd seen. I talked about the trip a lot,
and when Alex and Katya came back I sat around with them and re-
viewed it down to the smallest detail. I began to read all kinds of books
about Russia, at first ones about Lenin, and then moving on to Russian
authors—Zoshchenko, Kharms, Bulgakov, and others—I hadn't heard of
before. I found a recently emigrated tutor in Brighton Beach and went
back and forth on the subway in order to study Russian with her. I started
putting notes about Siberia in folders. In a sense, this book is the distant
result of an initiative for cross-cultural exchange proposed originally by
Sasha Khamarkhanov of the Ministry of Culture of Buryatia in 1993.

Chapter 4

One of my all-time heroes is a man I consider almost a relative, George Kennan. I'm not talking about George Frost Kennan, who died in 2005 at the age of a hundred and one. George Frost Kennan was a diplomat, an author, an expert on Russia, and the main architect of the policy of containment used against the Soviet Union during the Cold War. I admire him, but I think the other George Kennan, who I sometimes call the original George Kennan, was a cooler and wilder guy. The original George Kennan was born on February 16, 1845, in Norwalk, Ohio. The reason I feel I'm almost related to him is that many of my relatives on my father's side back to 1815 lived in that town. It's safe to say that most of them from there knew or knew of George Kennan. A relative named Sam Wildman was George's childhood friend. My three-greats grandfather, the editor of the local paper, was George Kennan's first publisher. And some years ago, when I was interviewing a very old and distant cousin named Winthrop Wickham (born 1901), he told me that as a boy he took piano lessons from George Kennan's sister. Some people who you read about you have a special affinity for; George Kennan I feel I know to the cowlick in his hair.

George Kennan, small-town Ohio boy, who Norwalk old-timers remembered getting a whipping from his father under the apple tree in the family's backyard or walking along Main Street from the telegraph office to the newspaper with the latest dispatches in his hand, went on to become the most famous Siberian traveler of the nineteenth century. Indeed, to this day, no traveler in Siberia has made a reputation to compare with Kennan's. It happened like this:

In 1828, a man named John Kennan came to Norwalk to take the job of principal of the Norwalk Academy. Ohio had been a near wilderness just a dozen years before, and the local boosters hoped that a good secondary school would add distinction and substance to their town. A Vermonter by way of New York State, John Kennan had recently graduated from Hamilton College. The year after he arrived, he married a Norwalk girl, Mary Ann Morse. They would have six children, of whom George would be the second youngest. John Kennan was of a type common on the frontier in that he tried many careers. He soon quit being principal, then opened a law office, ran a daguerreotype parlor, served as county auditor, put out a short-lived newspaper, and in the 1840s became fascinated with the telegraph, which was just beginning to spread itself across the country. After the line reached Norwalk, John was hired as the town's Western Union operator, a post he held for years.

John's enthusiasms included a weakness for bad investments. Eventually the family's finances declined to the point that George, who had shown an aptitude for the telegraph since he was small, left school at the age of twelve to help out at the telegraph office full-time. When the Civil War started, George's youth and physical frailness kept him at home, but he did participate through the telegraph, that war's essential mode of communication. In a letter of February 1862, Lucy Preston Wickham, one of the matriarchs of the town (and my three-greats grandmother), wrote, "George Kennan has just received a dispatch that Fort Donelson has been taken." For my ancestors, all of them vigorous supporters of Lincoln and the Union, the fall of Fort Donelson was the first substantial good tidings in the war, and seventeen-year-old George was its bearer. As the first to hear important news, and especially to take down the fearful lists of casualties—Norwalk lost many boys in the war—the Kennans became figures of some moment in town. George's skill at telegraphy soon won him promotions and transfers through the ranks of Western Union. He was sent to Cleveland, to Columbus, and to West Virginia. By the time he was nineteen he had been made an operator at the Military Telegraph Corps's central Midwestern station in Cincinnati.

Elsewhere, in the big picture, telegraph technology of that era had hit an obstacle. Wires had proved cheap and easy to string on land and had quickly crossed North America. Crossing the Atlantic Ocean to Europe, however, presented a tougher challenge. In 1858, a competitor of Western Union had tried to lay an underwater cable from Newfoundland to Ireland, but it broke. As an alternative, Perry McDonough Collins, an energetic American entrepreneur and promoter of the advantages of trade with Russia, proposed linking America to Europe by running a line to Alaska, across the Bering Strait (a much shorter and shallower water crossing), through Siberia, and onward to the west. The Russian government went for the idea and gave the necessary permissions and promises of help. Western Union liked the plan, too, and in 1864 acquired Collins's rights-of-way. As soon as George Kennan learned of this development, he wrote to his top superior and asked if he could join the expedition to survey and build the line.

In late September 1864, Kennan received a response asking if he could be ready to go to Alaska in two weeks. He had been declining mentally and physically in Cincinnati under the pressures of wartime telegraphy; he cabled back that he could be ready in two hours. Unfortunately, he then came down with typhoid fever and had to return to Norwalk to recuperate. His parents, still worried about his health, hesitated to give permission for him to go, but finally they did. Kennan sailed from New York to San Francisco in December, spent some months there, and in July 1865 embarked on a small Russian vessel bound for Kamchatka. By November he was driving dog teams across the tundra. He had not yet turned twenty-one years old.

Seldom has a trip had greater consequences. Work on the telegraph project was divided among a number of detachments, each assigned a section of the line. Kennan's party—four men, under the command of a Russian nobleman and major, Sergei Abaza—had to find a route and construct it over about eighteen hundred miles of tundra and forest between the Bering Strait and the mouth of the Amur River. To cover the territory, the party further split up into individuals or groups of two. Sometimes Kennan spent months by himself with just an interpreter and Korak or Yakut guides. His main responsibility was a five-hundred-mile stretch between the Anadyr River and the northern coast of the Sea of Okhotsk.

Much of what we know about the expedition comes from a book Kennan wrote, *Tent Life in Siberia, Adventures Among the Koraks and Other Tribes in Kamchatka and Northern Asia* (1870), a lively account whose good literary quality testifies to the soundness of the Norwalk primary schools, the author's only formal education. In *Tent Life*, Kennan dodges danger and has adventures of thrillingness or awfulness on almost every other page. We see him galloping along a Kamchatka beach in a race with the incoming tide for thirty miles fenced in by sheer cliffs, and climbing into reindeer-herder dwellings that can be entered only by the chimney hole, and being dragged nearly to his death by a runaway horse, and dancing with every woman at a ball in the Siberian village of Anadyrsk in the middle of winter, and almost losing his life when a small sailboat he's in becomes dismasted in the Sea of Okhotsk, and battling flights of mosquitoes that turned the tundra sky gray, and enduring a dogsled journey so cold and grueling that one of his comrades, having survived it, shot himself soon afterward. Despite all difficulties, Kennan's team made good progress, and eventually had poles and supplies in place to begin building the line.

Then in late May 1867, after two full winters in Siberia, Kennan and his coworkers learned from the captain of a New Bedford whaling ship coasting along the Sea of Okhotsk that a new Atlantic cable had been laid the year before. "Does it work?" Kennan asked with trepidation. "Works like a snatch tackle," the captain cheerfully replied. Not only that, but the previous, broken cable had been fished up and repaired, and it now was working, too. Kennan and the others understood what this meant. Some weeks later a Russian-American Telegraph Company ship arrived in the Sea of Okhotsk with the official announcement that the project had been abandoned and instructions that the parties in the field sell off all supplies, pay the remaining debts, and disband.

Kennan wound up the last of his business in the region and started for home across Siberia. First he traversed fifteen hundred miles of roadless wilderness to Yakutsk, then went by river to Irkutsk. In Irkutsk his route would join the Siberian Trakt, Russia's great trans-Asian road for mail, goods caravans, prisoners, and exiles. Irkutsk and its attractions—the city was then known as "the Paris of Siberia"—appealed to him, so he stayed awhile. There's no single moment in *Tent Life* when an overwhelming love of Russia bowls Kennan over, as it would later do under different circumstances to John Reed. Rather, throughout the book you sense Kennan's engagement with the country and affection for it growing as he goes. He admires unreservedly his superior, Major Abaza, a brave and funny guy, and describes the wilder-than-wild Siberian scenery with a grim relish, and gets a kick out of changing his worn-out American clothes for the hides and furs of the tundra. When he scandalizes the beautiful ladies at fancy dress balls in Irkutsk with his sled-driver version of the Russian language, he is definitely having a good time.

The book mostly omits the rest of Kennan's trip and concludes with him in St. Petersburg. Elsewhere he would describe how palatial and gilded and massive he found the city, with its extraordinary music and the sleighs dashing along the Neva and so on, all of it leaving him "in a state of boyish wonder." In a letter from St. Petersburg to his parents, he wrote of the city's sights, "You can imagine what an effect they produced upon me coming from the desolate steppes of Siberia." (And therein resides a truth: St. Petersburg looks most like itself not when you come to it from the West, an approach that might lead you to think St. Petersburg is merely the West's imitation; to be affected properly by St. Petersburg you must arrive from the vast East, where you have already conjured the city in your imagination over the course of four thousand desolate Siberian miles.)

By April 1868, Kennan was back in Norwalk. Since he had last been home three and a half years had gone by. Perhaps he felt strange, restored to his family and once again in his original town. He soon discovered that there really was not a lot for him to do. He tried being a traveling schoolbook salesman for a while. One career that no longer interested him was telegraphy; he had done all the sitting at a telegraph key that he wanted to. A few of the letters he had written to his family about the expedition had appeared in the *Norwalk Reflector*, and readers had praised them. Maybe writing was what he should do. At his father's law office in the Whittlesey Building in the center of town, George worked on *Tent Life*. Back then, travelers with interesting stories to tell made their money not so much by writing as by lecturing. Starting in 1869, Kennan explored the Midwestern lecture circuit that brought speakers to cities and rural towns. He gave his first Siberia lecture to a gathering of about fifty farmers and their wives in a church in the neighboring hamlet of Monroeville, down the road from Norwalk about seven miles.

. . .

In Russia, meanwhile, dedicated young people kept trying to kill the tsar. As a teenager, Tsar Alexander II had been the most beloved Romanov ever. On a grand tour he made as tsarevitch in 1837 at the age of nineteen, the people were smitten by his handsome bearing, his dark, liquid eyes, and the aura of hope he emanated. Across the empire, even in Siberia (where no member of the Imperial family had ever been), weeping, cheering throngs ran after his carriage. Alexander assumed the throne in 1855, and in 1861, as progressive Russians had been urging (when they dared) since the reign of Catherine the Great, he ended serfdom by freeing forty-eight million serfs from their bondage to the government or private landowners. The monumental nature of this act—the American Civil War freed a mere four million slaves—led to equally big problems, mostly having to do with the redistribution of land. The land problem was, basically, never solved.

In fact, by the time of Alexander II, Russia had become such a mess, with corruption and systematic repression and avoidance of policy questions neglected for generations already, that it's hard to see how any tsar would have known what to do. In his frustration, Alexander retreated to autocracy, believing finally that the mystical veneration of the people for their autocrat provided Russia's foundation. As reformers saw that he wouldn't change, and popular disappointment increased, he grew to be more hated than he had been loved.

Acts of antigovernment violence and terror soon became almost commonplace. In 1866, a young man named D. V. Karakozov fired point-blank at Alexander but missed. The American government, remembering Lincoln, sent a delegation to Russia to congratulate the tsar on his miraculous escape—but later did not repeat the gesture, due to redundancy. Other young men took shots at Alexander. In 1879, a member of the Land and Freedom Party fired five times at him; he again survived unhit. Other revolutionaries tried to derail his train. In February 1880, a conspiracy of violent radicals used inside contacts to plant a bomb in the Winter Palace in a room below a banquet hall, but unfortunately (from the conspirators' viewpoint) the bomb exploded before the dinner it was to disrupt took place.

Finally, on March 31, 1881, a terrorist from the People's Will movement, which was a more violent offshoot of Land and Freedom, threw a bomb at the tsar's carriage as it went along a street in St. Petersburg. The

bomb killed some bystanders and Cossack guards but did not injure the
tsar. Alexander, who by now was probably getting tired of this, stepped
down from his damaged carriage to see how his coachman was. When
he did, a Polish student named Grinevitsky, an accomplice of the first
bomber, emerged from the crowd, threw another bomb, and blew the
tsar apart.

His successor, Alexander III, responded as one would expect, by
making the government far more repressive than it had been already. No
one ever accused Alexander III of seeking popularity; all notion of reform was set aside, and emergency rule was declared in Moscow and
St. Petersburg and other places, suspending if necessary civil liberties
and the courts. That edict would remain in force until the upheaval of
1917. Under the new regime, arrests went way up, especially of young
people who might conceivably be revolutionaries. Police pulled them in
for plotting assassinations, for being present at meetings where authors
such as John Stuart Mill and Herbert Spencer were discussed, and for
offenses in between. Many ended up in Siberia under long sentences of
prison labor or administrative exile.

Tent Life in Siberia remained in print during these years. It did well
with critics and the public and even received some favorable notice in
Russia. The book, and Kennan's widening recognition as a lecturer, put
him at the top of American experts on Russia, the Arctic, and Siberia—
admittedly not a crowded category at the time. In his thirties he made
more trips to Russia (though not, then, to Siberia) and wrote articles for
newspapers and magazines. But the Russia beat did not provide him
with steady income, and so, like his father, he tried various jobs. His
brother John had a bank in Medina, New York, and Kennan worked
there. He then got a position in the legal department of the Mutual Life
Insurance Company in New York City. He had married in 1879 but he
and his wife had no children. Other members of his family kept needing
money, though, and he helped them. Abruptly leaving Mutual Life and
New York, he took a job with the Associated Press in Washington, D.C.;
there he found himself suited to daily journalism and he stayed with the
AP for more than ten years.

As America was recovering from the Civil War, it seemed unusually
disposed to daydream about places far away. In 1879, James Gordon
Bennett of *The New York Herald*, the same man who had sent Henry

Stanley to Africa in search of Dr. Livingstone, sponsored a voyage of a ship called the *Jeannette* to find the North Pole. Unlike Stanley, the *Jeannette* failed in her objective; she became frozen in sea ice north of the Siberian coast, drifted, broke up, and lost most of her men. A few survivors landed at the delta of the Lena River in 1881, from which after further hardship they eventually reached civilization and returned home. Continuing coverage of the fate of the *Jeannette* kept the idea of Siberia prominent in people's minds.

Newspapers regularly called on Kennan for advice and commentary when questions came up about Russia. Often he was asked about the Nihilists, a disturbing new phenomenon that sent half-pleasurable tremors down America's spine. The tone of Kennan's public discourse in those years was fully confident and scornful of any criticism of the Russian government. In his opinion, reports of the government's incompetence, and of its cruelty to Siberian prisoners and exiles, were worse than misinformed. In the early 1880s, he fought several battles in the editorial columns over these questions.

Because he thought a second book about Siberia would make the money he needed for his own financial security and that of his family, and because he believed that in Siberia he could talk to the frightening, fascinating Nihilists more easily than in Moscow or St. Petersburg, and because he wanted to see for himself how the Russians treated their exiles and prisoners, Kennan decided in 1884 to make an extended investigative tour. The *Century* magazine, circulation two hundred thousand, offered a contract of $6,000 for the articles he would write. His public championing of the Russian government meant that he had no trouble obtaining its official permission and letters of bona fides for the journey. He made a trip to St. Petersburg in early 1885 to set things up, came back, and in May set out again in the company of a traveling partner, George A. Frost, of Massachusetts, an artist who would do the illustrations of their journey. He had met Frost years ago on the telegraph expedition.

Kennan's first Siberian trip had been hard, but this one seriously challenged his health and shattered his nerves. Later he called it "the hardest journey and the most trying experience of my life." He and Frost covered eight thousand miles of Siberia visiting prisons, talking to prison officials, observing prisoners on the march or in transport barges or in the barracks or at work. The good credentials Kennan had been able to obtain from the government forestalled most interference from local officials and gave him a chance to visit political exiles of all kinds. Sometimes he and Frost traveled on the main road, the Siberian Trakt, and sometimes far off it, to places one could not reach today without helicopter assistance. They suffered from cold, lack of sleep, jolting of the wagons, poor food, and bugs. For almost four months, Kennan had bugs on his body or in his clothes. In the trans-Baikal city of Selenginsk, his face became so disfigured by bedbug bites that he was ashamed to go on the street.

None of these hardships wore him down as badly as did the constant exposure to human misery. He had started the journey ostensibly in sympathy with the government. A month or so into it he was wondering why a powerful country couldn't protect itself from shy young women seminarians of whatever political stripe without exiling them to the middle of an Asiatic desert. His progovernment sympathies reversed themselves, his indignation and painful empathy grew; hearing the exiles' tales he found himself weeping "almost for the first time since boyhood." Into this emotional fissure, the unhinging, reason-obscuring passion for Russia inserted its crowbar end. In *Tent Life*, Kennan had kept his tone jovial and wry throughout, but in *Siberia and the Exile System*, the book he wrote about this journey, strong feelings began to show, for example when he said of his meeting with the revolutionary (and terrorist) Katarina Breshkovskaya, "All my standards of courage, of fortitude, and of heroic self-sacrifice have been raised for all time, and raised by the hand of a woman."

Toward the end of *Siberia and the Exile System*, Kennan calls the revolutionaries he met in Siberia "the flower of Russian young manhood and young womanhood," and goes on, "I am linked to them only by the ties of sympathy, humanity, or friendship; but I wish that I were bound to them by the tie of kindred blood. I should be proud of them if they were my brothers and sisters, and so long as any of them live they may count upon me for any service that a brother can render."

Alongside his emotional involvement and growing fervor, Kennan kept his eye for Russian detail. He noticed the peddlers selling "strings of dried mushrooms, and cotton handkerchiefs stamped with railroad maps of Russia," and the outlandish colors the people loved (houses painted metallic green, shirts of violet and blue and crimson and purple and pink, gowns of lemon yellow, brightly colored fences even in graveyards), and the chained parties of convicts with one side of their heads shaved to identify them, their chains sounding like "the continuous jingling of innumerable bunches of keys," and the smell inside the prison barracks, a foulness so intense that the carbolic acid sprayed on him after he came out seemed like spirits of cologne by comparison, and the whitewashed wall around the barracks sleeping platform stained red by the blood of smashed bedbugs, and the glorious air of the steppes with its smell of wild honey, the carriage wheels crushing scores of flowers at every rotation.

Past Baikal, onward by horseback into untraveled places, Kennan and Frost continued to the farthest-flung exiles, finally reaching a remoteness known as the Kara mines, where prisoners and exiles in the dreariest of surroundings moiled in the silver diggings. Once when I was in Siberia and within (I thought) the vicinity of Kara, I looked it up on the map. No roads led to it; it really is the earth's end. Kennan found a few well-educated people there, and a copy of *Punch* in prison. Among the exiles he visited was a quiet, well-spoken young woman named Nathalie Armfeldt, who lived in a small room with her mother. Nathalie Armfeldt had been a friend of Tolstoy's, and she asked Kennan to see Tolstoy when he returned to western Russia and tell him what she was going through. Kennan promised he would. At Kara, Kennan and Frost had come to the turnaround. Kennan had been suffering for weeks with fever, and both men were weak and exhausted. From that point they retraced their steps, making their way back toward western Russia, encountering more physical and emotional trials. After much journeying, they gratefully boarded the train at its eastern terminus in the Ural city of Tyumen.

From Tyumen they went less strenuously to St. Petersburg, and thence to England. When Kennan's wife met him in London, he was so sunken-faced and wrinkled she hardly recognized him. Barely able to walk, he could "hardly express much joy at our meeting," she said. A doctor he saw feared Kennan would lose his mind.

Many observers of Russia in those days discussed the sad state of the country and debated (in the famous phrase) "what is to be done." Kennan's articles in the *Century*, appearing in nineteen consecutive issues starting in May 1888, poured a bucket of coal oil on those flames. Hundreds of thousands read the articles, or the book when it came out in 1891. In the auditoriums where Kennan lectured beginning in 1889, the crowds often were standing-room only. Democracy-loving Americans cheered for the success of the Russian revolutionaries, and opinion ran against the tsar's government so strongly that it enlisted anti-Kennan propagandists to counter the trend. People called Kennan's book "the *Uncle Tom's Cabin* of Siberian exile." In American cities, societies were established to encourage Russian freedom and to help Russian exiles, and Kennan traveled to speak before groups of prominent supporters of the cause. When he addressed the luminaries of the Washington Literary Society and vividly depicted the Russians' plight, Mark Twain, who was in attendance, stood up and said with tears in his eyes, "If dynamite is the only remedy for such conditions, then thank God for dynamite!"

Kennan kept his vow to Nathalie Armfeldt and spoke to Tolstoy about her troubles during a trip to Russia in 1886. Though he arrived unannounced, Tolstoy received him cordially, and the two talked from early morning until midnight, including during the evening when Tolstoy adjourned to his last and did his usual cobbling. The great man didn't want to hear about the Armfeldts, however. Nor would he listen to accounts of exile suffering, or look at manuscripts Kennan had brought to show him. Tolstoy said he felt sorry for the exiles but did not approve of their methods. "They had resorted, he said, to violence, and they must expect to suffer from violence," Kennan related in a footnote about the visit in *Siberia and the Exile System.*

But Tolstoy didn't forget Kennan, and he read his articles in the *Century* when they were smuggled into Russia. What Kennan had to report about the exiles and prisons aroused him to "terrible indignation and horror," Tolstoy wrote in his journal. Reading Kennan also inspired Tolstoy in his long piece of later fiction, *Resurrection*, which in an early draft has an Englishman who travels in Siberia in the attempt to refute Kennan.

Another Russian writer affected by Kennan's work was Anton Chekhov. Soon after the articles began appearing in the *Century*, Chekhov decided to make a journey to the Siberian prison island of Sakhalin and examine the conditions there. In the introduction to the book Chekhov wrote about the Sakhalin journey, he said that he did not intend to make the kind of study Kennan had done. Oddly, Chekhov's book is not nearly as good as Kennan's, and probably would not be known today had it been written by somebody other than one of the greatest short-story writers and playwrights of all time. Critics have wondered why Chekhov undertook this terrible journey, which occupied most of 1890 and exceeded the limits of his strength and no doubt shortened his life. For lack of a better, I offer this ham-fisted psychological explanation: Chekhov's beloved brother Nikolai had just died; Chekhov read or heard about the investigations of Kennan; weighed down by survivor's guilt, he resolved to use his art for the betterment of suffering humanity. Chekhov's Sakhalin trip, one may argue, is the only known instance of a Russian writer sending *himself* to Siberia.

After John Kennan moved to Norwalk in 1828, his two brothers, Jairus and George, came west also. Jairus settled in Norwalk and raised a family. Brother George continued farther, to the Wisconsin frontier, where he stopped at the town of Menasha. From him a Wisconsin branch of the Kennan family descends. The Wisconsin George Kennan had a son Thomas who had a son Kossuth. In Milwaukee in 1904, Kossuth and his wife, Sophie, had a son they named George Frost Kennan, in honor of his famous Siberian-traveler relative (the baby's first cousin twice removed, technically). By coincidence, George Frost Kennan was born on February 16, his namesake's birthday.

George Frost Kennan grew up to be a public figure so perspicacious and levelheaded that the twentieth century hardly knew what to do with him. He kept giving good advice and speaking the truth, often reviled or ignored, as events tumbled forward around him. He graduated from Princeton, joined the Foreign Service, observed the rise of Nazism from his posting in Berlin, and spent six months interned there after the United States and Germany went to war. When peace arrived, he helped design Allied policy for Europe and became deputy chief of the U.S. embassy in Moscow. A long memo he sent by telegram, later published anonymously in *Foreign Affairs*, provided the basis for NATO's policy of containment, the anti-Soviet strategy pursued in various forms throughout the Cold War. As a State Department official in Washington, he saw the approach of the Korean War and offered sound suggestions (unheeded) for avoiding it.

Appointed ambassador to the Soviet Union in 1951, he later made some overly frank comments about the virtual "house arrest" restrictions he and his family had to endure in Moscow, a misstep that led to the Soviets banning him from the country. Ill-suitedness to bureaucracy in general caused him to leave the foreign service for a position at the Institute for Advanced Study in Princeton, New Jersey, where he lectured and wrote voluminously for decades. Before almost anybody in the policy establishment, he knew America shouldn't be in Vietnam, and he stated his opinion publicly. At the age of ninety-eight he advised against the second invasion of Iraq. In his later years, an ability to restrain himself from constantly saying "I told you so" must be numbered among his most remarkable qualities.

He and the original George Kennan met only once, though their life spans had an overlap of twenty years. According to George F. Kennan's recollection, as a boy he was brought to meet his famous cousin; but the Siberian traveler, and especially his wife, were unwelcoming. Perhaps they feared making the acquaintance of more relatives in need of money. Afterward, the boy wrote a thank-you note to the Kennans, and was stung, he said, by Mrs. Kennan's opinion that it was the worst thank-you note she had ever received. Boy and man did not cross paths again.

The admiration George Frost Kennan had for his famous cousin remained great all the same. "I feel that I was in some strange way destined to carry forward as best I could the work of my distinguished and respected namesake," he wrote in his memoirs. "What I have tried to do in life is, I suspect, just the sort of thing the latter would have liked a son of his to try to do, had he had one." Being related to the traveler sometimes came in handy. During the younger Kennan's time in Soviet Russia, his name provided him a conversation starter with the old Bolsheviks who had survived. Mikhail Kalinin, a member of the Politburo and chairman of the Presidium of the Supreme Soviet under Stalin, told him that his relative's book about Siberian prisons "had been a veritable 'Bible' for the early revolutionists."

George F. Kennan did not lose his usual clear-sightedness when evaluating his adventurous relative, however. In 1958, the University of Chicago Press published an abridged edition of the 1891 two-volume *Siberia and the Exile System*, and George F. Kennan wrote the introduction. In it he talked about "the relationship of Kennan's work to the Russian political realities of the day." He referred to the wide diversity among the revolutionaries Kennan knew, and to Kennan's indiscriminate sympathy with them all. The fact that Kennan had claimed he wanted only to explain the terrorists cut no ice with his younger relative:

> One wonders today whether Kennan, moved as he was by the sufferings which befell these people in Siberia, took full account of the preposterous and indiscriminate campaign of terrorism they had waged against the government and of the extent to which they, by these reckless and certainly criminal actions, had provoked the regime and its police establishment to extremism of which many others, besides the terrorists themselves, were the victims. One wonders what would have been the effect in the United States of a secretly organized campaign of assassination of public officials comparable to that which was launched in Russia in the late 1870's.

One indeed might wonder how the original Kennan could not have seen what madmen (and -women) many of the revolutionaries were. A prominent émigré revolutionary with whom Kennan became friendly and whose agenda he tried to advance was Sergei Kravchinskii, known by the nom de guerre of Stepniak; Stepniak had personally assassinated the head of the tsar's secret police in 1878. Kennan welcomed Stepniak to America, raised money for him, introduced him around. As for the shy young women whose exile Kennan deplored, he must have been aware of individuals like (for example) Sophie Perovsky, involved in every one of the seven known attempts upon Alexander II's life by People's Will, the last made when she was still under thirty years old. And anyone who knew about Russia would have heard of Vera Zasulich, a woman from the lesser nobility who at the age of twenty-seven shot and mortally wounded General F. F. Trepov, military governor of St. Petersburg. Tried for the crime before a jury, she was acquitted and set free, her lawyer having argued that she acted politically and thus "had no personal interest in the crime." As terrorist violence accelerated toward the end of the nineteenth century, upward of four thousand local and national officials in Russia were pointlessly wounded and killed. You'd never guess that from reading Kennan.

But I don't really wonder at Kennan's credulity myself. I would have probably done the same as he did. In Siberia he was traveling far from home, in the cold, bugs chewing on him, misery all around. Americans believe in democracy and they like to fix things. There had to be a happy ending in here somewhere, some grounds for hope, a fair repayment for all the suffering he saw. Then in the middle of Siberia he met the idealistic young exiles; and Katarina Breshkovskaya said to him, "Mr. Kennan, we may die in exile, and our children may die in exile, and our children's children may die in exile, but something will come of it at last." Hearing that, of course anyone would say, "Yes!" And if at that moment you knew that Katarina Breshkovskaya had also smuggled bombs across the country, you might mentally push the fact to one side.

When Kennan set out on his journey to Siberian prisons in 1885, Joseph Vissarionovich Dzhugashvili, the future Stalin, was six years old. Vladimir Ilyich Ulyanov, the future Lenin, was fifteen. In 1887, while Kennan was preparing his articles for the *Century*, Alexander Ulyanov, Vladimir's older brother, a zoology student at Moscow University, pawned a gold medal he had won for his research on freshwater earthworms in order to buy dynamite, and then contributed the dynamite to fellow conspirators making a lead-pellet-and-strychnine bomb with which they hoped to kill Alexander III. Betrayed by an informer, Alexander Ulyanov and fifteen others were arrested. A court condemned five of them, including Ulyanov, to hang. Later the tsar offered to commute the death sentences if the perpetrators would say they were sorry and wouldn't do it again. Ulyanov and the other condemned men refused; Ulyanov explained that to say what he was required would be "hypocritical." And so Alexander Ulyanov and his comrades were hanged.

Did the tsar guess that the hanging of these young men would be an irrevocable step toward the end of his own line? Did he imagine that Alexander Ulyanov's little brother must be out there, getting stronger, aimed unstoppably at the next tsar? A police mug shot of the younger Ulyanov in his early twenties shows an implacably focused young face with no sense of humor at all. Perhaps the tsar suspected that something like Lenin awaited the Romanovs. A number of Russian thinkers knew disaster was on the way, as the sage Tolstoy saw that violence from violence grew. Everybody imagined too tamely and too small, however, and the wrath to come, like so much in Russia, turned out to be grotesquely large scale.

The original George Kennan's gift was not for prophecy. He had grown up in a young country pleased with the promising beginning it had made and eager to spread the good news of its political system. For Americans like Kennan, a hopeful future was unthinkingly assumed, leaving the present as the main item of business at hand. The American Revolution had been relatively benign; his view of Russian possibilities bent under the weight of his native optimism. The slippery Stepniak himself described Kennan as "deeply interested in the country [Russia], which he truly loves." But Russian politics and policy interested Kennan only on their surface. Better than any other American, or perhaps than any other non-Russian, Kennan registered the deeper Russian passions of his time.

The rest of Kennan's life is daunting to think about, as he continued his career as an expert on Russia through that murky and mad period in its history. For a few years after the publication of *Siberia and the Exile System*, the woes of multitudes seemed to cross his desk, with letters from exiles, requests for help, plans for escape or for entry into America. He spent a lot of his money on charitable projects and even had exiles staying at his house sometimes. By the mid-1890s, the excitement in America about Russian freedom and the Siberian exiles had tapered off, and his lecture bookings as well. Kennan's finances sometimes ran low. He wrote other articles and kept alert for opportunities. In 1901, he went back to Russia to collect information and was able to meet with liberals in St. Petersburg over a period of four weeks before the tsar's government found out and expelled him. THE FAMOUS NORWALKIAN— GEORGE KENNAN ORDERED TO LEAVE RUSSIA BY TEN O'CLOCK TONIGHT, the *Norwalk Reflector* blared; elsewhere it had proudly referred to him as THE PLUCKY AMERICAN WHO BEARDED THE CZAR IN HIS DEN.

Kennan's view of Russia in these years missed a lot, naturally. He never returned after his expulsion in 1901, so his news tended to be limited and out of date. When the tsar conceded in principle to government reforms in the October Manifesto in 1905, and events that would end in revolution gained a big lift of momentum, Kennan had reached the age of sixty. He seems never to have grasped the philosophy or appeal of Marxism; to appreciate that particular style of romance you needed a younger and more sophisticated sensibility, like John Reed's.

By the time of the Bolshevik revolution, Kennan was going on seventy-three. Like much of the world, he responded to this event with surprise and alarm. But the fact that he was old, possessed of fixed ideas, and increasingly conservative did not make him hopelessly wrong in his judgment of the Bolsheviks; on the contrary, he got them right at the first try. To him the Bolsheviks were a catastrophe unmitigated by anything, and he urged President Wilson's advisers, who periodically asked Kennan for counsel, to tell Wilson to oppose the Bolsheviks in any way he could, including militarily. Whatever were the emotions that had led him to overlook the crimes of the revolutionaries of his generation, these Bolshevik troublemakers young enough to be his sons or grandsons did not fool him at all.

In 1918, with much of Russia in armed resistance to the Bolshevik government, Wilson did order military intervention, but not in support of the goals advocated by Kennan. One expeditionary force, sent to Murmansk with the stated purpose of protecting Allied supplies from German capture, did join British and other troops in battling the Bolsheviks. A larger American force of twelve thousand men sent to eastern Siberia, however, attempted to remain neutral, pursuant to Wilson's idea that all warring parties in Russia, including the Bolsheviks, should sit down together and work out an agreement of some kind. The ridiculousness of this, given the Bolsheviks' ruthless methods and utter lack of compromise, drove Kennan up the wall. He protested and sent memos, to no avail. In the end, the net effect of U.S. and Allied intervention was to give the Bolsheviks a pretext for legitimacy without weakening them significantly either in the East or West. Most Allied troops had left Russian territory by the end of 1920, with the Bolsheviks solidly in control. That outcome probably would have been the same, intervention or no.

In later years, Kennan lived in Medina, New York, where he had once worked in his brother's bank and where his wife was from. But he always stayed in touch with his Ohio hometown, and he went back for visits. At his return to Norwalk for his sister's funeral in April 1923, the *Norwalk Reflector-Herald* did a story that laid on more rhetoric about him shaking the might of the Russian empire and the tsar putting a price on his head and so on. The story's quotes from Kennan sound aged and fond. He remembered the handwritten newspaper he put out with Sam Wildman when they were ten years old; the paper had three subscribers, he recalled, two of whom were himself and Sam. The *Reflector-Herald*'s reporter didn't ask and Kennan didn't say why he thought the dream of liberal democracy in Russia had so sadly failed. In anybody's life, plenty of dreams don't work out. He had gone on epic travels, he had written words that influenced Tolstoy and Chekhov, and he had helped shape tumultuous events on the other side of the world—not bad for a boy with a primary-school education from Norwalk, Ohio.

Chapter 5

For my own first solo trip to Siberia—unaccompanied by Russian friends—I decided to follow Kennan's earliest example and come at it from the West. Americans like to wester; but when you reach the Pacific, why stop there? If there's wilderness on the other side, might as well keep going. For starters I moved with my family from Brooklyn to Missoula, Montana. One reason I chose Missoula was that I had seen a brochure in the Missoula airport describing flights that Alaska Airlines had begun to make to the Russian Far East. Consulting the schedule, I saw I could fly from Missoula to Siberia with just one change of plane.

Not long after we moved, I read a story in the local newspaper about a recent evangelical meeting led by a traveling musician and preacher named Fred Brodin. Dr. Brodin is an Inuit whose grandfather was an Inuit from Siberia who crossed the Bering Strait and settled in Alaska in the early 1900s. The family still has relatives on the other side, and Dr. Brodin knows a lot about the region. The news story said that Dr. Brodin was raising money for an evangelizing expedition that would go by snowmobile across the frozen Bering Strait to native villages on the Siberian side. The boldness of this idea struck me, so I gave Dr. Brodin a call, and then drove down to see him in Kimberly, Idaho, where he lived. Dr. Brodin runs an organization called Indigenous Messengers International, which works to bring the Gospel to Inuit communities from Siberia to Greenland. He told me about that, and about the language problems involved—Siberian and Alaskan Inuits can talk to each other, but both have a harder time understanding Greenland Inuits—and about the up-coming snowmobile journey, which he said would go in February if they raised enough money and had thick enough ice.

A journey like the one planned had actually happened two winters before, though Dr. Brodin had not been on it. He said that five Quaker Eskimo missionaries had set out from the Alaskan village of Kotzebue and had driven west to the edge of Alaska, where a plane and then a Russian helicopter had ferried them and their snowmobiles across the strait. The helicopter set them down in Chukotka, the part of eastern-most Siberia that resembles a Rorschach-blot duplicate of Alaska. On Chukotka's Chukchi Peninsula, the men then made a thousand-mile cir-cuit by snowmobile, over the tundra from one native Siberian village to another.

Dr. Brodin told me that the leader of that trip was Robert Sheldon, a pastor in Anchorage and the superintendent of the Quaker Alaska Yearly Meeting. Robert Sheldon would be leading the next trip as well. Think-ing maybe I could go along, I asked Dr. Brodin to put me in touch with him, and he did. I flew up to Anchorage at my first opportunity.

Robert Sheldon turned out to be a powerfully built man of average height with sloping shoulders, short black hair that hugged his head like a bathing cap, and a mustache that went around his mouth and con-nected to a small beard. He had canny, humorous eyes; some pastors radiate naïveté, but Robert Sheldon seemed not at all that kind. Over breakfast one morning he described his trip to Chukotka. His compan-ions had been Roland Booth, pastor of the Friends Church in the village of Kivalina; Enoch Stalker, pastor of ditto in the village of Noatak; Nor-man Westdahl, a Quaker evangelist; and Rodney Jones, a student at the Friends Bible School. The group left from Kotzebue on February 22, 1993, driving five snowmobiles and towing sleds of fuel and supplies. They crossed Kotzebue Sound, went along the northern shore of the Seward Peninsula, and stopped at the village of Shishmaref because of a whiteout snowstorm. After a day or two they continued on to the village of Wales, at the peninsula's tip where the strait is narrowest.

Ice ridges and open water caused by currents between the continents made the strait impassable, so a twin-engine Beechcraft came to Wales, loaded men and sleds and snowmobiles (dismantled), and flew them twenty-three miles to the U.S. island of Little Diomede. That island is about a mile and a half from the Russian island of Big Diomede; the Russian-American border runs between. A little Eskimo village holds on to the western shore of Little Diomede. A Russian border post, invisible from the east except for a hut of a guard station, constitutes the only human occupation on Big Diomede.

Little Diomede has an ice runway in winter. The Beechcraft landed there, and then a Russian commercial helicopter—the fruit of complicated negotiations that had taken months—arrived. It packed the men and equipment into its large cargo hold and then flew west. Robert Sheldon said the entire round-trip fare for the Russian helicopter came to only $824.

Robert Sheldon kindly gave me a copy of the video he had made of the journey. The video's production values are shaky, but that only adds to its authority. At the beginning you see the five men and their wives and other relatives and friends in Kotzebue, a village of one-story houses, oil tanks, shipping containers, and dog pens linked by narrow paths in the snow. The men are lashing things to the sleds and smiling and blinking at the camera. Then they're sitting at a kitchen table eating scrambled eggs and pancakes; Robert Sheldon looks over his shoulder at the clock and says when they will go. Outside again, they pull on their long white parkas with fur around the hoods and cinch them behind. They say goodbye. Robert Sheldon's four-year-old son, Michael, has tears on his cheeks. The men jerk the starter ropes on their machines, swing aboard, and head off into the white yonder.

Snowflakes, close to the lens, then lots of white blankness and the pervasive chattering whine of the snow machines. Soon the men are in Wales; then they're airborne. A big moment comes—I pause the tape at this point—when the plane banks around Little Diomede and the camera sees Big Diomede for the first time. Impending out of the ice, the Russian island stands almost vertically, a rampart of rock and snow. The gloomiest and most Russian of minor chords, played by a full orchestra, would be appropriate here. Even a completely uninformed observer could not help but sense that at the icy shore of Big Diomede a major shift in philosophy begins.

The Siberian part of the Eskimos' journey, village to village on the Chukchi Peninsula, becomes sadder and darker the farther north they go. In the first village, Lorino, smiling kids sitting cross-legged in the

school gym hear their message and sing songs the Americans teach them.
But driving on in the Arctic night, the party comes across the vodka
wagon—big metal drums of vodka on sleds, behind Russian snow machines driven by itinerant vodka peddlers. In one or two of the northernmost villages, the population is so drunk that public assembly isn't possible,
and the Eskimos meet with villagers by twos and threes in their homes.

The whole journey lasted almost three weeks. At the end of the video,
the returning travelers are a few miles from Kotzebue when they see the
headlights of neighbors' vehicles lined up on the ice to welcome them.
The five men ride past the lights and then the scene shifts to indoors, as
they walk one by one through a front hallway and into a kitchen, unbuck-
ling and pulling off their several layers of outer clothes. Bravery and ac-
complishment radiate from them like heat. Robert Sheldon's little boy,
Michael, is now so happy he can't stop jumping up and down. Robert
Sheldon picks Michael up and holds him, then puts him back on the
floor, where he goes shouting and bouncing out of the frame.

As it happened, I never did go to Siberia by snowmobile. For reasons of
politics, money, and global climate change, the follow-up trip that Dr.
Brodin had been working on did not come to pass, and Robert Sheldon's
remarkable snowmobile journey remains the only one of its kind. But
after flying up to Alaska and talking to him, I modified my original plans
anyway. Something about the proximity of America to Siberia beguiled
me. I had not previously thought about the fact that the United States
and Russia share a border. In that part of the world you can be in one
country and then in the radically different other like slipping behind the
looking glass. Instead of making my first solo trip to Siberia in a long,
trans-Pacific swoop via Alaska Airlines, I decided to travel north, through
the former Russian America, and find out about crossing to Siberia there.

I ended up going to Alaska many times. On flights from Seattle to
Anchorage I always asked for a window seat on the right-hand side of the
plane, because from it (if the weather was clear) I could observe white
cruise ships on the deep blue of the Inland Passage, and the shrinking
bigness of the Hubbard Glacier (usually described as larger than Rhode
Island), and the delta of the Copper River with its glittering, complicated channels. I got to know the Anchorage airport well. In the big

hexagonal waiting room on Concourse B there is a mounted Kodiak bear on all fours next to a polar bear standing on its hind legs. Both bears look fierce, both are "record class" animals (according to the plaques), and both were killed by dentists.

In Anchorage, I came across books on Siberia I hadn't known about, many of them from the University of Alaska Press, as well as some obscure ones in the public library. In midwinter, when snow plowed up from the parking lots blocked the first-floor windows and a day from sunrise to sunset was just a few hours long, the whole dark world seemed to hover around the light on the page. At first I mainly read about the Bering expedition—how Vitus Bering led an expedition to the North Pacific in 1725, following the instruction of Peter the Great; how he was supposed to see if Asia and America were joined but did not sail far enough north to establish that for sure; and how he returned to Petersburg in 1730 only to be reproached by the authorities and sent back to try again. Crossing Siberia and sailing from Kamchatka a second time, he managed to reach the Alaskan coast in July 1740. Upon the first sighting of America his men congratulated him on his success, but Bering merely shrugged. He was becoming apathetic and strange. He turned back for home quickly, spending not even a night on the Alaskan mainland, thereby infuriating George Steller, the naturalist on board. Mishap then followed mishap for Bering. Almost everybody onboard, including him, got scurvy, the ship drifted helplessly, and finally it washed ashore on an island a few days' sail from Kamchatka. On that island, Bering died.

A team of Russian and American archaeologists began excavations on Commander Island (as it became known) in 1979. The Bering expedition had been a massive undertaking, involving thousands of people at its various stages, and it was well supplied, even oversupplied. A lot of the stuff Bering and his men had on the island was still there. The archaeologists found an optical lens from somebody's spectacles, and an iron rope-splicing tool, and sticks of sealing wax, and a silver kopek from the reign of Boris Godunov, and a bottle of turpentine, and four iron boarding axes, and flasks of pharmaceutical glass, and iron crampons for walking on ice, and a dog- or wolf skin with a crucifix sewn to it, and little iron hammers, and fragments of an hourglass, and a box of the type cannoneers wore for holding their fuses, and a large number of objects whose purposes were unknown.

In the roofed dugout Bering's men made for him, he lay on the floor, and the sand slid onto him. He said he didn't mind because it kept him warm. When he died he had to be dug up to be buried. In 1991, the archaeologists found his grave. He had been laid out facing east, Christian-fashion, with his head propped up against one end of the too-short coffin. He was five foot nine, slightly bowlegged, and in possession of all but six of his teeth. The archaeologists kept his skeleton whole, shrouded it in plaster, and sent it by ship to Petropavlovsk. From there it was flown to Moscow, speeding in hours over the Siberian expanses he had taken decades to cross and recross. In Moscow, scientists from the Research Institute of Criminal and Forensic Medicine examined the skeleton. After the studies were done, the skeleton retraced its route to Commander Island and was reinterred in a redug grave—all postmortem developments that probably would have been a surprise to the dour and incurious Vitus Bering.

Beyond Anchorage, I often continued another two hours by plane to the town of Nome, on the Alaskan coast where Norton Sound turns north to join the Bering Sea. I always looked forward to going there. Nome serves as a jumping-off point for destinations in Russia; the regional headquarters for U.S. Customs and Immigration are in Nome. Along the U.S.-Mexican border are numerous cities like Tijuana, and on the boundary between the United States and Canada you find many towns like International Falls, Minnesota. Nome owns the distinction of being the only U.S.-Russian border town.

During the early days after the fall of communism, when it looked as if a boom in Russian trade and tourism might replace the total shutdown of the border that had characterized the Cold War, some Nome businesses changed their signs to include both languages. Even today in Nome, a few remnant signs in Russian can be seen. In those heady years, some Nome merchants accepted payment in rubles, and when Russians did arrive these merchants amassed rubles by the sackful. Due to Russian currency laws, the bills turned out to be unredeemable. Now in Nome rubles are sometimes used as decorations, or are handed out to tourists as souvenirs. Also in the days of optimism, some men in Nome became aware of the short-skirted, high-heeled, thoroughly made-up Russian women who lived in Chukotka just a short flight away. That the women maintained this style even in the coldest weather won them much admiration. In time, international marriages resulted, and some Russian women relocated to Nome.

Nome does not go out of its way to be ingratiating. To an unromantic eye, the town in certain seasons may look like an expanse of mud with pieces of rusted iron sticking out of it. Trees in Nome are so rare that the town's official architectural walking tour features both of them; it is perhaps ungenerous to point out that in other places such landmarks would be considered shrubbery. During stays in Nome, I was usually depressed, in an uninterrupted and satisfying manner I never could have pulled off at home. Often I was waiting for a break in the weather so I could fly somewhere. I would emerge from my room in the Nome Nugget Motel in the morning to see what the chances were today, and I'd find the usual lowering, stormy sky draped above sea and land like a tent you have to hold up with your head to keep it from collapsing on you. On such days the best course was to return to the room, lie down, and stare up at the acoustical-tile ceiling.

Bering Sea waves the color of wet cement landed on the shoreline with dull thumps; rain slashed the windows. Eventually I would put on my rain gear and wander the town. Facing northwest on the beach—Nome's famed "Golden Sands," source of fortunes during the gold rush—I was looking directly toward Siberia. The border here is so unyielding, and the sea and sky and climate so forbidding in every way, it seemed that the line of the horizon, instead of being level, should go:

Nome is not the end of the road, because all roads connecting to anywhere have ended long before. The town is accessible only by ship, plane, or snow trail. The famous Iditarod dogsled race ends in Nome. Nome is the end, period. The whole continent, in a sense, makes a final diesel-fueled spasm in Nome. Its irregular waterfront lots accumulate crumbled-up Caterpillar treads, school bus hulks, twisted scaffolding in rats'-nest heaps, rusted gold dredges, busted paddle wheels, crunched pallets, hyperextended recliner chairs, skewed all-terrain vehicle frames, mashed wooden dogsleds, multicolored nylon cable exploded to pompoms, door-sprung ambulance vans, dinged fuel tanks, shot clutch plates, run-over corrugated pipe, bent I beams, bent rebars, bent vents. The pileup at land's end is almost audible, as if you could still hear the echoes of the cascade from the continental closet where all of it once was stored.

In general, people in Nome have time to talk. On my first visit, and often on later ones, I stopped in at a store on Nome's west side called Chukotka-Alaska, Inc. This store sells furs from Alaska and Russia (wolf, red fox, wolverine), Soviet army hats, Russian wood carvings (stork, moose), CDs of the Red Army chorus, etc. Behind the counter, among items and their price tags hanging around his head, sits the store's owner, Vic Goldsberry, a stocky, gray-haired man with a blunt nose.

Sensing my affection for Russia, Vic Goldsberry set out straightaway to disabuse me: "I don't think I'll be going over to Chukotka much anymore," he said. "In fact, I don't care if I never go over there again. Can't do honest business there. The governor of Chukotka just bought himself a one-point-three-million-dollar dacha in Miami Beach. He's already got a beautiful house in Anchorage and spends a lot of time there. He gave all his henchmen new Fords, so I don't think you'll hear them complaining, either. I just read in *Alaska Businessman* magazine that according to the Russian government, American businessmen won't have to pay bribes in Chukotka anymore—of course the person supposedly enforcing that is the governor's number-two man, who also spends a lot of time in Seattle, so we'll see what comes of that decree.

"It's not safe for a foreigner to travel in the Russian Far East. The governor has even said he doesn't want tourism, because tourists don't spend enough money. The only people the Russians want are Japanese nature-documentary crews, and there's an endless supply of them, and they don't blink at paying gigantic bribes. I never paid bribes, myself, and I resent people who do, because they're perpetuatin' the system. It won't really be possible to travel there until the system changes. Besides the Japanese, the only people who can travel there right now are criminals and missionaries. The criminals pay the bribes because they have no morals, and the missionaries pay because they think their higher purpose justifies the means.

"When the border first opened up after Gorbachev and everything a few years ago, you had thirty–forty flights a month from here to Provideniya and Anadyrsk, and people thought this border would become like the Canadian border. Now the bribery's got so bad—five hundred dollars and up just to get a visa—that the border's almost completely shut down. Customs and immigration here doesn't care about it and would like to close it and forget about it. Now there's maybe two–three flights a month, if that. The Russian Far East is a place without law and it's going to stay that way, far as I can see. Foreigners who go over there get beaten and robbed, Russians who live there get beaten and robbed. Some U.S. Coast Guard guys came in here last month. They'd been to Alaskan ports and then to the Russian Far East, and they said they were ashore somewhere on Sakhalin Island comin' back to the ship early one evening, not even drunk, when they met up with a big group of Russians who beat them senseless and took everything they had except their clothes. No law at all, just no law at all. Businessmen from other countries pay bribes up front and that gives 'em a competitive edge on Americans, because for us it's a federal crime to bribe a foreign official to do his job. Most travelers just accept the bribery, but that's not the kind of country we are—not yet, anyway. No, I won't do business that way."

The bell on the door jingled and an older couple I recognized from the motel came in. Like me they were grounded by weather and had taken a stroll. The woman said to Vic Goldsberry, "Oh, you have such beautiful furs here!"

"We have native crafts, books, and some Russian stuff," he said. "Everything here is one of a kind, and everything has its story."

"—And if it doesn't, you'll make one up!" the woman finished for him, cheerily.

Vic Goldsberry became grave. "No, ma'am," he said. "For that you'll have to go uptown."

The first time I went to the Chukotka-Alaska store, I bought an anthology of short works of Russian literature with notes in English for students. From the lessons I had taken at Brighton Beach, my Russian had improved enough that I could read some of the abridged stories, aided by the notes and glossary. The bad weather did not lift, so while the rain pelted I spent days on my bed at the Nome Nugget Motel slowly reading: first, "Taman'," by Lermontov, and then "Stantsionnyi Smotritel'" (The Stationmaster) and "Vystrel" (The Shot), by Pushkin.

Until then I had never got the point of Pushkin. Russians, of course, worship him, but I think I'm right in saying that he has not translated well to other languages, and thus remains above all a Russian poet. But for some reason, reading him there in the Nome Nugget—maybe because Russia was only a hop away, and Pushkin had promised that someday he would be read from one end of Russia to the other—I finally understood what was great about him, or thought I did. To explain, I have to describe the plot of "Vystrel." Russian readers who know the story, and those who do not wish its suspense ruined should they ever read it themselves, may skip the next few pages.

"Vystrel" is the story of a duel. Its main character is a strange, intense former army officer named Silvio. He lives in an out-of-the-way village where he often invites the officers of the local regiment to his quarters for supper, drinking, and cards. One of the officers is the narrator of the story. Silvio practices regularly with his pistols; the walls of his quarters are full of bullet holes from his target shooting. During a card game, a drunken officer insults Silvio. Everyone expects Silvio to challenge the officer to a duel, but he does not. The narrator cannot understand this, and although he had admired Silvio, after this incident he mentally dismisses him and considers Silvio's honor stained.

One day Silvio receives a letter that he reads to himself with great excitement. He then announces to the officers that he must leave the village right away, and he asks them to come over for a final evening at his place. Later, as his guests are departing, he takes the narrator aside and says he does not want him to have the wrong impression. He says he declined the duel with the drunken officer because he cannot risk his life until he finishes something he has to do. He then tells this story:

Some years before, when Silvio was still in the army, he developed a jealous antagonism against a fellow officer. The object of his jealousy was noble, rich, handsome, and gifted in every way. His witticisms were funnier than Silvio's. Women adored him. At a ball one evening, Silvio whispered a vile insult in this officer's ear, and the officer slapped him. A challenge was made and accepted, and a duel was arranged for the following morning.

Silvio showed up first, so upset and enraged he could hardly control his shooting hand. His antagonist, carefree as ever, arrived carrying his cap, which was full of fresh cherries. Winning the draw for first shot, the lighthearted young officer fired first and put a bullet through Silvio's cap.

(Here Silvio takes the cap from a box and shows it, and the bullet hole, to the narrator.) Then came Silvio's turn to shoot. As he sighted along his pistol, his enemy stood smiling, eating cherries from his cap and spitting the stones. Silvio stood for a moment, then lowered his gun. Depriving a person of life who had so little concern for it seemed pointless. Silvio told his enemy that he had decided not to fire just now; the young officer replied that Silvio was free to fire whenever he liked, and that he would be available at any future time Silvio chose.

Today (Silvio continues), he learned by letter that "a certain person" is about to marry a beautiful young girl. Silvio tells the narrator that he is leaving immediately to find his enemy—the "certain person"—and see if under his new circumstances he still does not care whether he lives or dies. At this point the carriage comes and Silvio rides off.

Time passes. The narrator retires from the service and is managing his estate in the country. He does not have much to occupy him socially, so when a countess comes to spend time at her estate not far away, the narrator goes to meet her. The countess is young and beautiful, and her handsome husband, the count, is a former army officer, thirty-two years old. The narrator is brought into the library, where he notices a painting on the wall with two bullet holes in it, one beside the other. He and the count begin talking about marksmanship. The narrator says the best shot he ever knew was a man named Silvio. The count says, "You knew Silvio!" The countess turns pale. The count tells the narrator this story:

He (the count) is indeed the same officer who had been the focus of Silvio's jealousy and had eaten cherries during their duel. Some years ago he and the countess married, and immediately afterward they came to stay at this estate. One afternoon they went for a ride. The countess's horse became balky, so the count rode home leading it, and she walked. When he got back he found Silvio in the library waiting for him. Silvio announced to the count that he had come at last to take his shot.

The count stood at one end of the room. Silvio paced off twelve steps and aimed. The count asked him to shoot quickly, before his wife returned. Silvio paused and said this seemed too much like murder. Another pistol was brought and loaded. They drew for the first shot. As in the first duel, the count won the draw. He fired at Silvio but missed and hit the painting.

Silvio aimed at the count. Just then the countess came in, saw what was going on, screamed, and clung to her husband's neck. Her husband told her not to worry, this was just a joke. Silvio said yes, this was much like jokes her husband enjoyed, slapping his face, shooting his hat, and shooting the painting just now. The countess threw herself at Silvio's feet. The count shouted at her to get up, wasn't she ashamed? After a moment, Silvio said that he had decided not to fire; now, he said, he was satisfied, having finally seen the count lose his nerve. Silvio turned to leave and, looking back, fired a shot through the painting right next to where the count's bullet had struck.

Nobody ever heard from Silvio again. Rumor said that he died in Greece while fighting in the revolution against the Turks.

I put the book down and went out into Nome's peculiar late-summer twilight. It arrived filtered through gray-white rain clouds that now were dropping a kind of floating mist. All the town's colors were gray's imitation of them—gray-red, gray-yellow, gray-blue—and yet the effect was still of twilight in summer, somehow. I'm not sure that the above summary of "Vystrel" makes it clear why Pushkin was great. I know that when I finished the story I was convinced that Pushkin was one of the coolest people who ever lived. Later I learned that in an actual duel Pushkin fought, he ate cherries from his hat while waiting for his rival to fire, just as his character does.

Across the street and a few blocks up from the motel, a neon Kirin Beer sign glowed fuzzily and vividly. The sign indicated the Szechwan restaurant where I ate most evenings. The place had good hot-and-sour soup, spicy double-sautéed pork, and a large television set that remained on all the time. I went in, sat, ordered. As I ate, I thought about Pushkin and watched network TV stars compete in group sporting events. One of the groups competing was Team Baywatch. Though I was, to outward appearances, still depressed, I had in some sense never been happier.

On the sidewalk on my way back, I passed several Native kids standing around by their bicycles and talking. A Native girl with frosted tips on her ginger-colored hair said to a slim boy, "I heard you were in an accident and had to be medevacked out."

"Yeah," the boy replied modestly. After a pause he added, "It was pretty cool."

· · ·

Another means of passing the time while socked in in Nome was to visit the office of the Chamber of Commerce on Front Street and read the local news stories it had collected in a file labeled RUSSIAN EVENTS. Many of these stories had to do with the adventurous or crazy people who travel through Nome en route (successfully or not) to or from the Russian side. Not many of the items predated 1987, the year the cold-water swimmer Lynne Cox swam the Bering Strait between the Diomede Islands and became the first American to legally visit Big Diomede since J. Edgar Hoover sealed the border in 1948. Her two-and-a-half-hour swim in 44° water left Lynne Cox more dead than alive when she reached Big Diomede. The feat attracted notice worldwide. At Gorbachev's historic meeting with Reagan in 1987, the Russian premier said that Lynne Cox's courage had shown Russians and Americans how close to each other they lived.

Item: Also around then, the ice in the strait froze thick enough that a Mexican illegal alien named Lazaro Castro, all on his own, was able to walk across. When he arrived in Big Diomede, the Russians arrested him, confined him, and afterward escorted him back to the United States, saying, "Next time . . . use the front door."

Item: In 1989, a joint U.S.-Soviet expedition traveled by dogsled and skis from Anadyr, on the Siberian coast, twelve hundred miles northeastward across the strait to the Alaskan North Slope and Kotzebue. The international trekking team then came to Nome. During a celebration marking the journey, two Soviet journalists, Anatoly Tkachenko and Alexander Genkin, defected to the United States at Little Diomede.

Item: In 1992, a doctor from Austin, Texas, looked into whether he could drive across the strait in his four-wheel-drive vehicle. And in 1996, Sir Ranulph Twisleton-Wykeham-Fiennes, an Englishman, listed in the 1984 *Guinness Book of World Records* as the "World's Greatest Living Explorer," announced that he would cross the strait on foot. (No follow-up, however, on how the plans of these two aspirants turned out.)

Item: In 1996, Dmitri Shparo, of Moscow, Soviet explorer and folk hero, winner of the Lenin Medal, became stranded with his two sons on an ice floe off the coast of Chukotka while attempting to cross the strait from Russia to America on skis. After extensive searches, a Coast Guard C-130 aircraft located the party, and a Russian helicopter rescued them from the floe. The next year Shparo and one son tried again, encountered better ice conditions, and crossed successfully to Alaska.

(During one of my later stays in Nome, I happened to be there at the same time as two young Englishmen who had built an amphibious vehicle in which they planned to go around the world. Because they imagined that the Bering Strait crossing would be a tricky leg of the venture, the Englishmen were trying out their vehicle first here. It was a kind of pickup truck on pontoons, with screws that looked like giant crayons on either side to power it through the water, and a paddle wheel arrangement on the front to help it, they said, "walk" from the water up onto any floating ice they encountered. They took the vehicle to Wales, drove off into the strait, failed to make sufficient headway, and soon became tightly frozen in ice fifty yards from shore. Eskimos from Wales cut them free with chain saws and hauled them back to land. When I saw the Englishmen on the streets of Nome in their bright red coats and black trousers, and they smiled by lifting their upper lips to expose their top teeth, I understood that *Monty Python's Flying Circus* had been simply a documentary.)

Most of the clippings in the "Russian Events" file were about the reopening of the border during the late Gorbachev and early Yeltsin years, and expressed the hopefulness of that time. In Wales, a sculptor named David Barr erected a big hand reaching toward the strait and Russia; he said he hoped to build an identical hand reaching toward America in the Russian coastal village of Uelen. In 1988, Alaska Airlines initiated its Russian Far East flights. That same year, a delegation of Alaskans journeyed to Provideniya on a "Friendship Flight," met Russian dignitaries, and discussed plans for Russian-American business cooperation. Delegations of Russians made return visits that year and in later ones. Bering Air, a small Nome airline, began flying to Chukotka in 1989. Trans-strait telephone connections, which previously had to go around the world to end up across the strait two hundred miles away, now were sent by a more direct route, via a switching station in Fairbanks and then a satellite.

Soviet Young Pioneers from Provideniya paid a visit to the Boy Scouts of Nome. A burn victim in Chukotka needing special medical care was flown to an Alaska hospital. People in Russia and Alaska began to discuss creating an intercontinental nature reserve to be called the Bering Strait Land Bridge Park. Basketball teams and dance groups from Chukotka came to Nome. Concerned citizens of Nome, learning of the hunger in parts of the Russian Far East, devised various projects for sending relief to their Russian neighbors. As the news stories moved closer in time to the present, however, the hope and anticipation evident in the events of the late 1980s seemed to have disappeared. The file contained no item later than 1995, presumably when the problems Vic Goldsberry had complained to me about became too great to ignore.

A story from *The Washington Post* of July 1, 1990, caught my attention. It mentioned the "palpable sense of giddiness" in the air in Nome since the border had been opened and quoted a lot from a Nome real-estate broker named Jim Stimpfle. He had all kinds of ideas. He described wonderful cruises from Nome to Chukotka that might be possible—a New Year's package, for example, in which celebrants would sail to Provideniya before the holiday, enjoy a New Year's Eve party in Russia, and then (thanks to the time change at the International Date Line, which here coincides with the Russian-American border) return to Nome for the repeat of New Year's Eve on the following day. Because of the ice conditions at that time of year, a Soviet icebreaker would be required, but that was a mere detail to Mr. Stimpfle. "Imagine," he told the *Post*, "you're soaking in a hot tub on the deck, sipping Stolichnaya and listening to the strains of Rimsky-Korsakoff. The Northern Lights are out. Polar bears are frolicking on the ice. And you are smashing your way to the Evil Empire. It's the last great trek on earth."

Somehow I got a feeling that in Mr. Stimpfle I had found a fellow sufferer of the dread Russia-love. I thought I should talk to this man. The lady in the Chamber of Commerce said that I might run into him in town anywhere and that he often had breakfast at Fat Freddy's, next door to my motel. On that first visit to Nome, I didn't see him, but on a later one, while eating reindeer sausage and eggs in Fat Freddy's, I heard a voice rise above the breakfast clatter, just as buoyant and visionary as it had sounded in the newspaper story.

I introduced myself, asked a few questions, and then hung out with Jim Stimpfle for a couple of days. Mostly we talked and drove around. I also helped him move some furniture. We went by his house and I met his wife, Bernadette, an Inupiat from King Island, and their three children. I accompanied him to the Nome City Jail—"voted the best jail in the United States by *Playboy* magazine," Stimpfle proudly informed me—so he could collect monthly rent from the warden, a house tenant of his. Stimpfle proved to be a rush-hour stampede of ideas for the betterment

of Nome and the improvement of relations across the strait. He looks a
lot like the German film director Erich von Stroheim. He has a thick
neck, a mostly bald head, and pale blue eyes that dart around in his glasses'
steel frames. He said, "I was named Alaskan of the Year by the Alaskan
Chamber of Commerce in 1989! But I've set my sights even higher!
I may be just a small-town Realtor, but I intend to win the Nobel Peace
Prize someday!" Stimpfle's laugh is a cackle of pure joy.

Born in Lenox Hill Hospital in New York City; father a dentist; raised
in Washington, D.C., area; graduated from George Mason University
with a degree in history, 1970; went through countercultural divagations
standard for the time; married; moved to Fairbanks; lived in a tent-
camper; had triplets (all boys); divorced; ex-wife went to work on the
Alaskan oil pipeline; Stimpfle stayed in Fairbanks; raised sons; worked as
janitor, forest-fire-fighter; trained as a drug and alcohol counselor (much
success at that; was told, "Jim, if you can talk a person out of drinking,
you certainly can talk him into buying a house"; agreed with this sentiment); met future wife, Bernadette, on a lunch line at the University of
Alaska when both were presenting educational programs; married Bernadette; got real estate license; moved to Nome and bought house in 1981.

Stimpfle had always wanted to be a diplomat; many of his father's
patients were diplomats in Washington. Thus, Stimpfle took great interest
in the first stirrings of Russian-American amity that began shortly after
he moved to Nome. When Lynne Cox swam the strait, Stimpfle managed
to be among the party accompanying her to Big Diomede, and there,
with the help of Alaskan Natives in the group, he made a lot of contacts
among Russian natives, and those led to communications with Soviet
mayors and other officials. Stimpfle wrote letters to people across the
strait and to officials in D.C. and received some replies. A man he knew
in the U.S. State Department said Stimpfle was having more luck getting
through to the Russians than official U.S. channels had achieved. The
"Friendship Flight" to Provideniya was largely Stimpfle's doing. In 1988,
he made a rousing speech before top management at Alaska Airlines on
the subject of why they should begin flying to the Russian Far East. The
airline decided he was right. (So, in a sense, it had been because of him
that I had happened to move to Missoula.)

Among Stimpfle's many visions for the future, three stood out. Having seen the failure of the Nome merchants' policy of accepting rubles

(he had accumulated, he said, fifty or sixty thousand worthless rubles himself), he thought travelers on both sides of the strait should use something called "smart cards," a kind of credit card able to exchange goods and services internationally, value for value, without any money changing hands. He explained this idea to me at length, but I never got my mind around how it would actually work. Eventually he admitted that his friends and family had grown so sick of hearing about smart cards that they begged him not to bring up the subject anymore.

Second, he touted the great regional benefits that would accrue from establishing an Alaskan-Chukotkan coastal and trans-strait ferry service. He said one of the small ships used for supply and transport to offshore oil-drilling platforms would be perfect for this ferry line. The ferry would go from community to community, carrying local passengers, bulk goods, and eco- or adventure travelers. The route would follow the Alaskan coast northward, cross to the Chukchi Peninsula, continue down the Russian coast, recross the strait, and begin the circuit again. He said he had talked to the Russian billionaire Roman Abramovich about the ferry idea, and Abramovich had asked him, "But Jim, will it make any money?"

The idea that gets Stimpfle the most het up concerns a proposed tunnel under the Bering Strait. One of the business cards he hands out identifies him as a director of the Interhemispheric Bering Strait Tunnel and Railroad Group. This trans-strait tunnel would be seventy-two miles long—only forty-one miles longer, Stimpfle points out, than the Chunnel between England and France. It would begin in the low mountain behind the village of Wales, seven miles back from the water, to achieve the proper slope, and would come out in Cape Dezhnev on the other side. Earthquakes would not be a problem for the tunnel, he said, because this is a seismically stable area, north of the Pacific Rim's high-quake Ring of Fire. And the Bering Strait tunnel, unlike the Chunnel, would need no lining, because it would go through granite all the way. Of course, extensive rail links would be required. Many billions of dollars would have to be spent, but that is not unthinkable when you consider the money governments throw around these days.

Stimpfle had driven us to the Nome dump to do one errand or another, and we had chatted for a while with dump manager Gary Hart. Then Stimpfle turned onto a high winding road in the hills above Nome, still talking about the tunnel. We stopped and got out on the tundra to better view the geography. "Asia's just over there!" he said, gesturing across the foggy strait. "Asia! The biggest continent, containing the largest population, in the entire world! If you had a Bering Strait tunnel, and railroad tracks to it and from it, think of the coal, the minerals, the grain you could move! Right now if you ship wheat from Kansas City to Bombay, it's going about twice the distance that it would be to send it through this tunnel. With this tunnel, a passenger, if he wanted, could travel on trains the entire way across North America and across Siberia from New York City clear to London around four-fifths of the world!"

Stimpfle raised both his arms in the air, enclosing the bleak surrounding Arctic sky, and his eyes increased their wattage. "This could be HUGE!" he cried.

Chapter 6

Everybody told me I should go to Chukotka with a group. That seemed sensible; not even George Kennan had traveled alone. The people at Bering Air recommended that I talk to a woman who runs a tour company in Anchorage. I called her, and after some months she found four other people who wanted to go. Arrangements were made, and she got me a visa. I paid my $3,000, bought the gear I would need, and went back to Nome. One afternoon in early August 1999 I was in a twin engine Beechcraft taxiing out the Nome Airport runway bound for the Russian city of Provideniya, 233 miles away.

Of the plane's twelve passenger seats, a few had been removed to provide extra room for eighteen fifty-pound bags of salt that the United States was giving to Chukotka. Late summer is the time for netting and salting down the winter's supply of salmon for residents of the Chukchi Peninsula, and salt is always needed. So far that summer, Bering Air pilots had ferried seven thousand pounds of it to Provideniya. In other passenger seats were: Karen, fifty-six, a high school counselor; Bill, forty-eight, her husband, a telephone lineman; Briggie, a former high school English and journalism teacher, in her early sixties; and Micky, Briggie's husband and Karen's brother, also in his sixties. When I asked Micky what he did, he said, "I'm semiretired. I manage my family's holdings." All were from California and enjoyed photography. They hoped to take pictures in Chukotka, and for that they had brought a lot of gear.

They had arrived at the Bering Air hangar in a deteriorating mood. Micky asked me if I had any apprehensions about this trip, and I said, "Well, let's just say I've never done this before." He said he was afraid of boats, his sister was afraid of bears, and his wife hated to fly in small planes. She sat gripping the armrests as we took off. The pilot, Larry, treated this journey as if it were a mail route he'd flown a thousand times. I peered out, wishing I could see Asia—the Chukchi Nos (*nos* means "nose"), the very tip of the continent—but the weather, though calm enough to fly in, was still densely overcast, so that even the ends of the plane's wings were obscured. No bells or sirens went off as we crossed into Russian airspace. I felt I was in an X-ray machine: a big change had taken place, but silently and invisibly.

I had a moment of exhilaration thinking how much my father, a dedicated wanderer and traveler, would have liked to do what I was doing now. He had made a point of taking the family on car-camping vacations as far as one could drive in North America—to where roads ran out in Alaska and to the end of the Overseas Highway in Key West, Florida. At proud occasions he used to point to my brothers and sisters and me and brag, "These kids have been to both ends of the road!" For me, getting beyond the end of the road had required some momentum, not to mention a major shift in history.

Larry was talking to the control tower in Provideniya. Someone there spoke English serviceably. I remembered the sculptor David Barr, who had wanted to build hands reaching toward each other on both shores. Still, I could understand why Micky was uneasy in the seat beside me. All those stories about corruption, bribes, mafia guys, beatings. Who knew what would be there? The tour company had sent a group to Chukotka for a short trip earlier in the year, and they'd had no problems. But in *The Gulag Archipelago*, I had read Aleksandr Solzhenitsyn's musings on the proper memorial for the forced labor camps of Stalin's time: "I visualize . . . ," Solzhenitsyn wrote, "somewhere on a high point in the Kolyma, a most enormous Stalin, just such a size as he himself dreamed of, with mustaches many feet long and the bared fangs of a camp *commandant*, one hand holding the reins and the other wielding a knout with which to beat his team of hundreds of people harnessed in fives and all pulling hard. This would also be a fine sight on the edge of the Chukchi Peninsula next to the Bering Strait."

We descended from the clouds and suddenly Chukotka appeared. We were flying at about four thousand feet and parallel to the shore. The scene had the basic color scheme of arrival—blue water, white surf, green hills. Just as at the landing at Omsk, someone said, dramatically, "Siberia!" This time it was Bill, the telephone lineman, providing narration for the video he was shooting through the plane window. On the barren shore I saw no crazed statue such as Solzhenitsyn had proposed, or indeed any sign of habitation at all.

Our approach took us along Provideniya Bay and over to the town of Ureliki, across the bay from the city of Provideniya. Ureliki used to be a major military base and is now a much smaller one, and commercial flights use its runways. The moment we landed, everything was different. The scene where we had taken off, just an hour before, bore virtually no similarity to the one where we came down. As we neared the ground, we flew just above fences with black fence posts shaped like upside-down L's and trailing broken strands of black barbed wire with big black barbs, like something from a World War II movie, maybe *Stalag 17*. And in America, when a plane crashes in or near an airport, management whisks the wreckage away, so as not to dishearten future travelers. Here, plane wrecks had merely been moved over to one side of the runway. We taxied by a couple of crumpled-up passenger aircraft and one crushed helicopter.

Then, the gizmos we began to see! As we neared the terminal buildings, we passed lots of old, Cold War, formerly high-tech electronic stuff, antennae and whatnot, all of it silhouette black and leaning one way or another, disconnected wiring dangling from it, and poles holding up wires in such quantity that they had to be strung on circular frames at intervals to separate them from one another, and stumps of poles, and guy wires running diagonally, and corkscrew-shaped contraptions dark against the sky—the total effect was as if a mad scientist in an old horror movie had done some of his monster-animating experiments here, and then had been discovered by the villagers and chased off, and all his mad-scientist equipment had been left out in the weather to fall apart gradually.

The colors, too, were of a different kind. Kennan had been right about that. Russia occupies its own universe, chromatically. Near where we taxied to a stop sat a Russian car of a particularly Russian version of green.

I guess it was an apple green, but to call it that is to reimagine the apple. It was a bright, bilious, chemical-spill version of apple green. Russian colors sometimes make my gums ache. And on our right stood the Aeroflot terminal, a building that appeared to have been constituted entirely of shiny chrome. It resembled a hugely outsized bumper from an SUV, only an SUV transported, in design terms, back to about 1963.

The plane door opened and two women soldiers in their twenties escorted us across the tarmac to the entry room for international passengers. The women wore camo jackets and square-heeled high heels with buckles in the shape of hammers and sickles. They were dark haired, pretty, and bored. (Of the beauty of Russian women I will say more later.) Strange bursts of gunfire, and louder explosions, sounded all around. Larry explained that the Russians were dismantling the military base and had begun to shoot off the extra ammunition rather than take the trouble to ship it out.

When I entered the cold terra-cotta-tiled room where we were to fill out our customs declaration forms, I encountered an old friend: the smell of Russia. How do they do it? Here on the edge of the Bering Strait, five thousand miles from Moscow, almost within wafting distance of the U.S.A., the Russia-smell is exactly the same! I breathed it deeply. Yes, it was all there—the tea bags, the cucumber peels, the wet cement, the chilly air, the currant jam. About the only point of similarity between this smell and the one I'd just left in Nome was the overtone of diesel exhaust. But, still fresh from America, I understood that America's essential smell is nothing at all like Russia's. America smells like gift shop candles, fried food, new cars. America's is the smell of commerce. The smell of Alaska that stays with me the strongest is that of the Cinnabon sweet rolls shop in the Anchorage airport; I'm sure the scent of Cinnabon is set adrift everywhere in that space intentionally, in order to ensnare passersby. The smell of America says, "Come in and buy." The smell of Russia says, "Ladies and gentlemen: Russia!"

And there at the top of a poorly lighted staircase (why not try using a bigger lightbulb every once in a while, guys?) stood an older lady, a customs officer, beckoning us along. She smiled. In the dimness, her single gold tooth flashed like a Russian Welcome sign.

• • •

Provideniya, a city closer to America than Dallas is to Houston, was built mostly in the 1930s by slaves. Or "convict laborers," as we were told by Tanya, the bibulous copper-blond former ballerina who introduced herself to us at the airport as our guide. The laborers would have been in the custody of Dalstroi, the giant prison and construction combine, a fiefdom of the KGB, that ran the entire Soviet Far East. Perhaps in revenge for how it was built, Provideniya was now falling apart sort of spectacularly. On our way from the airport we passed rows and rows of smashed-out windows, and cement buildings of four and five stories all abandoned and hollow eyed, crumbling like sand castles that had been rained on. From some entryways, small waterfalls flowed down the broken front steps and into the potholed road. Apartment buildings rose from the street front in long horizontal terraces, decay and disintegration apparent everywhere, with occasionally a window still intact and a sack of provisions dangling from it—evidence of someone still living there, Tanya said. She added that the city had not had coal for its central-heating boilers in seven months, since early February. I had been in a ghost town before, but never a whole ruined city.

The idea was that we would spend one night in Provideniya, visit the museum and the power station, and then travel by boat and off-road vehicle to a camp of Chukchi reindeer herders on the tundra, where we would stay in reindeer-skin dwellings called *yurangis*. From the reindeer camp we would continue to a Yupik fishing camp at the mouth of a river, where there were hot springs and a chance to observe interesting sea mammals. However, something had come up. In an office at the ethnological museum in the middle of the city, our real guide, Vladimir Bychkov, whom it turned out Tanya had only been filling in for, explained the problem to us.

Vladimir Bychkov has brown eyes and a well-trimmed dark beard, and he looks maybe Persian. He is the son of a former Soviet army officer and was born in 1963 at the military base at Ureliki. A geography teacher during the school year, he is a mild, sensible, and intelligent man. In good English and with a serious expression he told us that the day before, a party of thirty-seven Yupiks from the village of Novo Chaplino in Chukotka, who had been visiting their American relatives on St. Lawrence Island on the U.S. side of the Bering Strait, had set out on the sixty-five-mile journey home. Their visas were about to run out, so they took a chance with the threatening weather. Soon after they left port, a storm came up (the same one that delayed us in Nome). Many of the Yupiks were in small aluminum boats with low-horsepower outboards, and the waves had been too much for them. Some had been able to jump to the large whaleboats of their companions, but two Yupiks, a father and son, had drowned. Their family name was Severov. Vladimir had known them. Most of the group had arrived in Provideniya thirty hours after they had started. They had thrown their belongings overboard to lighten their boats and thus lost the stuff they were bringing back from America, a big objective of the journey. Also, three boats carrying a total of six men remained unaccounted for.

A few years ago, he continued, three American researchers at just this time of year had gone on the strait from the Russian side in a small boat and had swamped in a storm and drowned. In light of that, and because of this week's tragedy, the governor of Chukotka had announced today that August sea conditions were too unpredictable for tourist travel in small boats. That meant we could not get to either the reindeer camp or the fish camp, as we'd planned, because both excursions required going by boat some of the way. We would instead find things to do and see in and around Provideniya, Vladimir said.

The Californians and I were supposed to stay in the apartment of a woman named Nina. She lived a few blocks from the museum in a not-ruined building just like you might find in Moscow, down even to the English-language graffiti—RAP, and RAVE, and BREAK DANCING—in the dark, Russian-scented entryway. Nina, a large, blond, motherly woman with mournful dark eyes, had been the head chef at Provideniya's only hotel until it closed a few years before. At the table in her small kitchen she served us a supper of borscht with beef, pelmeni in sour cream, red caviar on slices of hard-boiled egg with mayonnaise, and a many-layered birthday cake (the birthday was hers) with buttercream frosting. After we had finished, I told her that the food was better than at Moscow Gastronome in Brighton Beach. She asked me please to say that to Vladimir, the guide, and to the Chukotka director of tourism whom we'd also met briefly that day. Micky pointed out that the menu did not conform to the low-cholesterol diet that the travel company in Anchorage had assured him would be available. Nina didn't know English, and I couldn't translate that.

After supper, both the California couples retired to their rooms. The room that was supposed to be mine, however, was unavailable, all its flat surfaces being covered with wet clothes and camera parts laid out to dry. Nina explained that a woman who had arrived early in the morning was staying there. My Russian quickly proved inadequate to understanding what was going on. Eventually I gathered I would be staying elsewhere, in the apartment of her daughter, or brother, or somebody. Miffed to have lost my spot, I took my bags and followed her out into the paths of coal soot between the buildings. There we were met by Ira, Nina's daughter. Ira resembled a beautiful young woman in a children's story—rosy cheeks, perfect skin, chestnut hair to her shoulders, dark eyes. She wore a V-neck aqua-colored fuzzy sweater, slacks, and high heels that made neat circular indentations in the black and oily ground.

Nina said she would see me at her apartment for breakfast the next morning and wished me a quiet night. Ira led me into another building, a more run-down one, and through some narrow halls, and then into a luxury duplex flat. The place had a large-screen TV, a sort of staircase balcony overlooking a spacious living room, and a kitchen twice the size of Nina's. Ira brought me up to the room on the second floor where I would sleep. I was understanding perhaps one sentence out of every ten she said. I couldn't shake the misgiving that some dangerous mafia over-boss lived here and would show up unexpectedly. Back downstairs, Ira asked if I'd like to watch a movie and I said yes. She put on a cassette she said she really liked. Its title was *Bolshee chem Zhizn'*. I looked at the box—I had seen this movie and liked it, too. In English the title is *Larger Than Life*. It stars Bill Murray and is about a man who inherits an elephant. My friend Roy Blount wrote the screenplay.

She followed the dialogue, reading the Russian subtitles though she already knew it pretty well. We laughed mostly in the same places. She said that Bill Murray was funny, and I agreed. After the movie was over, she showed me some walrus-ivory carvings a friend of hers had done. The skilled and intricate miniatures represented a money bag with a dollar sign on it; the "annuit cœptis" pyramid and its single eye, from the dollar bill; a piggy bank with a coin sticking out; a change purse; and the cartoon millionaire from the Monopoly game wearing his top hat.

In the middle of the night, thirsty from the caviar, I ventured downstairs in my pajamas to find a glass of water. At the kitchen counter

I met Ira's husband, Edward, a young man of perhaps twenty-five, sweet faced and not at all sinister-looking. This settled my mind considerably.

Walking around Provideniya one couldn't escape the notion that it had been destroyed in a war, as I guess it had. The constant gunfire and detonation of surplus explosives in the distance, like a skirmish in some tundra suburb, contributed to the effect. Tanya, again substituting for Vladimir as guide, gave us a tour of the sights: the empty community swimming pool, its lane ropes drooping to a few puddles on the bottom, formerly the best pool in all Chukotka; Provideniya's last restaurant, recently destroyed by fire; a Baptist church, founded a few years before by some Americans, now also a burned-out shell, possibly the victim of arson; and a shiny statue of Lenin striding ominously (from America's point of view) eastward from his pedestal on an eminence in the town. Tanya said there had been talk of pulling the statue down, but the citizens had decided that since Provideniya had no other statues they should keep this one and paint it gold instead.

Tanya told us she had a degree in chemistry and worked testing water samples at the power station. Eventually she led us there. We had to go up and down a number of stiles that provided crossings over the many insulated steam pipes along the ground. Provideniya's population used to be about seven thousand five hundred, she said, and the power plant's central-heating system heated the whole place. Now barely a third that many inhabitants remained (three thousand five hundred people, by contrast, live in Nome). The power plant's stack rose high above the surrounding buildings. Though out of coal, the plant was still burning oil for electricity. Inside, the works resembled an old Soviet poster of industry—huge pistons shiny with oil, hexagonal-headed bolts on sheets of steel, sharp lines of shadow, a sense of some further fire glowing within, and coverall-clad figures in antique hard hats manning the controls. The numbers and letters identifying various gauges had been painted in red enamel by hand. According to Tanya, nobody in her office had been paid in more than three years, and one of her coworkers had begun a protest, never leaving the office or eating any food for two weeks now. The money to pay them was there, she believed, but the boss would not part with it. With a careless toss of her head she said she did not know what would happen to any of them.

Back at Nina's apartment that evening for dinner, I finally met the woman who had taken over what I still considered, proprietarily, as my room. She was Heidi Bradner, an American photographer, and the reason her clothes and camera parts were wet was that she had come over from St. Lawrence Island with the Yupiks in the storm. While Tanya and the Californians drank tea and vodka in the kitchen, Heidi Bradner and I sat in the hall and she told me about the voyage. About ten days before, she had gone over to St. Lawrence Island from Nome to take pictures for a French magazine. When time came to leave, the Yupiks offered her a ride to Provideniya. She had doubts about their boats and so chose the most seaworthy-looking whaleboat and most competent-looking crew she could find. The group of boats hadn't gone halfway across when the storm hit, with rain, fog, and eight-foot waves. Boats began to get separated from one another. None of the Yupiks had radios or GPS equipment, she said, because Russian bureaucracy makes it hard for Yupiks to own or use them.

The Yupiks' little outboards couldn't do much in the waves, which were so steep that the propellers often weren't in the water. High swells flooding in astern caused the engines to stall. Boats began swamping and going down. Everyone was drenched, bailing, hanging on. A boat came alongside, and two men jumped into her whaleboat just as their boat disappeared beneath them in the sea. Her boat, now heavily laden, was riding low and filling up. None of the Yupiks were showing how scared they were, except by the speed with which they pitched duffel bags and outboard motors and nets and walrus ivory and all kinds of other valuables overboard. During the last part of the journey, the storm let up slightly. Her boat reached Provideniya harbor after fifteen hours. Other boats took twice that long. Then the Russian authorities made the Yupiks wait for hours to clear customs, while their wives and children and other relatives cried on the beach, wondering who had or had not survived. After Heidi had been processed through customs, she came to Nina's, where she dried off and made phone calls.

Of course I then felt dumb that I had begrudged her the room. When she finished her story, I asked her how old she was. She looked at me to see if I was being fresh, then understood I wasn't. "Thirty-five," she said.

"You are brave," I said, and reached out and tapped her shoulder. When a person does that, after a good play in sports, or when a king knights somebody, you assume that the power goes from the one doing the touching to the one being touched, but actually the opposite is true. The person touching does so in the hope that a spark of the other's bravery will jump across. Brave people are one of the glories of the world.

Heidi Bradner has long, wavy red hair, a high forehead, pale skin, and a photographer's large, long-fingered hands. She is five foot nine and slim, almost rangy. She grew up in Alaska; her father, Mike Bradner, was a state legislator and served as Speaker of the House. After graduating from Robert W. Service High School in Anchorage, she went to the University of Alaska, then traveled in Europe. During a trip to Moscow she decided she wanted to stay there awhile. The year was 1991, and what was going on in Russia then dazzled her. "It was like a huge treasure chest had opened," she later told the *Anchorage Daily News*. "History was changing before my very eyes."

She was living in an apartment not far from the White House in Moscow in September 1993 when fighting began between supporters of Yeltsin and those of Vice President Rutskoi and the Supreme Soviet, which Yeltsin had dissolved. During the time the White House was under siege, she climbed into it through a window to take pictures of the defenders inside. She also witnessed the fighting for the Ostankino TV station, where she was under fire. A *New York Times* photographer was shot through the lung and nearly died. "I was thinking I could not believe this," she said. "There were a whole field of dead people out there." Afterward, she traveled often to Chechnya to photograph the conflict there. For pictures she took in Chechnya and elsewhere in Russia she won the 1998 Leica Medal of Excellence, awarded by the camera company and *Mother Jones* magazine. Heidi Bradner lives in London now. She is one of the people I think of for reassurance when I reflect on my country's failings and despair.

Provideniya's attractions unfortunately could not keep the Californians and me fully occupied for long. Nightlife was limited, though apparently there was a bar, which I did not go to. I liked the ethnographic museum and listened with interest to Vladimir Bychkov's short lecture about the toggling harpoon point and its importance in history. The point, invented in the remote past by a forgotten Eskimo genius ivory carver, turns sideways on a kind of pivot at its base when it is embedded in a large sea mammal, so that the entire harpoon end is at right angles to the connecting line and thus holds the speared animal more firmly than a barbed point could. This invention led to an increase in the Eskimos' food supply and an all-around improvement in their lives.

The lecture, good as it was, did not give the Californians much to photograph. They preferred the performance of native dances and singing that three teenage Chukchi girls put on. One of the girls was green eyed, one had curly black hair, and one was tall and graceful with a heart-shaped face. The girls wore dresses of embroidered white reindeer hide and braids wrapped in ribbon with balls of white fur on the end. Some of their songs were tonal and some used only heavy breathing, or breathing and clicking in the throat combined. For a few of their dances they asked us to join in, but we were all too timid, until Bill stood up gamely and did a fair imitation of their moves. His hiking boots slowed him down a little, but still he looked admirable, striding on his long legs and concentrating to get the steps right. Chukchi girls dancing with a telephone lineman from California is a sight seen almost never, and then not more than once. For a moment the dancing caused the entire room to come into focus—the floors of bare wood, the beige curtains with their decorative pattern of cattail plants, and the cold silver radiators along the walls.

In the evenings I enjoyed hanging out with Ira and Edward and their six-year-old son, Igor, in the apartment where I was staying. To communicate we used a kind of level-one pidgin Russian, aided by hand gestures and maybe mental telepathy. Also, Igor had learned some English in his first-grade class. The first words he said to me in English he pronounced carefully and with a look of solemnity: "How. Do you. Do." I was surprised to learn that he had never heard of tic-tac-toe. (In fact, I've never met a Russian child who knows that game, and I believe it may not exist there.) We played page after page of it, and after a while he became skilled and could not be beaten but only tied.

The four of us watched a lot more videos, mostly American movies, although Igor also liked a couple that were Russian children's shows. Edward brought out a favorite tape and played it several times, with commentary. He had a job in the Provideniya customs office, and the video was one he and his fellow customs officers had made themselves during a recent camping holiday on the tundra. For transportation they had used *vezdekhots*—tracked vehicles sort of like tanks; their name means "go-everywhere." The video showed the customs officers, all of them young fellows of about Edward's age, motoring along on bare hills in the *vezdekhots*, occasionally firing celebratory blasts with their Kalashnikovs and drinking vodka from the bottle. Certain moments in the video struck Edward as so hilarious that he laughed and fell over, repeating the same phrase over and over. The specific joke eluded me, but I got the general one and laughed, too.

After much driving around (still in the video), the guys stop near a declivity thick with low-lying bushes, possibly willows. One guy walks into the bushes with a gun and then comes out carrying by the ears a tundra jackrabbit almost half as long as he is. More laughing, more vodka drinking, more firing of rifles into the air. The rabbit is skinned and cut up somewhere offscreen while the guys make a fire in half an oil drum. The rabbit reappears, now skewered on sticks, to be cooked as *shashlik* (like shish kebab). Edward paused the tape to tell me that if I wanted, he could provide a *vezdekhot* for me to drive, and that obtaining one would be very simple. I would have liked to try it, but I thanked him and declined. Vladimir had told us that vehicle tracks on the tundra take twenty-five years to heal. I figured it was okay if the Russians wanted to drive around out there—it was their tundra—but that wouldn't apply to me.

From time to time, Vladimir kept us informed about the search for the missing boats and the six Yupiks aboard. So far no sign of boats or men had been found. He said that all Chukotka was worried about them, and that the native villages were also in mourning for the two who had drowned. U.S. Coast Guard C-130 radar planes had looked thoroughly on the American side of the border and were confident that the Yupiks hadn't drifted there. Repeated offers on the Americans' part to cross the border and search Russian waters had been ignored or refused. Chukotka's governor, Aleksandr Nazarov, was said not to be sympathetic to the Yupiks' misfortune. What resources he had assigned to the search remained unclear. The Russians had no radar planes in the area to match the C-130 and apparently only a single patrol boat was currently searching the Russian side. Russian authorities had told the Coast Guard that another vessel was on its way from Vladivostok, but any ship that far off could not arrive for many days. Local seas were still rough and foggy, with a ceiling of a few hundred feet. Adding to the discouragement, no one could be sure that the lost boats hadn't simply gone down the first day during the storm. Chances of finding the missing men seemed small.

Chapter 7

One morning, for no known reason, the ban against sea travel as it pertained to foreigners had disappeared. We would be going to the fish camp after all. On the street in front of Nina's building, the Californians and I loaded our luggage and their photographic equipment into a Russian military vehicle for the first part of the journey. This vehicle had an olive truck cab, a school-bus-yellow back with bench seats in rows, three sets of wheels as tall as my shoulder, and six-wheel drive. Its driver was a short Russian guy with a cap like a lid, and nothing to say. Sitting with us in the back were Vladimir and three Chukchis: Gennady, Ivan, and Valentina.

These Chukchis were so remarkable that they should be introduced with some ceremony. Chukchis are generally reindeer Chukchis or sea Chukchis. The former herd reindeer and live inland; the latter hunt sea mammals and fish for salmon and live on and around the coast. Gennady, Ivan, and Valentina did both, but they spent more time on and around the sea. Both of the men walked with the rolling, bowlegged sailors' gait I had only read about in nineteenth-century nautical novels. They had killed whales. Gennady was a whaling captain and had the build of a middleweight boxer. He wore rubber boots, a black-and-bright-orange waterproof insulated jumpsuit, a blue Hollofil coat, and a blue denim porkpie hat with the front of the brim turned up. In his gear he carried a new palm-sized GPS navigating device, which he had received special permission, as a captain and guide, to own.

Ivan had served as Gennady's first mate and harpooner on whale hunts. He displayed the qualities of competent chief assistant and wise-cracking sidekick combined. His last name was Tanko (I never found out the other Chukchis' last names). Ivan didn't mind talking to me, despite my Russian. He had once been a local Communist Party official and had studied for three years at the Agricultural Institute in Leningrad. He wore blue jeans with the back pockets removed and then sewn over the knees for reinforcement, a short wool jacket under a heavy rubber rain cape, and a blue knit cap. He spoke in a low, hollow, hoarse voice, and he laughed hoarsely, too.

Valentina was the wife of Gennady. She was short and solid, but not heavy, with long hair and a round, pretty face. Whenever she noticed something in need of correction, she made a quiet comment about it in Chukchi to Gennady, or in Russian to Vladimir. She took care of her and Gennady's equipment immaculately. Valentina had come along to accompany Gennady and to cook for everybody.

Once we had loaded up, we drove north from the city for an hour or so. For many miles beyond the outskirts of Provideniya we passed the ruins of military installations, with the now familiar collapsing fences of black barbed wire, chipped concrete structures, and ramshackle mad-scientist paraphernalia. Here and there along the road guard towers appeared. Tanya had told us there had been gulag camps near Provideniya until not long ago; no, all the sites we saw had been merely military, countered Vladimir. After a while, the surrounding landscape left almost all signs of people behind, and we went through bare hills marked with rock slides the color of graphite and long, narrow swaths of old snow fitting themselves into hillside contours. The overcast sky came down to an altitude almost an arm's length above, and when the vehicle climbed to a stony pass through a range of hills, we got out and walked around in an assembly of clouds. Not fog, but individual white clouds like stage scenery, with edges you could touch and almost grab.

We continued down the other side, across open spaces that were gravel and sky and not much else, through a couple of small lakes about two feet deep, and out onto a long tongue of gravel that ended at a body of water like a fjord stretching out of sight. Families had set up tents and plyboard houses here, or were living in cars and vans, waiting for the start of the salmon run. We sat on some old concrete foundations and had a lunch of kielbasa, bread, and hot, sugared tea. The tea was served in steel cups which the Russians held bare-handed without comment and which we Americans could pick up only by wrapping our hands inside our jacket sleeves.

At the gravel beach nearby, four small aluminum skiffs with outboard motors awaited us. The Californians and I looked them over skeptically. Micky, with his fear of boats, stood shaking his head. Out of our party's heaped-up gear, I immediately chose a life jacket that looked new and dependable. Valentina saw this and came over and spoke to Vladimir; that life jacket, it turned out, was hers. I gave it up for a flimsier one, picturing the substitute bunched around my ears as I flailed and drowned. We stowed our bags and equipment and got aboard. Bill and I rode with a Russian-Russian guy and his wife, fish camp people we hadn't met before. The boat sat low enough in the water that the sea was at our elbows. Bill reached over and felt its temperature. "This isn't any colder than Tahoe!" he said. "I could water-ski this!"

We then bounced through medium-sized waves for about twenty-five miles. Foolishly, I had not brought along waterproof pants, and my drenched trousers were clinging to my knees. All around us, only blue-gray ocean and white cloudbanks could be seen. I preferred the cloudbanks with little strips of rock or beach showing at their bases; had it been up to me, and not impossible, we would have made this entire journey within fifty feet of land. For twenty minutes at a time we crossed long reaches of open water where the waves rose higher. After a while we were approaching a shore, where our boatman ran us up on a gravel strand with none of the other three boats around. This missed connection caused some alarm and the firing of a flare by the rest of our party down the shore a mile or two away. Our guy then set out again and dropped us off there, at what turned out to be the mouth of the Hot Springs River. Disembarked, we joined the three other Americans looking in puzzlement and suspicion at a surrounding landscape of nothing, apparently.

Or almost nothing. There was a long, tapering gravel spit, waves breaking on the seaward side of it, and a small bay formed by the river's mouth on the other side. On the high ground of the spit, no more than a few feet above the water, grasses and mosses grew sparsely. Near the end of the spit was a cabin made of drift boards, a flattop structure smaller than a two-car garage. A radio aerial extended twenty-five feet above its roof, with a second, shorter aerial alongside. As the taller aerial moved back and forth, it provided the only visible indication, besides the waves, of the force of the wind. A small drift-board storage shed flanked the cabin at one corner. Inland, a green tundra plain stretched away into the clouds and fog. At a cleft between two hills close by, where the river emerged, a steady breath of steam went up, evidence of the hot spring that gave the river its name.

On the gravel spit's highest ground, Vladimir began to set up our tents. They were not promising and appeared to have been bought at a Kmart in Anchorage; they had names like "Junior Outdoorsman." Bill and Micky and I helped him, Micky grousing quietly the while. He had not yet recovered from the boat ride—and now this. When we finished, I followed a path that led around the bay and onto the tundra. I had never been on actual Russian tundra before. First off, I found old *vezde-khot* tracks, a whole convention of them, wandering in different directions, and lots of the aluminum containers that Russian military rations come in. Also, inexplicable junk lying around: the handlebars and front-wheel fork of a bicycle, and a pile of heating-system radiators.

Mostly the tundra was low-growing birch trees that resembled ground vines, and hummocks of moss. I hadn't gone far across it when I started to see mushrooms everywhere. These were plump, big boletes, the smaller ones a clean mushroom-white on top and the larger ones as brown as a perfectly baked loaf of bread. Once I had noticed them, I realized that this place was in fact a boletes bonanza, like an Easter-egg hunt for three-year-olds, with the prizes barely hidden at all. I took off my baseball cap, filled it with boletes, and then began to put them in my pockets. Russians love wild mushrooms, and boletes often are edible, even tasty. I thought I'd present these to the residents of the fish camp cabin who were to be our hosts. Picking up a boletus bigger than any I'd seen in my life, I hurried back across the tundra to the cabin. Everyone in our party had gone in there to drink tea and vodka and get warm. I walked in—the small room was lantern lit, fogged with coal smoke, and crowded by a propane stove, a sleeping platform, and benches along the walls—and presented my mushrooms to the pregnant young Yupik woman standing by the stove. She took one look at them and laughed and said, "*Starii*," which means "old." I examined the mushrooms more closely and saw that they were indeed completely soggy from the recent rains, and starting to decay.

A problem for anyone writing about Russia is the fact that all Russians have the same name. Or, rather, they have one of about six names. The owner or presiding occupant of the fish camp cabin was another Vladimir, whom I will call Vladimir-the-Yupik. He was a relative of some of the Yupiks who had been caught in the storm. When I went outside to throw the mushrooms away, I met him standing with Vladimir-the-guide by the storage shed and smoking a cigarette he had made from loose tobacco rolled in the torn page of a book. Vladimir-the-Yupik was a slim, quiet young man, thin faced and light eyed, with a wispy goatee and mustache. I asked him what book his cigarette paper had come from—sympathizing with the author, I suppose—and he seemed embarrassed out of all measure to have been caught in such an act of desecration; he sucked a last drag and tossed the butt away.

Vladimir-the-guide told him I spoke some Russian, so Vladimir-the-Yupik asked me where I learned it, and I said in New York, and he said, "Brighton Beach?" Even on the farthest shores of Siberia, they know Brighton Beach. Then he switched to English, which he spoke well. Vladimir-the-Yupik told me he comes to this camp to fish for salmon every year. He lives in the village of Novo Chaplino, his son had come with him, and his wife, Cenia, was the pregnant young woman inside. The son, he said, had found a float from a whaling ship that day. An orange rubber ball maybe three feet in diameter, it lay on the ground nearby. He said it had belonged to a Japanese ship and was worth a lot of money. Then he told me that the fish hanging to dry on the outside of his cabin wall were called antler fish and tasted very good boiled in seal oil. He also enjoyed eating young cormorants, which he catches before they have all their feathers and are able to fly. He had shot three Dall sheep, another tasty species, on the far side of the inlet last year. "I like this country," he said, gazing reflectively at the foggy starkness around him and dragging on another book-paper cigarette. When he turned to go inside the cabin, I saw on the back of his softball warm-up jacket the words POLARIS BAR, NOME, ALASKA.

Supper was wild-mushroom soup, bread, and tea—not really enough, I thought. After it I walked on the ocean beach and watched Ivan, Gennady, and Vladimir-the-guide put out their salmon nets. The nets were about seventy-five feet long and eight feet wide, with floats along the top edge every six feet. Burlap sacks filled with rocks would anchor the nets to the beach and to the ocean bottom. Ivan produced the sacks from among his gear, unfolded them, and began to fill them with rocks. He asked if I wanted to help. I said yes, and he held the mouth of a sack open while I grabbed rocks from the beach and tossed them in. As I did, a line from one of my favorite works of Russian literature occurred to me, and I recited it out loud: *"Pushkin lyubil kidat'sya kamnyami!"* Ivan laughed hard at this and repeated it to Gennady and Vladimir-the-guide, who also laughed and repeated it. As we filled the sacks, everyone was saying, *"Pushkin lyubil kidat'sya kamnyami!"*

It is perhaps vain of me to mention this small linguistic triumph, but almost nothing is as satisfying as making someone laugh in a foreign language. *"Pushkin lyubil kidat'sya kamnyami"* (Pushkin loved to throw rocks) is from a piece by Daniil Kharms, the absurdist writer, who was killed by Stalin in 1942. The piece consists of seven short, numbered paragraphs and is called "Anegdotes from the Life of Pushkin." (The misspelling of "Anecdotes" is intentional.) The sentence about the rocks begins anegdote #6.

Once the sacks were ready, Ivan pumped up his little rubber raft and paddled into the waves, setting the nets perpendicular to the shore and adjusting them so that all the floats rode at the surface. There were four nets and he put them about a hundred yards apart. When he had finished with the last net, he was about a quarter mile upwind of where the rest of us were sitting on the shore; to return, he opened his cape wide with both arms, caught the wind in it, and sailed back, singing full-throated nautical songs.

The next morning the Californians awoke displeased. The night had gone badly. Rain had fallen nonstop. The tents leaked. High winds caused them to move around alarmingly. Then, trying to wash up with no facilities but the Bering Sea proved difficult. Breakfast was on the sparse side. On a walk across the tundra to the hot springs, Vladimir-the-guide showed us lingonberries, groundberries, and cloudberries of a lovely tequila-sunrise orange hidden among the greenery at our feet. Valentina identified a tiny wildflower, midnight blue with black pistils inside, as the *petushok*, a word that means a young rooster. The flower did look just like a rooster's comb in profile. At the hot springs, Karen and Vladimir-the-guide both swam, but the ground around the spring was so muddy it was hard to come out any cleaner than you went in. The party walked slowly back to camp, with the Californians' frame of mind unimproved.

As we sat drinking tea in the cabin after lunch, Karen and Micky began asking Vladimir-the-guide pointed questions about the tour's finances. Vladimir-the-guide said he had nothing to do with the money, he was just supposed to guide us in Chukotka. Karen persisted, and Vladimir said, "That's not my business," and stood up and went outside. With no other target handy, the Californians then for some reason presented their complaints to me: The tents, Micky said, were inadequate, and in fact were the kind children use camping in the backyard. We had been promised a visit to a reindeer camp, and no reindeer camp was now on the schedule. The food was not sufficient, and Micky's low-cholesterol diet requirements had been ignored. On top of that, photography, the whole purpose of the trip, was almost impossible in this coastal fog.

I told them they were right about the tents, and right in general—but what did they expect? This was Russia. Misrepresenting my own experience somewhat, I said that judging by the many Russian trips I'd been on, ours was about average so far. My answer calmed them only a little. It seemed that what really rankled was the money. Nobody likes to be ripped off. Exactly what had our $3,000 apiece paid for? The plane ride had been a puddle jump. We had stayed in private homes in Provideniya. The food couldn't have been that expensive, or the gas for the army vehicle or the boat ride. Where, they asked, had the money gone?

"That's simple," I said. "I'm sure most of the money was spent on bribes."

The Californians looked at one another. Bribes. These were honest and decent American folks. Such a thought had not crossed their minds. I then explained about the many important people who probably had to be paid off for our easy entry into the country, maybe even for our unexpected journey to the camp here. I told them about the widespread reputation of Russian officialdom and the way business here is said to be done. I could see them feeling a little better with every moment that passed. After this conversation, and for the rest of the trip, I can't say that they were exactly content, but the subject of where the money had gone did not trouble them anymore.

I was reminded of the old joke of W. C. Fields, famous comedian and drinker from the 1930s. Fields walks into a bar, and he says to the bartender, "Did I spend a twenty-dollar bill in here last night?" The bartender says, "Yes, sir, you did." "Oh, what a relief," Fields replies. "I thought I'd lost it."

During times when nothing else was planned, I walked the surrounding landscape for hours. I am susceptible to geography, and the idea that I was in a different country, continent, and hemisphere—with the United States forty-five minutes away!—stayed in the front of my mind. I felt I'd fallen down the rabbit hole, or stepped behind a secret sliding panel in ordinary life. Not that the scenery here on the other side offered much in the way of drama. Instead the fog, sea, beach, and tundra suggested drama of an undramatic kind, like the dull, flat paint jobs used to obscure the most expensive warplanes. I went high on the tundra hills, stepping from hummock to hummock in the rubber boots Vladimir-the-guide had provided me, and found thousands more mushrooms. This time I checked for water damage and tried to pick the newest-looking boletes, ones that maybe had popped up just that morning. Ivan Tanko, when I showed them to him, pronounced them *otlychnie grybii*—outstanding mushrooms—and Cenia, the young wife, strung them on thread and hung them from the beams of the cabin ceiling to dry.

I thought it somehow wrong that geography this momentous could begin without any sign or monument to commemorate the fact of it. Solzhenitsyn's statue on the shoreline had been just a fantasy, and the reaching-hand sculpture in Uelen merely a plan. But couldn't there be even a simple boundary marker of some kind? "Welcome to Asia," or something? I had read that during the reign of Catherine the Great, iron markers bearing the Russian Imperial double-headed eagle were placed all along the coast of Chukchi-land. As I walked, I kept my eyes open. Who knew? Maybe a few of those double-eagle signposts were still out there.

One day after a few miles of wandering I saw a pole or post on a seaside bluff in the distance and went to check it out. To my surprise it was indeed a monument. What I had taken for a pole was actually an iron whaling harpoon, the kind that's shot from a gun. It had a blunt-tipped, finned head, ugly as the point of a missile. A pedestal of rocks and cement supported the harpoon at the base, and an arrangement of whale ribs on the ground a pace or so away bracketed it. A plaque in Russian on the

monument read, IN MEMORY OF THE WHALING FLOTILLA "ALEUT,"
1932–1967. ERECTED BY THE CREW OF THE "CELESTIAL," SEPT.
1970. A smaller plaque said, HISTORY OF THE SOVIET WHALING IN-
DUSTRY IN THE FAR EAST. 23 OCTOBER 1932 THE FIRST WHALE
WAS TAKEN IN THE PACIFIC OCEAN. A list of flotilla names followed.
Waves broke against the stones at the bottom of the bluff and continued
to the horizon in foggy obscurity. In the surrounding vastness of sea and
hills I could not pick out a single other work of man. Never had I seen a
monument in a lonelier spot.

Aside from the rain and wind and chill, and the chronically damp clothes,
I enjoyed the fish camp. After salmon started coming to the nets, the food
improved. Valentina made sautéed salmon steaks, and a soup of salmon
heads and potatoes called *ukha*, and fried salmon liver and salmon milt
with kasha, and salmon eggs and butter on thinly sliced black bread. For
Valentina's birthday, Gennady shot a spotted seal. Some of us went along
in the boats to observe as he approached a small isthmus beside a bay,
slipped ashore, concealed himself behind one of the special stone cairns
built there for seal hunting, laid his rifle in a crenellation at the top of the
cairn, waited for a curious seal to pop its head up from the waves, and
shot the seal in that split second right in the head at a distance of more
than a hundred yards. And all this with iron sights and not a scope! The
dead seal drifted and its blood made a red plume in the blue water.
Vladimir-the-guide zipped over in his boat and picked it up. When we
returned to the camp, Ivan quickly and expertly butchered it—its cute
seal face looked strange cut up and reduced to a cubist jumble—and Valentina fried its liver and boiled its meat with angel-hair pasta for the
birthday dinner. Seal meat tastes like the beef of a cow fed on salmon.

Morning, noon, and evening I helped Ivan tend the nets. When the
nets' floats went under, the net was full and had to be retrieved soon or
little crabs would eat the catch and reduce them to limp, emptied-out
skin wrappings. We pulled the nets up on the beach, untangled the
salmon, and threw them into a heap by Ivan's salt barrels and cleaning
board. Most of the salmon were of two kinds, king and humpbacked;
there was also a shimmery, spotted char known in North America as the
Dolly Varden. The nets also caught many strange, spiky little fish that

Ivan called *bychki*. Later I learned that these fish are a favorite Russian snack to have with vodka. They come in a can, with a distinctive tomato sauce. Ivan disdained them, so we threw them away.

Ivan was fun to fish with. He and I talked a lot. Whole five-minute periods went by during which I understood nothing he said, but that was okay. He also sang folk songs and rousing Communist Party anthems he had learned during his student days in Leningrad. Taking a deep breath and throwing his head back, he belted out, *"Lenin, yeshcho zhivoi . . ."* (Lenin, living still . . .). Sometimes when pulling the net he recited lines from great works of literature, matching the recitation to the action. A favorite went, *"Tyanem, po-tyanem / Vytyanut' ne mozhem . . ."* (We pull, and we pull / We cannot pull it out . . .). He said this was from a fable called "Repka," about people trying to pull up a huge turnip. He said it was written by Pushkin.

Some of the other lines he spoke or half sang he also said were by Pushkin, but I didn't catch them or write them down. ("Repka," it turns out, is an old fable, not Pushkin's.) Maybe I had put Pushkin in Ivan's mind because of the joke about throwing rocks. Still, I thought again of the poem Pushkin wrote based on Horace's poetic claim, "I have built a monument more lasting than bronze." The Russian poet's prediction of his own literary immortality was in an unpublished work found among his papers after his death. That poem said he would live forever in his verses on the lips of living men, and his name would be remembered "wherever one poet is still alive." Across Russia, he foretold, all would know him, including

> *I Fin, i nyne díki Tungús,*
> *I drug steppéi Kalmík . . .*
>
> (The Fin, and the now wild Tungus,
> and the Kalmik, friend of the steppes . . .)

What a grand prediction for a young poet in a still-young literature to venture! And I can affirm that as regards the Chukchi, the spirit of it came true.

• • •

The Arctic summer twilight lasted in the evening until about eleven thirty and returned in the morning about four. Sometimes, during the latest or earliest hours of light, we heard the sound of Vladimir-the-Yupik's outboard motor growing louder or fading away. All six of the Yupiks missing since the storm remained unaccounted for; he kept going out to try to find them, the other Russians said. One morning just after dawn, he and his son came upon one of the Yupik boats washed up on a shore. No tracks on the beach or tundra indicated that any men had been nearby, so doubtless this boat had been among those abandoned in the storm when its owners jumped from it to another. Vladimir-the-Yupik towed it back to the fish camp and beached it on the gravel beside the cabin.

When I heard about it, I went to take a look. In its sea-battered state, the boat most resembled objects I had seen that were damaged by a bear. Its seat struts were broken, its seats crushed down, its oarlocks torn out, and its sides dented in. Pieces of Styrofoam-type stuff that had fit under the seats for added flotation had been knocked askew and shattered. Spills of gravel strewed the boat's bottom, along with sea plants, and pieces of wire, and a few chunks of dried salmon that were white and waterlogged. Natural disasters produce a special grunginess unlike that of human-made chaos, somehow. Observing all this I got a sense that the terror the boat's occupants had felt was still there.

On an afternoon jaunt with Gennady and Ivan and Vladimir-the-guide, I met more Yupiks who were searching for the missing men. The four of us had stopped at a calm, lee-side beach to have tea when two boats bigger than ours carrying six or seven native guys passed by. Seeing us they abruptly veered and came ashore. The sight of non-Yupik Russians whom they assumed to be on the same mission as their own cheered them, and they jumped from their boats and thanked us and shook our hands. Then they heard me say something in English to Vladimir-the-guide, and all did a triple take. Learning that we were in fact on an excursion of tourism, and not a search party, they cooled in their enthusiasm. But having pulled their boats up, they decided to take a tea break also. Gennady and Ivan joined them while Vladimir and I hiked along the strand to an ancient site nearby.

The site, as Vladimir explained to me, offered proof of the efficacy of the toggling harpoon point. Sea mammal hunters started living at an encampment here about five hundred years ago, several centuries after the toggling point's invention. On the long, grassy expanse above the seaside gravel, many large skulls of bowhead whales they had killed stood in an unevenly spaced line. Looking along the row from one end of it to the other, I absorbed the wordless impact of the site. In life these creatures would have been forty feet long and weighed fifty tons. The men who lived here pursued them aboard walrus-skin boats in water that was death even to fall into, and killed them with harpoons tipped with ingenious pieces of ivory. Vladimir said no one knew for sure if the skulls had had a ceremonial purpose, or perhaps simply served as stands on which to dry the skin boats and hold them ready for quick launching when whales were seen.

A distance away in the knee-high grasses, two whale jawbones of great length had been set upright; they curved toward each other like parentheses, making an almost-completed white arc against the hillside backdrop of green. To me, the minimalist eloquence of native sites tops the fanciest cathedral any day. Vladimir told me there was also a cemetery hundreds of years old on the crest of the hill above. While he took photographs of the skulls, I hiked to it—no easy deal, given the steepness and the thick growth of angelica plants. Here and there a large bear had preceded me, pressing down the plants and leaving tufts of ginger-colored fur. When I reached the cemetery, an unfenced saddle of bare ground inlaid with rectangular stone graves, I saw that the drop from it on one side was as precipitous as the first hill on a roller coaster. For a moment the clouds and fog over the ocean opened out and afforded a view that was, approximately, eternal. With just bare land, sky, and empty sea up ahead of me, I had for the first time an astronomical awareness that I was standing on a planet—perhaps the way a visitor would feel walking on Mars.

And then, when we returned to the fish camp, amazing news. The missing Yupiks had been found! Vladimir-the-Yupik had heard it over the radio on an Alaskan station within range of the cabin's long antenna. At six thirty on Saturday morning, the U.S. Coast Guard had received a fax from Moscow authorizing the Americans to search Russian waters. The Coast Guard immediately sent a C-130 plane equipped with radar, and it picked up blips from the aluminum hulls of two of the boats about thirty miles west of Provideniya that same afternoon. A few hours after this find, a Russian freighter spotted the other boat. All the men were swollen from exposure and caked with salt from four days at sea but had suffered no serious harm and in fact refused to leave their boats when Coast Guard helicopters appeared overhead. The men had all managed not to throw the valuables overboard and did not want to abandon the boats now. After some delay, Russian vessels arrived to tow the boats to port.

Good feelings from this turn of events made the rest of our trip go better. Afterward, every native person we met, and some Russian-Russians, smiled when they realized we were from America. The Californians had been agitating to visit a native village so they could photograph "the people and the faces," as Karen explained. I told her there were people and faces right here at the fish camp, but she was thinking in terms of volume. To satisfy their requests, one afternoon Vladimir-the-guide organized a full-scale expedition of the entire party, along with some Russians and their boats from another fish camp along the shore. At armada strength, we set out to pay calls on Vladimir-the-Yupik's village of Novo Chaplino and another village called Yndrekanute.

Along the way we stopped at the site with the whale skulls. For a change the sky had cleared to a bright blue, and in the sunshine the arrangements of ancient bleached bones looked even more impressive than before. Perhaps selfishly, I still preferred my previous viewing of it, when the day had been gloomy and no one but Vladimir and me there. While the others walked around and took pictures, Gennady and I hung out by the beach and he showed me the wonders of his GPS device. When he first turned it on he said, "We must wait for a sputnik." We waited, a satellite linkup occurred, and the GPS began to tell us where we were in relation to everything. I think we both got a kick out of doing this high-tech business next to the ancient skulls. Provideniya was 55 km (35 miles) by air to the southwest, Anadyr 596 km (370 miles) in the same general direction; I forget how far other landmarks in Chukotka were. Significantly, he had programmed the GPS only for places in Russia and had omitted all American destinations, maybe so as not to upset Russian authorities. Our own coordinates at that moment were 64° 38' 42" N latitude and 172° 31' 09" W longitude. Vitus Bering, in his inconclusive voyage northward between the continents, had turned back at 67° 18', about 160 nautical miles north of where we were now.

From the whale skull place—Vladimir-the-guide and other Russians called it Whalebone Alley—we motored on across calm water and through a small archipelago of islands that were mostly high black cliffs with green moss on their horizontal parts and white birds dispersing from them like pollen. Vladimir-the-guide pointed out the kittiwakes, jaegers, eider ducks, cormorants, and common merles flying by. Some little islands seemed to be all puffins. These squat, large-billed birds have wings that are set midway along their bodies and apparently perpendicular to them like the wings of bees. The puffin swarms almost seemed to buzz as they burst from the cliffs and went arrowing by. Then suddenly, among our group of boats, a gray whale surfaced, turned one flipper up, and dove back down. Instantly we all shouted, in at least two languages, "Whale!" The word "Whale!" like "Shark!" or "Fire!" is a word you don't say, it says you.

Motors idling, we sat and waited for the whale to reappear. From whale-watching trips I'd been on, I knew that it is possible to time a whale and predict the duration of a dive, so I asked a Russian guy in my boat how long the whale would stay under. "Until he comes up again," he replied. The wind had died completely, and lozenge-shaped spaces were swapping back and forth on the surface in the flat calm. The sea flashed colors of azure and green and turquoise with a swimming-pool allure, if you could forget how cold it was. Here and there curled white feathers dropped from the passing seabirds sat undisturbed like wood shavings on a shiny floor. Five minutes or more went by. Then a mile away a whale spout rose against the dark land beyond it. The spout shot white and unmistakable in the sky, then dropped back, leaving a veil of mist that hung in the air and drifted to one side.

At the first village we visited, Novo Chaplino, not a lot of people were home. Some had still not returned from the St. Lawrence Island trip and were stopping with relatives in Provideniya or elsewhere. Others had gone to tend the reindeer herds or catch salmon or hunt. A few of us drank tea with the principal of the local school, and then we all got back in the boats and continued to Yndrekanute, where more was going on. As our fleet came up the narrow bight leading to the Yndrekanute boat landing, a bunch of kids and young people ran along the shore beside us shouting and waving like in a scene from the travels of an old-time explorer. Some of the kids threw stones or shot at us with slingshots. After we disembarked, the Russians in our party spoke sharply to these boys, who hung their heads and smiled.

Yndrekanute had been created or expanded by the consolidation of a lot of small village groups into a single collective during Communist times. The recent disappearance of communism had left complicated ruins and a sense of "Now what?" The crater at the center of the post-Soviet wreckage was the late office of the Communist Party; this brick building had char marks around its broken-out windows, blackened wood and cinders inside, and spray-painted graffiti inside and out. The central-heating system for the village had quit long ago and its aboveground steam pipes were shedding pieces of insulation effusively. The village had formerly supported a reindeer-raising collective and a fox-fur-growing farm. Now the empty fox cages spread along a flat expanse below the town in disarray, all scattered and tumbledown. A whitened heap of bones of the whales and other sea mammals Yndrekanute's hunters had killed to feed the foxes resembled a junk pile of wrecked cars, and beyond the cages and boxes, discarded fifty-three-gallon metal drums were strewn into the distance in multitudes.

Our visit quickly became a mob scene. Crowds of Yndrekanute citizens of all ages gathered around us, thanking us for America's help, saying hello, trying to sell us stuff, or doing all three. The faces that Karen was hoping to photograph had to be shot at extremely close range. With prompting, some of the subjects did see the problem and stood back a few feet and posed. I broke away on my own and with a dwindling entourage walked the side streets of the village, which was in better shape all in all than its Soviet-era leftovers had led me to think. Most of the houses were of stucco and lath construction, trim and cozy looking, with salmon hanging all along the eaves to dry, wooden ladders leading to outside attic doors, and neat yards. Some had front walks made of the old rubber drive treads of snow machines. Chairs in front of many houses faced the village's sea view, a sweep of mountains and ocean widening eastward to a full Bering Strait horizon. I saw a row of chairs made of three linked folding seats, like in a theater, next to three stools made of whale vertebrae.

Along with photos, the Californians wanted souvenirs, and they had no trouble finding plenty among the crowd. Mittens, fur hats, toy dogsleds, sealskin boots—soon the Californians were loaded down. As they slowly wound their way back to the boats, they were a heavily laden parade, with villagers thronging around, bringing more stuff, laughing, calling out to one another. At the center of the excitement, Karen carried a set of reindeer antlers and wore her new hat of reddish-gray fox fur with big earflaps. She was smiling a triumphant smile.

We stayed at the fish camp another few days. We were there only about a week in all, but I felt I could have lived there for months. The routine of it suited me. I continued to keep an eye on the nets, and every so often I helped Ivan pull them and knock the accumulated seaweed off them with a tool like a carpet beater. I also read, ate Valentina's good cooking, walked. Growing tired of my leaky Junior Outdoorsman tent, I asked Ivan if he had room for me in his tent, and he said sure. His was a two-man Russian army model of heavy canvas, which he had floored with furs artfully piled one upon another so that when you lay down your head was higher than your feet. It's still the most comfortable tent I ever slept in. Another storm came, and the Russian flag he had erected on the beach nearby cracked like a whip as the wind swept by. I read by flashlight in the tent and drifted off.

On a morning when the sea conditions had moderated, we started back for Provideniya. I went in Gennady's boat and marveled at the exactness with which he turned into each wave we crossed, heading the bow at an angle that brought the crest of the swell within half an inch of the gunwale, and then angling back the other way as we descended into the trough. When we reached the take-out point at the end of the fjord and had to wait for the others, Ivan sheltered beneath a turned-over boat someone had left there. Then he produced a blowtorch, lit it, applied its flame to a blackened teapot, and boiled water for tea. The same military vehicle with the same no-comment Russian driver had come to pick us up. The driver joined us for tea and in a low voice asked Ivan what these foolish Americans had done at the fish camp—sit all day in the cabin by the stove? Ivan told him that this American (pointing to me) had walked farther and found more mushrooms than he, the driver, ever could. The driver looked at me. He showed an unpersuasive grin consisting of metals of different kinds and said no more.

Back in Provideniya, I spent another evening at Ira and Edward's watching videos and talking, as before. Edward told me that most people in Provideniya wanted to move to either Alaska or western Russia. He said it was possible to buy a big apartment in Provideniya now for just a couple of thousand dollars. Igor, their little boy, was ill with fever and did not come out of his room. In the morning I let myself out very early and walked the town—up Dezhnev Street, down Polarnaya, and along the waterfront. The tall row of cargo cranes by the docks stood rusting and idle; 150 ships used to come here every year, Tanya had told us, but this season the port had seen fewer than a dozen. And yet just outside the bay I could make out a long pennant of diesel smoke from an approaching cruise ship, part of Provideniya's new tourist equation. I wondered what the tourists would find to do.

At the end of a point of land, past a last crumbling high-rise, I happened upon a graveyard. Like many lonely places in Russia, it had weathered its share of drunken vandalism. Tiny pieces of liquor bottles that had been thrown hard against the stones gave a holiday sparkle to the ground. Memorial busts had been smashed, their noses broken off. Flower vases had been tipped over and cracked. Some of the grave markers bore enameled photo portraits of the deceased set into ovals in the stone. A picture of a woman named Elena featured those intense, empathetic dark eyes you sometimes see in young Russian women. She had been born in 1957 and had died at the age of thirty-six. Lots of the people in the cemetery had died in their thirties. At the foot of one marker, centered neatly on its broad stone base, sat a Russian military cap. It had a shiny black bill and one of those extrahigh fronts with an emblem on it—the kind of hat formerly seen on the heads of generals reviewing a May Day parade. I wanted to pick it up and examine it, but I let it be.

At Nina's, the Californians were getting ready for departure, saying things like, "Has anybody seen my black bag?" Nina told me a long story about another of her daughters, an unlucky young woman whose husband, she said, had tried to kill her. Amid the confusion, six-year-old Igor suddenly appeared; he had stopped by, Nina said, to tell me goodbye. Igor stood very formally with the top button of his shirt buttoned and his mouth held in a straight line. I asked him if he had recovered from his fever and he said, "*Konechno*" (Naturally). We shook hands and I promised I would send him some Legos. After I was back home I did send him some, but I don't know if they ever arrived.

At the airport, surprisingly, a line of people were already waiting at the outgoing customs checkpoint. Just ahead of our party stood some guys from Mason City, Iowa, who had obtained a quick-visit visa in Nome and had flown over in their own plane on a whim to see what Russia was like. They told us they didn't think much of it. From some inner airport office V——, the Chukotka minister of tourism, emerged with a couple of aides. The minister had curly blond hair, blue eyes, and the personable manner of a casino greeter. He spoke English well and asked the people in line if they'd had a good time. He got to our party right before we went through the door. In his spotless blue warm-up jersey and pants highlighted with parallel white stripes on the sides, he shook our hands and listened with his head cocked inquisitively. Seizing the moment, Karen said to him, "V——, Sandy here [indicating me] told us that most of the money we paid for this trip was spent on bribes. Is that really true?"

V—— replied without hesitation. "Yes, that's correct, bribes." He raised his eyebrows and looked at her, mildly curious about what the point of such an obvious question might be.

•

PART II

Chapter 8

In the year 1220, a Taoist monk named Ch'ang ch'un received a summons from Genghis Khan. The Mongol emperor, ruler of more earthly territory than any human before him, had a curiosity about spiritual things. He had heard of Ch'ang ch'un's reputation for wisdom and he wanted the monk to come to him so he could ask some questions. The rumor that the monk possessed medicine of immortality especially interested him. Ch'ang ch'un replied modestly, "I have grown old and am not yet dead. My repute has spread over all kingdoms; but as to my sanctity, I am not better than ordinary people, and when I look inwards, I am deeply ashamed of myself." Any request from the khan had to be obeyed, however, so with an entourage of disciples, the seventy-three-year-old monk set out from Peking in 1221 on a journey to Genghis's encampment far to the west.

Ch'ang ch'un and his companions went across much of Asia. Maybe they were in southern Siberia part of the way, maybe not. The disciples kept a diary; here is a sample: "There was a stony river, more than fifty *li* long, the banks of which were about a hundred feet high. The water in the river was clear and cold, and bubbled like sonorous jade." (One of the best river descriptions ever: *bubbled like sonorous jade*.) Crossing hot deserts in the cool of the night, they feared being charmed by goblins. The foods of the master's diet—rice, meal, vegetables—could not always be found. By the time winter came on, they had reached the city of Samarkand, north of the pass through the mountains that led down to present Afghanistan. Genghis Khan and his army were there, camped on a plain between Kabul and Andarab. The chroniclers note that in those years Genghis was fighting "the Mohammedan rebels in the mountains." The Mongols would not be the last army to give that exercise a try.

In May 1222, about a year and a half after leaving Peking, Ch'ang ch'un reached the camp of Genghis Khan. Out of respect for the Taoists, the Mongol courtiers did not make them fall to their knees and bow their foreheads to the floor—the practice called kowtow—as was customary. Genghis asked the monk about the medicine of immortality. Ch'ang ch'un replied, "There are means of preserving life, but no medicine of immortality." Genghis praised him for his honesty. The monk also got away with refusing to drink koumiss (fermented mare's milk), the Mongols' favorite alcoholic beverage and a part of their court ceremonies. Eventually Ch'ang ch'un explained Taoist doctrine to the khan, who was "highly edified" by this, and "the discourse of the sage pleased his heart." Ch'ang ch'un asked Genghis if he could go home now, and Genghis said they would travel together, since he was headed eastward also and had more questions in mind. After keeping the monk close at hand for almost a year, the khan finally let him begin his trip home in April 1223. Ch'ang ch'un was back in Peking by 1224. Genghis ordered a monastery to be built for him there. Ch'ang ch'un died three years later at the age of seventy-nine.

People think of the Age of Exploration as beginning in the fourteen hundreds, with various well-known voyages. In fact, its stirrings may be seen two centuries earlier, in epic pedestrian journeys like Ch'ang ch'un's. Other monks—Christian rather than Taoist though no less intrepid—traversed Asia in that time to visit the Mongol khan. The Christians, of course, started from the west rather than the east. John of Plano Carpini, a Franciscan and a companion of St. Francis, traveled from Lyons in April 1245 on a missionary journey in the pope's name. Carpini endured a hard trip, reached the khan in Mongolia, definitely did not convert him to Christianity, and arrived back in France in the fall of 1247. Six years after that, King Louis the Pious of France, hearing a report that some of the Mongols were Christians, sent another Franciscan, William de Rubruquis, with official letters requesting that Rubruquis be allowed to settle in Mongol lands and preach the gospel. Rubruquis took another couple of years in his travel and, like Carpini, did not succeed at all in winning souls. The most famous pedestrian explorer of the age, Marco Polo, made his trip to the court of Kublai Khan, grandson of Genghis, in 1271–75. In Polo's book, many in Europe would read about travels in Asia for the first time. None of these journeys would have been possible without the Mongols. Genghis's global conquests, and those of his sons and grandsons, not only opened up Asia but provided enough order so that people could travel there.

The Mongols were the last of the great solar-powered scourges who gathered strength on the grassland steppes of Central Asia and emerged in search of plunder and destruction. The invention of the bronze bit in about 800 BCE put the steppe dweller on horseback, and his mobility let him find new pastures to fuel ever-larger herds. Later advances in iron-working and weaponry made him a terrifying foe. The Greeks called these barbarians Scythians; Herodotus said they descended from Hercules' son, Scythes, inventor of the bow and arrow. Another name for the barbarians—Sarmatians—came from the Greek for "lizard-eyed." (Going by that description, there are still many Sarmatians in Russia today.) The Roman poet Ovid wrote of the dangerous steppe barbarians during his Black Sea exile in the first century AD: "When the fierce strength of the mighty Boreas fetters the waters, then at once the barbarian enemy rides along the Ister [Danube] . . . The enemy, mighty with horses and his swiftly flying arrows, lays waste the countryside far and wide."

Scythians, Goths, Huns, Magyars, Avars, Khazars—the waves of nomadic peoples of the grasslands came and went. The ever-renewing Central Asian pastures, and their wild horsemen, constituted one of the hazards of the planet for more than a thousand years. Attempts to fence the steppe barbarians out by means of walls, of which the Great Wall of China was only the most dramatic example, never did solve the problem. In the end, all that really worked was shooting the mounted invaders with guns. By the fifteenth century, fortunately for civilization, the improved battlefield efficiency of firearms had moved military advantage to the defenders' side.

But before the steppe barbarians receded into history forever, they produced a final, world-shaking spasm with the Mongols and Genghis

Khan. The Mongols were originally one of many tribes on the eastern steppes and Genghis only a local tribal leader. He was born with the name Temuchin in 1167 on the banks of the Onon River in the grasslands between Lake Baikal and the Great Wall. His mother, Alan-Koa, was said to have been impregnated by the sky god Koko Tengri entering her tent on a moonbeam and penetrating her womb with a ray of light. The clot of black blood the baby was holding in his fist at birth augured his future and the world's. By young manhood, Temuchin had fought and maneuvered his way to a chieftainship, employing remarkable gifts of organization and a knack for judging his comrades' character and inspiring loyalty. In 1206, the *kuriltai*, or gathering of tribes, elected him the Great Khan; "Genghis" means something like "oceanic." From that point his armies grew and added new and more-distant conquests every year.

Almost the only not-horrible thing about the Mongols was if you happened to be one yourself. Within the group they treated one another generously and fairly, following the legal code called the *yasaq*, laid down by Genghis Khan. Plus, there was the comradely fun of destroying and pillaging civilizations from Peking to Bukhara. A Muslim eyewitness to the invasion of the Irano-Mesopotamian borderlands told a Persian historian how the Mongols cheerfully mocked the Islamic cry *"la ilaha illa allah,"* shouting it when they were about to kill someone. "The massacre over, they plundered the town and carried off the women," the witness said. "I saw them frolicking on their horses . . . they laughed, they sang in their own language, and they said: *'la ilaha illa allah.'"* After victories, the Mongols sometimes put boards on top of their prisoners and had drinking contests on them.

Genghis Khan told the peoples he conquered that he was their punishment for the soft, luxurious lives they had been leading. Certainly, the Mongols' existence on the steppes had been the opposite of that. Physically, the Mongols were narrow waisted, small footed, with large heads; many had the bowlegs nomads acquire from growing up on horseback. The men shaved the crowns of their heads and left bangs hanging down in front and two long locks in back, which they braided and tied to their ears. They had thick eyebrows. Much of their lives was spent outdoors in the steppes' fierce climate, almost always on horseback. They would mount up and ride whenever they had to go a distance farther than a hundred paces. Observers said the Mongols would eat just about anything—mare's milk curds dried on rocks, roots, lice, dogs, rats, meat tenderized by being ridden on all day beneath a saddle. Marco Polo said they ate a lot of hamsters, which were plentiful on the steppes. Other observers noted that on long journeys Mongol riders would open a vein in their horse's neck and fill a small bowl with blood, or drink directly from the vein. They could endure extreme cold or heat while riding, Friar Carpini said, and after two days with no food "sing and make merry as if they have eaten their bellies full."

The heads of Mongol arrows were four fingers broad, to cause bigger wounds, and they kept them sharp with files. No Mongol soldier was without a file. Their arrows had very thin notches, too small for their enemies' bowstrings, so the arrows could not be picked up and shot back at them. Their bows were of horn and sinew on a wood frame and took two men to string. They wore iron helmets and armor made of polished iron sewn on leather; one observer described an army clad in this armor shining like the sun. On the open steppes, they tended to get hit by lightning. Thunder terrified them. During their long campaigns they carried all kinds of belongings with them—whole houses made of felt, on giant carts—with their immense herds of horses and oxen providing the transport. In the summers, when the grazing was the best, they journeyed most widely. A historian has written that in battle the Mongols "made the fullest use of the terror inspired by their physique, their ugliness, and their stench." Considering that in summer their diet consisted almost entirely of mare's milk, and that the *yasaq* had strictures against ever washing their clothes, that last point sounds plausible.

By the time of Genghis's death in 1227, the Mongols had subdued northern China, middle Asia, the Crimea, and the northern Caucasus; their empire stretched from the Caspian to the Pacific. In the process, they had killed tens of millions of people—more than eighteen million in China alone, over one and a half million in the Central Asian city of Herat, according to contemporary historians. A Persian chronicler said that in the Muslim countries Genghis invaded, "not one in a thousand of the inhabitants survived." These estimates are perhaps exaggerated, but they give an idea of how contemporaries saw the calamity. Rashid ad-Din, a Persian who is considered to be perhaps the best ancient authority on Genghis Khan, quotes Genghis's saying that the greatest pleasure in life is "to cut my enemies in pieces, drive them before me, seize their possessions, witness the tears of those who are dear to them and to embrace their wives and daughters." This, more than any Taoist precepts he might have acquired from Ch'ang ch'un, is the enduring wisdom of Genghis Khan.

And on the subject of embracing those wives and daughters: Genghis had hundreds of wives and concubines among different harems around his empire. Whenever women were captured, the most beautiful were presented to the soldiers' immediate superiors, who passed the most beautiful to their superiors, and so on up to the khan. The very fairest were called "moonlike girls." Genghis's sons and the subsequent princes in his line continued this practice. Of course, Genghis and his heirs fathered many children. A Persian historian writing about the Mongols in 1260 said that by then the Mongol leader had twenty thousand descendants living; the historian added that he knew he would be accused of exaggerating.

Recently, geneticists from Oxford University working with colleagues from China, Pakistan, Mongolia, and Uzbekistan spent ten years taking blood samples from men in Central Asia to study the Y chromosome, which is passed from father to son. The geneticists found that a distinctive cluster of Y chromosomes in the DNA of 8 percent of the men indicated descent from a single common ancestor about a thousand years ago. The geneticists believed that the ancestor was Genghis Khan (or rather, an eleventh-century ancestor of Genghis Khan). From this study they concluded that in Central Asia, about sixteen million men—or about one-half of 1 percent of the world's entire male population—is descended from Genghis Khan.

During Genghis's lifetime, the Mongols took only a passing interest in Russia. As I mentioned in chapter two, Genghis gave the western part of his empire to his eldest son, Jochi. In 1237, ten years after Genghis's death, Jochi's son Batu, whose name meant "hard or durable" in Mongol, set out at the head of a great army to bring Mongol rule to the Russian principalities. Batu chose winter for his campaign, and with horses and carts and men made his way along Russia's central rivers, obligingly level and hard frozen. As the army advanced, steaming, the prince of the city of Ryazan sent his son Feodor to meet them with presents. Batu accepted the gifts and told Feodor that he had heard that the prince of

Ryazan had a beautiful wife, a princess named Euphrasia. Batu informed Feodor that he would like to see this wife. Feodor said Christian princes were not in the habit of showing their wives to infidels. Batu then beheaded Feodor, and at the news of this Euphrasia jumped from an upper room in the palace to her death.

Batu sent envoys accompanied by an enchantress to Ryazan. The envoys asked the city to give them a tenth of everything—one in ten princes, one in ten horses, a tenth of all citizens, a tenth of all products. The leaders of Ryazan answered that when none of them were left alive, what remained would belong to Batu. The Mongols enclosed Ryazan in a wall, reduced it with siege engines that shot burning projectiles, and took the city in December 1237. Cinders, stones, and dead bodies strewed the ground when they were through. From Ryazan, Batu continued to Moscow, where he killed 270,000. Ordinary people were just killed, while those of distinction were flayed alive, crucified, or burned. At the city of Vladimir, Batu's next target, the Mongols overcame the defenses by building an earth mound higher than the walls and then crossing down into the city from it. When the Mongols finally departed Vladimir, there were no cries, because all were dead.

The Mongols—or Tatars, as the Russians and others called them, a generic term for Asiatic horsemen—returned to pillage Russia each winter after that for four years, taking the cities of Pereyaslavl, Chernigov, Smolensk, and Suzdal. When the Tatars approached Kiev, the most beautiful of Russian cities and the capital of ancient Rus, a contemporary chronicler wrote: "Like dense clouds the tatars pushed themselves forward towards Kiev, investing [surrounding] the city on all sides. The rattling of their innumerable carts, the bellowing of camels and cattle, the neighing of horses, and the wild battle-cry, were so overwhelming as to render inaudible the conversation of the people inside the city." When Kiev fell, the Tatars outdid themselves in killing and burning, and even opened the tombs to scatter the bones and crush the skulls beneath their heels. Five years later, when Friar Carpini passed by on his embassy from the pope, he saw "an innumerable multitude of dead men's skulls and bones lying upon the earth." After the razing of Kiev, the Tatar attacks stopped for a while; in most of southern Russia there was nothing significant left to destroy.

During these events, the rulers of the Russian cities did not particularly cover themselves with glory. Historians have noted that often a prince would find it necessary to be elsewhere when the Mongols came to attack his city, while the prince's family and subjects stayed behind and took their chances. Often the princes were hampered in their resistance by feuds among themselves, or would even side with the Mongols in order to eliminate a rival. After Batu's attacks of 1237–41, the Mongols settled in and oppressed Russia with varying degrees of severity for the next two hundred years; they were not totally removed as a force in the region for another hundred years after that. The western branch of the Mongols became known as the Golden Horde. In theory, the Golden Horde was subject ultimately to the Great Khan in Peking or Mongolia, but that tie weakened over time.

The Mongols did not like trees. A people who lived on horseback needed open space, as well as grazing for their animals. For his capital, Batu chose a spot in the steppe country of the lower Volga where he and his family lived in large linen tents previously owned by the king of Hungary. The Mongols called this capital Sarai; later they would move to a new site, also called Sarai, a bit farther downstream. From Sarai they pulled strings in the Russian cities to the north and west, using as their agents, instead of their own men, the Russian princes themselves. These princes often served as proxy Mongols, collecting taxes and tribute and enforcing Mongol decrees. Sometimes the cities rebelled, and the Mongols had to come back and show who was boss. For one political misstep or another, Moscow was sacked and burned many times during the Mongol years.

To escape the Mongol influence, a population shift took place in Russia, with people moving into the forests and northward to more remote cities where the horsemen were unlikely to come. Russian culture, too, stunned by the occupation, retreated into its spirituality, and into monasteries deep in the woods. Russia survived as itself mainly in the monasteries during this hard period. The Mongols, with their unlikely reverence for things of the spirit, allowed the institutions of the Orthodox church to be exempt from taxes; as a result, during these centuries the Russian church did all right. Some Russian historians say that the spiritual growth and sense of self that Russia found during the Mongol period formed the beginnings of the Russian empire, or that the later Russian state combined the continental vision inherited from the Mongols with Russian spirituality.

My own theory about Russia and the Mongols is more psychological or fanciful, and addresses the question I said I had stopped thinking about but actually can't help returning to: namely, how Russia can be so great and so horrible simultaneously. I think one answer is that when other countries were in their beginnings, developing institutions of government and markets and a middle class and so on, Russia was beset with Mongols. That is, Russia can be thought of as an abused country; one has to make allowances for her because she was badly mistreated in her childhood by the Mongols.

Whatever else the Mongols did to Russia, they turned her attention toward the east. When the Mongols first appeared, the Russians understood only that this nightmare had come from the eastern wilderness, as the church chronicles had prophesied that the savage tribes banished by Gideon would do in the final days. And after Batu's conquests, Russians began to make their first journeys deep into Asia—at Mongol command, and of course unwillingly. Thousands of Russian prisoners were sent eastward to add variety to Mongol harems or fill out Mongol armies. Russian princes, too, often had to cross Asia to present themselves to the khan, in obedience to a summons or to secure favor, on the general principle that it was somewhat better to visit the Mongols than to have them visit you.

Trips to Sarai, relatively close by on the Volga, were bad enough. But sometimes that show of submission did not suffice, and the princes had to go on to the Great Khan's capital, a city called Karakorum, perhaps a year's travel away in Mongolia beyond and to the south of Lake Baikal. When Friar Carpini was in the court of the Great Khan in 1246, he saw Grand Duke Yaroslavl of Suzdal treated with disdain, forced to walk behind and sit behind his Mongol attendants, pitiably waiting their pleasure. Yaroslavl died on that trip, possibly poisoned by a woman in the khan's retinue.

Yaroslavl's son Alexander, later called Alexander Nevsky because of his victories against the Swedes and the Teutonic Knights at the Neva River, knuckled under to the Mongols just as his father had done. Though later a saint of the Orthodox church described as possessing supernatural powers—he was said to have sailed up the Neva River on a grindstone—

Nevsky still could not get out of making many trips to Sarai, and also went on a journey to Karakorum that lasted for two years. It was on a trip returning from Sarai that Nevsky died.

Maybe the reason that no Russian tsar (until Alexander II) ever ventured east of the Urals, and that the tsars instead used Siberia as a place to send their enemies, was that they still had a historic memory passed down from medieval Russia of those cross-continental visits to the Great Khan.

In time, like a drunk forgetting some mischief he had set out to do, the Golden Horde and its oppression of Russia succumbed to entropy. Russians point to the defeat of Khan Mamai at Kulikovo Field in 1380 as the beginning of the Golden Horde's eclipse and the corresponding rise of Russian power. It is also true, however, that Tokhtamysh, a renegade general formerly under Tamerlane, defeated Mamai, took over the Golden Horde, and burned Moscow to the ground two years after Kulikovo. Real and lasting withdrawal of Tatar power dated from a century later, when Ivan III ("the Great"), prince of Moscow, managed a long standoff with Akhmet Khan and the reduced Golden Horde at the Oka River. When Akhmet finally withdrew without a battle, Tatar domination of Russia had come to an end.

By then the Mongol multitudes in much of Asia had been absorbed into the people they'd overrun, and had taken up the faiths they'd encountered—Buddhism, Islam, even Nestorian Christianity. As the Mongol empire shrank and the feared horsemen retreated to the steppes where the empire had begun, many Mongols converted to the Tibetan version of Buddhism, persuaded by its leader, Sonam Gyatso, the Dalai Lama, who made a missionary trip to Mongolia in 1577. According to Tibetan Buddhist belief, Sonam Gyatso lives today in the person of Tenzin Gyatso, his latest incarnation and the current Dalai Lama, known to many from his political activism and his computer ads. As Tibetan Buddhists, the Mongol descendants of Genghis's legions renounced not only warfare but all other forms of violence, including hunting and hawking. From being the most violent people on the planet in the thirteenth century they became, within a few hundred years, some of the most peaceable.

The influence of the Mongols on Russia was profound. Russians have long been proud to claim that by absorbing the worst the Mongols could do they saved Western Europe, and maybe civilization, from destruction. Slavophilic historians have also said that Russia should be grateful to the Tatars for keeping her from becoming subject to the Roman church and a kind of lame imitation of Europe; instead the Tatars "introduced into the Russian soul the Mongolian continental feeling," as one historian put it. Many Mongol words entered the Russian language. Often these were words like *yamshchik* (driver), *loshad'* (horse), *sunduk* (trunk or box), or *orlov* (from *orluk*, eagle), having to do with travel. As for spanning Asia, the system of post roads that Genghis Khan set up to provide communication in his empire, with relays of horses kept at a series of way stations each a regular distance from the next, continued to serve the Siberian part of the Russian empire in only slightly modified form until the building of the Trans-Siberian Railway. Some everyday Russian customs have Mongol origins—for example, the superstition against shaking hands or embracing across a threshold. Most Russians refuse to do that. Instead, they step all the way across the threshold and then shake hands and embrace, or insist that you first come inside. This custom is said to derive from the Mongols' extreme touchiness about stepping on, greeting across, or otherwise behaving carelessly at the threshold of their dwellings.

Mongol influence protected Russian literature, too, from being merely a European copy. Russian writers claimed Tatar ancestry to mark their distinctiveness, as the poet Anna Gorenko did when she became Anna Akhmatova, borrowing the surname from a relative of Tatar blood. Even Vladimir Nabokov, a writer as westernized as they come, said in an interview that his last name was derived from one Nabok, a twelfth-century Tatar prince, and that he, Nabokov, was thus directly descended from Genghis Khan (him and sixteen million other guys).

One of my favorite scenes in Dostoyevsky happens early in *The Brothers Karamazov*, when Dmitri Karamazov is telling his younger brother, Alyosha, about an encounter with the beautiful and proud Katarina Ivanovna some years before. Dmitri, in the army at the time, had just received six thousand rubles owed him by old Karamazov, their father; Dmitri also happened to know that his commander, Katarina Ivanovna's father, had been guilty of a financial irregularity involving the disappearance of four thousand five hundred rubles from the regimental accounts. When the commander is about to be disgraced, Dmitri tells Katarina Ivanovna's sister that he will give them the money to repay the

missing funds if Katarina Ivanovna visits his quarters "secretly." Katarina
Ivanovna has no choice, so one evening she appears at Dmitri's room.
The young woman is shaken and pale; but determined to sacrifice her
honor to save her father; Dmitri takes out a five-thousand-ruble note,
shows it, folds it, hands it to her, makes a bow, and opens the door for her
to leave. Katarina Ivanovna accepts the money and (Dmitri says), "All at
once, not impetuously, but softly, gently, bowed down to my feet—not a
boarding school curtsey, but a Russian bow, with her forehead to the
floor." *Not a boarding school curtsey*; that "Russian bow," one of the
most romantic, not to say erotic, moments in all of Dostoyevsky, comes
to Russian literature from the Mongols.

Finally, this thought on the Mongols: When you travel in Russia, especially in the cities, you see a lot of ravens and crows. The ravens are a
dark, shiny black, while the crows are duller, many of them with capelike
areas of gray on the breast and back. A jet-lagged traveler in Moscow
lying awake in the small hours remembers he's in Russia when at first
light he hears the crows' and ravens' raspy calls. The birds build large,
uncomfortable-looking nests of sticks, fight over crusts of black bread in
the snow, and spend much of the day checking out new developments at
the large communal garbage bins behind the big apartment buildings.
I've never seen the black-and-gray crows (called hooded crows, or jack-
daws) in eastern Siberia; with that exception, crows, and ravens are ubiquitous in Russia, I've found. In fact, there are so many of them that a
traveler interested in birds quickly learns not to get his hopes up when
seeing something flying in the distance, because at closer view it's almost
always a raven or a crow.

In America, ravens and crows have a shifty, raffish, troublemaking
quality; they're always looking for an easy score. The crows and ravens of
Russia, by contrast, are somehow more grave. Like buzzards, they appear ruminative, as if they know that all things will come to them in time.
I'd always found the Russian crows and ravens disquieting, though I
couldn't have explained why. Then one day I remembered a notable fact
about the small rural town of Hinckley, Ohio. Every year in March, on or
near the same day, flocks of buzzards arrive in Hinckley. Tourists gather
annually to watch this event, and over the years it has given the town
some small fame. People in Hinckley say that this convocation of buzzards began back in the nineteenth century, when Hinckley was a fron-

tier town. The local farmers, wanting to tame the still-wild neighborhood, staged a big encirclement and drove all the predators to the center, where they killed them in heaps. Soon news of this bonanza reached buzzards all over, and they came to Hinckley and feasted. They've been coming back in March ever since, just in case.

With the Hinckley buzzards on my mind, I wondered if that wasn't what troubled me about the crows and ravens of Russia: maybe someplace deep in their bird consciousness these carrion lovers cherish memories of the Mongols' glory years in the distant thirteenth century, and they know that if they are only patient, the Mongols will return.

Chapter 9

The Russian princes who hiked endlessly to appear before the Great Khan at Karakorum left no written descriptions of the experience, preferring to forget about it, no doubt. But after Russia was a country among others, and Muscovy had unified the princedoms and elevated the Muscovite prince to the eminence of tsar, he began to send out embassies. Ambassadors dispatched to meet with the Chinese emperor, six thousand miles away in Peking, wrote some of the first and best accounts of travels in Siberia.

The earliest of these travelers, in the seventeenth century, knew almost nothing about China. Russians of the time had heard that China was completely surrounded by a brick wall, so they assumed it couldn't be very large. Nicolae Milescu (sometimes called Spathary), a Moldavian-born Greek of great learning, spent three years on the journey and accomplished little besides annoying the Chinese emperor, K'ang-hsi, with arguments over protocol. Evert Ysbrantsoon Ides, a Dutchman sent in 1692, had better diplomatic success, and after his tedious twenty-month trek to Peking delighted in the food and entertainment there—"Soops and pottages . . . extraordinarily grateful to the taste," he wrote, as well as performances by trained apes and mice and rides on the emperor's elephants.

Like many high-ranking officials in tsarist Russia, these envoys and their suites tended to be foreign born. John Bell, a physician with the embassy led by L. V. Izmailov in 1719, was a Scotsman of a prosaic and down-to-earth sensibility who wrote an account described by a reviewer in 1817 as "the best model perhaps for travel-writing in the English language." I like Bell a lot, and think the almost-dour factuality of his prose argues for nonfiction being a particularly Scottish art. The Izmailov party left St. Petersburg on July 14 and by fall were waiting in Kazan for the roads to freeze. Setting off from there in late November, Bell wrote, "The roads were rough and narrow, lying through dark woods, interspersed with some villages and cornfields." Minus the now omnipresent power-line towers, that description would still fit the landscape today.

Going by sled for 250 versts from the city of Tyumen to Tobolsk, the Siberian capital, Bell and his companions covered the distance in thirty hours, which I figure equaled about five miles an hour. From Tobolsk they went up the Irtysh River and then across the Barabinsk Steppe, a dangerous region because of the Kalmuck bandits that roamed it. At the Ilim River they turned south and followed that tributary to the Angara, which led them to the city of Irkutsk, a big place even in that day, with two thousand houses. While in the vicinity of Lake Baikal, Bell learned of the existence of a personage called the Dalai Lama, and his mention of him is believed to be the first ever in an English text.

Between Baikal and the Chinese border, Bell reported "waste land enough to maintain, with easy labour, several European nations." He complained about the insects, like almost all travelers before and after. Headed south across the Gobi Desert he noted that European tents were useless, because the tent pins wouldn't hold in the sand. When in the distance the travelers saw, on the high hills, the windings of the Great Wall, one of them cried, "Land!" Like Ides, Bell noted the pleasures of Chinese dining, the "water-melons, musk-melons, sweet and bitter oranges, peaches, apples, wall-nuts, chess-nuts" he tasted, and the courses enlivened with "dancing and musick, and quail-fighting." He wrote, "The Chinese handle the two ivory or wooden pins, which they use instead of forks, with such dexterity, that they can even take up needles with them."

Lacking knowledge of each other's language, the Russians and the Chinese conducted their diplomatic business in Latin. Mandarin-speaking Jesuit missionaries in Peking—by then there had already been a Catholic missionary presence in Peking for almost four hundred years—provided the Latin-to-Mandarin translation. Adding to the difficulty of conversation was the Chinese belief that their emperor embodied God and thus could regard the Russian tsar only as a vassal. That meant the tsar's representatives had to kowtow; the awkwardness of this in terms of protocol had thwarted the Milescu embassy. Peter the Great, the tsar who sent the Izmailov party, really wanted it to make progress, especially in the establishment of regular trade. Peter had instructed Izmailov to kowtow if he had to. Peter even sent along, as a present for the emperor, a model of the Battle of Poltava, which he had carved himself.

K'ang-hsi, by the way, is considered perhaps the greatest Chinese emperor of all time. He occupied the throne for sixty-one years, from 1661 to 1722, and solidified the Manchu line, whose years in power (1622–1912) were almost the same as those of the Romanov tsars. K'ang-hsi consistently outmaneuvered and outsmarted the Russians. In the Amur River Valley, on China's northern border, he blocked Russian expansion and made the Russians formalize their withdrawal from the area in the Treaty of Nerchinsk (1689), the first-ever treaty between China and a European power. Because of that setback, Russia had to keep to the north in extending herself across Siberia and wasn't able to move into the Amur country until the nineteenth century. Had it not been for K'ang-hsi, Russia might not have gone so far northeastward or colonized Alaska.

The emperor's attitude toward foreigners may be seen in his Ministry of Foreign Affairs, whose name translated literally as "Office for the Regulation of the Barbarians." John Bell described K'ang-hsi sitting cross-legged on his throne and wearing no crown but "a little round cap" topped with "a large beautiful pearl in the shape of a pear." Of K'ang-hsi's power, Bell wrote, "It seemed somewhat strange to a Briton, to see some thousands of people upon their knees, and bowing their heads to the ground, in most humble posture, to a mortal like themselves."

Bell returned across Siberia to St. Petersburg without misadventure in 1722 and soon after accompanied Tsar Peter, whom he admired, on a trip to Derbent. In later years, Bell served as secretary to the British minister in St. Petersburg, married a Russian lady, and went home to Scotland in 1746. He wrote his book there, and it came out in 1763, forty-some years after his trans-Siberian journey. At the end of the book he remembered Siberia in terms that, for Bell, almost constituted praise: "From what I have said concerning it [Siberia] I presume it will be granted, that it is by no means so bad as is generally imagined."

. . .

The first book by a native-born Russian who went to Siberia was *The Life of the Archpriest Avvakum by Himself*. Written in 1672 or 1673, this book has been called the only significant work of Russian literature between the Old Russian "Lay of Igor's Campaign" in the twelfth century and the poetic predecessors of Pushkin in the later eighteenth. I think *Life of the Archpriest* is one of the best works of nonfiction I've ever read. It's vivid, hair-raising, and sometimes unintentionally hilarious. Avvakum Petrovich, a priest of the Orthodox church, found himself on the conservative side of the seventeenth-century dispute between the reformers of the church and what came to be called the Old Believers. For its time, this split was almost like the reforms of Peter the Great or even the Russian Revolution in the turmoil it caused. Changes that seem small now—crossing oneself with three fingers instead of with two—appeared huge and heretical to Avvakum and his followers, who saw in them the coming of the Antichrist and the loss of the possibility of salvation, in their hard lives the only enduring hope they had.

Today Avvakum seems like a complete fanatic, as indeed he was. He hated learning and rationalism, anathematizing what he called "almanack-mongers [who] say: 'We understand the things of heaven and earth, and who is equal unto us?' . . . Look then, proud almanack-monger," he went on, "where are thy Pythagoruses and Platos: they have all been eaten by worms, like so many swine." And when Avvakum got mad, he got really mad, as in his response to the reformers' excommunication of him from the Orthodox church: "My excommunication, it came from heretics and, in Christ's name, I trample it under foot, and the curse written against me—why, not to mince my words, I wipe my arse with that; if the heretics curse me, the saints of Moscow—Peter, and Alexis, and Jonah, and Philip—*they* bless me."

Yet somehow, for a fanatic, Avvakum kept his eyes open and saw what was in front of him and wrote it down. For his intransigency and vehement preaching, Tsar Alexei Mikhailovich exiled him to Siberia, along with his wife, Nastasia Markovna, and their children. In the lands beyond Lake Baikal—a region then called Dauria—he served as a chaplain to an expedition led by the Cossack Athanasius Pashkov, an unsympathetic type who burned and tortured people and even flogged Avvakum

seventy-two strokes with a knout. At one point Avvakum was riding on a
boat that got away in some rapids of a river, and he was running back and
forth, calling on God, weeping and beseeching the heavens. When the
boat finally passed through to safety, the Cossack said to him, "You're
making yourself a laughing-stock." Avvakum had enough sense of reality
to tell this story on himself. Sometimes, he reported, his family was reduced to living on fir cones and the bones of carcasses left by wolves.

When Avvakum and the other exiles eventually are marching back to
Moscow, and the months of journeying drag on and on, Avvakum records
a conversation between himself and his wife that is a Russian moment for
the ages. The two are among a group walking along on ice, unable to
keep up with the horses, and Avvakum says, "My poor old woman tramped
along, tramped along, and at last she fell, and another weary soul stumbled over her, and he fell too, and they both screamed, and were not able
to get up . . . And I came up, and she, poor soul, began to complain to
me, saying, 'How long, archpriest, are these sufferings to last?' And I said,
'Markovna! till our death.' And she, with a sigh, answered, 'So be it,
Petrovich; let us be getting on our way.'"

How long, archpriest . . . ? Both question and answer were apt. The
trip back to Moscow from Siberia took them three years. After Avvakum's
return, the tsar was hoping for compromise but met only continued resistance from Avvakum, whom exile hadn't softened. As the dispute over
reform became a full-scale schism, believers of Avvakum's persuasion
began starving themselves and committing mass suicide. Whole villages
shut themselves up in their wooden churches and immolated themselves
rather than submit to enforcement of the reforms. Historians estimate
that in these years about twenty thousand followers of the old way killed
themselves by fire. Avvakum, always the voice of moderation, wrote,
"You will not be very long burning in the fire—just the twinkling of an
eye—and the soul is free. Are you afraid of the furnace? Play the man,
spit at it, do not be afraid! Fear comes before the fire; but once you are
in it, you forget it all." For this kind of rhetoric he was again exiled, this
time to the north, to the Arctic coast near Nova Zembla, where he preached
that "the Gates of the Church had been forced by Satan." In 1682, after
sending an unusually violent letter to the tsar, he got his wish and was
burned at the stake.

Thousands of others who opposed the reforms ended up in Siberia,
either through exile or voluntarily. Old Believer villages remain in Sibe-

ria to this day. During the Stalin years, when Old Believers suffered new persecutions, some survived by going even deeper into the taiga. In 1978, a team of Soviet geologists prospecting by helicopter for iron ore happened to see garden rows on a mountainside in remote taiga 150 miles from the nearest village. Upon investigation, they found a family of five Old Believers who had seen no other humans for forty years. As the geologists and the family talked, someone mentioned Nikon, the patriarch of Moscow who had instituted the reforms more than three hundred years before; at his name, the family spat and crossed themselves defiantly with two fingers.

The inquisitive spirit of the eighteenth century desired more books about Siberia. Of course the Bering expeditions produced several. George Steller, the naturalist infuriated by Bering's quick decision to turn back, lived through the shipwrecked winter on Commander Island and wrote *Journal of a Voyage with Bering 1741–1742*, which described his journey and some of the flora and fauna. That book, and *Steller's History of Kamchatka*, came out before the century's end. An outspoken fellow, Steller angered the Russian bureaucracy and died in unhappy circumstances a few years after the expedition's return; I think of him when I'm in the American Northwest and I see the large and quarrelsome Steller's Jay. Sven Waxell, a Swede who served as Bering's lieutenant, not only survived that winter, but his twelve-year-old son, Laurentz, who accompanied him, made it as well. Waxell's account was written in 1758 but not published until much later.

Part of Bering's commission had been to send parties to far regions of eastern Siberia for exploration and mapping. In 1751, Johann Georg Gmelin, a German naturalist and coleader of the expedition's academic contingent, published his *Reise durch Sibirien, von dem Jahr 1733 bis 1743 (Travel in Siberia in the Years 1733–1743)*, a work that came to be widely read throughout Europe. It described Russia as a harsh and brutal place, and even more so in Siberia. The writings of Gerhard Friedrich Müller, the other coleader, portrayed Russia more upliftingly as the possessor of a continental empire. Müller was a member of the Russian Academy and a geographer and historian. In his travels with the expedition, Müller went to Siberian cities so remote that officials in St. Petersburg had little contact with them. In the archives of the city of Yakutsk, almost a third of the way around the globe from the capital, Müller found documents indicating that a group led by a Cossack named Semyon Dezhnev, seeking furs, had sailed from the Lena River delta around the Chukchi Nos to the coast of the Bering Strait back in 1648. In other words, Müller learned in Yakutsk that the main question supposed to be determined by Bering's expedition—whether or not the continents of Asia and North America joined—had already been answered in the negative by Russian sailors almost a hundred years before. Either the news had never gotten back to western Russia, or it had but then was somehow forgotten there. Müller published this scoop in his *Nachrichten von Seereisen* (Description of Voyages) in 1758.

After the second Bering voyage, travelers began to come to Siberia from all over. Among non-Russians, the English, French, and Germans predominated, though Swedes and Swiss and others traveled there as well. A Hungarian soldier named Benyowsky who had been captured while serving in the Polish army ended up in exile in Kamchatka and did a number of horrible things there; the book he wrote afterward falls into the category of Siberian adventures of questionable veracity. Nor were the travelers from Europe only. When a detachment of Bering's men explored the coast of Japan, a contemporary Japanese account recorded the event and described the appearance of these new strangers, noting that "their eyes were the color of sharks." In 1789, Japanese sailors who had shipwrecked on the Siberian coast were sent by the Russians to Irkutsk, and from there crossed Siberia and continued to St. Petersburg, whence four of them returned to Japan by ship around the world.

The first American to travel in Siberia was the famous John Ledyard, one of the most footloose souls who ever lived. (I have written about him in my book *Great Plains*.) Ledyard had sailed the Bering Strait and North Pacific with Captain Cook and apparently there devised the idea of exploring western North America by approaching it from Asia. Meeting up with Thomas Jefferson in Paris, Ledyard interested him in this notion, and Jefferson then sought permission from the Empress Catherine for Ledyard to cross Russia. Ledyard's journey would be Jefferson's first attempt at sending an expedition to the American Northwest, a mission later carried out successfully by Lewis and Clark. Catherine, however, hated all revolutionaries, Americans especially, and to Jefferson's request she returned a firm no.

Nothing daunted, late in the year 1787 Ledyard went anyway. Unable to cross from Finland because of ice conditions, he walked clear around the Gulf of Bothnia to St. Petersburg in the middle of the winter. Finding Catherine not in residence at the moment, he charmed some kind of permission from a high-ranking *chinovnik* and then set out. He had made it remarkably far—all the way to Yakutsk—before Catherine learned of this contravention of her wishes and fell into a rage. She ordered him brought back by closed conveyance, never stopping, to be questioned first and then expelled at the Polish border. The grueling return destroyed Ledyard's health and may have undermined his sanity. Soon after, he determined to explore inner Africa, and when he was in Egypt and a hitch came up in these plans he took too much emetic and died. There is a statue of him at Dartmouth College, which he had attended briefly before a journey called him away.

Almost twenty years after Ledyard, an American did cross Siberia from one end to the other, but going in the opposite direction. In this case the motive—Yankee determination to collect a debt—was perhaps a more compelling one than wanderlust or exploration. In 1804, a young sea captain named John D'Wolf sailed the 206-ton three-masted brig *Juno* loaded with trade goods and provisions from Bristol, Rhode Island, around Cape Horn and then north to the Russian settlements in Alaska. In New Archangel (present-day Sitka), he sold not only all his supplies but also the ship itself to Alexander Baranov, manager of the Russian American Company. Not having the $50,000 purchase price, Baranov gave D'Wolf a note payable at the company's offices at St. Petersburg. D'Wolf wintered in New Archangel. The next year, in a small ship Baranov provided, he sailed to Kamchatka. There he spent another winter. The next year he sailed to Okhotsk. While crossing the Sea of Okhotsk, he had the experience of running up on the back of a drowsing whale. The ship sat there for a while until the whale submerged.

From Okhotsk a sketchy and obstacle-filled road led inland. D'Wolf endured a journey of swamps, mountains, mosquitoes, and tedium. "At first I was quite pleased with the idea of this land excursion, but I found in a very little while that it was no joke," he wrote. In a month he had reached Yakutsk, and Irkutsk a month after that. From Irkutsk he followed the main road, the Siberian Trakt, and traveled joltingly by carriage for thirty-five hundred more miles, arriving in St. Petersburg about two

months later, at the end of October. Not including his sail from Kamchatka, his trip across Siberia had taken five months. When he presented
himself at the offices of the Russian America Company, he learned that
a duplicate note had reached his employers in Rhode Island by ship
sometime earlier, and they had already sent an agent to collect the
money, and the business had been concluded. D'Wolf's voyage and sale
of ship and goods had earned them a profit of $100,000. Contrary weather
and other delays kept him from returning home until April of the following year. He had been gone for three years and eight months.

A footnote about John D'Wolf is that he happened to be the uncle of
Herman Melville. D'Wolf's wife, Mary, was Melville's father's sister. Tall,
straight, long legged, with a crest of white hair, D'Wolf personified the
Yankee sea captain; he "made so strong an impression on me, that I have
never forgotten him," Melville wrote in his novel *Redburn*, adding inac-
curately that this uncle had been lost in the White Sea some years later:
D'Wolf was in fact alive when *Redburn* was written, and he died in the
bosom of his family at the age of ninety-two. Melville included the incident about sailing onto the back of the whale in *Moby-Dick*.

Many people who you might not think of as ever having been in Russia,
were. For example, Captain John Smith, of Pocahontas fame, served as a
mercenary in the army of the Holy Roman Emperor before going on to his
adventures in America. Captured by the Tatars in 1603, he escaped through
northwest Russia. John Quincy Adams, the future president, accompanied
the American government's minister to Russia in 1781 as his personal secretary and French interpreter; Adams was only fourteen at the time. He
returned to St. Petersburg when he was forty and the U.S. minister himself,
and remained for five years, through the Napoleonic wars. The democrat
Adams and the autocrat Alexander I got along fine. Another future president, James Buchanan, occupied the ministerial post in 1832 and 1833. A
Presbyterian from Pennsylvania, Buchanan was shocked at what he saw as
the irreligiosity of the Russians, and especially at the royal family's habit of
holding grand fetes and balls on Sundays. Alexander Herzen, the revolutionary thinker and hero, remembered as a young man seeing Buchanan at
some event and noticing how his plain black frock coat and top hat stood
out among the gaudy uniforms and court finery.

Samuel Colt, the arms manufacturer, attended the coronation of Tsar Alexander II; Colt made several visits to Russia, selling guns. While on the trip memorialized in *Innocents Abroad*, Mark Twain met Alexander II on the Black Sea in 1867. Twain compared him to "a tinsel King." Whistler's mother, of the well-known painting, got up from her straight-back chair long enough to go to Russia with Whistler's father, an engineer, who helped his hosts build docks and railroads. Dumas père, the Marquis de Custine, Admiral John Paul Jones, Théophile Gautier, Booker T. Washington, Lewis Carroll—a list of unexpected sojourners in Russia could go on and on.

The nineteenth century was the great age of travel, when private citizens made long journeys to distant and almost-unexplored parts of the globe. Among alluring destinations, Siberia rivaled Africa and western North America. Many dozens of books about travel in Siberia came out in those years and up to the Bolshevik revolution. Per usual, the English travelers outdid almost everybody else. Englishmen saw Siberia on foot, and by boat, cart, and sledge. As a title of a book by an Englishman, *Narrative of a Pedestrian Journey Through Russia and Siberian Tartary from the Frontiers of China to the Frozen Sea and Kamchatka*, by Captain John Dundas Cochrane, Royal Navy, gives the general idea. Soon after setting out on this cross-continental stroll, Captain Cochrane was accosted by robbers who took all his possessions and clothes, overlooking only his waistcoat; Cochrane tied the waistcoat around his middle and continued on.

Englishmen went to Siberia to examine mineral resources, visit prisons, look for trade opportunities, distribute Bibles, study the natives, hunt, botanize. Intrepid Englishwomen ventured far into Siberia as well. To cite another representative title, *On Sledge and Horseback to Outcast Siberian Lepers*, by Kate Marsden, of the Royal British Nursing Association, is the story of that lady's search for a miraculous root said to cure leprosy, and for the lepers themselves. Wealthy people in St. Petersburg gave Miss Marsden money, and eventually she located some lepers in the northern wilds and set up a leper colony. Breaking under the strain of the trip, she then returned to England and spent the rest of her life as an invalid. As far as I could find out, no book before or since has ever mentioned the Siberian lepers. Miss Marsden is also the only traveler I know of to express concern about the sufferings of draft horses in Siberia.

Experts from Poland came to oversee mines, Norwegians to work in the fur trade, Danes to help in the dairying in western Siberia. The German scientist Alexander von Humboldt traveled Siberia in 1829 to establish meteorological stations, by international agreement, and to do studies on terrestrial magnetism. He and others like him continued the tradition of German-speaking scientists in Siberia. Americans of any kind were rare in Siberia until after 1850; then they became almost as numerous as Englishmen. The Americans' main focus was on mining and trade, with some Christian evangelizing. Perry McDonough Collins, a businessman looking into commercial possibilities for the United States, went on a wide-ranging jaunt through eastern Siberia in 1860 and devised the transcontinental telegraph project that brought George Kennan to Chukotka. American aggressiveness in trade beat most competitors. By the end of the nineteenth century, American products, from canned goods to McCormick reapers, could be found throughout the habitable parts of eastern Siberia.

As usual, global ambition reached for more. China, having grown much weaker since the days of Emperor K'ang-hsi, could not keep an expansionist Russia out of the Amur Valley, and in 1856 Siberia's governor-general, Count Nikolai N. Muraviev, simply took it from China by fiat with a small force of gunboats and soldiers. This grab had the good (for Russia) effect of giving her river access to the Pacific and a vast valley of relatively temperate and arable land. Unfortunately, moving into the Amur also put Russia on a collision course with the other country expanding into the region—Japan. Eventually this would lead to the disastrous (for Russia) Russo-Japanese War. The early buildup to the conflict featured an obscure and intriguing episode of travel in Siberia: the long ride of Captain Fukushima Yasumasa. For the purposes of reconnaissance, this Japanese army officer traveled on horseback across European Russia, western and central Siberia, Mongolia, part of China, and the Primorskii Region northeast of Vladivostok in the years 1892 and 1893. Aside from a brief mention of this unprecedented feat, I can find nothing about it in English-language histories.

Another timely idea of Count Muraviev's was the Trans-Siberian Railway. Building a line from the Urals to Vladivostok made obvious sense for Russia, but it presented engineering problems that were difficult even in that optimistic age of railroads. Bridges had to be erected across five rivers wider than the Mississippi; swampy ground troubled the route for many hundreds of miles; and even with a shortcut across compliant China the track would have to extend for more than five thousand miles. Construction of the line was authorized by imperial edict in May 1891, and Tsarevitch Nicholas, visiting the Far East at the time, pushed a wheelbarrow of dirt along an embankment in Vladivostok to inaugurate the great enterprise. By 1898, the line building eastward had reached Irkutsk. By 1901, the tracks had been completed from one end of Siberia to the other, not including the section circumventing Lake Baikal (a huge ferry to take the trains across the lake served as a temporary measure; during the winter tracks were laid on Baikal's ice). Regular service began in 1903. The section around the southern end of Baikal required thirty-eight tunnels and wasn't opened until 1905.

In these early railroad years, when the Trans-Siberian was being built and just after, a lot of people from the American Midwest traveled in and wrote books about Siberia. As a Midwesterner myself, I pause to take note of this phenomenon. Adventurous sorts from Illinois and Indiana made trips by land, river, and rail, mostly for business but some for pleasure. The number of travelers from the state of Ohio alone is statistically off the charts. In 1898, John Wesley Bookwalter, an Ohio businessman, went on a summer journey of some length; his *Siberia and Central Asia* (1899) "intelligently comments on every aspect of life and includes hundreds of photographs," says a bibliography. (Bookwalter later ran for governor of Ohio.) George Frederick Wright, a professor at Oberlin College, published *Asiatic Russia* in 1902, about his trip of the previous year. Senator Albert J. Beveridge, of Indiana, went through European Russia, Siberia, and Manchuria to write his *The Russian Advance* (1903). Beveridge was born in Ohio. Henry C. Rouse, president of the Missouri, Kansas and Texas Railway, rode the Trans-Siberian in 1903 and wrote about it for the *New York Evening Post*. He also was born in Ohio. Ohio-born William Wheeler's *The Other Side of the Earth*, about his Siberian train trip ("extremely superficial," in the opinion of another bibliography), appeared in 1913.

That's five people from Ohio visiting and writing about Siberia in the space of fifteen years, or an average of one Ohioan every three years. How can this oddity be explained? Were these people all inspired in their youth by stories about George Kennan, and did they want to be like him? Or did the official closing of the American frontier at the end of the nineteenth century make them restless and eager to see some even wilder place, the "Wild East," said to resemble the now vanished Wild West in many ways? Or perhaps something unknown in the flat, open landscape of the middle of America produces in a few of its citizens a strange affinity for the vastnesses of Russia. Maybe that happened to me; in any case, I am now at least the seventh person from Ohio to travel in and write about Siberia.

All these previous Midwesterners, even if they went as late as 1913, may be said to have traveled in the nineteenth century. The Russia they saw was still the Russia of the tsars, despite its advances, and it was of course about to be thoroughly swept away. Had these travelers made their journeys in late 1917 or after, they would have had an especially vivid experience of a torn-apart country, because the chaos of revolution, when it came, swirled around and along the railroads. After the October Revolution ended Russia's participation in the ongoing European war, soldiers rushing home to claim the land the Bolsheviks had promised them overwhelmed the trains. An American Communist who was in Russia at the time reported that a representative from the YMCA told him he had seen a sign that said, *Tovarish Soldiers*: Please do not throw passengers out of the window after the train is in motion." Soldiers rode all over the cars, even on the tops; at the entrance to many tunnels around Baikal lay the bodies of soldiers whom the low ceilings had knocked off.

In Siberia, the civil war that followed the revolution was fought mostly on and near the Trans-Siberian. For the next few years, the death and horror there were unlike any previously seen. Armed bands of uncertain loyalties went up and down the tracks in trains fitted with machine guns and armor. Derailed locomotives punctuated the scenery here and there. Tsar Nicholas II and his family, who had been under house arrest since he abdicated early in 1917, were shipped east by rail across the Urals for strategic reasons that summer, and there they came to an end even more awful than was traditional for Russian rulers who ever set foot in Siberia. For a while the tsar and family and household were held in Tobolsk; then they were moved to a well-fortified mansion in Ekaterinburg. On July 17, 1918, in the middle of the night—maybe because anti-Bolshevik forces were approaching, or for a crazier reason, or for nothing resembling a reason at all—they were taken to the basement and slaughtered, every one, among screams and ricochets and flying plaster dust, by a squad of killers who used a variety of weapons including a Colt .45.

Meanwhile a force of about fifty thousand Czech soldiers from the World War's eastern front had started out on the Trans-Siberian with the goal of reaching Vladivostok, boarding ships, and making their way to Europe and the western front by sea. These former Allied prisoners of war hoped that by changing to the winning side they would gain independence for Czechoslovakia after the war. Their presence in Siberia was a wild card that would further destabilize the situation.

Because the Soviet government had signed a separate peace with Germany, the Czechs soon were halted on their eastward journey. The Czechs had guns and numbers, however, and they chose to fight the Red Army units that opposed them along the railroad, with the result that much of the Trans-Siberian was in Czech hands by mid-1918. Adding to the confusion, Admiral Aleksandr Kolchak, former commander of Russia's Black Sea Fleet, had recently appeared in Siberia as the minister of war in an anti-Bolshevik government that he then took over by coup d'état. As self-proclaimed supreme ruler, Kolchak hoped to fight his way through western Russia and overthrow the Bolsheviks. He crossed the Urals into the west and won a few victories, but the Red Army pushed him back, and he withdrew again into Siberia, where support for his White Army was supposed to be strong. Among his potential allies were worthies like the murderously anti-Bolshevik Cossack atamans Grigory Semeyonov and Ivan Kalmykov, who each controlled a stretch of Far Eastern railroad line. For public relations value, both these leaders had their drawbacks. Semeyonov claimed he couldn't sleep well at night unless he had killed someone that day, and Kalmykov was said to have shot members of an orchestra in a café for playing the "Internationale" instead of "God Save the Tsar." Around the cities of Chita and Khabarovsk they racked up many atrocities.

England and Japan, eager to help defeat the Bolsheviks, sent their own troops into Siberia in 1918. The British force was small—a mere one thousand six hundred men—but Japan upped the ante substantially with an army of seventy-three thousand. Together the British and the Japanese pressured President Wilson to contribute an American contingent, and finally he did, reluctantly. The stated mission of the twelve-thousand-man American Expeditionary Force, as it was called, was to protect Allied supplies in Vladivostok from capture, to aid the passage of the Czechs, and to make sure the Russian people had a chance for unco-erced self-determination. At a more basic level, the Americans probably intended to keep Japan from grabbing Russian or Chinese territory, and more basically than that, they didn't know what they were doing at all.

The English hated the Bolsheviks, plain and simple. The British com-mander, General Alfred William Fortescue Knox, had been a military attaché in St. Petersburg before the revolution, knew many former tsarist officials, and inspired little confidence in General William Graves, the American commander. Graves, of a devotedly democratic cast of mind, wanted the Russian people to choose their own system of government, and he feared Knox was maneuvering them back to monarchy. Graves was especially distressed by his English counterpart's referring to the Russian peasants as "swine." Knox and his fellow officers, for their part, thought Graves a pro-Bolshevik fool because he wouldn't join them in trying to eliminate the Reds. In this opinion the Japanese concurred with the British so vehemently that Graves had to cope with many news-paper stories in America reporting Japanese charges of his supposed Bolshevik sympathies.

Admiral Kolchak's hoped-for support in Siberia never materialized. Losing battles with Red forces and partisans, he retreated farther east-ward. Typhus hit what remained of his army, and dead and dying White Army soldiers by the thousands accumulated along the railroad line. Kolchak pleaded with the Czechs to help him, but by late 1919 his chance was past. Instead the Czechs turned him over to the Soviet government in Irkutsk, along with the half billion rubles in gold reserves Kolchak's train had been carrying. The Irkutsk Soviets gave Admiral Kolchak a quick trial, shot him, and shoved his body into the Angara River through a hole in the ice.

The American, English, Japanese, and other foreign intervention forces had left Siberia by the end of 1920; Red victories continued until most of Siberia fell under Soviet control, though in the Far East battles were still being fought until 1922. Some of the very last White forces escaped the region into China that year and ended up in northern Cali-fornia. Events of the civil war in Siberia produced heroes of Communist iconography—for example, Sergei Lazo, the partisan leader, whom the poet Vladimir Mayakovsky praised in verse for defying his Japanese captors and crying, "Long live Communism!" even as they poured molten lead down his throat. For a while the Bolsheviks allowed the Russian Far East to exist as a separate republic, called the Independent and Democratic Far Eastern Republic, with a president who had lived for many years in Chicago, and its own declaration of independence written in English. That sham government was soon dispensed with, and all Siberia officially became part of the Soviet Union.

During the Soviet era, the Trans-Siberian Railway would take on the dismal role of transport for millions of prisoners shipped eastward to camps in the gulag. Accounts of Siberian exile and prison under the tsars had always included a journey, usually on foot, along the Siberian Trakt. All twentieth-century descriptions of Siberian punishment would begin with a rail journey, usually torturous and long. Soviet-era prisoners who had read about prison and exile of tsarist times sometimes scoffed at how tame those former sufferings were compared to their own. In my catalog of travels and travelers so far, I have said little about Siberian prison journeys, labor, and escapes. I will talk more about those subjects farther on.

For the moment it is perhaps enough to say that in the years of Bolshevik rule the evil of the system was so dense that it distorted anything that came near. That was of course especially true of books about Siberia, a region used by the Soviets as a penal colony screened off from the world. Even relatively lighthearted books—*I Wonder as I Wander*, by the American poet Langston Hughes, about his round-the-world ramblings in the early thirties—take on a queasy air because of what we know was happening offstage. At least Hughes had a sense of humor and was no ideologue; foreign travelers (and Russians as well) writing in moods of political rapture, real or feigned, produced books about Siberia that are embarrassing to look at today.

Henry Wallace, a former U.S. secretary of agriculture who served as Franklin Roosevelt's vice president from 1941 to 1945, was a passionate believer in "the century of the common man." Born in Iowa, Wallace also had a bad case of the Russia-love that seems to strike Midwesterners, and he happened to catch it at an unfortunate time. As America's successful cooperation with Russia in the Second World War was growing, and Germany was falling back in retreat, Wallace urged Roosevelt to send him on a friendship mission to Siberia, China, and Central Asia; Roosevelt agreed. Wallace made the trip in five weeks during mid-1944, and in 1946 published an account, *Soviet Asia Mission*. Worse books have been written about Siberia, but Wallace's holds the distinction of being the worst that is also widely known.

By now Wallace, a decent and dedicated man, has already been kicked around enough for *Soviet Asia Mission*, and it is perhaps unsporting to pile on. He later admitted the book's failings himself, in an article titled "Where I Was Wrong." Still, one has to note that in his visit to Magadan, headquarters of the complex of Kolyma gold-mining camps that cost perhaps three million slave laborers' lives, Wallace did not grasp that he was seeing a Potemkin village tricked up temporarily just for him, with the barbed wire taken down and the watchtowers dismantled; or that his host, Ivan Fedorovich Nikishov, was not the mere "industrial boss" described. Nikishov turns up in his true capacity as bloody tyrant in a number of gulag memoirs; he was in fact a feared lieutenant general in the NKVD (secret police). Wallace's *Soviet Asia Mission* includes the sentence, "The larch were just putting out their first leaves, and Nikishov gamboled about, enjoying the wonderful air immensely."

As David J. Dallin and Boris Nicolaevsky wrote in *Forced Labor in Soviet Russia* (published 1947), "[Wallace] should have been aware that every yard of the ground of these cities and towns [Magadan, among others] was drenched with the blood of Russian 'common men.'" These authors identified Nikishov as the "NKVD chief and actual dictator of the Far Eastern slave empire." Elevated words about Siberia from a speech Wallace gave in Irkutsk—"men born in wide, free spaces will not brook injustice and tyranny. They will not even temporarily live in slavery"—were quoted back at him reprovingly by Dallin and Nicolaevsky. Of course, many well-intentioned people in America and elsewhere at that time were still optimistic about the Soviet Union and reluctant to hear about the gulag. Robert Conquest's *Kolyma: The Arctic Death Camps*, published closer to the end of the Soviet era, in 1978, blasted Wallace all over again and was accepted more widely.

Owen Lattimore, of the U.S. Office of War Information, who traveled to Siberia with Wallace, wrote an article for *National Geographic* magazine that came out not long after they returned. In it he said, "We visited gold mines operated by Dalstroi in the Valley of the Kolyma River, where rich placer workings are strung out for miles . . . It was interesting to find, instead of the sin, gin, and brawling of an old-time gold rush, extensive greenhouses growing tomatoes, cucumbers, and even melons, to make sure that the hardy miners got enough vitamins!" Lattimore later conceded that he was "totally ignorant about the actual situation" he encountered in Siberia.

Just as the twentieth century split the atom, it took apart the human soul; in the camps of the Siberian gulag the soul's reduction approached the absolute. Most of the prisoners dispatched to the worst of the Far Eastern camps died, and writers like Osip Mandelstam who might have described the horrors did not survive to do so. Among those who did survive, the experience usually depleted the residue of hope in them to a level where they didn't have much left to write with. Only a very few gulag prisoners (like Varlam Shalamov) came out sufficiently unimpaired to create literature from what they'd been through. In certain respects not even the sufferings inflicted by the Mongols had been as bad. The Mongols killed the body but generally left the soul alone.

Still, history kept revolving, and the nightmare years of the gulag receded, amazingly, into the past. The same Siberia the old-time travelers saw remained, in its broad characteristics of geography and nature. Again Siberia became a space connected to the rest of the planet—traversable, visible, relatively unveiled. Wreckage from the Bolshevik era lay strewn around the landscape like the morning-after relics of a debauch, and the environment had been damaged, and the threat of drastic climate change evoked fear of some new swerve of history waiting just down the road. Through simple luck, the present seemed to be a breathing spell, at least for a little while. Sometimes travel is merely an opportunity taken when you can.

Chapter 10

So I decided to cross Siberia. I had flown into it and out again, and that was okay. But as I read more and studied the journeys of previous travelers, I understood that Siberia belongs to the category of things (oceans, deserts) that must be crossed, just as mountains are to be climbed. In the genre of Siberia travel, flying in and out again doesn't qualify. Of course, flying across Siberia hardly counts at all; anyone could accomplish that in the course of a nine-hour snooze. Neither, by my judgment, does taking the train, for reasons of its claustrophobia and its speed. After some thought, I decided the best method would be to drive.

I wasn't sure how to go about this. I began in this way:

With my family I had moved back East, to New Jersey. My friend Boris Zeldin, who lives in Jersey City, not far from me, had been telling me how great Leningrad was. He grew up there. Previously the city I kept visiting was Moscow, which had continued to overwhelm me. Moscow is a megalopolis, like Los Angeles, and most of the money of Russia is there. Listening to Boris, I wondered if St. Petersburg (the former Leningrad) might be smaller and easier, and suit my purposes better.

In July of 2000 I went to St. Petersburg to check it out and suffered Russia-infatuation all over again. Moscow is crowded, dense, centripetal—a capital city of the world. St. Petersburg is less frantic and more open, with a contemplative feel. Built on a swamp, one of Russia's recurring motifs, it's a sea-level city of long horizontal lines anchored at intervals by statues of writers, explorers, and tsars. Canals in the older parts of the city reflect the Italianate architecture its builders favored and add watery ripplings to the style.

For travelers, St. Petersburg is like a platonic ideal; it was a mark on a map before it became a city. Vectors drawn on maps seem to converge invisibly above it, in its high, pewter-colored sky. I imagined sorcerers from Gogol's ghost stories riding in their cauldrons across the sky's emptiness, and crowds staring upward at the raising of the great obelisk on the twentieth anniversary of the Battle of Borodino, and searchlights piercing the darkness and throwing noir shadows during the nights of the October Revolution as described by John Reed. Exploring all day and staying by myself in the Soviet-era Oktyabrskaya Hotel, I was adrift in about a dozen works of literature simultaneously.

On one of my first wanderings I came across a museum called the Museum of the Arctic and the Antarctic. It immediately became one of my favorite museums ever. Of Soviet vintage, the museum is in a large, pillared building, crumbling on the outside, that used to be an Orthodox church. In the museum's center, formerly the nave, is a partial globe fifteen or twenty feet across. The unusual feature of this globe is that it represents only the top third of the world; set in a cylindrical base at about waist height, it allows a viewer to walk around the Arctic regions in a leisurely way and examine the world's northern geography from a top-down vantage.

Of course, a good part of this third-of-a-globe is Siberia. Little illuminated bulbs indicate all the far northern cities of Russia. I strolled semicircularly from the Urals to the Bering Strait, noting the bulb for Provideniya and the minute whorls of the Bering Sea coastline where I'd been. The globe made dramatic the closeness of Provideniya to Alaska— no Russian city is at all as near. Building renovation had blocked windows and transformed the old church's liturgical twilight into a simulated Arctic one. The display pictures of snowscapes and the hand-painted dioramas of polar weather stations with just a lone red light on the tiny airfields did a fine imitation of what I'd seen myself in the far north. Some of the exhibits required that the lights be darkened in the museum hall for full effect. When an old, hobbling lady guard saw me in front of the Northern Lights diorama, she asked if I would like the overhead lights out. I said yes and she hobbled over to the wall switch and flipped it. On

the exhibit's midnight-blue sky, iridescent Northern Lights began to pulse and flash in the dark. After what she deemed sufficient time she flipped the gallery lights back on.

Growing more familiar with the museum's layout, I walked up the stairs one afternoon to the director's office and introduced myself. The director turned out to be a young man named Victor Boyarsky. His name sounded familiar—then I remembered that I had come across it in stories about sled dog expeditions at the Chamber of Commerce in Nome. Victor Boyarsky attended the University of Minnesota and speaks English well. He even sounds slightly Minnesotan. For a while we talked about his sled dog journeys and the dog-trekking friends he keeps in touch with in Alaska and Minnesota, and the pleasures of Nome, a place both of us recalled fondly.

When I explained to Victor Boyarsky that I was planning to drive across Siberia, he told me he knew who I should talk to. He led me up more stairs to a larger office with many desks. Sitting at one of them was another Victor—Victor Serov, director of publicity for the museum. Victor Serov is a trim man in his fifties with ice-blue eyes and a blond mustache thick enough to hold the many icicles that have hung from it. Publicity director defines only one of his occupations; Victor Serov is also a guide who specializes in extreme adventure, and expeditions to most of the cold places on earth you can name. He has been to the North Pole twenty-two times, led a ski trek to the South Pole, and wintered in Antarctica twice. He also climbs mountains, and his skill as an alpinist is such that he leads climbs all over the world. When I said I wanted to cross Siberia by car, he said he could help me. He added, offhandedly, that he did not think such a trip would be difficult to do.

I was relieved to hear that. Up till then all my Russian friends who I'd told about my plan had informed me that I was crazy and if I went I would be robbed or killed. Later I understood that Russians from Moscow and St. Petersburg tend to have exaggerated ideas about Siberia.

Later my Russian friends also said, of Victor Serov, "How can you trust this guy? You don't even know him. Why do you believe he'll do what he says?" I said I didn't know, he just looked dependable. I paid him some money and he said he would handle the details. Basically, what Victor said he'd do, he did.

· · ·

January 2001 I spent in St. Petersburg. Through my friend Boris I rented an apartment a few blocks off Nevsky Prospekt near the middle of the city. The apartment belonged to Luda Sokolova, a sweet blond woman in her late fifties who worked for the equivalent of the city zoning board and is a friend of Boris's wife, Sonya. Luda owns other apartments and stayed at one of them while I was there. My purpose, first, was to have several meetings with Victor Serov to plan my trip's route, budget, and schedule. The rest of the time I would read books in English and (slowly) in Russian on the subject of Siberia at the Russian National Library, and study the language for three hours a day with a tutor some friends of Boris's found for me.

Now might be as good a moment as any to talk about what it was like learning Russian, or attempting to. We know that the language has the reputation of being difficult. When I was first memorizing the alphabet, I told my friend Saul Steinberg that some of the Russian letters were weird, and he said, "Those aren't letters, those are sneezes." Some of the language's sounds elude the English-speaking throat and tongue. To get the Russian *bI* sound—it's related, sort of, to our letter *y*—I had to sit down hard in a chair as I pronounced it. If you're middle-aged when you start learning, as I was, your brain is less receptive to languages, they say; I think another obstacle is that a grown-up's dignity stumbles on the preschool mnemonics you have to recite, and it fears the humiliation of being stuck for so long at baby-talk level.

My teacher, a woman in her thirties named Katya, was dark haired, dark eyed, and quick as light. She had taught many Americans and not only spoke English beautifully (with a British accent, like most English-speaking Russians) but also could imitate various American accents. Hearing Katya do a Texan was worth all the money I spent on tutoring and more. I mean, here's a Russian woman, dressed all in charcoal gray, quite serious and put together, and she starts in on, "Wall, as I was sayin' to mah good ol' buddy . . ." And she gets it right! I admired her elegant Russian, too, with its buzzing softness and the mouth-filling satisfaction of its one-syllable words—*grob* (coffin) and *grom* (thunder) and *kon'* (steed) and *zub* (tooth) and *lug* (meadow) and *les* (forest) and *dom* (house) and *Bog* (God) and *grad* (hail) and *lyod* (ice), and the long, unrolling ones like *spravadlivost* (justice) and *provolochnaya zagrazhdeniya* (barbed-wire entanglement). Sometimes lying awake I still go over a few of the sentences we used to illustrate the case endings of nouns: *Mamont lezhal v sinei peshchere* (The mammoth lay in the blue cave) and *Ochki vo mkhu* (The spectacles are in the moss) and *Lyudi moevo vozrasta lyubyat spat'* (People my age love to sleep) and *U vas nyet stradanii* (You have no suffering).

And *Mir zakonchitsya za odnu nedelyu* (The world will end in one week) and *Puteshchevstvennik videl zelyonii prud* (The traveler saw the green pond) and *On rvyot zabavnie pisma* (He tears up the amusing letters) and *Vdrug ya ispugaois' nichtozhestva* (Suddenly I am afraid of nothingness) and *Tserkov otkryta dlya poklonennii* (The church is open for worship) and *Utki vyletyat s Sibirskikh ozyor* (The ducks fly from the Siberian lakes) and *Krov' velikikh geroev otstroila gorod* (The blood of great heroes built the city) and *Ivan lovit rybu shlapoi* (Ivan catches fish with his hat) and *Boris zaplatil creditoram zdaniem* (Boris paid his creditors with a building) and *Mne skuchno, kogda elektrichestvo otkliochaetsya* (It is boring for me when the electricity is shut off).

I worked hard at first, but then the slowness of my progress disappointed me. Rather than stick closely to the day's lesson I preferred to talk to Katya about various subjects in my bad, slapped-together Russian of before. The constant errors in my speech made her wince like someone with perfect pitch listening to a clumsy beginner on the violin, but eventually with her linguistic ability she adapted herself, and we talked about all kinds of things. I told her about traveling in Chukotka (an exotic place to her, as to most Russians), and about my work, my family, and the book I wanted to write about Siberia. Katya talked about how the Russian language is being destroyed by poor education and by the sloppiness of nonnative speakers who ignore case endings and have no conception of verb aspects and don't care. You find the worst speech in the street markets, she said. She called the new, bad Russian that's spreading everywhere "market language" (*bazarnii yazyk*).

Both Katya's parents were doctors. Her father had been a doctor in the army, and she had spent some years on military bases in the south of Russia. The duty was hard; sometimes her parents had to work with patients suffering terrible illnesses caused by radiation. At a base in the Kazakhstan missile fields, her father had been the doctor for soldiers in charge of nuclear missiles, she said. I told her that when I lived in Montana I had gone down in a nuclear missile silo buried in the prairie near an air force base, and an officer there had described how the missiles were aimed at missile silos in southern Russia. That evening Katya mentioned this to her father, now retired, who lived in the same building she did. He told her to tell me that the missiles on his base in Kazakhstan had been aimed at the missiles in Montana.

Russian employs six different cases for nouns—nominative, genitive, dative, accusative, instrumental, and prepositional (also called locative)—depending on how the noun functions in the sentence. The nominative case is easy, because it corresponds to the basic form of the noun. In a month of lessons we barely got through the other five cases. Of course that left great, thorny expanses of the language largely unexplored. With discouragement tinged by irony, I gave Katya the excuse I had used before, about Russian being a hopelessly complicated language with no rhyme or reason and with more exceptions than rules. She said that wasn't so, because even the most complicated parts of the language made sense if you thought about them. She said being inside a language was like being in a person's house—after a while you came to see why the teapot was where it was.

And once in a while, after (for example) seven hours of working on the prepositional case, the beauty of the language's structure would emerge, and I would be transported by a vision of its elegant and meaningful intricacy. Of course the next day I would lose this vision and become aphasic and marble mouthed again. Overall, though, it was interesting to exercise my mind in this unaccustomed way; acquiring a language, a task usually accomplished unconsciously in childhood, has no real counterpart in the ordinary adult world of gain and loss. No matter how globalized our cultures become, language will always be their untransferable part. I would have paid plenty for a total-fluency Russian-language cassette I could just insert into my forehead. No such product being available, I had to take the slow and awkward path. Learning Russian (or trying to) showed me that in my everyday life, perhaps like many adults, I use my brain mainly for scheming.

One morning during that January I went on an expedition to Peterhof, the grand palace built by Peter the Great twenty-five miles west of the city on the Gulf of Finland. Night was still full when I left Luda's apartment at about seven thirty; at that time of year the sun would not be up for another couple of hours. On the slippery sidewalks, old women were sweeping away a light accumulation of snow using the kind of brooms that are associated in America with witches and Halloween. The air was clear and the temperature well below freezing. From various parked cars came little welcoming chirps as their owners approached to warm them up before driving. When I crossed a cloud of car exhaust, a deep olfactory memory came over me. Maybe because Russian gasoline still used lead, maybe because Russian emission laws are less stringent, the exhaust of cars in Russia smelled like no car exhaust in America has smelled since I was a child. Not quite awake, I lapsed briefly back to Cleveland, Ohio, and 1954.

At the cavernous train station, the Baltiskii Voksal, ceiling lights of pitiful feebleness pushed back just enough of the darkness that you could see to get around. Russians were congregating densely at the two open ticket windows in their usual free-for-all style. Somehow I purchased a ticket, divined the train platforms in the farther gloom, and boarded a train. That it turned out to be the wrong train came as no real shock to me. For twenty minutes the train kept going without pause. I could see nothing in the blackness out the windows. Finally I asked the woman sitting across from me if this was the train for Peterhof. She was young and pretty, with a face that tapered downward like a cat's. It expressed with minimal effort her complete disdain for me as she gave me the bad news.

When we finally did reach a stop, I got off. By now the night had been infused with a little bit of gray. As the train's back lights receded, I looked around: a narrow station platform covered with hard-polished snow; on both sides, fields bisected with lines of brush extending vaguely into the early dawn; and a village of eight or ten houses, with no lights showing, and snow draping roofs and fences as if it had been laid on in multiple coats every day since fall. At the platform's far end, a single figure approached, carrying a shovel. I walked over to him and asked if I could catch a train back to Petersburg here. He said I could, in half an hour.

With nothing else to do, I walked down some steps to the little road leading into the village. There were no tire tracks in the new snow, or tracks of any kind. The railroad-crossing barrier was stuck in the "down" position and its warning lights flashed a strong red in the landscape of gray and white. The houses in the village had no yards to speak of but sat hard by their fences along the road. The houses' construction seemed to have been a cumulative process, with afterthoughts of small side struc- tures stuck onto and obscuring their original frames, and the whole business sealed in place from above by its lavish and drooping cap of snow. As I came closer, I saw that there were indeed lights in some of the windows, barely more than peepholes in little angles of wall; also, that parsimonious breaths of smoke rose from two or three of the chimneys.

In fifty paces I had walked into and out of town. Ahead, the road set off across blank fields through a scraggly avenue of birch trees, without signs or markers of any kind. I continued along the road to the top of a little rise. When I looked back, two women in long coats and head scarves were slowly pushing a cart from the village toward the station. Thinking maybe I had misunderstood when the train would come, I hurried back to the platform. The women had just finished wrestling their cart up the platform steps. I went over to them, said hello, and explained I had taken the wrong train. The women were unmistakably a pair. Both wore two head scarves, a light one underneath and a heavier, coarser one on top. One woman was thin and her long wool coat was brown. The other woman was stout, and sturdy-looking as a bollard, and she wore a wool coat of a particular red I have never seen except in displays of British soldiers from the American Revolutionary War. Both had weathered, wrinkled-shoe faces, multiple warts, and lively pale-blue eyes.

They told me the right train to take to Peterhof and where on this railroad line to get it. The station I wanted was called Leninskii, they said. They were going to the market by Leninskii station themselves and would tell me when they were getting off. I asked them if they lived in this village, and they said they did. The village was called Little Verevo, they said, and it used to be an administrative center of Verevo oblast dur- ing Soviet times. There was also a South, an East, and a Big Verevo, they added. Having strained my conversational abilities almost to overheating, I thanked the women and moved down the platform, but in a minute the thinner one came to me and said I should stand with them, because only one door opened on this train, and it usually stopped with that door where they were standing. I rejoined them, and in another minute the train arrived. From the platform up to the train door was a giant step. I helped them get their cart aboard, lifting it from the bottom. The cart

was amazingly heavy. The stouter woman told me that the station platform sank lower and lower every year.

   In the dawn light as we approached Petersburg, I noticed many of
the same empty white fields that surrounded Little Verevo; then all at
once the fields stopped and the city began. You could see the exact building where that occurred. Arrived at Leninskii station, I again helped the
women with their cart, out of the train and then down a long flight of
stairs to the street. They showed me the direction they were going,
toward the Leninskii market. Afraid of seeming nosy, I didn't ask what
they had in that heavy cart to sell. Before setting out, the women told me
again what train I should take and where at Leninskii station it would
stop. As they walked away the thin one looked back at me and said,
"*S'Bogum*" (Go with God). As soon as I reached the platform, I became
convinced I had gone to the wrong one. I could still see the women proceeding slowly along the street, so I ran down and asked them again.
They replied with some heat that I had the right platform and I should
hurry back, because the train was about to come in a minute and there
would not be another for a long time.

   The train in fact came as I ran back; it was just pulling out as I reached
the top of the stairs. I waited an hour and forty minutes in the windy cold
for the next one. While I stood there, people kept coming up to me and
asking me when the next train to this or that destination would be. Maybe
they chose me because of my boots—I was wearing the same ones
Vladimir-the-guide had given me in Chukotka, and they may have made
me look as if I worked for the railroad, or something. To each questioner
I replied that I didn't know, I was a foreigner. After an hour or so I had
accumulated a group of five or six people standing in my vicinity who had
previously asked me about the trains. When a new questioner would
come along and begin to ask me something, the bystanders would cut
him off, saying, "Don't ask him—he's a foreigner. He doesn't know
anything."

Snow was falling hard as I crossed the spacious sculpture garden, bigger
than several parade grounds, that leads to the main palace at Peterhof.
The snowstorm made the palace look even more looming and impressive,
its ranks of tall windows sketching the principles of classical architecture

like an old drypoint drawing. I might have imagined that the gardens and the fountains with their statuary and the palace façade in the background, snow-blurred as they were, exactly resembled what a visitor would have seen on a winter day almost three hundred years before; but the quick blue-white flashes from tourists' cameras here and there restored the view to the present tense.

Long lines were waiting patiently in the snow for admission. Through the palace windows, what little I could see of the inside seemed filled with tour-group crowds. I decided to go to one of the smaller palaces first and come back here later in the day. The guidebook I'd brought mentioned a modest-looking residence of the tsars, the Kottadge Dvorets (Cottage Palace), a little over a mile away on the Peterhof grounds. I set out for it and found it after some wandering around. The Cottage Palace is a small château sequestered in the woods and behind gates like a mafia don's retreat on Lake Tahoe. I paid my admission, took off my snow-covered coat and hat, removed my boots, and put a pair of *tapichki* on my feet. (*Tapichki* are the slippers, often just boatlike pieces of felt stitched together at the ends, that many Russian museums require visitors to wear.)

Almost no other tourists had made the journey to this little place, maybe because it's no more impressive than a single-family house in a comfortable suburb. We few who did show up had the guide to ourselves. Not understanding much she said on the first go-round, I took the tour a number of times and with several guides. The Cottage Palace was built in the 1820s by Tsar Nicholas I, and he and the tsars who followed him spent a lot of time with their families here. The paintings on the walls depicted mostly humdrum seascapes, and the furnishings were nice but nothing the rich tastes of earlier tsars or empresses would have admired. Here, apparently, tsars of the nineteenth century indulged a longing to live like ordinary well-to-do people away from everybody else. And yet references to their vast and autocratic power could be seen even in the knickknacks. I was especially taken with an elaborate clock, presented as a gift to Tsar Alexander II in 1861; on the clock's large glass face were sixty-seven smaller clocks, each showing the time in a different one of Russia's sixty-six provinces and Alaska.

The real spirit of the Cottage Palace resided in its view. Though the house sat on an eminence, it featured only one, northward-facing vista: an exhilarating sweep of open meadow (now snow covered, crossed by small cross-country skiers) down a long and gentle slope to the storm-blue waters of the Gulf of Finland. All the major rooms of the house had been designed around big windows that framed this view. On the top floor was a snug, comfortably furnished room called the Morskoi Kabinet. (The name means "Sea Office.") This was like a study or an aerie for the tsar. Its intricately patterned parquet floor and the green trompe l'oeil curtains set off the soaring distance in its windows. Through wood-mullioned double French doors leading to a small roofed balcony, one looked both downward and dizzyingly far across the gulf. On a table before the French doors sat a long brass telescope and a speaking trumpet; sometimes the tsars directed naval exercises from the balcony, calling orders to aides who relayed them to the assembled fleet. When the weather was clear, the guide said, you could see all the way to Kronstadt from here. Kronstadt is an island in the gulf, site of a Russian naval base and former customs station for ships entering and leaving St. Petersburg.

Peter the Great built St. Petersburg to open Russia to the West and provide her a convenient port on the Baltic (of which the Gulf of Finland is an arm). In descriptions of St. Petersburg's history, the epithet "Window to Europe" is often used. To me St. Petersburg seems more like a hole in the corner of a sealed-tight packing crate that Peter crowbarred open violently from inside. Once the breach was made, the light flowed in, and it continues to flow. That mobile and constantly incoming western light may partly explain the watchability of the St. Petersburg sky. Joseph Brodsky, the Russian-American poet, said that when he and his friends were boys in Leningrad, they used to look westward across the gulf and pretend to see Sweden, and they took hope from the proximity. In the speech he made to the Swedish Academy and other attendees in Stockholm when he received his Nobel Prize, Brodsky said, of his childhood bedroom, "Depending on the wind, the clouds I saw in my window were already seen by you, or vice-versa." For Brodsky, Leningrad/St. Petersburg had kept its psychological status as a portal even in Stalin times.

By my fourth go-round on the Cottage Palace tour, the guides had become used to me, and one of them continued to guide me even as I put on my coat and boots to leave. I got the feeling she was glad to have a customer who didn't yawn at this middle-class place after gorging on the splendors and eccentricities of Peter the Great. Outside, where she followed me, she pointed out the house's vaulted windows in the Dutch style and the wild grapevines growing above them, and she described in some detail which improvements to the structure had been added by which tsar. Finally the cold affected her and she retreated back inside.

Before she left she said I should walk down the meadow and look at the house from there. I followed the path she had shown me across the open and snowy field. When I turned around after about half a mile, the house all by itself on the ridgetop rose with a dramatic presence. At the head of its long meadow cut through the shoreline trees, its sky-reflecting windows with the tsar's own window at the very top must have been hard to miss even from well out at sea. The Cottage Palace and the rest of the Peterhof complex is not as far west in Russia as one can go, of course. Still, for practical purposes, this place marked the symbolic westernmost point of Russia. And there at the western gate, in his Morskoi Kabinet with its commanding view, like a splendid sentry in a sentry box—the tsar himself.

At the end of my January in St. Petersburg, I flew back to New York. I spent February at home in New Jersey. In March, I traded in my accumulated frequent flyer miles on Alaska Airlines for another ticket to Nome. In all my previous trips to that city I had never had good enough weather for a trip to the Diomede Islands (the reader may remember that the Diomedes, Big and Little, are the islands separated by the Russian-American border in the middle of the Bering Strait). The sight of Big Diomede looming from the sea like a Russian boundary stone had persistently eluded me. I wanted to give it one more try.

First I flew from Newark to Minneapolis and from there to Anchorage; after a few days in Anchorage I caught an early-morning flight to Nome. The plane made a stop at Kotzebue, above the Arctic Circle. A Kotzebue resident named Roy Toruk sat beside me and we talked on the way. He knew two of the Eskimo evangelists whose snowmobile trip to Chukotka had aroused my interest in going to the Diomedes in the first place. As the plane descended to Kotzebue, I could not believe how little was there; all the works of man seemed as if they could be erased into the surrounding whiteness with one sweep of a hand. I asked Roy Toruk, "Does it ever get depressing, living here?" With a big smile, as if bragging of a remarkable local resource, he said, "It—sure—*does!*"

After unloading and loading in Kotzebue, the plane continued on, over endless bare white hills, until we were approaching Nome. Before, I had seen Nome only in its muddy phase. Now the town and its surroundings were mostly white with blue shadows. On the sea before the town, chunks of ice threw shadows as long as jet trails in the flat light from the horizon-hugging sun. The pilot said the local temperature was one degree below zero, with a forty-mile-an-hour wind making it feel like fifty below. As I stepped from the plane door, the wind hit like a cutting torch that cuts with cold.

On the phone in my old room at the Nome Nugget Motel, I began inquiring about flights to the Diomedes. I had two choices. A small Nome airline, Cape Smythe Air, flies to Little Diomede in winter when ice conditions permit. Unfortunately, so far this year the ice hadn't been thick enough to make a good runway, the person at Cape Smythe told me. She said she didn't think they'd be flying to Little Diomede this winter at all. The other choice, Evergreen Helicopter, also in Nome, provides service to Little Diomede whether there's an ice runway or not. Evergreen Helicopter is a two-person operation consisting of the pilot, Eric Penttila, and his mechanic.

Eric answers the phone himself. I had gotten to know him a little from previous planned-but-then-canceled trips to Little Diomede. I had gone out to the hangar where his shiny machines sat, rotors folded, between walls hung with flight suits, charts, and tools. Eric Penttila is a Vietnam War veteran. He had told me about his luck there when a helicopter he was piloting survived an attack while picking up troops on a battlefield. Several people in the helicopter were hit, and when he got back to base he found that the main control rod, a hardened aluminum tube, had taken an AK-47 round through its middle without snapping.

Eric seemed a peevish, worried, mournful fellow, knowledgeable about the world's wickedness and striving thanklessly against it. He also told me that a while back he had received a call saying that a small aircraft carrying evangelist missionaries who were returning from Chukotka had gone down in the Bering Sea. With his mechanic and a Nome volunteer firefighter, Eric had flown immediately to the site of the crash and located the missionaries and the pilot hanging on to five-gallon gas cans. Maneuvering carefully, he had taken the chopper down into the swells, keeping his tail rotor just above the water, while his companions straddled the floats and pulled the people aboard. Nome-ites had previously reported this story to me as a tale of heroism; Eric described it as just another of the vexing things he was expected to do.

Now when I reached him on the phone he allowed that he would probably be flying to Little Diomede on Wednesday, a couple of days away. He didn't sound at all happy about the idea. A front was supposed to move in later in the week, so maybe it would cloud up by Wednesday; he added this last with the gloomy optimism of one holding out a faint hope. He would be making half a dozen shuttles back and forth between Wales and Little Diomede carrying passengers, mail, and supplies. On one of those shuttles he would have room for me, but on the Nome-to-Wales leg of the flight he was full, he said, so I would have to get up to Wales on my own. I called Cape Smythe Air, and luckily they had a seat left on their flight to Wales on Wednesday morning.

During my many previous visits to Nome, the weather had never been remotely this clear. Now on the walks I took I saw geographic features up and down the coast that had always been obscured by clouds before. The only problem was the cold. It froze my pen tip when I tried to sketch or make notes, and if the wind caught me square in the face it almost flash-froze my eyes. Wednesday dawned completely cloudless and ten below. I called Eric Penttila at nine o'clock and he was still waiting for a weather report. In fifteen minutes he called back and said the weather would be clear all day, so he guessed he was going. This development annoyed him in the extreme. "Nobody should even be living out on that rock," he said. "We maintain those idiots out there. They ought to abandon that ridiculous place and move back to the mainland. They always need help and we're always ferrying people out there to help them. Today I'm taking a nun and a social worker and a physical therapist and I don't know who else, all to help those idiots out there."

A flight of about forty-five minutes in a Cape Smythe prop plane deposited me at the Wales airport. This establishment consisted of two wind socks, a snow runway, and a steel shipping container in which passengers could wait out of the cold. A halfhearted gas heater kept the container's interior above frostbite level, but its ridged steel floor, and the brown liquid—root beer?—frozen between the ridges, and the spoiled food smell, and the packing peanuts scattered around made it a place to go only as a last resort. I sheltered on its lee side and waited with the other passengers.

Little Sister Mary Jo was the nun Eric had mentioned. She stood less than five feet tall. At first I thought "Little Sister" must be part of her name, but she told me that the Little Sisters are a Catholic order. She came from Belgium and spoke with a French accent and had formerly lived on Little Diomede full-time for nineteen years. This visit would be only a short one. Every Native person who saw her, in Wales as well as in the Cape Smythe waiting room in Nome, embraced her. She was quite old and walked on the snow and ice with practiced care.

Passenger two, the physical therapist, was a young man named John who worked for the hospital in Nome. He had very red eyelids. He told me that a friend of his from the hospital had gone to Little Diomede earlier that winter just before a weather change and had ended up stuck there for thirteen days. The third passenger, a Native man named Erik, was the head of the tribal government on Little Diomede. He informed me I would have to pay a $100 arrival fee in cash at the tribal office when we landed. I was glad I'd brought that much with me. Under his coat he carried his son of about two years old. The little boy's nose was running copiously and he looked sad. "We lost his mother here just last year and now I take him everywhere with me," his father explained.

Suddenly, with a percussive wind, the helicopter arrived. Eric Penttila hopped out, flight-suited and goggled beyond recognizability. The other three passengers climbed into the helicopter's backseat, where they barely fit, and Eric opened the door on the helicopter's left side and gestured to me. I got in, then awkwardly climbed over some controls and into the seat on the right side. I had never been in a helicopter before and assumed the right was the passenger side. Eric came around and opened the right side door and said, through goggles and mask, "I was wondering why you climbed over here, unless you are going to fly this sucker yourself." Under the gaze of the others just inches behind me, I clambered back over to the left side. After a few minutes Eric got in on the right side and we took off.

Helicopters require more faith than airplanes. If something goes wrong with a plane, you imagine you could glide, but in a helicopter you must put from your mind the thought of how fast the earth will come up to meet you in an emergency. As we moved out over the strait, sea ice in many shades of blue and white alternated with sigmoid-shaped stretches of open water animated by sharp, swift ripples. In places where linen-white ice expanses met, the lines of crunched-up ice pieces were the exact same blue as Comet Cleanser. Around the ice floes that had been frozen in place the ice took on an unlikely Caribbean Sea hue, and sometimes a pale purple wash with no discernible source flickered over the whole scene.

From the Cape Smythe plane I had caught a glimpse of the Diomedes and of the coast of Asia beyond. Now, as the helicopter moved farther from land, the Diomedes approached on our left, with the much smaller and uninhabited Fairway Rock to the south of them; in the clear distance, just a few ticks to the right of dead ahead, the easternmost cape of Asia rose into view, gray and vast, disappearing around the earth's bend. Meanwhile, over our right shoulder, the Cape of Wales's white hills stood out vividly in the sun. Few travelers to the region have seen this sight. The ill-starred Vitus Bering sailed through the strait twice without guessing how close he was to land. Captain Cook's ships, on the other hand, happened to hit good weather when they came through in July of 1779. A journal of the voyage states: "The weather becoming clear, we had the opportunity of seeing, at the same moment, the remarkable peaked hill, near Cape Prince of Wales, on the coast of America, and the East Cape of Asia, with the two connecting islands of St. Diomede between them."

That view was before us now. Looking at one continent and then at the other, and encompassing in a glance the space between, gave a grand, globe-bestriding feeling. Of course human beings came from Asia to North America by this route! Of course Alaskan Natives traveled by boat to hunt walrus on the coast of Chukotka! Of course adventurers crossed on skis from one side to the other! *It's right over there!*

Soon Eric was banking around the northern tip of Little Diomede, and the massive front of Big Diomede filled the bubble window of the helicopter—but only for a second, as we swung past. Then we were landing on the helipad. I hopped out and someone showed me the way to the tribal office, where I paid my $100 and filled out some forms. The woman handling the paperwork was about to walk me through a sheet of complicated rules for taking photographs, when I told her I had no camera. I took my sketchbook from my pack and showed it to her and said I preferred to draw. At that she mentally slipped me into the harmless-nut category and sent me on my way.

First I went to the ice runway at the edge of the island. Pieces of it had broken off. Wales had been colder than Nome, and this place was colder than Wales. Sea currents sped by the ice runway's edge. In the narrow channel, a little over a mile across, ice floes jostled and slid onto one another as they hurried past at maybe seven knots, the wind and current pushing them hard. Above the lines of open water, wraiths of steam fifteen feet high whisked along next to the floes, leaning forward and rushing all in one direction like commuters. Beyond this fierce and wind-scoured zone, the lowering, black-gray rock of Big Diomede reared up immediately without beach or shoreline. This was what I had come to see, and I could barely face in that direction, with the wind belt-sanding the side of my nose and freezing the pen tip as soon as I took it out of my mouth.

Clouds caught on the peaks at the top of Big Diomede, then seemed to come loose and blow by. Somewhere along that ridgeline was a Russian observation post, but I couldn't pick it out with my eyes tearing so. The idea that any human beings inhabited that rock seemed a stretch, though I knew that a detachment of Russian soldiers, in a small base on the island's less steep northern side, were on duty year-round. I attempted a couple of drawings before my pen became useless. Then I returned to the village, grateful to turn my back to the wind.

Little Diomede, the village, was a hardscrabble place if I ever saw one. At the time its population was 178. Its public buildings and houses ascended the island's steep rock in a shallow out-of-the-wind indentation on its northwest side, one small structure mounting above another like the apartments of desert cliff dwellers. The village's vertical access ways were zigzag staircases carved into the cement-hard snow. I walked and climbed around the village for a couple of hours, stepping into a store or office now and then to get warm. I saw a frozen seal on the floor of the vestibule of the tribal health building, and a polar bear skin hanging on a wooden frame, and two boys shooting a small black dog out by the village dump, and a guy carrying cans of soda pop on his shoulders into the general store when the cans exploded in the cold and sent soda cascading all over him and down the back of his neck. I spent a good while examining a walrus-skin boat on a rack near a launching ramp at the bottom of town. Almost nobody makes skin boats anymore. Splitting the skins and sewing them require skills both physical and spiritual; you have to have absolute quiet in your soul to sew the skin covering to the willow frame. This twenty-foot boat, a museum-quality object, was obviously still being used.

Eric's helicopter had been landing and taking off on its shuttle runs all the while. Late in the day I heard it coming back and went down to the helipad. Looking back at the village I saw Little Sister Mary Jo, all four foot eleven of her, shoveling loose snow off the steps to the Catholic church building on the cliff face sixty feet above. I got in on the left, Eric loaded some stuff in the back, and we took off. Again I saw the globe-spanning view of the two continents and the strait in between. Then we turned toward Alaska; it grew gradually larger straight ahead. Soon we could make out the village of Wales, and the hill beyond it, and then some little specks at the hill's base—Wales's reindeer herd, Eric said.

I was glad, after so many tries, finally to have reached the Diomedes. In that winter of 2001 I saw Russia at both its westernmost and its easternmost end. In the summer, I would go on a nine-thousand-mile road trip to see what was in between.

PART III

Chapter 11

When I went back to St. Petersburg for a quick visit in June to take care of some final details, I learned that Victor Serov would not be guiding me himself. Victor would do the planning, he informed me, but his colleague, Sergei Lunev, would be the actual guide. Victor had worked with Sergei on other expeditions. He had been Victor's mountaineering coach at university, and together they had climbed peaks in the Caucasus and Crimea. Both had also climbed in Kamchatka, though on separate expeditions. Sergei was a "good man," Victor assured me, underlining his pronouncement with a brisk, military nod.

Zdravstvuite, Sergei! Greetings to you and family! I ended up spending more time at a stretch with Sergei than I ever have with anybody except my family. With nobody else except those closest to me have I ever been so deeply annoyed. Maybe he could say the same about me. Often I composed long and stern speeches to Sergei in my head, though I could translate only fragments of them. I saw more country with Sergei than I ever did with anybody, and eventually I agreed completely with Victor's judgment of him. Early on, I admired his ingenuity and toughness. Learning to trust him, though, took a while.

The impression I got when we first met did not help. Victor had said he would bring Sergei to Luda's apartment to meet me, and I had arranged to be waiting for them on Zagorodnyi Prospekt out front. They arrived in Victor's car and parked across the street. I crossed to that side to greet them, and before we'd even shaken hands Sergei came up close and grasped my elbow and steered me back across through traffic, like a Boy Scout helping an old lady. That sort of gave me the creeps (a word whose Russian equivalent, *murashki*, also means "small ants"). Later when I became upset with him, I sometimes felt a dark regret that I hadn't paid more attention to my first impression. Later still, I understood that the gesture hadn't signified much of anything, besides a certain exaggerated Russian deference and courtliness. It was just the way Sergei was.

Sergei Mikhailovich Lunev is a muscular and youthfully fit man in his midsixties. He looks like a gymnast, or a coach of gymnasts. He has a long, ectomorphic head whose most expressive feature is its brow, which furrows this way and that in thought, emphasizing his canny, mobile, and china-blue eyes. The neatly trimmed hair around his balding crown adds a professorial dignity—appropriately, because he is the head of the robotics lab at the St. Petersburg State Polytechnical University. He used to work in the Soviet space program before it was reduced in size; guiding is something he does for extra cash. After knowing him for a while I wondered if the discontent and suppressed anger that sometimes showed on his face were the result of taking on an additional job, one unequal to his talents. We did seem to get along better once I understood how prestigious the Polytechnical University and his real job were.

I had asked him and Victor to come to Luda's partly at her request. She wanted to have a look at these sharp characters who she was sure were taking advantage of a naïve American; she also wanted to quiz them about the Siberian perils into which they were leading me. She conducted the investigation over tea and snacks in her apartment. I followed only some of it, but I believe she went into the subject of bears, and particularly what the guides planned to do if bears bit the tires of our vehicle and punctured them. Victor laid out his and Sergei's credentials and answered all questions patiently and in detail. At the end of the session she was less doubtful, but only marginally.

From Luda's, Victor and Sergei and I drove to a labyrinthine warren of single-vehicle garages in a far section of St. Petersburg. I had wanted to buy a Russian all-road vehicle like a four-wheel-drive jeep Niva. Victor had said that was a bad idea, because Russian vehicles constantly break down. (On our journey, after I'd seen the thousandth Niva by the side of the road with its hood up and the driver peering under it, I appreciated this truth.) Instead, with $4,500 supplied by me, he and Sergei had bought a diesel-powered Renault step van. They promised me this car was far more reliable.

In the narrow, low-ceilinged garage where Sergei was keeping it, the Renault struck me as not Siberia-ready. It looked more suited to delivering sour cream and eggs, the job it had done until recently. Sergei backed it out and we went for a quick test-drive. Its shocks weren't much and its stick shift was stiff. Sergei said he would have it running smoothly in time for the journey. He said he planned to put an extra seat in the back and a place to store our stuff, and a table where we could eat when it rained. I noticed there were no seat belts and said that each seat must have one. Sergei and Victor conceded that seat belts could be added if I wanted them. They treated this as an eccentric special request. Russians in general do not use seat belts and consider them an American absurdity.

Sergei described how he would arrange the back so we could sleep in there if necessary. I didn't see quite how this would work, especially when I learned there would be three of us—Vladimir Chumak, called Volodya or Vitya, who was another past associate of Victor's and Sergei's, had been asked to come along as an assistant. Sergei and Volodya had been in Kamchatka together and had known each other since university. Victor said that three men were better than two for safety. That sounded sensible to me. Both my companions praised Volodya Chumak as a top-notch alpinist and great guy. He lived in Sochi, a resort town on the Black Sea, where he employed his alpinist skills in his regular job as a building renovator, rappelling down the façades of buildings he was restoring. I would not meet him until just before the trip began.

There are almost no motels in Siberia. Most of the time Sergei and Volodya and I would be camping out, or else staying in people's houses. Sergei and Victor would supply tents, propane stove, camp chairs, and other gear. I was to bring my own sleeping bag, eating utensils, personal items, etc. I asked if I should buy a travel directory of Siberian campgrounds, and Victor laughed. He said I would understand better what Siberia was like once I got there.

To celebrate, we then drove outside the city to Sergei's dacha. Just before it we passed a village that Victor said he remembered as a lovely place in his childhood, but Khrushchev ruined it. The remnants of the village could still be seen, crumbling at the feet of out-of-place and also crumbling 1950s-era high-rises. Sergei's dacha, in a woodland clearing filled with many other dachas, reminded me of family cottages in Ohio on the shores of Lake Erie before the modern age. It was a plain, unpainted board structure, just walls and a roof. Sergei's wife, Luda, met us at the door with their twelve-year-old grandson, Igor. We picked wild strawberries, walked to a pond; some of us swam. During a dinner of shashlik—marinated pork skewered on thin sticks and cooked by Sergei on a wood fire—Victor made an emotional toast to the great adventure Sergei and I would soon be embarking on. And while we were walking in the woods, Sergei came up beside me and said, with passion and sincerity, how happy he was to be going on this trip with me.

The reader may be wondering how I happened to have the money to pay for this expedition. The answer is that I received an expense advance from a magazine. George Kennan in 1884 financed his Siberian journey with an advance of $6,000 from the *Century* magazine in New York City. For my trip in 2001, I was advanced $22,000 by *The New Yorker* magazine. Kennan's trip was ten months long; mine would be about seven weeks. Six thousand dollars back then would be about $112,000 today.

The American dollars I imported strengthened the Russian market for used delivery vans, vehicle-interior improvements, diesel-engine parts, trip-consultant fees, groceries, motor oil, preowned GPS navigating devices, water jugs of flexible plastic, collapsible metal-and-canvas camp stools, pith helmets with drawstring veils of mosquito netting, and other Siberia-related miscellany. During my own preparations when I returned to New Jersey, more of the advance went for additional mosquito netting, olive-drab plastic bottles of high-strength insect repellent with DEET, a kit of camp toiletries, a small suitcase-load of presents (boxes of Legos, assorted Beanie Baby dolls, Statue of Liberty key chains, snow globes featuring the New York City skyline, pocket mirrors, bassfisherman baseball caps, Swiss army knives for the guides); also, iodine pills, new carbon filters for my water purifier, SPF 40 sunblock, ziplock bags, energy bars, pocket packs of Kleenex, a plastic tarp, a pen that can write in zero gravity . . .

Anybody going to remote parts of Asia is advised to get vaccinations of various kinds. At a travel clinic in New Jersey, I was administered shots for typhoid, hepatitis A, tetanus, and polio. Hepatitis B, also recommended, requires shots spaced six months apart for full effectiveness, so I skipped that one. A clinic doctor gave me prescriptions for Cipro antibiotic and said I should buy other medications also for intestinal ailments. He warned against tickborne encephalitis, a danger east of the Urals; he said there's no vaccine against it and no cure. Fortunately, the ticks that have it are infectious only in the spring. The doctor asked if I would be carrying firearms and I said the guides would be. This surprised him. He had never advised anybody going to Siberia before.

A big expense was the satellite phone. I didn't think I would need one, but my wife insisted. She took care of finding and buying it. From Outfitter Satellite in Nashville, she ordered an Iridium brand phone made by Motorola. Outfitter Satellite also handles the satellite linkage and gives you a troubleshooting number to call. In the event, I did use that number; deep in Siberia it was strange suddenly to be talking to a technician with a Tennessee drawl. This $1,000 piece of equipment, when it arrived in its foam-padded case, looked like a combination of a cell phone and a field radio. It had an extendable antenna shaped like a pistol barrel, and many accessories—batteries that cost $85 each, a battery recharger, two kinds of foreign-current adapters for the battery charger, another charger attachment that fit into the cigarette lighter of a car, a remote antenna for use on the roof of the car, and so on.

I wanted to make sure that the phone worked and I knew how to use it. I took the phone into our backyard, turned it on, waited for a satellite hookup, and made a call. The signal went from me to one of the system's sixty-six satellites in low-earth orbit about five hundred miles above. The satellite passed the signal to another satellite, which passed it to another, and so on, until it was relayed down to the Iridium "gateway station" in Tempe, Arizona, which then sent it along regular long-distance routing to my house. In about a second and a half, our downstairs phone rang. Looking at each other through the back window, my wife and I kept our conversation brief, because rates for this kind of phone are in the $4-per-minute range.

Victor had said that a trip later in the summer would avoid the worst of Siberia's insect season. The first week of August was when we planned to set out. On July 30, my wife arranged a farewell party for me at our house. Alex and Katya came, and Boris and Sonya, and our friends Mark, Caroline, and Bill. For the Russians, the evening was an occasion for minor-key histrionics and doom-predicting in their native fashion, along with excitement and hilarity. Katya said how bitterly she blamed herself for leading me into this Russian nightmare in the first place; the next minute she was saying what a great adventure this would be. Boris asked if he could have my car, in the event that I did not return. He added that he was saying this as a precaution only, because I would return, of course. Caroline, who is French-Canadian and observant of style, said she thought it was cheating for me to bring along a satellite phone. That was the only comment I took sort of seriously. What would George Kennan have thought of the satellite phone?

During my last two days, my wife helped a lot, buying hard-to-find travel items, packing the big trunk she found for me, checking off supplies one by one from the list Victor had e-mailed. I had fallen into a half-dazed state and could not have accomplished all that alone. On August 2, as I stood on the front lawn with my heap of stuff waiting for the car service to take it and me to the airport, I looked back at the house and at her and the kids and felt sorry for myself, ridiculously.

Travel, like much else in life, can be more fun to read about than to do. When I'm reading a travel book and the protagonist sets out on a journey and the harbor lights drop behind, I imagine enviously what a grand feeling that must have been. In actual travel situations, however, I've noticed that moments of soaring consciousness are rare. Worries and annoyances and trying to remember which pocket the passport is in tend to deromanticize the brain. But on that evening flight to Russia, after wrestling my stuff through customs and clearing security and waiting in the crowded boarding area and filing onto the plane and finding my seat; and after the plane pulled back from the gate and inched onto the runway and inched some more and finally took off, and I saw New York City receding below me and the tiny A train running out the causeway to Far Rockaway, and then we were over the Atlantic as it glittered widely in the orange sunset: At that moment I felt a blast of mental acceleration that would have made me shout with happiness if I'd been alone.

Again the Helsinki airport. Its employees had taken to zipping here and there on those little foot-powered Razor scooters, making the place somehow even more like purgatory. Again St. Petersburg's Pulkovo International, and the well-known smell, the sparrows in the concourse, the long line at Passport Control. Sergei and Victor were waiting on the other side of the doors beyond the customs officers. Sergei was beaming with excitement; a white point of light shone on his tanned and furrowed brow. They drove me to the city. For a reason I've forgotten, I spent that night in a hotel on the Neva just across from the *Aurora*, the Russian navy cruiser whose cannon had announced the beginning of the October Revolution. The Communists had made her into a museum; her guns were still trained on the Hermitage. I had a farewell dinner with Luda at a microbrew restaurant and then came back to the hotel. The room had become stuffy so I opened the high, narrow windows facing the river. Two or three mosquitoes flew in—the advance pickets of a vast, continental army.

The next day Sergei and Victor and I checked supplies, packed and repacked the van, and went over maps of our route. I participated mainly as an onlooker. When we were eating a midday meal at Sergei's apartment, Volodya Chumak arrived, to comradely demonstrations of joy. Volodya is a slim, broad-shouldered man who usually wears neat work shirts and pants in shades of gray. He was fifty at the time, with a full head of graying black hair, blue eyes, and the thin nose and chiseled features of his Ukrainian ancestry. For our trip, Sergei had learned some English, but Volodya spoke none. His everyday Russian hung up now and then on a slight stammer, though after a few beers the words flowed out swiftly and copiously, as if a hand brake had been released. With Volodya was his son, a handsome fellow in his midtwenties who managed breweries in Russia for Labatt, the Canadian brewers. He was traveling for his job and happened to be in town.

Volodya and I spent that night at Sergei's. Before bed, at what I thought would be an opportune moment, I presented both guides with their Swiss army knives. Volodya opened out all the blades and attachments, examined them, and slipped the knife into his work pants pocket. Sergei oohed and ahhed over the knife, feared to touch it, and put it in a place of honor on a high shelf in his apartment, where, as far as I know, it has remained ever since. Then I gave both guides one-third of their wages for the journey. This executive act of mine distressed Sergei enormously. His brow furrowed and refurrowed, and disapproval beyond the power of his English to express clouded his eyes. He explained to me that all payments of trip expenses from now on should be made by him. I should give him all the money now, he said, and he would provide me a full receipt at the end. I didn't go for this idea and tried to counterexplain why I thought all the money should remain with me. Awkwardness in each other's language (Victor had gone home by then) caused an impasse. Finally, I gave him enough money to last us, I figured, about half the way. Neither of us liked the compromise.

Early on the morning of August 5, Sergei and Volodya brought the van to the back of Sergei's building. We did our final loading, Sergei said goodbye to his wife and grandson, and we climbed aboard. With Volodya at the wheel, we drove to a meeting place on a highway along the Neva where Victor had come to see us off. We all got out and stood by the road and talked to him and his wife, Lena, for a while. Lena asked me in Russian if I was afraid. The optimism I had enjoyed on the airplane had vanished; I said I was, a bit. She asked the same question of Volodya and he replied, with a shrug, "*Na rabote,*" which means, approximately, "It's a job." Victor stood with Sergei and Volodya and me and shook our hands and wished us luck. He said he would see us again, "after your victory!" His eyes were shining, maybe with tears.

We drove off down the highway, Sergei leaning out the passenger-side window and videotaping Victor and Lena as they waved goodbye to us. Then we pulled over and Victor drove up beside us and Sergei handed him the video camera, and Victor and Lena stood beside the road videotaping us driving off while Sergei leaned out the window and waved goodbye to them. Then Victor drove alongside and returned the video camera, and we finally and actually said goodbye.

Setting out, I did not think about the enterprise before us or about our destination a third of the way around the globe. Instead I noticed that the rain, which had been sprinkling, had begun to pour, and the windshield wiper on the passenger side worked only intermittently. The driver's-side wiper worked all right. The gray Neva beside us reproduced the overcast drabness of the sky and the speeding traffic threw up rooster tails of spray. By the time we reached the city limits, the oil-pressure warning light on the dashboard had come on. I pointed it out to Sergei and Volodya. They said it was nothing.

The van had been built with the cargo area in the back lower than the front seats, which rested on a raised platform. In the seat Sergei had installed in the back, one therefore had to sit straight up and lean forward in order to see over the dash. For comfort this was not ideal, but I had no choice, because there were no windows on the van's sides in the back. About the time the oil-pressure light came on I also smelled a strange burning odor, mixed with diesel exhaust. When I mentioned this to Sergei, he rolled his window partway down.

Past the city we turned onto the Murmansk highway eastbound. Its four lanes soon became two. Trucks were speeding toward us in the downpour. I thought Sergei was driving too fast but I couldn't tell for sure, because the speedometer needle, which had been fluttering spasmodically, suddenly lay down on the left side of the dial and never moved again for the rest of the journey. After a couple of hours we came to the highway leading southeast to Vologda, and we pulled over at the intersection. The rain had let up by then. The intersection appeared to be a popular place to stop, with broad aprons of gravel beside the pavement and trash strewn around. We got out to use the facilities, which were bushes and weeds that had seen such employment before. Near the intersection stood a ruined brick church with grass and small trees growing from its upper towers and from the broken-off parts where the onion domes had been.

The Vologda road led through rural places with people selling potatoes along the narrow shoulder and irregularly shaped yellow meadows sometimes opening widely to the horizon. Then birch forest thronged close around, and Sergei said we were going into a huge swamp where many men had died in battles with the Nazis. People still go back in the swamp and find rusted grenades and skulls in helmets, he said. This conversation got Volodya talking about Ivan Susanin, the heroic Russian peasant who deliberately misled a Polish army deep into a swamp in order to save the life of the first Romanov tsar in the Time of Troubles, during the seventeenth century. The Poles, discovering the trick too late, killed Ivan Susanin before perishing themselves. He is the main character of Glinka's opera *A Life for the Tsar*, Volodya told me.

(At later moments I would have occasion to remember Ivan Susanin, and wonder if perhaps the Polish army was me.)

The woods continued; now we came to a rotary completely enclosed by forest. On a pedestal in the middle of the rotary, pointing nose-upward as if about to swoop into the sky, was a bright silver MiG fighter jet. I had never seen a MiG up close. We had passed no airbases or factories that I recalled, so I couldn't figure out what it was doing here. Sergei didn't seem to know, either. The shiny MiG was a strange object encountered inexplicably in a dark forest, spaceshiplike.

The Vologda road had become a spill of pavement, untrimmed along its edges, with scalloping where the poured asphalt had flowed. Small villages followed one after another at regular intervals, roadside signs announcing their names. Often I looked up the names in my pocket Russian-English dictionary to see what they meant. According to my translations (verified by Sergei), that day we went through villages named Puddle, Jellies, Knee, New Knee, and Smokes.

All along the road, sometimes to heights of ten or twelve feet, grew a plant Volodya identified as *morkovnik*. This plant resembles a roadside

weed in America called Queen Anne's lace—except that *morkovnik* is like our modest, waist-high plant drastically and Asiatically enlarged. Queen Anne's lace and *morkovnik* are in fact related, both belonging to the carrot family (*morkov'* means "carrot"). Along the route we traveled, *morkovnik* grows abundantly from one end of Russia to the other.

In a larger town, Pikalevo, we stopped to buy bread. When Sergei opened the van door, his cell phone, which he had said would provide a backup to my satellite phone, slid from the car seat and fell into a puddle. As far as I know, it never worked again. And when he returned with a loaf of bread tucked under his arm like a volleyball—in most Russian stores, you must bring your own shopping bags—he hopped into the driver's seat, turned the key, and received not a sound in response. Multiple tries produced the same result. The van would not start. A red film of rage crossed my eyes. How could he not have done a better job of checking out this vehicle before we left? I held my tongue for the time being. He and Volodya persuaded the driver of a passing microbus to pull us for a jump start. They crawled under the bumpers, tied a rope to the frames of both vehicles, and with a quick tug we were running again. Volodya and Sergei acted as if this were just the normal way you start a car.

In early afternoon we stopped at an informal rest area like the one at the intersection of the Murmansk and Vologda roads. Here for the first time I encountered big-time Russian roadside trash. Very, very few trash receptacles exist along the roads of Russia. This rest area, and its ad hoc picnic spots with their benches of downed tree trunks, featured a ground layer of trash basically everywhere, except in a few places, where there was more. In the all-trash encirclement, trash items had piled themselves together here and there in heaps three and four feet tall, as if making common cause. With a quick kicking and scuffing of nearby fragments, Sergei rendered a place beside a log bench relatively trash-free and then laid out our cold chicken lunch on pieces of cellophane on the ground. I ate hungrily, though I did notice through the cellophane many little pieces of broken eggshell from some previous traveler's meal.

After lunch Volodya and I traded places and I rode in front. Getting the passenger's-side seat belt to buckle took about ten minutes and the combined efforts of Sergei, Volodya, and me. (As for themselves, neither Sergei nor Volodya used their seat belts once in the entire journey, though they sometimes draped them across their shoulders when we passed by the checkpoints of the Dorozhnaya Patrulnaya Sluzhba—the DPS, or highway police.) To my complaint about the broken speedometer, Volodya had responded by duct taping the GPS to the dash and setting the digital readout so that it showed kilometers per hour. I asked Sergei please not to drive any faster than about 90 kph (about 55 mph). He smiled politely and agreed. The next time I looked at the dash he was going 110.

The GPS registered that we'd come about five hundred kilometers (about three hundred miles) when we turned off the road late in the afternoon at a village called Pestovo. Driving up and down the dirt roads of the village we found one called Ulitsa Kosmonavta—Cosmonaut Street—and we followed it until we came to a small, neatly kept log house with verdant gardens on both sides and a well with a shingle roof and a little bucket that you cranked up, like in a fairy tale. This was the house of Avdotia Fedorovna, Volodya's mother-in-law. Here we would spend the night.

Chapter 12

Avdotia Fedorovna was a short, wide, fiercely smiling old woman who
swayed from side to side when she walked. Probably she suffered from
stiffness of the joints; she appeared to be about eighty years old. Usually
she lived alone, but at the moment her daughter, Lena, and Lena's
daughter, Olya, had come from Kirov to visit her. Avdotia Fedorovna's
speech varied between a growl and a roar. Among these sounds I could
pick out almost no words or phrases I recognized, with the exception of
Velikaya Otchestvennaya Voina (Great Patriotic War) and *Baltiiskovo
Flota* (Baltic Fleet). That gave me more purchase than you might think,
though, because she used those phrases a lot.

The Great Patriotic War is what Russians call the Second World War.
The almost-inestimable sacrifices the Russian people made in that war
and the importance and greatness of their victory are facts everybody
can agree on. Every Russian village and town and city has at least one
memorial to the war, the way that every American town east of the Mississippi has its Civil War monument. The walls of the larger room in
Avdotia Fedorovna's house were the parlor equivalent of the outdoor
memorials to the war. Swaying from side to side, she led me from one
photo or medal or citation to another. Three of Avdotia Fedorovna's
brothers had died in the war. Pointing to each faded, milky portrait photograph, she told me his name and military record, and I'm not sure what
else. The recitation had a singsong quality from many repetitions, but

her growly voice broke in tears nonetheless a couple of times. Next to the brothers were framed documents and ribbons having to do with her own service as an officer in the Baltic Fleet. A large photo of her in her naval uniform showed a young woman whose features, determinedly set for the photographer, made parallel horizontal lines. She did not look like somebody you would want to mess with at all.

Lena, her daughter, was a quiet blond woman of forty-nine, just a year younger than I. After Avdotia finished, or paused in, her remarks about the war, Lena led me on a tour of the village. Many of the streets had names associated with the Russian space program. I remember Ulitsa Gagarina, after the pioneer cosmonaut Yuri Gagarin, and Ulitsa Tereshkovoi, after Valentina Tereshkova, the first woman cosmonaut. From a bridge over the river at the edge of town, we could see women and girls standing on a clothes-washing platform half submerged along the riverbank. They had their skirts up to their thighs and were splashing and treading barefoot on the clothes as the suds floated downstream. Lena showed me ruins of dairy barns and silos and said that agriculture in the region, which had flourished in her youth, had been disintegrating recently.

Hills rose above another part of town, and we hiked up into them on well-maintained asphalt lanes we had to share with young men and women speeding by on cross-country skis equipped with little wheels. I had never seen wheeled skis before and would not have guessed you could go so fast on them. The statuesque and sweat-glistening skiers thrusting powerfully with their rubber-tipped poles gave me a quick flashback to the state-engineered *Übermenschen* who were supposed to bury us during the Cold War.

Back at Avdotia Fedorovna's garden, as she and Lena gathered gooseberries, raspberries, parsley, radishes, and little yellow potatoes for supper, they talked about the Soviet aerodrome that used to be near the village. Planes used to fly from here to bomb the Germans during the war. Lena said she remembered when she was a girl there were big reunions of pilots who had been stationed here, and they sometimes did air shows and flew low over the dairy barns. Putting in my two cents, I added that some of the planes those pilots flew during the war had been built in the city of Detroit, not far from where I grew up, and that they had been flown here from Alaska and across Siberia as part of the Lend-Lease program. My attempt to join the Great Patriotic War conversation met with silence. America lost four hundred thousand people in the war, a frightening number; but Russia's dead numbered about twenty million. To many Russians, America's participation in the war was that of a bystander who holds the combatants' coats and steps in at the end to finish off the loser.

Sergei and Volodya and I spent that night in the front room with the war memorials. For a long time I lay awake while Sergei and Volodya snored. The bare floorboards I spread my sleeping bag on were hard, but I liked the feeling of the house overall. It had the folk-art, personalized appeal of an object made completely by hand. The trimmed logs of its walls were chinked not with plaster, as in log homes in America, but with moss. I had noticed the pale-green chinking and asked Lena about it. She told me what kind of moss it was and where in the forest it could be found, and said that this particular kind of moss resists insects and rot and mold. The back of the house gave directly onto a haymow where Avdotia Fedorovna stored bales of hay for the milk cow and calf she kept in a shed out back. Stuck through the rafters near the hay were a hand-carved hay rake and a yoke of peeled wood for carrying milk pails. The sweet smell of dried alfalfa faintly pervaded the house.

No matter how benign your surroundings, you can lie awake for only so long without going a little nuts. Worries about my satellite phone suddenly began racking me. I had plugged the phone in to recharge it, but I became convinced I hadn't connected it right, and now nothing would do but I must unplug it and make a call home right away to see that it was working okay. I had not yet used the phone in Russia. I put on my trousers and took the phone quietly outdoors through a side door and a storage room into the village's pale, dead-quiet dawn. I turned the phone on, found a satellite, dialed: no luck. Dialed again: ditto. Dialed another twenty times. My head was an implosion of frustrated cries and curses. Back inside the house I took out the satellite-phone manual and read it over and over. Had there been someone else available for me to blame for the nonfunction, I would have done so, but unfortunately the only fault here was that of my own denseness—a fact that aggravated me even more. Finally on the tenth reading of the manual I understood that I had been dialing one digit wrong in the international access code. I went outside again, dialed correctly, and found myself talking to my wife. We had a brief, affectionate, unsatisfactory conversation. With new respect for my own tech-support skills, I went back in and dozed successfully for a while.

When Sergei and Volodya awoke that morning and set out to buy groceries and fuel, the van wouldn't start. They strolled the village until they found someone with jumper cables. After a jump start they drove off and were gone for a long time. I sat around at Avdotia Fedorovna's and fooled with my stuff and fumed. When they finally came back, they were all smiles. Sergei proudly showed me some of his grocery purchases, including the real prize—little cartons of yogurt from Finland. "Ahhh, from Finland!" he said, displaying a sample carton for my admiration on the palm of his hand. Almost as an aside he mentioned that they had been to a garage, and all the problems of the van had been cured.

Unsurprisingly, that turned out not to be true.

Before we left, Avdotia Fedorovna gave us a midday meal of beef-and-potato stew, salad with fresh garden tomatoes, homemade cookies, and tea. After it, I made her a present of my extra pair of knee-high rubber boots. She put them on immediately and walked all around her garden in them trying them out and growling happily. To Olya, her granddaughter, I gave a few Beanie Babies and a New York skyline snow globe. Olya kept shaking it up and down and watching the snow fall among the buildings. With the delays because of the van and then this final socializing, we didn't get off until two in the afternoon.

Back on the Vologda road we continued in the direction of Cherepovets, where, Sergei said, we would take a side road to a famous monastery. He said the monastery would be interesting for me. The monastery hadn't been on my own itinerary, but I didn't object. After not many miles, the warning light for the engine generator lit up on the dashboard, making a companion for the oil-pressure light, which had never gone off. I expected that soon every warning light on the dashboard would be glowing. I pointed out the generator light to Sergei, and to humor me he said that we would stop and have the generator looked at in Cherepovets.

If that city consists of buildings, like a conventional city, you couldn't prove it by me, because all I saw of it was complicated highway ramps among a forest of power-line towers. The towers were everywhere, many stories high, sometimes clustering right up next to one another like groves of trees all striving for the daylight. Of daylight itself there was almost none; a tarpaulin of gray clouds overlay the entire scene. Somewhere Sergei spotted a garage in a roadside expanse of mud and gravel and pulled up in front of the bay door. Just at that moment the garageman came out, yanked a rope, and pulled the bay door down. He informed Sergei that the garage was now closed for the day. Then the garageman hurried to his car and sped away into the power-line forest. Sergei returned to the van, reseated himself behind the steering wheel, and turned the key. From the engine came no sound of any kind.

With this particular nonstarting of the van, we entered an odd zone—a sort of horse latitudes of confusion and delay caused by the mysterious problems of our vehicle. At low moments I thought I might bounce around in this zone and stay in western Russia forever. The episode comes back to me in flashes:

Here are Sergei and Volodya and me pushing the van away from the garage bay door, and then heaving and straining from behind to build up enough speed in order to start the engine by popping the clutch. Finally, at our breaking point, Volodya runs up to the open driver's-side door, leaps in, throws the gear shift into first, and the engine coughs alive.

Here we are in the city of Vologda, about eighty-five miles down the road, where Vyacheslav, the brother of a friend of Sergei's wife's, lives. Night has fallen. We are in a parking lot behind some buildings with our weakly idling van. Vyacheslav arrives. He is like a provincial nobleman from a nineteenth-century novel. He is tall and straight, with Tatar eyes, a round head, and Lenin-pattern baldness. He wears a well-tailored shirt of white, finely woven cotton; freshly pressed slacks; and polished brown loafers with silver buckles. His confident and peremptory manner shows not a particle of doubt. In the silvery aura of the headlights of his shiny new Volvo sedan, he says he knows an excellent mechanic who will repair the van tomorrow. For now, we will stay at his dacha, seventeen miles out of town. We will leave the van here in this parking lot overnight. Someone must stay with it to watch our things. This job falls to Volodya. He accepts it with a shrug.

Here we are—Vyacheslav, Sergei, and I—rocketing out of Vologda in Vyacheslav's car. He is going seventy-five miles an hour. He and Sergei are having a telegraphic conversation about mutual friends, impossible to understand. I am in the Volvo's backseat, down in the soothing leather upholstery. Little interior lights on various control panels glow comfortingly. None signal impending engine failure. Outside all is dark.

Here we are in Vyacheslav's large brick dacha, in a densely packed village of dachas. Vyacheslav's is set off from the others by a brick wall with a steel gate. On the other side of the driveway, but inside the wall, is a smaller dacha, which Vyacheslav has told me is the dacha of his security staff.

Here we are rocketing back to Vologda in the early morning. The faithful Volodya, when we find him, is walking up and down unhappily in the parking lot. He looks a bit worn from his night in the van. Vyacheslav's mechanic has been summoned and is on his way. Now, Vyacheslav tells us, we will go to a tennis exhibition put on by his son, a rising tennis star. Then we will take a tour of Vyacheslav's factory. Meanwhile Volodya will stay and deal with the mechanic and the van.

Here we are in Vyacheslav's factory. He owns a company called Start-Plus; it bottles a mineral water called Serebrenaya Rosa, which means "silver dew." The factory is a Soviet-era cement-and-brick pile reconfigured into a bottling plant, with many hallways, storerooms, catwalks. As we go through it, Vyacheslav tells me that he was trained originally as an engineer in metallurgy, but after meeting the founder of the first Russian bottled water company, he got the idea of starting such a business himself. With friends, he formed a company, hired a team of geologists to search for springs, found the water of one particular spring to be good-tasting and extremely healthful, and began to bottle it. The company's success has been enormous. He attributes this to the company's collective method of working, and to the water itself, which he says is better and purer than bottled water in America, where what is sold as spring water is actually fake—distilled, or piped from a public water supply. His bottled water is alive, he says, while bottled water in America is "dead water." In office after office, he introduces me to his employees, who stand at their desks and smile and say they are pleased to meet me.

Here we are in Vyacheslav's own office. His desk extends toward me in a sweep of warm, dark wood. Sergei has gone to see what is keeping Volodya with the van. Vyacheslav tells me he would like my advice about something. He has a new beverage, a lime-flavored mineral water, and he does not know what bottle would be right for it. A manufacturer of bottles has sent him five samples. Would I kindly examine the five samples and tell him which bottle I, as an American, would prefer to drink a lime-flavored mineral water from? Nothing loath, I look carefully at each sample bottle, examine them one more time, and gravely choose the bottle that somehow seems the best to me. Vyacheslav narrows his eyes thoughtfully, nods his head, and sets the bottle I have chosen to one side.

Here I am taking a walking tour of the city of Vologda with Stanislaus, a vice president of the Start-Plus company. The van, which we hoped would be fixed by now, has apparently presented some new difficulties. Stanislaus is in his seventies, with thinning blond hair combed back, faded blue eyes, and an easygoing style. He seems to have done this kind of duty before. He shows me a cathedral that Ivan the Terrible got built in record time by denying food to the workers when they progressed too slowly; soon after the cathedral was finished, it began to fall apart, and it wasn't consecrated for many years. Stanislaus also shows me the house of the first translator of Marx's *Das Kapital* into Russian, and the building where Lenin's sister lived while in exile, and a statue of Lenin that Stanislaus says is the only life-sized statue of Lenin in the world. It looks painful—as if the powerful Bolshevik had simply stood on a pedestal and been bronzed alive.

Now here I am with Stanislaus and Vyacheslav in a restaurant in Vologda having a late lunch. No word at the moment on the van. Vyacheslav asks me about the writing business in America. For example, how much do my books sell for, and what percentage of that price goes to me? He will publish my books in Russia, he says. Today he is wearing an even more elegant shirt than the one he wore the night before. This shirt has a collar and cuffs white as new stationery, and on the rest of it, a pattern like fine blue lines on graph paper. I tell Vyacheslav that his shirt is extraordinary. He agrees that it is and says, "I bought it in Paris. I go to Paris every week to buy my clothes."

"Remarkable!" I tell him.

"That is actually a joke," he says.

"A joke?"

"It is not a joke that I bought this shirt in Paris. But it is a joke that I go to Paris every week to buy my clothes."

Here I am turning down a tumblerful of the liter of iced vodka Vyacheslav and Stanislaus have ordered with our lunch. My refusal puts Stanislaus in a thoughtful mood. "I had heard that Americans no longer smoked, but I did not know they had stopped drinking, also," he says.

Here we are back in Vyacheslav's office. Sergei and Volodya have just arrived. The van is out of the shop and supposedly ready to go. A conference of the executives of the Start-Plus company has been assembled to determine what we travelers should do now. My own plan is simple: let's go. Oh, but that is an overly hasty idea, I am told. The afternoon is almost gone. We should not leave now, but instead stay another night at Vyacheslav's dacha. Sergei and Volodya both strongly favor this idea. What can I do but agree?

Even more important is the second order of business: What route should we take tomorrow when we do leave Vologda? I want to go straight east and get over the Urals to Siberia as expeditiously as possible. Again, this idea is ill considered, the Vologdans say. A Start-Plus executive with a pouchy face and hair dyed a bright mahogany shade has maps and papers assembled to demonstrate the proper route—namely, up the Sukhona River from Vologda to that river's meeting with the mighty Iug River, where the confluence of the two forms an even mightier river, the Severnaya Dvina. That, the executive says, is the route the early travelers to Siberia took. And, he adds, the city of Velikii Ustyug, at the confluence point, is one of the most beautiful cities in Russia and possibly in the world. A good road parallels the Sukhona all the way to Velikii Ustyug. Eventually, overwhelmed by popular opinion, I again agree.

Here we are at Vyacheslav's dacha that evening. Dinner has ended long ago, but still we are sitting at the table, drinking our fifth or seventh cup of tea; and I am thinking that Russians can sit at a supper table drinking tea and saying brilliant or ridiculous things longer than seems physically possible; further, this trait may explain Russia's famous susceptibility to unhealthy foreign ideas, with the postmealtime tea drinking providing the opportunity for contagion; and further yet, I am wondering whether tea perhaps has been a more dangerous beverage to the Russian peace of mind, overall, than vodka. At about midnight Vyacheslav brings down his semiautomatic rifle and begins to tell us his adventures hunting bears.

Here we are saying goodbye to Vyacheslav and his wife on the steps of his dacha the next morning. Perhaps tiring of my not-good Russian, he does an imitation of how dumb I sound. It is weird to hear myself imitated in a foreign language. Sergei walks over to the van. Against expectation, it starts. I am glad it has finally been repaired.

Of course the van's ills were not cured—not then, nor were they ever, really. As we continued our journey, and new problems arose, I sometimes raged inwardly at Sergei for attempting to cross the continent in such a lemon. In time, though, I quit worrying. I noticed that whatever glitch there might be, Sergei and Volodya did always manage to get the thing running again somehow. When the ignition balked, Sergei found a method of helping it along by opening the hood and leaning in with a big screwdriver from our gear. Soon his pokings with the screwdriver would produce a large, sparking *pop*, the engine would start, and Sergei would extricate himself from the machinery, eyebrows a bit singed.

Once after Volodya had accomplished a similar maneuver, I asked if he could explain to me just what *was* the matter with this car. He thought for a while and then said that what was wrong with the car could not be said in words. I recalled the lines by Tyutchev:

> *Umom Rossiyu ne ponyat',*
> *Arshinom obshchim ne izmerit';*
> *U nei osobennaya stat'—*
> *V Rossiyu mozhno tol'ko verit'.*

> (Russia cannot be understood by the mind,
> She cannot be measured by ordinary measure;
> She has her own particular stance—
> All you can do is believe in her.)

So we drove through Vyacheslav's steel gate, which he closed behind us, and we retraced the seventeen miles to Vologda, and then we wandered in and near the city looking for the Velikii Ustyug road. Finally we found a northeastward-tending two-lane so level and straight that it had to be the right one. Seldom had I seen a more monotonous road. It ran without variation in direction or grade for hour after hour through an unchanging forest of birch and conifers. From the middle of the windshield, the view up ahead was an X: the lines of the highway made the letter's bottom half, and the horizon of the trees along the road made its top.

We were all happy to be going nonetheless. Volodya had replaced his gray work shirt with a brown T-shirt that said (in English) EXCEPTIONAL HIMALAYA EXPEDITION. And I had been pleased to find in my research notes the information that many early Siberian travelers had indeed gone by way of Vologda and Velikii Ustyug on their passage through western

Russia. Evert Ysbrantsoon Ides, for example, went from Vologda to Velikii Ustyug by sled on his diplomatic mission to Peking in March 1692.
The forest then must have looked about the same as it does today. Few
villages interrupt its silence. The only billboards, popping up infrequently along the road, urge the traveler to visit Velikii Ustyug and see
the birthplace of Ded Moroz. Sergei and Volodya explained that Ded
Moroz (Grandfather Frost) is the Russian Santa Claus.

When we reached Velikii Ustyug in the late afternoon, it turned out
to be so lovely that I was sorry I had doubted the executives of the
Start-Plus company for even a second. River-junction cities are often
grand, and here the wide waters of the Iug and the Sukhona come together to form the Severnaya Dvina, whose name—literally, "Northern
Double"—gives a notion of its amplitude. From this junction the river
traveler from western Russia could go north to the White Sea, back to
the south, or east toward Siberia. After the closed-in forest where we'd
been, the openness of this place, with the pale sky spreading not only
above but also reflected expansively at one's feet, was like an unhooding.
On a rise above the river, the city itself shone in a profusion of gold onion
domes, which the smooth water also doubled, so that they seemed to
span heaven and earth like an Orthodox mystic's dream.

In the city's historical museum, the guide was a young woman whose
occasional self-conscious smiles redeemed her rapid-fire, rote delivery.
She told us there were forty churches in Velikii Ustyug. Many of their
domes had recently been regilded, which accounted for their celestial
gleam. In the seventeenth century, enriched by trade in Siberian sable
and porcelain from China, Velikii Ustyug for a while became the greatest
city in Russia. It has monasteries dating to the twelfth century. When
Russians took to the forest to get away from the Mongols, Velikii Ustyug
(then called just Ustyug) was one of the places they retreated to. Even
during Stalin times, its remoteness helped save it; the fact that until
1970 no train line went here may have kept the more ambitious of the
demolition-minded Soviets away.

Near the river at one end of the city stood a memorial to the explorers
who had come from Velikii Ustyug. The monument represented a ship's
prow with (confusingly) a modern cosmonaut in a space suit on the bow-
sprit. Among the honored names were those of Siberian adventurers like
Vladimir Atlasov and Yerofey Khabarov, who could also be characterized

as pirates and murderous thieves. According to the monument, Semyon Dezhnev came from Velikii Ustyug. (Actually, scholars say he came from a village on the Pinega River some three hundred miles to the north.) Almost certainly, Dezhnev passed through here in the 1630s and saw this river junction on his eastward journeys that would take him eventually around the Chukchi Nos on the farthest eastern tip of Asia.

Deciding against a visit to the spot where Ded Moroz, the Russian Santa Claus, was born, I instead sat with Sergei in the van writing in my notebook while he added up how much we'd spent so far and Volodya went to the post office to call his wife. As we scribbled, not saying anything, one beautiful woman after the next walked by. We found we both were looking up every minute or so. I remarked on this phenomenon to Sergei and he agreed it was surprising. After half an hour I concluded that Velikii Ustyug has more beautiful women per capita than any other city in the world.

That night we camped out for the first time. From a policeman who stopped us at a checkpoint—coincidentally, his name was Khabarov, the same as the explorer-pirate—Sergei learned of a good camping place on the river a few miles from town. Following Khabarov's directions, we went from pavement to gravel to a deeply cut track that probably had been a dirt road for centuries. It also constituted the only street of the village of Esiplovo, a row of humble one-story houses with sheds and small barns attached to them and fenced enclosures that allowed the animals to drink at the creek out back. Sergei said that many northern villages were like this one.

Past the village, the road ended at the Severnaya Dvina River, and we turned into a field and drove along the bank to a bluff offering a broad overlook and a light, mosquito-dispersing breeze. The river stretched perhaps half a mile wide and seemed not to move at all as it reflected the lavender evening sky. The sun had approached the horizon and it burned a hole through the branches of a windbreak of conifers at the field's far end. Sergei set up the two-man tent for himself and Volodya and the one-man tent for me, and laid out our sleeping pads and bags. Volodya started preparing dinner on a plywood board resting on two milk crates. I put on my swim trunks and went into the river with a bar of soap to wash up. The water was warm and the bottom muddy to the point of in-extricability. As I came out I found several ink-black leeches dangling from my legs. When I brushed them off, the holes they left bled impressively.

Farther along the riverbank, on the horizon, the onion dome of a church stood high above a grove of surrounding trees. Against the sky, the Orthodox cross and the silhouetted dome presided quietly in the evening light. No other structures anywhere around interfered with the impres-sion this lone church made—the whole view was just church, fields, and sky. (At dawn the next morning I sketched this scene.) Volodya said din-ner would not be ready for a while, so I bandaged the leech bites, changed into dry clothes, and hiked over to the church to check it out.

When I got to within shouting distance, I saw that it was another ruin. The grove it occupied not only surrounded it but also sprouted from parts of the building itself. One of the lower towers had a broken dome and a good-sized birch tree growing straight up through it. The front steps had been trashed so thoroughly that going up them was like climb-ing a rockslide. On the wall of the narthex someone had spray-painted in Russian I STILL BELIEVE IN GOD. DO YOU? The church's nave, which was high and narrow and ascended into the central tower, had been stripped of most of its frescoes. I recognized the stripping method that had been employed, because I had used it myself to expose the brick of an industrial loft where I lived in Manhattan years ago. Whoever had done the stripping here had used a broad-bladed chisel and a hammer and had chipped away the fresco plaster with blow after blow, leaving an array of chisel-blade lines on the brick.

This kind of plaster removal is disagreeable work. You have to wear goggles to protect your eyes from the flying fragments, and stuff gets in your mouth and at the roots of your hair and inside your nose. Whoever had undertaken this task must have used a scaffold to reach the higher areas, and eventually he or they had abandoned the job. Toward the top, a faded saint or two the chisel hadn't gotten to still held his hand up be-atifically. But in the lower reaches, the chisel marks made a pattern of swerves and sworls, as if the wielder of the chisel had leaned into the work with real enthusiasm. Other than a lust for icon smashing, I could see no possible motive for the destruction. What a people—to devote all the energy and expense it must have taken to build this lovely church out here in the middle of nowhere, and then to spend such passion in de-stroying it!

From the weedy, rubbish-strewn churchyard I saw Volodya in the distance waving his dish towel, so I started back for supper. When I turned around for one more view, the church's onion dome and its cross looked so mild and benevolent against the pale sunset that I imagined somehow it had had the final word, in a turn-the-other-cheek kind of way.

Chapter 13

For days we motored eastward toward the Urals. Though the road went on and on, it never settled down and became what I would consider a standard long-distance highway. You never knew what it would do next. Sometimes it was no-frills two-lane blacktop for hours. Then without any announcement it would change to gravel degenerating into mud and enormous potholes, and I learned the word *yama*, meaning "hole." Arriving in a village, the road might lead straight into an Olympic-sized mud puddle or lose itself among streets apparently based on cattle paths. Many stops to ask directions would be required before we could pick up its thread again.

On long, desolate sections with no villages nearby, people sat along it selling things, or not. You might see a very fat and not-young woman in a bright yellow dress sitting on a folding chair and reading a newspaper, with nothing visible to sell; then a half mile later, a group of little boys with several buckets and a sign that said RAKI. I knew that *rak* means "cancer," but Sergei said that here it was also the word for crayfish, which the boys catch in nearby creeks and swamps. Day after day men and women waited beside cardboard boxes filled with newspaper cones of mushrooms, gooseberries, strawberries, fiddlehead ferns, and cedar nuts. The term for these forest products is *podnozhnii korm*, Sergei told me; it means, literally, "feed found underfoot." Regularly we passed women standing all alone and giving each passing vehicle a sideways, hangdog stare. When they realized the driver wasn't stopping, they would turn away with their eyes cast down. They reminded me of fallen women from an old novel; I had never seen prostitutes acting ashamed before.

Wherever we stopped to refuel, the stations were as minimal as could be. A couple of fuel pumps on a gravel apron and a sheet-metal kiosk with a glass or plastic pay window so thick and opaque you could hardly make out the attendant inside comprised the total of their amenities. No advertising banners, vending machines, drinking fountains, or restrooms cluttered up this just-the-facts approach. Of course no bucket or squeegee was available should your window need to be cleaned. We had entered a buggy part of the journey, and our windshield was usually covered with splattered insects. No problem: Volodya took some water from our supply, gave the windshield a few splashes, crushed an unfiltered cigarette in his fingers, and using the tobacco as a solvent washed the bugs from the glass with big sweeps of his hand. Sergei, meanwhile, removed the wiper mount from the windshield-wiper arm and with the blade of the wiper squeegeed the windshield dry and clean.

One day—a Saturday—we drove through five weddings in the course of the afternoon. I couldn't tell whether the bridal couples had actually been married on the highway or were just having their receptions there. In either case, a lot of participants and guests had showed up, their numbers perhaps swelled by curious passersby. The celebrants stood on the pavement and along the roadside, clutching champagne bottles by the neck, photographing one another, and shouting remarks. Late in the day we came upon the biggest and most sociable wedding yet. The bride and groom themselves were square in the middle of the road with the wedding party milling around them and backing up traffic in both directions. A young woman in a fancy dress came to the passenger-side window of our van and, talking fast, said we must give money to the newlyweds. Volodya handed her a few kopeks, and she said with indignation that that was not nearly enough. He asked how much and she said, "Ten rubles, at least." He found a ten-ruble bill and gave it to her. She then handed in a tray of little plastic cups of vodka, which Volodya declined, saying we were drivers on our way to the Far East. She sang, "I don't believe you!" and turned away. With some cajoling, Sergei finally got the party to let us through. In the opposite lane, a young man in a disarrayed tuxedo was holding back a semitrailer truck with his outstretched arms across its radiator grille and his feet spread and planted on the road.

Volodya said we had been lucky to get by. Once in the Caucasus, he said, he had been stopped on the road and forced to drink at a wedding for an entire afternoon, and he had heard of people who had been taken off by weddings and detained for days.

Cities came and went—Kirov, then Perm. Both were big, gray, and industrial. We struck Kirov at rush hour. Everywhere, little groups of people were leaning from the tall roadside weeds to see if their trolley-bus was coming. When we approached Perm, about a day's drive farther on, we stopped outside the city and camped next to the Kama River, another wide and apparently unmoving stream. Hot and dusty from the road, we swam in the Kama and bathed in it. In the morning we used its tepid, gray-brown water to shave.

In Perm itself we visited the city museum and saw, right by the door, a large exhibit about the terrible industrial pollution in the Kama, complete with formaldehyde jars of deformed fish and amphibians found in it. A case nearby displayed pieces of Francis Gary Powers's U-2 spy plane, from the well-known Cold War incident. The plane had been shot down near Perm. Exiting that city after an hour or two, we covered a fair amount of it while searching for the right road. I remembered reading somewhere that the three sisters of the Chekhov play had lived in a provincial city based on Perm. Now the main motivation of the plot made more sense to me.

For a while the scenery had been getting hillier. Sometimes the road ran on ridgetops above pine forests, and beyond Perm the land reminded me of the Rocky Mountain foothills along Interstate 90 near Bozeman, Montana. Just when I was expecting the sight of the mighty Urals themselves rising above their hilly prologue, we were on flat ground again. The Ural Mountains had been crossed. If there had been a moment when we crested the continent-dividing range's summit, somehow it had slipped by me. Then almost immediately we were coming up on Ekaterinburg, considered the westernmost Siberian city; here the road did one of its quick-change acts to become a crowded and roaring multilane highway with furniture-store billboards alongside, and broken-down vehicles, and extralarge heaps of trash, and stooped figures poking through the heaps with old umbrella handles. In the midst of all the highway miscellany I glimpsed a monument, and thinking this a strange site for one I asked Sergei to pull over.

He didn't like the idea, and liked even less my darting across the four lanes to find out what the monument could be. He followed, yelling for me to be careful. And what it turned out to be, here beside this busy commercial highway on the outskirts of Ekaterinberg, was a monument to victims of Stalin's Terror. The inscription read: "Here lie the remains of thousands of dead, our innocent compatriots who were shot. The truth of the places of the mass burials and the cause of death was hidden for many years. Slow your steps, bare your head before the fraternal grave."

When Sergei saw what the monument was, he told me I should not spend time on this sort of thing. His face assumed an expression of great displeasure and distaste, and as I began to write down the first of the thousands of names inscribed on the rows of sandstone plaques—

AALTO, E. K.	1906–1938
ABAZAPULL, E. P.	1907–1937
ABAIDULLIN, SH. G.	1897–1938
ABAKULEIS, I. S.	1892–1938

—I could feel him trying to move me by telekinesis back into the van and the hell out of there. I knew how angry he must be. I have felt the same way in America, especially out West, when I've encountered the reproachful glances of French and German tourists reading the inscriptions on monuments to American Indians massacred by my fellow citizens of the U.S.A. The foreigners' condemnation was justified, of course, but on the other hand, what business did a Frenchman have in judging me? Or (worse!) a German? Then again, what business did I have here?

ABAKUMOV, G. G.	1872–1938
ABAKUMOV, Z. A.	1889–1937
ABAKUMOV, I. P.	1886–1938
ABAKUMOV, T. G.	1867–1937
ABAKUMOV, F. E.	1916–1937
ABATUROV, A. K.	1906–1937

I got no further in copying the list before Sergei's intense and silent disapproval overpowered me and I retreated to the van.

Having read a lot about the end of Tsar Nicholas II and his family and servants, I wanted to see the place in Ekaterinburg where that event occurred. The gloomy quality of this quest further depressed Sergei's spirits, which had not rebounded from our stop at the memorial, but he nonetheless drove all over Ekaterinburg searching for the site. Whenever he stopped and asked a pedestrian how to get to the house where Nicholas II was murdered, the reaction was a wince. Several people simply walked away. But after a lot of asking, eventually Sergei found the location. It is on a low ridge on the edge of town, above railroad tracks and the Iset River. The house, known as the Ipatiev House, no longer stands, and the basement where the actual killings happened had been filled in. I found the blankness of the place sinister and dizzying. It reminded me of an erasure done so determinedly that it had worn a hole through the page.

The street next to the site is called Karl Liebnecht Street. A building near where the house used to stand had a large green advertisement that said, in English, LG—DIGITALLY YOURS. On an adjoining lot a small log chapel kept the memory of the tsar and his family; beneath a marble-faced pedestal holding an Orthodox cross, peonies and pansies grew. The inscription on the pedestal read, "We go down on our knees, Russia, at the foot of the tsarist cross."

At a little gift shop connected to the chapel, I bought a book called *The Last Act of a Tragedy*, by V. V. Alekseev. It is a collection (in English translation) of original source documents and commentary having to do with the fall and execution of the tsar, and the fate of his and his family's corpses and jewelry. The book came out in 1996. While Sergei and Volodya bought supplies and did other errands in Ekaterinburg, I read it with fascination. I found myself feeling sorry for the foolish, overmatched tsar, and particularly for his worries about Alexis, his hemophiliac only son, who was nine. The accounts of the men who actually committed the slaughter are full of detail. They describe how the tsar, unsuspecting, carried his son in his arms into the execution room, because the boy had earlier injured his leg; and how fierce one of the killers looked beforehand with three revolvers stuck in his belt ("We could not help smiling at his warlike appearance," another killer recalled); and how surprised and dismayed the doomed ones were as they met their ends; and how in the finishing-up afterward a Red Guard soldier brought out Princess Anastasia's lapdog impaled on his bayonet.

Nobody can beat the Russians for horror combined with ghastly slapstick. What happened later to the bodies is a ghoul's miniseries in itself. The corpses were partly burned, thrown down a well, taken out of the well, burned again, doused with acid, buried in the middle of a swamp road because the truck that was carrying them happened to get stuck there; I forget what else. Rumors and lies about the fates of the Romanovs clouded the question for sixty years.

In the early 1970s, some of the bodies were discovered in a forest grave, and in 1991 the discovery was made public. Forensic work set about to determine if they actually were the tsar and the others, and DNA tests soon proved that the grave had contained the remains of nine of the eleven people murdered in the Ipatiev basement, although two of the tsar's five children were still unaccounted for. More tests found out which fragment had been who. In 2007, the charred bones of the two missing children turned up in a grave about seventy yards from the first. Eventually the remains of Nicholas and his wife and children were given a ceremony of public interment in Sts. Peter and Paul Cathedral in St. Petersburg.

The cruelty visited on the Romanovs, exceptional even in the history of regicide, provided an unmistakable hint of the horrors to come. From the sad piece of ground on Karl Liebnecht Street to the names of Stalin's victims on the monument across town is a short and straight line. Whether Lenin and the other Bolshevik leaders in Moscow directly ordered the tsar's execution, or whether the hard-nosed Bolsheviks of the Urals acted mainly on their own, or whether the two somehow combined with the prevailing madness of the time, remains unknown. The Ural Bolsheviks definitely had been in communication by telegraph with Lenin and with Yakov M. Sverdlov, chairman of the All-Russian Central Executive Committee, in the days before the killings. Six years after the tsar's death, the city of Ekaterinburg, named originally for the Empress Catherine I, received a new name: Sverdlovsk. The city remained Sverdlovsk for sixty-seven years, until 1991, when the name was changed back to Ekaterinburg.

Beyond Ekaterinburg the road lay straight through grain fields like Nebraska's or Iowa's, and the sky unfolded itself majestically outward and higher. Vistas kept appearing until the eye hardly knew what to do with them—dark green tree lines converging at a distant yellow corner of the fields, and the lower trunks of a birch grove black as a bar code against a sunny meadow behind them, and the luminous yellows and greens of vegetables in baskets along the road, and grimy trucks with only their license numbers wiped clean, their black diesel smoke unraveling behind them across the sky.

And everywhere, the absence of fences. I couldn't get over that. In America, almost all open country is fenced, and your eye automatically uses fence lines for reference the way a hand feels for a banister. Here the only fenced places were the gardens in the villages and the little paddocks for animals. Also, here the road signs were fewer and had almost no bullet holes. This oddity stood out even more because the stop signs, for some reason, were exactly the same as stop signs in America: octagonal, red, and with STOP on them in big white English letters. Any stop sign in such a rural place in America (let alone a stop sign written in a foreign language) would likely have a few bullet holes.

Because I knew the 1885 route of George Kennan, I generally had it in the back of my mind. Though the human geography had changed in 116 years, I was confident Kennan had traveled quite near where I was right now. Kennan and George Frost, his travel companion and sketch artist, arrived in Ekaterinburg on June 13, 1885, and left there soon after. Kennan wrote, "When we passed through the gate of Ekaterinburg, we were on the 'great Siberian road'—an imperial highway which extends from the mountains of the Ural to the headwaters of the Amur River, a distance of more than three thousand miles."

During Frost and Kennan's first day on the Siberian road (also called the Sibirskii Trakt, the Moskovskii Trakt, or just the Trakt), they saw 1,445 freight wagons. The Trans-Siberian Railway had not yet been built, so the Trakt served as Siberia's main artery. Traffic crowded it, especially the tea caravans, which were among its chief nuisances—the great throngs of carts and wagons loaded with crates of tea from China moving in herd formation all over the roadway at the will of their driverless horses loosely controlled by a few caravan masters. For centuries the tea trade enriched cities in Siberia. Tea that came overland was said to have a more delicate taste than tea that had suffered the mists and fogs of a sea journey.

Of course, much of the Trakt's eastbound traffic consisted of exiles. Shackled or not, sometimes accompanied by their families, always under guard, parties of exiles journeyed to their various Siberian destinations on foot for most of the way. In tsarist times, many thousands of exiles walked the Trakt every year. It officially crossed into Siberia 150 miles east of Ekaterinburg, where the province of Perm, a western Russian province, met the Siberian province of Tobolsk. A square pillar of stuccoed or plastered brick marked the spot of this continental transition. One side of the pillar bore the coat of arms of Perm province, and the other side that of Tobolsk. Of this marker, Kennan wrote:

> No other spot between St. Petersburg and the Pacific is more full of painful suggestions, and none has for the traveler a more melancholy interest than the little opening in the forest where stands this grief-consecrated pillar. Here hundreds of thousands of exiled human beings—men, women, and children; princes, nobles, and peasants—have bidden good-by forever to friends, country, and home. Here, standing beside the square white boundary post, they have, for the last time, looked backward with love and grief at their native land, and then, with tear-blurred eyes and heavy hearts, they have marched away into Siberia to meet the unknown hardships and privations of a new life. No other boundary post in the world has witnessed so much human suffering, or been passed by such a multitude of people.

At this pillar, Kennan said, exiles were allowed to stop and make a last goodbye, to press their faces to the ground and pick up a little of the earth of western Russia to bring with them. Beyond this spot they were, in a sense, jumping off into the void.

Naturally I wanted to find this pillar and see what it looks like now. If I stood beside it, I would be in an exact place where the famous traveler had been. I explained about the pillar to Sergei and we kept our eyes open. Kennan had said that the pillar was two days' travel from Ekaterinburg, between the villages of Markova and Tugulymskaya. I noted a large town named Tugulym on the map, but Markova was either too small to be included or didn't exist anymore. Then about 145 miles from Ekaterinburg, on the right-hand side of the road, there it was: Markova, barely a hamlet, just some houses and a sign. A short distance beyond it, tall markers announced the boundaries of two *raioni*, or districts. The marker facing westward said Tugulymskii Raion and the eastward-facing marker said Tapitskii Raion. We got out at the wide place in the road there. Pistachio shells and a Fanta Orange can littered the oil-stained ground, the trucks blew by, the trees leaned overhead. But no sign of Kennan's fateful pillar could be seen.

A woman in a roadside café nearby told Sergei that the road we were on was the new road. The previous one, the original Trakt, used to run through the woods just to the north. She had never heard of any pillar such as Kennan had described. Following her directions, we went down a brushy lane until it ended at a collection of trash piles, and then Sergei and I continued on foot into deep forest with weeds and underbrush over our heads sometimes. Rain had fallen the night before and our clothes were soon soaked through, while grass seeds covered us all over. The woman had said that exiles who died along the road were buried beside the old Trakt, and you could still see the mounds. We did find mounds on either side of a declivity among the trees, and its barely visible path could once have been a roadway. But the mosquitoes were coming at us so madly that we had to wave our hands before us like windshield wipers on the fastest setting, and I soon decided that Kennan's pillar, if it did perhaps exist somewhere in these thickets, would not be found by me.

Back on the road, we drove slowly and asked people along it if they'd ever heard of the pillar—none had—and if they could show us sections of the old Trakt. Everybody we talked to pointed out pieces of the Trakt right away. Sometimes it was on one side of the new road, sometimes the other. Where it crossed grassy fields you could still see the deep depression the road had made in the ground. A man selling carrots on the new road told us that the Trakt had been the main street of a tiny village nearby called Maltsevo. Leaving the pavement and rambling along mud paths, we came upon Maltsevo in its backwater where the new road as well as the railroad had passed it by. Every one of the dozen or so houses in the village was made of wood, and every piece of wood was the same shade of weathered gray. The houses' logs, thin pieces of overlying lath, decorative scrollwork, and plank window shutters all seemed to be in a slow-motion race to see which would be the first to fall completely down.

The single distraction that kept the village from epitomizing the dreary Russian peasant village of all time was the loud rock-and-roll anthem reverbing from speakers somewhere invisible but quite close by. I recognized the song as "It's My Life" (in English, the original) by Bon Jovi. As we stood on the town's one street, a small, unshaven, dark-haired man came walking along. He had on two sweaters whose several large holes almost did not overlap. We asked him where the Trakt used to be and he immediately said, "Right here!" gesturing backhand at the ruts at his feet. "Also there," he said and gestured far to the west. "And there!" This final gesture, to the east, was like an overhand throwing motion, and it pantomimed a hopelessness at even imagining how far the road went on.

I turned to where he gestured—first, back to the west, where the old road came on snakily but straight, a pair of muddy ruts in a wide and worn bed. The ruts entered the village, barely deigning to notice the weak attempt at domestication alongside, and then headed straight out of town. Across another field they dwindled eastward to the horizon and forever. I had seen some lonesome roads, but this one outdid them all. I stood looking at it with Sergei and Volodya and the man wearing two sweaters. For a moment I got an intimation of the sadness Kennan had been talking about—the deep and ancient sorrow of exile.

Chapter 14

Siberian exile began almost as soon as there were tsars. In a document dated 1592, Tsar Theodore, son of Ivan the Terrible, ordered that a prince being sent to build the Siberian city of Pelym take with him one Ignati Khrypunov "and his wife and children and whole household," deposit Ignati and family in the new city of Tobora, and not let him go from Siberia without an order from the tsar. The offense of the unfortunate Ignati is not mentioned. During those years of the late sixteenth and early seventeenth centuries—including the period of turmoil over succession and false tsars known as the Time of Troubles—many people were exiled to Siberia. Boris Godunov, the regent and actual power during Theodore's reign, was said to have executed or exiled the whole town of Uglich for rebelling against his rule. And because the town's church bell had rung to call people to insurrection, Godunov sent the bell to Siberia, too.

A number of books about Siberia mention this bell. Godunov dispatched it to the city of Tobolsk. Valentin Rasputin, in *Siberia, Siberia*, says that the bell may have melted there in a fire in the seventeenth century. According to another book, it was hanging in a Tobolsk church tower in 1850 when its ringing greeted Fyodor Dostoyevsky as he arrived on his way to labor-camp exile. George Kennan visited the belfry in Tobolsk where the bell hung in 1886. He reported that the city of Uglich now wanted its bell back, but the mayor of Tobolsk had replied that the bell was sentenced for life and therefore its term of exile had not yet expired.

When I was in Tobolsk, I saw what I took to be the original Uglich bell in the museum, but it turned out to be a replica. According to the website of the city of Uglich, a vigorous local campaign for the bell's return succeeded in bringing it back in 1892.

Exile became an official form of punishment under the Code of Laws of 1648, during the reign of Tsar Alexei Mikhailovich. Within fifteen years, there were seven thousand four hundred exiles in Siberia. Peter the Great, Alexei's son, made many new laws that his subjects did not want to obey; Peter exiled hundreds of people at a time. In that era, Russian corporal punishment was so brutal, with whippings, brandings, and mutilations, that exile also served as a way of removing the disfigured from public view. In 1753, Empress Elizabeth had replaced execution with permanent exile to Siberia, and from this came a system whereby there were four classes of exiles: prison convicts, sentenced to hard labor and banished for life; penal colony settlers, also banished for life; banished people guilty of lesser offenses, who did not have to live in prisons or penal colonies; and families who chose to accompany any of the above. The first two classes of exiles wore iron shackles on their legs and sometimes on their arms, and they had their heads half shaved to identify them.

In *The House of the Dead*, Dostoyevsky recalled how he and other prisoners had half their heads shaved every Saturday when "the battalion barbers washed our heads with soap and cold water and scraped them mercilessly with the bluntest of razors. The memory of this torture still gives me gooseflesh." To avoid this weekly experience, Dostoyevsky found a convict with a better razor who shaved him for a kopek. On some convicts the shaved part went from the front of the head to the back, on some it went crosswise.

Of course the exiles of all classes suffered other miseries as well— filthy quarters, hunger, cold, all kinds of bugs, diseases, beatings with the knout. The convict-executioners who wielded that instrument, which was a handle with leather thongs, had been instructed to distribute the blows around a central point on the prisoner's back so that the scar they left looked like an asterisk. Sixty blows in a single beating were enough to kill a man. The authorities ordered Dostoyevsky flogged twice in prison—once for complaining about a "lump of filth" in a fellow prisoner's soup, and once for saving another prisoner from drowning after he had been ordered not to. The second flogging put him in the hospital, and when he got out and rejoined the other convicts, they nicknamed him Pokoinik, the deceased.

Dostoyevsky had ended up in Siberia because he belonged to a Fourierist discussion group, and because at a meeting of the group he read aloud a letter by Vissarion Belinsky, the banned literary critic. Nikolai Gogol, during the more eccentric later stage of his life, had published an antiliberal pamphlet in which he praised the monarchy, the church, and serfdom; Belinsky, then living in Paris, attacked him in a letter that became the reformers' rallying cry. Betrayed, arrested, and convicted, Dostoyevsky received a sentence of death. He was at the place of execution when an order from the tsar commuted the sentence to prison labor in Siberia followed by four years of service in the army. The close call gave him a certain perspective on his Siberian sojourn and no doubt contributed to his sense of plot.

From the beginning, exile was the punishment for imaginary and real misdeeds of all kinds. During the years of schism in the Orthodox church, believers set out for Siberia voluntarily, to get away from heretical practices, or under compulsion, as was the case with Avvakum. Even expressing doubt about the truth of Greek Orthodoxy could result in exile to Siberia. In the seventeenth century, according to Kennan, you could be exiled for fortune-telling, prizefighting, vagrancy, taking snuff, and driving a horse with reins instead of sitting on its back or running alongside. Usury, debt, drunkenness, trespassing, salt gathering, wife beating, and begging when not in distress were all infractions worthy of exile. At times when Russia was fighting wars with Sweden and other countries, thousands of prisoners of war were sent to Siberia, and many lived out their lives there.

People in power often used exile to get rid of personal enemies and those they felt threatened by. An exile in the time of Peter the Great wrote that Peter had sent Prince Dolgoruky to Siberia merely because he was too popular with his soldiers. Abram Petrovich Gannibal, the black African valet and secretary to Peter, incurred the displeasure of Alexander Menshikov, Peter's high-ranking counselor, who had him sent to Irkutsk (Gannibal would be better known in later years as the great-grandfather of Alexander Pushkin). Menshikov himself, one of the great grafters and rakes in Russian history, spent his last days in the tiny Siberian village of Bereyozov, above the tundra line, where he went around in a peasant smock and a long beard and soon died. He had overreached in his arrogance after Peter's death and angered Peter II, who exiled him. When Peter's youngest daughter, Elizabeth, became empress in 1742, she lost no time in exiling Natalie Lopukhin, the French wife of a general in St. Petersburg, because Mme. Lopukhin was too beautiful and copied Elizabeth's dresses. For good measure, Elizabeth branded her rival's tongue. By the time her successor, Peter III, pardoned Mme. Lopukhin twenty years later, presumably that lady's charms were not so threatening.

Catherine the Great, who followed Peter III, changed the government substantially by giving the nobility more power and freeing them from obligatory government service. The glory days of the Russian nobility began with Catherine. As part of the new arrangement, small disputes and violations of the law would be decided by local councils run by the nobles, and among the punishments available to them was exile to Siberia. In effect, a local nobleman could send a serf to Siberia because he didn't like his attitude—bad conduct, general worthlessness, being "incompatible with public tranquility" or "prejudicial to public order" were sufficient reasons for deportation. Catherine's new laws encumbered the serfs even more than they'd been oppressed before, and as a result many took off for Siberia on their own. Serfdom, as an institution, did not exist east of the Urals.

The wretchedness of the serfs' condition under Catherine troubled the conscience of a nobleman named Aleksandr Radishchev, who became the most famous exile of her reign. Radishchev's offense was to write a book called *A Journey from St. Petersburg to Moscow*, a passionate unmasking of the evils of serfdom that is sometimes compared to *Uncle Tom's Cabin*. Scholars consider Radishchev's book to be the beginning of the literature of social protest in Russia. Radishchev, born in 1749, was an official of some rank who had served as a clerk of the Senate and chief of the St. Petersburg Customs House. Ideas of freedom and justice shared by his contemporaries in other countries inspired him; his idol was George Washington. *A Journey from St. Petersburg to Moscow* describes a semifictional trip between the two cities during which the narrator sees and is told about a horrifying array of local injustices and crimes caused by serfdom.

The book came out in 1790, and he published it himself. Following the usual procedure, he first submitted the manuscript to the censor, who told him he must take out a lot of it. Radishchev agreed, went home, and on his own printing press published the whole book uncut as he had written it. Then he brought the bound book back to the censor, who did not bother to reread it before stamping "With the permission of the Department of Public Morals" on the last page.

When a copy of this combustible samizdat fell into the hands of Catherine, indignation sharpened her critical faculties, which were considerable to begin with. She read every page of the book, writing down her comments as she went along (an English-language edition, published in 1958, includes them). She notes the book's illegal parts—"on p. 36 there begins an illegal discussion"—but other of her objections are only literary or commonsensical. Even a reader completely sympathetic to Radishchev might find some of Catherine's comments hard to argue with. "Arbitrary, quasi-philosophical ravings," she says of one passage, and I had to agree. In fact, Radishchev's book is kind of a mess, like a screed written by a junior high student against the school administration. Of one heated thirty-page section, the author says he found it written on a single piece of paper: "Here it says that everything written above was found on a piece of paper which he picked up in the road," Catherine dryly remarks. And yet the book is also bold, shocking, and moving—not to mention morally right.

The name of the author does not appear anywhere on the title page or in the text, but Catherine knew enough about the people in her government to have a fair idea who had written it before she was a fifth of the way through. Brought in by the police, Radishchev was imprisoned in the summer of 1790 and quickly sentenced to death. In September, Catherine commuted the sentence to ten years' exile in Ilimsk, a settlement on the Ilim River three hundred miles north of Irkutsk. The convict lost his noble title and rank in the government service, though he was not stripped of his property. His deceased wife's sister took care of his children, and then with them followed him into exile and married him. They had three more children in Siberia.

Catherine the Great died in November 1796. Her son Paul, who succeeded her, hated her and tried to undo many of her acts. She had been dead less than three weeks when he eased the punishment of Radishchev, allowing him to return to his estate in Kaluga province and live there under the observation of the provincial governor. For this news to reach Radishchev and for him to make the journey back home took eight months. His wife died on the way. After Paul was assassinated in 1801, the next tsar, Alexander I, indulging liberal leanings that he would later lose, freed Radishchev from all remaining restrictions and restored his rank and titles.

When Alexander set out on his early path of reform, Radishchev was honored by being made a member of the Commission on Revision of the Laws. At one of the commission's meetings he got carried away and brought up his old opinions from his *Journey from St. Petersburg* days. This lack of caution surprised Count Peter Zavadovsky, chairman of the commission, who genially reproved him, "Eh, Aleksandr Nikolaevich, do you still want to talk the same old nonsense? Or didn't you have enough of Siberia?" Radishchev took this as a threat; upon returning home, he killed himself with poison.

Catherine had ordered that all copies of Radishchev's book be destroyed, and most were. *A Journey from St. Petersburg to Moscow* became a dangerous book to own, though a few daring souls managed to hang on to theirs. Pushkin, born three years before Radishchev died, kept a copy in his library. Eighteen copies of the 1790 edition exist in Russia today, and two in the United States. I have seen one of those, in the Houghton Rare Book Library at Harvard University. The book is bound in red calfskin, with gilt lettering on the cover, a red morocco label on the spine, and the edges of the pages stained red. The faded clarity of the hand-set type, the craft of the book's binding, and the courage and crazy hopefulness of the author make this an object to bring tears to one's eyes. (In the documents of provenance tucked into the book's protective sleeve, I noticed that this copy had previously belonged to Serge Diaghilev.) Throughout the nineteenth century, the Russian government continued the ban against Radishchev, with the result that no new edition of his book would be published in that country until after the Revolution of 1905.

As usually happens, being forbidden increased the book's reputation. The fact that someone had spoken out for liberty, however futilely, put the subject on the table. Radishchev's idealism became one of the inspirations for the Decembrists, Russia's first revolutionary generation, whose move against the government was smashed on December 14, 1825. (Over one hundred of the Decembrists ended up in Siberia; I will say more about them later on.) Alexander Herzen, the Socialist and progressive

whose influence would be important to a later generation of revolutionaries, was fourteen years old and living in Moscow when five of the Decembrists were hanged. Herzen and his friend Nikolai Ogarev heard the
Te Deum sung in praise of the tsar on this occasion, and afterward, on
the Sparrow Hills overlooking the city, promised each other they would
dedicate the rest of their lives to the Decembrists' cause.

No radical of any consequence in the nineteenth century could avoid
being sent to Siberia sooner or later, and Herzen's turn came when he
was a student at Moscow University and a member of a group (like
Dostoyevsky's) that discussed illegal literature. Herzen's punishment
was a term of exile in the city of Viatka, where he was given a job in the
provincial government. Herzen happened to be a brilliant man and a
natural organizer, well suited for the job. Though a convict and an exile,
he had a lot of responsibility. In *My Exile in Siberia*, he says, "I am certain that three-quarters of the people who read this will not believe it,
and yet it is the downright truth that I, as a councillor in the pro-
visional government, head of the Second Department, counter-signed
every three months the *politsmeyster's* report on *myself*, as a man under
police supervision."

Later Herzen was allowed to return to Moscow. After he had inherited a fortune from his father and endured another period of exile, he
decided to emigrate. He established himself in London, and while living
there published a magazine, "*Kolokol*" (The Bell), which in smuggled
form became the main voice in Russia for liberal reform in the years
leading up to the freeing of the serfs in 1861. As part of this movement,
Herzen also published in England a new edition of *A Journey from St.
Petersburg to Moscow*.

George Kennan's trip to meet and talk to Siberian exiles turned up
many stories reminiscent of Herzen's. Political exiles and prisoners were
filling the system by that time, when a person could be sent to Siberia for
lending money to a revolutionary, holding a package for one, or just being related to one. Prince Peter Kropotkin, a political exile whom Kennan met in Tomsk, had been arrested, the first time, for possessing a
copy of Ralph Waldo Emerson's *Self-Reliance* and refusing to say where
he got it. Then there was the man whose term of exile specified that he
never stay longer than ten days in any one place, and who spent the rest
of his life wandering; the druggist who threw a rock with a petition wrapped

around it through the window of a government minister, for which he was sent to live in a Siberian village that the authorities did not know no longer existed, so the druggist had to keep looking for it for thousands of miles; the woman who almost died trying to reach Verkholensk, the place she thought her husband had been exiled to, but actually she had two letters of the name wrong, and instead he was in Verkhoyansk, two thousand six hundred miles farther on, at which news the woman went insane and later died; and the man exiled for possessing a manuscript of a newspaper article that he later saw published without objection or alteration while he was in Siberia.

Did any exiles or prisoners ever escape? A reader cannot help hoping that somehow some did. The historian S. V. Maksimov, in his *Sibir' i Katorga* (Siberia and Prison), tells the story of a prisoner named Tumanov who, during a display of gymnastics before the regional governor, leaped from the top of a human pyramid and landed outside the prison palisades and got away. The escapee left behind part of his costume, a flax beard, which the prison commander was forced to wear until his dying day. Some of those who had been sent to Siberia did in fact manage to sneak off and start the long walk back to western Russia after winter was over, when the cuckoo began to sing in the spring; this annual throng, for whom sympathetic peasants sometimes left food by their doorways or on their windowsills, were known as General Cuckoo's Army. Kennan mentions certain indefatigable souls who made the westward trek repeatedly, only to be recaptured and returned. An officer told him of a prisoner who had done the round-trip journey sixteen times. Among prison guards the saying went, "The Tsar's cow-pasture is large, but you can't get out of it; we find you at last if you are not dead." And yet two of the exiles Kennan met did eventually escape and leave the country. One of them ended up in London and the other in Milwaukee.

For a wild and woolly story about escape from Siberia, perhaps the best is that of Mikhail Bakunin, the anarchist and revolutionary. Bakunin belonged to a type that had not been clearly identified in his lifetime; I like him because he reminds me of a 1960s hippie radical from my youth. He was a voluminous talker, a sponger, a permanent adolescent, an effusive smoker, with cigar ash all over himself and tea stains on his papers, subject to mad enthusiasms and exalted monologues. Minna Wagner, wife of the composer, whose guest Bakunin had been, recalled how shocked she was at the way he ate meat and sausages in huge chunks and gulped brandy by the glass. He was very fat, with unbarbered black, curly hair.

After driving his family close to nervous collapse and being disinherited by his exasperated and formerly liberal aristocratic father, Bakunin caromed around Europe and England, mooching off friends and fomenting rebellion. The tsar stripped him of his title and banished him to Siberia in absentia for his exploits, as if such correction could deter him. In the late 1840s, he was stirring up revolutions in France, Saxony, and Austria. The latter two states rewarded his efforts by sentencing him to death. Extradited from one to the other, and then back to Russia, he was imprisoned at the Sts. Peter and Paul Fortress in St. Petersburg. Nothing about prison life agreed with him; he developed piles and scurvy, lost some of his teeth, and fell into such a state of apathy as to alarm his mother, who petitioned and repetitioned the tsar to grant him clemency. Finally the tsar yielded and offered Bakunin a choice: stay in prison or be permanently banished to Siberia. Bakunin did not find the decision a difficult one.

Though his assigned place of exile was Tomsk, Bakunin thought he would prefer to be in Irkutsk, and here he had some luck: the governor of Siberia, Count Nikolai Muraviev, who had just wrested the Amur Valley from China, happened to be Bakunin's second cousin. By then Bakunin was forty-three and had an eighteen-year-old wife whom he had met when he was hired to tutor her in French. Through Muraviev's intercession, Bakunin not only got his wish and moved himself and his wife to Irkutsk, but he also began a job with the newly formed Amur Company, a trading firm. Part of his duties with the Amur Company involved traveling throughout eastern Siberia.

In 1861, Count Muraviev (by then Count Muraviev-Amursky) retired and went to Paris, there to spend the rest of his life. Bakunin, seeing ominous prospects for himself in this development, determined that this must be the year to make his escape. Accordingly, he cooked up a scheme whereby he would go down the Amur River and investigate trade possibilities on behalf of merchants in Irkutsk and elsewhere, and he presented such a persuasive case for his fake enterprise that he was able to raise a good amount of cash. Taking his wife along would of course look suspicious, so he solved that problem by leaving her behind. On June 5, 1861, Bakunin departed Irkutsk and traveled overland to Sretensk, on the Shilka River. A steamboat carried him down the Shilka to the Amur, another brought him all the way down the Amur to Nikolayevsk, at its mouth. By now officials in Irkutsk had decided he might be making a break, but the letters sent after him warning of this were miscarried or arrived just after he had gone.

In Nikolayevsk, Bakunin took ship on a Russian vessel bound for Kastri, another Russian port on the Pacific. To ease his hard-to-explain exit from Nikolayevsk, the cash raised from his fellow merchants almost certainly came in handy for bribes. En route, the ship for Kastri met and took in tow an American ship, the *Vickery*, bound for Japan. Bakunin, wasting no time, simply transferred to her and was free. Yet even this remarkable lucky break did not induce him to be careful. After the Russian ship put in at Kastri, and as he proceeded down the coast on the *Vickery*, Bakunin went ashore at the little Russian port of Olga and stayed overnight with the local commandant—assuming, correctly, that at this remote place the news of his escape would not be known.

Deposited in Yokohama by the *Vickery*, Bakunin found another American ship, the *Carrington*, which was bound for San Francisco, and he booked passage. While the ship waited in port before departing, the Russian consul general in Yokohama came aboard for dinner. He asked Bakunin if he planned to meet up with the Russian fleet, which was also in the harbor, and return with it to Nikolayevsk. Bakunin said he'd like to see a little more of the country first. The *Carrington* sailed the next day.

On the way to San Francisco, Bakunin borrowed $300 from an English clergyman on board. He went by steamer from San Francisco to Panama and took another ship from there to New York City. After about a month in New York, he sailed for Liverpool and arrived before the year was out—not quite seven months after he had left Irkutsk. His old friend Herzen, who like many people had assumed Bakunin was permanently buried in Asiatic exile, was understandably surprised when the long-lost anarchist popped up in London. According to one account, "after a stormy, moist embrace [Bakunin's] first words to Herzen were, 'Can one get oysters here?'"

For the leaders of the Bolshevik revolution, time spent in Siberia was an important highlight of their résumés, a proof of authenticity, just as going to jail has been for certain rap stars. I have mentioned Lenin's Siberian period, and the six escapes claimed by Joseph Stalin. In 1901, a revolutionary named Leib Bronshtein, not yet possessing a catchy moniker, found one when he escaped from Irkutsk with the aid of a blank passport on which he had inscribed the name of the man who had been his jailer back in Odessa, Leon Trotsky. After the Bolsheviks had finally won and the Soviet system was locked in place, exile became almost the easiest among the horrid array of punishments it employed. And during Soviet rule, successful escapes—from Siberian exile, from prison, from anywhere—happened only rarely, if at all.

Varlam Shalamov, the prose writer and poet who survived seventeen years in the murderous gold-mining camps of the Kolyma, noted in his prose piece "An Epitaph" that the daily quota of dug-up earth for a Kolyma miner was about 267 times as much as the quota had been for a Decembrist prisoner laboring in Siberian mines about a century before. Both the nineteenth-century and the twentieth-century prisoners had essentially the same tools—-shovels, picks, wheelbarrows. And after he finally got out of the Kolyma, Shalamov wrote, "I read memoirs of persons who had been sent to exile in Siberia under the czars. I found their escapes from Yakutia and Verkhoyansk bitterly disappointing: a sleigh-ride with horses hitched nose to tail, arrival at the train station, purchase of a ticket at the ticket window . . . I could never understand why this was called an 'escape.'"

We know the Soviets killed or jailed people for offenses even more bizarre than any the tsars dreamed up. Biographical notes about Shalamov don't say why he was sentenced to the Kolyma mines the first time, in 1937, but in 1943 he was given an additional ten years for, among other things, expressing the opinion that Ivan Bunin, a recent Nobel Prize laureate, was "a classic Russian writer." People slaved in the gulag camps for five, ten, or fifteen years because they had used fake ration cards, or worked for the American Relief Organization during the famine that followed the First World War, or stolen a spool of thread, or perpetrated a "facial crime" (such as smiling during a serious party lecture), or inquired about the cost of a boat ticket to Vera Cruz, or studied Esperanto, or possessed a piece of Japanese candy (proof of spying for the Japanese), or danced the decadent Western dance called the fox-trot.

A single ill-considered remark could be enough. An actor named Shirin, of the Lenin Collective Theater, landed in a labor camp for bursting out, "Don't feed us Soviet straw; let's play the classics!" A woman got ten years for saying that a recently convicted enemy of the people, Marshal M. N. Tukhachevsky, was handsome. A man spoke of the tragically deceased hero of the revolution, "Sergo" Ordzhonikidze, with apparent reverence ("Let's remember his soul") but unwisely happened to be in a bathroom at the time . . .

Stalin, with his wide-screen approach to governing, moved not only individuals but also entire populations around his empire like pieces on a game board. In those years people were even exiled *from* Siberia. As part of the Soviets' campaign against religion, the Tibetan Buddhist High Lama, Agvan Dorzhi, was deported from Buryatia to Leningrad. Solzhenitsyn tells of a Yakut native who was relocated from the Kolyma district to near Leningrad for the crime of rustling reindeer. After his release from exile and return home, the Yakut said to prisoners whom he met in Kolyma, "Oh, it's boring where you come from! It's awful!"

During the Second World War, tens of thousands of citizens of Korean background were shipped from Vladivostok and environs to Central Asia because of fears for their loyalty. A large number of Chinese were rounded up in Russian cities along the Chinese border and moved north to Yakutia for the same reason; most of them died as a result. Whole trainloads of German-speaking Estonians were given one-way passage to the Barabinsk Steppe, in the middle of western Siberia, because they were thought to be sympathetic to the Nazis. And so on.

Stalin's death in 1953 marked an end to the large-scale deportations. Nikita Khrushchev denounced the wrongs and excesses of Stalinism in his famous speech at the Twentieth Party Congress in February 1956. The following year, after winning a struggle for power with fellow Stalin-era holdovers among the party leadership, Khrushchev did not have his main rivals shot, as Stalin would have done, but instead made Vyacheslav Molotov ambassador to Mongolia and sent Georgi Malenkov to head a Siberian electrical-generating plant. In the later years of the Soviet Union, and certainly after its fall, one heard less often about enemies of the government being sent to Siberia. And yet in 2005, when President Vladimir Putin brought down the politically inclined oligarch Mikhail Khodorkovsky on charges of bribery, theft, and fraud, the defeated billionaire was sent not to some minimum-security jail in greater Moscow, but to Penal Colony Number 10, southeast of the Siberian city, of Chita. That city, many miles east of Lake Baikal, was where Tsar Nicholas I had sent the most dangerous of the Decembrists—or rather, those he had decided not to hang.

· · ·

Some of the above ran through my mind as I stood in the village of Maltsevo looking at the old Trakt running eastward out of sight. In the road's
deeply worn ruts I tried to picture its former magnitude. This had been
a continental highway, after all, a road of empire. I imagined parties of
prisoners tramping along it, chains jingling, and sleighs slipping by in
winter, and imperial couriers on horseback bound for Peking, and troops
of soldiers, and runaway serfs, and English travelers, and families of
Gypsies, and hordes of tea wagons in clouds of dust. If there were a museum of the great roads of the world, the Sibirskii Trakt would deserve
its own exhibit, along with the Via Appia and the Silk Road and old U.S.
Route 66.

In America we love roads. To be "on the road" is to be happy and alive
and free. Whatever lonesomeness the road implies is also a blankness
that soon will be filled with possibility. A road leading to the horizon almost always signifies a hopeful vista for Americans. "Riding off into the
sunset" has always been our happy ending. But I could find no happy-
ending vista here, only the opposite. This had also been called the Convicts' Road or the Exiles' Road. Not only was it long and lonesome, but
it ran permanently in the wrong direction, from the exiles' point of view.
Longing and melancholy seemed to have worked themselves into the
very soil; the old road and the land around it seemed downcast, as if
they'd had their feelings hurt by how much the people passing by did not
want to be here.

Using a place as punishment may or may not be fair to the people
who are punished there, but it always demeans and does a disservice to
the place.

Chapter 15

Eleven days from St. Petersburg we were well into the swampy flatlands of western Siberia. Now we were camping out every night. In a country without fences or No Trespassing signs, we had an abundance of camping spots, but every one required a certain amount of searching nonetheless. Sergei sometimes spent an hour or more in the evenings looking— stopping, getting out, walking around, then trying somewhere else. He wanted ground that was dry, not too low, not too many trash heaps, near water if possible, away from the road but not too difficult to get to. When he was satisfied with his find he would pronounce it a "khoroshoe mesto," a good place.

The country's swampiness did not manifest itself in great expanses of water with reeds and trees in it, like the Florida Everglades. There were wide rivers, and reedy places, but also birch groves and hills and yellow fields. The way you could tell you were in the swamp was, first, that the ground became impassibly soggy if you walked at all far in any direction and, second, by the mosquitoes.

I have been in mosquito swarms in beaver meadows in northern Michigan, in wetlands in Canada, and near Alaska's Yukon River. West-ern Siberia has more. On calm and sultry evenings as we busied our-selves around the camp, mosquitoes came at us as if shot from a fire hose. Usually mosquitoes cluster in a cloud around their targets, but as Volodya made dinner I observed a thick and proximate cloud surround-ing him head to toe, and then a whole other sort of candidate swarm around that inner swarm, and then more in all directions, minutely enlivening the sky.

With such astronomical numbers, Siberian mosquitoes have learned to diversify. There are the majority, of course, who just bite you anywhere. Those are your general practitioner mosquitoes, or GPs. Then you have your specialists—your eye, ear, nose, and throat mosquitoes. Eye mosquitoes fly directly at the eyeball and crash-land there. The reason for this tactic is a mystery. The ear mosquito goes into the ear canal and then slams itself deafeningly back and forth—part of a larger psyops strategy, maybe. Nose and throat mosquitoes wait for their moment, then surf into those passages as far as they can go on the indrawn breath of air. Even deep inside they keep flying as long as possible and emitting a desperate buzzing, as if radioing for backup.

Nothing short of a good breeze keeps Siberian mosquitoes down. They laugh at organic-based repellents. Strong repellent with DEET is disagreeable to them, but they work around it. Thick smoke can be effective, but you have to stand right in it. In past times, native peoples and Russians wove fine netting of the long hairs in a horse's tail and wore the nets throughout the summer. Members of a tribe called the Tungus carried smoke pots with them wherever they went, while another native people, the Voguls, retreated into smoke-filled huts for the summer months and became dormant, doing most of their hunting and traveling in the wintertime. The sheer volume of mosquitoes might cause an observer not to mention the gnats, flies, and tiny biting insects (known as no-see-ums in America); there are plenty of all those as well. Sometimes in the evenings I imagined I could hear the great insect totality tuning up all around, a continent-wide humming.

The mosquitoes kept tabs on us vigilantly everywhere we moved, indoors as well as out. Because all our campsites were just places along the road, the bathroom arrangements had to be of the walk-off-into-the-bushes variety. Tending to necessities while under insect attack was a real experience. I recalled what a Siberian traveler named Hans Jacob Fries had written about this problem more than two centuries ago: Fries was a Swiss doctor whose book, *Reise durch Sibirien* (Travel in Siberia), described a journey he made in 1776 and, incidentally, became one of the earliest books to use that serviceable title. Fries wrote that during his passage through western Siberia he was bitten on a "delicate portion of my privy parts . . . so severely by a horse fly . . . that for three days I didn't know where to turn on account of the pain, and I had the greatest trouble to prevent the setting in of gangrene." The recollection of Fries's misfortune filled me with caution, not to say fear.

Sergei had provided each of us with a special antimosquito hat, called a *nakomarnik*, that was draped with netting and resembled something a beekeeper might wear. When the mosquitoes were the worst, we wore those hats, and gloves, and we tucked our pant legs into our boots. Dressed this way we could move around and perform most essential activities. I found sketching and taking notes difficult with gloves on. Also, the no-see-ums got through the holes in the netting and were hard to swat once inside. A few mosquitoes always sneaked in, as well, and whined maddeningly. As Volodya cooked meals on the propane stove, mosquitoes attracted by the rising vapors flew over the pot, swooned from the heat, and fell in. When we ate our oatmeal in the morning there were often a few mosquito bodies in it. Most of them we just ate, but sometimes there were ones that had bitten somebody and were full of blood . . .

Bugs are just part of the Siberian situation, as inescapable as distance and monotony. That long-suffering traveler Chekhov described a cockroach-infested room in the jailhouse where he spent the night in a tiny settlement on Sakhalin: "It seemed as though the walls and ceiling were covered with black crepe, which stirred as if blown by a wind. From the rapid and disorderly movements of portions of the crepe you could guess the composition of this boiling, seething mass. You could hear rustling and a loud whispering, as if the insects were hurrying off somewhere and carrying on a conversation."

Vladimir Arsenyev, the Russian army officer and explorer who mapped some of the most inaccessible parts of the Primorskii Krai north of Vladivostok, wrote about flies that fell so thickly that they put out his campfire; Dostoyevsky waxed lyrical about the blessed moment in the cool of predawn in the prison barracks when the fleas stopped biting and the convicts could sleep; and John Bell noted that his ambassadorial party bound for Peking changed its route across eastern Siberia partly because they were "much pestered by gnats and muskitoes." The swarms afflicted animals, too—descending on young foals in such numbers as to kill them, suffocating reindeer in Yakutia by clogging up their nostrils, tormenting

cattle on the Barabinsk Steppe so that the herdsmen had to paint them
all over with tar. Some of my Siberian notebooks still have squashed
mosquitoes between their pages. The Lonely Planet guidebook to Russia that I referred to before I went on my journey states, in the section
about Siberia, "By August, the air has cleared of mosquitoes." From my
experience, this is no longer the case.

After about two weeks on the road, Sergei and Volodya and I had been
together enough that the official politeness among us had worn off and
we were all acting like our ordinary selves. I sometimes withdrew into
moodiness and silence; Sergei said nothing for hours at a time and looked
grim around the eyes. I glanced at him every so often trying to detect
his mood. Meanwhile Volodya leaned back in the passenger seat, comfortably unencumbered by a seat belt, eating hard candies and listening to the radio. He and Sergei often talked so fast and allusively
between themselves that I could not extract a clue as to what they were
saying.

Now that we were unmistakably in Siberia, I had got the idea that I
should set about finding some prisons and had broached this possibility
to Sergei. He had taken an even dimmer view of it than he had of my
writing down the names on the monument outside Ekaterinburg. He
folded his brow into its deepest furrows and winced and shook his head
and gave me fragments of reasons why this search for prisons could not
be done. Then he continued driving at sixty miles an hour. During our
earlier, polite phase, I had had the illusion that I was in charge of this
expedition. Now I began to feel that they were the ones taking the trip
and I was along for the ride.

As we followed the banks of the Tura River going northeast, we came
to the village of Pokrovskoye. I had wanted to check this village out because it was the hometown of Rasputin—not Valentin Rasputin, the
writer, but the original unhinged self-described holy man Grigory Rasputin, abettor of the downfall of the Romanov line. The village was all
gray wood and stretched along the river for miles. Sergei did not care to
look for Rasputin memorabilia—an old church associated with Rasputin,
perhaps, or a Rasputin museum. And unlike Ded Moroz, Rasputin was
not the kind of celebrity whose homeplace seemed eager to claim him;
no signs anywhere, including at either edge of town, mentioned his name.

Later I heard that there is a small Rasputin museum in Pokrovskoye, but you have to make arrangements in advance. Sergei drove straight through the village without a pause while I fretted and said nothing.

Rasputin, it was said, gave off a powerful odor of goat. What a museum you could make about a guy like that! Oh, well.

A few hours later we came to a river I'd long wanted to see—the Tobol. This is the river that Yermak, the almost-mythical conqueror of Siberia, traveled as he approached his decisive battle with the Siberian khan. The problem was, we could glimpse the river only off in the distance, because for most of its length it's really more like a deeper part of a continuous swamp. Trying to get close to it in the late afternoon, we drove up on a small hill. Birch groves and a meadow of long grasses covered the hill, which on its far side ended at a cliff, descending steeply to the Tobol itself. Here the view swept far around a long continuation of the cliff, enclosing a wide swath of water made by a sharply turning river bend. This seemed an ideal camping place. Sergei parked the van back from the cliff, in a clearing in the birch woods, and set up the tents for the night.

Along the cliff a mile or so away, the roofs and smokestacks of a village mingled with the silhouetted trees. According to somebody we had asked on the road, the village was called Berezovyi Yar (Birch Cliff). A breeze rendered our supper pleasantly mosquito-free. After the meal, as the light was declining, Sergei and Volodya proposed that they walk over to the village, buy some bread, and find out information about the area. While they were there, I would keep watch over the camp and the van

I did not like being left in camp, but I had brought that duty on myself. What with my awkwardness in the language, and the fact that I didn't drink, I sometimes preferred to stay in camp and read a book while Sergei and Volodya were hanging out and socializing with people they'd met along the way. But that does not quite describe the problem, either. By now we were in remote places where the arrival of a vehicle with St. Petersburg license plates was news. Even the highway police, when they waved us over at checkpoints, were a bit wide-eyed as they examined our documents—"Where do you live in America? What do you do?" and so on. One young policeman, before he saw my passport, asked wistfully, "Is it expensive to live in St. Petersburg?" And this curiosity seemed to affect the local women even more strongly than it did the men.

I'm not saying that women paraded through our campsites wherever we happened to be, but they did show up occasionally, even when we were camped far from any village. A few nights before, in a glade well off the road, I had just got into my sleeping bag when Sergei rousted me out so I could meet two women whom he described as schoolteachers eager to meet me. Dutifully I got up and emerged and made conversation with the schoolteachers for a while. They had wanted to see the American, and I think Sergei had felt compelled to prove that he really did have one. Then he and Volodya and the schoolteachers went off—to a birthday party, Sergei said—at a picnic spot nearby. I demurred and returned to my tent. The idea of chasing women in Siberia would have made me nervous even had I not been married. Sergei and Volodya found my reluctance mystifying.

In any event, that night after supper on the banks of the Tobol, Sergei and Volodya trooped away single file down the narrow path along the river on their fact-finding mission to Berezovyi Yar, and I sat on a folding chair and read until the twilight became too faint. They had said they would be back by ten o'clock. I turned in and dozed for a while. At about midnight I stuck my head out of the tent. The campsite was quiet; no sign of the guys. From somewhere came the sound of singing. Restless, I got up and walked around the camp. Because of the clouds, no moon or stars could be seen. Darkness in rural Siberia is a serious business, with no streetlamps or brightly lit gas stations or city glows on the horizon to break the spell. All around was only dark, with the wind in the trees, and the soundless river flowing by.

Maybe Sergei and Volodya weren't coming back at all. Maybe at this moment they were plotting with confederates—somebody else they'd known back at university, now residing in Berezovyi Yar—to return to our camp when I was asleep and rob me. Maybe my Russian friends in America had been right, and I had naïvely walked into my doom. I know that I sometimes have a tendency to lose my head and think panicky things. I went back into the tent and zipped everything up tight and burrowed into my sleeping bag and tried to calm down. A few minutes later as I lay there, lights swept the top of the tent. Then a distant engine roar began, and grew louder. The lights vanished, then came back again on the other side of the tent. I put my head out the tent flap and caught a glimpse of headlights swooping and bouncing through the trees. There followed some whoops and more engine roars. It seemed someone was out in the birch forest at midnight driving around.

The headlights approached, retreated, approached again. That part of the night passed slowly. I kept the tent flap open, prepared to bail out if it appeared that the car or cars were about to run me over. For a while the shouting became more intense, and the engine roared louder. I imagined that the car must have run itself into a wet place and bogged down. Finally the lights and the noises faded away, as if all had been swallowed by the swamp. The coal-cellar darkness prevailed again, and the river's faintly lapping quiet. A dog barked and then howled. I couldn't decide whether it made sense to try to sleep. I just lay there.

Then there was a throbbing, a rumbling as if of something rising under the ground below me. The throbbing got more powerful. Suddenly the whole side of the tent lit up with a blue-white light that magnified the shadows of nearby weeds and sent them sprawling across the nylon. Wanting at least a glimpse of what was about to crush me, I looked from the tent and saw, coming up the river, a barge about a hundred feet long followed by another barge just like it, both of them pushed by a tugboat that was churning water in a surf behind; on the front barge, at its blunt bow, a searchlight the size of a tunnel entrance was swinging the white pillar of its beam over the river, right bank, left bank, trees, and sky.

This floating apparition took a few minutes to pass. After the bow searchlight had gone by, I could see the flat, featureless surfaces of the barge dim in the beam's shadow. No human forms could be distinguished anywhere. In the tug's high pilothouse only a blue glow comforted whoever was within. As the tug came alongside, the throbbing of its engines filled the night. Then tug and barges receded, and the bow light could be seen careening through the dark in the distance for ten minutes or more, while the river continued to slosh at the bank below like a bathtub someone had jumped into. Then the dark and the quiet returned.

When Sergei finally came back, at about three thirty, I yelled at him. Giving up on sleep, I had sat waiting for him in a camp chair getting madder and madder. At my tirade, he tried to soothe and reassure me. The memory is humiliating. Why did I let him see that I'd been scared? Rather than wait up, I should have just chilled and gone back to sleep. The chances of anything happening were remote. I should have understood that while I was basically semifearful and watchful most of the time on our journey, Sergei and Volodya were having a ball. In this land where I never stopped feeling strange, they enjoyed perfect ease and even a sense of glamour, of being welcome everywhere they went. When they said they were coming back at such and such an hour, they meant if no interesting opportunities arose. What did I expect? Sergei didn't even wear a watch. I should have been happy to be the originator of their good time. Still, I had not liked being by myself in camp in the middle of the night.

Tobolsk, our local destination—a must-see as far as I was concerned—was about an hour and a half away. In the morning Sergei announced that we would drive to Tobolsk now, spend the day there, then come back here and camp for another night. (The main road, like the old Trakt and the route of the Trans-Siberian, runs a few hundred miles to the south of Tobolsk, bypassing and isolating the former Siberian capital, so we would have to go by here on our return to the main road anyway.) I gave the plan my okay. Rather tiredly, he and Volodya broke camp and packed the van. Then we drove off, with a first stop at the village, where three women were waiting for us. The youngest of them, a sturdy, round woman of about thirty with blond-streaked hair, came up to Sergei and took his hand. She seemed delighted with her luck in having met him. The other two women were in their late fifties or early sixties and did not appear to have been principals in last night's socializing. These two women were sisters. One of them was the blond-streaked young woman's mother, the other her aunt.

Both the aunt and the mother had brown, deeply weathered faces. The mother wore a brown cloth Lenin-type cap, a dark gray overcoat-smock with holes in it, brown bloused pants with red-brown patches, and knee-high rubber boots. The aunt was dressed similarly, but she had a head of wiry hair dyed yellow-orange. Both carried big galvanized pails. They were on their way to pick berries, and we were going to give them a ride to the berry patch a couple of miles away. The mother started right in talking to me. Sergei must have told her that I was interested in Yermak, because she informed me that Yermak and his men had camped at the exact spot where we were last night. I asked how she knew this and she said, "It's a fact, everybody knows it," adding that the aunt had even written a paper about this subject. The aunt nodded her head in confirmation. The mother went on to tell us about the aunt's paper, and what it said, and where it was published. With more verifying nods, the aunt backed up each detail. I asked the aunt what her job was. "She's a philologist," the mother said. With matter-of-fact pride the aunt nodded again.

At the berry patch, the mother showed me what they were picking—a small, round berry growing close to the ground on a plant with leaves like strawberry leaves. It looked like a holly berry and was very sour but sweet, with a big stone. There were thousands of them. The mother said its name was *kostyanika* (the name means "stone berry"). She said they made a jam of it to put in tea.

As for her information about Yermak, later I read in a Russian chronicle from the late seventeenth century that the Cossack leader and his men, having fought one battle with the warriors of the khan of Sibir, "sailed on the 8th day of June down the river Tobol, fighting and living on the alert. When they reached the landmark of Berezovyi Yar [!] a great battle was fought lasting many days. The infidels were like sheep rushing out of their folds but with God's help and the manifestation of heavenly hosts they too were defeated."

The chronicle is called the *Remezov Chronicle*, after its author, Semyon Remezov, of Tobolsk (born 1648), who was also Siberia's first cartographer. His account of Yermak's conquests consists of small blocks of text, each of which is accompanied by a schematic and cartoonlike drawing of the action described. Downstream of Berezovyi Yar, Khan Kuchum and his forces barred the Russians' way with chains across a narrow part of the Tobol. Yermak defeated this tactic by manning his boats with stuffed dummies, while he and his Cossacks detoured around on land and surprised the enemy from the rear. Farther down, the Tatars set another ambush along the shore, and the picture accompanying this text shows Jesus himself carrying a sword in the sky above Yermak's boats: "then all the infidels saw how along that bank there appeared on clouds the great and wonderfully beautiful king in a bright light with many winged warriors flying and bearing his throne on their shoulders . . . O wonderful miracle! According to the infidels' own accounts, the arms of those strong in archery who shot at him from afar went dead by divine fate and their bows were shattered."

The chronicler notes that even before Yermak came, the Tatars had been afflicted by a disturbing premonition, in the form of "a vision of a shining Christian city up in the air, with churches and a great ringing of bells." The site of this imagined city was the geographic eminence soon

to be occupied by Tobolsk. Now, as we drove toward Tobolsk from Berezovyi Yar, I had an envisioned city in my mind, too—something striking
and celestial along the lines of Velikii Ustyug. Many cities today are just
denser parts of a big sprawl, and dull to look at. The closer we got to
Tobolsk, the more I feared that's what it would be. Cement fences and
cement-block buildings and the usual decrepit Soviet high-rises seemed
to be all there were, until unexpectedly we passed through that zone and
came to the *kreml*—the walled city—of old Tobolsk. It's the oldest stone
kreml in Siberia, built beginning in 1587, and on its promontory two
hundred feet or more above the floodplain of the Tobol and Irtysh rivers
it rises skyward like the fabled crossroads of Asiatic caravan traffic that it
used to be.

What I want in a city is partly a miragelike quality, an elusive shim-
mering you can see and dream on from afar. The old part of Tobolsk
provides that, with the *kreml* visible at a distance and the humdrum
structures of the city not prominent at all. The walls of the *kreml* are
white, fifty feet high, with conically shaped towers at each corner.
St. Sophia Cathedral, inside the wall, has a large central tower and three
subsidiary ones, and their main domes are a light blue with gilded dots
on them and gold filigree at the top and bottom, and above are smaller
gold domes supporting tall Orthodox crosses. And above all that is the
sky and its suggestion of limitless Siberian space, more breathtaking
than any modern building could make it seem. As we parked in the parking lot near the *kreml* and walked toward it, I noticed that one end of the
structure was under renovation, and the scaffolding erected for it was of
planks supported by tall, narrow fir-tree trunks with their bark still on.
When the *kreml* was first being built, the scaffolding used then probably
looked just the same.

At the walled city's completion, believers saw the vision made real—
"A shining Christian city up in the air, with churches and a great ringing
of bells." The new dispensation had arrived, because Yermak's victory
over Khan Kuchum hadn't been only that of Cossack over Tatar, but of
Christian over Muslim. (Though just how Christian the piratical Yermak,
or any of his men, really was is another question.) In a wider context,
Russia's expansion into Siberia can be seen as one of the many struggles
between the two religions at the time, and its success partly counterbal-
anced the blow Christianity suffered when the Ottoman sultan captured
Constantinople from Orthodoxy almost 130 years before.

Russian art and popular history tend to depict Yermak's Tatar enemies generically, just as has been done too often with American Indians. Because of that, I had wondered who Kuchum and the subjects of his khanate really *were*. The Kraevedcheskii Musei (Regional Museum) within Tobolsk's *kreml* complex offered some clues. Right by the entry were stone tombstones from after the time of Yermak; they commemorated the lives of Tatar noblemen departed into immortality, and they were in Arabic, with many flourishes and swirls, beautifully carved. Arabic is the liturgical language of Islam. Since the thirteenth century, most of the Tatars of Central Asia, including the Mongols and the Genghisite nobility descended from them, had been of the Muslim faith. Khan Kuchum was from a noble family known as the Shaybanids, who traced their lineage back to Shaybani, a brother of Batu. (Batu, you will remember, was the Mongol general and grandson of Genghis Khan who caused the Russians such misery between 1237 and 1241.) The Shaybanids often fought with the Taibugids, a non-Genghisite family also of western Siberia. Kuchum had killed the Taibugid khan, Edigei, and taken over the Siberian khanate not long before Yermak and his men arrived.

During the time of Kuchum, an Ottoman historian wrote a description of these Siberian Muslims. The historian, a man known as Seyfi Çelebi, reported that the leader of these people, Khan Kuchum, of the race of Genghis, was a Muslim of the Hanefite school. Hanefite teachings comprise one of the four schools of Islamic law and differ from the other schools in that they pay more attention to the law's spirit than to its strict word. Thus the Hanefite philosophy is more congenial to non-Arab, far-flung parts of Islam because of its flexibility in accommodating local customs. Seyfi Çelebi said that near Khan Kuchum's country there were bizarre people without religion, whose language no one could understand—he meant Siberian native peoples, many of whom would join Kuchum in his fight against Yermak—and he added that at certain times of the year in these lands the nights were so short that for twenty-four straight days it was impossible to finish evening prayer before the first rays of dawn appeared.

Yermak defeated the Tatars partly because his Cossacks had "arquebuses," while the Tatars used mainly arrows and spears. In the climactic battle by the Irtysh River, Yermak's men not only won, but then made a captive of the Tatar general, who happened to be Khan Kuchum's nephew, Mametkul. Afterward, Yermak sent Mametkul under guard to Moscow.

I earlier described how Khan Kuchum rallied, defeated the Cossacks, killed Yermak, and drove the Russians out, only to lose these gains as the Russians came back and reconquered the strategic points of western Siberia one by one. Forced to flee, Kuchum took refuge among a northern tribe called the Nagai, who soon killed him.

He might have had better luck surrendering to the Russians; with many of the captured Tatar nobility, the Russians did as they had done with Mametkul and sent them back to Moscow. There the tsars took a lenient, even generous attitude toward their brother nobles from the East. Mametkul was made a general and survived to serve under Boris Godunov. Ivan the Terrible gave the Tatar princes revenues and estates, and many became the founders of Russian noble families. Of course a condition of the tsar's largess always was that the captured Tatars renounce Islam and convert to Christianity.

The Tobolsk museum had a lot of cool stuff. Besides the replica of the Uglich bell, there was a display about Tatar villages that had existed in the Tobolsk area during the time of Yermak. At or near the site of Berezovyi Yar had been a village called Tarkan-Kala. A large case contained chains worn by Siberian convicts, such as the leg-and-arm chains, the *dvoinie kandali* (double chains), a contraption that must have weighed twenty-five pounds. Another exhibit detailed the life and career of Dmitri I. Mendeleev, the chemist who devised the periodic table. Born in Tobolsk in 1834, Mendeleev is the most famous person ever to come from that city.

In fact, Mendeleev is probably the most famous person ever to come from Siberia, period. After I learned about him, I was always on the lookout for other well-known Siberians, and I found that there aren't many. Admittedly, Siberia's population has never been large, but somehow I expected it to have more famous sons and daughters than, say, Cleveland, Ohio. The goatish and wicked Rasputin I have mentioned already; he falls into the "infamous" category. Many people know that Boris Yeltsin, Russia's first elected president, came from Ekaterinburg. Raisa Gorbachev, wife of the father of glasnost, was from the city of Rubtsovsk in Siberia's mountainous Altai region in the south. And on the still-active list of the politically inclined, Kim Jong-Il, the seriocomic dictator of North Korea, was born in 1942 in a wartime internment camp for Koreans near the Russian Far East city of Khabarovsk.

Among famous people in the arts, the ballet dancer Rudolf Nureyev also qualifies technically as a Siberian. Nureyev was born in 1938 in the vicinity of Irkutsk on an eastbound Trans-Siberian train. His parents, Hamet and Farida Nureyev, were Tatars, and Nureyev was raised Muslim. In later years he said that coming into the world while in transit contributed to his feeling of never belonging to any home or country. A more patriotic Siberian was Vasily Surikov, the nineteenth-century painter whose large-scale historical canvasses have become part of Russia's cultural memory; Surikov was born and grew up in the city of Krasnoyarsk, on the Yenisei River. His dramatic painting of Yermak's battle with the army of Khan Kuchum bristles with the generic Tatars I was talking about before.

The poet Yevgeny Yevtushenko, whose work is closely associated with the 1960s and the warming of the Cold War, came from Zima Junction, a village on the Trans-Siberian about two hundred miles from Baikal. Yevtushenko has said that his nineteenth-century ancestors were exiled to Siberia for burning down their landowner's house, and that his great-grandmother had also killed a village constable with a single blow of her fist. A lesser-known writer, Esphyr Slobodkina, the children's book author and illustrator, was born in 1908 in the western Siberian city of Chelyabinsk. She immigrated to America with her family in the late 1920s. If you have children, you might know her book *Caps for Sale*. It's about a monkey who steals hats from a hat peddler and goes up a tree. For a while, I was reading it to my kids almost every night.

Yul Brynner, the late stage and screen actor, is the only Siberian-born celebrity I ever saw in person. His grandfather Yulius Brynner was a Swiss merchant who owned a large trading company in Vladivostok. Yulius married a woman described by the family as "a Mongolian princess" descended from Genghis Khan, thus making Yul Brynner distant cousin to Vladimir Nabokov, Khan Kuchum, and half of Asia. People remember Yul Brynner mainly as the king in *The King and I*, a role he played for a record-breaking 4,633 performances, one of which I saw. In the sixties he met and palled around with Rudolf Nureyev, thus creating a very rare conjunction of Siberian-born celebrities. To resolve Nureyev's passport problems, Brynner even considered adopting him, but nothing came of the plan.

As we were leaving the Tobolsk museum, an Englishman, overhearing me speaking Russian to Sergei, came up and asked in English where I was from. I told him I was from London, England. He eyed me skeptically and asked where in London. I said from a little neighborhood down by the Thames that he'd probably never heard of. I didn't even bother to put on an accent. He let that go by and asked what I was doing in Tobolsk, and I told him we were driving across Siberia, and so on. He asked me some other questions. I really enjoyed talking English with him. After a few minutes he smiled and said, "You know, I'm going to put you in my book!" I don't know if he ever did. According to my notes, his name was Simon Richmond. I would not run into another anglophone for the next three thousand miles.

Sergei and I walked around old Tobolsk, looked at the hill beside the *kreml* that is said to have been the site of Yermak's great battle, and attended part of an afternoon service at the St. Sophia Cathedral. The congregation consisted almost entirely of old women. Then we met Volodya back at the van and retraced our route to the previous night's camping place at Berezovyi Yar. When we arrived there, Sergei and Volodya could hardly wait to finish putting up the tents and eating supper before taking off for the village. This time I didn't pay their absence any mind. For one thing, the wind had died down and the mosquitoes of Berezovyi Yar exceeded all the Siberian swarms we had seen before. Mainly I kept moving, trying to create a slipstream effect that made it harder for the fiends to land. In the evening I did a sketch of the Tobol River, hopping and bobbing and feinting all the while. Then I noticed that the river's surface was alive with little circles made by rising fish. Setting up my fly rod, I cast a tiny minnow imitation to a few of the rises and immediately caught several pike, none of them longer than five inches. As I was fishing, a Tatar family drove their car down to the shore and two of the men took out a seine net of monofilament woven into a very fine mesh. Casting the net, they began to haul in load after load of baby pike and then empty the pike into big plastic paint buckets. In Russia, people will catch and eat fish no larger than a little finger.

Later I stayed up and looked at the stars. I could not believe the depth of the sky. In modern-day, lit-up America, almost none of us sees the stars anymore. Here on the Tobol, the bright multitude of stars and planets overwhelmed me so that I'm not sure I even found the North Star. Every now and then I did see a satellite go over like a lone car on a remote stretch of road. For fun I took out my satellite phone and called home,

where it was midmorning of the previous day, and I imagined that the call went streaking upward to the satellite I could just see coming into view. I found my wife and kids sitting around the house on a Thursday morning.

We talked about ordinary things. Here in this place that used to be beyond the beyond, I was having a conversation with my wife in New Jersey about getting our front porch steps repaired. My daughter told me about her dance class, and my son described his new video game, "Angry Angry Aztecs." The conversations lasted for a long time, racking up a bill. Then I said goodbye and crawled into my tent and slept peacefully, with no interruptions or alarms.

Chapter 16

The next days took us to and through the city of Omsk. I had been there twice before, but only at the airport. Omsk presented the usual row on row of crumbling high-rise apartment buildings, tall roadside weeds, smoky traffic, and blowing dust. For a moment we passed an oasis scene—a crowded beach beside the Irtysh River, kids running into the water and splashing—before the city's grittiness resumed. Solzhenitsyn wrote that he spent time in an ancient prison in Omsk that had once held Dostoyevsky, and that the prison's ten-foot-thick stone walls and vaulted ceilings resembled a dungeon in a movie. I had wanted to explore Omsk looking for this prison but forgot that idea entirely in our collective eagerness to get out of Omsk. We stopped just to buy groceries, then sped on.

We were hungry and wanted to pull over for lunch, but the roadside was strewn with trash for a long way outside the city. Finally Sergei chose a place that appeared from a distance to be less trashed but actually wasn't. When we got out of the van and looked around, I noticed that the dumping here seemed to have been mostly industrial—empty spools of wire, frayed pieces of cable, broken fluorescent lightbulbs, and big heaps of curlicue-shaped steel shavings from a metal lathe mingled with the luxuriant ground foliage. There was also a felled telephone pole, convenient to sit on, so what the heck, we stayed and broke out the eats. The treat that Sergei had planned for us that day was thick slices of freshly baked black raisin bread on top of which he put chunks of canned mackerel dripping with oil and garnished with peeled cloves of garlic cut in half. Raisin bread, mackerel, and garlic. As he handed me my portion, my stomach hesitated. I ate it all, however, and then washed it down with tinny-tasting canned orange juice from Georgia—in retrospect, another mistake.

After lunch I strolled around in the trash-filled grove. My objective was to subdue a queasiness that had grown stronger, but the more heaps of steel shavings I came across the shakier I felt. The heaps were so springy-looking, so sort of alive, with the weeds growing through the coils. They seemed such horribly *Russian* trash, somehow . . . After we were back in the car and driving, I expected the breeze to revive me, but unfortunately the exhaust fumes had recently become more eye-watering in our not-perfect vehicle, and I felt woozier still. After an hour or so, Sergei stopped to videotape a landscape in which a field of bright neon green adjoined a brown field and a meadow of normal, grassy green. I looked at the neon field, and I thought of the weird name of the plant— rape (*raps*, in Russian)—growing in it. The neon green of the rape was so penetrating, and the accumulated impressions of the afternoon so nauseating, that I went into a birch grove and was sick for a while.

Sergei and Volodya followed me into the trees, their faces worried, but I waved them away. All at once I had reached a moment of overload, as if the toxicity of Russia had finally filled me right to the eyebrows. Between retching bouts I looked up from the birch I was leaning against and saw Sergei and Volodya hovering outside the grove. They really were good guys. Eventually I felt better, though I was light-headed and had a sore throat. I emerged and got back in the van and we drove to a nearby village to refill our water jugs. While Sergei and Volodya did that at the communal well beside the main street, I paced up and down on the gravel and breathed deeply, still recuperating. A distance away I noticed a road sign announcing the village's name. I went closer until I could read what it said: NEUDACHINO, which means "Unhappyville." Sergei took a picture of me next to the sign.

Rather than drive much farther, we made camp that afternoon in a nearby field with fresh haystacks in it. Leaning face-first against a haystack and breathing the hay smell restored my spirits completely, though I still trusted neither my stomach nor the next ingenious concoction Sergei might serve. For supper I had only tea with honey. Something about the picturesqueness of the haystacks in the long rays of the declining sun gave the campsite a Gypsy feel. After supper, Sergei, not usually one to recite poetry, started in on some verses he said were translated from an Islamic poet of the eighteenth century:

> Shto op'yanyaet sil'nee vina?
> Zhenshina, loshad',
> Vlast', i voina!

> (What intoxicates more strongly than wine?
> A woman, a horse,
> Power, and war!)

Lying down to sleep, I recited the lines over and over to myself. I think of this as the poem of the haystacks camp.

The hard-to-comprehend vastness of the Barabinsk Steppe, which we partly crossed the next day, kept the verses running through my mind. A man on horseback in such a landscape could hardly help but dream of women, power, and war—and, indeed, many former travelers here probably had. For hours at a time the land was so empty and unmarked that it was almost possible to imagine we weren't moving at all, and I often had trouble staying awake. Lenin himself had declared this a land "with a great future," but what I saw resembled more the blankness of eternity. And yet it was not like other flat places I've seen. The Great Plains of America tend to undulate more than this steppe does, and when the Plains are flat-flat, as in southwest Texas, they're also near-desert hardpan with only stunted brush and trees. On the Barabinsk Steppe, by contrast, stretches of real forest appeared here and there, intruding into the flatland like the paws of a giant dog asleep just the other side of the horizon.

In the place's enormous vacancy, any signs of human presence seemed to take on extra significance. At an intersection, on top of an iron pillar about twelve feet tall, the drastically crumpled remains of a car sat totemlike against the sky. By the base of the pillar, two steel markers provided the unelaborated facts. One marker read, ZYKOV, ALEKSANDR VASILEVICH—24 X 1953–12 III 1996; the other, OLIFER, ALEKSANDR

IVANOVICH—20 XI 1959–12 III 1996. The wayfarer who stopped to look could imagine the two men, maybe friends, maybe both called Sasha, maybe drinkers, and could almost hear the violence of the crash that had destroyed both of them one March day.

The villages now were fewer, and their names seemed to reach new levels of strangeness. In far-apart succession we went through Klubnika (Strawberry), Sekti (Sects), and Chertokulich (hard to translate, but something like "Devil Bread," according to Sergei). In the village of Kargat (meaning unknown, probably a Tatar word) we stopped for a break in late afternoon. I sat in the van with the window open and my feet up, watching. First a man went by on a motorcycle with a sidecar. In a few minutes he passed by going the other direction with the sidecar now full of hay. A flock of sparrows burst from a cluster of bushes by the corner of a house with a noise like heavy rain. A moment later a small hawk hopped from the bushes onto a nearby pile of firewood, looked around, hunched down, and flew off after them.

A motorcycle again came by with its sidecar full of hay. I looked closely. It was definitely not the same as the previous motorcycle. This motorcycle's driver was wearing an aviator's hat with goggles, and the sidecar was blue, not brown. As I considered that, a tall, shapely woman came walking from a long distance up the road. She wore a plain dress and had curly black hair. She passed the van and I smiled at her. She did not smile back. Then a beat-up car lurched into sight towing an even more beat-up car. As the cars came near, I saw that they were connected back to front by a loop made of two seat belts buckled to each other. That was the only time I ever saw a Russian use a seat belt for any purpose at all.

Beyond the Barabinsk Steppe lay the city of Novosibirsk. Travelers who crossed Siberia before 1893 made no mention of any city at the place where Novosibirsk is now, because none existed. The settlement begun in that year at the point on the Siberian railway where a long and technically challenging bridge crossed the immense Ob River was originally named Novonikolaevsk, after Nicholas, the emperor. Novosibirsk became the city's name in 1925. Most of its growth has been since the Second World War. Novosibirsk's tall steel-and-glass buildings, including a strange blue one with sort of knobs at the top that give it the look of a two-pronged electrical plug, form an impressive skyline above the Ob's eastern shore and its complicated crosshatching of cargo cranes. Boosters of Novosibirsk point to its domed opera house in the classical style, its up-to-date underground metro system, and its population of almost a million and a half. Here in the not-quite-middle of Siberia it is the third-largest city in Russia.

Normally Sergei liked to stay clear of cities. Spending an hour or two in a city was okay, but after that he was eager to motor on and leave city headaches and city prices behind. I had suggested several times that we find a good, affordable hotel, just for a change of pace and the opportunity of bathing elsewhere than on a riverbank. But hotels meant cities, so Sergei would never agree. What changed his mind with regard to Novosibirsk was, first, he wanted to see a friend who lived eighteen miles outside the city in the prestigious "science city," Akademgorodok; and second, in Novosibirsk he intended to carry out what might be called a plan of camouflage he had long had in mind.

Sergei's friend in Akademgorodok was a tall, careful-spoken mathematician named Sergei Prigarin. I'm not sure how the two knew each other. I think technically they were friends of friends. A professor at Novosibirsk State University, Sergei Prigarin looked the total scientist, with short curly hair and metal-rimmed spectacles and features as distinct as if rendered by a very sharp pencil. His English, spoken without effort or mistake, had a slight German accent. Prof. Prigarin's field of mathematics is stochastic systems, i.e., randomness. Recently he had been working on stochastic simulations of waves on the sea. His book *Spectral Models of Random Fields in Monte Carlo Methods* is available in an English-language hardback edition from Amazon.com.

You'd think in a place that must attract plenty of visiting academics you could just walk into a hotel and get a room. But no—finding a hotel, or the correctly priced hotel, took both Sergeis an hour or more. On various backstreets, they led us from one unlikely looking building to the next, conferring at each with people who appeared to be mere passersby. Finally we ended up in a hotel that showed no outward indication of being one. The first floor of the high-rise it occupied was a day-care center, the second floor a medical clinic, the third some kind of store. The hotel consisted of part of the building's seventh floor and offered cabinet-sized guest bedrooms, a sitting room with a television and two chairs, and a communal shower. The beds were comfortable, though, and the older ladies who ran the place attentive and kind.

After we brought up our bags and checked in, Sergei P. took us to a special luxury *banya* for scientists at his institute. For a pricey $50 or so, we travelers could have the use of it for two hours. Sergei and Volodya had been looking forward to this. They loved any and all *banyas*. I had become not so keen on *banyas*, myself. Being enclosed in a small space with large amounts of hot steam had begun to seem too culinary for me. This particular scientists' *banya* had an electric heater shaped like a short and squat Soyuz spacecraft. Once activated, it glowed as if nuclear fuel were involved, and then began hissing and pumping out industrial quantities of steam.

As it happened, my sore throat of the day before had become laryngitis, and now I could barely speak. Sergei and Volodya knew that the cure for this was honey, combined with a thorough, pore-cleansing *banya*. On the road to Novosibirsk they had bought an amphora-sized glass jar of honey from a roadside seller. To loosen me up, they first struck me repeatedly with leafy, freshly cut birch branches. Then they laid on the honey in big handfuls all over my neck, back, and chest. This honey was not your store-bought pasteurized product; it still had bee legs and pieces of weed in it. I sat, honeyed and steaming, for some time. Then I was instructed to dive into a pool of icy-cold water in the anteroom, and I did, leaving a honey slick on the surface. Then I exited the *banya* chamber, showered, and drank mineral water in the return-to-normal room.

Supper that evening was in Sergei P.'s mother's apartment in a high-rise development among tall fir trees. We sat at a small table laid with pickles, herring strips wrapped around pieces of red peppers, cold sliced chicken breast with dill, potatoes also with dill, and plates of radishes and cucumbers from the family's dacha garden. Tea after the meal came with the usual unbelievably delicious strawberry jam. I could eat that jam every day of my life. The conversation went off into realms social and philosophical, also as usual, interspersed with lively narratives from Volodya on the subject of the construction business in Sochi. Sergei P.'s mother—a pretty, red-haired woman, who looked almost too young to have grown-up offspring—spoke about the economic sufferings of the time. She also said that when she was younger, working on the Soviet space program, she and her colleagues had considered Americans the enemy. Something in her quiet, firm manner suggested that her views on this had not yet entirely changed.

Seeing that I was disadvantaged by my low comprehension and not-yet-cured laryngitis, Sergei P. kindly provided a side commentary for me in English. "Some people here in Russia refer to the events of the last ten years as the Third World War," he explained. "They say that Russia lost the war, and you Americans won. And if you just look around you almost anywhere in Russia, except in the biggest cities, it's obvious that this country lost a war. Many people have left Novosibirsk, just as people are trying to leave all parts of Siberia. Some have even gone to America, of course. I do not have any interest in leaving, however. Life anywhere in Russia is more interesting than in the West, because here it is more unpredictable—more stochastic, if you will."

I croaked that Russia's unpredictability must make it an ideal place for a mathematician of stochastic systems to live. Prof. Prigarin laughed briefly, as if excusing a pun. "Well, you could describe Russia itself as a stochastic system, definitely," he said. "But I think stochastic systems develop probabilities as they increase in size, so in this sense you could say that I believe a greater order exists in the stochastic system that is Russia. The situation now in the country is not good, but I think it is tending in a direction that is better. I believe in an optimistic kind of stochastics, both for Russia and the world. Humanity, in my view, is only at the stage of a very young child who cannot yet see its parents. As we get older in civilization we will see that our parents created life and continued it, and are still watching over us, and won't let things turn out badly."

"By parents, do you mean like . . . space aliens?"

"That I don't know, of course, but greater beings of some kind, yes. Beings that give form to my optimism. My belief, as much as I have one, is in a certain optimistic stochastics as the main force in the universe."

For simplicity's sake I have been leaving out the various minor breakdowns and nonstartings of the van. Sergei and Volodya had dealt with them all in their unflustered way. In Novosibirsk, however, more serious engine problems arose. After a night in the hotel, Sergei woke up and told me, "Today we go to auto shop." Then he disappeared with Volodya out the door. Later, as I was sitting on a lawn near the hotel building and sketching, I saw the van go by behind a tow truck. An hour passed, then two, then three. I sat on the bed in my room and wrote letters. In the early afternoon, still with no sign of the guys, I decided to wash some laundry in the sink in the communal bathroom. After rinsing and wringing out the clothes, I draped them on the railing of the porch outside the TV room to dry. But I had forgotten the wind, which in just a few minutes had blown the clothes off the rail, whence they had fallen six stories onto the roof of the building's entryway.

I ran to the elevator and went down to the first floor and outside. My clothes were on the middle of the entryway roof where I couldn't possibly get them. I rode the elevator back upstairs depressed about the shirts, socks, and underwear I would be leaving permanently in Novosibirsk. But when I looked half an hour later, I saw that the wind had swept them away yet again, and they were now scattered on the sidewalk and across the lawn. People were walking around them. I hurried down and collected them.

After Sergei and Volodya came back, we drove in the once-again-functioning van to a historical park outside town. Sergei P. and his mother, who had suggested this outing, led us to it in their car. His fifteen-year-old daughter, Sveta, and her friend Maria came along. A few minutes after we all arrived and got out in the parking lot, an old lady, the park's lone guide, hurried up the hill toward us, breathing hard and striding briskly as if she feared we might escape. Still panting, she introduced herself as Galina. She seemed not to have guided anyone in a while. Her hair was long and gray and unrestrained, but her prim blue blouse with white lace at the collar and down the front offset this rather wild look, as did her matching blue skirt and brogan-style walking shoes.

Eyes alight with excitement at what she was going to show us, she shepherded us to the park's main exhibit—a tall, narrow church made of logs. It rose high and dark and somber above the sunny meadow that stretched all around. While unlocking the door, our guide swung into her narrative about how this church had been built in the town of Zashiversk in 1700 on the Indigirka River far to the northeast; and how in those days trade fairs for all northern Siberia took place in that town; and how after a fair a mysterious wooden trunk was left behind, and a local shaman warned the villagers that the trunk was cursed and they should take the trunk and cut a hole in the ice and throw the trunk in it, but the church's

Sasha Khamarkhanov and his son, Tioshi

George Kennan, from the frontispiece of his book *Siberia and the Exile System*

Along the eastern shore of Lake Baikal

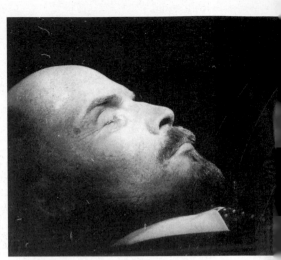

V. I. Lenin when he was still V. I. Ulyanov, at the time of his Siberian exile

Lenin as he looked in 1941, when he returned to Siberia (AFP/Getty Images)

Katarina Breshkovskaya, the nineteenth-century revolutionary and Siberian exile; later called "the little grandmother of the Russian Revolution"

Georgette Mossbacher, New York City socialite; risked "social Siberia" with plan for party (New York Daily News)

City of Provideniya in Chukotka, across the Bering Strait from Alaska

Whale jawbones at old Eskimo village site, Chukotka

Siberian boundary post, 1885; from *Siberia and the Exile System*

Boundary post at same approximate spot, 2001

Sergei Lunev, guide extraordinaire

Vladimir "Volodya" Chumak, his assistant

DECEMBRISTS

TOP: Prince Sergei Trubetskoy; Ekaterina Trubetskoy, his wife

MIDDLE: Ivan Dmitrievich Yakushkin

BOTTOM: Maria Volkonsky; Prince Sergei Volkonsky, her husband

Our Renault step van (with МЧС insignia added)

Tearing down statue of Tsar Alexander III after the 1917 revolution

Tearing down statue of Feliks Dzerzhinsky, first head of Soviet secret police, after the fall of Communism

Ice road, Lake Baikal

Landscape in northeast Yakutia, near the village of Topolinoe

Abandoned prison camp on the Topolinskaya Highway

Prison camp barracks

Varlam Shalamov, the writer who survived the Kolyma gold-mining camps

priest said it would be better to throw the shaman himself through the ice, so the people opened the trunk, and the curse came out, and the church's entire congregation fell ill and died of smallpox, except for one girl who survived; and how the town was then abandoned, and soon only the church remained, perfectly preserved; and how the church was then discovered by A. P. Okladnikov, the famous anthropologist, and other scientists on an expedition from Akademgorodok in the twentieth century; and how the scientists had the church brought here in pieces and reconstructed so that everybody could see what a beautiful wooden church in far northern Siberia looked like long ago. To move and reassemble the church cost so much, she said, that each log might as well have been made of gold. Galina added that when the scientists were first taking apart the church, they found the body of the girl who had survived the smallpox, frozen in the ice beneath the altar. She was wearing a beautiful dress and many costly jewels.

The starkness of the church's all-wood interior reminded me of old-time Protestant churches on the American frontier. And yet somehow the structure's high central space, which rose from the nave like a big wooden chimney, did not inspire in me the soaring feeling Orthodox church naves often do. Centuries spent in the far north had left their chill in the old church's bones, I imagined. Either that, or the dark of the winters, the long silence after the last prayer died, had leached into them like tannin. Frontier religion is sometimes the most desperate kind; and I am not the first to point out that harshness of doctrine and coldness of climate often keep each other company.

Our guide had no interest in any gloomy theologizing as she showed us the skill of the nail-free peg-and-groove carpentry and the plain-style beauty of the church when viewed from outside. Gradually her spiel began to move into areas of autobiography. Telling us again that her name was Galina, she pointed down the hill to where she said she lived in her own *izba* (cabin) with a small black dog and a milk cow. She asked us if we liked poetry. She wrote poetry herself, she said; now we would hear her read her poems. The next we knew we had been walked from the church down to her cabin, which was a tiny, rustic affair with grass growing on the roof and a door frame barely taller than she was. How she had emerged from such a primitive place looking so neat (except, perhaps, for the hair) was puzzling.

Still laughing and talking without a pause, Galina went into the cabin and brought out a big pitcher of milk that she said she had got from the cow just that afternoon. In her other hand she carried a plate of chocolate cookies and a thick sheaf of handwritten poems. None of us visitors were eager to drink unpasteurized milk, so we left the glasses she poured for us untouched. I ate a few of the cookies, though, and they were not bad. Meanwhile, Galina began to declaim her poems after first announcing to us the quality of each one. Some she described as "very good," some merely as "good." The sonorousness of her reading reverberated pleasantly in the little open-air roofed shelter where we were sitting, but the poetry's style was antique and I couldn't understand a word. After each poem she nodded her head appreciatively while we smiled and murmured praise.

The two Sergeis, from whom the rest of us were taking our cues, listened politely as she read. Rain, however, had begun to spatter on the shelter roof, and soon Sergei and Sergei interrupted Galina to tell her that, sadly, we had to be going. She walked us back to our cars, still reciting poems, still talking, still full of good spirits from the day. The rain was falling harder. A groundskeeper had locked the parking lot gate while we were down at the cabin, but fortunately Galina had a key. The rain was pouring now, so we jumped into the vehicles and started to leave. Galina, by now drenched to the skin and with her hair streaming, stopped us for a last word to me. I rolled down the window. "You are an American, so I want to tell you this," she said through the torrent. "Two Englishmen were here earlier this summer, and when they were leaving, one of them said to the other, 'That is an amazing church, and an amazing old lady!'" Still laughing, and shaking her head ruefully at how wet she was, she waved us on our way.

Sergei P. and his mother had warned us that the road would become more dangerous beyond Novosibirsk and farther into Siberia. Sergei P. said to me, "I think you will find as you continue your journey that conditions will become even more stochastic than those you have encountered so far." This prediction worried me, coming as it did from someone not in Moscow or St. Petersburg but closer to the scene. When I mentioned my concern to the other Sergei, he said he had already thought of a plan. From here on, he said, we would travel under colors that would guarantee our safety.

Back in June when we were planning the trip, Sergei had told me that he and Volodya were members of an organization called МЧС (an acronym pronounced "Em Che Ess"). The letters stand for Ministerstvo Chrezvychainym Situatsiyami, which means "Ministry of Extraordinary Situations." МЧС is a well-respected organization with branches all over Russia, and its mission is to provide rescue service and emergency assistance of all kinds. You have to pass demanding mental and physical requirements to be in МЧС. Afterward, as I traveled, I met other МЧС members and they all were tough and competent-looking fellows like Volodya and Sergei.

The МЧС uniforms sort of resemble those worn by some emergency medical services staff in the United States. The МЧС jacket and pants are blue, with white and orange stripes. Sergei and Volodya had brought their МЧС uniforms along and they also had their identification cards. Now in Novosibirsk they would make their МЧС affiliation clear by putting identifying markings on our van. From the local МЧС office Sergei obtained the necessary symbols, emblems, and stripes for the van's sides, and one morning he spent a long time carefully applying them to the vehicle as МЧС rules prescribed. He said that should I need an МЧС jacket, he had one for me, too. I saw the logic in all this—from now on we would be driving across Siberia in the apparent equivalent of a fire-department rescue vehicle—but I was kind of bothered by the semideception, too. We had no rescue equipment, per se, in the van. What if we actually had to save somebody? Sergei and Volodya were qualified, I had no doubt. But how would an unfortunate person who needed saving feel about having to depend, in any way, on me?

While that rebranding was going on, I walked around downtown Novosibirsk, which reminded me of Seattle with Lenin statues. At the Vladimir Mayakovsky Kinotheatre, two movies were playing: *Crocodile Dundee in Los Angeles* and *Scary Movie 2*. The air that gusted out of an entrance to the Novosibirsk metro when a train went by smelled just like the Moscow metro two thousand miles away. Then Sergei and Volodya picked me up in the van and we drove back to Akademgorodok for a last meal with Sergei Prigarin at the cafeteria at his institute. Afterward, we bade him farewell, he wished us safe travels, and we headed east from greater Novosibirsk under the flag of the Ministry of Extraordinary Situations.

Chapter 17

Now, a short interlude of traveling music on the balalaika, and a few images from the road in no particular order, movie-style:

TRASH: The more of it I saw, the better I understood how it differs from American roadside trash. Russian trash has less paper. Paper plates and paper cups, especially, are almost never seen. The basic and most common item of Russian roadside trash is the handmade plastic drinking cup, which is improvised on the spot by cutting off the bottom quarter or third of a plastic bottle that formerly contained water, soda, or beer. Some of these bottle-bottom cups are neatly trimmed at the lip, but most look ragged and slapdash. The sturdier ones are made from bottles with thicker sections of black plastic reinforcing their bases. After use, the cups are naturally left where they were created, along the road or at the picnic grounds. In more frequented parts of Siberia from the Urals to the Pacific, you see these cups along the roads everywhere.

RAVENS AND CROWS: I have mentioned that the gray-and-black hooded crows, and their all-black companions, the ordinary crows and ravens, seem to be awaiting the return of Genghis Khan. For weeks as we drove, the flocks of ravens and crows remained a constant—ubiquitous in western Siberia no less than in St. Petersburg. On the Barabinsk Steppe, collections of all these birds sometimes wheeled in great numbers that vivified the blank sky above the wide-open horizon. Past Novosibirsk, however, it suddenly occurred to me that although I was still seeing black crows and ravens, I hadn't seen any hooded crows for a while. I began keeping a special watch for hooded crows and did see a few stragglers. But after another hundred miles or so, no more of them appeared. Beyond the city of Krasnoyarsk there were none, though the ravens and other crows continued all the way to the Pacific. As an observer of Siberian fauna I have nothing to add to the tradition of Müller, Pallas, Steller, and others beyond verifying or reverifying the fact that the hooded crow is not to be found in Siberia east of the Yenisei.

PRISONS: Sometimes I caught a glimpse of a prison, but invariably it went by too fast. Prisons cropped up in unexpected places on the outskirts of a city. Suddenly I'd see a guard in boots carrying a machine gun and standing on a catwalk directly above an exercise yard. But always, it seemed, we were in traffic and couldn't stop. Outside Novosibirsk I saw derelict guard towers, tumbledown buildings, and drooping barbed wire in a broad, open place beside the road. Whenever I pointed to such a site, Sergei and Volodya would say "military" without even turning their heads. My ongoing search for prisons did not sit well with either of them. After a while I decided that pursuing it too much was impolite, and I let it drop for the time being.

PIGS: Although roaming herds of pigs were occasional in villages in western Siberia, east of Novosibirsk they became more common. Now every village we went through seemed to have big gangs of them. Because the weather was so hot, the pigs had generally been wallowing in a mud hole just before they got up to amble wherever we happened to see them ambling. Evidently, the wallowing technique of some pigs involved lying with just one side of themselves in the mud. This produced two-tone animals—pigs that were half wet, shiny, brown mud, and half pink, relatively unsoiled original pig. The effect was striking—sort of harlequin. The other animals that roamed the villages in groups were geese. When a herd of pigs came face-to-face with a flock of geese, an unholy racket of grunting and gabbling ensued. I wondered if the villagers ever got tired of the noise. Whether challenging pigs or not, the village geese seemed to gabble and yack and hiss nonstop. The pigs grunted and oinked almost as much, but always at some point the whole herd of pigs would suddenly fall silent, and their megaphone-shaped ears would all go up, and for half a minute every pig would listen.

BIRTHPLACE OF VOLODYA: About a half day past Novosibirsk we passed close by a village called Yashkino. Seeing it on our road map, Volodya remarked that he had been born there. His mother's people were originally from this area, he said. His father, a tank officer who had been stationed in the Far East at the end of the war, had met his mother while crossing Siberia on his way back to western Russia. Volodya was still a baby when he and his parents left Yashkino, so he had no memory of it; no relatives he knew of still lived there. He felt no need to go there.

COTTAGE CHEESE: Called *tvorog* in Russian, this was a favorite lunch of Volodya's and Sergei's. Usually it could be obtained in very fresh supply from the grannies along the road, who dispensed it in small sacks of clear plastic. Sergei and Volodya especially liked their *tvorog* drenched in *smetana* (sour cream). I got to like it that way, too. Sometimes we had *tvorog so smetanoi* not only for lunch but also for a snack later in the day. The only drawback to this diet was that it made us smell like babies. And as we were able to bathe only infrequently, our basic aroma became that of grown-up, dusty, sweaty babies—the summertime smell of Mongols, in other words.

TALK RADIO: There is talk radio in Russia just as in America, and call-in radio shows, and shock-jock hosts who say outlandish things. Sergei and Volodya enjoyed listening to these shows sometimes. Usually I understood nothing that was said on the radio, except for one time when the host told a joke that Sergei and Volodya both laughed at. I picked out the word "*Americantsi,*" so I knew the joke was about Americans. I asked them to tell me the joke, but they wouldn't. I kept bugging them, but Sergei said the joke was not important. Finally when he was off doing something in the campsite I asked Volodya about the joke again, and he told it to me. The joke was: "Why do American men want to be present when their wives are in childbirth?" Answer: "Because maybe they weren't present during conception."

(Many Russian men think American men are unmanly for letting their women push them around with demands like helping with the housework and being present in the birthing room during labor. I believe this opinion is also common worldwide.)

I found the joke funny, too, after a fashion. Generally I regretted not being able to joke around more with Sergei and Volodya. Conveying humor in either direction across the language barrier was hard. Once I was riding in the back of the van and I happened to think of my friend Bryan DiSalvatore, a writer who sometimes did movie reviews for the local paper in Missoula, Montana, and of his pronouncement that the latest *Beavis and Butt-Head* movie was "flawed." The memory made me laugh. Volodya asked what I was laughing about. I tried to explain.

Until we left Novosibirsk we had seen none of the large-scale environmental damage Siberia is famous for. Then we hit the small, smoky city of Kemerovo in the Kuznetsk Basin coal-mining region. Russians don't bother to hide strip mines with a screen of trees along the road to spare the feelings of motorists, as we Americans do. Beyond Kemerovo the whole view at times became the gaping pits themselves, sprawling downward before us on either side while the thread-thin road tiptoed where it could between. Strip mines are strip mines, and I had seen similar scenery in North Dakota and southern Ohio and West Virginia, though never quite so close at hand. Often through this Siberian coal region, the road strayed and forgot its original intention, and more than one fork we took dead-ended without warning at a city-sized strip-mine hole. We meandered in the Kuznetsk Basin for most of a day and drove until past nightfall in order to camp on the other side.

After the Kuznetsk Basin, a long interval of meadows followed. We saw dark-clothed people working the hayfields in big groups like in an old bucolic painting, or riding to or from the work in horse-drawn flatbed wagons whose hard rubber wheels bouncing on the uneven pavement made the flesh of the passengers' faces jiggle fast. In this more peaceful region we camped one night on the banks of the Chulym River at a popular spot with a gravel bank more convenient for bathing and washing than the usual swampy mud. While we ate supper, a group of Christians waded in not far from us, some of them in flowing white baptismal clothes. The worshippers sang songs accompanied by a guitar, held hands in a circle, swayed. A man in the middle of the circle took another man and woman and two girls in his arms and then immersed them one by one.

More people and cars were scattered along the bank for maybe a half mile. At dark, almost everybody had gone. I walked into an adjoining field a distance away from our tents to call home on my satellite phone, and I had just begun talking to my wife when a guy who must have seen my face in the faint blue light of the phone's display screen popped up from the

darkness beside me. Drunk and talking fast, he asked me a question involving his car. I went back to the tents and got Sergei. It turned out the
guy wanted a jump start. Sergei agreeably drove the van over to the guy's
car and jump-started it. Meanwhile I continued a distracted conversation
with my family. My whole body was still twanging. The guy jumping
from the dark like that startled me almost out of my shoes.

Environmental grimness resumed the next morning as we approached
the city of Achinsk. Never, under any circumstances, go to Achinsk. I'm
still coughing Achinsk out of my lungs to this day, probably. During Soviet times, 95 percent of everything—buildings, roads, bus shelters,
playgrounds, fountains, telephone booths, lampposts—was made of cement. A particular kind of five-foot-by-eight-foot cement panel often
used in fences and walls seems to be the basic visual element of urban
Siberia.

Well, all that cement, or a hell of a lot of it, is made in Achinsk.
Achinsk has mineral refineries, too. The thick, dusty air of Achinsk coats
grass blades to death and desertifies everything in a wide radius around
the city. Still forty minutes away from it, we rolled up the windows and
sweltered in the van rather than breathe the emanations of Achinsk.
Skirting the city at a far remove, we never actually saw it but only its
cement-dust cloud, which densified to a dark gray at what I took to be
the city's middle. For a second or two a haze-blurred smokestack could
be seen.

Our passage through this almost-dead zone heightened the surprise
a few hours later when we reached the river city of Krasnoyarsk. The
name—from *krasnyi*, "red," and *yar*, "cliff"—refers to the red cliffs nearby
the city that give the landscape with its broad valley a slightly out-of-
context look, as if this place might be in eastern Wyoming or South Africa. The city occupies a prominence above the Yenisei River just upstream
from where a series of mountainous, tree-covered cliffs along both sides
of the river suddenly descend to level ground. Chekhov judged Krasnoyarsk the most beautiful city in Siberia, and he was right, from what I'd
seen. Many buildings in the city center were from the later nineteenth
century and of a style of brickwork done decoratively, almost whimsically.
Recent renovations had emphasized a color scheme perhaps based on the
earth-toned reds of the Yenisei cliffs, and with white or light blue trim
for intensity. The downtown boutiques, restaurants, clothing stores, and

galleries called to mind shopping districts in any of a thousand gentrified antique-ish towns and small cities in America. And although a line of storefronts bearing the logos of Wrangler and Reebok and Benetton and Nike would not gladden me if I encountered it in New Jersey, seeing it in Siberia did, somehow.

Krasnoyarsk opens onto the Yenisei the way St. Petersburg opens onto the Neva. And the Yenisei here is huge, more like an estuary than a river. Many of Krasnoyarsk's streets end at the water and route its amplified daylight into the city; I recalled a similar effect on the streets of older Mississippi River towns. To get a better look at the whole picture, Sergei drove us to a scenic overlook he knew of on some heights west of town. This particular vantage dominated a graffiti-covered stone outcropping above a small parking lot. As we climbed up to it, a wedding party was coming down with surprising agility in their tuxedos and high heels. The viewing promenade, when we reached it, was strewn all around with shattered champagne flutes from their just-completed toasts. While we stood there, a storm came up the river, and you could see almost its entire extent—the dark clouds, the advancing netlike pattern of smooth and rippled water beneath the clouds, the wispy paleness of the rain. The city itself, off in the distance, was only a thumbnail-sized patch of the scene's immensity.

The long view also revealed that Krasnoyarsk puts out an impressive smoky haze of its own. During Soviet times, a lot of heavy industry relocated here. The first thing you see in the main hall of Krasnoyarsk's regional museum is a banner with a slogan intended to inspire Krasnoyarsk's factory workers during the Cold War. In large white letters on a red background, it reads, DOGONIM I PEREGONIM AMERIKU! (We Will Catch Up to and Overtake America!).

Sergei had been asked to say hello and deliver a present to a friend of Victor Serov's wife, Lena. This friend lived on Krasnoyarsk's main drag, Prospekt Mira. After driving us back to the city, Sergei carried out that errand while Volodya and I killed time downtown. I walked around for a bit, then sat in the van. Soon I saw a lissome blonde in tight pants with a beeper at the waist walking lissomely by to use the pay phone in a little plaza across the way. A few minutes later she returned to the phone with a dark-haired woman as attractive as she and made another call. The two had a girlish, conspiratorial air; whatever they were up to, they were having fun. Looking around, I noticed that beautiful women were in fact walking everywhere, as if I had wandered onto the set of a science-fiction movie about a city inhabited only by beautiful women. The number of beauties in Krasnoyarsk would put even Velikii Ustyug in the shade.

It still strikes me as strange that during the Cold War we in America liked to believe that Russian women were not beautiful at all. Longtime fans of professional football in the United States may remember a light-beer commercial of twenty-five or thirty years ago that involved an imagined Russian beauty contest in which very fat, be-warted, missing-toothed women in bathing suits promenaded down a ramp before judges and flashbulbs: "And now, contest in svim vear!" I forget what the point of the commercial was, aside from its generic beer-commercial comedy, but it reflected the prevailing attitude of the time. How, I wondered, could we have got the facts so wrong? Maybe the misconception grew out of the Second World War propaganda posters of our Soviet allies, with their images of beefy Russian women working at war-industry jobs. Or maybe it had something to do with the Iron Curtain, which kept almost all women but the wives of the highest Soviet leaders from the eyes of the West. Those wives were older, like their husbands, and tended to be equally blocky and stone-faced.

Or maybe the error goes back to John Quincy Adams. In the second volume of his memoirs, Adams describes the five years he spent in St. Petersburg during the eighteen teens as America's first official ambassador there, and he mentions repeatedly how ugly the Russian women were. Other American observers in the nineteenth century followed Adams's lead, declaring that Russian women were too manlike, rough, and otherwise unattractive to appeal to American tastes. This assessment makes me more inclined to distrust the messengers, however, when I recall that perhaps the best foreign observer of Russia in that century, the Marquis de Custine, viewed the subject differently. Custine was the most famous French homosexual of his day, and his journals of his Russian travels (published 1843) report on what he saw there with intelligence and specificity. Of the Russian peasant women, Custine wrote that handsome ones were scarce among them, "but when they are handsome, their beauty is perfect." He went on: "They possess all the vague and shadowy delicacy of the women of the north, united with all the voluptuousness of Oriental females."

A later American ambassador, Cassius Marcellus Clay, who represented the United States in St. Petersburg during the American Civil War, and who believed that he personally had won that war by enlisting the tsar's support on the side of the North, and whose ghost, wherever it may be, I feel sorry for because his name will always be associated with a man greater than he, wrote in a recollection of his ambassadorial career that he had known "many hundreds, almost thousands" of beautiful Russian women, and he added, "so many wonderfully fine women can hardly be seen in any country in one assemblage." A scholar who quoted this in a book published in the 1930s cautioned that Clay's opinion should not be taken seriously because of "his egoism and his sensitivity to women." But on the question of the beauty of Russian women, it seems only common sense to rely on Clay and Custine rather than J. Q. Adams.

The first time American men met Russian women in large numbers, the statistics offer evidence on the side of Clay. Of the twelve thousand soldiers serving with the American Expeditionary Force in Siberia from 1918 to 1920, 6 percent—more than seven hundred men—married Russian women. After the American withdrawal was announced, Orthodox priests were marrying as many as thirty couples at a time. General William Graves, the AEF's leader, disapproved of all this romance and made a rather killjoy report to his superiors in which he said, "Entirely too many of these women would not, under the law, be permitted to enter the United States." If a bride was found to be of poor moral character (by Graves himself, presumably), he wanted the army to deny her transportation. Higher-ups countermanded this idea.

My friend Alex Melamid points out that one saw almost no beautiful women on the streets of Moscow when he was growing up in that city during the 1950s and '60s. Alex agrees that now all over the country there are millions of them—the Ukrainian city of Kiev, he says, is also amazing in this regard—but he thinks they have appeared only since the fall of the Soviet Union. He guesses that the end of the Cold War and the emergence of Russian female beauty are connected in some way, but he doesn't know exactly how.

Puzzling over this mystery, I one day happened upon a possible answer in a book by an American economist named Alexander Blakely. As a young entrepreneur, Blakely witnessed the birth of Russian capitalism firsthand in the 1990s when he tried to establish a chocolate factory in

Novosibirsk. He puts forth an explanation based on market forces. In his book *Siberia Bound*, he compares the women he observed in Siberia to one-crop farmers in a stable economy. Their crop is their beauty, which they overproduce in pursuit of limited demand, thus increasing the supply, thus driving down the value even more, thus increasing the supply further, and so on. The women's object in all this is, of course, to gain economic advantage, which to them means somehow getting out of Siberia. Blakely says that whenever one of these beauties flirted with him, he would tell her that he loved Siberia and planned to live there forever. Usually, he recalls, she would turn on her heel and walk away without a word.

Today, many hundreds or thousands of websites show photos of Russian women and other information about them. The purposes of these postings are mixed, no doubt, but certainly a great amount of heartbreak and hope is involved; also, one can't avoid sensing the women's danger. Articles in newspapers and magazines warn us regularly about the rise of international sex trafficking. One article I read said that a sex trafficker can make $250,000 from each woman sold. Slavery, ineradicable as all human evils, appears to be going strong in the world once again. A large number of the women taken by sex traffickers to destinations around the world are from Russia and the former Communist bloc nations of Eastern Europe. Once again the beauties of Russia are being shipped away in bondage almost as in Mongol times. A Russian friend told me, half seriously, that women have become Russia's second-leading export, after oil.

From Krasnoyarsk we drove southeast to the Mana River and camped on a wide stretch of bank across and just upstream from a village called Ust'-Mana. All three of us were tired and the weather had turned sunny, so we decided to spend the next day and night there. We lounged around camp, bathed in the river, washed our clothes, spread them to dry on the wild rosebushes along the shore. The forest that covered the nearby hills and extended beyond in mind-numbing immensity was an original-growth combination of sky-high cedars, with less-huge firs, birches, and pines. I made a few forays into it. There were no trails, just little pathways that went for a distance and then petered out. Gazing at it from our camp during supper, I asked Sergei and Volodya if this forest qualified as taiga. They looked at it, thought for a minute, and then Sergei said, "No. That is not real taiga." Volodya agreed. Later I learned that no matter the forest and no matter the Russian, if you ask him or her if a forest is taiga, he or she will always look at it, pause, and say, "No. That is not real taiga."

For me the big event of our lazing-around day was the attack of the cows. Sergei and Volodya had gone off somewhere and I was a hundred yards or so away from the camp when I saw a small herd of cows heading for the tents at a trot. Without stopping, they went into the camp and began to rip it apart. One stuck her head into our cardboard box of provisions, ate half a cabbage in a couple of bites, nosed open the oatmeal box and slobberingly ate several mouthfuls. Another came to the table on which Volodya had left a round loaf of bread and licked it fast all over, causing it to spin. Another bumped her head beside the head of the first cow, who was still neck-deep in the provision box. By the time I ran up, the table was knocked over, the chairs were scattered or down, tent pegs were pulled up, and oatmeal flakes had been strewn everywhere. I hissed at the cows with a snakelike sound that always used to scare cattle years ago when I was a ranch hand in Wyoming. These Russian cows just looked at me from the corners of their eyes. I shouted and waved my arms, and they did me the courtesy of stopping what they were doing to look directly at me, still without backing off. Only when I picked up a chair and threatened them with it did they huffily and slowly retreat.

A footnote regarding the village of Ust'-Mana for students of Russian cinema: scenes from Vladimir Nazarov's *Khozyain Taigi* (Master of the Taiga) and Nikita Mikhalkov's *Sibirskii Tsiryulnik* (*The Barber of Siberia*) were filmed in and around Ust'-Mana, local people told us.

The next morning when we started out again, the road, which had been getting worse since Krasnoyarsk, deteriorated thoroughly. Long unpaved sections with many big rocks and *yamy* (holes) made for a bumpy and dusty ride. The van's low clearance underneath, which I'd worried about before, now caused problems as we began to scrape, and we almost high-centered from time to time. A boulder in the path knocked away a foot or so of tailpipe. A worse bump on an uphill grade crushed and scraped away the remaining two or three feet, leaving no pipe extending from the muffler's outlet to carry off the exhaust fumes. Immediately the air in the van, which had never been good, became unbearable. Now I could detect an actual blue fog. I tried to remember what the signs of carbon monoxide poisoning were. Sergei, as expected, refused to go to a garage or muffler shop and do anything about the problem. That was not necessary, Sergei announced, sitting beside his open window and its plentiful incoming dust. Finally Volodya, the swing vote among us, switched to my side and told Sergei that we had to fix the tailpipe right away or we'd all suffocate. Sergei said he would fix it, and with some annoyance he pulled over to the shoulder.

He got out. Volodya and I watched. Sergei was just wandering around a weedy patch of ground that paralleled the road, looking down and kicking occasionally at the dirt. After a minute or two he bent over and stood up with something in his hand. It looked to be a piece of pipe. We got out to see what he'd found, and he showed us a somewhat rusty but still serviceable yard-long piece of tailpipe that must've fallen off another vehicle. It was exactly the same width as the one we'd lost. With Volodya's help, Sergei scooted under the van and wired the length of the tailpipe in place at the muffler outlet and other points leading to the rear bumper. When we started driving again the fumes were much better, though not by any means gone. Still, I had to praise Sergei for what an ingenious guy he was.

Beyond Krasnoyarsk the road also began to run closer to the tracks of the Trans-Siberian Railway, crossing it over and back from time to time. Each crossing was watched over by a guard in a small shed. When the guard, usually a short, stout woman, saw a train coming, she would walk into the road, wave a flag to stop the cars, and lower the barricades. If the train was a long and slow one, as many were, the people in the waiting cars would unpackage drinks and snacks, throw their doors open, stretch out their legs, and get comfortable. After the train had gone by, the guard would walk onto the tracks, look both ways to make sure all was safe, raise the barricades, and wave the cars through with her flag. At regularly spaced intervals on the road, piles of snack remains showed where each car had been.

Sometimes in the evening we camped not far from the tracks. During lulls in the train traffic, I climbed up the stones of the roadbed and looked down the rails to where they disappeared around a distant bend. As on the old Sibirskii Trakt, phantoms thronged along the railway. I pictured the flag-bedecked, celebratory trains that passed by here when

the railway was first completed in tsarist times, and the soldiers of the
Czech Legion in their slow-moving armored trains in 1919, and the
White Army soldiers dying of typhus by the thousands along the route,
and the slave laborers who laid the second set of tracks in the 1930s, and
the countless sealed Stolypin cars of prisoners dragged along these tracks
to the deadly gulag camps of the Soviet Far East. Osip Mandelstam, the
great poet on his way to death at the Second River transit prison in Vladivostok, had gone along this line. The ties and the steel rails and the
overhead catenary wires all leading determinedly eastward still had a
certain grimness, as if permanently blackened by history.

One afternoon a few days out of Krasnoyarsk, we stopped to buy our
tvorog so smetanoi for lunch in a village called Kuskun. I had made a
note of Kuskun while reading Kennan. He and Frost came to this village
(then called Kuskunskaya) on the return leg of their journey during a
night when the temperature was forty-five below. Both men were wretch-
edly uncomfortable and about played out. On a narrow plank bench in
the post station, Kennan threw himself down and fell asleep and had
a nightmare to which he devotes a detailed description. He says he
dreamed that he had been invited to give a talk to a Sunday school of a
church called the Holy Monopolists. He asked the congregants who the
Holy Monopolists were and was told that "they were a new sect consisting of people who believed in only one thing." He did not know what the
one thing was, however, and was afraid to ask. The Sunday school superintendent, in front of all the students, asked him a question to which he
did not know the answer: "Who was the first progressive euchre player
that after his death was brought back from Alaska amid the mourning of
a nation?" Unable to find the answer in a soda biscuit the superintendent
handed him, and deeply ashamed of his ignorance, Kennan awoke.

In all of the books of Siberian travel I read, this is the only recorded
nightmare. Kennan goes on about it for two pages. Probably it struck
him so forcibly because it was an advance tremor of an oncoming nervous breakdown, one he only narrowly avoided. (Frost, for his part, did
not fare as well, and in the journey's later stages became crazed and
paranoid.) No darkness can match Russian darkness, as Kennan's unconscious was perhaps discovering. Of course every dream is unique
in its particulars, and Kennan's nightmare is doubly removed from us
because it is a nineteenth-century nightmare—a sort of antique. The

Holy Monopolists sound plausible as a frontier American sect, progressive-euchre players are seldom mentioned anymore, and Sunday school superintendents, awesome figures in their day, have lost their power to terrify.

Kennan identifies the Sunday school superintendent in his nightmare as "a well-known citizen of Norwalk, Ohio, whom I had not seen since boyhood," but he does not give the man's name. A local historian in Norwalk, Henry Timman, whom I once asked about this mystery, guesses that the superintendent in Kennan's dream might well have been Cortland L. Latimer, for many years superintendent of the Sunday school at the Presbyterian church in Norwalk, which Kennan's family attended in his youth. Presbyterian children had to be well prepared for Mr. Latimer's questioning about the weekly Scripture lesson, and they spent their Saturday evenings going over it before bed. Latimer was also a banker and a lawyer in the town, so he seems to have been suitably austere for his nightmare role. Whoever the actual superintendent was, he attains a strange, twilit immortality in Kennan's Kuskunskaya nightmare.

The day we were in Kuskun, the village could not have been more unlike the lonely and winter-besieged place where Kennan stopped. Kuskun's older part, with its houses of gray logs below moss-covered roofs, had grown a several-mile stretch of newer village that extended on either side along the old Trakt. At a wide place where a turnoff led to the present highway, babushka ladies had set up a bazaar of farm- and home-made goods. Sergei bought our lunchtime *tvorog* while I talked to a man in a Boss T-shirt and to some other locals who said that most of the village had been built after the war. Zinnialike yellow flowers on high climbing bushes perked up the fences and housefronts with their bright blooms. They're called *zolotie zhari*, golden balls, a woman told me. Some of the gaily painted houses had radio antennae on high poles in their yards, or birdhouses, or nonfunctioning cars; one had a horse-drawn hay rake parked out front. A man stood cooking soup in a big black kettle resting on bricks above a fire next to the road. A woman with her hair in a topknot bent over in a garden. The village seemed to be in full summer mode.

At one end of the village, the old Trakt crossed a small river called the Esaulovka on an ancient, ruined bridge. Its gray wooden crossbeams supported the ricketiest of planking; the planks were sawn lumber but the beams showed only the marks of a bladed tool like a froe or an adze.

Perhaps those old beams had been here since Kennan. From a hempen rope tied around one of the beams, some village boys in shorts or under-pants were swinging and dropping into a deep part of the river. The water was clear and tannin tinted, and it had a visible current, a rarity in Siberia. I thought of going out onto the bridge but decided the planks looked risky. A minute later an old, stooped peasant woman approaching from the other side hurried across the bridge without looking down or breaking stride. She told Sergei she crossed over it and back every day to buy bread in the village.

More cities: after Kuskun we went through Kansk, which was hot and dusty and sprawling like a west Texas cattle town, and Nizhneudinsk, where we passed more prisons, including an abandoned one with its high steel gates gaping wide. Outside the small city of Tulun, our jury-rigged tailpipe came off the muffler outlet and began to drag on the road as the van refilled with fumes. Sergei and Volodya parked on a gravelly place in Tulun and crawled underneath to wire it back on. When Russian cities are uncheerful they don't fool around, and Tulun was as uncheer-ful as they come. Here the usual dust and heat and drabness were abet-ted by a special, extramiserable quality I couldn't put my finger on. Close to where we pulled over, a train station stood on a hill, and people drained of all expression were walking down its dusty slope like souls in the underworld.

   I sat with my back against the van's front bumper and did a quick sketch of Tulun. For the first time I really noticed the wires. More than

any place I've ever seen, Russia is bedecked and bedraped with wires. It's like a house with not enough electrical outlets, in which extension cords and multiplug connectors are everywhere. Competing with the festoons of wiring, the city's central-heating steam pipes, which in this region cannot be buried underground because of the permafrost, add their own vermiculate wanderings to the mixed-up scene. One of Lenin's famous sayings was, "Communism equals Soviet power plus electrification of the whole country." Though I'm not sure exactly what that means, I think its real-world consequences can be seen in a mare's nest like the skyline of Tulun.

The urban or semi-urban landscape we had entered now became continuous. Soon we were in the valley of the great Angara River, approaching Irkutsk. The air turned smoky and gray, and extensive industrial plants began to parallel the road. I couldn't decide if the region actually qualified as industrial, because sometimes farm fields came right to the factory walls, and haystacks poked up beneath tall chimneys spewing smoke. Traffic began to roar in many lanes alongside us. Aiming toward city towers ahead, we pinballed through a skewed grid of smaller streets until we finally arrived at the center of Irkutsk, the onetime Paris of Siberia.

Chapter 18

We reached Irkutsk on the afternoon of August 27. Since leaving St. Petersburg, we had been on the road for twenty-two days.

One of the first places we went in Irkutsk was to the house (now a museum) built in 1854 for Prince Sergei Trubetskoy. He was one of the leaders of the revolutionaries whose failed uprising of December 14, 1825, earned them the name Decembrists. Had the revolution succeeded, Trubetskoy was supposed to become the country's interim dictator until a constitutional government could be set up. Many of his comrades saw him as a George Washington figure. By logic, after the movement was crushed, Trubetskoy should have been among the ones hanged. The loftiness of his family—in nobility, the Trubetskoys ranked just below the tsar—and the fact that his mother was a lady-in-waiting to the tsarina no doubt saved his life.

Like many other Decembrists, Trubetskoy was sent to Siberia. His wife, Ekaterina, followed him into exile. For twelve years he served his sentence of hard labor in prison fortresses east of Lake Baikal, and in 1839 he was allowed to relocate with his family nearer to Irkutsk, where he later moved and built this house. Though it may have been one of the grander houses of Irkutsk in its day, it is not overly fancy but rather suggests the elegance of curtailed excess and of cultured taste making the best of materials at hand. The house has a brick foundation supporting smoothly joined logs that have been planed square and fitted together horizontally. Single-story wings on either side balance a central, peaked-roof section that rises to a tall second story. The overall effect is of an eccentric Greek Revival style married to the skill and intricacy of Russian-village woodworking. I thought I'd never seen a better-looking house. I wanted to find out what it was like inside, but unfortunately it was closed for renovation when we were there.

A block away is another Decembrist house-museum. It was the house of Sergei Volkonsky, whose importance to the Decembrist movement and nobility of birth almost equaled Trubetskoy's. The Volkonsky family descended from a prince, later a saint of the Orthodox church, who fought the Mongols in the fourteenth century; Sergei Volkonsky's mother, Alexandra Repnina, also happened to be the tsar's mother's highest-ranking lady-in-waiting and closest friend. Like Ekaterina Trubetskaya, Maria, the young wife of Sergei Volkonsky, voluntarily shared his exile. Nikolai Nekrasov's poem "Russian Women," in praise of the Decembrist wives, compared Maria Volkonsky to a saint. Pushkin rhapsodized that her hair was more lustrous than daylight and darker than night. Tolstoy, whose mother was a Volkonsky and who came from the generation that followed the Decembrists, thought so highly of Sergei Volkonsky that he is said to have based the character of Prince Andrei Bolkonsky in *War and Peace* on him and to have used the letters and journals Volkonsky wrote during the Napoleonic Wars to help create the character.

The Volkonsky house-museum is large and imposing, in a Russian château style, though it's not a work of art like the Trubetskoys'. Its displays consist mainly of portraits and photographs of the Volkonsky family and the families of other Decembrists. The elderly lady guide who took us through gave us the biographical details of everybody. Zinaida Trubetskoy, born to Sergei and Ekaterina in Siberia in 1837, survived to 1924, long enough to receive a government pension granted by Lenin himself in honor of her revolutionary father. Among the ancillary characters, the museum also had the only picture I've ever come across of Georges-Charles d'Anthès, the French army officer and ballroom roué who killed Pushkin in a duel. Had there been matinee idols in d'Anthès's day, he could have been one, with his wavy blond hair.

For a while Tolstoy planned to write a book about the Decembrists, but he set the idea aside because all official papers relating to them were in secret archives and thus unavailable for his research. After the Revolution of 1905, when documents withheld under the tsars became accessible, Tolstoy was seventy-seven years old and no longer able to take on such a big project. Why the Decembrists interested him is easy to grasp. Though their revolution fell apart and though their punishment was a humiliation and a waste, the Decembrists were inspiring nonetheless. Of the hundred and some Decembrists judged most culpable by the Committee of Inquiry that followed the suppression of the uprising, only three were over forty years old. Almost all the Decembrists were of the same youthful generation in 1825; and if I had to pick one generation as the greatest in Russian history, theirs would be it. Alexander Herzen hailed them as "a perfect galaxy of brilliant talent, independent character, and chivalrous valor—a combination new to Russia." Of those Decembrists declared the most dangerous—in other words, the most prominent among them—the greater number would live out their lives imprisoned or exiled in Siberia.

They began their young manhood by beating Napoleon. Most of them were or had been officers in the army of Tsar Alexander I, who could claim to be the liberator of Europe for outlasting the French emperor's invasion of Russia; following up the French retreat with his army of 110,000; fighting Napoleon at Vitebsk, Vilnius, Lutzen, Dresden, Kulm, and Leipzig; contributing to the French defeat at Waterloo; and winning for Russia the top position among the allied nations that finally brought down the Napoleonic Empire. Throughout the war, Alexander's officer corps performed outstandingly, its members vying with one another in acts of bravery. The young lieutenants and captains and adjutants were proud of their country and loved their emperor. When they led their troops in the grand victory march down the Champs-Élyseés, no Russian officers in history had ever enjoyed such glory.

Being in France during the four-month occupation dazzled them, too. When it came to ideas, the countries they had liberated were far more up-to-date than their own; now the Enlightenment, which previously had been allowed to penetrate Russia in only the tiniest doses, belatedly hit them head-on. They had been educated well, if narrowly, in Russian military academies. They knew classical authors, and like most of the Russian gentility spoke fluent French. Their travels in the war opened them to writers like Adam Smith, Condorcet, Benjamin Franklin, Montesquieu, Walter Scott. In France, their emperor magnanimously dissuaded the other allied powers from punishing the conquered country with harsh conditions, and he let the French choose the type of new government they preferred. Away from home, Tsar Alexander acted like a liberal monarch. He even talked about ending serfdom in his own country, a passionate cause among many of his young officers.

Then the occupation ended, the officers went back to Russia with the army, and the door of their oppressive country slammed shut behind them. For young men who had just been in the sunlight for the first time, the experience was especially painful; having brought freedom to Europe, they could enjoy little of it themselves. Their emperor, once again in his own country, reverted to despotic type, shutting down their informal discussion groups, saying what they could and could not read, and making them report to martinet superiors. The officers found their situation degrading, intolerable.

Among the principal Decembrists, there are a lot of guys to like—for example, Sergei Muraviev-Apostol, who led the December uprising in the south and took full responsibility for its failure, and who remarked, when the wet rope attempting to hang him slipped off his neck and dropped him on the ground, "Poor Russia. We don't even know how to hang people properly"; or Mikhail Lunin, who betrayed none of his comrades during his interrogation and who vowed in old age that as long as he had even one tooth left in his mouth it would be directed against the tsar; or Nikolai Bestuzhev, a sweet and companionable fellow who refused to allow the boy cadets from the Naval Academy to follow him when he led his men to the Senate Square on the day of the rebellion, thus saving the cadets' lives, and who made clocks and taught agriculture and painted portraits and generally ameliorated life for everybody with him in Siberian exile.

The Decembrist I especially like, though, is Ivan Dmitrievich Yakushkin, a guards officer of wide acquaintance and popularity, whose memoir gives a vivid picture of the movement and the later sufferings that he and his comrades endured. Near the beginning of his book, Yakushkin tells of the moment during a parade in St. Petersburg when he and another officer fell out of love with their tsar:

[We] were standing not far from the golden carriage in which sat Empress Maria Federovna with the Grand Duchess Anna Pavlovna. Finally the emperor appeared, leading the guard division, on a glorious chestnut horse, with unsheathed saber, which he was ready to lower before the empress. We joyed at the sight of him, but in that very minute almost right in front of his horse, a peasant went running across the street. The emperor put spurs to his horse and sprang after the running peasant with unsheathed saber. The police corralled the peasant among their nightsticks. We could not believe our own eyes and turned away, ashamed for our beloved tsar. This was my first disillusionment with him; involuntarily I was reminded of the cat magically transformed into a beautiful woman, who, however, could not see a mouse without pouncing on it.

Progressive reforms that Alexander had been considering before Napoleon's invasion stayed on the shelf after the war had been won; instead the tsar now busied himself with drilling his army, and with a road-building program that exacted onerous sacrifices from peasants and landowners alike, and (most unpopular of all) with a plan to militarize whole regions of the country under a system of military settlements whereby every male citizen would be a soldier and wear a uniform while the women grew provisions to supply the army. Peasants who hated and resisted the plan were attacked by troops, and many were killed. Officers in the tsar's retinue reported his oft-stated contempt for his subjects. Alexander also spent a lot of time abroad or away from the capital and left the country in the charge of his cruel deputy, Count Aleksei Arakcheev. Russian tyranny has produced many creepy henchmen, from Ivan the Terrible's feared toady Maliuta-Skuratov to Stalin's NKVD chief Yezhov, but of them all the dread Count Arakcheev possessed the most poetically sinister name.

An Arakcheev story, in passing: Herzen tells of the time the president of the Academy of the Arts proposed that Count Arakcheev be made an honorary member of the academy. When Alexander Labzin, the academy's secretary, inquired what Count Arakcheev had contributed to the arts, the president didn't know what to say. Finally he offered that Arakcheev was the man closest to the tsar. Labzin replied that, by similar reasoning, the tsar's coachman, Ilya Baikov, should also be a member. "He is not only close to the Tsar, but sits in front of him," Labzin noted. Evidently this *mot* later got back to Arakcheev; he ordered that Labzin be exiled to the city of Simbirsk in southern Russia.

Like many of the Founding Fathers in America, many of the Decembrists were Masons. Officers saw one another at Masons' meetings, at meals in the officers' quarters while on duty, at social events in the capital and in Moscow, and during long visits to friends' estates in the country. Among themselves they talked endlessly about what was wrong with Russia and how it could be reformed—about the evil of serfdom, the wretchedness of the peasants' condition, the unfairness of the common soldiers' twenty-five-year service terms, the corruption of public officials, the disrespect for the individual, the ignorance and reactionary attitudes of the old guard. One day a small group of intimates during such a conversation resolved to form a secret society whose goal would be to work with all its strength for the good of Russia. Specifically, the secret society would strive for the emancipation of the serfs and the introduction of constitutional monarchy.

From this beginning, the secret society grew and spread and evolved over the course of nearly a decade. Hundreds of young men—many more than were involved in leading the events of December 1825, or than went to prison afterward—would belong to the organization over that time. For some years in the beginning, the society was called the Union of Salvation. Then that organization was dissolved, a new constitution replaced the previous one, and the name became the Union of Welfare. Officers transferred to serve in the south of Russia started a branch of the secret society there. Its members had less patrician origins than their friends in St. Petersburg, and the two groups' political philosophies differed in ways that were never reconciled. Both agreed on the need for overthrowing the tsar at the first opportunity. The two branches were known as the Northern Society and the Southern Society.

Pavel Pestel, an officer who had been seriously wounded at the Battle of Borodino, became the moving spirit of the Southern Society. Of all the Decembrists, he was among the very few who could qualify as a political thinker. Pushkin called him "one of the most original minds I know." Many of the members of the Union of Salvation could not stand him and dissolved the organization partly so that Pestel would think the movement was over and go away. He just kept on working with his comrades in the south, however. In testimony after his arrest, Pestel said that he had been very influenced by antimonarchical theories of government put forth by Destutt de Tracy in his book *Commentaire sur L'Esprit des Lois de Montesquieu*. Scholars believe this book to have been partly or largely written by Destutt de Tracy's collaborator, Thomas Jefferson, who also saw to its publication. With such politics, Pestel could be described as well to the left of most Decembrists. Herzen summed him up as "the socialist before socialism." He wanted no kings and a republican form of government. Yakushkin said of Pestel, "Of all of us he alone in the course of ten years, not weakening for a minute, labored diligently in the business of the Secret Society."

The Northern Society, in keeping with its aristocratic membership, met less often and did less in general than its southern counterpart. The Petersburg members at the society's core were Yevgenii Obolensky, Trubetskoy, Nikita Muraviev, Nicholas Turgenev, Mikhail Lunin, and the poet Konrad Ryleev. The new Russian constitution that Nikita Muraviev drafted for the Northern Society had been modeled directly on the U.S. Constitution. It called for a federation of thirteen states and two provinces. Pestel did not like that constitution, saying it favored wealth.

The maneuverings and debates and membership changes of the Union of Welfare in its northern and southern branches are more complex than I'm going into here, of course. Essentially, the movement drew the most talented and energetic young men in Russia, men eager for change without knowing exactly what it would be or how to bring it about. Their moment of political activity would be brief. But they would prove to be mythopoeic out of all proportion to their political success. Their lives and times would provide a source of poems and short stories and novels, flowing into the great nineteenth-century surge of Russian literature that began with Pushkin. In that richness they resemble the American cowboy, whose actual existence on the plains of the West was small compared to the myths he spawned.

The officers were dashing, in other words. So well did the adjective apply to them that these dashing young officers might be said to have epitomized the phrase. Officers would continue to be dashing for a while after the Decembrists' generation, until perhaps the arrival of motorized warfare; I don't believe young officers are ever described as dashing today. Like few young officers before or after, those of the Decembrists' generation dashed. They drank champagne, went to balls, broke hearts and had theirs broken, gambled away their estates on the draw of a card. Though dueling was illegal, they dueled. Some of their personal dramas were great romantic tragedy but enacted in real life—for example (and most famously), the Novosiltsov-Chernov duel.

Alexei Novosiltsov and Konstantin Chernov were brother officers and friends. Novosiltsov came from a high-ranking and wealthy family, while Chernov's family, though noble, was poor. Chernov had a beau-

tiful sister, whom he introduced to Novosiltsov. The two fell in love. Novosiltsov told the sister he would marry her, and then went away with
her, and they lived as man and wife. Soon after, he informed his mother
of his decision to marry Mlle. Chernova. The mother, appalled at the
match, said no. Thus brought to heel, Novosiltsov suddenly became unavailable to his one-time intended. To numerous pleas from both Chernov and the young woman, he made no reply. Chernov, having no other
choice, then challenged Novosiltsov to a duel. Novosiltsov accepted and
the duel occurred. Each man fired to kill; each mortally wounded the
other. Afterward, from their deathbeds, each man sent a message forgiving the other and declaring friendship. The young woman entered
a convent.

Her desolation, and that of Chernov's mother, can be imagined. The
mother of Novosiltsov mourned her only son by building two churches,
one on the site of the duel and another on her estate. She had pictures
of the young man all over her house, and drawings done by him, and a
full-length portrait of him in her parlor. Nine years after his death she
was still deep in mourning, with "her affections . . . fixed on another
world," said James Buchanan, the U.S. ambassador; during his time in
St. Petersburg, the future American president met and became a friend
of the bereaved Mme. Novosiltsov. Whether by then she had decided
that her son might have been better off disadvantageously married but
still alive Buchanan did not say.

Sworn oaths meant a lot to these young men. How seriously they took
them might be hard for us to understand today. In fact, sometimes they
went overboard. Yakushkin laughed about how some of his comrades in
the secret society became caught up in devising obsequies for the induction of new members, with "exorcist-like oaths" and swearing on the
Gospels or on the sword—"comical in the extreme," Yakushkin said.
From the outset, all the society's members had agreed that, given the
horribleness of the current tsar, to whom they had already promised
their allegiance, they would under no circumstances swear allegiance to
the tsar who succeeded him.

Unexpectedly, this resolve met its test in late November 1825, when
Tsar Alexander I died of malaria during an inspection tour of his troops

in the Crimea. At the news, everybody in the society understood that now they must act, although they were not really prepared. Adding confusion to the moment was the fact that Russian officialdom did not know who Alexander's successor would be. Alexander had no children, so his successor should have been his younger brother, Konstantin. Konstantin had secretly renounced the throne, however, back in 1823, the memory of the murder of his father, Tsar Paul, evidently having dampened his enthusiasm for the honor. Nicholas, the third brother, had been designated as heir, but for some reason Alexander had not announced the decision publicly. And on top of that, Nicholas himself was at first hesitant to take the throne. As a result, for almost three weeks Russia had no tsar. Some of the troops had already been administered the oath of allegiance to Konstantin. Then Nicholas decided he would be tsar after all. A new date for the oath-taking ceremony, this time to swear allegiance to Tsar Nicholas I, was set for December 14.

On December 12 and on the evening of the thirteenth, uproarious meetings of the secret society took place in members' apartments in St. Petersburg. In Yevgenii Obolensky's rooms on December 12, the suggestions or objections of people who tried to speak reason in the clamor met with the shout-down, "You can't have a rehearsal for an enterprise like this, just as if it were a parade!" Konrad Ryleev rose to new levels of eloquence, as his stirring words, "A beginning must be made," cut through the noise. At the meeting in Ryleev's rooms the next evening, the poet's face, "pale as the moon but lit up by some supernatural light, would vanish, reappear, and vanish once more in the stormy waves of that sea in which simmered various convictions, many passions," a participant later recalled. Prince Trubetskoy drew up a manifesto to be read in the Senate following the seizure of power and made plans for the takeover of the palace and the arrest of Nicholas and his family. A character named Yakubovich, whose violent temperament many of his comrades had feared to unleash, promised to kill the tsar himself. Prince Alexander Odoevsky cried, "We shall die, oh, how gloriously we shall die!"

Of course they failed—disastrously, spectacularly. Almost better to avert your eyes. None of them even managed to die gloriously. When the time came they did not do one thing right. The wife of the British ambassador, traveling the city's streets after the event, was horrified to see the "pools of blood on the snow, and spattered up against the houses." But the blood was not the conspirators'; in St. Petersburg the major ones did not suffer any serious injury, so more likely the blood belonged to the deluded soldiers whom they had persuaded to follow them to the Senate Square with the lie that the rebellion was to reinstate the rightful emperor, Konstantin. The soldiers, who revered the tsar, probably would not have gone along otherwise.

Prince Trubetskoy, the designated dictator, turned out to be a no-show. On the fateful day, he inquired about taking the oath to Nicholas, then sought refuge in the Austrian embassy. Yakubovich, the implacable assassin, wandered around the square cheering for Konstantin, then said he had a headache and left. Then he came back, dithered some more, and left again. None of the other rebel officers had the rank of Trubetskoy, so no one knew who should take command. A firebrand named Kakhovsky shot and killed the redoubtable governor-general of St. Petersburg, M. A. Miloradovich, when he tried to talk the troops into laying down their arms. Kakhovsky killed another high-ranking officer after that. The standoff in Senate Square lasted for hours, and as the day was waning, one of Nicholas's generals told him he must clear the square with gunfire or else abdicate. Reluctantly, Nicholas gave the order, and canister shot tore the Decembrists' troops apart. Soldiers who tried to escape across the frozen Neva were drowned when cannonballs shattered the ice below them. Bodies littered the square. *"Voilà un joli commencement du regne!"* said Nicholas.

The Southern Society's rebellion had a better chance of success because its planning had been more thorough and more troops followed the conspirators. But in the south the government got lucky by arresting Pavel Pestel on December 13, before the uprising began. With him gone, Sergei Muraviev-Apostol's troops turned on him, while his brother Ippolit and an assistant, Kuzmin, shot themselves; et cetera, until the southern uprising's complete collapse.

Sergei Volkonsky, a leader in the Southern Society, did not know what to do after the arrest of Pestel. After some confused attempts to rally his soldiers, and further zigging and zagging, Volkonsky realized the rebels' cause was lost, and he decided to see his wife and family on his estate not far away one last time before the government caught up with him. When he arrived home, he found a sleigh with two police officers and a government official waiting for him. They had come all the way from St. Petersburg. He was arrested immediately and taken to prison there.

Generally incompetent and corrupt as the tsar's government tended to be, it did a thorough job with the subsequent inquest, trial, and punishment. All of its highest pomp and dignity was brought to bear. True, when the mostly elderly and occasionally drowsy officials who conducted the trial proceedings assembled in full plenum and announced the conspirators' sentences, some of the culprits spoiled the mood by starting to laugh. But that was just a minor hitch. Bureaucracy had seen to it that all prisoners were questioned, depositions taken, confessions made, lists of additional suspects drawn up, and priests dispatched to the jail cells of individuals whose spiritual condition seemed particularly in need. Yevgenii Obolensky went through a religious epiphany that called upon him to provide the investigators with the names not only of the members of the society whom he had associated with personally but also of members he had heard of from years in the past. Tsar Nicholas conducted many of the questionings himself. Prince Trubetskoy, whose uncle had turned him in, threw himself at the tsar's feet and pleaded for his life: *"Ma vie, sire!"* (this according to Nicholas's memoirs). Kakhovsky, the cold killer of Gen. Miloradovich, entered into a correspondence with the tsar and through it discovered a deep love, understanding, and respect for his sovereign.

Ivan Yakushkin, whose head seemed always to stay on straight, described an exchange early in his own inquisition, when he was refusing to name names:

After about ten minutes the door opened and Levashev made a sign to me to come into the hall in which the interrogation had been. By the card table stood the new emperor. He told me to come closer, and he began in this manner:

"You broke your oath?"

"I am guilty, sovereign."

"What awaits you in the next world? Damnation. You can despise the opinion of people, but what awaits you in the next world must terrify you. However, I do not want to completely destroy you: I will send you a priest. How is it you do not answer me?"

"What would you wish from me, sovereign?"

"I, it seems, am speaking to you fairly clearly; if you do not want to ruin your family and be treated as a swine, then you must unburden yourself of everything."

"I gave my word not to name anybody; everything that I know on my own, I already told to his excellency," I answered, indicating Levashev who was standing a ways off in a respectful posture.

"Don't give me 'his excellency' and your vile word of honor!"

"I cannot name anybody, sovereign."

The new emperor recoiled three steps back, gestured toward me with his hand, and said, "Put him in irons so that he cannot budge."

Per Nicholas's orders, Yakushkin was held in leg and arm fetters while locked in his cell in the Sts. Peter and Paul Fortress. Mikhail Lunin, for similar defiance, was not only chained but also forbidden to have anything with him in his cell. Baron Andrei Rozen was allowed no books for his first four months in prison. During the blank hours, Rozen suffered at the sound of the man in the cell next to him, Mikhail Bestuzhev-Ryumin, turning the pages of his French-Russian dictionary. Bestuzhev-Ryumin did not speak his country's language well and needed the dictionary to compose a full confession in Russian as the court required.

He, Kakhovsky, Sergei Muraviev-Apostol, Pestel, and Ryleev were sentenced to be drawn and quartered. Trubetskoy and thirty other lesser offenders were to have their heads cut off. After review, the tsar, in his clemency, reduced the sentence of the first group to hanging and of the second to prison labor followed by exile for life in Siberia. A ceremony in which the guilty officers' uniforms were burned in a pile and their swords broken over their heads did not come off as impressively as hoped, and again was marred by laughter; the hanging, conducted in a drizzle of rain, did not go smoothly, either, and Muraviev-Apostol, Ryleev, and Kakhovsky had to be hanged twice. In July of 1826, small groups of those sentenced to Siberia began to depart on their journey east. Histories say that as the wagon carrying Sergei Volkonsky rolled out of St. Petersburg past the palace, his mother was inside at a ball, dancing with the tsar.

During Ivan Yakushkin's removal to Siberia, the authorities allowed him to meet his family at a stop in Yaroslavl and spend six hours with them. He had had little contact with home, and when he learned from his wife that she had been given permission to join him in exile, but only if she left the children, he made a quick decision that she should stay behind. He thought the children too young to be without their mother— wisely, as it turned out, because young children of women who did go off to join their husbands did, in several cases, die. Yakushkin and his wife never saw each other again. He wrote that when he parted from her and his children, "I wept like a child from whom they have taken his last and favorite toy."

His simile was well chosen; the failure of the uprising, and the experience of being arrested, jailed, tried, and sentenced, seemed to reduce most of the bold and dashing Decembrists to the psychological status of boys. For a modern observer this is perhaps the most painful aspect of their story. Tsar Nicholas treated the men who had tried to overthrow him the same way he would treat miscreant sons gone terribly astray. And the Decembrists, for all their energy, sophistication, and idealism, somehow couldn't help but accept that narrative. They loved their country, it was their fatherland, the tsar was the father of Russia . . . In prison and in exile, their high-flown plans of bringing justice and freedom to Russia disappeared. Of all the Decembrist prisoners, only Mikhail Lunin kept objecting and resisting, and as a result he endured punitive downgrades in his imprisonment, until he ended his days at the horrid silver mines at Akatui.

Deep down, they simply could not imagine themselves the equals of the tsar. Everything in their upbringing, religion, military training, and sense of duty obstructed that idea. During the uprising, Nicholas brought out his seven-year-old son, presented him to a battalion of loyal troops, and let some of them hold him: how strongly that act would have resonated with his honorable young adversaries, and shaken their will to follow through! With the Decembrists as a point of comparison, I have increased my respect for America's Founding Fathers and the men they led, who seem to have believed even in their unconscious that King George III of England really was no better than they were. They were fortunate, perhaps, that to them King George was kind of a theoretical idea, being so distant from them physically. True equality is a difficult concept to hold in the mind. I believe we Americans have lost our grip on it today. I know that in my case, I can tell myself that I'm just as good as a billionaire and even believe that it is true. But when I'm in the actual presence of a powerful person, my own concept of equality gets blurry, and I have a regrettable tendency to truckle, if only to be polite.

To drive his paternalistic point home even further, Nicholas put the Decembrists in Siberia under the immediate command of a respected, experienced, and quite old general named Stanislaus Leparski. After a large number of Decembrists had been concentrated at a prison in Chita, General Leparski arrived to run it and see to their rehabilitation. The principle here was analogous to sending a difficult teenager to live under the supervision of his stern but lovable grandpa. Leparski reported that he had little trouble controlling the men, but he did say that dealing with the wives of the Decembrists who had found dwellings near the prison became a dreaded part of his job.

Though the Decembrists had fallen into political helplessness, and the reforms they had dreamed of were probably dead for the rest of their lives, they resolved to treat one another decently in their imprisonment, at least. Indeed, these idealists' true greatness may be said to have emerged most clearly during their time in Siberia. To begin with, they threw out all recriminations about anyone's behavior under questioning. As N. V. Basargin wrote, "Though many of us had made careless statements, and had this or that 'lack of firmness' on one of our comrades' part to thank for our present state, no one allowed himself even a comment as to how others had behaved during the trial and enquiry. It was as though all hostile thoughts had been left behind us in the cells, and only mutual liking remained." In Yakushkin's memoir, he spends pages explaining the "artel" system the prisoners devised whereby everybody, those receiving generous stipends from home as well as those receiving little, contributed to a common account to ensure that no prisoner ever had to be in need.

The "hard labor" of the Decembrists' sentences not being all that hard, the convicts also had time to write letters and poetry, give lectures to their comrades on subjects of personal expertise, cultivate a vegetable garden, play musical instruments, tinker with mechanical ideas. After they had been released from prison and assigned to their places of exile, some of them started schools, experimented with new crops, studied the native peoples. Nikolai Bestuzhev taught the Buryats how to grow tobacco, and in the early twentieth century there were still old Buryat men who could recall studying in Bestuzhev's school. In general, the Decembrist exiles greatly raised the tone of Siberia. Travelers through the region sought them out; though under police supervision, and still forbidden to do things like attend a public concert, they became Siberia's unofficial first citizens.

The Decembrist Dmitri Zavalishin described their local appeal in this way: "We [Decembrists] were the first to appear in Siberia as people of the higher class, entirely approachable and . . . with rules totally opposite to those which the inhabitants were accustomed to see in their superiors and officials: in us they saw sympathy and the performance of good instead of oppression and extortion. For this reason no one ever kept a secret from us . . . Therefore we could study the country in its true light."

Not surprisingly, the wives who followed their husbands to Siberia and became pregnant there had a lot of children who died. The seven wives of Decembrist prisoners in the trans-Baikal prisons lost twenty-two children among them. But many Siberian-born children survived, as well. Paulina Gueble, who married Ivan Annenkov while he was imprisoned in Chita, bore him eighteen children, of whom six survived. The Volkonskys had a healthy son, Mikhail, in 1832, and then a daughter, Elena, in 1834. Yakushkin's wife back in western Russia died in 1845 or '46, but both his sons survived to adulthood and eventually came to Siberia and joined him.

In various places of exile throughout Siberia, the aging Decembrists endured their sentences and carried on their reduced and humbled lives. Meanwhile, the affection their fellow citizens had for them began to grow. These men had acted only out of love of their country, after all. And unlike so many other important figures in Russia's past, they were not horribly drenched in blood. They had been passionate young men, and their passions had cost them their youth. The ideas they had fallen in love with remained hopeful and deserving of men's devotion. Over the years, the Decembrists' reputations rose and rose; Russians still think of them fondly today. Streets named after them during the serious revolutionary times of the twentieth century were not renamed when that era had passed. In a country where icons are built up and smashed down with regularity, the Decembrists' position seems secure.

Tsar Nicholas never forgave his antagonists of December 14 for what he saw as a family betrayal, but late in his life even he allowed himself some sentimentality about them. Discovering the corruption of members of his administration during the disastrous Crimean War, he was reported to have said, "Pestel and Bestuzhev would never have treated me in this fashion."

Nicholas became bitter and depressed toward the end and died in March 1855. His son, Alexander, was believed to have a kind regard for the Decembrists. During his triumphal national tour as tsarevitch in 1837, he had let it be known, as he passed through western Siberia, that he wished local Decembrist exiles to be present when he worshipped at a church in Kurgan. They came, and he looked at them during the service with tear-filled eyes. When he became Alexander II after Nicholas's death, many people thought he would pardon the Decembrists right away. Months passed, though, and Alexander took no action. Then on the occasion of his coronation in August 1856, Alexander issued a Proclamation of General Amnesty for all those who had been convicted in connection with the December uprising. In Siberia, only thirty-four of the original hundred-some sent there were still alive.

Sergei Volkonsky, still living in Irkutsk, was now an eccentric old man with a long beard. His son, Mikhail, now twenty-four, had been allowed to go to officers' school in Moscow, and at the time of the tsar's amnesty was living there. He and his sister Elena attended Alexander's coronation and sat in the official section because of Mikhail's recent appointment to the famous Governor-General Muraviev-Amursky's staff. After the ceremony, Mikhail and Elena returned to her apartment. At about six o'clock in the evening the doorbell rang. A messenger had come to summon Mikhail to the Kremlin. There, Prince Dolgoruky, the tsar's chief military officer, handed Mikhail a parchment copy of the Manifesto of Amnesty: the tsar had requested that Mikhail's father be the first Decembrist exile to receive the news. Mikhail left for Siberia that night in a tarantass (a springless carriage) and covered the distance from Moscow to Irkutsk in fifteen days.

No doubt Mikhail traveled with a courier's *podorozhnaya*, a pass that gave the bearer the highest priority on the road and the first pick of horses at every way station. Fifteen days is remarkably fast nonetheless. Had Mikhail started not from Moscow but from St. Petersburg, as Sergei and Volodya and I did, the extra distance would have cost him another day or two. And of course my companions and I had also gone on side journeys, and visited people, and waited out breakdown delays. Still, in a horse-drawn vehicle on nineteenth-century roads, feeling so happy he barely stopped to rest, Mikhail Volkonsky made the journey from western Russia to Irkutsk five or six days faster than we did in our van.

Chapter 19

Irkutsk *does* kind of look like Paris, it turns out—if you can imagine a Paris with the Seine gigantically expanded to the horizon-filling width of Irkutsk's Angara, and with diminished buildings and steeples poking up along the river's distant margins on either side. We drove down the Street of the Events of December, we parked, we bought supplies. But the afternoon had gotten late, and Sergei, as usual, was in a sweat to escape the city limits and find a good camping spot. He said he knew of an ideal place on the shores of Lake Baikal, thirty or forty miles away. Before we set out for it, I stipulated that we return to Irkutsk the following morning; there was more here I wanted to see.

Sergei's camping spot was in a little regional park above the fishing town of Nikola. Centuries ago, eastbound travelers used to stop at the monastery there and pray at its church dedicated to St. Nicholas for safe passage across the lake. The park is on a hillside, and as Sergei navigated the van up its incline, he made a sharp turn that came within a breath of tipping the vehicle onto its side. He then stopped, backed down, found a less-steep route, drove to the campsite, and set up the tents without comment. This was the first "improved" campsite we had been in. Each site had a fire circle surrounded by stones, an iron grate for cooking, and two benches made of wood.

When I awoke the next morning, Sergei and Volodya were not around. Two young men and a woman at the campsite just across the way were shouting and playing loud music and drunkenly carrying on. I stuck my head out of the tent flap and saw one of the guys in the process of breaking up the benches in his campsite. Loud splintering sounds accompanied this. He then began to heap the more manageable fragments in the fire circle, where a few logs from the night before still smoldered. I crawled back into the tent and slept awhile longer. When I got up an hour or two later, Sergei and Volodya had not yet returned. I walked around and stretched. Then I took out my kit and hung my shaving mirror on a tree and began to shave.

I was about half finished when a young man in what I took to be a park ranger's uniform walked up to me as I squinted in the mirror and asked me if I knew anything about the benches that had been destroyed. I saw his truck parked nearby. Evidently he had been driving by and noticed the pieces of the bench scattered around. I said I did not speak Russian very well and he should wait until my friends returned. In a tough-cop manner he asked me a few more questions; he seemed to find something fishy about me. Half covered in shaving cream, I pleaded ignorance of everything. After a while he gave up on me and went over to the tents of the neighbors, who had retired to sleep it off.

Hollering into the tent, the ranger flushed them out into the daylight. I heard his loud questions and their sullen-sounding replies. Suddenly the ranger grabbed one of the guys around the neck and began to beat him on the head. He slapped and cuffed and knocked him around like a boy pummeling his little brother. The victim covered his head with his arms and did not resist, as if this was just part of the drill. I guessed that being beaten by a public official was an experience he had been through before. After a few last boxes of the ears, the ranger went back to his vehicle and drove off. The guy and his companion then began throwing the pieces of bench out of their fire pit—the punishment for their vandalism being that they could not enjoy the results of it, apparently. Soon after that I saw them putting the pieces of bench back in the fire pit again.

Sergei and Volodya did not return until the day was too far gone for us to pack up and make the trip to Irkutsk we'd agreed on. This development was predictable enough that I didn't even waste much time being mad. Sergei said that he and Volodya had spent all morning climbing the cliffs above Baikal, and these cliffs were so beautiful that I must see them immediately. After lunch he led me there. We climbed past the

camp and well beyond the village to a point where pale, columnar cliffs rose spirelike above. Single-file, we started up. The rock had interstices and eroded places through which a hand's-breadth of trail snaked, mostly along the side closer to the water. I admired Sergei's quick footwork; mine was more uncertain, and at one or two places I got down on all fours. Lake Baikal, immensely blue, occupied the entire space on our right-hand side clear to the horizon. At the top of a spire we stopped, and directly below us, maybe fifteen stories down, a naked couple was swimming in water of a clear, almost tropical greenish-blue. We could hear the woman laugh; her figure was Rubensian. In another moment they ducked into a grotto, maybe realizing we were there.

At a distance in from the cliffs, a gravel lane ran along the lakeshore to a bluff where a gray-and-white observatory, all angles and planes, like a piece of modernist sculpture, leaned its notched profile to the sky. I said we should check out this observatory and Sergei said sure, so we hiked up to it and knocked on the door. An astronomer named Elena Kossumova answered and invited us inside. She had short, honey-blond hair, wore a white lab coat, and spoke the flawless English I now expect from every Russian in the sciences. Her colleague, Victor Trifonov, a thin man with prominent teeth and a big smile, wore a baseball cap with FSB on it and below that, FARMERS STATE BANK; he said he had been given the hat on a trip to Athens, Ohio, the year before.

The observatory's purpose was to study the sun. It had been built here because this part of Baikal's shore gets more than two hundred days of sunshine a year. Victor Trifonov had designed the telescope himself. This telescope sees the sun's surface; another, in an observatory on the next bluff to the north, sees its atmosphere. Victor adjusted the eyepiece of the telescope so Sergei and I could look. First the bright red sun, a bit yellow in its outer margin, filled the view. Then an enlarged part of the sun's lower left section emerged in more detail. Elena pointed out a solar flare, two or three times the size of earth, on that southern edge. She said that the sun becomes active with solar flares every eleven years. We were now in a very active part of the cycle, and when that happens, studies have found that there is more human turmoil on earth and more earth-quakes and storms. A less active period was expected to return in about two years. She said that if people do unkind or violent things during a time of solar activity, it's not really their fault, it's the sun's.

Possibly as a result of this visit to the observatory, later that afternoon Sergei and Volodya made the acquaintance of a lady geologist who lived in the village of Nikola. I think she was a friend of the astronomers. Anyway, this lady geologist had a friend, etc., and Sergei and Volodya stayed out that evening until the small hours. I woke the next morning at five thirty, took a bath in Baikal in the quiet dawn twilight with no one yet around, and agitated my sleepy guides awake much earlier than they wanted to be. I was not going to miss Irkutsk a second time. We had packed and were on the road by nine. Only a short way down the Irkutsk road, the van, perhaps growing bored with its everyday tricks, tried a new one and caught fire. The back filled with black smoke and a trail like that of a shot-down fighter plane could be seen in the rearview mirror streaming behind.

We pulled to the shoulder and I undid my seat belt and came hopping out on the double, remembering the two big tanks of propane we were carrying. I found a place to watch about a quarter mile away. Meanwhile Sergei braved the smoke to look under the hood and beneath the dash. Somehow the flames went out after a while and the smoke disappeared. Sergei explained that the fire had been caused by the automatic locking device on the steering column. After some tinkering, he assured me that he had completely fixed the problem and the van would not catch fire again; and he was right. That would be the only time it caught fire.

Seen close up, the city of Irkutsk resembled the Baikal cliffs' ancient and weather-beaten windings. During its early centuries, Irkutsk had grown unplanned, like coral, and when civic improvement tried to bring some order to the confusion, the crews sent out for that purpose sometimes sawed houses in half to make crooked streets straight. In much of the city they still aren't. A sense of almost microscopic embroidery fills the town's windingest lanes, where log homes sunk halfway to their eaves in the permafrost draw your attention with decorative wood carving on shutters and doors and windows as ornate as the finest carved birch jewelry box. And yet almost every house also looked gray and older than old, though never as decrepit as the defiantly ugly high-rises that confront you whenever a big open space from Soviet times scissors across the network of lanes.

Elsewhere on my Irkutsk ramblings I came across the graves of Ekaterina Trubetskoy and three of her children at Znamensky Monastery.

In the first years of the Decembrists' imprisonment, Katya Trubetskoy had been everybody's morale builder, with her good humor and level-headedness, but after her children began to die and her own health failed, she became indifferent to life, and she died about two years before the amnesty. Her death stunned her husband; when he went back to western Russia in 1856 he said goodbye forever to her grave.

In advertisements posted around the city I also noticed that Admiral Kolchak, the White Army leader whose attempt to overthrow the Bolsheviks ended in Irkutsk with his capture and execution, is now a beer. Admiral Kolchak Beer is brewed locally. I picked up an empty bottle of it that I found. The label has a portrait of the admiral in his white naval uniform and even provides the history-minded beer drinker with a brief bio, which plays up his heroism in the Russo-Japanese War and World War I, his polar explorations, and his contribution to the Russian navy, but makes no mention of his violent exit. A beer garden on Irkutsk's Angara riverfront sports a long striped awning with the Kolchak Beer logo repeated prominently all along it; maybe the awning is within sight of the place where the corpse of the unlucky admiral was shoved through the ice back in 1920.

That night we again slept near the shores of Baikal. This time, due to bad planning, we camped on the grounds of what was billed as a resort. It had a gate, cabins, picnic shelters, and washroom conveniences best left undiscussed. Its strewn heaps of trash were extreme, even for Russia. Somebody who saw this campground without context or explanation might come to the conclusion that a group of confused people had mistakenly gone on vacation at the town dump. The woman who ran the resort had been driven to a near frenzy by how awful it was. We discovered this when Sergei invited her to have tea with us after supper, and she told us, with great drama and forcefulness and scorching irony, about the difficulties of her job. By one o'clock her monologue had worn me out and I retired to my tent. Sergei had to evict her bodily at two thirty. At an even later hour than that, when he and Volodya were again off somewhere, I came awake to a loud conversation between two passing drunks who were debating whether to do something or other—I did not recognize the verb—to our tents. Fortunately, the milder of the drunks prevailed after a while and they went away. Cars then blasted up and down the resort's dirt lanes for an hour or so, blowing their horns. Just after dawn, the Big Brother–like speakers of the public-address system wired to nearby trees began playing bad music from many different cultures while exhorting everyone to get up and exercise.

Sergei assured me he would find us a better place on Baikal, and the next day he did. We drove around the southern end of the lake and then followed the railroad tracks that ran between the road and the shore. At a place where a creek went under a railroad bridge there was enough dry ground on one side for the van to squeak through, and we emerged onto a beach of small, smooth rocks with no sign of people anywhere for two or three miles. Sitting on the beach with nothing to do but look at the lake, I finally got the point about Baikal.

I knew that it's the largest body of freshwater in the world, that it contains about 20 percent of the world's freshwater, that it's more than a mile deep at its deepest, that it was created by continental landmasses moving apart, that it has species of animals found only here. But, beyond its facts, Baikal really does have a magic to it. Travelers who wrote ecstatically about it in the past were not exaggerating. Most of Russia's inland water is sluggish, swampy, inert; Baikal's is quick. For sparklingness and clarity it's the opposite of swamp water. The surrounding hills and cliffs that funnel winds along it keep it jumping. It reflects like an optical instrument and responds to changes in the weather so sensitively that it seems like a part of the sky rather than of the land. And along with all that, Baikal is distinctly Asiatic: if a camel caravan could somehow transport Baikal across Siberia to Europe, and curious buyers unwrapped it in a marketplace, none would mistake it for a lake from around there.

When a wave rolls in on Baikal, and it curls to break, you can see stones on the bottom refracted in the vertical face of the wave. This glimpse, offered for just a moment in the wave's motion, is like seeing into the window of an apartment as you go by it on an elevated train. The moon happened to be full that night, and after it rose, the stones on the bottom of the lake lay spookily illuminated in the moonlight. The glitter of the moon on the surface of the lake—the "moon road," Sergei called it—fluctuated constantly in its individual points of sparkling, with a much higher definition than any murky water could achieve. Light glitters differently on water this clear. I understood that I had never really seen the moon reflected on water before.

This camping spot was so great we decided to stay another day. True, trains did go by almost constantly just the other side of some shoreline trees, but the sound was not bad for sleeping at all. In the morning, a fisherman who put his boat in at the mouth of the creek brought us some *omul'* he had just caught. To reciprocate, I opened my stash of presents and got out a New York City snow globe, some Beanie Baby stuffed animals, and two folding pocket mirrors to give to him. He liked the snow globe and he accepted the Beanie Babies, but he gave me back the mirrors, saying he had no use for them. This made Sergei indignant and he scolded the guy for being a rude person who didn't know how to behave with foreigners. Chastened, the guy took the mirrors. I remembered I had a baseball cap with the logo of the Bass Anglers Sportsman Society on it—the logo shows a leaping bass, in bright green—and I gave him that, too. He put it on and examined it in the mirror, and above his broad face and brown bib overalls it looked exactly right. I liked the idea that I had successfully launched a BASS hat on the waters of Baikal.

Volodya took the fish the guy had brought and gutted them, split them to the backbone, filled them inside with slices of lemon and garlic and handfuls of coarse salt, and tied them shut with string. At the end of the day he cut the string, removed the lemon and garlic and salt, scaled the fish, rinsed them quickly in the lake, and cut them into half-inch slices for sushi. They tasted wonderful, though you had to watch the bones. *"Esh' akkuratno"* (Eat accurately), Sergei advised.

All day the lake was covered with the kind of whitecaps that indicate good sailing, but in late afternoon the wind dropped off to nothing. The whitecaps disappeared, and the waves, now forceless, kept rolling in. The sound they made when they landed on the small pebbles at the edge of the beach—a sound like setting down a canvas sack of change—started me thinking about when I used to hear the same sound on my grandmother's beach on Lake Erie. Often in the evening the lake would get calm like this, and each wave would land just a bit more gently than the one before it, and the time for rounding up the children and preparing to go home would begin. Now the sun was going down across Baikal just at the angle it would be at my grandmother's beach this time of year. I sat

on the stones and thought about my family of forty years ago and grew
lonesome and melancholy.

Before we left the next morning, I took out my satellite phone and called
my friend Jamaica Kincaid in North Bennington, Vermont. She said she
was having a dinner party. We talked for a while and then she passed the
phone around the table. I talked to Howard Cohen, her rabbi, and to
Howard's wife, Gail; to our friends Annie and Gordie Thorne; to Meg
and Rob Woolmington, friends who live near Jamaica; and to her son,
Harold. I could imagine the smell of the poached chicken on a bed of
lovage that Jamaica had prepared, and the West Indian pastels of the
walls in her kitchen, and the evening primrose opening its yellow blos-
soms in the dusk outside the windows. In fact, I could picture being
there more clearly than I could picture being here on the stony beach
where I was.

I waited a few minutes for my thoughts to reassemble themselves and
then I tried again to call Sasha Khamarkhanov in Ulan-Ude. I had been
hoping to see him when we passed through Ulan-Ude that afternoon.
Every time I had dialed his number before, it had been busy, and I got
the same result this time. I should have sent him an e-mail saying I was
coming. I had forgotten to do that before I left home, and I hadn't
thought of it the last time I was near a computer, in Novosibirsk. I had
not handled this intelligently at all. Even worse, now I had misplaced
Sasha's address. I knew Sergei would not want to tarry in Ulan-Ude, eager as he always was to get beyond urban areas. All the same, as we approached the city I insisted that I remembered where Sasha's apartment
building was and that we had to look for it.

Surprising both of us, I found the building almost as soon as we drove
into Ulan-Ude. I recognized a street, a row of buildings, and the place
where we'd loaded up the minibus for the trip to Baikal. I don't know
how that discovery happened because Ulan-Ude is not a little place
at all. We pulled over. Walking around one of the buildings I saw a
familiar-looking entryway. I went up several flights of stairs, saw what
seemed to be the correct door, knocked. Tania, Sasha's wife, opened it.

I was not the person she had been expecting to see standing there.
She was amazed for a few seconds and then not amazed in the least. She

asked us in (Volodya had accompanied me while Sergei stayed in the van) and didn't know what to do after that. She said she should make us a big dinner; I said we couldn't stay long. Dropped in on as she was, she didn't have the time or supplies to do very much anyway. When I had seen her before, I had been mute in her language and now I could talk a little. She asked if I still had that funny picture of my baby. On my previous visit I had been carrying a wallet-sized photo of my daughter at age eight months or so wearing a bright orange shirt-and-pants outfit and sitting in the corner of our dark-colored sofa. She had her arms akimbo and was looking up suspiciously. I told Tania I had forgotten to bring it with me.

"And how is your thumb?" she asked. "I remember that you cut it at Baikal while you were making a fishing rod, and you thought you were about to die!" I assured her the thumb was fine, and I showed her the scar, which she said she could not see.

Sasha Khamarkhanov, as it turned out, was in the hospital. Tania said he'd just undergone a small operation on his hand. Apparently he had other health problems, too, but I didn't understand when she explained them to us. Later when I asked Volodya what she'd said about that, he wasn't sure, either. Sasha's condition remained a mystery. We could go and visit him if we wanted right now, she said. She would come along and direct us to the hospital. First she tended to an elderly parent—hers or Sasha's, I'm not sure—in a little bedroom off the living room. Then she loaded a bag of things to take to Sasha, and she and Volodya and I went downstairs.

As I'd expected, Sergei was not keen on this hospital visit. He asked Tania where the hospital was and seemed unhappy to learn it was clear across Ulan-Ude. He drove us there a bit dourly; this was more entanglement than he'd bargained on. The hospital occupied a narrow ridge with a road running along it and open sky all around. Tania and I went in while Sergei and Volodya parked in a lot and waited. Families and patients, mostly Buryats who looked to be in bad shape, stood at the waiting room entrance and sat in little groups on the bare furniture inside. Some had dried blood and bruises on their faces and staggered around. The waiting room with its low-watt bulb was dim as a cave. On the wall, a phone from fifty years ago seemed to be the only way to reach the hospital's interior. Tania picked it up, talked for a few minutes, then disappeared through a door and up some stairs. After a short while she and Sasha came down.

His face looked longer and thinner and he walked more like an old man. He wore a short-sleeved shirt and dark trousers, just as before, and not hospital garb. I didn't notice any sign of doctoring on his hands. He seemed genuinely glad to see me and he spoke with the same diffident, cheerful demeanor I remembered. I would have enjoyed our meeting more if anxiety had not been distracting me. The fact that he was always kind to me even when I was not quite present due to interior static makes me like him even more in retrospect. I had to explain to him twice why my friends and I couldn't stay for longer than this quick stop. Meanwhile, I was calculating: I could stay that night in Ulan-Ude in a hotel— clearly I couldn't stay in his apartment, with the invalid parent there, and Sasha himself in the hospital—and Sergei and Volodya could camp somewhere outside the city, as Sergei would no doubt want to do, and then tomorrow evening they could come back in and pick me up . . . Nahh, too complicated. Anyway, truth was, I had the same traveling fever that gripped Sergei. I wanted to move on. And maybe the Khamar-khanovs would be relieved, afterward, not to have visitors to worry about just now.

Dropping in on people is always a mistake. I should have tried harder to get in touch with Sasha beforehand.

Still, he was glad to see me, and I him. I told him that I'd been reading about Mikhail Küchelbecker and Barguzin, and that thanks in part to him, Sasha, I'd begun working on a book about Siberia. We moved from the waiting room to the hospital's front steps, a less gloomy place to talk. He asked after Alex and Katya and Vitaly Komar. I inquired about his children; Sasha's daughter, Arjenna, had gone to Moscow to study. Tioshi, his son, was in school in Ulan-Ude. We began to walk to the van. Sergei and Volodya, who were standing in the parking lot and eating ice cream cones, did not immediately come over to greet us as we walked up. I wasn't sure what, if any, social dynamics were going on.

In a minute they did walk up and introduce themselves to Sasha, and a rather distant and disjointed conversation ensued. I had to explain yet again that because of our schedule we needed to keep going and get back on the road before the end of the day. Sasha laughed and shook his head, as if quietly amused by it all. I told him and Tania I'd tried to call them, and showed them the slip of paper with their telephone number; I had a digit wrong. They told me the correct number and I wrote it down, and we did the usual business of exchanging addresses and e-mail. Sergei took a picture of me standing between the Khamarkhanovs. They gave us directions to the road, not nearby, that led east from Ulan-Ude. Tania said she didn't need a ride back to their apartment, because she would stay with Sasha and take the trolleybus home. We said goodbye and I shook Sasha's hand and wished him luck and good health. He wished us safe travels and waved his thin hand. They were walking back to the hospital as we drove off.

Navigating Ulan-Ude's rush-hour confusion, we got lost almost right away. While we were meandering, the van, as if showing its new command of special effects, sprang a leak in the radiator and began to billow forth clouds of steam. But as usual it proved no match for Sergei. In the random tumbledown district into which we had wandered, he immediately found a radiator-repair place. It was really more of a radiator-repair hovel—a small corrugated steel structure filled to and beyond the doors with used radiators. Sergei and Volodya took out our busted one, put in a used one, paid what I am sure was a not-exorbitant price, and received directions to the eastbound highway. A few hours of light were still remaining when we reached the road we wanted and went spinning up the valley of Ulan-Ude's wide and stately river, the Selenga.

Of the 437 rivers that are said to flow into Baikal (only one, the Angara, flows out), the Selenga is the principal stream coming from the south. Its origins are in the steppes of Mongolia. Genghis Khan made his capital, Karakorum, near a Selenga tributary called the Orkhon. The Selenga was the most authentic-looking Siberian river I'd encountered so far. Up to now I'd seen swampy rivers and ones bordered by mountains and trees; the bare hills along the banks of the Selenga and the wide-screen vistas of river and open country spoke of Asian steppes expanding to the southeast. After the busy streets of Ulan-Ude, we seemed to have crossed suddenly into a depopulated region. Again, the fencelessness of the land amazed me. At a place where wheel tracks led through the sparse brown grasses beside the highway we drove down a hillside and stopped beside the Selenga to make that evening's camp.

The fact that the wheel tracks ended at the edge of the river should have tipped us off that this was a ferry crossing. We didn't notice that until the tents had been pitched. Then from the other side of the Selenga arose the sharp rat-a-tat of an unmuffled engine whose sky-filling volume seemed out of proportion to the little craft that was its cause. In another few minutes the sound came nearer as a short, stubby power launch angled across the current with a small fenced raft in tow. On the raft sat a truck of the kind that carries troops, its box back enclosed by an awning. The launch approached and then executed a neat, sharp turn that swung the tow rope and the ferry raft at its end into an unfurling arc that ended with the front of the raft wedged against the shore. Someone undid the raft's gate and the truck drove off onto the bank, and a dozen or so passengers jumped from the raft into the back of the truck. It revved its engine smokily for a few minutes and then motored away.

Meanwhile, a few cars had arrived to go aboard for the return trip. I pointed out to Sergei that this traffic was likely to continue into the night, so maybe moving camp would be a good idea. My chronic fear of being run over while asleep in my tent had begun to flare up. Sergei replied that we had nothing at all to worry about, and not wanting to be difficult, I went along. In fact the traffic did keep coming and going until late, and began again just at dawn, but its orderly rhythms didn't trouble me. I even found them comforting, somehow.

While Volodya was fixing supper, I went a distance down the bank and sat on a camp chair and admired the view. To the north, or downstream, the river spread so far from bank to bank that it seemed more like a landlocked sea. Facing that way I did a sketch of the river and of the ferry launch arriving. In the other direction, upstream, a rock cliff came down to the water and cut off the vista that was beyond. I hiked a bit to get a look around the cliff and discovered only more cliffs and hills, and a narrowed river slipping out of sight among them.

In that direction—south—lay China. Here the Selenga used to be a highway. Travelers bound from Russia for Peking often went by river along this stretch until they came to the Chinese border. (Now it's the border with Mongolia.) A city called Kyakhta grew at the border and flourished on the Russian-Chinese trade before faster routes replaced this one. The naturalist George Steller, while crisscrossing Siberia as part of the Bering expedition in the 1730s and '40s, made a detour to the border to replenish his supply of paper. Past Kyakhta, travelers journeyed in a southeasterly direction for another fifteen hundred miles to Peking. First they had to cross the Gobi Desert, a tough six- or seven-week trek, and then for a couple of months they continued through a thinly settled outlying region before coming to the Great Wall. From the wall it was usually only another week's travel to Peking.

Our route didn't lead south, toward China, but veered away from the Selenga and to the northeast. We spent the next day climbing out of its watershed through hilly country of mixed taiga and steppe. The many hilltop vantage points revealed one view after another, with endless uplands and ridges and low mountains; Sergei kept stopping and getting out to sweep the video camera slowly across the scene. Many trees in this part were dead and gray, I assumed from some infestation or disease. At first I thought the cause might be the pine beetle, as in similar forest die-offs in North America, but I saw many dead birches, too.

Now we were passing fewer cars, people, and villages than at any previous stretch of the trip. I had rarely seen country this unused and empty anywhere. At midday we stopped in a village called Desyatnikovo to buy potatoes. An old woman there told us that this was an Old Believer village, but it was dying. She said that houses with the shutters closed meant that no one lived there now and the people who used to live there had died. She showed us her own house, a brightly painted cabin of trimmed logs on the central street with shuttered houses on either side. The old woman seemed to be in permanent mourning; she told us she was very sad. The somewhat younger guy we bought potatoes from said only old people lived in the village nowadays. There is no work, so young people move away, he said.

We kept climbing, descending, climbing again. One hilltop overlooked a span of the Trans-Siberian Railway on which a train consisting entirely of black oil-tanker cars stretched as far as one could see, west to east; it must've been two miles long. At about three o'clock in the afternoon, Sergei informed me that according to the map we had just crossed the divide between the watershed of central Siberia and the basin of the Amur River. The M-55 highway goes over this divide near the village of Tanga. From that point the road began to descend until it dropped into the broad valley of the Ingoda River—a familiar name. When the Decembrists were imprisoned in Chita, they bathed in the Ingoda.

In late afternoon we found a good place to camp on its banks. The Ingoda is a pleasant, small river with a brisk flow and a bottom of sand and gravel in the parts I saw. Some boys near our campsite who came by to check us out told Sergei you could catch plenty of fish in it using crickets. I set up my fly rod and tied on an all-around attractor fly. Casting into slack water below some riffles I got a lot of splashy strikes, but the fish were too small to fit their mouths around the fly. Finally I hooked a flipping and flopping six-incher. It had delicate yellow markings on its side like little reef fish I'd caught in Florida. I don't know what kind of fish it was.

I showed it to Volodya and he said he'd fry it up for an appetizer before supper. Then I waded back into the river and cast some more. Far downstream, I knew, the Ingoda joined the Onon to make the Shilka, which joined the Argun to make the Amur, which eventually emptied into the Pacific, which extended all the way to Dockweiler State Beach, in Los Angeles, where my sister-in-law brought her children to swim. In theory, from here I could take the all-water route home.

Chapter 20

I was becoming numb to scenery. My stock of landscape adjectives was running low. On the road paralleling the Ingoda, the panoramas just kept coming at us as if they were being brought to the windshield by a conveyor belt somebody had forgotten to turn off. The road was gravel and dusty, the sky blank and bright. From it a hawk flared suddenly right in front of us, its belly feathers white, and then was gone. In every direction the land rolled on—unfenced, untenanted, unvaried, still apparently unused. The idea of "scenery" implies a margin, a frame. What we were seeing had neither, and I couldn't exactly situate it in my mind.

After a hundred miles or so we reached the city of Chita. The name is pronounced with a short *i* and the accent is on the final syllable: Chi-TAH. The sound itself is like a fading cry from far away—"Chi-*tahhhhhh* . . ." Perhaps as a symbol of how remote the city is from anywhere, its central square is huge; it practically has its own horizon. Overseeing the square at about the halfway point, a tall, dark-gray Lenin stands with the tails of his long coat flared to one side as if blown in that direction by the wind, or by the motion of the planet through space. In Chita, as usual, the plentitude of beautiful women overwhelmed and swamped description. I even gave up trying to decide if the number of beauties in Chita was greater than in Krasnoyarsk or Velikii Ustyug or anywhere. There were just a hell of a lot of them, is all. In straight lines that followed no pattern, they crossed the square's vast concrete reaches, their stiltlike heels clicking sharply.

Since Irkutsk, Sergei had decided that the book I was writing was about the Decembrists. That is what he now started telling people. Maybe the Decembrists, as a subject, was easier to explain than if he had said "a book about Siberia." In any event, when the van blew a radiator hose, or something, in Chita, and Sergei flagged down a passing МЧС truck, and his brother МЧС guys led us to a repair place, and they and Sergei and Volodya fell into conversation, Sergei told the МЧС guys that I was writing a book about the Decembrists. The МЧС guys responded to this with enthusiasm and told me I must see Chita's Decembrist museum, the best of its kind in Russia. After whatever was wrong with the van this time had been dealt with, they escorted us there.

Because I was expected to, I went through the museum item by item and evinced interest in everything. I didn't have to fake much. We never would have found the place had the МЧС guys not told us about it; it was in a tall wooden church dating to 1776 that used to be the highest point in the city, though now your standard-issue high-rises ringed it around. It had also escaped the notice of my guidebook. The Decembrist prisoners in Chita had been housed just a short walk from the church and had used it for worship regularly. When state prisoner Ivan Annenkov married Paulina Gueble in this church, he was allowed to have his chains taken off, but only for one hour. Mlle. Gueble, a Frenchwoman, had made the journey to Chita to join her lover after receiving special permission and financial assistance from the tsar; later the couple would have many children, and later still they would provide Alexandre Dumas père with the inspiration for his (or his ghost writer's) romantic novel *The Fencing Master.*

I tried to explain to Sergei and the Chita МЧС guys that my book would not be about the Decembrists only, though the Decembrists would be *in* the book, of course. I got almost nowhere with that, and the failure of communication worsened my already bad mood. All of us— Sergei, Volodya, and I—were out of sorts at the time. We had been on the road for four weeks. Travel weariness had set in. Our dirty-baby smell had worked its way into the seats of the car, into our sleeping bags. Washing in muddy rivers gets you only so clean, and the same goes for clothes. Little things had begun bugging me—for example, discovering while drinking tea in the morning that the cup I was using had recently held Gillette's lemon-lime shaving foam. One of Volodya's molars had started to ache and he was able to continue at times only because of extrastrength aspirin. To make all this worse, I was fretting again about not seeing enough prisons. The worry seems dumb to me now, but somehow it kept enlarging itself in my mind. I could sense the stubbornness of Sergei's resistance to the whole idea and that made me determined to be stubborn right back.

As we were leaving Chita, I got a chance to show how serious I was. We came around a bend, and on the other side of the road directly in front of us I saw a prisonlike accumulation of buildings and guard towers with a fence and barbed wire around it. I asked Sergei to pull over, grabbed my camera, and got out. Then I started taking pictures of the supposed prison, ignoring Sergei's yelling from the van to stop. Perhaps to prove he wasn't kidding, he drove off as if to leave me there, but a short distance down the road he pulled over again. As I approached the structure more closely, I saw warnings to stay away spray-painted on its battered steel gates. The place looked decidedly grimmer the closer to it I came. In another minute or two I jogged back to the van.

Sergei was shouting at me the moment I opened the door. He spoke harshly and yelled and gesticulated like a completely different person, someone I'd never met before. He said that what I had done was very bad and very dangerous and could get us all in trouble. I yelled back at him, but I forget what. Even Volodya, usually mild mannered, added his own accusatory comments and seconded Sergei with disapproving shakes of the head. Sergei kept repeating that I must never do anything like that again. I heard him out angrily but refused to say I would not.

Sergei and I were sort of not speaking to each other for a while after that. Following this incident, I became deeply uncertain of everything around me and briefly considered asking Sergei to drop me off at a train station so I could continue on my own. At the next police checkpoint where we were stopped, the DPS officers detained us longer than usual, and a strange, skinny woman hanging out with them asked if we could give her a ride. Sergei refused her. I wondered what that was about. I wondered about everything. I thought maybe I should take the film with the prison photos out of my camera and throw it away; in the next moment that seemed absurd, and then not absurd the moment after that. At the evening's campsite, in a cow pasture near a village, Volodya silently endured tooth misery while Sergei and I went about our business close-mouthed and shut down.

. . .

This remained our general frame of mind the following afternoon when we reached Chernyshevsk, an important point on our journey. I had been half dreading Chernyshevsk, because beyond it the road became undrivably bad for the next five hundred miles. Due to the swamps and the lack of local population and the difficulty of maintenance, from Chernyshevsk to the town of Magdagachi, a long way to the east, there was in effect no vehicle road. Therefore, all cross-country drivers had to stop in Chernyshevsk (or, if westbound, in Magdagachi) and load their vehicles onto Trans-Siberian car- and truck carriers in order to traverse the roadless stretch by rail.

This situation had created a bottleneck at Chernyshevsk, where traffic backed up like leaves in a storm drain. The place was really just a village beside a large Trans-Siberian Railway train yard, and it offered travelers—who routinely had to wait forty-eight hours before an available transport appeared—almost no lodgings, no bathroom facilities you would want to enter without protective gear, and almost no restaurants. Meanwhile the trucks and cars kept arriving.

We joined the queue of waiting vehicles beside the train station at about two in the afternoon. Asking around, Sergei learned that we would be able to get on a train leaving that night at nine thirty. If I thought I could pleasantly while away the afternoon reading, sketching, and jotting in my notebook, I was mistaken. The misery bubbling up everywhere in Chernyshevsk blotted out any idea of calm. Sitting in the van was difficult because of the heat. The widely strewn trash and garbage guaranteed every person an individual corona of flies. Strange guys in warm-up suits loitered the premises at large and hit on any stranger they saw. Even Sergei and Volodya, when they strolled from the van, had to dodge them. The couple of times I ventured among them I was like a crouton in a goldfish pond. The public bathrooms had overflowed some long time before, so most people who needed them employed instead whatever out-of-the-way or not-so-out-of-the-way corner of Chernyshevsk they could find. The train station itself was devoid of services or information of any sort. Apparently all departure and arrival announcements were relayed solely by word of mouth.

Every fifteen minutes or so, a gang of begging children descended upon the vehicle queue. They rapped on the van's windows and pleaded and cajoled. One of them was a girl with a scar on her face, close-cropped auburn hair, and surprisingly fashionable hoop earrings. The first time they came, Sergei assembled them around him and gave them a short lecture about the shame of begging compared to the honorability of work. Sergei offered them, instead of a handout, a decent amount of rubles if they would wash our car. The kids loved this idea and went immediately and found a whole slew of cut-off bottle bottoms and other vessels among the ambient trash and filled them at a public tap. Then they washed the car, every inch. In our stuff, Sergei found some rags for them to use for polishing. They polished like demons, climbing all over the van. When they had finished, Sergei examined the work, paid them, and complimented them highly on their job. They ran off, and in fifteen minutes were back begging again.

Late in the afternoon, a train hauling vehicle transports arrived from the east. The transports carried used Japanese cars, most of them Toyotas, with their front ends covered in masking tape, like bandaged noses, to protect them from flying gravel on the road. So far I have not described this important aspect of Siberian trade: throughout the year, but especially in the summer, guys ride the Trans-Siberian to Vladivostok, buy used Japanese cars there, and drive the cars west across Siberia for resale. Cargo ships full of these vehicles arrive in Vladivostok all the time. A used car bought in Vladivostok for $2,000 can be resold farther west in Russia for three times that much. The entrepreneurs who drive this long-distance shuttle tend to wear muscle shirts, shiny Adidas sweatpants, and running shoes, and their short, pale haircuts stand up straight in a bristly Russian way. On the road they are easy to recognize by the tape on their vehicles and the fact that they speed like madmen. The faster they finish each round-trip, the more trips they can do and the more money they can make.

One of the drivers debarking in Chernyshevsk told Sergei that this load of cars and drivers had had to wait five days in Magdagachi for transports, and then spent forty-eight hours on the train. In Chernyshevsk, the unloading had to be done one car at a time. Some of the drivers, when they finally did emerge with their vehicles onto the cracked pavement of the Chernyshevsk parking lot, shifted into neutral and raced their engines in automotive howls of liberation or rage. The appearance of each vehicle caused the crowd of begging children to swarm around it. Some drivers honked and yelled at the kids to go away, others rolled their windows partway down and held out little pieces of leftover food. I saw the girl with the hoop earrings trot to a window and snatch the back end of a kielbasa that a driver offered her. At a more aloof distance, but just as attentively, the loitering guys also gathered around.

As the unloading was going on, I thought I'd take advantage of the moment's distraction to attempt another exploratory stroll of Chernyshevsk. When I walked onto the main street, the latest driver to zoom his vehicle from the parking lot spotted me and pulled over alongside. Hopping out and locking his car, he said, "You are an American, right? I love Americans. America is the best. I'm going to get something to eat. Come and eat with me. We'll drink vodka and get drunk." The guy was big, large bellied, bristly haired, and his T-shirt said, in English, KALASH-NIKOV: THE GREATEST HITS. Above the words was a picture of a Kalashnikov rifle, and below them a list of the "Greatest Hits," i.e., wars in which Kalashnikovs have been used. I thought I should accept the guy's invitation, in the interest of writerly curiosity, but somehow I couldn't bring myself to. I pretended I didn't understand and wandered away.

In a little memorial grove of pines growing from the scuffed, hard-packed earth beside the station platform, I came upon the village of Chernyshevsk's main—indeed, only—point of interest. Here a tall statue of Nikolai Chernyshevsky, the nineteenth-century writer after whom the village was named, stared broodingly across the train yard. Made of pewter-colored metal and standing perhaps ten feet high, the statue embodied the most heroic of socialist realist styles. Straight Prince Valiant–like hair just past the collar framed the writer's determined chin, noble nose, and deep-set eyes. He wore a long coat, unbuttoned, over a waistcoat and cravat; his left hand, curled like the hand of a discus thrower in classical Greek statuary, held not a discus but a thick sheaf of manuscript pages. By his aspect one could imagine him waiting forcefully here for a train to take him to the offices of his publisher, where his recently completed oeuvre would be turned in. Adding to the realism was the fact that none among the station's passersby, even its pigeons, seemed to pay him any mind.

From what I knew about Chernyshevsky I would hardly have pictured him as such a handsome or dynamic-looking guy. He lived from 1828 to 1889, and in 1862 and '63 he wrote the utopian socialist novel

Shto Delat'? (*What Is to Be Done?*). Next to the Bible, *Shto Delat'?* was the most widely read book in Russia in the 1870s. Later it would be the favorite novel of both Lenin and Stalin. Its author, the son of an Orthodox priest in the Volga River city of Saratov, wrote it during four months when he was imprisoned in the Sts. Peter and Paul Fortress in St. Petersburg. A mix-up within the censorship bureaucracy allowed it to slip through, and it was published in three installments in *Sovremennik* (The Contemporary), a St. Petersburg journal. It had already come out as a book by the time the authorities discovered their mistake and banned it.

Shto Delat'? is about liberated women who defy social expectations by living unconventional lives, and who put their politicoeconomic theories into practice by establishing a sewing collective. The novel also has male heroes who are revolutionaries and who interact with these women. One of the male heroes, Rakhmetov, became the basic ideal that every male revolutionary in Russia aspired to be. Here is some sample dialogue:

> "You haven't heard?" he said aloud. "There's an experiment at putting into practice those principles recently developed by economic science. Do you know about them?"
>
> "Yes, I've read something. That must be very interesting and valuable. Can I really take part in it? Where can I find it?"

Scholars say that after Marx and Engels, Chernyshevsky was the writer who had the most influence on the generation that made the Russian Revolution. Many revolutionaries of the late nineteenth century knew the book practically by heart; some even tried to set up collective commercial enterprises like the one in the novel. Lenin said hundreds of people became revolutionaries as a result of reading *Shto Delat'?* After Lenin's brother Alexander was executed, Lenin reread the book because it had been among Alexander's favorites. "[Chernyshevsky] plowed me up more profoundly than anyone else," Lenin said later. "I sat over [*Shto Delat'?*] not for several days but for several weeks. Only then did I understand its depth . . . It's a thing that supplies energy for a whole lifetime."

Almost unanimously, world literary opinion has disagreed with Lenin's rave review. Though Chernyshevsky admired Tolstoy, Tolstoy did not like him and rejected his principles. Turgenev and Herzen, both early acquaintances of Chernyshevsky, came to find his writing coarse and simpleminded. In the twentieth century, the philosopher and critic Isaiah Berlin, while acknowledging the "literally epoch-making effect" of *Shto Delat'?* pronounced it "grotesque as a work of art."

After being convicted of subversion in 1864, Chernyshevsky was sentenced to seven years of hard labor in Siberia, to be followed by permanent exile. The punishment only enhanced his revolutionary mystique. As the popularity of his book grew with young radicals, a few of the more daring among them set themselves the task of finding its imprisoned author and spiriting him to freedom. In 1875, a student named Hypolite Myshkin almost succeeded in this attempt by impersonating a gendarme sent to convey Chernyshevsky to another prison. Another would-be rescuer was Boleslav Shostakovich, grandfather of the composer. Because of Chernyshevsky's popularity as a rescue target, the prison authorities moved him from one prison mine to another, and when the time came to exile him, they shipped him to the far north, to the town of Viliusk in Yakutsk province, where he was permitted to move about as long as he stayed within five hundred yards of the stockade.

Prison life had broken Chernyshevsky thoroughly by then. Scurvy, malaria, stomach ulcers, and rheumatism afflicted him. In Siberia he wrote almost nothing of note; even his letters descended into repetition and confusion. His wife visited him only once, for four days, while he was exiled. In accordance with his principles he had wanted her to have complete freedom, and she willingly took him up on the idea. In 1883, his sons succeeded in persuading the government to grant him amnesty, and he was then allowed to return to western Russia. In 1889, gravely ill, he received permission to go back to Saratov, where he died the same year.

Shto Delat'? had been partly a response to Turgenev's *Fathers and Sons*; in turn, other important books of the time, particularly Dostoyevsky's *Notes from the Underground*, were written in reply to *Shto Delat'?* Chernyshevsky's theories of aesthetics, laid out in two widely read essays, would provide the basis for the Soviet style of writing, painting, sculpture, and cinema that was formally labeled socialist realism during Stalin's time. Certainly Chernyshevsky played an enormous part in the intellectual turmoil of his era and after. But having read *Shto*

Delat'? I can only say that the title is excellent, but the book goes down-hill from there. One of Chernyshevsky's biographers, trying to give him a fair hearing, nevertheless has to conclude, "He had some grasp on many things, but ultimately, Chernyshevsky's thought was fudge." Cher-nyshevsky's life illustrates the unfortunate fact that a writer can hope and strive and suffer, and in the end even give his life, for work that turns out to be not good.

Beyond the statue, the platform's broken asphalt stretched on and on, like those train platforms in movies that people run along while wav-ing goodbye. A few tracks to the side, a line of olive-colored train cars with bars on their doors and windows sat as if waiting to be taken some-where. In one of the windows, a man wearing a sleeveless undershirt took a drag on a cigarette and looked at me and blew a plume of smoke through the bars. At the platform's end I left the station and turned onto the main street of the town. When I came to the town's last house, I cut across an empty field and hiked into the low brown hills that enclosed Chernyshevsk from that angle. Nobody bothered me, and I was much less troubled by flies. Just being able to sit and think without low-grade harassment was a relief. I had brought along my sketchbook and I did a drawing or two. But the worry that the train would suddenly begin load-ing, and Sergei and Volodya not be able to find me, got me moving again. I walked along the side of the hill until I was close enough to the town center that I could see the vehicle queue. The van was still there, in the same place as before.

I sat down and began another sketch, but in this new spot I stood out more conspicuously, and the begging kids saw me and came bounding up the hill. Closely encircling me, they asked what I was doing. I showed them my drawing, and one of the older boys examined it, looked at the actual scene before us, then back at the drawing. *"Pohozhe,"* he said, meaning "It looks like it." Then he and all the others stuck out their hands and demanded, *"Dai mne ruble!"*

I asked them first to sing me a song, and they sped through a ditty about somebody named Yanni who gets *p'yanyi* (drunk). Then out came their hands again: *"Dai mne ruble!"* Inches from my face, each little hand was grimy as a curbstone. I took all the change I had in my pocket and parceled it out, ruble by ruble. At the end one little boy, smaller than the others, did not get a coin. I had to tell him that was all, I had no more. An

expression of wrenching, almost grown-up disappointment contorted his kid's face and he began to weep with large tears and wails of heart-felt misery.

Once the kids had discovered me, they kept coming back and swarming, so I had to return to the van. By then it was almost nine thirty in the evening; Sergei said he thought our train would be loading soon. But at about ten thirty, the stationmaster, a blocky woman with dyed red hair, a dalmatian-spotted blouse, and an orange workman's vest, appeared among the vehicles and told us all that there would be no train tonight. Nor would there necessarily be one tomorrow, she added with keen enjoyment disguised as nonchalance. The quiet way she savored giving out this disappointing news was a wonder to see. Maybe a train would come along tomorrow night, she speculated; but then again, maybe it would not.

As we considered the prospect of spending the night in Chernyshevsk in the van, Sergei again showed his mastery of difficult situations. By distributing a small amount of cash to the drivers immediately in front of and behind us, he held our place for tomorrow. Then he backed out of the queue, sped away from Chernyshevsk, and found us a place to camp beside a quiet and clear and relatively untrashed stream a few miles outside town. I was so grateful for this smart move that I put aside any beef I had against Sergei. We set up the tents, ate supper by lantern light, and turned in for a good sleep. In the morning I took out my fly rod and caught a couple of little fish in the stream. Volodya made breakfast, then drove to Chernyshevsk to monitor what was going on. He returned in haste, saying the train was about to leave and we must get back there begom—"at a run."

The train was not about to leave, as it turned out. To my surprise, though, it had arrived. We spent another afternoon in the vehicle queue waiting to load. I had understood that we would be going on a vehicle transport, the usual open-air affair, where we would just sort of hang out like train-hopping hoboes until we reached Magdagachi. But Sergei had something better in mind. There was a guy he had heard about who had his own train car. The guy, a short, dark-haired, bushy-eyebrowed, villainous-looking party, appeared at the loading ramp surrounded by a small entourage. Yes, he did have his own *vagon*—a long, windowless boxcar with room inside for four ordinary-sized vehicles. This *vagon* represented the high end of Chernyshevsk vehicle transports. Sergei negotiated to ensure that our van would be one of the lucky four, and the guy agreed, for $200.

For some reason I have never figured out, the $200, which Sergei hurriedly paid so as not to lose the place, seriously upset his economy. After concluding the negotiations, Sergei came to me and cried, *"Ty mne dolzhen dvesti dollarov!"* (You owe me two hundred dollars!). When I couldn't understand why this was, he just kept repeating that I owed him $200. Finally I told him to calm himself and handed him ten twenties.

Then our van was locked in the guy's *vagon* for a few hours while the train made up its mind about leaving, and we had to fend for ourselves in the Chernyshevsk train station with no vehicle to retreat to. I just kept moving, strolling and taking evasive action so as not to be swarmed on. Finally we were let into the *vagon* and it somehow got hooked up to the train; and later, hours later, sprawled in the van, I felt the first few blessed inchings of forward motion. When a conveyance you are riding in fails to move and fails to move, and you hope and pray and apply all your mental powers in an attempt to get it rolling, and it finally *does* move, that's one of life's sweetest feelings. When the train at last left the yards after all that time in Chernyshevsk, I relaxed as if the sedative had finally reached my veins.

Just before we started moving, I happened to look over at Sergei and he was pale and sweating. "I am sick," he announced. "I have a high fever. I am sick, and I cannot be sick." With that he took out his sleeping bag and, standing on the rear bumper, unrolled it on the roof of the van. Then he climbed up, got into his sleeping bag, and lay there in the three-foot space between the van's roof and the ceiling of the *vagon*. From time to time he shivered so violently that I could feel the shakes in the front seat below him.

The *vagon*'s luxuries did not include interior lighting. Small planes of daylight came through narrow slots at the top of what might once have been windows; otherwise the space was completely sealed. Once darkness had fallen, everything in the *vagon* grew dim, except at the front end, where a glow came from an open door. Inside the door, the guy who owned the *vagon*—its *khozyain*, as he repeatedly instructed me to call him—occupied a sort of stateroom.

Past his room was a small between-cars passageway with doors on either side that opened at the top so you could look out. This place was great for fresh air, an antidote to the claustrophobia of the *vagon*. The *khozyain* kept his stateroom door open, and as I went by he would hail me, "Hey, comrade writer!" Sometimes we had short conversations. Generally he was drinking vodka from a large bottle while lying on a bed that fit into the stateroom's corner. Beside him lay a blond woman so large and rumpled she seemed to be part bed herself. A TV sat on a shelf opposite them, playing a Russian movie, and they were passing back and forth a sunflower blossom the size of a party pizza, pulling seeds from the blossom's center and chewing them and spitting the shells into cups.

Very late at night as I sidled past, the *khozyain* appeared in the doorway, maintenance-level drunk and in a confidential mood. "Comrade writer," he stopped me, "you are writing a book about the Decembrists, right?" (At some point Sergei must have passed along this news.) I began my explanation about how the book would not be about the Decembrists only, but he cut me off. "I know many things about the Decembrists, comrade writer," the *khozyain* disclosed in a gravelly voice, pointing his finger at his own chest. "I know many secrets about the Decembrists which other people do not know." He beckoned me until I was leaning close to him in the half-light. "I know . . ." he said, "I know where is the grave of Mikhail Lunin. I—I—can take you to his grave."

In every trip there is a hump that must be gotten over, a central knot to be worked through. For us that knot pulled tight in the Chernyshevsk–Magdagachi part of our journey. Through these days we took things minute by minute and sort of struggled along. First came the delay and vexation of Chernyshevsk, then Sergei's sickness, then the twilit strangeness of the sealed car as the train progressed so slowly it seemed it might fail entirely and start slipping backward to Chernyshevsk. Sergei lay on the van roof with his teeth chattering. Whenever Volodya or I offered to get him something, he replied that he was doing all right. Volodya's molar pain had let up a bit; he drank shots of vodka with the *khozyain* and one or two of the passengers and afterward dozed in the back of the van.

Being sealed in the *vagon* soon got to me. I mean, here were four vehicles parked inches apart in a closed space, maybe twenty gallons of gas in each vehicle, and there were no windows, no fire extinguishers on the walls, no Exit signs, the *vagon*'s back doors secured tightly from the outside . . . Safety is never the Russians' primary concern. Meanwhile the guy in charge of the *vagon* is drunk and watching TV. Of course I understood there was no point in mentioning any of this to anybody.

Besides our van, the *vagon* carried two Japanese-made SUVs driven by families on their way back to their home cities in the Sakha Republic, in northeastern Siberia, after their summer vacations. One family consisted of a hard-drinking dentist and his fourteen-year-old daughter, Kira. The other family was a mother and father, a young son, and a fourteen-year-old daughter named Olya. The two girls lived far apart and had never met before. They hung out together in the passageway and talked, and when they found out I was from America they had a lot of questions for me, mostly about Jewel (the singer), Sylvester Stallone, and the Hard Rock Cafe. Both girls said that Yakutsk, the capital of the Sakha Republic, was a really boring place. Olya gave me a piece of paper with her address and wrote "Write to me!" all over it; naturally I lost it soon after. At one point I was sitting in the van and I took a nervous look behind us—making sure no wisps of smoke were rising, signs of coming inferno—and Olya happened to sit up in the front seat of her car where she'd been napping, and she smiled at me so beautifully that all my malaise lifted for a while.

The guy in the fourth car, a Russian vehicle right in front of the van, was a scuba diver. He said he worked on oil platforms and also gathered shellfish off the coast of Sakhalin Island, to which he was returning. He was wiry haired and ruddy and he wore a vest of black leather. With other people and by himself, he drank vodka night and day. Our first morning in the *vagon*, after I'd slept pretty well on the front seat of the van complicatedly propped between the door and the steering wheel, I sat up and rubbed my eyes. The scuba diver woke at the exact same moment and got out of his vehicle rubbing his eyes. He saw me, broke into a huge grin, and made the do-you-want-a-shot-of-vodka? gesture, tapping his throat below the jaw with a flip of his fingers. From his car he pulled a half-full bottle of vodka to show me. I shook my head politely; it was about eight in the morning.

Quietly, I slid from the van and went to the passageway for a look outside. The sun had risen on a cool, clear day in early fall. Our train was making a steady twenty miles per hour through taiga mixed with hayfields. During the night a heavy frost had covered the countryside. It rimed the leaves of the birch trees, some of which had already turned yellow, and made the needles and knobby branches of a tree I took to be a larch a soft white. At this speed I could see the trackside weeds curved like shepherds' crooks by the spiderwebs attached to them, the frost on the web strands glistening in the sun. When the tracks went around a bend, the rest of the train was revealed extending far ahead. Our *vagon* was the second-to-last car. A broad hayfield we passed had just been cut. The short stubble, all frost-white, lay like carpet among the haystacks spaced regularly across it. In the cool morning air, the top of every haystack was steaming, and each wisp of steam leaned eastward, the direction we were going.

All day the train moseyed on. During stretches where the track was really bad, it slowed to walking speed. It stopped, it started, it waited on sidings, started again, stopped. In our *vagon*, a temporary lobotomy seemed to have leveled everybody. Sometimes as the train sat awhile at a station I got out and walked around, never wandering too far, from fear of being left. Every station I observed was dark, cracked, in the process of being colonized by weeds, and with the lights of its platform broken.

People thronged the stations nonetheless—old ladies selling *pirozhki* (pies of cabbage or meat or mushroom), skinny guys with big bottles of foamy, off-color beer, girls displaying boxes made of birch and carved wooden shoes on pieces of carpet, vodka sellers with their bottles lined up in rows on folding card tables. Here and there, black electrical wires drooped above the assembly. The *khozyain* and the scuba diver, hopping down for quick vodka runs, were the only ones in our car who got off besides me. Volodya dozed in the van, and Sergei stayed in his sleeping bag on the roof hour after hour. At least he had stopped shivering.

The day went by, and again the twilight in the *vagon* dimmed to almost darkness. I ate an energy bar I'd brought along and experimented with new sleeping positions in the front seat. If I hit upon a workable one, I could get an hour or so of napping time, provided the train kept up its regular motion. When it stopped I grew restless and thrashed around.

During a long stop in the middle of the night, I emerged into consciousness with a sense of something being different now. I got up, opened the van door, walked to the passageway. As I stepped out onto it, my awareness of space expanded enormously: our *vagon* was sitting by itself in a vast, irregularly lighted train yard. This must be Magdagachi. In half a minute the *khozyain* joined me, looking a bit rusty from the entertainments of his journey, and confirmed that we had arrived. Suddenly a beam of light swung down on us, backed up by a resounding diesel noise. Behind the light I could just make out, by shading my eyes, a train engine's massive form. Out of the brightness, stepping onto the coupling at the engine's front, the engineer appeared.

Without preamble the engineer began to yell an abusive stream of complaint or instruction at the *khozyain*, who yelled even more heatedly at him. Amounts of rubles were shouted back and forth. Then the *khozyain* went into his stateroom and reemerged, cursing, with a wad of bills. He handed it to the engineer, who counted it in the engine's headlight, then put it in his bib. I was told to get out of the way. The engine was then maneuvered around and the *vagon* coupled to it. In another minute we had been pulled up to the unloading ramp. All the drivers in the *vagon* woke up, the sealed-shut back doors opened, and the vehicles rolled down the ramp into the Magdagachi night.

Chapter 21

At the wheel of the van sat Sergei, a bit puffy in the face but feeling fine after his thirty-one hours on the roof. He told us that he had recovered completely. "I could not be sick," he said. "I gave my body the message that I could not allow it to be sick, and it understood. I am better now."

It was one thirty in the morning when we emerged from the *vagon*. We knew nothing about Magdagachi except its name. The hard-drinking dentist, father of fourteen-year-old Kira, told Sergei that he could lead us to a fuel station that he thought would be open, so we followed him there. He also said that he knew how to find the road out of Magdagachi, but after he had fueled up he drove off without waiting for us, and when we tried to make our way by the directions the fuel-station man had given us, we soon were meandering on roads and nonroads in Magdagachi. Finally we got so turned around we were driving on gravelly nothing zones between unlit buildings, and Sergei pulled over in a weed lot where we spent another few uncomfortable hours attempting to sleep in the van.

A little after dawn, we awoke and set out again, and with more people available at that hour to ask for directions, we did find the road. Driving in our dusty, exhaust-fume, no-shock-absorbers van seemed like carefree travel after the gloomy limbo of the *vagon*. A leisurely two hundred miles or so farther on we stopped in the early afternoon and camped on the banks of the Zeya River outside the city of Svobodnyi (Free). I had not used my satellite phone since before Chernyshevsk, and I took it out and got a strong connection.

The phone had a feature providing free text messages up to 160 characters long that you could bring up on a display screen as soon as you made your connection. Every day my friend Bill in North Bergen, New Jersey, would e-mail me (via the satellite phone website) the punch line to a joke. Not the whole joke—just the punch line. Things like "And the kangaroo said, 'So's mine!'" or "Hell, find my car keys and we'll *drive* out!" A half dozen punch lines had accumulated since I'd last looked. I read them over as the call went through to my family. After I was done talking to them, I gave the phone to Sergei and Volodya and they each called home, too. Neither had spoken to his family for a while and of course on the riverbank there were no public phones around.

From the Zeya we took a detour off the main road in order to see the Amur River and the city of Blagoveshchensk. *Blagoveshchenie* means "annunciation," and the name is not too lofty for the city, which I thought the handsomest we'd been through since St. Petersburg. Blagoveshchensk is fortunate for two reasons—its light, and China. Something about the Pacific Ocean, maybe, gives a reddish-gold tint to light that spreads up the river and this far inland. The benign and hopeful sunniness of Blagoveshchensk reminded me somehow of Palo Alto, California. Blagoveshchensk and other Amur River cities could be the Golden East, as California was the Golden West. Or maybe this notion was just my homesick imagination. Still, the sun and blue sky and reddish-gold light as we drove around Blagoveshchensk struck me as imported, not quite Russian.

Second, China: the Chinese industrial city of Heihe is just across the Amur. Our radio had begun picking up Chinese radio stations. On the other side of the pale-brown, slow-moving, dauntingly wide Amur, the tops of the tallest buildings of Heihe could be seen. Like other Amur River cities, Heihe and Blagoveshchensk participate in an agreement that locally suspends certain visa and customs regulations for the purposes of encouraging trade. I saw several big buildings under construction in Blagoveshchensk, a rarity in these remote areas, and Chinese laborers working on them. The hard hats the workmen wore were made of wicker. A lot of the smaller structures in the city were new. Some had pagoda-style roofs. No thickets of *morkovnik* or other weeds grew along the streets, and the usually omnipresent trash, in heaps or promiscuously strewn, seemed to be gone.

Sergei and Volodya were talking about finding a place in Blagoveshchensk to buy a pistol. Kolya, the scuba diver, had told them that someone had pulled a pistol on him a couple of weeks ago when he was in a store in Irkutsk oblast. For protection we already had Volodya's shotgun, but maybe we needed a concealable gun to carry around, Sergei said. I said I didn't think we needed to carry a pistol. Sergei said we probably would only buy an air pistol, just to frighten people with if necessary. I said he knew best, but I didn't think we should buy one. He said he and Volodya would look for one that afternoon.

Again I made my first stop at the regional museum. Blagoveshchensk's was full of Chinese tourists trailing behind Chinese-speaking Russian guides. These were young women, and when one tour group passed another, the guides exchanged glances and rolled their eyes. Unlike any other museum I'd seen so far, the Blagoveshchensk museum had a display about the region's gulag camps. It said there had been several around Magdagachi, where prisoners had worked in cobalt and iron mines. A short biography of an Orthodox priest and pioneering mathematician named Pavel Florensky said he had died in 1937 after being imprisoned in a camp at Skovorodino. That was one of the stations where I had gotten out and walked around on the Chernyshevsk–Magdagachi run.

As I idled along, Sergei interrupted me, very stern in the face. We had to leave immediately, he said. Volodya's tooth had suddenly become so bad that he must take care of it right now. I had thought that I would stay with the van, as Volodya had been doing, while he and Sergei went in search of a dentist. But Volodya hurried off on his own, Sergei stayed at the van, and I wandered Blagoveshchensk's immense riverfront public square. From a distance I noticed a big memorial marker on the wall of a fancy redbrick building with arches and turrets near the shore of the Amur. The marker turned out to be a bas-relief bust of Chekhov wearing spectacles and holding a finger to his cheek as if in thought. Its inscription said, HERE ON THE 27TH OF JUNE, 1890, A.P. CHEKHOV STAYED. The building, formerly a hotel, now housed geology and hydrology offices of the Russian Academy of Sciences. Empty spaces nearby seemed to indicate that buildings contemporary with this one had been torn down. The great writer's single-night visit had evidently inoculated it against destruction.

By the time I came back, Volodya was sitting in the van's front seat drinking a large can of malt liquor. He had found the name of a dentist by asking at a hotel, gone to that dentist, presented his passport, sat down in the chair. The dentist yanked the tooth and charged him 135 rubles, about $4.50. The extraction had cheered him up wonderfully. He opened another can of malt liquor and talked about the dental history of his family. As we drove out of Blagoveshchensk in its California evening light, Volodya said he didn't mind losing teeth and was surprised to have so many of his own still remaining. His father and uncles had lost all their teeth long before they were Volodya's age. He said losing teeth just ran in the family.

The tooth incident diverted the guys' attention from buying a pistol. When I mentioned it to Sergei, he said that after thinking about it he had decided we didn't need a pistol after all. I was relieved to hear this. We settled back for a few hours of driving in what remained of the day, but the road we were on—a major road, and in fact the only one here that continued cross-country, a road marked in red on the map—suddenly came to an end. It reached the Bureya River and just quit. Reexamining the map, I noticed that the red of the highway did become a dotted line for a very short span at this spot. There was no bridge, no nothing. I had never known a major road to do that before. After a bit of searching, however, we found a ferry landing, albeit sans ferry. The ferryman had apparently taken the ferry to the other side of the Bureya, and no one among the two dozen waiting cars knew when he might return. Sergei backtracked up the road to look for a camping spot, figuring we'd just wait till morning. All we could find were small openings in the thick woods where the weeds grew six feet high. Finally we plunged the van into an out-of-the-way opening, tramped down some weeds beside it, and pitched our tents.

At the ferry landing the next morning there were only a few cars, but still no ferry. Soon more cars and several trucks showed up. Always sociable, Sergei and Volodya circulated among the other drivers and made conversation, but they could learn nothing definite about when the ferry might come. I preferred to sit by the van and let the waiting bother me. Volodya noticed my mood and said, "Call your wife." That was always his solution when he saw me in the dumps. I took out my phone and called, a bit self-conscious because of the three or four waiting people nearby who came closer and stared at me. When my wife answered she was making dinner. I complained to her about having to wait for the ferry.

Finally it came, loaded a few cars and our van with great slowness, and slowly took us to the other side. A lot of other vehicles were waiting there for the return trip. I could not understand why this one river should be without a bridge; clearly, some of the people in the queue would be there all day. But we seemed to have entered a forgotten zone. As we continued on this alleged cross-country highway, it quit trying altogether and became little more than a swamp lane. On its rare paved stretches you couldn't get too comfortable, because in another moment you'd have to slow down and negotiate mud holes in lowest gear.

Half a day of this brought us to the border of Birobidzhan, the Jewish Autonomous Oblast. Under Stalin in the 1920s and '30s, the idea of setting aside this region in the drainage of the Bira and the Bidzhan rivers for a Jewish homeland attracted support among Jews in the Soviet Union, America, and elsewhere. Here sparsely occupied land extending for two hundred miles along the Trans-Siberian Railway offered the advantages of plenty of room and no unwelcoming nationalities who needed to be removed. On the other hand, Birobidzhan is a swamp in the middle of nowhere. Although tens of thousands of Jews, including groups from America, did move here, almost all of them left within a few years. Today, Birobidzhan's Jewish population is about 2 percent.

In Birobidzhan's only city, also called Birobidzhan, we stopped to buy supplies. The place looked run-down and disheartened; a single figure on a bicycle teetered across a deserted square, and in the cement-gray storefronts I saw one Yiddish sign.

That evening we camped at an intersection of off-road tracks in an expanse of agricultural fields. Near where we pitched our tents, a field of squash had begun to bloom, their cream-yellow flowers abundant on the ground. At this campsite, the mosquitoes were the worst of anywhere on our journey except for the second night at Berezovyi Yar. We had to put on our beekeeper hats again, and gloves. Because it's impossible to eat while wearing a beekeeper hat, we removed the hats for supper and could finish it only while pacing and dodging around. Though we zipped up the tents tight for sleeping, the mosquitoes squeezed through tiny openings, no doubt forced by the pressure of the infinite mosquitoes behind them. Several times I woke up to smash mosquitoes on the inside of the tent by flashlight. They left bloody smears. The dish of eggs, potatoes, onions, and peppers Volodya made for breakfast in the morning had mosquito bodies sprinkled through it like coriander, and the harvesters in the potato field we drove through on our way out were bundled in thick, dark clothes despite the heat.

About an hour down the road was a place I really wanted to see—Volochaevka, site of the last battle of the Russian Civil War on February 12, 1922. By 1922, Bolshevik forces had secured all of Russian territory except out here, where a White Army resurgence had recently recaptured strategic points including the city of Khabarovsk. The victorious Whites, led by General Viktorin Molchanov, continued west along the Trans-Siberian until they reached Volochaevka, where they were crushed by forces of the People's Revolutionary Army under the command of General Vasily K. Blyukher. The Soviets never again faced a serious internal military challenge to their power. Older Russians still remember the popular song inspired by the victory, "*Volochaevskie Dni*" (Volochaevsky Days).

The Battle of Volochaevka converged on a hill that rises above a small village of the same name. As a battle site, Volochaevka is picturesque, iconic—the partly forested hill topped by a silver marker dominates a broad and level landscape of fields and tree lots, with the tracks of the Trans-Siberian curving along the hill's base. Soviet-era remembrance has terraced one side of the hill with steps of white cement, amphitheater-style. Leaving Volodya and the van in the parking lot, Sergei and I climbed the steps, which were crumbling and had weeds growing in their cracks. The hilltop memorial, fenced in by iron palings bearing Soviet emblems, had suffered similar neglect; its cement and stone were slowly going back to dust and pebbles. On the base of the statue—a silver soldier holding a silver rifle upraised—was inscribed, "Here lie the bodies of a hundred and eighteen fighters for the victory of the Soviets in the Far East, brave men fallen in the struggle with the White Guards and the Interventionists during the assault on the fortifications at Volochaevka on February 12, 1922. Eternal glory to the heroes!"

Near this monument stood a pedestal with a bust of the victorious general, V. K. Blyukher. To one side, a small biographical display on some all-weather material described selected events in the general's life. As Sergei looked at the Blyukher part of the memorial he became increasingly sad. His aunt's husband, his uncle Nikolai, had been Blyukher's driver in the 1930s, he said. The family had admired Blyukher and thought he was a great man. "It was terrible what happened to Blyukher, terrible," Sergei said, shaking his head. A historical darkness that I recognized came over him and he did not want to talk about Blyukher anymore.

At the time of this battle, Blyukher was thirty-one years old. His youth, competence, toughness, and Civil War successes brought him a hero's status in the early years of the Soviet Union. G. K. Zhukhov, the most famous Soviet general, said in his memoirs that when Blyukher came to Zhukhov's cavalry regiment on an inspection in 1924, even the cooks were delighted to shake his hand. Blyukher quickly rose through the army's ranks until he reached the top one, marshal, of which there were only four.

When Stalin's purges began in the mid-1930s, Blyukher remained untouchable for a while. The Japanese in Manchuria were making sorties across the Amur, and Blyukher, commander of all Far Eastern forces, could not be spared. But then in 1938 these hostilities eased and Blyukher received a summons to come to Moscow. Accused of being a Japanese spy, he was interrogated for days without interruption and beaten until he was "unrecognizable." He died in prison without signing any confession in November 1938.

The only other visitors at the monument, an older couple from Khabarovsk, told Sergei that there were White soldiers buried here, too. After the battle, the dead from both sides were put in a common grave. The memorial made no mention of the enemy dead, or of Blyukher's opposing commander, Viktorin Molchanov. After Molchanov's defeat here, he withdrew into China, then sought asylum in the United States, and eventually wound up with other White Russian refugees in Petaluma, California, where he became a chicken farmer. Molchanov died in San Francisco in 1974, just shy of his eighty-eighth birthday.

Blyukher's wife, Glafira, who was arrested when he was, spent seven months in Lubyanka, the NKVD headquarters in Moscow, and then eight years in prison camps. Evidently Glafira survived to see the post-

Stalin rehabilitation of her husband. An inscription at the Blyukher memorial noted that it had been given by his wife, children, and grandchildren.

All the way across Siberia I had certain books at the back of my mind. In western Siberia the main book I took my bearings from was of course George Kennan's, and it stayed with me, along with Avvakum and Yakushkin's memoirs and some others, until well past Baikal. Now, though, I was farther east than any of those eastbound travelers had gone, and a new book took over as my mental accompaniment—or, rather, a book combined with a movie. For this part of farthest Siberia, the book was *Dersu Uzala*, by Vladimir K. Arsenyev. Though the English-language edition I had read was published as part of the Soviet Literature for Young People series, *Dersu Uzala* is neither ideology nor a book only for teenagers; it's a timeless wilderness adventure story, and a classic Russian expression of a genre that goes back to James Fenimore Cooper (whom Arsenyev himself mentions as an influence).

Told in the first person, *Dersu Uzala* begins in 1902, when Arsenyev is a young army officer assigned the job of exploring and mapping the almost-unknown regions east and northeast of Vladivostok, including Lake Khanka and the upper watershed of the Ussuri River. The name for the whole area is the Primorskii Krai—the By-the-Sea region. It and much of the Khabarovskii Krai, just to the north of it, consist of a unique kind of Pacific forest in which tall hardwoods hung with vines grow beside conifers almost equally high, and where the lushness of the foliage, especially along the watercourses, often becomes quite jungly. In Arsenyev's time, this jungle-taiga was full of wildlife, with species ranging from the flying squirrel and the wild boar to the Siberian tiger. Back then tigers could be seen even on the outskirts of Vladivostok, where they sometimes made forays to kill and carry off dogs. Arsenyev describes how tigers in the forest sometimes bellowed like red deer to attract the deer during mating season; the tiger's imitation betrayed itself only at the end of the bellow, when it trailed off into a purr.

The only humans one was likely to meet in this nearly trackless forest were Chinese medicine hunters, bandits, and hunter-trappers of wild game. Dersu Uzala, a trapper whom Arsenyev and his men come upon early in their 1902 journey, is a Siberian native of the Gold tribe whose wife and children have died of smallpox and who now is alone. After their meeting, Dersu becomes the party's guide. The book is about Arsenyev's adventures with Dersu on this journey and others, their friendship, and Dersu's decline and end.

In the 1970s, a Soviet film studio produced a movie of *Dersu Uzala*, directed by Akira Kurosawa. It won the Academy Award for Best Foreign Film in 1975. The movie is long and slow paced, like a passage through the forest, and wonderfully evokes the Primorskii country. I own a cassette of the movie and in my many viewings of it even picked up some useful fractured Russian from the distinctive way Dersu talks.

Khabarovsk, the city, figures importantly in the movie when Dersu, whose sight is failing, moves to Arsenyev's house in the middle of town. Finding the house where Arsenyev lived in Khabarovsk was another of my Siberian goals. Sergei and Volodya completely approved, for a change; they are even bigger fans of Dersu and Arsenyev than I am.

From far off, Khabarovsk looks nothing like the trim little community of the movie. The city occupies one of the great river junctions in this part of the world: at Khabarovsk the Amur River, having been the border between Russia and China for about a thousand miles, turns left, or northeastward, and crosses Russian territory for the rest of its course until reaching the ocean. Meanwhile, the Ussuri River, joining the Amur from the south, takes over as the Russian-Chinese border. Travelers coming to Khabarovsk from the west cross the Amur on a bridge that goes on and on. Sergei said it was the longest bridge in the country. Up ahead, spread out in a succession of ridges above the confluence, Khabarovsk seemed endlessly large. With its tall sky and sprawling landscape it could have been a city designed for animals considerably larger than humans—mammoths, maybe, or midsized dinosaurs.

I soon learned that Arsenyev's house no longer stands. An exhibit about Arsenyev in the regional museum said that an Intourist hotel had been built on the spot where the house used to be. The exhibit had a photo of Arsenyev—a slim, well-built man in an army uniform—along with his notebooks, compass, and eyeglasses. The glasses showed hard use and had been repaired at the bridge with twine or wire. Nearby, a 360-degree painting of the Battle of Volochaevka on the wall of a circular room devoted to war memorabilia put Sergei back into his historically sad frame of mind. He remained somber and withdrawn as we left the museum and went for a walk along the riverfront esplanade. Today was Sunday and the populace had all turned out on this early fall afternoon. I noted, as had become routine, the great number of beautiful women. I thought I observed a more windblown, "California-girl" look among them here. From the esplanade I climbed up to a prominence where a heroic statue of Muraviev-Amurski, China's bane and the cousin of Bakunin, stood high against the blue of the sky surveying his self-appropriated empire. I could see the crowds along the esplanade, and speeding motorboats, and, far into the distance, the Amur whipped to waves by the breeze.

Before we left town, Sergei and Volodya stocked up at a gastronome and we had a late lunch at the van. Opening the side door, Volodya set the stove on the milk crates to boil water for tea. He offered to prepare for me some of what he was eating—bread and butter topped by a thick, white slice of pork fat. I said I couldn't eat that stuff because pork fat was horribly bad for you. Volodya said I was wrong about that; when the pork fat—its name is *salo*—is followed by several cups of very hot tea, the tea melts the fat and renders it harmless in the body. I was unpersuaded, although I'd never heard that hot tea theory before.

(Readers who might want to rent the movie *Dersu Uzala* some-day and do not want to know how it ends should skip the next three paragraphs.)

After Dersu moves in with Arsenyev and his wife and son in Khabarovsk, he spends his days indoors, homesick for the forest. When he goes out, he is unhappy to be told that he cannot take his gun. One day Arsenyev is informed that Dersu has been arrested for chopping down a tree in a city park, and Arsenyev has to get him out of jail. Finally Dersu tells Arsenyev that he can no longer stand this life and must go back to the forest. Arsenyev gives Dersu his new rifle, saying that its ac-curacy will make up for his poor eyesight. Dersu thanks him, says good-bye to Arsenyev and his family, and leaves.

Soon after, Arsenyev is notified that Dersu has been found murdered beside his campfire. The only identification on the body was Arsenyev's visiting card. Arsenyev takes the train to the tiny village of Korfovskii, south of Khabarovsk, where the murder occurred. He arrives just as a police officer is overseeing the burial of the body. The policeman tells

Arsenyev that Dersu's new gun was never found and speculates that its robbery was the motive for the killing. When the workmen finish filling in the grave, Arsenyev sees Dersu's old walking stick on the ground and plants it beside the dirt mound. From the scene at the beginning of the movie we know he will return to Korfovskii and be unable to find the grave. The last shot is of Dersu's walking stick.

I wanted to take a look around Korfovskii myself, especially since it was right on our way as we headed south from Khabarovsk. Maybe modern admirers had put up a marker of some kind. Korfovskii is only about twelve miles south of Khabarovsk—poor Dersu had not gotten very far—and it now appears to be mainly a village of weekend dachas for Khabarovsk residents. The traffic coming back into the city on a Sunday evening was intense. Sergei wanted to keep going and locate a good camping place before dark, so we gave the village only a quick drive-through. Some of the dachas were fancy and large, or under elaborate construction; the place seemed to be in the middle of a dacha boom. If there was any monument to Dersu Uzala, we didn't find it.

That night we camped on a gravel bank beside the Khor River. *Khor* means "chorus," but this river was about as mute and languid as most of the other Russian rivers I'd seen. The setting sun silhouetted the arch of a nearby bridge across it, and the line of trees beyond, and the boom of a construction crane; after dark an orange half-moon rose. At bedtime, the air became chilly, and when I bathed in the river in the morning, a cold mist lay on the water and made the stones of the gravel bank wet with dew. By breakfast the sun had come over the trees and the day quickly got warm. While Sergei broke camp, Volodya gave the van a wash. We set out and continued southward, passing villages called Roskosh (Luxury), Zvenevay (Small-Group Town), and Tigorovo (Tigerville), and rivers called Pervaya Syedmaya Reka (First Seventh River) and Vtoraya Syedmaya Reka (Second Seventh River).

When Sergei went into a store at noontime to buy bread in the small city of Bikin, he soon returned and asked me to come inside. He had told one of the salesladies that he was traveling with an American, and she had asked if she could see me. Obligingly, he presented me to her. This saleslady was another Russian beauty, though not at all the kind who wears low-rider jeans and pinpoint high heels on the streets of St. Petersburg or Chita. Instead she brought to mind the heroic ladies on Communist posters extolling motherhood—she was matronly, pink cheeked, with vivid dark eyes, and the tunic under her clean white apron left her big, strong-looking arms bare.

She and I talked for a while. She asked me where I was from and I said New Jersey, and she asked if that was a city. I said it was a state, not a city, but it was very near New York City. She had heard of that. She told me that she had seen many Americans in the cinema and on television but I was the first American she had ever seen *zhivoi*—living, in the flesh. She thanked Sergei for bringing me in. Then she asked us to wait and went into the back room and brought out a kielbasa too special to be put out on general display, and we bought it from her.

Like most cities of military importance, Bikin had been closed to foreigners until after the end of Soviet times. With the Chinese border only twelve miles away, Bikin formerly was fortified with active military installations all around it, and now their barbed wire dangled and their concrete works had turned ramshackle in predictable post-Soviet style. And yet Bikin still had the cloistered feel of a garrison town. Afterward I read that during the Great Patriotic War, a husband and wife in another closed city of the Far East had given Stalin their fifty-thousand-ruble family savings in order to pay for a tank to fight the fascists; their patriotic gesture received much publicity, as did the couple's being allowed to operate the tank themselves against the Nazis. After the USSR entered the war against Japan in 1945, a mechanic in Bikin, inspired by this couple's example, donated his life savings to buy a tank so he could personally fight the "samurai." Unluckily for the Bikin mechanic, however, Japan surrendered soon after and he never got his chance.

Past Bikin we entered the Primorskii Krai and the last leg of our journey. If we kept going south on the road we were on we would arrive in Vladivostok in a day or so. But what then? At Vladivostok we would have reached our destination and our trip would be done. And probably we wouldn't stay in Vladivostok; our money had begun to run low, making Sergei even more opposed to the idea of paying for a room. And camping places within range of a city that size were unlikely to be too good.

None of these end-of-trip complications seeming attractive, I agreed with Sergei's suggestion that instead we turn east, cross the Sikhote-Alin Mountains, and arrive at the Pacific (more precisely, its Sea of Japan) in a less-inhabited place on the mountains' other side. We'd certainly find better camping spots along the shore. And, that way, when we finally did get to salt water, it would be the open ocean, not the domesticated and no doubt dirty version of it in Vladivostok's harbor. We could always see Vladivostok later when we were about to go home.

Soon after Bikin we suddenly entered a weird all-watermelon area. Watermelon sellers crowded both sides of the road under big umbrellas in beach-ball colors among wildly painted wooden signs. Sergei pulled over and bought a watermelon for a ruble, but as we went along, the heaps of them kept growing until melons were spilling into the road and the sellers were giving them away. A man with teeth like a crazy fence hailed us and in high hilarity thrust two watermelons through the passenger-side window. By the time we had emerged at the other end of the watermelon gauntlet, we had a dozen or more in the van. The watermelons were almost spherical, antifreeze green, and slightly smaller than soccer balls. We cut one open—delicious. This was not a part of the world I had previously thought of as a great place for watermelons.

V. K. Arsenyev, when leading his Sikhote-Alin expedition in 1906, took the railway south to just beyond the Ussuri River bridge. Then he disembarked from the train and headed east through the taiga. We turned east about seventy-five miles farther on, at the town of Spassk-Dalnyi. The Sikhote-Alin mountains, once we were among them, seemed more like hills, and not very forbidding, but the depth and silence of their forest made up for that. Arsenyev had described the taiga here as "virginal, primeval timberland." From the height of the trees and the venerable length of the vines depending from them I would guess that the taiga we saw was still original growth. That night we camped above the small gorge of a river named for Arsenyev—the Arsenevka. The sound of it was pleasant to sit beside; this was our first genuinely rushing stream. I stayed up for a while after Sergei and Volodya had gone to bed, listening to it and looking up at the stars and at the satellites tracking past.

The next day we continued winding generally eastward through the Sikhote-Alins. I noted villages called Uborka (Harvest), Shumnyi (Noisy), and Rudnyi (Oreville). Now we were in Arsenyev's very footsteps. A little beyond Rudnyi we crossed a mountain pass that hardly looked like one. This was the divide between the waters that flow roundabout to the Pacific via the Ussuri and the Amur, and those that drain down the front of the Sikhote-Alins into the Pacific directly. At the crest of the divide, back among the roadside weeds, stood a cement obelisk on which was inscribed (in Russian) CROSSED OVER THIS PASS: M. I. VENYUKOV 1858; N. M. PRZHEVALSKII 1887; V. K. ARSENYEV 1906.

Sergei did not know who the first guy, M. I. Venyukov, was. Later I learned that he was a major general who traveled all over Asia and Japan and harbored revolutionary opinions, secretly reporting for Alexander Herzen's magazine, *Kolokol* (The Bell), and finally emigrating for good in 1877. N. M. Przhevalskii, Sergei said, was an Asiatic traveler best known for his explorations of deserts and steppes, and for discovering a kind of steppe horse that is named after him. Przhevalskii bore a strong resemblance to Joseph Stalin, and was even rumored to have fathered the future dictator while traveling in Georgia. The rumor is ridiculous, however, Sergei said.

V. K. Arsenyev's passage across this divide happened during the mapping expedition guided by Dersu and is described in detail in the book. Arsenyev continued from here until he came to the Pacific and the port village of Olga, where he was resupplied. Sergei said we would also aim for Olga and camp near there.

Often the taiga stood so close to the road that the vines almost touched the side of the car, and on the upgrades we were looking into the canopy. At one point in the movie *Dersu Uzala*, a tiger stalks Arsenyev's party, and the Siberian tiger used for the scene was a splendid animal, all liquid motion and snarling growls. Though near extinction, the Siberian tiger has not yet been wiped out, and the thought that this Pacific forest—reminiscent in some ways of the American and Canadian Northwest—had tigers in it gave the shadows far back among the trees a new level of authority. I had been in a few forests that held grizzly bears, but a forest with tigers in it seemed even more mysterious and honorable.

Rather than go straight to Olga, we turned off at a little road where a sign pointed to Vesyolyi Yar (Merry Cliff). This road as it led eastward and Pacific-ward was not particularly merry. The closer we approached the coast, the more falling-down military structures cluttered the scene. Overhead the sky got bluer and lighter simultaneously in an ever-brightening expansiveness that could only be a reflection of the Pacific just beyond. At the top of each rise I thought I'd see it. Then we came over a crest above an unusually steep descent, and there ahead, in the notch between two hills: the Pacific Ocean. Against the green of the trees it was a deep pelagic blue, with many white waves.

Past a few more hills and an abandoned gate-checkpoint, and then we were on a level, sandy road that served as the main street of another military ghost town. On either side of the road, block after block of three- or four-story cement residential buildings with most of their window glass out showed only occasional signs of human presence. An onshore breeze rattling through the ruins smelled like the sea and made the vacant place spookier.

I saw the water just in glimpses between the buildings, but then the road bore left and we were driving alongside the shore. We stopped and got out. Here we had arrived not at a regular beach, with big rollers coming in, but at the semifortified shore of Vladimirskaya Bay. The Pacific rollers I had hoped for could be seen in the distance, at the bay's entrance between its northern and southern headlands. Here there was no strand, just rocks and broken cement and pieces of rusted iron, and a small black cow looking for something to eat among them. Between the road and the water, a twelve-foot-high observation tower leaned to one side; the hulks of two wrecked ships, one still with her stacks and superstructure, sat grounded and tilted over not too far out in the bay.

On the ocean-facing side of a big rock, someone had spray painted the NY logo of the New York Yankees and the LA logo of the Los Angeles Dodgers. Also in big white letters on the rock was the word RAP.

We drove along the shore a little farther until there were fewer ghost buildings. In this part, the beach was more beachlike and offered a better setting for our momentous arrival. Wave-smoothed stones and actual sand inclined down to clear and cold waves that were breaking hard on this windy day. Long fronds of kelp lay here and there like pieces of reel-to-reel tape. I put my hand in the water and cupped some of it and tasted salt. Sergei immediately stripped down to his briefs and dove in and swam. Volodya recorded the event with the video camera while I made a sketch of the bay and the ocean and the sky. During his dip, Sergei stepped on a sea urchin spine, a painful development, but he mentioned it only in passing among the shouting, hilarity, and mutual congratulations. Finally we were here. Today was Tuesday, September 11, 2001. We had crossed Russia by land from the Baltic Sea to the Pacific Ocean in five weeks and two days.

Chapter 22

Perhaps the reader is curious about how this trip ended and how I got home.

When I called my wife the next morning, September 12, I checked first to see what new punch lines Bill had e-mailed me; there were none. Instead I found a message from my wife saying she and the kids were all right. Then the call went through and I learned what that meant. In New York it was still the previous day, about seven o'clock at night. At that point no one knew how many thousands had died. My reactions to the news were the same as tens of millions of other people's; the only difference was that as the lone American in this obscure corner of the Primorskii Krai I constituted a nation of one, my country's lone representative. I told Sergei and Volodya what had happened, and they were great. They kept an eye on me without being overbearing as I retreated to my tent for a while and then wandered the near vicinity trying to begin to think about what had occurred.

We had made camp at the next bay down the shore from the ghost military base. This bay, called Olga Bay, had fewer military fortifications, and a river called the Avvakumovo came into it from the southwest. Spawning salmon were proceeding up the Avvakumovo in steady twos and threes. At the mouth of the river, near where we pitched our tents, an old drift log with many branches lay on the shore. All day long and into the night, local guys drove up in beat-up Japanese cars and then hung around for hours at the drift log. I could not figure out what these guys were doing. They just sat on the branches or the trunk and smoked cigarettes and drank beer and looked out over the water, and then sometimes they would all leave.

A day or two after the attacks, a deputation of these guys came to Sergei with a freshly caught salmon for him to present to me as a token of their sympathy for what had happened in America. The fish was a large female, maybe nine pounds, and with Volodya's cooking skills it would provide us several good meals and fresh salmon eggs, too. When Sergei brought the fish to me, I felt actual love for the drift-log guys and was moved to tears.

After we'd been at the camp for another couple of days, I finally learned (Volodya told me) what these guys were up to. They were watching for the appearance of the fish inspector. Only a tiny number of fishermen had the necessary permits to put nets in the bay. The fish inspector, a dogged-looking person in a small aluminum outboard, came by often to make sure no unlicensed nets were out. As soon as he left the bay, the guys would go to their own boats hidden somewhere nearby, speed out into the bay, set their nets, and catch a few before he returned. They were poachers, in other words, and we were probably breaking the law merely by possessing the illegally caught fish they had given me. Somehow this discovery made their gift even more touching.

I tried to catch a salmon myself, without success. In the clear water I could see them just like in an aquarium. Occasionally they would jump just a few feet away from me, popping up in full profile like toast from a toaster. But they had no interest in any of my flies or lures; when one of my offerings came too near they would shy abruptly to one side. The Avvakumovo River was full of fish. Schools of a fish broader than a salmon, but not as long—shad? striped bass?—were also spawning there. In slower water a bit upstream from the mouth, these fish followed one another around and around in rings until some point of tension was reached and they exploded from the formation with a splash that stirred up mud on the river bottom. Then the fish would regroup and start circling again.

On the surface of this slow place there were a lot of round, black water bugs. They resembled water striders, but they hopped across the water rather than strode. When the circling fish occasionally exploded directly beneath these water hoppers, I was sure I saw some of the bugs go under. I watched and watched to see if any of the bugs ever came back onto the surface from under it. As far as I could tell, none did. It is my opinion that no water strider or similar water-surface insect can return to the surface if it ever is unlucky enough to go under.

There were thousands of littler fish, too, hitting the surface constantly and leaving small round ripples like at the beginning of a rainstorm. Shorebirds ran along the bite-sized beaches the waves had cut into the birch and pine and swamp-maple forests that grew all the way down to the bay. Terns and gulls dove on the little fish with feathery splashes. Sometimes two mature bald eagles glided back and forth above. And as usual, we were under the supervision of a flock of crows and ravens, who walked more than they flew and provided commentary.

One afternoon Sergei and Volodya and I drove eighteen miles upstream on the Avvakumovo to explore. There the river ran through windings and pools of swimming-pool blue under old-growth taiga. The bottom was dark granite and gray gravel, devoid of all trash. This was a river you could have used on a fly-fishing calendar, with plentiful animal tracks in the sand and even a structure of sticks that could have been a beaver lodge at one of the pools. Volodya loaned me his hip boots and soon I was wading and casting flies to likely looking trout water for the first time on our journey.

For a while I fished deep and caught only a few brown minnows with big heads, similar to what we call sculpins in America. I had seen a few grasshoppers along the bank, so I switched to a large, bushy dry fly that I've had luck with in Montana during grasshopper season. My first cast with it produced an enthusiastic little strike. Laying the fly in a seam between fast-moving water and slow-, I got a swirl from what appeared to be a real fish. By the color on its side I knew it had to be a trout. A cast or two later I dropped the fly next to a half-sunken log and something sucked it in. The hooked fish veered out into deep and heavy current and held there awhile before I could lead it to the shallows. It was not huge— nine or ten inches at the most—but it was a trout, unmistakably. The name for it in Russian is *forel*, which is only the Russian version of the German *Forelle*, which means "trout."

I held the fish just above the water on my wet palm. I had never seen such a fish. Its sides were a burnished silvery-gold and had big, almost oblong patches of a pale camouflage-olive color, with little black dots along the back. The dots all leaned toward the tail, as if they'd been tilted in that direction by hydrodynamics. The fish's sides changed color depending on how you looked at them—they appeared platinum-silvery when viewed from above, but greenish-silver when you saw them from below. The *forel* reminded me of the little optical-square toys that used to come in cereal boxes, those whatnots that showed one picture from one angle and a different picture when turned the other way. With this fish in my hand I felt as if I'd captured an imaginary creature, a living distillation of Siberian forest light. I unhooked it without damage and set it back in the Avvakumovo.

Basically I was marking time. After the attacks I had decided to fly home from Vladivostok at the first opportunity. But no planes were flying into or within the United States, so like many travelers all over the world, I waited.

My thoughts about what had happened on September 11 swirled around without settling anywhere or producing any insight, except for one or two blunt ironies. Some of my friends had told me before I left that I was setting out on a foolishly dangerous journey, and as I went across Siberia I kept waiting for the disaster I had let myself in for. But I had reached my destination and no disaster had occurred. Meanwhile, a real nightmare that history held in store hit just a few miles from my supposedly safe starting point, and thirteen people from my suburban town of Montclair died in the attacks; and Merle Gehman, the local Boy Scout leader, father of my son's best friend, Christian, had gone to work in the south tower of the Trade Center that morning, and escaped after the plane hit, and lost his IDs, and the next day, as he and his wife were getting his driver's license replaced at the Bureau of Motor Vehicles, my wife picked up Christian and our son after school, and Christian said, of his father's escape, "He had blood all over him, but it was somebody else's blood!"

Also, I remembered that when I used to live in downtown Manhattan, I often took visitors from Ohio to look at the city from the observation deck on the top of the north tower. The view from there was actually a bit disappointing, and nowhere near as good as the Empire State Building's, because from the lower end of the island you could see mainly water, and the unimpressive buildings of Wall Street, and the green of New Jersey across the Hudson River. But that was the direction my guests and I naturally looked anyway—westward, toward Ohio, and home, and the American continent stretching beyond. For us the building we were standing at the top of was the World Trade Center in the same sense that America's baseball championship was the World Series. To us, "World" meant "American"; in fact, we thought not at all about the rest of the actual world.

But out in the rest of the actual world, people were thinking about us, in the larger sense, and specifically about this building. The attacks that targeted it represented not so much the beginning of a new war as a cruelly and ingeniously updated new wrinkle in an old, old war, one going back almost to the beginning of Islam. The recently ended Cold War, in whose ruins Sergei and Volodya and I had been wandering, would have been difficult to explain to ancient ghosts who knew nothing about twentieth-century physics. But the September 11 attacks would have made perfect sense to, say, Saladin: the flying machines, the proud towers, the slaughtered innocents, the suicidal believers, are a simple story that exists out of time. To Yermak and the other Christian conquerors of Siberia's Muslim khan, September 11 would have been easily understandable, and perhaps a further inducement to victory, had they heard its story while gathered around their smoky Tobol River campfires.

Sergei and Volodya, those party guys, had met two attractive widows at a birthday picnic near our campsite. Sveta and Natalia lived in the nearby village of Olga. Sveta, a sturdy, dark-haired, vivid-featured woman with a musical laugh, was charmed by Volodya's tales. As Olga's pharmacist, she had a position of importance in the town. Natalia, ginger-haired and blue-eyed, taught kindergarten and resembled a soft-spoken suburban mom. She gravitated toward Sergei. Each widow lived alone in a large apartment in the village. After we'd been at the campsite for several days, they invited us to stay with them. Sergei and I went to Natalia's, Volodya to Sveta's.

At Natalia's I saw TV coverage of the attacks. The images looked even more chaotic and bizarre on Russian television. The pictures veered and tilted and went out of focus, with quick glimpses of familiar places and buildings careening by like objects being dumped into the trash. To judge only from the Russian coverage, you'd think the whole city had been destroyed. The Russian TV plotline seemed to be that the United States had started the whole problem in the first place by getting involved with bin Laden during the Soviet Afghan War. Then the station broke away to show President Putin's speech to the Russian people about the attacks. Putin talked in subdued, concerned tones, as if he really did sympathize. He said that Russia was sending help to the United States immediately and that the two countries must work together to fight Islamic terrorism.

Natalia, with a schoolteacher's patience, often took time to talk to me. She told me her two sons were serving in the military, one in Chechnya and the other I forget where. Her husband had been a school bus driver. She showed me his photo—he was a long, slim fellow with blurry features and straight brown hair. After his second heart attack he had quit his job and spent all his time at home making wood carvings of tigers and repairing clocks. The apartment was full of clocks he had fixed and they rang and buzzed and chirped at various intervals.

Natalia gave me one of his carved tigers as a present and I gave her my last two Beanie Babies for her grandchildren. I asked her, just by the way, if she had ever seen a real tiger in the forest. She said she'd never seen one in the forest, but not long ago a tiger had walked down her street in Olga. She had taken a photo of it. The tiger in the snapshot she showed was skinny and shambly looking, walking along the pavement with its head to one side. Natalia said the tiger was sick and the police had shot it soon afterward.

With groceries we contributed, the widows made us dinners of red caviar, blini, cabbage soup, borscht with beef, pelmeni with sour cream, carrot salad, beet salad, cake, and the unavoidable endless cups of tea. I was sort of a fifth wheel during these evenings, and when my comprehension of what everybody was talking about went blank, I just sat there and brooded or daydreamed. Then every so often I would understand something they were saying, and I'd pitch in an observation or two, and they would think I'd been understanding all along. Once Sveta's cat jumped in my lap and began rubbing against me and purring, and Sveta said, "Oh, that's very strange, because usually that cat only likes women and doesn't go near men." I replied, *"Da, i Ya nastoyashchii mushchina,"* which means, "Yes, and I am a real man." I mention this one-liner, self-indulgently, because it was only the third or fourth time in my life that I made Russian friends laugh in Russian when I was trying to.

The village of Olga seemed snug and cozy or bleak and end-of-the-line, depending on my mood. Woodsmoke hung in the air and the crowing of roosters echoed among the houses and small apartment buildings set at different levels on the hills above the harbor. From certain angles the village looked like a little port city from a former time. But many of its houses had been abandoned, with doorways burned out and windows boarded shut, and though the harbor's good situation among flanking hills kept its waters glassy calm, I didn't get a sense that it enjoyed much ship traffic, aside from vessels like the small cargo transport at a timber company dock being loaded with logs for (I was told) export to Japan. Along the waterfront I saw chickens scratching at an oily beach, and a truck or two going by, but not much that could be described as bustling activity. It was hard to imagine a passing ship stopping in today just for a visit and her passengers disembarking to make a social call on Olga's commandant, as (the alert reader will remember) Mikhail Bakunin daringly did here in 1861 while sailing by during his globe-spanning escape from Siberia.

I took walks around the village, made a few sketches, visited the local museum. The museum director, who carefully marked her place in the translated Stephen King novel she was reading when I walked in, was a bespectacled woman of late middle age named Revolutsia. Her parents, ardent Communists, had given her the name; she said most people just called her Lutsia. Neither of us being in any hurry, she led me through a detailed tour of the museum's three small rooms, one of which consisted mainly of drawings by Olga schoolchildren. Lutsia discoursed on the Stone and Iron ages in the Primorskii Krai, and on several stone sculptures from a Chinese empire that had extended this far north in the time of Kublai Khan, and on Olga's all-time richest man, a nineteenth-century tycoon who made his fortune harvesting sea cabbage along the shore and selling it to Japan. I told her about our just-completed journey and she asked if she could write an item about it for her museum newsletter. Sergei, who had showed up, cheerfully obliged by describing some of our adventures and the book I was writing about the Decembrists.

At Olga's post office, a room of wooden phone booths scarred by decades of use carried a distinct, lingering atmosphere of the old-time Soviet blues. Sergei and I stopped by there sometimes to phone Vladivostok and see what was happening with flights from that city or into the United States. The ban on U.S. air travel had not been lifted. My wife had been trying to get me a reservation from Vladivostok to New York via Korean Air, and I stayed in touch with her by satellite phone.

When, after a few more days, I finally did go home, it was with the dreamy swiftness of zipping through a half dozen TV channels at a single touch of the remote. My exit happened like this:

One evening I called home and my wife said planes were supposed to start flying again the day after tomorrow, and she had made a reservation for me on Korean Air. At the post office, Sergei called Vladivostok and confirmed it. We had a farewell dinner with the widows, and the next morning we packed the van, said goodbye to them, and drove all day on small roads through mountains to the Razdolnaya River, about thirty miles from Vladivostok. (*Razdol'naya* means "free," as in "free and easy.") We camped near a bridge over it, and early the next morning I washed in the Razdolnaya and dressed in the clean clothes I had saved for the plane. I told Volodya I couldn't believe I would actually go home that day and he said he had no doubt I would.

The morning was foggy. We broke camp and then drove through fog for a couple of hours to the Vladivostok airport, where I presented myself at the Korean Air window. Barely looking at me, the sallow-faced Russian woman behind the thick glass said she had never heard of my reservation, although it didn't matter anyway, because all the planes were full. She advised me to come back in a week. At this, Sergei, standing by my side, leaned into the window and offered the woman 150 rubles, about $5. After a moment the woman told us she had searched again and this time had found my reservation after all. I handed Sergei the fare in dollars, he pushed it under the window, and in fifteen minutes she gave us the ticket—from Vladivostok to Seoul, from Seoul to Anchorage, and from Anchorage to JFK Airport in New York. To fly all that way cost $890.

Now I didn't have enough cash left over to pay Sergei and Volodya what remained of their wages. Anticipating this, I had asked my wife to wire me money to Vladivostok by Western Union. We drove from the airport into the city. Vladivostok is hilly like San Francisco, and many of its buildings recall the cast-iron architectural style popular in American cities in the late 1900s. In the middle of downtown we found a bank with a Western Union sign. The woman who took care of us—a lacquered, helmet-haired functionary with unflappable poise—drew out every part of the transaction to its maximum extent, even allowing herself recesses to chat with her colleagues. As this went on, Sergei said to me, "Sandy, we must hurry, because your plane leaves in two hours!" I, always the careful Russian student, looked at my watch, calculated, and said, "No, Sergei, my plane does not leave for three hours and forty-five minutes." He glared at me; he had only been trying to hurry her along. She favored each of us with a small smile and continued taking her time.

After we finally finished there, we became lost looking for the road out of town and ended up back where we began, in the middle of the city. At the intersection of Svetlanovskii and Okeanskii Prospekt, maybe the busiest intersection in Vladivostok, Volodya double-parked and hopped out to ask directions. He then returned, explained to us the directions he'd been given, and turned the key in the ignition. The van did not start. He turned the key another dozen times. No dice. And recently it had been running so nicely! Doubtless this special last nonstarting was a farewell performance it had saved up just for this occasion. Through the obligatory raising of the hood, the tinkering, the application of the big screwdriver, and the turning and re-turning of the key, the van's engine made a teasing click or two but no other sound.

Nothing to do but try a jump start. Unfortunately, Volodya had double-parked facing uphill on Svetlanovskii, one of the city's steepest streets. Pushing the van forward would be impossible. We would have to jump-start it in reverse. To go in that direction would mean backing up into oncoming traffic. By now our distress had attracted the attention of a small crowd of well-dressed Vladivostokians amused at the sight of this supposed rescue vehicle helplessly broken down in the middle of the city.

Volodya took the wheel. Sergei and I went to the front of the van, ready to push. Volodya adjusted the outside rearview mirror, gauged the traffic, stepped on the clutch, put the van in reverse, and gave the signal. We pushed. The heavy van quickly picked up speed downhill. We kept pushing, and the oncoming cars swerved around us in a wailing of horns. Volodya popped the clutch. The van lurched, the engine started, the van accelerated faster into the honking, swerving cars. Volodya dodged through them by rearview mirror until he was able to scoot around a corner into a quieter street, where by exquisite footwork he kept the engine alive. Running and out of breath, Sergei and I finally caught up with him. I describe all this in detail because it was the most outstanding feat of driving I have ever seen.

Back to the airport. In the parking lot we settled our accounts, and Sergei wrote me out a receipt the length of a mini-essay on a sheet of typing paper. I separated my stuff from the pile of gear in the back of the van. We stood around for a few minutes and took a few last photographs. Then I embraced Volodya and thanked him and said goodbye, and did the same with Sergei. With Sergei I even became emotional, saying what a good job he'd done even though I'd gotten angry at him sometimes. He beamed back at me, as if only happy thoughts remained. Across the lot I saw some guys disembarking from cabs at the entrance to the international building. By their bulk, their clothing, and the fact they carried fly rod cases, I guessed they were Americans. These were the first Americans I'd seen since St. Petersburg, almost seven weeks ago and more than six thousand miles away.

Now the speedy, channel-changing part began. Sergei helped me with my heaviest bag to customs, where the customs guys were so nice to all us Americans that the newness of it was disorienting; this was still during the period when people all over the world had sympathetic, kindly feelings toward Americans. Something about crossing the official boundary into the global, channel-changing zone made me almost go to pieces with intense jumpiness, and in the customs area I actually managed to lose the notebook in which I'd been writing my observations since Khabarovsk. One of the fly fishermen found the notebook on the floor among the X-ray machines, and he held it up and yelled, "Does this belong to anybody?" I consider losing my notebook almost a shooting offense, like an infantryman's losing his rifle. I retrieved it in embarrassment. The fly fishermen were friendly, outgoing West Coast guys. They had caught lots of trout and sea-run salmon in Kamchatka and were still in the mellow mood that follows angling success.

The flight attendants on Korean Air treated us Americans even more gently than the Russian customs people had done. All the Koreans spoke to us in the quiet, careful manner one uses with the recently bereaved. In a seamless rush, the flight from Vladivostok became the empty Seoul airport became an almost-empty 747 crossing the Pacific bound for Anchorage. My seat was way in the back of the plane with no other passengers for thirty feet around. As we approached American airspace, a shiver of patriotism pulsed through me and I began saying, quietly, "Self-evident! 'We believe these truths to be *self-evident!*'" trying to give the phrase the same inflection Martin Luther King did in his "I have a dream" speech. In America there are still truths considered to be self-evident. Russia is older, crookeder, more obscure; not much in Russia is self-evident, certainly not to me.

In Anchorage we had to deplane and reclaim all our luggage so each piece could be searched. Then immigration officials interviewed each passenger individually. I had to explain why my passport showed no entry into any foreign country besides my many visits to Russia. My attempt to describe my spiritual-mystical attraction for that country puzzled the immigration guy. Then the handful of New York–bound passengers boarded another huge, empty plane for a nine-hour nap across Alaska, the Northwest Territories, Alberta, Saskatchewan, Minnesota. Eventually the in-flight screens showed we were over greater New York. Now special security measures sent us on a slowed-down detour out to the end of Long Island and back before we were cleared to land.

JFK Airport, when we deplaned, was semideserted, its bare hallways still giving off a post-apocalyptic feel. I strolled almost alone through places where normally you'd have to wait a half hour in line. Because of the time difference between here and where I started, I walked out of the Korean Air terminal and onto the curbside pickup area at about nine in the evening of the same calendar day that I'd begun by bathing in the Razdolnaya River east of Vladivostok.

Alfred, a driver for Black Car Service in Montclair, was waiting for me. Black Car is now out of business, but I always used to use it because its drivers were West Indian and I enjoyed talking to them. Alfred was a very big man in a shiny black suit and he drove a large black Oldsmobile. He greeted me with a grave West Indian politeness, which was perhaps the Caribbean version of the Russian solicitousness and Korean tact I'd seen earlier in the day. I was happy to be home and I had a sudden upsurge of transnational affection for Sergei and Volodya and the Russian customs guys and the Korean flight attendants and the American customs guys and Alfred and everybody.

We stowed my luggage in the trunk and slammed it shut. I went to open the car door and then I stopped and looked around. The sun had set, but the heat of the day was still radiating everywhere. I smelled diesel fuel, bus exhaust, and a whiff of Jamaica Bay not far off. The speedy channel-changing in my head slowed to a stop, and all the ordinary JFK Airport surroundings seemed to settle on my shoulders like an old coat. In my gratitude I did not fall to my knees and kiss the ground. But for a moment I did squat down and touch the warm, black, grainy, pebbly asphalt with the fingers of one hand.

PART IV

Chapter 23

New York City, near where I live, is like an international capital. I believe every place on earth has representation of one kind or another in New York. Every place has its own consulate there, or landscape paintings of it in the museums, or displays of its works of art, or scientific exhibits about it, or its own cultural center, or ethnic food store, or emigrants' society, or some combination of these. The rule holds for Texas or Antarctica or Mongolia or Chad or anywhere. It's less true, though, for Siberia. There are no Siberian wildlife exhibits, for example, in the city's immense American Museum of Natural History. The best—and, as far as I know, only—New York spot connected to Siberia is the fur department on the second floor of Saks Fifth Avenue department store in Manhattan. When I want a local intimation of Siberia I go there and look at the stoles and jackets and floor-length coats made of Siberia's oldest, most numinous export, the fur of the Siberian sable.

The depth of Siberia's winters is in its sable fur. Animals in countries with the coldest winters produce the best fur, but that is only a small part of sable's allure. When you hold sable fur in your hands and look into it, there's an endlessness, an inward glimmering that pulls you. Like diamonds or gold, sable has a quality that locks into a strange susceptibility in human beings and half hypnotizes them. And yet sable isn't mineral, it's animal, like us, and affects not just our sight and our imaginations but also the senses of touch and smell and even hearing, in the ineffable soft swish of it against your skin. Plus, sable is warm; for that practical reason, it has probably been beguiling humans for longer, historically, than gems or gold. And when, beyond that, you combine the beauty of sable fur with the loveliness of Russian women, you approach the region of fairy tale.

Around the sable coats of Saks Fifth Avenue, Siberia itself seems to materialize vaguely in the air. The first village I ever visited in Siberia was the trading and exile village of Barguzin; the highest-quality sable that Saks sells is known by the commercial name of Barguzin sable. A sable stole at Saks costs twenty-five thousand dollars, a jacket eighty-five thousand, and a full Barguzin sable coat one hundred and eighty thousand, marked down from two-twenty-five. I know fur trapping is cruel, but I can't keep that fact in front of my attention when I'm staring into the deeps of Barguzin sable. If I had the money, I'd be grabbing hundred-dollar bills by the fistful from my shoulder bag and handing them to the sales clerk without taking my eyes away.

Books about Siberia often bring up the sable early on, mainly because of its usefulness for explaining how the region from the Urals to the Pacific was explored. The sable is a species of marten that lives also in the northern parts of western Russia and in Finland. It is about two feet long, with a tail half again its length, and it mostly eats smaller animals, nuts, and berries. Years when there is a good crop of cedar nuts— the small, husk-covered nut found in the cones of cedar trees—usually are good years for sables. The rich mahogany-brown of the cedar nut mingles with the blue-black of a northern night in the fur of the black sable, the most prized kind.

In trade, medieval Russia had little of value to offer the rest of the world besides slaves and furs. Most long-distance trade during the Middle Ages was in luxury goods. Along with sable, the furs that Russia exported included ermine, fox, beaver, and northern gray squirrel, known as miniver. Kiev, the chief city of medieval Rus, served as the center of the fur trade not only for Russia but also for the contemporary world. After the Mongols destroyed Kiev in the thirteenth century, it lost that distinction, along with much else, and the center of the fur trade moved north, first to the city of Novgorod, and then to Ustyug (later called Velikii Ustyug). With its prime water route location at the confluence where the Iug and Sukhona rivers combine to make the Severnaya Dvina, Ustyug remained Russia's fur trade capital for more than two hundred years.

When Ivan the Terrible captured the city of Kazan from the Tatars in 1552, he opened the Kama, the river it controlled. Now fur-seeking adventurers could go up that centrally located river and follow it eastward to the Urals. From the Kama they could continue east on its tributary, the Chuvosia, then cross the Urals and drop down into the drainage of the Tura, and thence to the Tobol, the Irtysh, and the Ob, the westernmost great river of Siberia. Yermak followed some of that route when he led his Cossacks on the expedition by which Russia would take possession of Siberia. Ivan the Terrible's initial anger at Yermak for stirring up trouble in that part of the world abated after he saw the captured supply of sable furs Yermak sent him.

The men who led the search for furs across Siberia were called *promyshlenniki*, a word that then meant "trader" and today is closer to "manufacturer." It was easier to catch sables along the main watercourses than hunt for them in the hard-to-reach regions in the interior, so these men went from one Siberian drainage to the next, hitting the prime locations and moving on. Though they sometimes trapped and skinned the sables themselves, the more usual method was to find a convenient tribe of native people, capture hostages from them, and demand payment in sable furs for the hostages' return. The natives naturally objected to this and resisted when they could. Semyon Dezhnev, the *promyshlennik* generally credited with the discovery of the separation of Asia from North America, described in a petition to the tsar the wounds that had been inflicted on him while he was pursuing the sable trade: Tungus arrows in his left knee and right elbow; one Yukagir arrow in his left shoulder, another in the muscle of his right arm, another completely through his left wrist; an iron-tipped Yukagir arrow in his head; and, as he was attempting to seize a hostage of the Chuvanskiye tribe, a knife wound in the chest. After Russian rule became more firmly established in Siberia, every able-bodied adult male native who had not converted to the Orthodox church was required to give the authorities a certain quota of sable skins annually, under a system called *yasak*. That word, from the Mongol, originally applied to the tribute Russians had to pay their Mongol overlords.

So headlong was the Russian hunt for furs that it had propelled the *promyshlenniki* as far as the Tunguska River drainage in central Siberia by 1626. In 1642—just sixty years after Yermak's victory on the Tobol—

839 men seeking furs passed through customs at the fort of Yakutsk on the Lena River about twenty-three hundred miles east of the Ural Mountains. By 1647, Russian fur seekers had gone all the way to the Pacific Ocean, where they founded the settlement of Okhotsk; Russia thus had an outlet on the Pacific before it had ports on either the Baltic or the Black seas. (Although Okhotsk, more than four thousand miles from western Russia, was not the handiest port in the world.)

When the *promyshlennik* Dezhnev sailed around the Chukchi Nos at the end of Asia, his purpose was to find new sources of sables and walrus ivory in the delta of the Anadyr River. During that voyage, Dezhnev's party lost four vessels that were never seen again. In 1937, remains of a three-hundred-year-old settlement consisting of thirty-one dwellings of European origin were found on Alaska's Kenai Peninsula. Historians have speculated that this site was settled by Dezhnev's lost companions. Therefore, it is possible that Russia's fur-seeking explorations in the first half of the seventeenth century deposited a Russian settlement as far east as North America, almost halfway around the world from Moscow and almost a hundred years before Alaska's official discovery by Europeans.

Sables equaled money, literally; for centuries Russia was poor in precious metals and sometimes used furs as a medium of exchange. Only in the fifteenth century did silver begin to replace furs as currency. A large proportion of the sable furs coming out of Siberia ended up in the Kremlin, in the tsar's sable treasury. By 1586, just a few years after Yermak's expedition, the treasury received two hundred thousand Siberian sables. The *promyshlenniki* were obliged to give the tsar one sable out of every ten they obtained, and his agents could also buy any additional furs they chose, mostly taking those of the highest quality. On top of that, all furs collected as *yasak* also went to the tsar. During Ivan the Terrible's reign and after, sable fur formed a main part of the wealth of the Russian state. One historian says that by 1660, a third of the state's total revenues came from sable fur.

The exact worth of sable as a commodity back then is hard to assess. Certainly it was valuable out of all proportion to its bulk and weight. A bundle of forty sable skins—called a *sorok*, a *sorochek*, or a *zimmer*—would have been enough to make the fortunes of maybe half a dozen ordinary people. A hundred rubles was a fortune then, and each sable fur, depending on quality, was worth from ten to twenty rubles. Sables provided the Russian state with its most in-demand and portable form of wealth. Diplomats took sables with them on foreign embassies to pay expenses and to give as presents. When Ivan the Terrible was pestering the young Queen Elizabeth I of England with letters and inquiries about a possible marriage to one of her relatives, he sent her a present of sable furs. In 1676, Tsar Alexei Mikhailovich, father of Peter the Great, paid ten *soroks* of quality sable furs for one unicorn horn. That horn, presumably from a narwhal, thus would have been enough to support eight hundred ordinary people for life.

Sables were prized by non-Russians everywhere. The Chinese wanted them because of the lack of good fur-bearing animals in their country and traded the finest silks for them; silk was easy freight for trans-Asiatic caravans and highly valuable in the West. Turks accepted sable fur for prisoner ransoms. The Greek Orthodox bishop of Gaza, after requesting financial help from his Russian Orthodox brothers, received sables from them worth eleven hundred rubles. Representatives of the tsar paid sables to the Cossacks in the Ukraine who defended Russia's border from Tatars, and bribed the Tatar khan of Crimea with sables to restrain his warriors after Cossack raids. When Emperor Rudolf II of Hungary requested the assistance of Tsar Boris Godunov in fighting the Turks in 1595, Godunov sent him 1,003 *soroks* of sables, and tens of thousands of other furs, in lieu of soldiers and money.

The sable has been considered an almost magical beast throughout history. The learned Nicolae Milescu (also known as Spathary), leader of one of the first embassies to Peking from the tsar, believed the sable to be the actual Golden Fleece of classical mythology. A black sable cloak figures importantly in the story of Genghis Khan: his main and original wife, Börte, brought the cloak as her dowry at their marriage, and Genghis later used the cloak as a gift to solidify an alliance with another chieftain at a crucial moment in the unifying of the Mongols. Genghis's grandson Kublai Khan was reported to have an audience tent lined with sable pelts; Vladimir Monomakh, Grand Prince of Kiev, whose city the Mongols destroyed, wore a crown of gold, jewels, and sable. The Caliph of Baghdad, Haroun al-Rashid, the most famous of all caliphs and the hero of the *Thousand and One Nights*, dressed in robes and shoes of silk edged with sable.

In 1189, before the Third Crusade, Richard I of England and Philip II of France vowed not to wear their sables or ermines on the campaign. They wanted to make clear the seriousness of their purpose and ensure that the knights would follow their example; any finery the king didn't wear his inferiors couldn't, either. In 1465, Edward IV of England decreed that no one below the rank of lord was allowed to wear sable. Similar laws regarding sable and other luxuries, called sumptuary laws, existed in many countries. Hans Holbein did portraits of both Thomas More and Anne Boleyn wearing sable. King Henry VIII, who ordered the execution of More in 1535 and of Anne in 1536, possessed a gown of damask and velvet embellished with 80 sable pelts, and a black satin gown to which were affixed the pelts of 350 sables. Kang H'si, the Manchu emperor whose geopolitical skills in the 1680s thwarted the Russians in the Amur River Valley, wore a "short loose coat of sable" over a tunic of yellow silk embroidered with five-clawed dragons, and received audiences while sitting cross-legged on a seven-foot-high throne covered with black sable furs.

According to a photographic history published in 1994, only six women in the world then owned coats of black sable: Elizabeth Taylor, Jacqueline Onassis, Elizabeth II of England, and Valentina Tereshkova, the cosmonaut, who had received the coat as a reward from the Soviet government after she became the first woman in space (the two other women were not revealed). After protests against the wearing of furs began picking up speed, owning furs (at least in America and Europe) lost some of its glamour and took on a slightly unsavory, clandestine quality. Nowadays you almost never see a celebrity wearing a fur in a photograph. Mary Tyler Moore, an anti-fur celebrity best known for her TV sitcoms, donated a brand-new, $112,000 coat of Russian sable to PETA, People for the Ethical Treatment of Animals. PETA then bedecked the coat with animal traps, electrocution devices, and other equipment of the fur processing business in order to make a point outside a show of fashions of Arnold Scaasi, a designer who sometimes worked in fur.

Saks Fifth Avenue keeps its fur department low profile, in a less-trafficked corner of the store. Tiffany's, the luxury jeweler just up the avenue, doesn't hesitate to show flashy gems in its store windows, but you never see a sable fur in the window of Saks. Whenever I stand at the racks of sables admiring them, I have a sense of being elsewhere—in a Siberian winter, in the past, generally out of the modern mainstream. Most shoppers who walk by smelling the perfume samples recently sprayed on their wrists never stop to check out the absurdly expensive furs made from this little Siberian animal on which worlds have turned.

So far I had not actually been to Siberia in the winter. When I told people I had traveled there, they almost always asked, "Is it cold?" and I would answer that the Siberia I saw in August was hot, dusty, buggy, and so on. Then the next person I told about my recent trip would ask, "Is Siberia cold?" I had *seen* Siberia in the winter—that time I flew by helicopter from the Alaskan mainland to the Diomede Islands, when I got a brief view of Siberia's easternmost end—and it certainly *looked* cold. But from firsthand experience that was the best I could do.

This answer always seemed to disappoint my questioners. How could I have gone to Siberia and not been cold? In people's minds, the two things most closely associated with Siberia are cold and prisons. I had not really seen prisons, either. Any book about Siberia should have cold and prisons in it. I began to think about making a winter journey.

As I did, I kept going over my 2001 trip with Volodya and Sergei. By its end I had been pretty fed up with Sergei, and now I couldn't decide whether to attempt another journey with him. After I had returned I had not e-mailed him for a while; I remembered his high-handedness, his evasiveness, his veiled or unveiled disdain. Going through customs at Vladivostok, I recalled, I had felt a great relief at finally being on my own.

In late May 2003, I returned to St. Petersburg to write a magazine article about the city's three hundredth anniversary. I stayed in Luda's apartment, as before, and she mentioned that just a week or so earlier Sergei had called to ask after me. By this time my anger was fading and I was recalling his good qualities—his all-around competence, his occasional sweetness, his love of adventure, his toughness. After the four-day tricentennial celebration was over, I stayed on in St. Petersburg for several days, and on one of them I gave Sergei a call. He responded effusively, said I must come to see him that very evening, said his wife would make a big dinner for me, said he'd been hoping I would call.

Late in the afternoon I rode the metro to the stop closest to his house and he met me at the top of the escalator. He embraced me, said he had been dreaming of this moment, said our trip together had been the greatest experience of his life, said over and over how happy he was to see me. He rejoiced like I was his long-lost son. At his apartment, his Luda had prepared a many-course meal and I ate a huge amount. Then we drank tea and watched excerpts of the videos he and Volodya had made of our journey (carefully edited, of course, to remove the widows and other women encountered along the way). We told each other stories (also edited) about our trip and generally had a fine time. At about ten o'clock he drove me back to the metro and we parted with promises to be in touch.

That night in Luda's apartment I was by myself; she had gone to her dacha for the weekend. At about midnight, soon after falling asleep, I awoke in awful pain. At first I thought I was having a heart attack, but then the problem became vomiting, then diarrhea, then dysentery accompanied by chills and a high fever. The symptoms got worse and worse. At about five thirty in the morning I found the name of a nearby clinic for foreigners in an English-language newspaper I'd picked up somewhere, and during a respite between vomiting spasms I made my way to this clinic, walking shakily on the sunny, empty streets of early June. I presented myself to the nurses at admitting with the statement "*Dumaio shto Ya umeraio*" (I think I am dying). They took an imprint from my Visa card and admitted me; a doctor named Vyacheslav Zuev examined me and hooked me up to an IV. After some tests he informed me that I had either cholera or salmonella poisoning. He added that cholera was less likely, because they hadn't seen a case of it at the clinic in about a week. I asked if I would live, and he said he thought so. Later he said it was definitely salmonella but he didn't know which kind.

After my symptoms let up a bit, I spent the day lying on a comfortable bed with the IV in my arm, staring at the large clock on the wall. The bedsheets and pillowcases were of crisp, heavy white cotton, a kind seldom seen in America anymore, and the nurses wore striped blouses, white cotton aprons, and high, peaked nurses' caps, Florence Nightingale–style. Their voices cooed mournfully as they drifted in and out. I knew they were beautiful without looking up and I carried on drowsy, simple dialogues with them. As I began to recover, my mood swung strangely toward euphoria, tinged with revived Russia-love. At about ten in the evening I felt well enough to leave. Dr. Zuev recommended I stay until morning, but he agreed to discharge me. I returned to Luda's, went to bed, and slept soundly through the night.

I didn't know what had made me sick, but I suspected a kielbasa the color of machine grease that I'd scarfed down the previous afternoon. I'd gone for a stroll, had a couple of beers, and bought the kielbasa on impulse at a really unpromising shop. Or maybe I got sick from something I ate at Sergei's. Whatever the cause, the salmonella episode erased any last bad feelings I'd harbored toward him. For some reason, after that illness I completely stopped worrying about him and how we had or hadn't always gotten along. He was just who he was, a Russian guy—bad in some ways, worse in others, and totally clever and dependable under it all. He and I had driven across Russia together and had more or less accepted each other by now. After I got back to New Jersey, I e-mailed him and asked if he would like to go on a winter trip to eastern Siberia with me.

I wanted to see places I hadn't been to before. I wanted to see the northern city of Yakutsk, on the Lena River, and the cloud of human breath that travelers said hangs over the city on the coldest mornings. I aimed to visit Oimyakon, the coldest spot in Siberia, northeast of Yakutsk by six hundred miles, where the temperature has gone down to –96°. I had heard about the north-south *ledyanaya doroga*, or ice road, on Lake Baikal's frozen surface from December to April, and I wanted to drive on that. I wanted to ride the Baikal–Amur Magistral, or BAM, Siberia's other cross-country railroad. The BAM runs roughly parallel to the Trans-Siberian an average of about three hundred miles north of it and reaches the Pacific about seven hundred miles north of Vladivostok. And this time, I had to be sure to see a few prisons. As with my 2001 trip, Victor Serov helped me plan. I told him to make clear to Sergei how important seeing prisons was.

With one thing and another, a year went by, so I missed the winter of 2003–2004. In the winter of 2004–2005, Sergei and Victor and I were e-mailing back and forth with scheduling details. They said the best month for the journey would be March, because by then the midwinter dark has lifted but the snow and ice and cold are unchanged. As with my previous trip, I bought a lot of stuff. I asked Victor if Siberia had begun to have warm winters like other parts of the planet, and he said, "No, Siberia is still cold." We would be in −40° temperatures for much of the journey. I bought French-made snowmobiling overalls, and Canadian-made long underwear of thick polyester-spandex, and skiers' gloves, and snowmobiling mittens, and the heaviest down coat L.L. Bean had for sale. (The coat was, in fact, so stuffed with down that the weight of it pulled the shoulders flat, causing my top third always to become cold; a cinch inside the coat was supposed to counter this problem but I never managed to adjust it right.) From Sorel Boots I bought a low-temperature design called the Glacier Extreme, big and clunky as the shoes of Frankenstein's monster, and a slightly less heavy boot called the Mounty. The best feature of the Mounty was its wide soles studded with dozens of rubber posts for traction. These snow-tire-like boots were the best single purchase I made, because the streets of Siberian cities in winter are all snow compacted to the slipperiest sheen, and walking on them in ordinary footwear is impossible.

On this trip, I would go the opposite direction from in 2001—east to west, rather than west to east. Retracing the route of my 2001 return, I would fly from New York to Vladivostok via Anchorage and Seoul. In Vladivostok I would meet up with Sergei, and we would proceed from there by various means of transportation to places mostly far to the north of where we went last time. Eventually we would wind up in Yakutsk and then fly to St. Petersburg. After a few days in St. Petersburg, I would fly home. The trip would take about a month. Because we would not be driving ourselves or camping out, one guide—Sergei—would be enough to handle everything.

For about nine weeks before I left, I worked on my Russian in an intensive course run by Boris Shekhtman, a virtuoso of language instruction who has taught scores of journalists and government employees. Boris lives outside Washington, D.C., and I began my study by staying in his house for five days. (After that I continued with teachers in his program in New York.) Boris is a hypersmart guy, with ears that listen so attentively they're almost prehensile, and features as vivid as the masks of comedy and tragedy combined. To anything you say, the high drama of his expression in response works as a powerful mnemonic. I got to see a wide range of those responses when he picked me up at the train station and we began by speaking only Russian. As I talked, he winced, his eyebrows shot up, his eyes narrowed in puzzlement, comprehension dawned, he winced again. After about ten minutes of this he switched to English. He said, "You know, I understood everything you said, and I think you basically understood me. But what is this Russian you're talking? It's not Russian, it's *hooligan* Russian—and I don't mean you talk like a Russian hooligan, either."

Studying with Boris turned out to be some of the best fun I've ever had. We started with basic grammar and quickly moved forward into memorizing poetry and composing autobiographical paragraphs. Sometimes I worked with one of his assistants, Dina or Luda, or with both of them together, or with him and both of them. We acted out everyday situations—street encounters, hypothetical phone calls, pretend interviews. Once he paired me with another semibeginning American student. She had adopted a Russian child and wanted to learn the language so she could speak both English and Russian with him, and Boris told the two of us to carry on a "who are you, where are you from?" basic conversation in Russian, without using a word of English, as he and the other teachers looked on. My face turned red from the exertion and self-consciousness and oddness of the exercise, as did hers. I couldn't remember the last time my mind had sped that fast.

Boris had me practice situations I might find myself in on my upcoming journey. He and I also talked about Sergei, and the nuances of my relationship with him. Boris suggested I refer to Sergei as *"moi collega"* (my colleague) rather than *"moi voditel'"* (my driver)—a smart and tactful idea. At the end of the nine weeks, Boris and the other teachers gave me an oral exam like the one they give to State Department employees. The exam rates the student from levels one through five—one being no proficiency at all, and five being Native-Speaker Proficiency. I was hoping to achieve level three, which is General Professional Proficiency. I was doing okay until near the end of the exam when Boris was asking about my future trip, and he said, "If you are so sure you will come back safely, then what is that ghost I see standing behind your chair?" The word he used for ghost, *prividenie* (its meaning is sort of like "ghostly sight" or "apparition"), confused me by its similarity to Provideniya, the city I had visited in Chukotka, which I had just been talking about, so I bluffed an answer having to do with that. For my mistake, and for bluffing rather than asking what in the world he was talking about, he lowered my final rating from a three to a two-plus. He'd thrown me a trick question, but I think in any case I didn't deserve a three.

At the beginning of March, I assembled my gear and went over it and started to pack. I got my satellite phone turned back on. A familiar excitement and dread began to build, with dread predominating. Boris's remark about the ghost standing behind my chair stayed in my mind, while my Russian friends were again murmuring about the dangers. It is a disappointment to me now, going over my notes, to see how reluctant I was at the time to make this trip, and how eagerly I looked ahead to returning home. But in every book about Siberia the author must at some point be there in the winter, and be cold. On March 6, a breezy, almost spring day in New Jersey, I left for the airport and Vladivostok.

Chapter 24

Passage through the zone of airports—New York, Anchorage, Seoul—was as undifferentiated and dreamlike as usual. Because of the time we took off, we remained in darkness for almost twenty-four hours of flying. A weak daylight caught up with us during the Seoul-to-Vladivostok leg; the plane came out of gray clouds and descended over a landscape that appeared to be from before color TV. The scene revealed itself in shades of gray and broad patches of white. In the field just before the airport runway, snow had risen to the tips of the weeds, which stuck out like a two-day growth of beard. Grayish footpaths wandered across the field, and on one of them, maybe ninety feet below the wing, a woman was trudging along carrying a shopping bag with handles. She did not look up

A stout woman employee all in white with a dark babushka drove the vehicle with the boarding stairs up to the plane door. A black dog with four white feet stood next to this vehicle; the dog waited as the vehicle waited to approach the plane, and when it advanced, the dog advanced also, just up to the plane and no farther. The stout woman, job accomplished, climbed down from the vehicle's driver's seat and walked back to the terminal, and the dog walked back to the terminal in step beside her.

Sergei was there to meet me when I came through customs, as I'd expected. We had planned for him to fly from St. Petersburg to Vladivostok before I arrived. But as I hadn't expected, he was accompanied by

Volodya. In all the e-mailing back and forth, neither Sergei nor Victor had mentioned that Volodya was living in Vladivostok now. Our 2001 trip had uprooted Volodya's life. After getting deeper into his romance with Sveta, the pharmacist of the village of Olga, he had decided that he must leave his family in Sochi, and he had moved to Vladivostok in order to be closer to her. When Sergei filled me in on these details later he expressed sympathy for Volodya's wife, whom he knew from university, and said he thought this move was a bad idea. Now Volodya was trying to find work in Vladivostok restoring building façades. He lived in an apartment in a high-rise on one of the city's many hills, and we would be staying there.

On my previous trip I had sort of skipped Vladivostok, and I wanted to make up for that. I walked all over the city's center, with the guys and by myself. The city's older, more elegant part is walkable, with buildings of painted stucco and ornamental brick and a different aspect of the port at the foot of every hill. At one dock we saw a freighter being unloaded of those used Japanese cars that the cross-country drivers would speed back to more western parts of Russia for resale. Blackened ruts of ice ran down the middle of many streets and the sidewalks were all hard-polished snow. So many high heels had walked on this snow that it was riddled by the small round holes the heels had punched; it looked like a ceiling of acoustical tile. At a short distance from the city's central part, the trash-strewn places began. Next to heaped-up trash bags that had been slashed open by beaks, all-black crows and ravens flipped through refuse scraps and croaked their raspy cries. Meanwhile the usual Russian Miss Universes, some in really unseasonal outfits, went step-stepping along.

Volodya didn't yet have his own car, so his friends Genia and Roman drove us around. The farther we went from Vladivostok's relatively well-kept downtown, the stronger was the overriding sense of Russian chaos almost out of control. Proceeding along the coastline we passed a beach that was all trash, then miles of mysterious seaside slag heaps lining the road. Then there was a huge factory or power plant spouting smoke from sky-high stacks, and a compound triple-wrapped in razor wire, and a building with scorching around all the smashed-out windows, and ice-locked blackened yards beside tall black houses, and a water tower with a giant tuberous icicle leaking out its side, and clotted accumulations of power lines and insulators at black transformerlike convergence points, and more wires streaking out from them in every direction, and wires not even on poles but strung through the branches of trees. Long lines of gray-faced, black-clad citizens stood waiting to cram themselves into tiny *marshrutka* public transportation vans, amid trailing smoke and roadside mud spatter and engine noise.

Then more trash crowded close all along the road, and a whole huge shoreline of trash cliffs beetled down to the sea on our right, like the Trash Cliffs of Dover, with seagulls flying figure eights above. A few miles beyond the trash cliffs, Genia said he had something he wanted to show me. We pulled over at a much-used parking area of fragmented and flattened trash beside the road, and there was a sign: MUSOR NE BROSAT' (Do Not Throw Trash). Just past the sign was a path leading to an ocean cove with a beach maybe two hundred feet long and fifty feet wide. The beach was composed entirely of broken glass. Genia said it was called the *steklyannyi plyazh*, the glass beach, and it was a famous spot for Vladivostokians to visit. Every square foot of the beach was small, water-smoothed pieces of glass, mostly bottle glass by appearances, and most of it a sea-worn bottle green.

How the beach had come to be I am not sure. Genia explained, but I missed some of what he said. I think he said people have been stopping at this cove to drink and smash their empty bottles since Vladivostok began. Whatever its origins, the beach was gorgeous, like a shattered church mosaic glittering in the light, constantly agitated at the water's edge by the waves. Each wave as it curled on the shore picked up a load of water-smoothed, shiny-wet glass fragments and then tumbled them and set them down and spread them out. Green and amber and blue and pink and brown and clear glass fragments lay ankle-deep everywhere and lifted and fell in the waves, sand slowly returning to sand.

Genia was a heavyset man in his forties with straight dark hair and a drooping mustache. Roman, his younger associate, had a thin face and curly dark hair and wore a black leather coat and a leather driving cap. Usually when we rode in Roman's car, he played American rap and rock music on tape cassettes that you might find in the 99¢ bin at an American flea market. He sometimes talked to me about the music he played. One afternoon as we were bouncing and zooming in his little car on a Vladivostok street broken to pieces by ice and thaws, he put on a cassette by Kid Rock. I would not have recognized the artist, but Roman told me who it was. "I love Kid Rock's music," he said, "but I don't know what his words mean."

I listened for a while to the song. "Well, here he's saying that he wants money in order to make his life better," I explained.

"Oh, I understand," Roman said. Then, "Kid Rock is a scandalist, yes?"

"Yes, I think so. He was married to Pamela Anderson, of *Baywatch*."

"Ah, yes. I know *Baywatch*. Pamela Anderson—she is also a scandalist, I think."

Just then the car hit a big bump and all of us ricocheted off the ceiling. Roman said, "Oh, these roads!"

"Dorogi, i duraki" (roads, and idiots), I said. (This is a famous saying, attributed to Gogol, who once noted that in Russia the two biggest problems were the roads, and idiots.)

Roman laughed. "Yes," he said. "And they never repair either one."

On the campus of Vladivostok State University of Economics and Service, beside a busy highway, there's a tall black statue of the poet Osip Mandelstam in a long overcoat. His eyes are closed, his head is raised, and his right hand is pressed to his breast. When we were there, a white Star of David defaced the statue's base, spray-painted beside the days, month, and years of the poet's life; Mandelstam died on December 27, 1938, at the age of forty-seven. The bare inscription did not mention the place of death—the Vtoraya Rechka (Second River) transit camp at the north end of the city. A similar mood of sorrow hung over the V. K. Arsenyev memorial museum, which occupies the middle-sized frame house in an older part of Vladivostok where the writer and explorer lived with his family during his later years. The museum has several good photos of Arsenyev with Dersu Uzala, who was stocky and gnarled, about a foot shorter than his Russian *kapitan*. Arsenyev luckily died of heart failure in 1930, soon enough to escape the worst of the Stalin-era horrors (though by then he had been accused of being a Japanese spy and had himself accused others of having Japanese sympathies). After his death, his wife (also featured in museum photos) was imprisoned and then shot, and his daughter went to prison for ten years. The daughter died in 1970 at the age of forty-nine.

Thoughts of fate and finality made the stately old Vladivostok train station a somber place, as well. At the station's main platform (so a prom-

inent sign proclaimed), 9,288 kilometers of the Trans-Siberian Railway
came to an end. A paved walkway between two sets of tracks emphasized
the sense of extremity: lampposts down the center of the walkway dwindled to smallness at the station's distant end, where the walkway itself
pinched to a point as the disappearing lines of tracks converged. The effect was to make one contemplate Russia's deadly vastness, and the silent accumulation of crimes this railway had seen.

At nights I lay awake in Volodya's apartment and listened to the little
Japanese cars of his neighbors racing their engines as they struggled up
streets of refrozen meltwater. The bass throbbing of the music on the
cars' speakers vibrated the apartment's window glass and faded away.
These occasional disturbances only heightened the night's quiet; unlike
in American cities, in Russian cities you almost never hear sirens at night.
From Volodya's balcony during daylight you could see two nearby hills
and the hollow between them filled with low apartment buildings, scraggly trees, and a scattering of little garage-boxes for individual cars On
one hill, high-rise buildings perched right at the edge as if defying any
earthquake to topple them, while on the other hill, radio and TV and
power-line towers in sizes ranging from small to medium to skyscraper
high clustered like a throng of black steel church steeples. The dark
clouds moving over them had the rolling momentum of weather just
come in from the sea.

Volodya had furnished his apartment with a basic bachelor function-
ality indicative of an expectation that he would usually be somewhere
else. In this new life he still had his easygoing charm, but he was dealing
with a lot of unwanted free time, it seemed, and he sometimes looked
lost and forlorn. Once as we were walking downtown, he observed some
workmen redoing a building front. He pointed out to me that they had
their ladder set wrong, and then with professional courtesy he went over
to inform his fellow building restorers of this fact. The boss guy among
them quickly gave him back a sharp answer and told him to be on his
way. Volodya rejoined me with a crestfallen expression. *"Ne deli dobra i
zla ne budet"* (Do no good deeds and there will be no evil), he said. In
his bare rooms in the evenings he made telephone calls to Sveta, still living in Olga. The conversations were long and (at his end) pained and
explanatory; it didn't sound as if things were working out.

Several times over the winter Volodya had gone hunting in remote
parts of the Primorskii Krai for wild boar and *kosulya*, a small taiga deer.

For our supper or dinner he fried up steaks from a *kosulya* he had killed, and told us his adventures. While hunting northwest of Olga in January, he said, he had come across the tracks of a tigress and two cubs in the snow. The tigers had approached very near to the village of Serafimovka and then had headed back into the taiga, where they made a circle six or ten miles around to hem in their prey. More recently, when he was hunting in the Nakhodka region closer to Vladivostok, he had seen the tracks of a male tiger. (The tracks of males are about four and a half inches long; of females, three to four inches, he said.) An American expedition just a month before had done a regional census and had counted 450 tigers in the Primorskii Krai. Volodya said that whenever he saw fresh tiger tracks he quit hunting, because he knew he'd be unlikely to find wild boar or *kosulya* if there were tigers around.

Overall, I couldn't help but feel kind of sad for the guy. Volodya and I are about the same age. I know that as you reach your fifties, a powerful restlessness and longing can shake your life. That restlessness, or something akin to it, had agitated me to Russia, where my trajectory had assisted in knocking loose a fellow restless fifty-year-old from the place he had occupied before. But unlike me, Volodya had ended up living the lonesome consequences for real. I pictured him going out hunting by himself in a dark winter forest with tigers in it and then returning to this apartment. When Sergei and I departed Vladivostok, I accidentally left behind my brand-new fleece jacket. I berated myself for my carelessness, but later I was glad Volodya had the jacket, because we're about the same size.

Flying out of Vladivostok took two tries, a not uncommon occurrence in Siberian air travel. When we went to the airport on a Tuesday afternoon for our scheduled flight to Irkutsk, no personnel of the airline seemed to be around. Eventually a guy showed up and put a sign in the ticket window that said RAIS OTMENYON (Flight Canceled). A great deal of further waiting was required while Sergei attempted to find someone who would either rebook us on another flight or give our money back. Neither could be done. The airline, Kras Air, had no other available flights for a week, and it turned out that the tickets could be refunded only at the place of purchase, which was St. Petersburg. Eventually, from another airline, we bought tickets for an Irkutsk flight leaving in two days.

We knocked around Vladivostok for another forty-eight hours—I found the house that the young Yul Brynner had lived in, among other minor accomplishments—and on our next attempt the plane left when it was supposed to. The funny thing about forgetting my fleece jacket (to return to that subject) was that I actually forgot it twice. When we went to the airport for the first flight, the canceled one, I left it at Volodya's, and after being upset with myself for that I somehow managed to leave the jacket at his apartment *again* when we went to the airport the second time. At some level that had to be intentional, I believe.

Flew to Irkutsk, vexed because two biggest drunks on plane sitting in front of me. For distraction, read review of Steve Martin's latest book, *The Pleasure of My Company*, in arts section of *Konkurent*, a Vladivostok newspaper handed out to each passenger. Needed help of Russian-English dictionary for translation. Among new words and phrases learned: *khokhot* (laughter) and *spuskat' shtany* (to drop one's trousers). Review very favorable. From time to time, looked out window. Icy almost-all-white Siberian landscape below—corrugated hills, scattered wiry conifers. Little change in scenery for hours.

At Irkutsk airport, horrible taxicab guys. Drivers shouting back and forth in Russian slang sometimes known as *Mat'*, in which most vocab and syntax derive from three or four basic obscenities. Sergei chose least criminal-looking driver. Other drivers shouted to us as we loaded bags in trunk, *"Yob' tvoiu mat'!"* (Fuck your mother!), with hearty good cheer.

Hotel Angara, Irkutsk. Marble facing of columns in front of hotel held on, in places, with clear plastic packing tape. Hotel guests mostly respectable types—Asian businessmen in suits, Russian technicians in shirtsleeves, a girls' volleyball team. At buffet breakfast, volleyball girls tall and gawky-graceful as sandhill cranes in a grain field. In Irkutsk, finally, true Siberian cold (Vladivostok, by contrast, more temperate, with more southern location, ocean nearby). Angara River frozen three-quarters of way across: in sun, frozen part blinding white, open part vivid blue. New statue in riverfront park: Tsar Alexander III, much larger than life, in full military splendor, gleaming imperial black against the surrounding white. Also, at Znamensky Monastery, statue of martyred Admiral Kolchak, also new. Statuary Kolchak bareheaded, heroic, shoulders back, in long coat, with White Army soldier and Red Army soldier supporting statue's base. In our day of wandering, finally got to see inside of Trubetskoy Museum, closed when we in Irkutsk before. Prominent in Trubetskoy parlor: Miller foot-pump organ, made in Lebanon, Pa.

After two days left Irkutsk, rode train twenty-four hours around southern end of Baikal to Ulan-Ude. Sergei and I in spacious sleeping compartment with big window. Ravens flying alongside train out of Irkutsk station like gulls escorting ship. Light glinted off lead raven's hard black beak as it opened to cry. Outside city, in deep forest, snow whiter and whiter; its lavishness like on cover of album *Peter and the Wolf*, childhood favorite of mine. Through complicated high hills—most difficult part of entire Trans-Siberian to build—tracks followed serpentine route. Famous crossing of great valley (Angasolka Loop) took train far up side of one height, around turn, then far down side of other. Baikal often visible on left, sometimes immediately beside train. Lake stretching white to apparent infinity; across its foreground, tiny red auto inching along.

Ulan-Ude sooty and gray, as before, but now fiercely cold. Short cab ride from train station to Hotel Geser. Long wait at check-in; Sergei negotiated red tape, I watched Russian infotainment program on lobby TV. Interview with Sylvester Stallone, overdubbed in Russian, promoting new magazine, *Stallone*. Undeniable fact that Sylvester Stallone most popular American in Russia, maybe most popular there of all time. Hotel Geser unusually posh for Siberia. Large banquet hall, restaurant with dinner dancing, disco ball. At next table during breakfast, young couple by selves, saying grace. Woman had on sweatshirt said TEXAS A&M. When she standing next to me at buffet, I asked if she an Aggie. She blushed and said she was. She and husband here to pick up baby they adopting from Ulan-Ude orphanage. Both husband and wife soft-spoken, born-agains. They had been in Russia just a day or two, would meet with Russian judge that afternoon. If all went well, flying back to Texas with new baby tomorrow. Both knew almost nothing about where they were. Intense, determined people, engrossed in their private moment, both just kids themselves.

In Ulan-Ude—to drop the telegraphic style—I made many calls to Sasha Khamarkhanov from the hotel phone but never managed to get through. Sergei tried, also unsuccessfully, and then when he was going out to do some errands he said he would call Sasha from a post office pay phone. In half an hour Sergei returned. He had called information and found that Sasha had a new number, and when he called it he reached Tania, Sasha's wife. She told him that Sasha had died the previous December. She did not say what he died of, only that she was surprised his friends in America had not heard.

After that news I made an effort to call Tania myself but kept getting a busy signal and finally gave up. I had no confidence in my ability to offer condolences on the phone in Russian, anyway. Instead I wrote her a letter and asked Sergei to check it. Whether she ever received it, I don't know. I mailed it from the same post office where I'd gone with Sasha and bought postcards of Ulan-Ude twelve years before.

In all my life I saw Sasha only twice and conversed with him only imperfectly, but somehow he is clearer in my mind than many people I see regularly. I still have the copy of *The Secret History of the Mongols* (in Russian and Buryat) that he gave me as a present when I left Ulan-Ude the first time. Inside its front cover he wrote, in English script, "That is history my tribe (clan)." I understand now that Sasha was a Mongol, of the peaceful, post–Mongol Empire kind. Back in the early thirteenth century, at the time *The Secret History* was written, the Mongols adopted Uighur script and so began to be literate even before they had taken up the various faiths—Islam, Buddhism, Nestorian Christianity—that would mostly replace their own sketchy shamanism. I remember Sasha because in remote Siberia he was a devoted man of letters, true to his Mongol soul.

The giant head of Lenin in Ulan-Ude's central square looked even weirder in the winter. In the summer, the green, well-tended plots of lawn and flowers and the enclosing hedges on either side of it softened the effect of its massiveness and gave it the appeal of a beloved, garlanded monster. But in the winter there's just the snow-covered square, a few sticks of hedge, dark gray surrounding buildings and . . . The Head. Many city buses and vans begin their routes at that square, and I imagined that on a dark winter evening as you stood waiting for your ride home, that giant-featured face looming over you could wear on the nerves.

From Ulan-Ude, Sergei and I rode a bus six and a half hours north along Lake Baikal to the town of Ust-Barguzin. We woke up before six, packed, and made it to the Ulan-Ude bus station by taxi in plenty of time. We had presented our tickets and found seats on the bus when Sergei discovered he still carried the plastic room key card from the Hotel Geser in his pants pocket. He told me to tell the driver to wait for him and he went back to the hotel to return it. He's sixty-one years old, no cabs in sight, so he runs the two-mile round-trip on icy streets in just under twenty minutes, and he's back before the driver has started counting heads and making ready to leave. Sergei wasn't even terribly winded. I told him that in America no one thinks twice about walking off with those keys. That's what I would have done. Sergei said that the woman at the reception desk was very grateful to him because she would have lost her job for not making sure he had returned the key card when he checked out.

Our route that day followed the same road I'd been on with Sasha Khamarkhanov when we went to Lake Baikal years before. Now, though, deep snow had altered everything; I guessed that garbage in a landscape may not seem like such a big problem if it's buried under snow for eight months of the year. The ride was uneventful, even though four kids who looked to be no more than fourteen were drinking two-liter bottles of beer in the backseat. When we stopped for a lunch break at a little café on the way, all four kids were still able to walk. They disembarked, and then got back on carrying more two-liter beers in their arms, their eyes bright with anticipation, like kids on a school trip to an amusement park. As the bus continued, two of the kids almost passed out, and the other two, although more functional, were keeping their comrades upright and requesting emergency stops so they could help them off to vomit. I was impressed at how quiet and relatively well organized they were.

Ust-Barguzin is a large village at the mouth of the Barguzin River, where it flows into Lake Baikal. The location is only about thirty miles from Barguzin, the village I'd visited before. Sergei discovered when we arrived that Ust-Barguzin has no restaurants and no hotel, so after everybody else had gotten off, he and I remained on the bus and asked the driver what he recommended we do. For a small amount of rubles he drove us around the village while Sergei kept asking people on the street if they knew of anyplace we could stay. Again, Sergei's МЧС connections came in handy. The village, with its good harbor, has a large МЧС station whose main business is doing rescues on the lake. Even in winter, a lot of МЧС guys were on duty. We got out there. One fellow I talked to said that he was in Ust-Barguzin on a six-week assignment and that he lived usually in Chita. The МЧС guys made some calls and found a family who said we could stay at their house for the night.

Later, after I got back home, I sent a Christmas card to our Ust-Barguzin hosts, Sveta and Tolya Belov, so they could put it in one of the scrapbooks they keep of cards and photos they've received from people from all over the world who have stopped at their house while visiting Baikal. The guest book they showed me, only their most recent one, contained names and comments in many languages and handwritings. Just glancing through I noted that a Rose Bodette, of Toledo, Ohio, had stayed with the Belovs, as had a Mr. Nofziger, of Liberty City, Ohio. I would never have guessed Ust-Barguzin to be such a crossroads.

The Belovs' house was several small houses grown together into a rambling big one. They had eaten supper already, and served us a meal of *omul'* and pelmeni and pickled wild mushrooms and fresh-baked bread. Afterward, Sergei and I went to their backyard *banya* for a sweat and a wash. In the cooling-down room, the Belovs brought us a chilled beverage made of cranberries and water from a healthful spring. The rest of the evening we sat around their kitchen table and drank tea and talked. Tolya Belov was a truck driver who drove a regular route between Ust-Barguzin and Ulan-Ude hauling freight for a local home-furnishings company. Sveta ran an after-school program teaching kids about ecology. Tolya was big and barrel chested, she smaller and dark haired. The previous fall they had gone on a vacation trip by car to China, where they had filled their vehicle with fabric items they had bought for unbelievably cheap. Sveta showed us bath towel after bath towel. Tolya said it takes them several days to drive to Heihe, the Chinese city across the Amur River from Blagoveshchensk. He said he loves to eat in the restaurants there because the portions are so big.

I gathered that a part of the Belovs' income also relied on out-of-nowhere travelers like us. Tolya told us about a Russian couple who were taking a Siberian motor trip the summer before, and as they passed along the shore of Baikal, a rock rolled down a cliff and hit the car and broke a part in the wheel. The couple hitched a ride to Ust-Barguzin, where they ordered a new part from Germany on the Belovs' phone. They stayed with the Belovs for a night or two, then hitched back to their car and camped by it in the forest for a month until the new part arrived. The man installed it in the wheel and the couple went on their way.

Calls came for Sergei throughout the evening from his new friends at Ust-Barguzin МЧС. The next morning at seven, a four-wheel-drive jeep-style Niva, an official МЧС vehicle, pulled up out front with two drivers. Sergei had arranged for them to drive us on the ice road for two hundred and thirty miles to Severobaikalsk, a city at the north end of the lake. He loaded our stuff in the back of the Niva while I was still in the Belovs' vestibule trying to pull on my extreme-cold Frankenstein boots. I just could not get them on. I fell over onto the cement floor in the attempt, but kept on pulling. Sveta came out while I was doing that, and she looked down at me in surprise. I guess that's not how Russians put their boots on.

After goodbyes to the Belovs, Sergei and I climbed into the Niva's cramped backseats. For a few miles we drove on a narrow trail through shoreline forest to the point where the trail came out onto the lake. Ahead was Baikal's blank white surface with faint wheel lines on it running onward into the distance. We pulled onto the ice and stopped. Aleksandr, the driver, flipped down his visor against the glare and put a cassette of a singer named Mityaev on the tape player. We sat idling for a moment waiting for the tape to catch. The first song was "Zdorovo!" one of Mityaev's hits. Aleksandr turned the music up and we sped off across the lake.

Chapter 25

"*Zdorovo!*" means "Cool!" It's a general expression of approval, defined in older Russian-English dictionaries as "Well done!" or "Splendid!" Recently the more hip and casual meaning has taken over. The song's chorus goes "*Zdorovo, kak zdorovo . . .*" (Cool, how cool . . .). The song is your basic pop earworm, upbeat and irresistible, a good driving song. But I thought I also heard deeper Cossack strains in it well suited to a day in a heavy-duty vehicle on a Siberian road of ice. The drivers replayed the song many times.

At first we headed west, to get around a peninsula north of Ust-Barguzin called Svyatoi Nos (Holy Nose). Then we turned northeast, paralleling the coastline. During parts of the day, snow and mist filled the air and we could not see land. At other moments we came in close to the shore and rambled around in coves and bays. Both drivers—I didn't get the other one's name; he was a stocky Buryat with a short beard, one missing tooth, and nicotine-stained fingernails—wanted to see the caves along the shore and talked a lot about them. From close up, the cave formations with their icicles like stalactites hanging down and folds of snow partly veiling their entrances suggested a complicated stage set for some Wagnerian fable. In most of the bays we explored we saw no tire tracks besides our own, and no signs of people among the tall firs and cedars on the hillsides.

Out in the middle of the lake the wind picked up; I remembered reading about horses in the old days that were pushed by strong winds for great distances across Baikal's ice until they fell and slid into fissures and drowned. I did not understand how the Niva was maintaining traction on ice that looked sheer. But when I got out to examine the roadway, I saw that it had a more granular surface than I'd thought, and in its heavily traveled sections the tires had roughed it up, so I couldn't slide on it if I tried. Just a short distance from the roadway on either side, the ice was pristine. Several times when we stopped, I lay face-first on it and looked down. Within the ice I could see planes like in a cracked cube of crystal extending for six feet or more, and milky white fracture lines, and bubbles the size of baseballs or peas, and somewhere deep below, the blue darkness of unfrozen water.

Baikal's ice road usually lasts from mid-December until mid-April, so this one still had about a month left. Trucks passed us coming the other way; several were huge industrial contraptions with giant tires. At this stage of thickness no vehicle would be too heavy for the ice. But the surface also had occasional big cracks, some of them miles long and new enough that they had not yet refrozen. Water was sloshing out of them in places. These cracks made me nervous, especially when Aleksandr and the other driver got out and began stomping beside them to test the ice's strength. We had reached the biggest one of these so far—they're called *treshchiny*—and had stopped to examine it when a small bus filled with Buryats approached from the other side. The Buryats got out, reconnoitered, and then all but one of them jogged up to the fissure and hopped over. The remaining Buryat got back in the bus, backed it up, sped toward the crack, and jumped the bus across. After seeing this, we backed up and jumped it at the same spot.

Sometimes tree branches set in holes in the ice marked the roadway on either side. Maintenance of the road seemed to be handled by the travelers themselves. Certain of the smaller cracks had been bridged with scraps of carpet onto which buckets and buckets of water had been poured, creating ice-rug patches of surprising sturdiness. On the lake surface within sight of the main north–south road, a lot seemed to be going on. Often we passed little gatherings of cars clustered around ice-fishing holes. Other random locations had been used, apparently, as party spots, where a half dozen or more seats made of blocks of ice cut from the lake formed loose rings, and beer and vodka bottles were scattered around.

The weather cleared and then lowered again; as clouds moved in at low altitudes, a fine snow fell, blurring the already minimal scenery. The Niva ran all right in the 5° cold, but its heating system was insane. Furnace-hot air from the dashboard and backseat vents blasted our top halves so we sweated and suffocated, while from hidden gaps in the vehicle's lower parts, air as cold as the outdoors, or even colder because of our speed, shot at our legs and feet. The Russians did not find anything strange in this. I was glad for my Glacier Extreme boots, but no readjustment of my gear could warm my thighs, shins, and knees. In midafternoon we stopped for lunch and ate our kielbasa, bread, and hot, sugared tea off the Niva's back bumper. In the wind the food tasted delicious, seasoned with cold and engine exhaust. I was glad to be standing up and moving around.

Not much daylight remained when we saw the skyline of Severobaikalsk on the shore ahead. Driving up from the lake into the regular streets of a city was a peculiar, abrupt experience, and mildly disorienting. Our drivers said they knew of a good resort where we could stay. It was several miles outside the city, in a forest. They took us there and we got out and unloaded our luggage, and Sergei paid the drivers $350 in American cash—a dollar a kilometer. They turned right around and started back to Ust-Barguzin. Sergei went in to the resort office and talked to the manager, who showed us the cabins he had. They were more like sheds—pretty rustic, designed mostly for summer, and not what we needed at all. We carried our gear to the highway and boarded a local bus going back to Severobaikalsk. Again Sergei gave the bus driver some money at the end of the route and he drove us here and there, finally depositing us at what he said was the best hotel in town.

In fact it was not a hotel but a *profilaktorii*—defined by my Russian-English dictionary as an "after-work sanitorium"—for workers on the Baikal–Amur Railway. This *profilaktorii* had doctors' offices, a clinic, pools for hydropathy, an exercise room, a cafeteria, and quiet bedrooms, a few of which it rented to travelers when vacancies opened up. I've almost never stayed in a more restful place. Its atmosphere was calm and soothing, with a kind of low hum, like a test pattern on TV; even the entrees in the cafeteria were peaceful, down to the mild cream sauce on the cutlets and the vaguely sweet tapioca dessert. You couldn't walk in the *profilaktorii* door without the lady security person telling you softly to stop and take off your coat and hat—as if all troublesome rustling must be left outside. And right next to the building, just below the window of our room, the train yard of BAM's Severobaikalsk station gently sighed and creaked and rattled with trains moving back and forth all night.

Only one off note jarred the mood, and that was the safety posters in the halls. These posters warned against drunkenness and other kinds of inattention on the job by showing their grim consequences, in the form of train wrecks. Such hair-raising photographs! There were engines crashed head-on into other engines, and jumbled-up derailments with shredded passenger cars accordioning into one another and bodies spilling out, and freight cars tumbled like toys in a deep ravine, and so on. It made a person think twice about going for a sightseeing jaunt on the BAM. You could understand why this railroad might need a sanitorium.

The *M* in BAM stands for *Magistral'*, which means "highway," "railway," or "main line." It's a word of suitable grandeur for the Baikal–Amur enterprise. The idea of building a second railroad across Siberia to the Pacific dates from before Soviet times. As conceived (and eventually more or less built), the route of the Baikal–Amur Railway would begin at the city of Taishet in central Siberia, where the Trans-Siberian angles toward the southeast. Branching off from there, the BAM would head more directly eastward, go around Lake Baikal on the north side just as the Trans-Siberian does on the south, continue through remote and mountainous country until it intersected the northeastward-flowing section of the Amur, cross that river, and eventually meet the Pacific Ocean at the port city of Sovietskaya Gavan. This route would traverse fastnesses where even sending the surveying teams would be a challenge. Some surveyors had to be flown in, some traveled by reindeer. Only small progress in actual construction was made before the Second World War. A north–south line connecting the central BAM city of Tynda with the Trans-Siberian was completed in 1940, but in 1942 it was dismantled and moved west to provide ties and rails for tracks bringing Soviet trains to the Battle of Stalingrad. That Tynda section would not be reconstructed for thirty years.

Two hundred miles of railway, from Taishet to Bratsk, were finished in 1947. Surveying of the route continued in the 1950s, but not much additional track got built. Then in the '60s, more mineral deposits were discovered in the parts of Siberia accessible to the BAM route, and hostilities between the USSR and China demonstrated the need for a second line across Siberia, one not so near the Chinese border. In the early '70s, the Soviet government restarted the building project with full and official enthusiasm.

President Leonid Brezhnev told the country that the BAM project would be "a great labor exploit of our people," while the deputy minister of railways said it "outranks every other project in the history of railroad building anywhere in the world." "The track we are laying," said the deputy minister, "passes through a wide and rich range of practically every element in Mendeleyev's table." BAM's engineers studied the four-thousand-plus bridges that would have to be built along the line's two thousand miles and the dozens of tunnels—one of them almost ten miles—that would have to be dug through mountain ranges. Other giant projects, like the Magnitogorsk Dam at Bratsk or the Dnieper Hydropower Project, were referred to for comparison and inspiration. Nor were BAM's promoters exaggerating; the building of this railroad would turn out to be the last great construction project of Soviet times.

It also would be the last great Soviet enthusiasm among the country's youth. After the authorities of the BAM project announced that it needed young workers, tens of thousands of them left everything and headed for Siberia by any means they could, even on foot, to be a part of BAM. Those who went by the Trans-Siberian to Taishet were greeted with brass bands and cheers at every station. BAM wanted construction workers, welders, carpenters, lumberjacks, ironworkers, chemists, teachers, machine-tool builders, geologists, electricians, truck drivers, tailors, laundresses . . . Early arrivals lived in tents or in dugouts in the ground. Uplifting slogans proliferated, such as "We are building the Baikal–Amur Railway and the Baikal–Amur Railway is building us." Official artists were shipped in to record the glory on epic spreads of canvas. Different cities and regions of Russia sponsored different sections of track and settlements along the route. Moscow sponsored Tynda, Leningrad sponsored Severobaikalsk. For motivation, people recited this rhyme:

> Let us warn you, friends,
> Answering the taiga's call,
> The railway wants no
> Chickening out at all.

Somehow everything built in Russia looks as if it has been made by hand. Even in the most generic industrial structures, the concrete looks hand poured, the corners as if shaped, sometimes clumsily, by individual hands. To me, BAM had the one-of-a-kind appeal of a completely hand-made railroad. No book in English exists describing the construction of BAM from beginning to end, so I have no way of knowing, for example, the numbers of workers who died in the labor. Individual sacrifice and effort are evident everywhere. Work on the BAM project went on for seventeen years, and although it was supposed to be completed in 1982, the railroad didn't officially open along all its length until 1991, the year the Soviet Union disappeared.

Government support for Siberian enterprises dried up after that, and people started leaving the remote places. By 1994, instead of the predicted flowering of cities and resource extraction and industry along the BAM route, fewer people occupied the 580,000-square-mile region served by BAM than had been there in 1991. As a result, the great achievement of building this railroad got buried in events and forgotten. Nowadays you often hear of impressive feats of construction in the world—in modern China, especially—but after BAM I can't think of another grand construction project that was carried out with so much soul.

Take the city of Severobaikalsk. It doesn't even qualify as a city, really; its highest population level, about thirty-five thousand, had dropped to less than half that in recent years. But the people who planned and built Severobaikalsk had cared about it, you could tell. No settlement at all existed on this site in 1973. The next year the first work crews came out and lived in tents and railroad cars and cleared the timber. On the ceiling of our room at the *profilaktorii* hung a light fixture of an elaborateness beyond the needs of the situation. As I lay in bed I contemplated the fixture's embellishments of leaflike metalwork, scrolled tracery, and small cascades of faceted glass lusters. It reminded me of similar extravagances I'd seen out West in America—those almost heartbreaking domestic items

(a spinnet, a chiffonier) that the pioneers brought from their former homes in the hope that fanciness would civilize the wilds.

This city, or town, was as charming as any Soviet-era relic could be. Its street grid had been laid out satisfyingly and comprehensibly. The lakefront and the hills around the town had prevented the characteristic Soviet-era gigantism from spreading too far. There was the usual wide central avenue, the public square, and the drab bureaucratic buildings, but all within a small-town radius and scale. In the telephone building, the room of phone booths of hand-carved wood had a pleasantly over-heated stuffiness after the cold, and a woolly, intimate, school-coatroom smell. In the post office, an ingenious system had been devised where people waited sitting down, sliding along benches one after the next in sequence as they moved up to the front. When I went in to mail some postcards, almost everyone waiting was an old or middle-aged woman.

At the head of the wide central street, the Severobaikalsk train station dominated the town. The station was another work of wilderness-defying whimsy. A guidebook said that the station's design was supposed to suggest a sail, in tribute to the great port city of Leningrad/St. Petersburg, sponsor city for Severobaikalsk. Once I'd read that, I could see the station as a sail, or sails, but what it had first reminded me of was a dramatic wide-brimmed hat like the Three Musketeers wore. A narrow middle part corresponded to the high crown, and the sweeping, upward-tending parts on either side were like the flaring of the brim. The brim, or sails, made the station's roof, and glass panels that came all the way from the brim down to the ground were the sides. The spirit and strangeness of the structure drew your eye wherever in town you happened to be; it cried a bold modernist *yawp* into the land's wide silence. Of all the pieces of Soviet architecture I've ever seen, this was the only one I'd describe as fun.

On our first day in Severobaikalsk, Sergei took a bus to some slopes outside town and spent the afternoon skiing. The return bus broke down, so he didn't get back until evening. Meanwhile, I geared up for the cold, put on my snow-tire boots, and explored the town. The day was sunny, clear, and calm. By taking occasional breaks inside warm public places, I had no difficulty staying outside for long strolls. Beyond the central administrative area, the town looked ramshackle, like a Western mining town. On some of the houses, sections of railroad cars had been used to add a room, or repairs had been improvised with sheets of corrugated iron. Most of the buildings in town were blocks of apartments, usually four stories high. I sat in front of one for a while and sketched the many kinds of antennae on its roof. In ninety minutes of sketching, I froze so I could no longer draw and had to start walking again. On a hill above town, I came upon the ruins of an amusement park with carnival-type rides lying around in pieces, and benches and walkways deep in snow. In a sort of cove of benches near one dismantled ride, a group of teenage girls and boys were smoking cigarettes and drinking from plastic liter-bottles of beer. The gust of alcohol breath and cigarette smoke and pheromones that came from them was more pungent for being concentrated by the cold.

One of the guidebooks had mentioned a museum in the middle of Severobaikalsk devoted to the construction of BAM. I hunted all over for this museum. Finally a lady at the coat check in an unidentified public building told me the BAM museum was closed for *remont* (repair), but

the place I was now in contained another interesting attraction—
Severobaikalsk's winter garden. I checked my coat and she showed me to
it. The reason I hadn't noticed it from outside was that its floor-to-ceiling
windows were obscured by condensation. I stopped short at the hot,
moist air suddenly engulfing me. From the name "winter garden" I
hadn't pictured what this would be. Here in the frozen-solid center of
Siberia, Russian romanticism or BAM pride or both had created a tropical oasis, with burgeoning greenery and a waterfall and a small tiled pond
and birds flitting about in the upper stories.

There were ficuses, banana plants, wild grapevines, cacti, pineapple
plants, and lemon trees growing this way and that in the bath of heat.
The gardener, a woman of late middle age named Marina Tabakova, met
me at the entrance and took me around. She had a broad face, blue eyes,
and brown-and-gray hair. She wore a blue blouse with white stitching
and carried a pair of yellow gardening gloves. Marina Tabakova told
me that she used to teach elementary school but had recently retired.
She and her husband had come out to work on BAM in the 1970s and
had raised their children here, and now their children were grown and
she had two grandchildren—a girl, seventeen, and a boy, twenty. Her
husband, who still worked part-time for BAM, was the handyman for
the garden. She said she loved showing people the garden. The last
writer who had visited it, she said, was an Irishwoman named Dervla
Murphy who had arrived in Severobaikalsk two summers ago riding
a bicycle.

We had been talking only a short while when Marina Tabakova's husband arrived to take her to the pharmacy. She said she had more to tell
me and I must come back later in the afternoon. I said I would, and then
I walked around town some more, browsed in a bookstore, and returned
to the *profilaktorii* to pick up my tape recorder. When I came back to
the winter garden at four o'clock, Marina Tabakova was there. I turned
on the recorder, and this (translated and somewhat edited) is what
she said:

"The winter garden was organized fifteen years ago. It moved here
from Novosibirsk. All the plants were small then. They were planted in
the ground, and over these years became so big." [Me: "Were you the
gardener then?"] "No, I was always a teacher. I'm not a gardener. But
nobody wanted this job, they paid little. But I love it, and I took it. I have

been working here for three years. I considered I was just obliged. This garden that people have made, I want to support in the way that it was when I got it, not to let the plants perish. Plants are like people, they love when somebody talks with them and communicates. Each has its own name. This is a rubber plant, this is yucca, this is monstera (aronia), these are small lemon and orange trees. What else? Well, a fig, a spiderwort . . . well, in general, every one has its own name . . .

"Here is the story I want to tell you. You know, there was a very unusual situation, two years ago, in 2003. The city of Ust-Kut, west of here, on the Lena River, have you heard of it? So, if you go down the Lena River to the north of Ust-Kut there is a small village called Verkhnemarkovo. On November tenth of that year it was very cold there, minus twenty-five degrees centigrade, ice already stays on the river. Some boys went fishing along the river. And suddenly from the sky this bird fell on them—a flamingo! A flamingo falls on them from above! It's snowing, ice all around, and this bird is falling. The boys picked up this bird and brought it home, started to treat its frostbitten toes, even some of its small feathers have fallen off.

"So they took care of it, and cured it, and in January of 2004 they brought it here to us in the winter garden, and the flamingo lived here in our garden. Crowds of people, everybody came here to look at this miracle. Here the flamingo became so beautiful and haughty. Our flamingo was shown on TV, they spoke about it on the radio, it was in newspapers and magazines. It is a real celebrity, a superstar, our flamingo. We fed him minced fish made in a meat grinder, carrots, all vegetables, whatever you have. But he was not pink, but gray. Flamingos are pink because of the pink in the hermit crabs and shrimps they eat, but Baikal has no shrimps, so he didn't have those, and that's why he was so grayish. But so beautiful, haughty, independent he was.

"The flamingo stayed with us for seven months and then we forwarded it to the Krasnoyarsk zoo. And now the flamingo is in the zoo, it lives there, and everything is okay. But you know, nobody can explain the reason for this bird's appearance in Siberia, in the north—a bird that lives in the south and does not fly so far, they are not migratory birds. Geese and ducks do arrive in our area, we admit, but this bird lives only in the south.

"But this is not all yet.

"Last year, also in November, on the Yenisei River in the north near the city of Yeniseisk, in the same way boys also find a second bird—*another* flamingo! This second flamingo was also frostbitten. It also was rescued and sent to us, and this other flamingo we also warmed up and caressed, and it too was then taken away to Krasnoyarsk. Now there are two of them there. Our first is called Phila, and the second Phima. Only, I do not know what they are, girls or boys, because they still are baby birds, little ones. Such a wonderful story. You are a writer—isn't it a most unusual story? How would one explain this occurrence? How come that the flamingos appeared here? I'll show you a few photos, just look."

She took a few snapshots from an album on a garden bench. The pictures of the flamingo—the first or second one, I'm not sure which—had the radiant, revelatory quality of icon paintings. They showed the flamingo standing in the winter garden's tiled pond and regarding the photographer with an expression that was, indeed, haughty. He (or she) looked as if he had just planted the flamingo flag and claimed this place for Flamingo. Though kind of gray, he was definitely a flamingo. He seemed to have become comfortable with his singularity, and to accept as a matter of course the attention focused on him. Naturally he would find a tropical forest in the middle of Siberia, and naturally it would need a flamingo.

When I left the winter garden, darkness had fallen and the lights had come on in the town. The temperature had dropped a lot; the snow underfoot was so cold it creaked.

Sergei returned to the *profilaktorii* in a great mood after his day of skiing. Aside from the bus breaking down, all had gone excellently. He had been able to rent a good pair of skis, and he had deep, fresh powder snow and the slopes almost to himself. The only other person skiing at the resort that day was the mayor of Severobaikalsk, he said. In between runs, Sergei and the mayor had talked. Sergei said the mayor was rather discouraged with life. The mayor had told him that Severobaikalsk now had very few jobs, and the railroad, the only employer of consequence, had begun to cut back and lay people off, and many people were trying to move away. (I could believe that, having seen signs advertising apartments for sale all over town.) The reason nobody else was skiing was that almost everybody in Severobaikalsk is old, the mayor said. He told Sergei that Severobaikalsk was dying.

Chapter 26

From Severobaikalsk we traveled east and then north to the city of Ya-kutsk—by train for about fifty-three hours, then by hired car for another eight. I became punch-drunk from travel well before we got there. First we rode on the BAM in a comfortable sleeping compartment with a big window and two berths. We boarded it at the Severobaikalsk station, whose mad modernism and vaulting windows gave the departure a sense of real moment, as if we were stepping from the mother ship into empty space. How to describe this train's slowness, its endlessness? The compartment window slowly fed the snow and forest into the past. Where the trees stood far apart, each had its own perfectly rendered shadow on the snow beside it, but where they grew thickly, their shadows lay jumbled together. I had never seen a more Christmassy landscape, except there were no little lit-up village churches, no Budweiser sleighs, no red ribbons, and, for great stretches, no sign of human or animal life of any kind.

A village we went through not long after Severobaikalsk appeared to be leaning uniformly to the right—fences, buildings, light poles and all—with the wind and the weight of the snow. I noted a sign with the village's name: KHOLODNAYA (Cold). We crossed the upper Angara River, a lake-wide plain of ice, where sharp-tipped icy mountains ranged like fence palings to the north. We disappeared into long, dark tunnels, including the ten-mile one. Occasionally the bigger BAM towns had a railroad station even wackier than Severobaikalsk's. These stations sported turrets, semicircular windows, conning towers, and giant clocks, among other flights of sub-Arctic surrealism. At several stations I got off and walked around. The way the arrival and departure announcements echoed in the boundless emptiness gave a new dimension to train yard solitude. Temperatures were holding at about −10°F; perhaps a frozen silence is a more profound kind. Occasionally, children's voices would rise from someplace in the vicinity, or a distinct and singular clink of metal would ring out. Sounds of hissing would burst suddenly from the train, followed by more deep-taiga silence.

Cylindrical, squat coal stoves at each end of the train-car corridors provided the cars' heat. Sometimes at a station a tractor-drawn wagon would pull up next to the car and a guy in the back of the wagon would shovel coal into big buckets the car attendants brought to him. If the attendant was a woman, the guy in the wagon would hop out and help her lift the coal buckets into the door of the train car. Then the wagon would pull ahead to the next car. The long-handled dustpan our attendants used to scoop the coal dust and tracked-in snow from the car's entryway had the cartoon characters Snoopy, Woodstock, and Linus on the pan's flat part; Snoopy was holding a banner that said "Rah." The attendant used a broom made of broom sedge wrapped with black electrical tape for a handle.

For a day or so the attendants in our car were a young husband and wife with a four-year-old daughter named Sophia. She could say, "What is your name?" in English. Sophia and I also talked a little bit in Russian. She kept referring to me as "the Chinese man." Her mother explained that almost every foreigner Sophia had seen so far in her life had been Chinese, so she had concluded that all foreigners must be of that nationality. At a high and bleak and snowy pass, the train stopped so workmen could crawl under the cars with hand axes and chop away the accumulated ice. While we were waiting for this to be done, Sophia's mother dressed her in her snowsuit so she could go out and play in the snow. As she climbed down from the train-car steps, she looked back at me and asked her mother, "Will the Chinese man come with us?"

All along the route I watched from the train window for wildlife or for animal tracks in the snow, but mostly I saw neither. It seemed unlikely to me that such a huge piece of country could be so unoccupied. I kept on looking, and all of a sudden in the middle of the same unchanging scenery I spotted a large bird sitting on a tree. The bird was brown, had a delta-shaped tail, and resembled a cross between a buzzard and a peacock. As the train passed by, it hopped from its branch and flew off with an impressive display of wingspan. We were beyond it before I could point it out to Sergei, but I described it to him, and he said it must have been a *glukhar'* (my Russian-English dictionary defines the word as "wood grouse"); the *glukhar'* is a prized game bird, said to be good to eat. I remembered I have a Russian children's book in which a boy gets lost in the Siberian taiga because he is pursuing a *glukhar'* deeper and deeper into the trees. During our entire sixty-one-hour journey to Yakutsk, through God knows how much forest, that was the only wild animal I saw.

Sergei and I had packed various nonperishable stuff to eat, like kielbasa and cookies and tea, but after a while our supplies began to run low and the packages they came in, brought out for the fourth or fifth reprise, looked less appetizing. At the train's longer stops, Sergei made quick canvasses of stores in the station vicinity in search of fresh bread or other additions, but there wasn't much to be had. Often he would come back having found nothing but bottled water of dubious origin or even-more-suspect kielbasa. At the Tynda station we had a longer stop than usual and he tried more shops. Most of them were closed, the rest almost empty, but he did find a few hard-boiled eggs, a small jar of mayonnaise, and two cans of pickled sea cabbage. He presented these finds to me triumphantly, then chopped the eggs, opened the tins of sea cabbage, and mixed these ingredients with the mayonnaise for a salad. The dish tasted only vaguely like food, but I was hungry, so I ate. Then I rebuked myself for my greed. Ever since I'd had food poisoning in St. Petersburg, I'd been afraid of getting it again, and now I'd walked into it with my eyes open. For a long while afterward I sat in the compartment waiting for the action to start. I pictured myself somehow rushed back to the Severobaikalsk *profilaktorii*, this time for real. After eight hours had passed without serious complaints, I figured I had gotten away with it.

The large town of Tynda is considered to be the capital of BAM, and the Tynda train station is another modernist fandango, its many bold architectural statements cramming themselves into one structure with an energy and incoherence difficult to summarize. Much clearer in my mind is the station's interior, which was a sort of mall of empty shops along hallways to nowhere radiating from the station's busy and relatively crowded central area. The interior's focal point was an improbable and elaborate fountain. In the middle of the Siberian winter, inside this not-warm train station, the fountain flowed and burbled. A water nymph, or maybe Venus herself, poured water from the fountain's high point down a cascade and into its broad basin. At the edge of the fountain, *Sibiriaki*—Siberian guys—were standing around in their heavy, multi-layered winter clothes. One was carrying a large steel ice auger, the kind used for drilling fishing holes.

At Tynda, the train turned north and took us another couple hundred miles to the coal-mining town of Neryungri, where it left the sleeping-compartment car by itself in the middle of a train yard. We sat there all night with no electricity, the coal fires dying in the corridor stoves, and the bathroom locked. I went out and made a few tentative explorations of the train yard in the dark; throbbing diesel engines hemmed us in like a sleeping elephant herd. In the lee of an engine I called my wife on the satellite phone. I had to take off my gloves to dial in the icy half-light; I found her running out to do errands on a balmy afternoon. The next morning another train came and hooked us to it and pulled us slowly north, although not all the way to Yakutsk, because the tracks don't go that far. The last three-hundred-some miles to Yakutsk beyond the tracks' end must be navigated by motor vehicle on a semiwilderness highway.

We took a cab from the town of Aldan, shortly before the end of the train line. A driver came into the train car while the train was stopped there, offered us a good price to Yakutsk, and the next minute we were loading our stuff in the trunk of his little Toyota. I sat in the middle of the Toyota's backseat, Sergei on my right, and on my left a thin old woman with dark eyes and a beaklike nose. As we left the town she argued and complained about the fare with the driver, a good-natured guy in a black turtleneck and a black leather vest who called her "babushka" (grand-mother) and parried her thrusts unperturbedly. In the passenger seat in front was a young Moldavian woman named Vera who was going to Ya-kutsk to visit her brother.

I had on my heavy down coat with its pockets full of notebook, sketch-book, disposable camera, documents, etc. After the babushka tired of ragging the driver, she started in on how the fat American was crushing her. I was doing all I could to keep from leaning on her, but I had no seat belt and nothing much to hold on to, and the driver drove fast, and sometimes I lurched. A sign at the side of the road said YAKUTSK 490 KM. The babushka muttered, complained, and groaned. Warming to her theme, she expounded at every swerve on how she was being pummeled, and what huge things I must have in my pockets, etc. About halfway to Yakutsk we stopped to get something to eat at a roadside café. While the others went in, I stayed outside for a moment, savoring the cold and the stars. The next day someone in Yakutsk told me it had gone down to forty below that night.

The café was a small cabin structure with steps leading up to it from the parking lot and an igloo-style entry chamber with an outer and inner door. When anyone opened the outer door, a big cloud of steam burst forth, and because of that a white horse-collar of fine-crystal frost had grown all around the door frame. I went inside, pulled the door shut, and opened the inner door. I found the babushka, my accuser, waiting for me. "There he is, the fat American!" she announced to the other diners. "See how big he is, in his big American coat? This is the one who crushes me! This is what I must endure!" and so on. Then she cackled a gap-toothed, beady-eyed old-lady laugh. I laughed, too. Everybody in the café laughed.

After supper, Sergei, Vera, the driver, and I were all in the car ready to go, but the babushka was not around. Then she emerged into the car's headlights, stepping from the trees beside the parking lot. She looked into the lights with her head cocked to one side. "Baba Yaga," said Vera, and with her skinny legs, knee-length coat, head scarf, and beaked nose the babushka did look like that witch from the children's story. Back in the car she once again set up such a grumbling that the driver, who had been remonstrating with her, finally pulled over and considered what should be done. Vera, in a sweet and respectful voice, asked the babushka if maybe she would like to switch with her and ride in the front seat. The babushka agreed readily and took Vera's place, where she chatted with the driver, perhaps about her recipes for boiling small children. Meanwhile, Vera and Sergei and I quit trying not to lean on one another and rode all bouncing around in the swerving car, which by now was following a nerve-racking shortcut atop the frozen Lena River, where the swerves greatly multiplied. Vera told me not to worry about leaning on her, and Sergei said, "Don't pay any attention to what the babushka said. You're a normal-sized person."

After the black darkness of the previous three hundred miles, the lights of the city of Yakutsk suddenly rose around us like fireworks in the sub-Arctic night. At about midnight we rolled up in front of the Sterkh Hotel, one of Yakutsk's fanciest, and Sergei went in to check out the room rates. Vera got out to look for a pay phone to call her brother. She soon came back because none of the pay phones worked. She was at a loss. I took out my satellite phone and offered to try Vera's brother's number with that. At first I couldn't make the phone work at all. Then somehow the satellite connection improved, I dialed again, and the brother answered. I gave Vera the phone and it vanished into the thick fur around her hood. Her happiness at hearing his voice was like a sweepstakes winner's. Five minutes later the brother arrived in his car in front of the hotel and Vera said goodbye to all of us and left with him. I felt a small uptick of patriotic pride that I kept to myself. Bravo, American technology! Bravo, Iridium Communications, Inc., of Bethesda, Md.!

. . .

Yakutsk is the capital of the Sakha Republic, sometimes called Yakutia. The city lies between the latitudes of Anchorage and Nome. The Sakha Republic is about the same size as India, but has a population of one million compared to India's 1.3 billion. That is, India has 1,299,000,000 more people than the Sakha Republic on about the same amount of land. Many of the people in the Sakha Republic are natives—Yakuts, Evens, Evenks, and Chukchis. Many native people live in taiga villages and follow their reindeer herds from place to place for parts of the year. Others have moved to Yakutsk and smaller cities. As we stood in the cold outside the Sterkh Hotel and Vera talked on the phone, young native women came and went, apparently from a party inside. The women wore short fur jackets, sparkly jeans, and leg warmers, and a few had glitter in their blond-streaked black hair.

When Wendell Willkie, the American politician, visited Yakutsk in 1942, he said it reminded him of Elwood, Indiana. Willkie grew up in Elwood and thus is another on the long list of Midwesterners who have traveled in Siberia. He came here because of the war. Although Willkie lost to Roosevelt in the 1940 presidential race, he was credited afterward with helping to unify America behind the war effort, and in that capacity he made a round-the-world tour in a U.S. bomber to represent his country and demonstrate the Allies' mastery of the air. The part of Yakutsk that specifically evoked Elwood for him was the boardwalks on the bigger streets; his hometown had board sidewalks when he was a boy. Willkie also spoke more generally about the heartiness of Yakutsk's citizens, the simplicity of their tastes, and the place's "tremendous vitality." He said, "The town itself seemed, in many ways, like a western town in my country a century ago."

As possibly the only person on earth today who has actually seen both Yakutsk and Elwood, Indiana, I think I understand what he meant. The Yakutsk Willkie visited was a frontier city, as the Elwood of his youth was a frontier town. Both were lively settlements far from their country's center (though the one, obviously, much farther than the other). Observers before and after Willkie noted the many similarities between the Siberian and the Western American frontiers—from the hogs running loose in the villages, to the smallpox epidemics that hit the natives, to the rumors of tribes descended from the ancient Hebrews somewhere out in the wilds, to the environmental problems of overplowing and dust storms that came with development, and so on. Willkie's trip also took him to Cairo, Baghdad, Moscow, and Peking; he stopped in Yakutsk partly because he was going that general direction anyway, and of all the cities he saw, this raw metropolis in the dark of the forest no doubt did look more like someplace in America.

But today I don't think anyone who saw Yakutsk would be reminded of Elwood, or of anyplace like it. Elwood is another small American town that has passed through stages of early settlement, enthusiastic development, industrial boom, and recent decline. In those terms, its frontier years ended ages ago. Yakutsk, on the other hand, is still a frontier place, still hanging on to the writhing wilderness by its fingernails. The Lena River, which Yakutsk is technically on the left bank of, has moved away from most of the city, and even to get to the river heading due east from the center of town you have to cross a no-road zone of islands and former river channels and oxbow lakes. The river itself, once you do reach it, is at least four miles wide. There is no bridge across it at Yakutsk, nor is there any farther downstream; upstream, the closest bridge is more than seven hundred miles away. To travel from Yakutsk to Nizhni Bestyakh, just on the other side of the river, you go by ferry in the warmer months and by ice road in winter. When the river is not yet frozen but too dangerous for boats because of the floating ice, people either don't go, or fly.

All of Yakutsk rests on permafrost, which extends thirteen hundred feet down. The city's average winter temperature is −42°. "The climate of Yakutia is the severest of the inhabited world," says the Encyclopaedia Britannica. Nome, Yakutsk's almost colatitudinist, has a population of about 3,500; in 2002, the population of Yakutsk was 210,642. The city has Orthodox churches with shiny onion domes, and big hotels, and an expressway along the (former) bank of the Lena, and a branch of the Russian Academy of Sciences, and a university, and a public square with, in winter, giant ice sculptures (Great Patriotic War tableaux; knight of medieval Rus on horseback), and one of those enormous, skyline-dominating, two-and-a-half-times-the-height-of-anything-else TV-radio towers that Russian cities can't seem to do without. This far north, in this drastic a climate, there is no other city of Yakutsk's size in the world.

Another difference between Yakutsk and present-day Elwood: in downtown Yakutsk I saw signs for a Gap clothing store, a Benetton, a Baskin-Robbins, and Wrangler Jeans. In Elwood, many of the stores are empty, mainly because the town's citizens now tend to go to the malls of Indianapolis or Muncie or Kokomo to shop. None of those familiar commercial logos may be found on signs in downtown Elwood, Indiana.

While in Yakutsk, you can (or could) visit the Museum of Music and Folklore of the Peoples of Yakutia, which is hidden behind a fence on Kirov Street; you can study the exhibits about Yakut authors in the Yakut Literature Museum, whose collections are partly housed in a giant cement yurt; or admire the traditional log construction of the old Orthodox church on Petra Alekseeva Street; or check out the regional museum, which has a skeleton of a whale; or look through the furs and hand-carved objects for sale in various shops; or attend a performance at the Government Ballet and Opera Center; or stroll the campus of Yakutsk University; or schedule a tour of the subterranean laboratories of Yakutsk's Permafrost Institute, where many important discoveries have been made.

Sergei and I skipped all that, however—too cold. Instead, the first day after we got to Yakutsk we mostly stayed in and watched TV in the hotel room while recuperating from our recent long time on the road. Sergei was a fan of the American sitcom *Mad About You*, and we happened to catch the episode in which Helen Hunt and Paul Reiser accidentally lock themselves in their bathroom. Overdubbed in Russian, the comical dialogue sounded better. The Russian TV news had a long feature about the red-tailed hawk known as Pale Male who with his mate had built a nest on a ledge of a Fifth Avenue apartment building in New York. Also, there was chaotic-looking coverage of an antigovernment uprising currently going on in Kyrghyzstan.

On other days he and I hung out with Dr. Sergei V. Shibaev, director of the Siberian Geophysical Survey at the Russian Academy of Sciences, in downtown Yakutsk. Sergei Shibaev was a dark-haired, young-looking guy with a high forehead and a quick, untrammeled laugh. Sergei had known him from university. We met him at the Academy of Sciences headquarters, a large and undistinguished government building with an entryway smelling strongly of heating oil, and sat in his office with him and some of his colleagues.

Nowadays many geologists do their work on computers and seldom venture into the field. Geology, formerly an outdoor profession, has become not necessarily that anymore. In my own limited encounters with geologists, I have found that they have differing opinions about which kind of geology, outdoor or indoor, is superior. From the look and atmosphere of the Academy of Sciences geology offices, I understood that Sergei Shibaev and his colleagues were the outdoor kind. Maps of Yakutia covered the office walls, rock samples and geological gear lay here and there on the desks, and one long wall of the central office was covered with a detailed multicolor map of the geology of the Russian Federation from Baltic to Bering Strait. Most of the geologists in Sergei Shibaev's department, he said, spend some or all of the warmer months in the taiga.

Maybe because of this focus on the actual land out there, Sergei Shibaev took a proprietary interest in the question of where in Yakutia Sergei and I might go next. The two Sergeis put their heads together, consulted maps, made calls, and (of course) looked up information online. I could not contribute much to this, so I fell into conversation with a geologist named Anatoly Firsovich Petrov. He was a white-haired, balding fellow, seventy-one years old, whose sturdy-looking build and general appearance brought to mind Nikita Khrushchev. He wore a blue suit jacket, a dark tie, gray trousers, and a light gray sweater-vest, and on his lapel he had two small round pins bearing emblems of his profession. From his somewhat oratorical style of speaking I gathered that he was the memoirist and philosopher of the department. After a while I asked how he had come here and what his work in Yakutia had been. He said he'd be happy to tell me. We went down the hall to his own office, where we could talk more easily, and he began:

"I am a specialist in plate tectonics, so I am interested in the structure of the earth's crust—in how the earth develops, and why the seas are where they are, and what influences what, and where earthquakes come from. You understand that everything depends on the interactions of the plates. Here is our map [indicating a map on the wall]. You see in this map of Yakutia that we have tectonic plates coming together, so we have many earthquakes, here in the region north of Baikal especially. These are the lines where the earth's crust breaks.

"I learned geology at Saratov State University, in that city, which is on the Volga River. My special diploma work was about a small river, the Markha, which is in Yakutia and which runs into the Vilyui River. I was here first in 1954 to study the geology of this river, and after finishing my diploma I became attached to all this open space in Yakutia. I am a nature fan, my soul strives not to destroy but to create. To protect nature. I do not say this to flaunt it, I say it sincerely.

"My father was completely illiterate, and although it is necessary to say that we blame Soviet authority from time to time, and that there were a lot of bad things, like gulags, on the other hand neither my father nor my mother ever had a chance to finish even a single grade of school. They were poor, and there were three of us children in our family, and all three, my sister and brother and I, all of us received a higher education at federal expense. There were many like us in the Soviet Union. Please, don't take it as my approval of Soviet authority. But really, 'Uchit'sya, uchit'sya, uchit'sya' [Study, study, and study], as Lenin told all young Communists—this really existed! Yes, in a way I was like Lomonosov, another poor boy who studied and who became a scientist.

"I arrived here in Yakutia to live in 1958. I was twenty-four years old. Here in Yakutia I liked, first of all, the purity of the country. Second, in Yakutia there were then comparatively few people who had studied at university, and most of the geology of Yakutia was unknown. Therefore I understood I had an opportunity here for interesting work. A new place, new people, and three hundred million square kilometers in Yakutia. Well, one can only dream about such work. At first the aim was as follows: to search for diamonds. We used various indicators as are found in South Africa, where so many diamonds are on the Kimberley plateau, and we looked for similar geologic structures. Basically we were searching for kimberlites.

"I don't exaggerate when I say I really loved the geologists who came here and who I worked with. I loved the tribe of geologists here—quite seriously, sincerely, from the bottom of my heart. Mutual assistance, one should save a friend even at the expense of your own life. Sharing even the last piece of bread. I lived in Yakutsk but I worked in Yakutia everywhere. In summers we geologists went in groups for four months, maybe five or six months, living in tents in the taiga, in totally different places. Well, you can imagine, during half a year with the same people, you live and work like brothers and sisters.

"Well, it was very complex work. I was engaged in everything, maybe it is not necessary to tell you about all of it, but I was involved in every sort of thing—both oil and gas prospecting, iron ores, gold and diamonds and whatever. In the taiga we transported all our cargo on reindeer. We put twenty kilograms on a deer, there were sixty deer in a team, and a deer driver. Sometimes deer would fall. Very difficult work.

"Geology is not a profession, as we say, but a way of life. That attracted me, and I stayed. We were constantly studying the geological configuration of Yakutia, and as a result we made some unique discoveries. Not all the deposits we found were in this category, but some were absolutely unique. Udokan copper, for example, located in the Chita area on the border with Yakutia—this is one of the largest deposits of this copper in the world. Also of course there were very rare stones that we found. The best example is charoite. Three of us discovered charoite together—two Irkutsk geologists and I. I was the chief of the geological party that conducted the geological shooting of the formation where we found the charoite. Some eroded deposits in this formation looked unusual to us, so we hit them with a hammer—a geologist is always with a hammer—and we gathered samples of stones that we then brought back to Yakutsk, and our colleague, Vera Parfentyevna Rogova, named this stone 'charoite.' Since then it has been determined that charoite is a previously unknown stone. Also, no other deposits of charoite have been found anywhere in the world. Well, it is a very beautiful stone, it has been made into beautiful vases, some rich people even make basins for baths out of it.

"You ask what is my most favorite place in Yakutia, and I would not say that I have a most favorite, but there is a very beautiful river, the Chara. Charoite is named after it. The word means 'a charm,' or in plural, *chary*, it is sorcery, witchcraft. The rocks along this clear and pure Chara River are crumpled in folds, various and multicolored, green, blue, red, all capriciously bent. I have gone on vacation on a Danube River cruise, and people admire that river, of course. But the rocks there are gray. On the Chara there is such a combination of rocks! Do not think every cook praises only his own broth. I agree that the Danube is a good river, but the rocks on our Chara are more beautiful, in my opinion.

"I spoke earlier about Yakutsk as a clean place, and I can repeat: I have read much on ecology from meetings and international conferences, and I know there are problems of great importance for the whole globe. Let's take oxygen, this is most important, its consumption still increases, but natural places that produce oxygen become always fewer and fewer. Yakutia is notable for huge areas occupied by woods. This is true of all Siberia, in fact. Approximately 85 to 88 percent of the Siberian woods is still intact. In Yakutia we have a strong movement for leaving Yakutia as an ecological oasis. Leave it untouched—woods, moss, tundra (which makes oxygen, too). That is first. Second, there are a lot of rivers here, with excellent pure water. There is certainly pollution, as in the places where steamships go along the Lena River. But all other rivers in Yakutia are extremely pure, with reserves of water for all mankind. There is also a deficiency of freshwater today on the planet, as is known. We in Yakutia have freshwater here. By preserving woods here we preserve these rivers. If we cut the woods down, the rivers will dry up, speaking simply. We are convinced that the main riches of Yakutia and Siberia in general are woods and pure water.

"Certainly, you know, there are minerals here about which I have already spoken, and maybe it is also necessary for mankind to extract them. I myself discovered deposits, I feel we cannot do without them, without them there will be no money, and people need somewhere to work. But how to organize this extraction? We have a proverb: *I volki sytie i ovtsy tselye* [The wolves are fed and yet the sheep are whole]. We will try to do both, extraction and preservation, but we believe our main task is the preservation of riches for generations to come.

"I assure you, I give my word to anybody, that 90 percent of our taiga territory today is absolutely pure. That is, there is no infection, no illness, no pollution. I can sincerely tell you, I worrylessly take a mug, or a cup, or a glass, and I come up to any puddle, and I scoop and drink, and I am not afraid. All of us who journey in the taiga do this, and not a single time was anybody poisoned. I actually put bread right on the ground. I put sausage on moss. All of us agree—as soon as we leave the city we can put anything on the grass. Do not think that we are savages. No. We understand that in other places there is infection and pollution. But here in our taiga I am sure I won't be poisoned. In this sense Yakutia is good for tourists who want to look at nature and not be afraid. We have plenty of such completely clean places here."

• • •

Somewhere along the academy's dim corridors were two museums, one devoted to the geology of Yakutia and the other to its paleontology. Both opened to visitors only by invitation. Sergei Shibaev said we should see them and he made a call, and an elderly female curator with an assistant appeared. The geology museum resembled a cross between a museum and a packed-full storeroom, with exhibits and wooden storage cases crowding one another along narrow aisles. Anatoly Petrov, who accompanied us, proudly produced a box of samples of charoite, which is a gaudy purplish stone, exactly in keeping with the country's overall color scheme. Studying a photo display on the wall, I tried to make visual sense of the big black-and-white panoramas of Yakutia's Mirny diamond mine, which appeared as a giant, tiered, conical hole in the earth with tiny trucks spiraling down into it. The curators passed around glass-topped wooden boxes divided into compartments, each of which contained a Yakutia diamond. The diamonds came in many sizes, from lima bean to regular aspirin pill size, and their tints ranged from clear to pewter to champagne. They rattled richly in their boxes when shaken.

I asked our guides who the dark-featured nineteenth-century fellow in a large oil portrait was, and they identified him as V. A. Obruchev, the pioneer geologist of eastern Siberia. As it happened, I had read some of Obruchev's memoir, *Moi Puteshestviia po Sibiri* (My Travels Through Siberia) when I was in St. Petersburg; at the time, I had the unachievable ambition of reading at least some of every known book with "Siberia" and "Travels" in its title. V. A. Obruchev first came to Siberia in the fall of 1888 to take a job with a newly established government department for geological explorations in Irkutsk, and he brought along his wife and seven-month-old son. The parents bundled the baby carefully for the journey in an inner sack of oilcloth and an outer sack of rabbit fur, with a down cap on his head. In the book's photographs the faces of the Obruchevs are hard to make out in the depths of their winter clothing.

The paleontology museum, down another twilit corridor, brought to mind the controlled confusion of an auto parts shop, with various sections of fossilized mammoths instead of radiators and transmissions lying around. I have already mentioned the museum's mammoth leg, with its well-preserved long hair, and the fossilized mammoth stomach cut cross-section to reveal the packed grasses of a last meal fossilized inside. There were mammoth tusks curling like untrimmed parentheses, and mammoth teeth, and pieces of fossilized mammoth hide with fur still on them, and a photo on the wall of a famous "mammoth graveyard" along a riverbank, where thousands of specimens had been found. A big part of the room was taken up by the outsize skeleton of a prehistoric rhinoceros (*nosorog*, in Russian) that had been found in Yakutia and that represented, according to the curator, the most complete skeleton of this animal in the world. On the wall above the rhino hung a bison skull resembling in every detail (ghostly eye sockets, tapering nostrils, scaly horns) any bison skull one might see in an Indian museum in the American West, except this skull was at least half again as large. It had belonged to one of our American bison's Siberian ancestors in the millennia before the species crossed the Bering Land Bridge, adapted to the American environment, and shrank in size.

Chapter 27

I had wanted to go from Yakutsk to the village of Oimyakon, said to be the coldest place on earth outside Antarctica. After looking into the details of this journey, the two Sergeis advised against it. The distance to Oimyakon was about six hundred miles, many of them on difficult, mountainous roads, and by the time we got there the village would be in the middle of its *Polus Kholodnii* (Pole of Cold) Festival, which might create problems finding a place to stay. Time and money considerations seemed to put Oimyakon out of reach.

The Sergeis suggested that instead he and I go on that same northeast-bound highway out of Yakutsk, only not as far, and make our first stop at the village of Khandyga. From Khandyga we could continue to the village of Tyoplyi Kliuch (Warm Spring), where we could visit a museum about the gulag. Past Tyoplyi Kliuch, a smaller and less-traveled road branched off heading farther north. This road went about 125 miles to a village called Topolinoe, which was a Even settlement where we could see reindeer and native performances and dances. I agreed to this second plan. What decided me was that along the Topolinoe road, they said, we would pass the ruins of gulag labor camps.

At nine o'clock on a Wednesday morning, with the temperature at –25°F, a Russian-made jeep called a Uazik (after its initials, UAZ, which stand for Ulianovskii Avtomobilnyi Zavod, or Ulianovsk Automobile Works; the first word comes from Lenin's original last name, Ulianov) arrived in front of the Sterkh Hotel to take us the two-hundred-some miles to Khandyga. Of the Uazik's driver, I find I have preserved nothing in my notes except his cigarette; the smoke and the diesel fumes in the jeep had me hacking for days.

Just outside Yakutsk, the road descended to the surface of the Lena River, and then it continued on the ice for about twelve miles. On Lake Baikal's ice road, I recalled, we had seen other vehicles only occasionally. This Lena River ice road roared like a major highway, with a heavy traffic of cars and trucks going in each direction. Slowdowns at bumps or cracks made the flow bumper-to-bumper sometimes. Baikal's frozen surface could have been a salt flats or an endless snow-covered parking lot, but on the Lena, with its windings and the way the land was, you never forgot you were on a river. No matter how slow the traffic, almost no cars veered from the established roadway to take shortcuts across the ice.

After an hour or so, the traffic thinned out. We had left the river and were driving fast on a road of gravel covered with snow in a countryside sort of like Wisconsin's, with white fields, gray forests, and low hills. And, of course, completely lacking in fences. A brown sleigh full of round hay bundles zipped along the snow beside the road, the hooves of the shaggy horses tossing up clods of dirt and snow. In some fields the same kind of horses, hippie-haired in the mane and equally shaggy on the sides and in their tails, grazed the snow-covered ground with their heads buried up to the ears. The few cows we passed looked cold and resentful, breathing out steam, while ravens with no apparent purpose hopped and made random miniflights along the roadside.

At about two hundred miles from Yakutsk we came to the Aldan River. Aside from the tire tracks on the river's surface where we were about to drive across it, the Aldan showed no sign at all of human presence. Its wide floodplain, its long, uneven shoreline in the far distance opposite, and its border of dark or bare-branched trees in the winter haze could have been a Missouri River landscape from the days of Lewis and Clark.

We arrived in Khandyga at about five thirty in the afternoon and pulled up in front of the village's central administration building, into which Sergei and the driver disappeared. I stayed in the Uazik, and after a minute a *marshrutka* public-transport van parked beside me. On the van's sliding door was written:

Nu vy blin daete
khlopnesh' Dverio—
Umryosh ot montirovki.

With nothing else to do right then, I took out my dictionary and tried to translate that. Literally, it said, "Well you darn give a slam with the door—you die from being mounted." When Sergei came back, I asked him about the last words and he said they meant "from being hit with a tire iron."

Recently Sergei had started acting sullen and fed up again. We had been traveling together for almost three weeks; conceivably, I was getting on his nerves. I asked him if we were going to visit the gulag museum in Khandyga now and he said, "What gulag museum? Did you read there was a gulag museum here? Where did you hear there was a gulag museum here?" I said Sergei Shibaev had been talking about the Khandyga gulag museum yesterday. He said, "There is no gulag museum here. The gulag museum is another hundred kilometers from here." In fact, I had forgotten that the museum was not in Khandyga but in Tyoplyi Kliuch, sixty miles farther up the road. The waspishness of his reaction caused me to worry I was being taken on a snipe hunt, and I would once again see no prisons or evidence of same.

Khandyga had been a major military base until a few years before, and part of the village was still set off behind high fences made of those prefab cement panels that are everywhere in Siberia. The Aldan River ran beside the town. A wide and much-driven-on ramp of ice-covered earth led from the village down to the river's surface. On a stroll I took in the light remaining that afternoon, I went down the ramp and suddenly had to hop aside to avoid an empty coal truck as it sped around a corner. The truck descended the ramp and drove onto the roadway leading across the Aldan. Soon after that a truck came along in the opposite direction, crossing the river and climbing the ramp to the town. The incoming truck carried a full load of coal.

Khandyga ran on coal, it devoured coal. A tall brick stack above the village emitted, nonstop, a towering conical billow of dark gray, as one would expect on a $-22°$ afternoon. The usual insulated steam pipes laced the village with their meanderings, and where the heat was escaping from the more run-down houses you could tell the location of the cracks by the elaborate, pure-white excrescences of frost that had built up around them. Some of these frost blooms were huge, like an outsize bole or a clot of dried sap on the side of a tree.

Because of the constant fall of coal soot, the crust of the snow in the village was a crystal amalgam of ice, snow, and dust. Over the winter the snow had piled up until it was maybe four feet deep in the uncleared and untrodden places. Snow topped the village's many abandoned cars with Elvis-like coxcombs. Where shoveling had dug pathways, you could see the individual snowfalls delineated like layers of sediment in a road cut. After every snowfall, evidently, enough coal dust had fallen to leave a black residue. Then the next snow had arrived, and atop that a new layer of coal dust had accumulated, and so on. Seen in cross section, the snow of Khandyga was striped black and white like a torte.

Noting, as I often do, whatever happens to be on the ground at my feet, I came across a piece of litter in Khandyga that I nominate for special international recognition. This particular item, which I picked up and saved like a botanical specimen, was a pill packet formerly containing individually wrapped pills, each in its own bubble of foil affixed to the packet's cardboard backing. I know I can find a similar piece of litter— same cardboard (or plastic) backing, same little foil bubbles with the foil torn and the contents removed—anytime I want on the streets near my house in New Jersey. Because I've encountered it close to home, and all over Russia, and in Khandyga at the almost end of the earth, I assume that item of litter to be a globally universal thing. Its ubiquity has caused me to wonder what it is called. Among manufacturers of packaging, the name of this object is the "blister pack." I believe the blister pack might be the most widely distributed single item of litter in the world.

Khandyga's hotel turned out to be a long two-story building with a torte-snow roof and an abandoned car out front. Torn-open trash bags spilled their contents on the hard-packed street snow, attracting the customary businesslike ravens. Nothing about the exterior of this establishment identified it as a hotel, but inside it was warm and clean, and laid out more like a rooming house than a hotel. Men slept in one big room, women and young children in another. Each of these rooms had five or six narrow beds. A kitchen next to the men's sleeping room provided refrigerator, stove, and cookware. The hotel also offered one or two single bedrooms, but they had already been taken, so Sergei and I put our stuff in the men's bedroom and claimed beds. We found nobody in there except a Yakut teenager drinking a Coke and playing a Game Boy as he sat cross-legged on his bed.

A stocky, blunt-faced young woman with short pale hair ran the hotel. We talked to her while Sergei made us dinner—frozen pelmeni that he bought at a local shop, boiled, and served with sour cream. I asked the manager what people found to do in Khandyga. She said she and her husband loved to fish and caught many fish in the summer in the Aldan. I was pleased to notice that she spoke with an accent, pronouncing some words differently and dropping the endings on others. I had known there were Siberian accents but had never been sure I was hearing one before. As I ate the pelmeni I found a thick black hair in it and added that, mentally, to the rock I'd bitten down on while eating a beet salad a few days earlier in Yakutsk. This latest surprise put me on a food-poisoning watch again. It would've been bad to get sick in this hotel, with twenty-some guests and only one bathroom. And throwing up, etc., outside would have been awkward, too, given the nighttime temperatures. Luckily no postmealtime consequences ensued.

In Sergei's current brisk and uncheerful mood, he had stopped telling me what was going on. I was retaliating by not deigning to ask. We had discussed the route and the expense in proceeding beyond Khandyga, and I had given the okay for it. But just how this next leg of the journey was to be accomplished I didn't know; the car that had brought us from Yakutsk had gone back to the city with a return load of passengers, leaving us without wheels. I knew Sergei must be planning something, from the calls he made at the phone in the hallway. I tried to eavesdrop on him, but he talked too fast. As far as I knew, when morning came we might be continuing on from Khandyga . . . or not. I sat on my bed writing in my notebook and trying to seem above it all. Sergei lay on his bed reading a Russian newspaper similar to the *National Enquirer*.

At breakfast he told me to be packed up by eleven, when our ride would arrive. I got ready, but then nobody showed. Sergei accepted this without comment and I made no inquiries as I waited in full cold-weather gear (minus coat and boots) and paged through my notes. At about eleven forty-five the phone rang; more negotiations about itinerary and price. Soon after, Sergei summoned me to the front hallway, where he introduced me to the woman who would be our guide over the next days. Her name was Galina Dmitrievna Gotovtseva and she came originally from the village of Topolinoe, our final destination. Now she lived in Khandyga and had some official position in the village. She certainly looked official, even ambassadorial, with her high, arched eyebrows; long face; narrow, fitted red coat going all the way down to her ankles; and tall hat of black fur.

Galina Gotovtseva told us she was a Even; so were the other passengers we would be traveling with. The Even (pronounced Yev-YEN) are similar to the Evenk, though I couldn't tell you the differences between the tribes. In former times the Even were called the Lamuts and the Evenk the Tungus. Both are reindeer-herding tribes. After we had loaded our stuff into the back of the buslike van waiting outside, Galina introduced us to the other passengers: first, Aleksandr Gavrilovich Sleptsov, the driver, an equanimous, broad-faced man in his midthirties; then Gavriil Dmitrievich Sleptsov, a rangy older fellow, the driver's father; then Andrei Petrovich Struchkov, a smooth-featured, athletic-looking man in his late forties. All these she identified as reindeer breeders and herders. Andrei Struchkov, she added, was also a famous reindeer racer.

With Andrei Struchkov were his wife, Rosa Dmitrievna Struchkova, whom Galina identified as a *chumrobotnitsa*, a word whose meaning is like "housekeeper," except the house in this case is a *chum*, a reindeer herder dwelling made of hide and resembling a tipi; their daughter, Varvara Andreyevna; and Varvara's daughter, Regina, who was two years old and watched everything. Also there was a small boy of maybe nine or ten who was related to the driver and did not feel well. I missed his name.

Out of politeness to the foreigner, our hosts had me sit in the front seat. I was happy about this, because the driver, after a few friendly questions, seemed content not to talk, and I could sit and daydream without my usual language struggles or worries that we were about to fall through the ice or skid off the road. We proceeded along the wide, well-graded, straight gravel highway, and the younger Sleptsov drove both quickly and with care. I felt comfortable in the vehicle, too, because this kind of microbus—it's called an RAF—which resembles the old dependable Volkswagen bus, is of a sound, wide-wheelbase, low-to-the-ground design, and is the only Russian-made passenger vehicle I've heard praised by Russians themselves. A spell of thinking about nothing during this trouble-free ride revived me better than a nap.

Two officials—a hefty, pretty, middle-aged woman and a slim, smiling young man—met us in Tyoplyi Kliuch and led us to the Tyoplyi Kliuch Museum of the Magadan Highway. From our reception I assumed that this was an open-to-the-public attraction associated somehow with the local government. However, the museum, which commemorated the settlement's history and the prison workers who built the road we were on, appeared to be entirely the work of its curator, Valentina Gerdun, who met us at the door. She was a short, well-dressed, soft-featured woman of seventy-four with a gold tooth in the lower right corner of her smile. She identified herself as a poet, and as she led us around, her passion for the museum she had made bordered on the ecstatic.

The Magadanskaya Trassa (as the highway we were on was called) had been built by prison labor in the 1930s to provide a land route to Magadan, capital of the Soviet slave-labor gold mines of the Kolyma Valley. Magadan is about nine hundred miles from Yakutsk, on the Pacific Ocean's Sea of Okhotsk. The highway runs through the coldest inhabited places on earth—Oimyakon is in its vicinity—and during its early years of construction, workers on its Kolyma section north of Magadan almost all died before the road was done. At the peak of operation in the thirties and forties, the mines of Kolyma produced perhaps 50 percent of all the gold being mined at that time in the world. By comparing the number of deaths in the Kolyma mines with the corresponding output of gold, historians have estimated that each ton of Kolyma gold cost between seven hundred and a thousand lives, or about one life for every two pounds of gold. The gold, sometimes carried out of the hills in backpacks, began its journey to western Russia along this highway.

Valentina Gerdun's museum displayed photographs of prisoners who worked on the road, along with short biographies of them, articles of clothing and other small mementos, and poems they had written. The museum's general tone was not at all accusatory, however; rather, Valentina Gerdun celebrated the highway as a great achievement of the Russian people. As in many Russian museums, a lot of this one celebrated the country's victory in the Great Patriotic War. The village—also known as Posyolok Dorozhnikov, or Roadbuilders' Settlement—had been the site of an airfield on the Alaska–Siberia transfer route, a Lend-Lease program that brought almost eight thousand fighter planes and light bombers from American factories to Russia's Eastern Front, thereby helping to win the battles of Kursk, Kuban, Stalingrad, and the war itself. Four hundred and fifty prisoners, two hundred horses, and fifty trucks and other machines built the Posyolok Dorozhnikov landing strip during August, September, and October 1943, she said. For finishing this air-strip ahead of time, many NKVD officers and a few civilians received awards, although no awards were given to the prisoners.

This air-transfer arrangement was perhaps the greatest single work of collaboration between Russians and Americans in history. Congress had voted the Lend-Lease Act into law in March 1941 with the intention of providing war matériel to America's allies, particularly England, for use against the Germans. After Hitler broke his nonaggression pact with Stalin and attacked the Soviet Union on June 22, 1941, the United States and the Soviets signed a protocol whereby the Lend-Lease plan would be extended to that country as well. At the start of the war, the Soviet air force had a third fewer planes than the Luftwaffe, and many of those were prewar canvas relics. Attempts to ferry U.S. aircraft quickly to Russia by a North Sea route or from the south, via the Persian Gulf, did not work well, so Lend-Lease planners came up with the idea of sending the planes to the Eastern Front by going west, across North America and Asia. The idea irritated the Russians, apparently, and at first they presented bureaucratic obstacles, but by late in 1942 the route was in operation. American P-39 and A-20 fighter planes and A-29 light bombers began showing up in air combat on the Eastern Front in early 1943.

To cross the continents, the air-transfer route needed many primary and secondary airfields and hundreds of pilots. Disassembled planes went by freight car to northwest Montana, where local workers put them together and got them fully ready to fly. Young Montana women had the job of painting on the Red Star and other Soviet insignia. American pilots then flew the planes by stages into Canada and across the Canadian Northwest—to Edmonton, Dawson Creek, Fort Nelson, Wilson Lake, Whitehorse—ending at Fairbanks or Nome. In Alaska, Russian pilots took over and flew the planes, also by stages, the rest of the way. (American pilots sometimes accompanied the planes into Siberia and beyond for training purposes or as technical advisers.) Of the 7,994 aircraft that traveled the Alaska–Siberia route, 73 went down, with the loss of 114 men. The leg that crossed the coldest part of Siberia, from Chukotka to Yakutsk, was the most difficult and dangerous of the route. Although the planes America sent were not its most up-to-date, and the P-39 (called the Airacobra) was considered obsolete by 1943, Soviet pilots became skilled in flying them. In the Battle of Kuban, the pilot Aleksandr Ivanovich Pokryshkin scored twenty Luftwaffe kills in a P-39.

When the war was over, Soviet historians said little about the contributions of the Lend-Lease aircraft. The omission was understandable, considering the overall Russian sacrifices and the fact that Lend-Lease planes were just a fraction of those the USSR, with ramped-up production, was able to put in the sky by war's end. But the planes from America, and other Lend-Lease goods and matériel, made an unforgettable impression on average Russians. Joseph Brodsky remembered treasuring empty tins that Lend-Lease Spam had come in, Kolyma prisoners marveled at the amazing American white bread "that produced no bowel movement worthy of the name," and boys who saw Americans for the first time in the pilots who stopped at their Siberian transfer-point villages thought the yellow boots those pilots wore were about the coolest thing in the world.

Valentina Gerdun's exhibits on the air-transfer route bore the heading "The Route of Courage," and as she showed them to us she said she had written a poem about this subject, which she always recites. Then she set her feet, threw back her head, and declaimed:

> Ty pomnish', moi drug, svintsovoe nebo
> I gorod pod nami, bagrovyi zakat,
> Marshrut ot Alyaski do dal'nei Sibiri
> S toboi nam doverila Rodina-mat'
>
> I smelo veli po vozdushnomy morio
> Rossiiskie sokoly—gordost strany
> Kingscobry i Mitchely, Duglasy, Bostony:
> Pobedu i slavu velikoi voiny.
>
> Byvalo, byvalo, shto v skhvatke c prirodoi
> Teryali my vernikh, otvazhnikh parnei.
> Nedarom nazvanie "Muzhestva Trassa"
> Potomki sevodnya prisvoili ei.

A nynche vzletaoit krylatye ptitsy
S Rossiskoi emblemoi drugikh obraztsov.
I v pamyat' o proshlom slagaiotsya pesni
I pishutsya knigi o slave otsov.

(You remember, my friend, the leaden sky,
And the city below us, the crimson sunset,
The route from Alaska to distant Siberia,
Which our Motherland entrusted to us and to you.

And bravely those Russian falcons—the nation's pride—
Through a sea of air they commanded
Kingcobras and Mitchells, Douglases, Bostons:
To victory and glory in the great war.

It happened, it happened, that in struggle with nature
We lost many devoted, faithful guys.
Not without reason was the name "Route of Courage";
As their descendants have called it today.

And now winged birds fly up
With a Russian emblem of other kinds.
And in memory of the past, songs are composed
And books are written of our fathers' glory.)

Valentina Gerdun paused for a moment to bow and receive our applause. "In August 1945, the Route of Courage ceases its operation," she continued, "and in 1953 the leader of our people, Stalin, dies. In 1954 the gulag in this area is liquidated and Dalstroi is dismissed. All the settlements along the Magadan Highway go to 'free existence.' Many people come here to live in the nineteen fifties and nineteen sixties.

"Here you can see the exhibit I made of this time—'How Young We Were, How Sincerely We Loved, How We Trusted in Ourselves.' This is about those people who came for a new life to Tyoplyi Kliuch. Some came to earn big money, some were assigned a job here, some came 'for the fog'—for the romantics of it. Many of these have now been here essentially for all their lives and many, of course, are no longer living. But the memory of them has remained in these photos, and their children, grandchildren, and great-grandchildren still are here.

"Dear friends, our settlement certainly reached its peak, its apogee, in the nineteen eighties and nineties. That is indisputable. Almost two and a half thousand people lived here then. With perestroika, of course, we felt a recession here, as well as everywhere in our country. Now one thousand people live in our district. But I want to tell that last year we witnessed very positive events. Due to our regional president, Mr. Vyacheslav Anatolyevich Shtyrov, our new school was constructed. The school is remarkable, full of light, equipped according to European standard, and everything is at a modern level. In this connection, our village library has moved to a very good place there, and my museum has found larger accommodations in this present building also. Before, my museum was in the old school.

"A few of the original inhabitants remain in this community. For example, Irina Nikolaevna Yemelanova, arrested as a girl of thirteen and sent to work on the road for theft of frozen potatoes remaining in the field after harvesting. Also, we are proud of the fact that one of our village inhabitants, Klavdiya Nikolaevna Ilyna, was a firsthand participant in the 'Route of Courage' who worked at the meteorological station at Seymchan. From 1943 to 1945, she was the weather forecaster who gave the okay for the planes to start.

"Also, in this village is the department called DSU-4, road-building management, which is responsible for road and bridge construction, as well as the agency responsible for federal roads. And while I am finishing my talk, I want to say that no matter how political and social conditions will vary, our village of Posyolok Dorozhnikov was and will be, because the road operates, and the road is necessary for the state. There are such words in the song I wrote in honor of the sixtieth anniversary of settlement:

> *Doroga, doroga, taiga i morozhy,*
> *Ty lentoi lozhish'sya po zhizni moei.*
> *Doroga, doroga, liobov' i trevoga;*
> *Ty stala, doroga, moeio syd'boi.*
>
> (Road, road, taiga and frosts,
> You are a ribbon lying along my life.

Road, road, love and anxiety;
You, road, became my destiny.)

"And really, for many people who live in this village, for those who
built the road, for those who provide its maintenance and even now are
constructing it, this road really did become their destiny."

Then we had tea and snacks and watched a short black-and-white
film about the highway. Many of the images were of prisons—barbed
wire, gates, barracks, grounds. Valentina Gerdun said that there had
been a main *lager* (prison camp) at Tyoplyi Kliuch, and *lagers* every six
miles along the road. On the screen appeared photos of road-worker
prisoners taken at or around the time of their arrest, and clips of the
same people as old men and women in more recent years. Other parts
of the footage had been shot during construction, on bald tundra hills
where the roadbed edged around curves with steep drop-offs beside
them, and teams of workers pushed barrows up ramps, and a wrecked
tractor-trailer lay on its side in a valley far below the roadway like a tiny,
two-dimensional object. The film compared the highway to the Alcan
Highway, the road that goes from Canada's Yukon Territory to Fairbanks.
Valentina Gerdun pointed out that the labor to build the Alcan Highway was expensive, while the labor to create this highway had cost nothing. When the film ended, she told Sergei and the assembled Eveny that
the Magadan Highway should make them feel proud, because it tied
their big country together and showed that its people were Russians
above all.

Chapter 28

Eighteen miles (twenty-nine kilometers) past Tyoplyi Kliuch, we turned onto the Topolinskaya Trassa—the Topolinskaya Highway. I traveled many thousands of miles in Siberia, and this is the most remarkable road I was ever on. The main aspect in which the Topolinskaya Highway resembled a regular highway was in its name. As a highway, so designated, it reminded me of the famous knife of the surrealists—the knife without a blade, whose handle is missing. The Topolinskaya Highway began at its junction with the Magadan Highway and ended at the Even village of Topolinoe, 189 kilometers—about 117 miles—away. At every kilometer, a numbered marker indicated how far along it you'd come. According to my Russian road atlas, this road was a hard-surface, year-round thoroughfare. Whoever put together that map cannot have seen this road even in a satellite photograph.

Better to describe the Topolinskaya Highway as a transportational antique, a relic and a ruin from Stalin times. Building it had been Stalin's idea. He had planned this and at least one other Siberian north–south route to continue past the Arctic Circle and clear to the country's northernmost shore. Presumably he just drew a line on a map and left the details to subordinates. The Topolinskaya Highway was abandoned in 1954, after Stalin died, and the camps of the prisoners who built it were closed. For much of its route, the road—or what remains of it—follows the valleys of the Olchan and the Topo rivers and winds back and forth among them. Most of its bridges have fallen down, so for many years the road has been drivable only in months when the rivers and the creeks that run into them can be crossed on the ice.

If most Russian construction looks handmade, this road appeared to have been beaten into the earth by hands, feet, and bodies. Almost unaided, human beings had forced it through the wilderness. To the right and left, the roadside showed none of the healed-but-still-visible gouges you see along roads built by earthmoving machines. There were many steep drop-offs—and as we continued, the drop-offs got steeper and longer—but not a single guardrail. All the bridges, even the longer ones, were made of logs. Aleksandr Sleptsov, the driver, had been over the road many times and dared to try some of the bridges whose roadways had not entirely fallen down. He steered deftly along board tracks not much wider than the tires themselves. From my front-seat vantage I couldn't always see the boards, but the gaps showed the ice and the rocks of the river below.

Sometimes we proceeded at little more than crawling speed. Attaining the next kilometer marker was an event. Particularly interesting kilometers got their own mention in my notebook. Near km marker 33 we came upon a tipped-over truck. I had been wondering what a vehicle with a smaller wheelbase-to-height ratio than ours would do about some of the deeper potholes, and here was the answer: trying to go around a washed-out place, a truck had put its right-side wheels too far up on the road bank and had tipped over on its left. It had been there awhile. The driver had unloaded its cargo of canned goods in cardboard boxes and now sat beside a fire of sticks he had made in the middle of the road. We didn't stop to see how he was doing but swerved to the left, climbing into and out of the hole and going on.

At km marker 55 we descended from the road to the riverbed and stopped beside the biggest bridge so far. The boy who wasn't feeling well had to get out, and I walked down to the river surface for a better look at the structure. The span of the bridge rested on high, square-sided, upward-tapering log cribs filled with boulders. Its overarching supports were also of logs, and their cross bracings had been carefully engineered. It resembled any large rural bridge you might see, except that instead of steel girders its main structural element was peeled gray logs. It vaulted over the canyon notch and stood out against the backdrop of dark firs with the hopefulness bridges often convey. Can an object created by slaves be beautiful? Unusable but still standing, this handmade log bridge from the early 1950s struck me as a road-building wonder of the world.

Sometimes the dark forest crowded around and met above the road as it burrowed a straight path through. Between km markers 77 and 78 I saw a sable. Or, rather, I SAW A SABLE!! The amazingness of this had me bouncing and almost hyperventilating in my seat. As the animal ran along the road ahead, I knew from a distance what it was. It moved as gracefully as a cat, though it had the overall shape of a squirrel. But it was substantially bigger than a squirrel, with a longer, bushier tail. Its fur gleamed a sort of bluish-brown, darker and more lustrous in the wild than on a hanger at Saks Fifth Avenue. As we came up on it, the sable sprang onto the snow berm and ran along parallel to the car. It looked like running gold.

Aleksandr pointed to it and said, "Sobol'!" I was shouting, "A sable! A sable!" to Sergei. For a few seconds it was right beside the car and I saw it clearly. In past centuries sables had the reputation of being merry creatures, maybe because of the wealth they possessed in their fur. This sable did seem to have a playful expression as it bounded briskly along, the arc of its tail duplicating its hops. Then it veered into the forest and was gone. The gigantic dimension of all the sable represented, historically and so on, was overwhelming me. I turned to Sergei and the Eveny in the backseats and tried to convey how wondrous seeing this animal was. They all smiled and nodded, indulgently, but I think they did know what I was talking about.

We came out of the thick forest into a mountainous section where the road had more windings, and drop-offs that sloped uncomfortably from the outside edge. At km 96 we met another tipped-over truck. This upset seemed to have occurred at higher speed, and the damage was worse than the previous truck's. The sides of the trailer were bent and the top split open. Again, the cargo of boxes had been stacked in the road. A Russian jeep had stopped to help. We did not, but kept our momentum and motored on.

At another stream crossing we paused again so the boy could get out. By now I had been rather shaken by the road's apparent dangerousness and I used the stop to pen a farewell note to my family, just in case. I was scribbling in my notebook by the front-seat overhead light (darkness had fallen), and I didn't notice the boy get back in. After a few minutes, Sergei said, gently, "*Sandy, oni zhdut . . .*" (They're waiting . . .). I looked up and saw all the Eveny patiently gazing at me. In Russia, writing is so revered that no one had had the nerve to interrupt me in what might have been an act of literary creation.

At km marker 122 we passed a sable hunter's cabin. It was a log hut with an overhanging roof and a stone chimney, set back from the road against the hillside. Tree branches hung low over it, its single window was dark, and no smoke came from its chimney. I don't know why cabins in the woods in Russia have a more enchanted quality than their counterparts in America, but they do. A full moon had risen and it hung just above the low, treeless, snow-white mountains. A few last streams had to be crossed—some of the creeks flowed so fast they hadn't frozen, and Aleksandr felt his way through the shallow fords, the water thrusting against the wheels—and then the road carved a narrow, curving terrace along the higher hillsides with the valley of the Olchan River beside us on our left.

At km marker 126 Aleksandr touched my arm, gestured to the valley, and said, "*Lager*." I leaned over and looked down and saw it. The fences, the barracks, and a few other smaller buildings occupied a level space in the crook of the river. All the structures in the long-abandoned prison were black, white-roofed with snow, and had not a light anywhere. Just the moonlight shining blue-white on the snow. The scene would have suggested the coziness of a ranch and outbuildings sheltered in some remote valley in the Rocky Mountains, except that wasn't what it was. The coziness here was only additional cruelty, a further guarantee of the place's inescapability. I wanted to get out and hike down to the *lager* despite the darkness, but no one else thought that was a good idea. The evening was late and the Eveny wanted to get home. I was told I would see more *lagers* on the trip back tomorrow.

Farther and higher into the mountains, the road went over pass after pass. Each unnerved me worse than the one before it. In my mind I still picture them—guardrailless, downward sloping at the outward edges, sidewalk-narrow above drop offs of thousands of feet, with Tinkertoy wrecked vehicles at the far, far distant bottoms. (My fear may have supplied the Tinkertoy wreckage, though I'm sure I did see a lost truck or two.) Meanwhile, Aleksandr, growing bored, began making conversation by asking where I lived in America, where I'd been in Siberia, etc. He asked about this present trip and whether it was *komandirovka*, a business trip. I was glad I'd learned that strange word in Boris Shekhtman's class. At a pause on level ground he told me that the village was now only five kilometers away. I asked, *"Yest' yeshcho pereval?"* (Is there another pass?), in what I thought was a neutral voice, but my real feelings must have come through, because all the Eveny listening in the backseat laughed. He assured me there was not.

Our arrival in Topolinoe village set the dogs to barking. They were everywhere in the dark; as we went from one small apartment house to the next dropping off passengers, the previous barking dogs faded out and new ones joined in. By now it was about nine o'clock. No one had been expecting us, evidently. Our guide, Galina, had to go several places to find the key to the rooms where we would stay. Then Aleksandr brought us to what was presented as "the hotel," and we unloaded our luggage in the forty-below night.

Galina led us through this establishment's entryway, which was a cavernous unheated two-story room hung with icicles and frozen cascades as if it had been hit by an ice tornado. At the top of the staircase at this room's far end she unlocked a door. Down a barely lit hall she unlocked another door and ushered us into our rooms. There was almost nothing in them except for heat, a feature that made up for a lot. After saying she would see us in the morning and wishing us good night, she disappeared.

Somewhere in our stuff we still had a lint-covered kielbasa from our train journey, and a few other semi-edibles. We made a supper of those, drank some bottled water, used the john (there was a john), and turned in—if that's an accurate description of what I did, which was to lie carefully on a shaky thin bench a few inches too short for my legs and pretend it was a bed. No other furniture was available, so the bench had to do. Sergei applied his own imagination to the bench in an adjoining room.

All night the bench kept jolting me from sleep with wobblings that threatened to pitch me onto the floor. I would have just let it, and tried to sleep there, had the floorboards not been gritty with tracked-in mire. At first light, about five o'clock, I came awake permanently and lay on my back worrying about one thing and another. When the morning was full light, I sat up and examined the room. Floor-to-ceiling windows filled the wall opposite, showing a view of a hillside, a couple of small buildings, and many conifers bent over with snow. Snow glare cast a brightness on the room's ceiling. On the wall behind me were many holes made by nails or pushpins, and a large, color-enhanced poster of a misty white waterfall falling into an impossibly green pool surrounded by palm trees. Contemplating it, I finally grasped a principle of Siberian interior decoration. The halls of our hotel in Yakutsk had been perked up by similar posters, and I had in fact noticed tropical-themed posters often on my travels. I believe the tropical poster is the most common indoor decoration in Siberia.

Without needing to, Sergei had refrigerated our remaining foodstuffs by putting them in the space between the indoor and outdoor windows in his room, and they had frozen solid overnight. Our breakfast was the same as supper the night before, only colder and crunchier. He broke off pieces of kielbasa for us to gnaw on. After this attempt at a meal I took the satellite phone outside to call my wife. She was sick, as were my son and daughter, all laid up with the flu. I couldn't hear well because the dogs discovered me immediately and gathered around to bark and howl. Ignoring my wife's difficulties, I moaned plenty about my lot, accompanied by dog howls. All in all, a regrettable performance on my part, and one my wife has not forgotten.

Overextended as I was, I suddenly lost my command of Russian. Even the simplest words had deserted me, I discovered. As Sergei and I set out on our schedule for the day, he noted my new aphasia and looked at me in alarm. Naturally our first visit, escorted by Galina, was at the office of the mayor of Topolinoe, whom I now learned I was supposed to interview. We went into his office, introductions were made, we sat at a long table, I opened my mouth, and nothing came out. Sergei was nudging me, whispering, "Say something! Ask him something!" Eventually I stuttered a phrase or two and like any competent politician the mayor began to hold forth. He was a middle-aged Even with abundant gray hair, and he wore a blue blazer and a gray shirt. People in the village were not making any money, a reindeer herders' festival was to take place in the village in April, the village was working to get Internet access. On the wall behind the mayor was a very large portrait of Lenin done in different natural shades of wood inlay. The mayor stopped to draw breath and everybody looked at me for the next question. Luckily Sergei supplied it.

Next stop: the village museum. Its floor had just been painted and the paint hadn't dried, but because of our importance we were allowed to walk on it anyway. Each step was like pulling your foot off a Band-Aid. Here my new tunnel vision centered on just one area—a small display case of objects found at the site of the crash of a Lend-Lease airplane in the tundra. There were headphones, bullets, a spark plug, a spoon, a flashlight, and a twisted metal label that said, "Briggs Manufacturing Co. Airplane Parts Division/Detroit, Michigan." Unsticking my feet from the floor, I thought what a whirlwind the world is, to take that little piece of metal from Detroit and toss it way up here.

In the village square, an obelisk commemorated the crash. It had occurred on May 25, 1943. The pilots were Pesnikh, Sivelgin, and Vedmitskii. Reindeer herders from Topolinoe had found the remains.

As we stood in the square, which was achingly bright with the morning sun on the snow, a troupe of thirty or forty children came running in a line from the school building and formed two concentric circles. They all had on traditional Even costumes of reindeer hide and fur, and reindeer boots with fur at the top. They presented themselves to Sergei and me, did a kind of curtsy, and began a back-and-forth, wheel-within-wheel dance to a song they sang. Sergei videotaped everything, circling around them, and I tried to remain inconspicuous behind a fixed smile. The Even schoolteacher in charge of the kids watched them closely and applauded when they finished. The kids seemed relieved at that. The sweetness of their smiles made me rebuke myself for how dull I had become. Then the teacher asked all the kids to tell us their names. Each said his or her last name first, followed by first name and patronymic.

An older Even woman named Kristina Mikhailovna Zakarova joined us after the dance. She was a Even poet, she told us, as well as a performer of Even songs and an author. She and Galina led us past the main government building, with its giant statue of a reindeer out front. We paused a moment to admire it. Continuing through the village, they then brought us to the apartment of the reindeer racer and his wife, whom we had met the day before. As we were ushered in I said to Sergei, aside, that we could stay only a little while. He shrugged to indicate helplessness in the face of hospitality. Andrei, the reindeer racer, seated us on the living room couch and began piling framed diplomas in our laps for us to look at. Sergei exclaimed politely over them, but I had no idea what they were. On the living room walls from ceiling to floor hung thick carpets, and stuffed toys were piled around the room. Andrei and his wife then presented their two-year-old granddaughter, Regina, dressed in reindeer-hide hat, coat, and boots. They said the little girl had ridden on a reindeer for three hundred miles wearing those clothes just a few months ago. Regina posed and turned so we could see the outfit from all sides.

Tiredness and hunger had reduced my concentration to practically none, and I just wanted to sit in a daze. Andrei produced some of the prizes he had won for reindeer racing. There were elaborate medals and ribbons. When the prize had been an appliance, and he had given it away to someone in the village, he had kept the box it came in. In a storage room he had a number of these boxes, including one for a TV set and another for an Electrolux refrigerator. The Even poet, who had disappeared into another room, now emerged dressed entirely in reindeer-hide clothing she had sewn and beaded herself. We sat again in the living room as she began a speech that sounded memorized.

I was thinking that we would probably be here forever, that time had become stuck with us in it, and we would remain here until the sun finally burned out and this place got really cold for a change. The poet bowed her head and collected herself and then sang a mournful song about a bird. Her strong, pure voice filled the room. As I followed the plaintive halftones, the music's risings and fallings carried me and caused the time-lock sensation to fade away.

Tea was ready. Sergei told Galina that we had to go, but she replied that we absolutely must stay for *obed*, lunch. We were brought into the apartment's small kitchen and seated at a table; on the walls were posters of tropical fruits, in a close-up, color-enhanced view, hyperrealistically photographed. A platter of large grayish pieces of boiled reindeer was set before us. We were given plates, sharp knives, and forks, and told to cut ourselves a piece. Another platter held thick slices of home-baked bread. I took some bread, speared a slice of meat, and carved off a chunk. The reindeer was fresh and tender, completely delicious, and the bread accompanied it perfectly. I ate one big piece of reindeer and then a cou-

ple more, as did Sergei. We'd had no real food for a while. Following the
meat came the soup course—a clear reindeer broth, very hot, brimming
with tiny noodles. To finish off we had squares of German dark chocolate
and hot, strong *kitaiskii chai,* Chinese tea. Immediately my stupor lifted
and I thanked our hosts many times. This was among the top two or
three meals I ever had in Siberia. I enjoyed it all the more because from
the first bite I knew I could relax in the certainty that it would not give
me food poisoning.

After lunch we left the village and headed back to Khandyga. This
haste was my doing. For me the main purpose of the Topolinoe journey
had been to see the abandoned prison camps along the Topolinskaya
Highway. If we stayed too long in the village we would again traverse
that road in darkness. I wanted to get to at least some of the *lagers* in the
daylight, and I had told Sergei that several times. Evidently the message
had gotten through. After finishing our tea we looked out the window
and saw Aleksandr and his minibus waiting outside. This time the passengers, besides us, were the reindeer racer; our guide, Galina; the Even
poet; and several other Eveny bound for Khandyga or beyond. Gavriil
Sleptsov, the driver's father, had dislocated his shoulder, and he was being taken to the clinic at Khandyga. Aleksandr asked if I would mind if
his father sat in the front seat so he would have more room for his arm.
The only way Gavriil Sleptsov could hold his arm without great pain was
directly out from his body at shoulder height. I agreed and took a window seat in back. At each bounce in the road, the jolt to his shoulder
caused his face to clench and contort, but he never made a sound.

We set out from Topolinoe with the sun still high. Evidence of prison
camps began to appear at about twenty-five kilometers from the village.
There were old fences and guard towers back in the trees, and small
buildings. I was surprised at how much I had missed in the darkness the
night before, even with the full moon. A building on the left-hand side
close to the road had been the bakery for several *lagers,* Aleksandr said.
We passed more guard towers, more small log buildings. At km marker
136—marker 53, measuring from Topolinoe—Aleksandr pulled over
and said there was a *lager* just down the hill on the left. From the road
all that could be seen was part of a snow-covered roof and the top of
another guard tower. Sergei and I got out and started down the hill in the
thigh-deep snow.

Chapter 29

The *lager* lay in a narrow valley between sparsely wooded hills. The gray, scraggly trees, which did not make it to the hills' higher slopes, grew more thickly near the *lager* and partly surrounded it; a few small birches had sprung up inside what had been the camp's perimeter. Their bare branches contrasted with the white of the snow on the roof of the barracks, whose wall, set back under the eaves, was dark. In the whiteness of an open field, a guard tower tilted sideways like someone putting all his weight on one leg. A ladderlike set of steps still led up to it, and two eyelike window openings added to the anthropomorphic effect. In the endless and pristine snow cover, I saw no tire tracks, road ruts, abandoned oil drums, or other sign that any human had been here since the camp was left to the elements half a century before.

At first view the camp looked as I'd expected. There were the fence posts shaped like upside-down L's, the ink-black barbed wire, the inch-long barbs shaped like bayonets. Some of the posts leaned one direction or another, and the barbed-wire strands drooped or fell to the ground; the fencing, and the second line of fence posts several yards beyond, and the low, shameful barracks with its two doors and three windows fit exactly with the picture of a Siberian prison camp that one has in the mind. Sergei had drifted off to the left to videotape the *lager* from the side. I went in by the front gate, which was standing open. When I was inside the perimeter, the camp lost its genericness and became instead this particular Russian structure of its own.

To begin with, the whole place was as handmade as a mud hut. The fence posts shaped like upside-down L's weren't factory stock that had been produced elsewhere, but plain logs, peeled and smoothed, with narrow boards atop them to complete the L. And the side of the barracks wall, which had appeared from a distance to be stucco, was actually a daubed plastering over thin strips of lath that crossed each other diagonally like basketwork. I broke a piece of the plastering off in my hand; at one time it had been painted a pale yellow and it crumbled easily. It seemed to be nothing more than a spackle of mud and river sand.

Aside from the nails and the barbed wire, I could see almost no factory-made product that had been used in the construction. Next to the windows were white ceramic insulators that had probably held electrified wire; no trace of mullions or window glass remained. The roof beam ran parallel to the building's length, and along the slope of the roof at each end a facing board about five inches wide had been nailed. These boards covered the raw edge of the roof and extended from beam to eaves, and at the end of each board a very small swirl of scrollwork had been carved. The embellishment was so out of place it caught the eye. I wondered what carpenter or designer had thought to put a touch of decoration on such a building.

Regions of deep cold preserve antiquities just as hot deserts do. Had the climate here been temperate, moisture and vegetation would have consumed this structure long ago. But in northern Siberia, with only a dozen or so weeks of reprieve from intense cold every year, and nothing below but permafrost, the old prison camp had hibernated into the present more or less unchanged. Around it, like a bubble of prehistoric air frozen inside a glacier, a familiar atmosphere of 1954 endured.

Maybe one reason I am susceptible to the dread Russia-love is that Russia evokes childhood for me. In the 1950s, when I was a boy, adults talked and worried and wondered about Russia all the time. For anyone who grew up then, Russia might have been the only other significant country in the world. I was six years old in 1957 when the Soviets launched Sputnik, and I remember the interest my father took in that event. Dad was a chemical engineer and he had a keen admiration for mechanical ingenuity of every kind. After Sputnik first went up, he used to bring my younger siblings and me into our front yard at night before bedtime to try to show us the satellite as it passed by. At his research lab in Cleveland—he worked for Standard Oil of Ohio—he and his colleagues rigged a radio dish on the roof of the building so they could pick up Sputnik's transmissions. Some evenings after dinner, Dad would put on his long coat and his fedora—the style of hat almost every man wore then, from Eisenhower to Clark Gable to Vyacheslav Molotov—and he would drive back to his lab for a night of listening for the satellite. The air of mystery and excitement he gave off as he left made an impression on me. I could tell he got a kick out of this, like a do-it-yourself spy—and in fact, with the Cold War secrecy surrounding Sputnik, the tracking data he and his colleagues compiled was for a while the only public information about Sputnik available in the United States. When he explained the satellite's orbit to me, I thought about Ohio's actual location on the planet for the first time.

The day the Soviets sent up the rocket carrying Yuri Gagarin, the first man in space, I came in from playing in the yard with my friends on that spring afternoon and found my father dejectedly hanging up his coat in the front hall closet. I asked what was wrong and he said the Russians had just launched a man into space, and now we would never catch up to them in the space race. I asked why and he said because their scientists were so much smarter than ours, because their country was so much bigger than ours that they had many more brilliant scientists to draw from. Also, he said, their kids were better at science than our kids were. I took this last to be aimed at me; I had never been as good at math and science as he had hoped. My father always tended to give in to his bad moods and indulge them. He had a flair for gloom and doom.

Years later when I was walking in Moscow and I saw in the distance a big upward-swooping statue with a cosmonaut at the top, and the Russian friend I was with told me it was the Yuri Gagarin monument, I knew for sure that the date on the statue's base would be a date in the spring. I remembered how Dad's dejection had contrasted with the spring day. And of course I was right—Yuri Gagarin's flight had occurred on April 12, 1961.

Dad used to tell my siblings and me—and my mother, too, I suppose—that we had no idea what the rest of the world was like. In our happy Ohio existence we would never understand the war, or the Depression (my mother had lived through the Depression, too), or countries not like America, or how people in places like Russia lived. The

word "sheltered" came up a lot. Dad could portray remoteness and im-
ponderability better than anyone else I've known. His voice would become sort of furry with melancholy as he said, "You'll never know how
they live, or what they went through in the war. Life under somebody
like Stalin is so totally removed from your lives." He would shake his
head at our innocence and say, "No, it's not anything you'll ever know. It's
another world." And truly, in Hudson, Ohio, in the 1950s, a prison camp
like this one in the fastness of northern Siberia would have seemed as
remote from us as the grave of the *Titanic* at the bottom of the sea.

Sergei came wading through the snow on the other side of the barracks.
He had stopped videotaping and was stepping quietly, almost tiptoeing.
I knew he didn't approve of my interest in this sort of thing, and I felt
some guilt that I had made him see it. But his face as he approached
showed no rancor, only a sort of wide-eyed, watchful awe. We didn't say
anything to each other. Slowly, simultaneously, we moved to see what the
place was like inside. Sergei went in at a door. I stayed outside and looked
in at a window. I didn't want to seem to be poking around (though of
course I was). Going in seemed to be something for him to do rather
than for me; he was next of kin, in a sense, while I was merely a foreign
observer.

The floor of the barracks was worn planking, tightly joined and still
sound. I saw nothing on it but a few twists of straw and the wooden sole
of a shoe. A short, cylindrical iron stove rusted near a corner. Its stove-
pipe was gone and the hole for it in the plank roof above had been covered over. Prisoners who had lived in barracks like this reported that the
stove usually heated a radius of fifteen to eighteen feet. As this building
was maybe thirty feet from end to end, areas of it must have always been
cold. From inside you could see the logs that the walls were made of.
The cracks between the logs had been chinked with moss. The barracks
space had been divided into several rooms, with bunks set into the walls.
The bunks also were made of bare planks—some planed on both sides,
some planed on only one. Planks with the bark still on them had been
fitted into the bunks so that the bark side faced down.

This interior offered little to think about besides the limitless periods
of suffering that had been crossed off here, and the unquiet rest these

bunks had held. Often prisoners in places like this had to sleep on the unimproved planking, or on thin mattresses stuffed with sawdust. For covering they might have had a single blanket, or nothing besides the clothes they wore during the day. Mornings began as early as 4:00 a.m., when the guards would awaken them by pounding with a hammer on a saw blade. That wake-up alarm, and the screeching of the guard dogs' chains on the wires stretched between the guard towers as the dogs ran back and forth, were characteristic sounds of the camps. Before the prisoners went out to work they were given breakfast—usually soup with a small piece of fish or meat, and bread. Even in 1977, not a lean time, the diet in Soviet strict-regime camps provided only two thousand six hundred calories per prisoner per day, less in the punishment blocks and sick wards. The international standard for a person actively working is three thousand two hundred to four thousand two hundred calories per day. Like almost all labor-camp prisoners, the ones in this barracks would have been hungry almost all the time.

Hunger in the camps made people eat many things. In the camps of the Kolyma during the warmer months, some of the prisoners ate grass. Intellectuals, for unknown reasons, were more subject to that malady. People who ate grass generally did not live long. Varlam Shalamov, the writer who survived seventeen years in Kolyma, wrote about prisoners there during the war who ate half a Lend-Lease barrel of machine grease before the guards drove them off with rifle shots. The prisoners had thought the machine grease might be butter; they said it tasted about as much like butter as American bread tasted like bread. They showed no ill effects afterward. In *The Gulag Archipelago*, Solzhenitsyn told of a work detail in Kolyma who were doing excavations when they came across a frozen-solid, perfectly preserved ancient stream complete with prehistoric fish and salamanders. He said that a magazine of the Soviet Academy of Sciences reported that unfortunately these interesting specimens could not be studied, because the workers who unearthed them ate them on the spot. He said the magazine did not identify these workers as convict laborers, though from that detail an astute reader would understand they were.

After breakfast in the *lager* came inspection, and then the prisoners would be lined up in the camp yard to receive orders for the day. If they were to be sent on a timber-cutting detail, the best assignment was that of taking the smaller limbs trimmed from the downed trees and feeding them to the fire. If their day's job was to work on the road, breaking a path through the snow with their bodies for horses and vehicles to follow, the assignment you wanted least was to be the man who walked on point, ahead of the others. Usually prisoners received no food during their twelve-hour workday. Guards watched them the whole time, and they had to keep within a boundary indicated by pieces of red cloth or other markers distributed around the work site. Any prisoner who crossed the boundary area would be shot, and the guard who shot him would get a day or two off. Sometimes guards tried to fool prisoners into going over the line just so they could shoot them. If the prisoners were doing road building, they toiled with picks, sledgehammers, shovels, and wheelbarrows. Even in forty-below weather the work caused them to sweat heavily. Back at camp at the end of the day, they had to stand in formation for another roll call while the sweat froze in their clothes. Then they marched into the barracks for a supper that was similar to breakfast, followed by a brief time for personal activities like letter writing and reading the little mail they were allowed. Then sleep.

As a bizarre extra, some camp systems maintained small orchestras. Occasionally in the mornings as the prisoners marched off to work, and in the evenings when they returned, the orchestra would be at the *lager* gate encouraging them with upbeat melodies.

Of course the death toll was cruelly high. More than a million died in the camps just in 1937–38, the Great Purge's peak years. A main goal of the Soviet labor-camp system was to take those citizens the Soviet Union did not need, for political or social or unfathomable reasons, and convert their lives to gold and timber that could be traded abroad. Almost from the beginnings of the camps, people outside the country knew or suspected what was going on in them, but the Soviet government simply denied all accusations and the subject receded from view. In 1941, after the Soviet Union joined the Allies and had to release its Polish prisoners, some of these survivors with firsthand experience told what they knew, and the ongoing horror of the camps became established beyond reasonable denial.

When the war was over, and the United States made agreements with Stalin whereby Russian P.O.W.s brought from France and Germany at the end of the war would be repatriated, some of those slated for return committed suicide in places of temporary confinement like Ellis Island and Fort Dix, New Jersey, rather than face the gulag. As Russia retook Poland, many Poles once again wound up in the gulag. Some who had lived through the Nazi occupation said Hitler was nothing compared to this, and they now wished they had fought on Hitler's side. A prisoner who had survived Dachau hanged himself when he was shipped to Kolyma. Gulag prisoners who knew the novel *Uncle Tom's Cabin* regretted that fate had put them in this time and place, and not in slavery in the American South a hundred years before. As Negro slaves, they reasoned, at least they would have lived someplace warm, and would have been whipped and branded but not worked to death outright. In 1945, news reached the camps that the United States now possessed the atomic bomb. According to Solzhenitsyn, this unexpected development gave hope to many prisoners, who began to pray for atomic war.

As I looked at the tiers of bunks I pictured male *zeks*—the word for gulag prisoners—lying on them, but the prisoners here might have been women, too. Female *zeks* worked in timber-cutting camps and on road-building details, and even mining gold. Their resilience was greater than men's, as was their ability to withstand pain. Or perhaps this barracks had been one of those occupied by and completely under the control of criminals. This distressingly numerous class played the camp system to exempt themselves from labor and, with the encouragement of the authorities, preyed on the political prisoners. The criminals' ethics and speech seeped into everybody's life. Political prisoners later said that the criminals in the camps were more dangerous than the meager food and the killing work conditions. The gulag also had *lagers* for children. Eugenia Ginsburg, who served fifteen years in the camps of Kolyma, wrote that when a camp of children prisoners in Magadan was given two guard-dog puppies to raise for a while, the children at first could not think of anything to name them. The poverty of their surroundings had stripped their imaginations bare. Finally they chose names from common objects they saw every day. They named one puppy Ladle and the other Pail.

Unlike the prisons of the tsars, the *lagers* of Soviet Siberia (or Soviet anywhere) were virtually escapeproof. To anyone sizing up the surroundings of this camp on the Olchan River, it would have been obvious that the country was tough traveling even for a well-equipped nonnative; for

a ragged escapee being hunted by guards who feared for their own lives
if they failed, the cold and geography constituted a fearful prison in
themselves. Stories of the very few who did get away, even temporarily,
became legends in the camps.

Shalamov told the story (a fictional one, like all Shalamov's Kolyma
stories, but based on fact) of a prisoner named Krivoshei who escaped
from a Kolyma camp by impersonating a geologist. Krivoshei was fortunate in that he had a helpful wife on the outside who kept him supplied
with money. One summer day, Krivoshei walked away from his work
team, hired some native assistants, and with a geologist's hammer and a
few other props continued slowly out of the region, collecting rock samples as he went. Occasionally he would stop and ship crates of random
rocks to the Academy of Sciences in Moscow.

Krivoshei was an educated and self-possessed man, quite believable
in his role as a scientist, though he knew nothing about geology. In a
month or so he had crossed the mountain chain that separates Kolyma
from Yakutia, and in time he made his way to the city of Yakutsk. To keep
up his disguise, he paid a visit to the local scientific society (this was in
Stalin times, before the geologists I met were there), and the directors of
the society were so impressed by him that they begged him to give a
lecture about his geological discoveries. Having little choice, Krivoshei
agreed, cautioning the directors that he must keep certain details secret
on orders from Moscow. Then he winged a lecture as best he could,
somewhat mystifying his audience. They asked him to repeat it for the
local students, and again he obliged. He managed to leave Yakutsk with
his cover intact, and he made his way to a small city in western Russia,
where he established himself and disappeared from view for a while.
The authorities tracked him down as a result of the correspondence he
had maintained with his wife, and Krivoshei was rearrested and shipped
back to Kolyma. He had remained at large for two years.

The sun shone brightly in the blue sky, the snow at my knees was a light
and fluffy powder, and my breath froze on the fur around the hood of my
coat. In dimmer light inside the barracks, Sergei was just standing, not
saying anything, getting a sense of what it felt like to be in there. I walked
a distance away to see what the barracks looked like from the back. In

that direction the fences were more tumbledown and I moved carefully, not wanting to trip over any of that wicked barbed wire in the snow.

The greatest discovery my father's research lab made in the 1950s, or ever, was of a revolutionary new process for manufacturing a plastic called acrylonitrile. In its fibrous form, this plastic is good at retaining heat, so a packing of acrylonitrile fibers can be an effective substitute for wool or down in cold-weather clothing. Once the process had been perfected and patented, it worked so well and so cheaply that anyone who wanted to make this plastic had to use it. Countries as well as companies lined up to pay the licensing fee. My father's former boss, who had been the head of the research lab at the time of the discovery, once told me that the Soviet Union had been among those countries, and that it had paid the $15 million licensing fee in gold. In those years most Soviet gold would have come from Kolyma, whose camps were deadlier than timber-cutting or road-building camps like this.

What I'm trying to say is that although the labor camps of the gulag were indeed far from our 1950s lives, they didn't exist on another planet entirely. For example, some of the barbed wire, a product vital to the camps, might have been of American manufacture; barbed wire was among the 9.2 million tons of Lend-Lease goods shipped from the West Coast to ports of the Soviet Far East. During the thirties, Dalstroi used some of its gold to purchase machinery and gold-mining equipment from America. American firms sold handcuffs to the NKVD in the Far East. Varlam Shalamov wrote about a time in a camp of the Kolyma when a mass grave of *zeks* who had died some time ago came sliding down a mountainside; the cold had kept the bodies undecayed, so that faces could still be recognized. After the bodies were reburied by a Lend-Lease bulldozer, Shalamov wrote, "On the mirror-like blade there was no scratch, not a single spot." Robert Conquest describes a large Marion excavator disintegrating in a mine-tailings dump, broken and rusted, after having been ruined by *zek* operators. Marion earthmoving equipment was made by a company in the town of Marion, in north-central Ohio.

Simply in geographic terms, many of the worst gulag prisons were closer to America than they were to Moscow. I have already mentioned the prisoner-built city of Provideniya, a seventy-five-minute plane ride from Nome. In other parts of Chukotka there were said to be prison camps so dreadful that very few prisoners sent to them survived. Anchorage is closer to Magadan (1,962 miles) than it is to San Francisco (2,005 miles). Magadan is 3,673 miles from Moscow. Even in these camps on the Topolinskaya Highway, the distance to America is about 1,600 miles shorter than the distance to Moscow.

Prisoners who suffered the terrible fate of being sentenced to work in the gold-mining camps of the Upper Kolyma, in the far north where that river empties into the Eastern Siberian Sea of the Arctic Ocean, went by train to Vladivostok, and there or in the neighboring port of Nakhodka boarded slave ships that could carry thousands of prisoners for the long voyage northward along Siberia's Pacific coast, through the Bering Strait, and westward along the Arctic coast to the Kolyma River delta. These ships sailed with their decks battened down, few lights showing, and the prisoners kept below in conditions that survivors described as something out of Dante. One method of controlling the prisoners in their cold cages was by hosing them down with seawater. As the reach of Stalin's police began to expand in the early 1930s, more prisoners were sent to the Far East, and the slave ship traffic increased.

In the fall of 1933, a ship loaded with thousands of prisoners bound for the Upper Kolyma left Nakhodka Harbor. The ship's name was the *Dzhurma*. At about the same time, a scientific research ship named the *Chelyuskin* sailed eastward from Murmansk to do studies along the Arctic coast. Winter came on suddenly that year, and in early December the *Chelyuskin* became stuck in the ice off Chukotka. Soviet newspapers reported extensively on this crisis, and people all over Russia and around the world followed the *Chelyuskin's* predicament.

Eventually the scientists and crew were rescued by Soviet pilots in a daring operation, widely trumpeted in the Soviet news. Other nations had offered to help the *Chelyuskin*, but the Russians refused all assistance. Years later, observers of the USSR guessed why. As it turned out, the slave ship *Dzhurma* had also become frozen in the ice and was just two hundred miles from the *Chelyuskin*. Doubtless the Soviets had not wanted the world to know that the slave ship existed at all. What happened on that icebound ship, with food gone and hope of rescue lost, is still only hinted at today. It is said that the dead were eaten by the living. When the ship finally reached port the following spring, some of the surviving guards and crew had gone insane, and none of the prisoners were still on board.

The Kolyma slave-ship voyages, among the grisliest of the many grisly events of Soviet times, also came the closest to American shores. Sailing through the Bering Strait, the ships would have passed within about twenty-five miles of the U.S. border. Under just the right conditions, a person standing on U.S. soil would have been able to see the ships as they passed by.

While Sergei and I were exploring the camp, the driver and the other passengers waited for us in the vehicle. We could not delay them much longer. Sergei had already started up the slope, walking backward and videotaping as he went. I took another turn around the inside of the perimeter and then exited at the gate. I now saw that what had once been the *lager*'s driveway curved to the left through a denser stand of trees, and I followed it, knowing it would soon intersect the road. Before the trees obscured the view, I stopped to look at the camp one last time.

What struck me then and still strikes me now was the place's overwhelming aura of absence. The deserted prison camp just sat there—unexcused, un-torn-down, unexplained. During its years of operation it had been a secret, and in some sense it still was. Horrors had happened here, and/or miseries and sufferings and humiliations short of true horrors. "No comment," the site seemed to say.

I thought this camp, and all the others along this road, needed large historical markers in front of them, with names and dates and details; and there should be ongoing archaeology here, and areas roped off, and painstaking excavation, and well-informed docents in heated kiosks giving talks for visitors. Teams of researchers should be out looking for camp survivors, if any, and for former guards, and for whoever had baked the bread in the bakery. Extensive delving into KGB or Dalstroi files should be showing who exactly was imprisoned here when, and what they were in for, and what became of them. The *zek* engineers and builders who made the hand-constructed bridges should be recognized and their photographs placed on monuments beside the road, and the whole Topolinskaya Highway for all its 189 kilometers should be declared a historic district, and the graves, of which there may be many, should be found and marked and given requiem.

Beneath a surface layer of unbelief or Orthodox Christianity, Russia is an animist country. Ordinary physical objects are alive in Russia far more than they are in America, and however Russia's religious or political currents flow, this native animism remains strong. Trees, streets, utensils, groves, machines—each has its own spirit and its own personality, like the cabin belonging to the witch Baba Yaga that could get up on its chicken legs and run around. A Russian telephone isn't just a phone, it's a being. Once at Alex Melamid's mother's apartment when I was having trouble dialing her phone, she showed me how, explaining, "He likes to be dialed *slowly.*" In Russia, alarm clocks don't ring, they burst into rooster crowing or songbird calls. My friend Luda had a clock that announced the hours in an old-lady voice: "The time is one o'clock exactly!" Luda referred to the clock as *moya tyotka*, my auntie. When you pass the turnstiles on the St. Petersburg or Moscow metros without paying, there's not a siren sound, as in New York, but a frantic chirping, as if you'd just trod on some creature's nest. In Russia the windshield wiper on your car isn't called a mechanical name—it's a *dvornik*, a word whose more common meaning is "custodian." What we call a speed bump in America the Russians call *lezhashchii politseiskii*, which means "lying-down policeman."

The animism applies especially to buildings. In Russia a building is regarded as and spoken of not just as itself but as a manifestation of the will of the person who ordered its construction or who held power when it went up. The church I was shown in Vologda, for example—the one constructed at the command of Ivan the Terrible, who denied food to the builders in order to get them to work faster—doesn't merely evoke the memory of Ivan the Terrible, it *is*, in a sense, Ivan the Terrible. The echo of his capricious and brutal spirit may be said to inhabit it as long as the church stands. And certainly no other individual personality in history has ever occupied a city as thoroughly as Peter the Great occupies St. Petersburg. Pushkin imagined a deathless bronze Peter on his bronze horse chasing citizens down the city's wide streets. In Peterhof, the palace compound Peter built west of the city, there is to this day a grove of metal trees that can be made to squirt water at unwary passersby just as they used to do in Peter's time. Whenever a tourist gets soaked, the wild tsar's laughter resounds in a neighboring dimension, intangible but full of his presence, that hovers all around.

By this metaphysic, the camp I was looking at, and all the camps along this road, and the road itself, were Stalin. His was the animating spirit of the place. The road project and its camps had come into existence by his fiat, had continued to exist in fear of his will, and had ended like a blown-out match with his death. The fact that the world has not yet decided what to say about Stalin was the reason these camps were standing with no change or context; the sense of absence here was because of that.

The world more or less knows what it thinks of Hitler. Stalin, though, is still beyond us. As time passes, he seems to be sidling into history as one of those old-timey, soft-focus monsters—like Ivan the Terrible, like Peter the Great—whose true monstrosity softens to resemble that of an ogre in a fairy tale. Hitler killed millions, and we have a rough idea how many, but the millions of victims of Stalin are still difficult to count. There were the millions his policies starved, and the million-plus whose executions he brought about, and the millions he sent to death in the camps. Historians estimate that anywhere from fifty-five to more than sixty million Russians died by unnatural causes as a result of the Bolshevik revolution, from its beginning in 1917 to the fall of communism in 1992. A large fraction of those deaths must be blamed on Stalin.

And yet somehow Stalin gets a pass. People know he was horrible, but he has not yet been declared horrible officially. Hitler's minions were tried and convicted and (some of them) hanged, but the only trials examining the crimes of the Stalin regime were the absurd and obscene show trials he staged to reinforce his power and give himself a cover for murdering more. Perhaps the world has even bought the PR he engineered about himself, with the photos of him holding smiling children on his knee (children whose parents he later killed), those happy photos of him with a twinkle in his eye. The ogre's twinkle seems to have achieved its purpose. During American elections, TV and other commentators sometimes quoted Stalin's famous remark, "It's not the people who vote that count, it's the people who count the votes." As a comparison, is it possible to imagine any commentator under any circumstances quoting a witty remark of Hitler's? In the 1960s, Stalin's daughter, Svetlana Alliluyeva, came to America to live, and was accepted here, and even wrote a bestseller; would any of that have been possible for a daughter of Hitler, or of any famous Nazi? America had to be civil, at least, to Svetlana Alliluyeva; her father had been our ally. He appeared on the cover of *Time* magazine eleven times.

Further complicating the problem is the fact that Stalin's popularity continues to grow among the Russians themselves. On the subject of the greatest leaders in Russian history, public opinion polls regularly rank him at or near the top. No doubt he benefits from the camouflage provided by Russian leaders who went before; Hitler's crimes seemed unique in European history, but Stalin could be seen as another bloody tsar, or as an Arakcheev with industrially augmented killing power. Stalin was actually incomparably worse than his predecessors all the way back to Khan Batu, but the illusion of continuity makes him look less bad. On top of that, he killed far and away more Russians—of many ethnicities and regions, but Russians all the same—than he killed foreigners. If now his countrymen, his principal victims, don't want him and his era brought to account, and are praising him instead . . . well, then what?

Stalin never saw this or any Siberian gulag with his own eyes. Once he had attained power, he seldom left western Russia, preferring to stay in or near the Kremlin most of the time. Perhaps the unhappy fate of every Russian ruler who set foot in Siberia gave him pause. Although he had passed through western Siberia often as a young man (those alleged six escapes), neither then nor afterward was he ever east of Baikal. His underlings must have occasionally shown him charts of this Topolinoe road and its system of prison camps, and maybe they even showed him photographs. But for him this camp would have been only a point on a map, a detail of a plan. The strange feeling of absence that prevailed in the frozen silence here had to do with the secrecy and evil of the place's conception, and with its permanent abandonment, in shame, after its author was gone. Now the place existed only nominally in present time and space; the abandoned camp was a single preserved thought in a dead man's mind.

Back in the minibus, I didn't ask to stop at a prison camp again, though others appeared along the road. I had no desire to explore any more of them. In daylight, the road's high passes bothered me less than they had at night. Instead my worry now focused on the driver's father with his dislocated shoulder in the front seat. His fortitude, and the silent contortions of his face every time we went over a bump, made me wince.

When we stopped for a break at a frozen river beneath another log bridge, I took my suitcase out of the back and found my bottle of Extra Strength Tylenol Gelcaps. I shook two into my palm and gave them to the driver and said he should tell his father to take these now. Then I handed him another two and said his father should take these in four hours, per the directions on the bottle. Here a language problem created what became an afternoon of drama for me, though I told no one about it. The Russian phrases for "in four hours" and "at four o'clock" resemble each other, and though I had meant to say the first, I accidentally said the second. The father took the first pair of pills at about three forty-five. Promptly at four o'clock, the son picked the second pair of pills from a small can by his seat, handed them to the father, and the father swallowed them.

This caused me no small anxiety. Should I say something? Would an overdose of this size hurt the old guy? Should I tell them to stop so he could throw up? Would that be an insane American overreaction? I didn't know. Probably, a double dose of Tylenol, even extra-strength, could not do any serious harm. For the rest of the ride I held my breath and watched. Soon at each bump in the road, the old reindeer herder was swaying forward, swaying back. Sometimes his forehead almost touched the windshield. Sometimes he would slump way down to the side. He always righted himself, though, and kept his stoic dignity. I had to admit that at least he did not seem to be feeling as much pain. By the time we reached Khandyga, in the evening, he had stopped swaying and looked okay, and both he and his son thanked me with big smiles when we said goodbye. I was glad to have no worse outcome to my attempt at doctoring.

Sergei and I again spent the night in the hotel in Khandyga, in the same communal bedroom as before. A local guy with a Uazik was driving us back to Yakutsk the following morning.

The only excitement of that trip happened on the Lena River. Our driver was a skittish, skinny kid who drove fast, kept to no particular lane, and often hit potholes dead-on. Duct tape held the windows in place, the door handles came off in our hands, and the whole vehicle tended to shimmy to the left or right, crabwise. Sergei sat in front and I sat in back with three other passengers—a mother from Khandyga and her thirteen-year-old son and nine-year-old daughter. The ride soon made the little girl carsick, which caused the driver concern. He was solicitous when he had to stop for her to throw up, and he sometimes screeched into the parking lots of roadside cafés to buy her tea with lemon and sugar for the purpose of soothing her stomach. Then he'd hop back in the car and we'd go racketing off again.

When we turned onto the Lena River, the driver explained that this new route was longer than the previous ice road because there had been an accident on the previous road a month ago—several cars had broken through the ice and six people had drowned. The southbound lane on this new road had a fair amount of irregularities in the ice, and as we were rattling over them the Uazik suddenly sputtered and stopped cold. Traffic backed up behind us immediately with a great honking and roaring that did not let up as people drove around us on the ice. The mother from Khandyga was worried because from here it was several miles to land. I told her not to disquiet herself because Sergei could fix anything. He and the driver were peering under the hood. The driver seemed overwhelmed, but Sergei had taken a piece out of the engine and was strolling on the ice, hunting around.

The mother told me they had lived in Khandyga for seventeen years and often made this trip to Yakutsk. I asked about the coal dust in Khandyga and she said it was a real problem because clothes got dirty so fast. She and her husband had moved there because of the military base, which back then had more than four thousand vehicles. Her husband was a mechanic, the best one in Khandyga or anywhere, and he believed in repairing vehicles as his mission in life. The village was poor now, with much unemployment, she said, and her children could no longer get a good education there. Sometimes there was not much food in the stores, the streets melted into the permafrost every summer and had to be re-paved, and winter was dark and sooty and very cold. She said she loved Khandyga anyway, especially in the summer, a beautiful time of year, when she and her husband and children sometimes went on four-thousand-mile drives to see relatives in Kazakhstan.

After more tinkering by Sergei, the driver turned the key and the car started and ran at a rough idle. The mother from Khandyga exclaimed in joy, and I said, "What did I tell you?" Later I asked Sergei to describe how he had done it, and he said, "When the Uazik died at approximately four o'clock in the afternoon in the middle of the great Lena River in traffic, the driver opened the hood and found with horror that in a most important part of the engine—the carburetor—a piece was missing. A screw had come off and the small rod that held the float regulating the gasoline level of the carburetor had fallen out and disappeared. Thus, the gasoline stream flew into the carburetor as if from a hose, gasoline was spilling on the ice, and naturally the car would not run.

"What was to be done? I looked all over on the ice road in the hope of finding our missing part. Instead of our part I picked up about half a bucket of other parts, but not the one needed. I then disassembled the carburetor and it appeared that all we needed was to find a piece of wire or a nail of the right diameter in order temporarily to replace that rod on which the float of the carburetor was set. I did find such a wire nearby on the ice, I cut off a piece of this wire, and I inserted it where the missing part should be. I found a bolt of approximately the right size belonging to some other machine under our car's wheels, and with this bolt's help I fixed the rod in place. In truth, the carburetor did not work so well as before, but nevertheless we were able to drive from the ice road and reach our hotel. Thus I was once again convinced that the Russian car is the most reliable in the world, because it is possible under necessity to replace any part in it with a piece of wire or with a nail."

Sergei and I left Yakutsk for St. Petersburg at ten the next morning. First we flew to Irkutsk, where the plane developed mechanical problems. I had an aisle seat and the action happened to be beneath the floor next to me. A bunch of jumpsuited technicians came on board, took up the aisle carpet, and lifted a panel in the floor. They all looked down into the hole, then left in a body. Then one of them returned with a flashlight and peered around inside some more. Bored children had begun to wander the aisle, and as the technician was looking in, several boys squatted down by the hole and looked into it next to him. Some were asking him questions, which he answered patiently without shooing them away. Then he left again and returned with a part that resembled a microfilm reel, and he installed it out of sight in the hole. Then he replaced the panel, laid the carpet back down, and left. The plane took off after about another hour and a half.

At the next stop, Krasnoyarsk, we disembarked and sat in a large waiting room filled with silent travelers while no announcements of any kind were made. At my prodding, Sergei asked around and learned that passengers for St. Petersburg were waiting for a plane that had been delayed from Kamchatka. I passed the time writing in my notebook. A girl with black hair and dark eyes and her head wrapped in a scarf was sitting next to me and observing me. When she asked me a question I didn't understand I said, *"Ya Amerikanets"* (I'm an American), and she replied, *"Ya Azerbaijanka"* (I'm an Azerbaijani). She was nine years old, in the third grade at school, and on her way back to her home city of Baku with her father, mother, and sister, who were sitting on the bench nearby. She was small for a nine-year-old but she had great self-possession. She came around to where she could watch me writing and after a minute she said, *"Molodets!"* The word means something like "Good lad!" It's what a teacher says to a student when he gives the correct answer.

After we'd endured more waiting and a risky meal of cutlets in the airport restaurant, the Kamchatka flight arrived. We boarded, sat a long while, and finally took off. Almost no one was on the plane and from my empty row of seats I looked out at western Siberia. Traveling in the same direction as the sun, we kept up with daylight for the whole five-hour flight. Late in the afternoon we crossed the Urals, which from this altitude resembled blistered white paint. At about seven in the evening, eighteen hours after leaving Yakutsk, we landed in St. Petersburg.

Again I had arranged to stay in the apartment of my friend Luda. A friend of Sergei's brought us in from the airport. After a long sleep in a bed with fresh sheets, I woke the next morning and took a stroll around the city, and a powerful new spasm of Russia-love came over me. There was no reason for it—I could think of plenty of good arguments against it—but I still could not stop a slide into exhilaration. In the cold sunlight, St. Petersburg seemed glorious. Everything about it aided the impression—the façades of the buildings in their faded Easter colors with their complicated veining of cracks, the strangely apt banners advertising superglues above the Nevsky Prospekt, the empty beer bottles frozen cheerily upright in the ice of the Griboyedova Canal, the brown haze of dust in the sky from the sand spread on the streets' winterlong accumulation of ice . . .

Newly arrived from Siberia, I saw that St. Petersburg is not a European city but an Asiatic city with European architecture. Its physical structures imitate Europe's, but its enormous sky is Asia's. St. Petersburg is a stop, or a station like those wacky modernist railroad stations on the

BAM line beyond the middle of nowhere. Arrivals and departures are its point. It's a caravanserai, like those cities (Tobolsk, Kyakhta) sprung up in the Asiatic emptiness where tea and silk caravans from China traveled, or like the sprawling tent cities the Mongols improvised on the steppes using felt from their animals and white linen they had plundered somewhere. Though far away, Siberia is an unavoidable part of this place. When Ivan Borisovich Pestel (father of the Decembrist) was governor-general of Siberia, he directed the affairs of his immense and distant province while comfortably ensconced in St. Petersburg. The joke about Governor Pestel went that one day when he and Count Rostopchin were dining with the tsar, the tsar looked out the window and asked, "What's that on the church, the black thing on the cross?" Count Rostopchin replied that he couldn't make it out, and then added, "You must ask Ivan Borisovich, he has wonderful eyes, for he can see from here what is being done in Siberia." The story speaks to a psychological truth: with the huge sky and long-distance vistas in this city, it almost seems as if he could have.

St. Petersburg is also connected to Siberia by the tendency of wilderness to make people who are in it long for civilization. On this flat site beside the Neva, the city rises against the sky like the final realization of the mirage that travelers saw constantly receding up ahead of them as they crossed the Siberian wastes. I remembered how as a kid I discovered that the deeper I went into the woods, the more I wanted the most unwholesome and delicious foods at McDonald's or Dairy Queen. Now I was experiencing a continental version of the syndrome: St. Petersburg may look unexceptional if you come to it from someplace else in Europe, but after Siberia it was sweet.

I went to a wonderful pastry shop on the Nevsky Prospekt with Luda and I overspent in bookstores. I took a day by myself wandering the Hermitage at random, and I decided that what makes that museum great is the bright, watery light from the Neva River that pours through its tall windows, and the endless profusion of paintings that were apparently acquired by wealthy, unschooled people who compensated for not knowing exactly what to collect by collecting everything. I checked out the Jordan staircase—the scene, I thought, of a struggle between Bolshevik supporters and palace guards during the October Revolution, and of Eisenstein's recreation of that struggle for his movie *October* (based on John Reed's *Ten Days That Shook the World*). Actually, the real-life struggle took place on a different, less-impressive staircase. For its cinematic reenactment Eisenstein instead used these more majestic stairs, and a huge cast of extras, some of whom carried live ammunition, with the result that more people were shot in the filming than had been shot in the event. The plasterwork I examined along the wall revealed no bullet holes.

I asked at the information booth where the room was in which the bomb went off when terrorists were trying to kill Alexander II during a banquet in 1871; nobody knew. I also asked where to find the painting "The Holy Family," by Domenico. I wanted to see it because in January 1826, my favorite Decembrist, Ivan Yakushkin, was held briefly in a room in which that painting hung. Before his interrogation by the tsar, Yakushkin had the cool-headedness to examine and admire that painting while a lesser official questioned him. Nobody in Information knew anything about the painting, either, except that it was not on display. Later I found out that Domenico Beccafumi's "The Holy Family with St. John the Baptist and St. Catherine" is in the museum's collection. I think they should put it up again, with a long label explaining about the Decembrists and Yakushkin.

In the evening, Luda and I got tickets for the ballet at the Mariinsky Theatre. With a Russian love of chicanery, Luda urged me to give her the money so she could buy both of us the low-price tickets reserved for Russians only. This was dishonest and cheesy of us, not to mention stupid. The old ladies who take tickets at the door of the Mariinsky are impossible to fool. They spotted me for a foreigner from ten feet away and indignantly turned me back. I had to go to the end of the long line at the foreigners' ticket booth. I felt mortified.

Near the ticket booths there's a small-scale model of the theater's interior with tiny numbers on every seat so that purchasers can see what tickets they're getting. Whoever made the model had a gift for that sort of handicraft. It is a gem in itself, and it accurately conveys the small-town intimacy and imperial elegance that the Mariinsky combines. Gilded tiers of box seats rise one above another on the theater's back and side walls, with a large box formerly belonging to the tsar in the center at the back. The arrangement emphasizes and somehow makes more charged the small enclosed ocean of space between the audience and the dancers on the stage.

People who go to the ballet tend to look like one another, and when many of those people are Russians and thus look a bit like one another already, the effect is that of being at an extended-family reunion. Interspersed among the reunion attendees are foreign tourists speaking many tongues. In the crowd I heard, mixed with the prevailing Russian, bursts of French, Japanese, German, English-English, and of course American. Suddenly from the babel an American sentence would jump out: "I wouldn't do law school, though I like the *idea* of law school," or "I just discovered I'm wearing my T-shirt inside out!"

The Mariinsky is another excellent setting in which to remark on the beauty of Russian women, but I will pass up the opportunity, except to mention the woman in the box next to ours wearing the black top and midriff-baring pants who had long honey-blond hair to the middle of her back and a lithe ease of movement that was a distraction to be near. Before the lights went down, I noted the many varieties of Russian dress-up attire, something I'd seen almost none of in Siberia. Not too many women here wore plain furs, but there were plenty of dyed ones, often attached here and there to garments in erratic places, adding furry patches of purple or burgundy or blue. There was a lot of leather, most of it black, with silver chains used as decorations on vests or pants; also, many silver-gray-black techno colors, sequined fabrics, and weird, out-of-nowhere design motifs. I saw a woman in a brick-red sheath dress with the logo from the movie *Who Framed Roger Rabbit* printed on it over and over. The hard-to-avoid suspicion that international trademark and copyright laws had not been strictly adhered to in the creation of this garment gave it a certain extra Russian panache.

Because of my usual difficulties understanding and being understood, interactions involving the Russian language always involved frustration, like using a telephone with a bad connection. I got so accustomed to the frustration that I almost forgot it. But when the lights went down and the ballet began, I felt relief at the wordlessness of it. For the moment I could be sure that I and everybody else were experiencing what was before us in more or less the same way. The Mariinsky's proscenium and its tiers of boxes give the impression of the theater's being gigantically high, so the dancers perform in what appears to be a sky-high column of space. The ballet that evening was *Manon Lescaut*, with music by Puccini, which is about a woman who is so incredibly sexy that she ruins other people's lives and her own and then dies. In the opening scene, Manon arrives at a country inn, and the trees above the square where she gets out of the coach went up and up, more toweringly than real trees.

Russia-infatuated as I was, I looked up into all that vertical space and saw Siberia even in the ballet. I remembered the girl dancing before the large-screen TV to the theme music from *V. I. Warshawsky* at the resort on Lake Baikal; now I reflected that Russians might not be such fabulous dancers if their country did not include Siberia. Dance is bodies moving through space, and the Russians perhaps think of their own bodies in relation to their immense, continent-wide swath of it. Nureyev, the greatest dancer of modern times, was born on a train crossing Siberia. Mikhail Volkonsky racing across the country from Moscow to Irkutsk in fifteen days in a springless carriage was a kind of nonfiction Russian dance. The gallantry with which these people fling themselves at their big—too big, really—country is played out in how they dance.

And I mean, these people can really *dance*. No two ways about it. I remember at the New York City Ballet years ago I saw a ballet choreographed by George Balanchine, the great Russian-born choreographer, in which six or eight women did a delicate and controlled number for the first movement of a piece, and a similar dance for the second, and then before the third and last movement, which had a much faster tempo, the women went offstage and loosened their hair from the tight coifs it had been in, and when they came out for the final movement their hair was flying everywhere, and those girls—by that time they were girls, not women—danced to shake the paint off the walls.

Well, in this ballet, *Manon*, the whole corps danced like that. In the crowd scene they let go like kids at a rock concert, while staying technically accurate and hitting their marks (as near as I could tell) the whole time. The Mariinsky audience was with the dancers every second. Perhaps some of the tourists were a bit abstracted, but the Russians themselves—the old-lady balletomanes on the parterre; and the middle-aged folks in the boxes; and the rich, gaudy young couples; and the little girls with bouquets of flowers—none of them could take their eyes away. At intermission I was on a staircase and I happened to look down at the crowd milling in the second-floor lobby, and I noticed six or eight little girls here and there trying out ballet steps for one another and for small knots of grown-ups looking on. During the last act when the stage lights were bright and spilling out into the audience, I observed the audience's faces and they all were pointed intently at the stage, each with the devout, rapt, out-of-body expression of somebody watching the enactment of a deeply remembered dream.

Afterward, Luda and I jostled through the remarkably long and slow line of people returning their rented opera glasses, and the equally full line at the coat check, and then we were outside in the cold among dissipating perfumes and faint cigarette smoke, and snow was falling steadily straight down. It was billowing in the streetlights overhead and making cones of the lights of the waiting taxicabs, and as we stood deciding whether to walk or take a cab, snowflakes came to rest among the fibers of fur in her hat. Each flake was small but unbroken, and detailed as a cutout snowflake made in school.

The next morning or the one after, I flew back to New York. A rough pat down by security in Helsinki, clouds over the North Atlantic, clear skies over Canada revealing forests chewed up by harvesting for the paper mills; then the coast of Maine, the high-rise apartment buildings of the Bronx, the cranes and stacks and cargo containers of New York Harbor, the row houses before JFK Airport; then home.

PART V

Chapter 30

I went back. When the subject of Siberia came up, people always asked me if I had plans to go back, and for a long time I didn't know if I would. At what point can you say you have traveled in Siberia enough? I had done most of what I wanted to do there. But I kept wondering and thinking about this question, and I decided that if I was thinking about it so much, probably I should go. "You should do it, if only just to breathe the air," my friend Katya said. For some reason her advice scaled it. In the fall of 2009, I started making plans for my fifth (and shortest) Siberian journey.

Meanwhile, like Governor Pestel, I had been observing Siberia from afar. Think about a name like Siberia long enough and your eye begins to pick it out at a glance among columns of newsprint even when you're not trying. Siberia is one-twelfth of the land on earth, and I came to suspect that it appears in one-twelfth of all news stories, also. Its use as an expression of failure or ineptitude is growing. Expressions like "pop-music Siberia," "career-counseling Siberia," "dental-care Siberia," "footwear Siberia," etc., all indicating complete out-of-it-ness in those various areas or categories, are a big percentage of what the eye pulls up. And the name has become almost obligatory in restaurant reviews: reviewers now routinely note, along with the quality of the service and the price range of the meals, the location of the restaurant's Siberia.

The real story, the one the papers were most excited about, had to do with oil and natural gas. To my mental map of Siberia with its rivers, swamps, taiga forests, and expanses of essentially nothing, I began to add the Siberian oil and gas fields appearing in the news now all the time. There were the two huge fields offshore of Sakhalin Island, called Sakhalin I and Sakhalin II, and the Kovytka natural gas field near the Chinese border, which the Chinese hoped the Russians would attach to them by a pipeline (much of which China offered to pay for), and the rich Khanty-Mansiysk oil and gas fields along the middle reaches of the Ob River, and the Verkhnechonsk oil fields near Irkutsk, and the tough-to-drill-in Yamal Peninsula fields in the Siberian Arctic, and the Vankor field, in the Far East, the largest Russian oil-field development since the end of the Soviet Union.

Lukoil, a Russian oil company flush with cash, bought Getty Oil, and began to turn Getty gas stations in the United States into Lukoil stations. Oil-policy analysts thought this was a good idea, because Russian energy clearly was going to be an important future source of American supply, and if a Russian company had stations here Russia would be less likely, for coercive or other reasons, to turn off the tap. President Vladimir Putin himself showed up to inaugurate a new Lukoil station at Tenth Avenue and Twenty-fourth Street in Manhattan. Vagit Y. Alekperov, the president of Lukoil, and the New York senator Charles Schumer were there, too. Putin held a cup of coffee and a Krispy Kreme donut in his hands.

Soon afterward, all the gas stations on New Jersey's Garden State Parkway, which runs a mile from my house, turned into Lukoil stations. The first three letters of Lukoil's name come from three fields the company has in western Siberia—the Langepaz, Urengoi, and Kogalym petroleum fields. Now when I want a whiff of distant Siberia, I need no longer travel into the city and breathe the scent of the sable furs at Saks Fifth Avenue. I just go to the nearest Lukoil and fill 'er up.

That particular Lukoil, by the way, offers no restrooms for customers. Large signs on the highway inform motorists of the fact. I found this innovation worrying. What other Russian bathroom customs might Lukoil be importing?

When Saudi Arabia reduced its oil production in 2005 and 2006, Russia became the largest oil-producing country in the world. Russia's known petroleum reserves of 79 billion barrels were well behind Saudi Arabia's 264 billion, but Russia also had the largest amount of territory whose energy resources remained unexplored. Most of those places were in the Russian Arctic and Siberia. Experts estimated that at least 80 billion barrels of Russian oil were yet to be found.

The maneuverings that Putin and his loyalists went through to take advantage of Russia's strong position in the global energy market were complicated, and tiring to think about. Basically, they renationalized the oil and natural gas industries. Oligarchs who had previously dominated the business were forced to submit to the new order. Those who didn't left the country or, like Mikhail Khodorkovsky, one-time head of Yukos Oil, ended up in a Siberian jail. Gazprom, the giant Russian natural gas company, of which the government owns more than half, grew to be the third-largest company (behind ExxonMobil and General Electric) in the world.

Key to the strategy of Putin & Co. was their focus on delivery. Primarily this meant pipelines, the traditional pinch point of the oil industry. If you wanted to move oil or natural gas out of the country, the Russian government was going to say how you did it and how much you paid. The United States, which now wanted to do business with Russia, seemed to forget that twenty-some years previously, during the Reagan administration, American sanctions had tried to block the completion of a Russian natural gas pipeline from Siberia to Western Europe. Reagan had feared the political power the Soviets might gain by it. The pipeline, and others, got built anyway. Gazprom became the chief supplier of Western Europe's natural gas. German homes were receiving 40 percent of the gas they heated and cooked with from Russia (that is, mostly from Siberia). All of the natural gas burned in Finland and the Baltic countries had the same source. In 2004, Hungary, Poland, and the Czech Republic bought three-fourths or more of their natural gas from Russia; Austria and Turkey imported almost as much. France and Italy were at 25 percent and 27. (All these numbers are unlikely to be much different today.)

Consumers across Europe came to the uncomfortable realization that Russia, the chronically semifailing state, had now acquired the position of mean landlord in Europe's basement. Now it could turn off the heat at will, depending on its mood. Marshall I. Goldman, an expert on Russian energy issues, has written that because of its control of the supply of natural gas "Russia is in a stronger position relative to Western Europe than it has ever been in its history." To quiet people's fears, Russian oil executives and high government officials swore that they would always stick to business agreements completely uninfluenced by political considerations of any kind. Dmitry Medvedev, a Putin appointee to

Gazprom's board, reformed top management at the company. In 2006, its deputy CEO promised, "For us, contracts are like a Holy Bible."

Medvedev, of course, later moved from Gazprom to take over (sort of) from Putin as Russia's president. Although the following fact has little to do with anything, I think it worthwhile to note that *The New York Times* has reported that President Medvedev's favorite band is Deep Purple.

When oil prices were up, Russian money flowed. For the first time almost ever, you saw groups of ordinary Russian tourists on the streets of New York. Russia paid off multibillion-dollar debts ahead of schedule and piled up a $300 billion hard-currency reserve. Putin considered using oil revenues to finish old Soviet-era projects, like the Boguchansk hydroelectric dam in eastern Siberia, or the few unbuilt parts of the Baikal–Amur Magistral. Russian collectors bought twenty-some of my friend Alex Melamid's paintings for a bundle. In rural America, fur trappers found themselves with unexpected windfalls, as the Russians, always big fur consumers, bought more and more furs. Roman Abramovich, the wealthy entrepreneur and one-time governor of Chukotka, sold his oil and gas company, Sibneft, to Gazprom for $13 billion, thereby becoming Russia's richest man. Then he moved to England and, upon arrival, became the richest man in England.

Oil prices went down again and the exuberance slowed; clearly, though, they would have to rebound. India needed oil, China was headed for U.S. levels of consumption. In Russia and outside it, Putin got a big amount of credit for Russia's newly established energy strength. Among his countrymen his approval rating was high. He had been lucky to have in place the network of pipelines that the Soviets built in the Brezhnev era, and even luckier in the unpredictable rise of the price of oil.

His focus on Siberia and its wealth seemed more than accidental, though. Soviet leaders like Brezhnev used to visit Siberia only slightly more often than did the tsars. Putin, on the other hand, showed up there all the time. He skied in the Altai, he attended the opening of the new Chita–Khabarovsk highway (a road replacing the undrivable section where Sergei and Volodya and I had traveled by *vagon*), he went down to the bottom of Lake Baikal in a minisubmarine. He laid a wreath on the grave of Victor Astafiev, the twentieth-century Siberian author, in Krasnoyarsk. When the European Union wanted to meet to discuss energy issues, he invited them to the oil town of Khanty-Mansiysk, or to Omsk. Putin made a trip to Yakutsk in January to talk about mineral extraction and reported that it wasn't very cold there yet—"It was minus 45 degrees in the morning and now it has become 'warmer' to minus 42 Celsius," he joked.

Russia had been in bad shape when Putin first took office in 1999. A currency crisis had occurred the year before, the country had defaulted on debts in the billions, millions of people lost their savings, the banking system became insolvent, foreign investors fled, etc. In those years every news headline about the plight of the country seemed to be RUSSIA ON THE BRINK? Financially, at least, Putin's actions and the price of oil had improved Russia's prospects a lot. From a wider-angled view of history, the country's turnaround recalled other times (the Time of Troubles, the Great Patriotic War) when Russia's fortunes had been saved by the resources of Siberia.

Once tapped and flowing, these resources seemed endlessly rich, even profligate. The Chernogoreft and Priobskoye and Yuganskneftegaz fields in western Siberia, the Samotlor and Berezovskoe fields, the Talakan field in Yakutia . . . Drillers of oil wells outside the gas-pipeline network had no use for the gas their wells might happen to extract, and so it was vented through pipes and burned at the well sites. This practice is known in the business as flaring. Enough gas to supply whole American cities was being flared every year. In 2006, the Environmental Protection Agency estimated that 426 billion cubic feet of methane were escaping annually from wells in Siberia (Gazprom countered it was only half that). Siberia, formerly an almost-all-dark swath of the nighttime planet in satellite images, now blazed with gas flares across the wilderness—"like cities on fire," according to one report.

This trip I would be by myself—without the company of friends, a tour group, or guides. My own command of Russian would have to do. Luda Stiler, a travel agent at Margo Travel in Manhattan, handled visa and reservations, as she has done for me many times. Luda is a kind and friendly woman, born in Leningrad and uninterested in going back. She regards my desire to travel in Russia as a mystery. I had decided to go to Novosibirsk because I'd seen not much of it in 2001, and it's relatively

easy to get to. In Novosibirsk I would stay in the Hotel Sibir, because
of the name. Aeroflot offered the cheapest fares, New York–Moscow–
Novosibirsk. To travel twenty-two time zones, there and back, cost
$1,183.10.

I had not flown Aeroflot since the nineties. Now the complete absence of smoking, in accordance with revised policies, made a real change
in the airline's tone. Russians not smoking! I wanted to congratulate and
console them. I was touched. Everything about the Boeing 767 we flew
in was better than what I remembered of their former planes. Now they
had real seats, not lawn chairs. Nothing about the interior looked beat-up
or shabby. The passengers, almost all Russians, boarded with the happy
boisterousness of people going home after a long time away. Many of
them had been shopping. Amid all the Russian conversation, some of it
deep voiced and sonorous, some of it shrill, they set about stowing their
shopping bags in the overhead bins. Many of the bags were from Macy's,
whose design, for the 2009 holiday season, featured a single large red
star on a white background. The Russians laughed and talked about one
thing and another, stowing their red-star bags.

Some years ago, a British public relations firm did an overhaul of
Aeroflot's image. Thus the plummy-voiced British recording that gave
the English translation of the Russian announcements. Thus the Scottish
plaid of the blankets that were passed out, and the stitched floral pattern
on the pillows, and the less hostile attitude of the in-flight personnel.
The stewardess who served our aisle had refined her instinctive contempt for the passengers into something transcendent and soulful. She
looked a lot like Babe Ruth, only with a slightly bigger hairdo, and she
mugged like Chaplin as she indicated approval, disapproval, commisera-
tion, and various other responses to each passenger she served. Sometimes she turned her face upward, saintlike, and rolled her eyes and
sighed.

I felt I was already back in Russia just being on the plane: the way
everybody ordered tea after dinner, and saved their dessert to have with
it; the men going to sleep with the plaid blankets wrapped around their
heads; the lustiness of their snores; the unmistakable hint of Russia-smell
in the cabin's recycled air . . . Not all the in-flight announcements were
translated by the plummy-voiced recording or by the pilot and crew.
One of the untranslated announcements informed passengers that this

Boeing 767 airplane was named in honor of the Russian writer Ivan Bunin.

No other country but Russia would name a commercial airliner after a writer. Just knowing I was flying on the *Ivan Bunin* gave me a small thrill. I recalled what had happened to Varlam Shalamov for saying, back in 1943, that Ivan Bunin was "a classic Russian writer." On the airport runways after we landed, I saw Aeroflot planes named after Dostoyevsky, Tolstoy, and Ivan Krasheninnikov (an explorer of Kamchatka who wrote a book about it). The plane I flew home in was the *Alexander Sergeevich Pushkin*. Naming planes after Russian writers may have been the British PR firm's idea. If it was, it had the intended effect on me.

My layover in Moscow was ten and a half hours. In the waiting room at the Sheremetyevo 1 terminal, I sat and watched, and sat and did nothing. For a while a teenage girl next to me was reading a book of short stories by Somerset Maugham. In English. Then she put it away and began to read Shakespeare's *Julius Caesar* (ditto). I hadn't wanted to bother her, but finally I asked, in Russian, what grade she was in. She said she was in the tenth. Here is something that would happen seldom or never in American air travel: in millions of air miles, you would be unlikely to sit next to an American tenth grader reading, in any language, the stories of Somerset Maugham. I told the girl that. She seemed puzzled. "But it is very interesting for me," she said.

From time to time airport security guards walked by with German shepherds trained to sniff for illegal substances. Scent-trained dogs in America walk more or less normally when they're working, but these dogs tracked their noses back and forth in the air and kept their bodies close to the floor, like snakes with legs. Flights departed for Samara, St. Petersburg, Chelyabinsk, Volgograd. The girl reading Maugham left, after saying a polite "Goodbye" in English. A middle-aged woman replaced her. When she got up after boarding was announced for the flight to Petropavlovsk-Kamchatka, I asked if she lived there. She said yes. I said, "That's very far," and she replied, "It's nothing! A nine-hour flight!" At one of the gates the microphone didn't work and the gate attendants were making the boarding announcements without it. A flight was leaving for Yuzhno-Sakhalinsk. It was strange, and moving, to hear the final summons for a place more than four thousand miles away called out by an unaided human voice.

Finally the flight for Novosibirsk began to board. It took off at about ten thirty at night. The plane was a brand-new Airbus 321, and its interior design featured Aeroflot's updated color scheme of orange and blue, exactly like the colors of the New York Mets baseball team. I dozed off, then woke after a couple of hours. From my window seat I could see nothing but blackness below—probably clouds. Then I started seeing occasional small knots of silvery-blue lights here and there, the lights of towns. Then suddenly big reddish-orange lights appeared, dotting the land's darkness in random profusion, often in clusters of twos and threes. I couldn't figure out what they were. Then I realized they had to be oil well flares burning off natural gas—those new irruptions of light into the Siberian wilderness that I'd read about. I don't know what oil field they were part of. I imagined how the taiga or swamp around them looked, weirdly illuminated in their flames. After a while they were fewer; then, none. For an hour before Novosibirsk the ground was mostly dark again.

I had wanted someplace cold, dark, remote, and hibernating. Novosibirsk at five thirty on a November morning seemed to be all of those. The temperature was –8°F. A layer of new snow covered everything, ready to stay. Around the airport, vehicles and workmen and the drainage grates in the runways all emitted steam. Along the top of the newly refurbished airport building (oil money, probably) ran a streak of midnight-blue neon that highlighted the blue-black of the sky. In the company of Anatoly, the bright-eyed, long-nosed, pixie-haired taxi driver who had claimed me, I came out the airport doors and into the parking lot, where other taxi drivers were standing around smoking cigarettes next to their idling cars. The hoarfrost in which each car was covered resembled a fur of white iron filings. My lungs filled with a familiar, delicious Siberian combination of secondhand smoke and bitter-cold air. One basic purpose had been accomplished. I had breathed the air.

Anatoly did not have enough left on his parking-fee card to get through the exit gate, so he had to back out, go to a lonesome kiosk in the lot, and buy a new one. While I waited in the backseat he bounded out of the car, bounded back in. Everything he said he delivered in the ex-

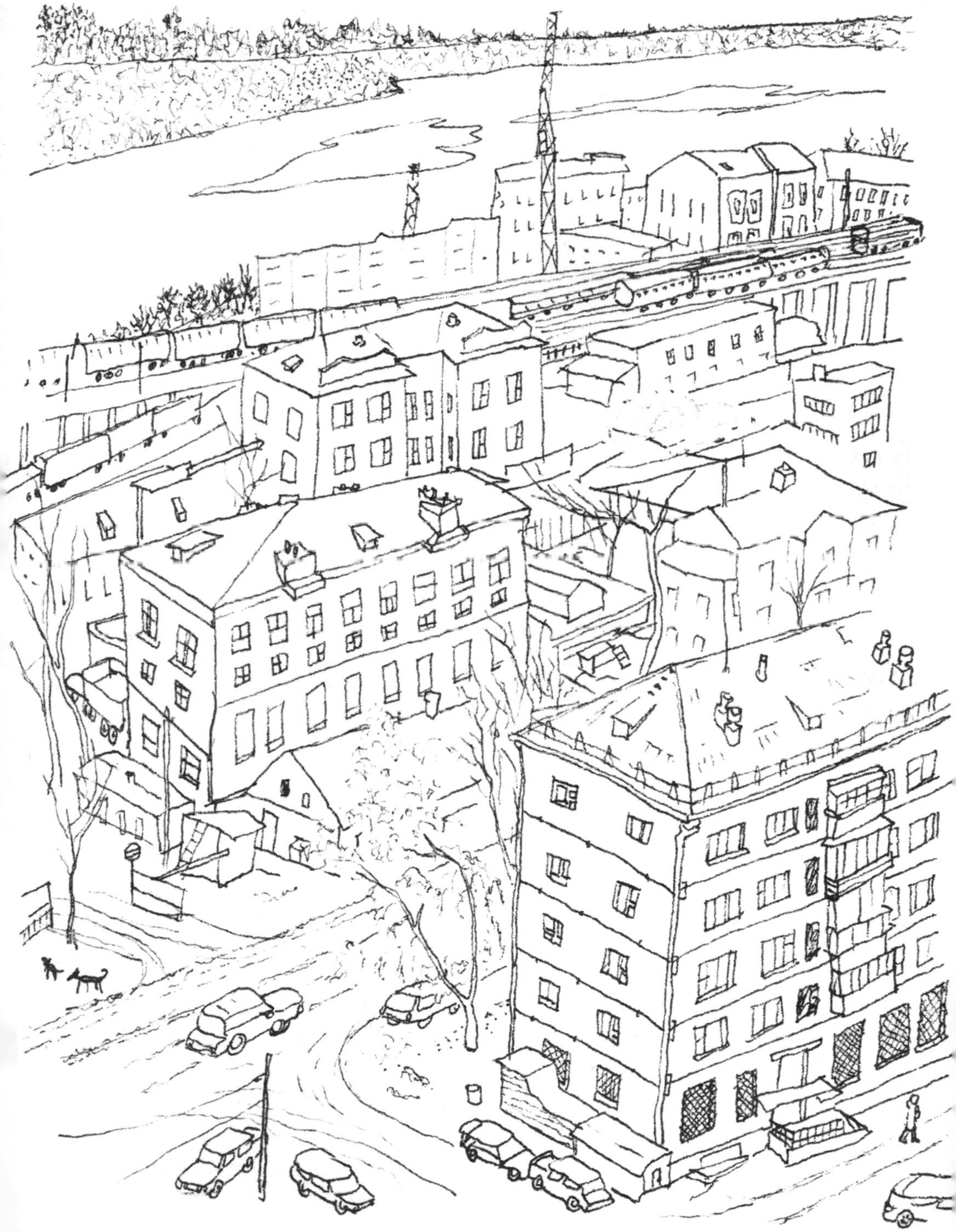

clamatory rhythms of taxi drivers. "No problem! I'll just get a new card! Please wait a moment! Do you think this is cold? To us this is completely normal! In Novosibirsk we are used to this! Where are you from?" and so on. The theatricality of it made his Russian easy to understand.

As we proceeded to the city, mercury lights along the highway held the darkness at arm's length, just barely. On the long bridge over the vast, dark Ob River, it pushed closer on either side. An icy mist on the river's far bank fogged and further dimmed the scene, and on the city streets, our headlights showed the few pedestrians only from the knees down. Tall fir trees along the Hotel Sibir's entryway had been covered in holiday lights of the same locally popular midnight blue, to which the mist had added its pointillism. Bounding from the car, Anatoly carried my bag into the intimately lit lobby and saw that I got checked in. I had a comfortable room on the twelfth floor, with a view of the train yard and the Ob River.

During my first days in Novosibirsk I was in darkness most of the time. Daylight itself usually was tamped down under clouds and falling snow, but I was awake for only a few hours of it, my internal clock having been turned around by all the time zones I'd crossed. Unable to sleep, I put on my full cold-weather outfit and walked the city in the early hours. A bank display on Ulitsa Lenina showed the temperature to be −18° (Celsius) at 5:18 a.m.; a light wind coming down the packed-snow sidewalk reinforced the cold. Nobody was about, for good reason. In the clear sky, a thumbnail-paring of a moon sat just above the horizon. To see the Big Dipper I had to crane my neck far back. At a few degrees lower than directly overhead, the North Star hovered like the point of a pushpin.

Novosibirsk is just that—*novyi*, new. A hundred and fifteen years ago most of the city site was virgin taiga. All its big buildings are from the recent era when it became okay for buildings to look strange. Novosibirsk has buildings in the shape of triangles, hexagons, spheres; also, there's the one whose top is like a two-prong plug, which I mentioned before. In the middle of the city, on a traffic island on one of the main drags, is a small Orthodox chapel that is said to sit at the exact middle of Russia. Actually, the chapel originally built there was supposed to be the geographic center of the prerevolutionary Russian empire. Whether this spot is the geographic center of the Russian Federation as constituted today is less sure. The original chapel was torn down in Soviet times and replaced with a monument to Stalin, which was torn down and replaced with the chapel that's there now.

Like most Soviet cities, Novosibirsk has its Lenin Square. At some moment since the Soviet Union ended, city officials must have decided simply to leave their Lenin Square alone. A huge columned opera house like a domed mosque anchors the square at one end. White lights bathe the dome at night, and at this time of year the dawn comes up behind it. From the opera house stretches a long and wide promenade, and at its terminus Lenin stands on his high marble pedestal, facing forward, one arm upraised, commanding the encircling space. Nearby on his right and at a lower altitude, three soldier-workers back him up, casually holding rifles; on his left, two Soviet citizens, a man and a woman, lift their arms in heroic poses. This Lenin statue is of the genre in which the tails of his topcoat are blown sideways by the winds of history. Less grandly, melt-water had run down his front and then refrozen in small icicles at the bottom of his vest for an unfortunate pubic effect. Snow had accumulated on the statues' shoulders and mustaches and in the crooks of elbows. The figures appeared to be stone but were actually rough, dark-gray steel, which gonged hollowly when rapped upon.

Six o'clock on a weekday morning and still almost nobody out. The subway began to operate, rumbling under the square's emptiness, but the few dark-clad passengers who emerged seemed to dissipate and become microscopic as soon as they did. Two or three widely separated women in city-employee garb were picking up trash, sweeping snow from the subway entrance steps, and scraping at scabs of ice with shovels. In the rotary zone around the square where occasional cars and buses passed, men in orange jumpsuits near vehicles with blinking lights were scraping also. Russia does not use salt on its roads. Another ambient sound came from the square's billboards, which changed their advertising every few minutes with a rustling of metal as the vertical panels turned. At the tops of buildings, a few international commercial logos in neon lights—NOKIA, SAMSUNG, DOUBLETREE HOTELS—added their usual cold comfort.

I wondered what other stars I might be able to see here. Across from the square I went into a city park where the snow on streetlights and fir trees was so picturesque as to seem fake. As I stared upward, not distinguishing much—the rising dawn had already hauled most of the stars out of sight—I was thinking about an unusual incident that had occurred some months before. The reader will remember that on earlier travels in Siberia I had used an Iridium satellite phone. On clear nights I would sometimes pick out a satellite passing overhead and imagine that my call was going by way of that satellite back to New Jersey.

Well, on February 10, 2009, an Iridium satellite crashed into a Russian satellite over northern Siberia. Perhaps I should say that again: an Iridium satellite and a Russian satellite crashed into each other. The collision happened in an orbit 491 miles above the earth, at 72° 5' north latitude and 97° 9' east longitude, over the Taimyr Peninsula. The Iridium satellite weighed 1,235 pounds, and the Russian Cosmos, an inactive communications satellite, weighed about a ton. Each was going about seventeen thousand miles an hour. The collision produced more than one thousand nine hundred pieces of debris large enough to be detectable by radar (larger than a baseball). Experts think that the impact was glancing, and that the Cosmos's long stabilizer boom probably hit the Iridium satellite's array of solar panels. Before this incident, even with the tens of thousands of orbital objects now in space, there had never been a collision of satellites.

When I used to watch satellites going by, I had never considered that one of them might run into something. They seemed to have a pretty clear field. And my notion that occasionally I might be watching an Iridium was mistaken; every satellite I saw was going east–west, while the Iridium orbits are circumpolar. The system divides its sixty-six satellites among eleven orbits that enclose the globe like the bars of a spherical birdcage. Because the earth spins under them, the orbital paths relative to it turn like candy striping. The collision did not interrupt Iridium's service. Other Iridium satellites were able to take over for the one that had been destroyed, and a spare satellite (the system also orbits eight spares) was maneuvered into its place within two weeks.

Navy Captain Paul "Mack" Insch, now retired, was chief of staff of the Joint Functional Component Command for Space of the U.S. Strategic Command (Stratcom) when the collision occurred. This command tracks objects in space for civilian purposes as well as for the military. Some months after the incident I gave Captain Insch a call. He told me that when Iridium lost contact with the satellite, the company informed

Captain Insch's department, which used radar sensors to search the area where the satellite was supposed to be. "We got what we call a multiple head count," Insch said—many pieces, indicating that a collision had occurred. The number of the destroyed satellite was Iridium 33. Following 33's path backward, Captain Insch's group found that a Russian Cosmos, number 2251, would have come close to 33 at the time of the collision. Looking at 2251's orbital path, they found another debris field. Some of the satellites' debris had been knocked into higher orbits, some into lower. In time the debris fields in their orbital paths spread out to encircle the world; they will remain up there for many decades, at least.

After the collision, people wondered what the risk might be to the Hubble Space Telescope, which orbits at 350 miles up, and to the Space Station, at 220 miles. "I don't believe there is a statistically huge increase in risk to either of them from this event," Captain Insch told me. "Human grasp of these spaces is inadequate—the magnitude of volume we're talking about. But you also can expect one result of this kind of impact to be a lot of pieces that are utterly invisible to our radar or optical sensors. I wonder about those pieces we can't see. Whenever the astronauts take space walks I always think what guts they have. One little paint fleck to the visor, at those velocities, and you're dead."

Maybe the meeting of Iridium 33 and Cosmos 2251 will turn out to be just a footnote, nothing anybody need worry about. Or maybe it was the first of more to come, with multiplying fragments hitting other orbiting objects in a chain reaction that turns certain orbit levels into dangerous and useless junk zones. If so, the fact that Russia and the United States, the space race's Cold War competitors, should be the first participants in this futuristic smashup, and that it should begin in the sky over Siberia, somehow stands to reason.

Things to do in Novosibirsk:

You can visit the Novosibirsk Regional Museum, a redbrick building with white trim near Lenin Square. When I was there, the museum was having an exhibit of mummies, or maybe I should say "mummies," because the mummies weren't real but replicas—or, more properly, "replicas," inasmuch as the originals of what the replicas represented may never have existed to begin with. It was scary, though! Along with human mummies, there were cat mummies, dog mummies, crocodile mummies. There was a mummy of an Italian bishop, in front of a perhaps real picture of a cathedral filled with monks who had had themselves mummified in emulation of him. The tour of the exhibit concluded inside a pyramid made of plywood in which dwarfish mummy-skeleton guys held torches next to a mummy of a pharaoh. Kids thronged all over. Out front the sign advertising the exhibit was in Cyrillic, of course, but with letters that wavered and dripped blood—the universal mummy typeface.

Up the street a few blocks, the Novosibirsk State Art Museum occupies an immense classical-style building from Soviet times. This museum has the usual large number of good paintings by Russian painters you've never heard of. Nicholas Roerich, the painter and guru/mystic who lived for a while in Novosibirsk, gave two dozen or so of his idealized mountain landscapes to the museum. In one of them, a sharp-eyed Genghis Khan sitting on his pony on a high ledge looks off to the left, as if there's something in that direction he can't wait to despoil. One of the museum's more recent paintings (not by Roerich) had a baffling title: "*Stakan Fanti*." The first word means "glass," but my pocket dictionary did not list the second. I looked more closely at the painting. The liquid in the glass was orange. "*Fanti*," therefore, must be the genitive singular of Fanta, the orange soft drink: "Glass of Fanta."

For a moviegoer, the Pobeda (Victory) theater, on Ulitsa Lenina, is both familiar and not. The ornate and columned building, formerly a Soviet movie palace, has been turned into an ordinary multiplex, but with the old high ceilings and triumphalist moldings mostly unchanged. One afternoon there I saw the just-released *Tsar*, about Ivan the Terrible. I found it almost unwatchably horrifying, though not inaccurate about Ivan's life. People in the movie are tortured in various ways, enemies of Ivan are eaten by his bear, monks are burned alive in their churches. The plot concerns Ivan's attempts to coerce Philip, the Orthodox metropolitan, into blessing Ivan's wicked schemes. When a monk who has refused to implicate Philip in a crime is beheaded, the executioner holds the head in front of Philip's face, and Philip takes the head by its cheeks and kisses it on the lips. Just another escapist costume drama, in other words.

If you like Cold War relics, the Museum of Siberian Communications, on the second floor of a brownstone by the Novosibirsk post office, is the place to go. This museum is sponsored by a Siberian telecom company. You have to ring a buzzer to get in. The humorous blond woman with Nefertiti eyes who showed me around laughed about the huge old radios, the suitcase-size adding machines, the bulbous green telephone that had come from East Germany, the almost-primitive Yenisei TV set made in Krasnoyarsk, the Brezhnev-era TV that was the size of a desk and that everybody in the 1970s dreamed of owning, and the 1950s TV that many older Russians remember because it had a tiny screen over which was superimposed a large magnifying lens that had to be filled with special distilled water.

In front of a display about old-time satellites and their orbits—concentric circles of colored lights, blinking in sequence around a globe—I asked the guide if she had heard about the American satellite and the Russian satellite that collided over Siberia. She said she certainly had. The crash was in the newspapers and on television and on the radio for days, she said. People weren't too sure exactly where it had happened, but they thought it must have been someplace just above them. She said old ladies in Novosibirsk were afraid that pieces of the satellites would fall on them.

When my friend Alex Melamid was a member of the Soviet Artists' union, back in the early seventies, he was sent from Moscow to work on some murals in Novosibirsk. The work required that he stay in the city for several months. At the time, as it happened, the region was suffering from a shortage of matches, so Alex had brought a supply of matches with him. He recalls that whenever he stopped to light a cigarette on the street, passersby would immediately hurry over to him holding out unlit cigarettes of their own.

Today Novosibirsk has its own giant shopping mall, with matches and more—in the event that you have come to Novosibirsk to shop, you'll be fine. I had found the claim hard to believe when I read it in *The New York Times*, but there it was: "Siberia, where Russians waited in long lines to buy food with ration cards not long ago, is the improbable epicenter of one of the biggest mall booms in history." The story cited "trickle-down petroleum money" as the cause and mentioned the new mall in Novosibirsk.

One morning I set out to find this mall. I had heard it was on the city's outskirts, so I went down into the Lenin Square metro, boarded a subway train, and rode to the last stop. The weather was as cold as usual but the station was heated to stuffiness. A drowsy warmth filled the subway car, too—until the train emerged onto the bridge over the Ob River, supposedly the longest subway-train bridge in the world. I noticed the passengers all rebuttoning and adjusting scarves. After a few minutes, the car's temperature dropped to the subzero cold outside, and everybody was breathing steam. In another few minutes, the train went back underground and the car became warm again.

I got out at the end of the line and wandered a shabby square where pieces of broken produce crates strewed the gutters and sidewalks. Maybe a farmers' market gathers here. Vans and buses idled in long lines at the curbs, and on the sides of some of the buses I noticed ads for the Mega-Ikea. That's the Novosibirsk mall's name. Mega is a developer of malls in many Russian cities, and Ikea is—do I need to say what Ikea is? A behemoth, world-devouring home furnishings store? I asked a guy in the square how to get to the Mega-Ikea, and he told me what buses went there. He was wearing a jacket with the Dannon Yogurt label on it in Russian, so I figured he'd know.

When I asked the bus driver to tell me when we reached the Mega-Ikea, he only shrugged. I soon understood why. The Mega-Ikea mall dominates its blank surroundings like a beached aircraft carrier, impossible to miss. Its huge parking lot lacks cars and thus presents the approaching mallgoer with a flat Siberian snowfield across which footpaths serpentine. I debarked with almost all the other passengers and took the footpath originating at this bus stop. Up ahead, I could see, the path would converge with others from other bus stops, aiming for what had to be the colossus's entryway.

Of the mall itself, little need be said. Any reader can supply his or her own generic experiences of malls and be not too far off. Perhaps the Novosibirsk Mega-Ikea is bigger than most malls—with its hallways as wide as airplane runways, etc.—and its customers correspondingly smaller-seeming and more scattered. Perhaps the Mega-Ikea's background Muzak is more bizarre—unthreatening American country songs, in a style that might be called shopping country. Considering that this is a mall in the Siberian taiga, I found "On the Banks of the Ohio" (sung in English) a confusing tune. The only part of the mall I really liked was right at the door, in the rush of heated air that pushed back against the exterior cold. Mixed with that air, a strong scent of Russian diesel blasted a muscular alternative to the retail atmosphere.

Certain of the mall's architectural elements had not been thought through. At the end of one airplane-runway hall, a floor-to-ceiling window opened a vista on the countryside. Malls in America do not have windows. For a mall to be a true mall this law must be observed. Here, a large sofa upholstered in blue denim sat in front of the window with its back to it, but the gesture was too late, the damage done. Inescapably the eye was drawn outward, where it met a small, drab village of wooden dachas, snow-covered roofs against dark-brown walls, and beyond, the taiga tree line's front rank, winter-cold and gray to the horizon.

On the Novosibirsk metro, the station closest to the Mega-Ikea mall is Ploshchad Karla Marksa, Karl Marx Square.

Another day, I took a bus to Akademgorodok, where I'd stayed on my 2001 trip with Sergei and Volodya. This time I went there to meet Ivan Logoshenko, a friend of Rob Carcy's, my brother-in-law. Rob got to know Ivan some years ago when both were doing experiments with the alternating gradient synchrotron, a particle accelerator at Brookhaven Laboratory on Long Island. Rob had told me that Ivan, called Vanya, is a prince of a guy, and he is. He holds the rank of "leading scientist" at Novosibirsk State University, where he heads his own *katedra*, or department, in the field of computers and physics. Vanya grew up on Sakhalin Island, in the city of Yuzhno-Sakhalinsk, but he speaks American English not much differently than Rob and I do.

Akademgorodok must have been designed to look its best in winter. I remembered it as being green and somewhat weedy, with apartment buildings and tall fir trees rising from the undergrowth. That was in August. Now, a thick snow mantle subdued the "science city," rendered it into a sharply focused two-tone photograph, made it look reasoned and disciplined. At a T intersection where a street met an avenue, the bus stopped and began to idle. The driver leaned back and lit another cigarette, blue lassos of smoke snaking around his rearview mirror, while all the twenty-somethings piled out. I figured this must be the center of town. The snow here had a packed-down, much-trodden patina and people were hurrying past, pushing kids in strollerlike conveyances that had sled runners instead of wheels. A group of boys, all of them about nine or ten years old, horsed around while waiting for their mothers to pick them up.

I called Vanya and told him where I was and he said he would be there in five minutes. The boys continued to play all around me, oblivious, like fish around a scuba diver. One kid climbed partway up a nearby fir and began to shake snow down on his companions. This got a laugh. Then a boy who was hopping here and there doing karate kicks happened to kick an aluminum light pole. Atop the light pole was a shade like a broad, flat hat, carrying a tall accumulation of snow. The kick sent some snow down on another kid's head. Great hilarity. All the kids then began karate kicking the light pole, which responded with satisfying dull *bongs* and cascade after cascade of snow. Meanwhile, several mothers pulled up in their cars and were chatting with one another, occasionally interrupting themselves to tell the boys to quit kicking the light pole. The boys only kicked more, and finally one of the boys, with high exuberance, began singing "Jingle Bells," in English, in time to his kicks. Snow tumbling off the light pole in showers, "Jingle Bells," *bong, bong, bong*, great laughter. He knew the words and sang them perfectly, without accent.

Vanya arrived in his Toyota with its steering wheel on the right-hand side, and he drove me around the town. This was a totally pleasant afternoon. Knowing that so many great brains were on the premises, in the apartment buildings and institutes and cottages distributed throughout the snowy landscape, gave the place a certain romance. Playing off that, the restaurant where we went for lunch had been designed around a science theme. Its decor featured elaborate scientific formulas in Russian handwriting on the zinc walls, and abstruse charts and graphs on the floors, and combinations of actual brass-and-steel gears set into the paneling above the booths. The check, when it came, was in an old Russian textbook of differential equations.

As Vanya and I sat and talked, I felt normal. I had never felt just that—normal—in Russia before. I had been making trips to Russia and working on this book since 1993. In those sixteen years I had been to Siberia five times, to western Russia five or six more. Never in all those travels had I felt merely normal. At the beginning, when the Soviet Union had recently disappeared, everything was giddy, in flux. A person you met might be your new best friend or a complicated criminal. The rubles in your pocket might be devalued overnight. Though the Soviets themselves were gone, the Soviet relics had not been hauled away, and

Cold War mirror images were everywhere. Back then the whole country was, to me, toxic as well as wonderfully new. I was both dazzled and on my guard constantly.

Now things had sorted themselves out, more or less. Once again Russia was not a democracy. People seemed to have accepted that. Absorbent of other cultures, as always, the country had taken in global capitalism and made its own version of it, in some ways a grotesque. English could now be found throughout the country, and Cyrillic signs, when sounded out, often were English, too. I noticed this restaurant offered a special БИЗНЕС ЛУНЧ—phonetically, "biznes lunch." I had seen similar signs around Novosibirsk. Vanya said the "biznes lunch" had become common some years ago. Like the Hotel Sibir and the Aeroflot planes and this restaurant, parts of Russia were now almost indistinguishable from their equivalents in America. I couldn't even find old Soviet postcards anymore. Those funny, drab, literal-minded cards of former times had been replaced with high-production glossies you might buy at Disney World or anywhere.

What to make of this remade, hybridized country? From what you heard and read, Russia was a bigger disaster now than it had been under communism. Russians today were dying faster than they were being born. The population, descending at a rate of 4 percent annually since 1993, was down to 142 million. At this rate it would go below 100 million in eight years. And yet, as mentioned, Russia had become the leading energy-exporting nation in the world. But that was bad for the country, too, given its unhealthy dependence on this single, unrenewable source of income. Russian men now were living, on average, only fifty-nine years—a life expectancy worse than in 165 other countries, and just above Gambia's. The World Health Organization noted that Russians were consuming twice as much alcohol as the amount considered dangerous for health. Three and a half times as many people were dying in car wrecks in Russia (twenty-one per hundred thousand) as were dying in car wrecks in Germany (six per hundred thousand). Three times as many Russians as Americans or Europeans were dying of heart disease.

And yet, in 2009, Russia passed De Beers as the world's leading producer of diamonds. And yet, Russia now supplied Boeing and Airbus with over half the titanium used to build their airplanes. And yet, Norilsk Nickel, in the far north, was producing a fifth of the world's nickel. And yet, Norilsk's smelters also were producing more sulfur dioxide than the entire nation of France. And yet, United Energy Systems, Russia's electrical monopoly, was putting almost as much carbon dioxide into the atmosphere as was the entire nation of Great Britain. And yet, a Russian billionaire who made a lot of money from Norilsk Nickel had just bought the New Jersey Nets basketball team. And yet, a Russian oil billionaire had just brought some very large bells back to the Russian monastery from which they had been removed years ago, and had compensated the bells' owner, a Harvard dormitory house, by providing duplicate bells, at great expense. And yet, a Russian aluminum billionaire had merged his aluminum company with two others to create the largest aluminum company in the world, explaining that he could make aluminum more cheaply because of the vast hydropower resources of Siberia; in fact, most of the money and resources currently enriching the billionaires, and Russia, had their origins in Siberia. And yet—

And yet Russia was a mess. Once again it was killing its writers; although, in keeping with the previous century's tilt toward nonfiction, reporters had become the victims now, while poets and fiction writers seemed to be exempt. Investigations of the Soviet past had been clamped down upon. The archives of the KGB, open during the Yeltsin years, were unofficially reclosed. Researchers seeking access to them met bureaucratic delays and other obstacles impossible to go around. In St. Petersburg, masked men of the Russian General Prosecutor's Office forced their way into the offices of Memorial, a research and information center devoted to studying the Stalinist repressions. The government men confiscated hard drives and CDs containing Memorial's entire files. These included databases of victims, letters, photographs, memoirs, and documents relating to the Terror and the gulag. Prosecutors said they were investigating Memorial's connection to a newspaper article that incited racial hatred—a claim with no foundation, Memorial's supporters replied.

Each year the long-dead Joseph Stalin continued ascending in the estimation of his countrymen. Putin himself sometimes made favorable comments about him, even referring to him once or twice familiarly as "Iosif Vissarionovich." In 2008 a Russian television station conducted a poll to find out which Russians were considered by their countrymen to be the greatest of all time. Millions voted in the poll, and Stalin came in third.

Alexander Nevsky, the thirteenth-century prince who later became a saint, was first, and Pyotr Stolypin, the prime minister who worked for reforms under Nicholas II and died by assassination in 1911, was second. Among the top twelve, the others were Pushkin (#4), Peter the Great (#5), Lenin (#6), Dostoyevsky (#7), A. V. Suvorov (famous general; #8), Mendeleev (the only Siberian on the list; #9), Ivan the Terrible (#10), Catherine the Great (#11), and Alexander II (#12). In light of how hated Alexander had been in life, and how hard his enemies had worked to kill him, his appearance in the top twelve was something of a surprise.

Snow was falling when Vanya and I emerged from the science-themed restaurant, and the snow on Vanya's car had to be removed with a snow scraper, while big snowflakes continued snowing down snowily. A heavy snowstorm, in other words, in this already snow-covered place. Vanya offered to drive me back to my hotel; as I said, he's a prince of a guy. I hesitated to accept his offer, knowing he would be driving forty miles in the snow. But accept I did.

Cars were going slowly on the road between Akademgorodok and Novosibirsk as Vanya told me about the first time he left Russia, back in the early nineties. He had won a prize of three months' study in Switzerland for being first in physics in his graduating class at Novosibirsk State. The difference between Zurich and anyplace in Russia at that time was enormous. On the crowded and snowy highway, traffic slowed more, then stopped. Vanya said this is the only road from Akademgorodok to the city and it gets busier all the time. I remembered locals telling me, back in 2001, that Akademgorodok was losing population; now, Vanya said, Akademgorodok had become fashionable, rents were rising, new apartment buildings were going up. Old-time residents had begun to worry about conserving the town's character, its forests and open spaces. Rich apartment buyers from Novosibirsk were moving in. Maybe in the future the scientists for whom the place was designed would no longer be able to afford it.

In a Siberian snowstorm, we were having a conversation about real estate—for me, another feature of normality. I continued to feel normal for a while after Vanya dropped me off at my hotel. Snow fell all night and for the next few days. The snow was pleasant to look at from my room, though hazardous to walk on as it piled lightly on the already slippery sidewalks. On every surface it settled in and soon became a Styrofoam-like substance that squeaked underfoot. After another solitary hike or two around the city, my feeling of normalness faded out, and I fell into a jumpy state again. I decided I kind of preferred it, overall.

The regional museum, where the mummy exhibit was, had a gift shop I remembered as a place in which I might find some presents to bring home. There was a whole shelf of refrigerator magnets. When I went back and looked at them again, I saw that the magnet facings with engravings of mammoths were made not of wood, but of mammoth ivory, and I bought a half dozen, happy to participate in the mammoth-ivory trade. Since an international ban on buying and selling elephant ivory was enacted in 1989, mammoth ivory from Siberia has taken over as a legal substitute. Japan and China are the chief importers; in those countries people often use ivory seals on documents in place of signatures. In the West, a pound of mammoth ivory can go for $800. Russia's mammoth-ivory exports increased from two tons in 1989 to forty tons in 2007. Mammoth ivory fifteen thousand or more years old, a part of Siberian commerce for centuries, became a sought-after product of the taiga again.

Some people hunt mammoth ivory professionally. It also provides an income source for oil-field workers and reindeer herders who trade in it as a sideline. Scientists estimate that the Siberian permafrost holds the remains of 150 million mammoths—or about 8 million more than the 142 million Russians aboveground in Russia today.

Sergei Prigarin, the mathematician whom I'd met on my trip in 2001, was not at home in Akademgorodok this time. By e-mail he informed me that he and his wife were staying in Munich while he worked on a meteorological project involving stochastic simulations of clouds. Sergei said his daughter, Sveta, was living in Akademgorodok, spoke fluent English, and would be glad to meet with me. Sveta had been only sixteen when we came through here in 2001. She and her friend Maria had gone with us to the outdoor museum with the restored wooden church. The truth was, I did not really remember them. Vaguely I recalled that they were cheerful and friendly kids and I'd talked some English to them.

On this trip, Sveta and I were in touch first by e-mail, and then arranged by cell phone how we would meet. I took a van to Akademgorodok and kept a window scraped clear of frost so I could see out. As the van came into the town limits, we passed a sign by the roadside: MOGU-CHESTVO ROSSII PRIRASTAT' BUDET SIBIR'IO! Many Russians know this saying, which was made by Mikhail Lomonosov, the first Russian genius in science, in the eighteenth century. It is the most succinct expression of the eastward-looking, pro-Siberia point of view, and the biggest sign in Akademgorodok, as well. It means, "The Power of Russia Will Grow from Siberia!"

Again I got off with everybody else, but the van had taken a different route than the bus did when I came to visit Vanya. I could not see any landmarks in the surrounding forest. I went with a flow of pedestrians along a snow path until it ended in front of what might have been a student union or a dorm. By my sketchy description over the phone, Sveta figured out where I was. In twenty minutes she showed up—a tall, slim young woman with long dark hair and dark eyes. She recognized me before I recognized her.

I had wanted to check some facts about the wooden church we'd visited in 2001. On the Internet she had found a three-page history of the church in Russian, and she brought it with her on a memory stick. She took me to a nearby minimall and got the history printed out at a copy shop, and then over coffee she translated the text for me. She also had a good recall of the visit and of Galina's, the guide's, speech, and filled in blanks in my notes. While I had been so distracted by my own concerns that I almost didn't notice her, she had been remembering everything.

Sveta had finished high school, attended Novosibirsk State, and graduated in 2008 with a degree in psychology. So far she had been unable to find a job and was taking classes in origami. She told me about growing up in Novosibirsk, and about a dacha the family has nearby, and she described the many mosquitoes around there. One summer, she said, a local pharmacy was offering $100 a pound for dried mosquitoes. Apparently they have some pharmaceutical qualities. Inspired by the big price, Sveta and her friends tried to catch and collect a pound of mosquitoes, but quit in despair after finding out how many it took to equal just a gram.

When I left, Sveta gave me an origami globe of pink and orange paper flowers she had made, and a cardboard candy box to carry it in. At JFK Airport, on my way home, a young woman police officer with a beagle trained to sniff for illegal substances walked by as I was standing near the luggage carousel. The candy box was in a plastic bag on the floor beside my briefcase. As the beagle trotted past, it suddenly stopped short and "indicated" at the plastic bag, scratching and whining and straining toward it. The officer asked me what was in the bag. I took out the origami globe and showed it to her. She smiled and said, "Wow!" and then she and the dog walked on.

From time to time I contemplate the phrase "the incomplete grandiosity of Russia." I'm not sure who said it originally, or how I happen to have it in my head, but it describes the country. Russia's grandiosity, good or bad, doesn't end. It just trails off into the country's expanses, like Kutuzov's army evaporating before Napoleon. The incomplete grandiosity pursues its incompleteness out there in Siberia somewhere. In past times there were stories of Russians who went so far into Siberia, and stayed so long, that they forgot the Russian language. Travelers who came upon them found them not really Russian anymore, speaking an unknown tongue. Incomplete grandiosity is the voyage of Semyon Dezhnev, who sailed around the eastern end of Asia, proved the continent was not connected to America, told his superiors of this epochal discovery—and then they mislaid his report. Incomplete and cruel grandiosity are the roads to the Arctic Circle that Stalin wanted people to build and that they quickly and gratefully gave up on when he died.

What I'd seen of Siberia was only a tiny part. The grandiosity extended constantly onward, out of the view. I hadn't seen the hydropower dam on the Angara River near Bratsk, which stoppers one of the largest man-made lakes in the world; or the Sayano-Shushenskaya Dam on the Yenisei, which blew a water conduit leading to a generating room in August 2009, killing more than sixty workers, and leaving in doubt the future of the dam, and of many other dams, as the Soviet-built infrastructure continues to decay. I hadn't seen Vissarion, the Siberian messiah figure who formerly was a traffic cop known as Sergei Torop; nor his village, called the Abode of Dawn; nor any of the forty villages his five thousand followers have built around it in the taiga while they wait for heaven on earth to arrive.

I hadn't seen a reindeer herd in Siberia, or witnessed the animals made frantic by mosquito swarms that seem to be fiercer and to stay around longer every year. I hadn't been to Siberia's Arctic coast, now with less ice in the summer than anybody can remember, and I didn't observe the German cargo ships *Beluga Fraternity* and *Beluga Foresight* when they went along that coast on the first-ever successful commercial voyage through the Northeast Passage, during the summer of 2009. From Europe to China or Japan via the Northeast Passage along Siberia is more than four thousand miles shorter than going through the Suez Canal; the opening of this passage as the climate warms is expected to change the shipping patterns of the world.

I never came across an American oil-field worker in Siberia, though I did see and talk to one in the Seattle airport while he waited for a plane to Kamchatka, from which he would fly to Sakhalin. I never talked to any climate scientists, though they must be the second most common kind of Americans, after oil people, currently in Siberia. The oil people think in terms of decades, to keep the oil flowing, and the climate scientists think in terms of centuries and the global damage the oil is doing and will do. I never saw the bubbles of methane rising in sheaves from the thawing sea floor along Siberia's Arctic coast, as documented by scientists from the University of Alaska in 2008. The amount of methane in permafrost in Siberian lakes is said to be ten times as much as the earth's atmosphere holds now; I never saw climate scientists lighting methane bubbles effervescing from a lake, though scientists do that sometimes. As a heat-trapping gas, methane is twenty times more potent than carbon dioxide; I never saw a Siberian lake where the stream of methane bubbles from the thawing permafrost on the bottom created a roiling action that kept the lake from freezing throughout the winter, though I've read that happens, too.

As the winters are getting shorter, sleep-deprived bears can't hibernate, and roam the forests of southern Siberia into November, frightening the local population; but I never saw those bears, or any others. I did not see or smell the forest fire as big as Italy that burned in Siberia in '06, or the yellow snow caused by the dust storms from the former Aral Sea that fell on Omsk and Tomsk in '07. When I swam in Baikal, I did not realize that it had warmed 2.8 degrees in the last century, or that the amount of chlorophyll was three times what it used to be.

I never came upon what is known as a drunken forest—a forest in which the thawing of the supporting permafrost causes the trees to lean every which way. The entire Siberian permafrost is starting to thaw, scientists say, and when it does it will release seventy-five times as much carbon as is put into the atmosphere every year by the burning of fossil fuels; I've seen plenty of Siberian swamps, but no clearly identified thawing permafrost, except under certain buildings, which are melting it themselves. For weeks and weeks I traveled through the taiga, most of which in Siberia rests on permafrost. Because the permafrost covers four hundred thousand square miles of Siberia to an average depth of eighty-two feet, and because the end of a drunken forest is a dead forest is a swamp, most of the taiga I saw may be future swamp. A melting of the permafrost will add gigantically to Siberia's already plentiful supply of swamps. All these signs and portents of future climate disaster are out there, unseen by most people, somewhere in Siberia.

The Decembrists, the historical Russians I admire most, were incomplete grandiosity personified. Their revolution failed, their idealistic plans for national reform remained dreams. The serfs, whom they had wanted to free, were freed eventually, but only after most of the Decembrists were dead. The Decembrists' reputation has survived so well, perhaps, because the grand intentions of their youth were never realized and tarnished. Their lives were noble, epic, partly finished sketches, backlit and sanctified by suffering.

Ivan Yakushkin, the clear-headed memoirist, returned to Moscow in 1856 following the amnesty and died eight months later. He was sixty-four years old. Prince Sergei Trubetskoy died of "apoplexy" in 1860 at the age of seventy upon hearing of his daughter's death from TB. Prince Yevgenii Obolensky married an illiterate servant girl and died in Kaluga, near Moscow, in 1865. The Annenkovs moved to Tobolsk, where he became a civil servant, and then to Nizhnii Novgorod. Baron Andrei Rozen lived to be eighty-four and fasted on the anniversary of the uprising every year. Nikolai Bestuzhev, the kindhearted officer who had refused to let the young cadets accompany his soldiers to the Senate Square, died in Siberia in 1855. His death was the result of a cold he caught from riding on the outside of his carriage so friends of his could ride inside.

Prince Sergei Volkonsky, after receiving the news of his pardon brought to him by Mikhail, his fast-traveling son, packed up the household in Irkutsk and left for Moscow. They made the return journey at a leisurely pace because of his age. Back in western Russia, the long-bearded prince, who had gone around in tarry clothes in his exile and enjoyed philosophical conversations with his fellow workmen and farmers, reassumed the air of a distinguished aristocrat. Observers remarked on his pale skin, silvery locks, and saintlike, biblical appearance.

For a long time the prince and his wife, Maria, had led mostly separate lives. She remained slim and lovely into her fifties and her lustrous hair never turned gray. She died of kidney disease at the age of fifty-eight at their estate in the Ukraine. Volkonsky was staying at his son's estate on the Baltic, and not well enough to go to her. Eighteen years her senior, he outlived her by two years. After her death he went into a decline, but despite his frailty and his confinement to a wheelchair his mind remained keen. Now as the end of his life was approaching, he set about to write his memoirs, and on November 28, 1865, while working on them, he died. The last words he wrote were,

The Emperor said to me, "I

NOTES

SELECTED BIBLIOGRAPHY

ACKNOWLEDGMENTS

INDEX

Notes

CHAPTER 1

3   During Soviet times: Stephen Waltrous, "The Regionalist Conception of Siberia, 1860 to 1970," in Diment and Slezkine, *Between Heaven and Hell*, p. 116.

3   Newspaper gossip columns: Lloyd Grove, "Lowdown: /40 Park Hits Roof over Book Party," New York *Daily News*, October 6, 2005.

4   latitudinally for thirty-six hundred miles: Lengyel, *Siberia*, p. 15. Siberia is one-fifth of the total forested area of the world. It contains more than half of the world's coniferous forests and two-fifths of its temperate forests. See Kotkin and Wolff, *Rediscovering Russia in Asia*, p. 257.

4   the Urals aren't much: The English traveler John Dundas Cochrane wrote, "The ascent and descent [of the Urals] are so nearly imperceptible, that were it not for the precipitous banks every where to be seen, the traveler would hardly suppose he had crossed a range of hills" (*Narrative of a Pedestrian Journey*, p. 122).

4   about three thousand miles beyond the Urals: From the Urals to Chukchi Nos, the easternmost tip of Siberia (and of Asia), is 3,562 miles; from the Urals to the Sea of Okhotsk is 2,771 miles, and to Vladivostok is 3,174 miles.

5   for as much as 250 miles: Lengyel, *Siberia*, p. 14.

5   The steppes were why: Gryaznov, *The Ancient Civilization of Southern Siberia*, p. 133.

5   "To the rescue, Kamchatka!": Pasternak, *Safe Conduct*, p. 69.

7   with only five portages: Sutherland, *Princess of Siberia*, p. 111. On the river portage system of Siberia, see also James Forsyth, "The Siberian Native Peoples Before and After Russian Conquest," in Wood, *History of Siberia*, p. 78.

7   more than four hundred years old: Tobolsk was founded in 1587, Surgut in 1594, Ketsk in 1602, Tomsk in 1604, and Turukhansk in 1607.

7   the largest swamps in the world: Diment and Slezkine, *Between Heaven and Hell*, p. 71; also Sinor, *The Cambridge History of Early Inner Asia*, p. 23.

8   the rivers run muddy: Barratt, *Rebel on the Bridge*, p. 153.

8   the lowest on the planet outside Antarctica: Forsyth, *A History of the Peoples of Siberia*, p. 9; also Pipes, *Russia Under the Old Regime*, p. 3.

8   the *Los Angeles Times* estimated: "70 Years' Worth of Waste Has Remote Region Over a Barrel," *Los Angeles Times*, September 13, 1997, p. A2.

9   Its coal reserves: See Kotkin and Wolff, *Rediscovering Russia in Asia*, p. 188: "Today, the West Siberian Basin remains the world's largest storehouse of hydrocarbons."

9   minerals like cobalt: See Hill and Gaddy, *Siberian Curse*, p. 81; also Encyclopaedia Britannica online, s.v. "Asia Mineral Resources."

9   about half the gold then being mined: Dallin and Nicolaevsky, *Forced Labor in Soviet Russia*, p. 146.

10   Geologists have always liked Siberia: Facts about Siberian plate tectonics come from Dr. Sergei V. Shibaev, chief of the Siberian Department of the Geophysical Service of the Yakutsk Branch of the Russian Academy of Sciences, in Yakutsk, Republic of Sakha. Dr. Kenneth Deffeyes, professor emeritus of geology at Princeton University, kindly passed along to me details about the Permian extinction and the Siberian Traps.

10   Paleontologists come to Siberia: For information about Siberian paleontology, I am grateful to Ross MacPhee, of the American Museum of Natural History in New York.

11   mammoth ivory became a major export: See Bobrick, *East of the Sun*, pp. 310–11.

11   cloud-free for more than two hundred days a year: Irkutsk, near Lake Baikal, has more hours of sunlight than anywhere else in Russia (Mowat, *The Siberians*, p. 61). Viktor D. Trifonov and Elena Kossumova, astronomers at a solar observatory on the shores of Baikal, told me the observatory was there because of the two hundred days of sunshine the lake receives annually on its western shore.

11   In the early morning of June 30, 1908: Gallant, *Day the Sky Split Apart*.

11   Travelers who crossed Siberia: The observations in this paragraph are found in Pallas, *A Naturalist in Russia*, p. 91; Bell, *A Journey from St. Petersburg to Pekin*, p. 59 and passim; Fries, *A Siberian Journey*, p. 108; and Strahlenberg, *Russia, Siberia, and Great Tartary*, pp. 371, 438.

12   At times Siberia has supplied: Leonid M. Goryushkin, "Migration, Settlement and the Rural Economy of Siberia, 1861–1914," in Wood, *History of Siberia*, p. 149.

12   Sentenced to three years' exile: Florinsky, *Russia*, 2:1149; also Lengyel, *Siberia*, pp. 147–48.

12   a government stipend of twelve rubles a month: Solzhenitsyn, *The Gulag Archipelago*, 3:342.

13   a rich distiller named Iudin: Lincoln, *The Conquest of a Continent*, pp. 217, 268.

13   translated a book by the English Socialists: Lengyel, *Siberia*, pp. 147–48.

13   inspired by the great Siberian river: Fischer, *Life of Lenin*, pp. 4–5.

13   Russians who had seen him both before and after: Melamid and Komar, *Monumental Propaganda*, p. 51.

14   in a sense, unkillable: "Siberia also meant greater security from enemy attack. 'Russia lacks a heart at which to strike,' the late German Marshal von Hindenberg insisted" (Lengyel, *Siberia*, p. 8).

14   "I am not afraid of military reverses": Florinsky, *Russia*, 2:675. Tsar Alexander I said

that rather than cede the country to an invader, he would withdraw to Kamchatka (ibid., p. 638). A similar strategy was employed as recently as 1993, when Boris Yeltsin, threatened by a putsch within his government, made a contingency plan to relocate the government near his home city of Sverdlovsk (now Ekaterinburg), east of the Urals. See Remnick, *Lenin's Tomb*, p. 472.

14   administrative capital and ecclesiastical seat: Ides, *Three Years' Travels*, p. 11; also Armstrong, *Yermak's Campaign in Siberia*, p. 80.

14   "crippled by its expanse": The historian Nikolai Berdayev, in Remnick, *Lenin's Tomb*, p. 523.

14   a road leading nowhere: "The Czars' Russia . . . wanted, above all, to break down the cruel barriers that contained her within a continent-wide blind alley" (Lengyel, *Siberia*, p. 6).

14   two public-policy experts: Hill and Gaddy, *Siberian Curse*.

14   Those on the positive side of the argument: See, e.g., Trubetskoy, *Legacy of Genghis Khan*; Rasputin, *Siberia, Siberia*; and Hill and Gaddy, *Siberian Curse*, pp. 170ff.

14   resources and hard-to-subdue vastness: Hosking, *Russia and the Russians*, p. 142.

14   "Russia is an Asiatic land": Lengyel, *Siberia*, p. 384.

15   escaped from Siberia six times: Sebag Montefiore, *Stalin*, p. 24; see also Lengyel, *Siberia*, p. 178.

15   style himself officially as tsar: *The Treasures of the Golden Horde* (St. Petersburg: Slavia Publishing, 2000), p. 51.

15   "Lord of All the Siberian Land": Armstrong, *Yermak's Campaign*, p. 3.

15   In 1552, Ivan led a large army: Grousset, *The Empire of the Steppes*, p. 475.

15   had his clergy sprinkle the streets: Lantzeff and Pierce, *Eastward to Empire*, p. 67.

15   Farther to the east, the khan of Sibir: Armstrong, *Yermak's Campaign*, pp. 1–2; also, Lantzeff and Pierce, *Eastward to Empire*, p. 70.

15   In 1581 and 1582: Armstrong, *Yermak's Campaign*, pp. 5ff.

15   a rich tribute of sable furs: Lantzeff and Pierce, *Eastward to Empire*, p. 110.

15   His mother, Ivan said: Izhboldin, *Essays on Tatar History*, p. 31.

15   a progenitor named Pruss: Florinsky, *Russia*, 1:186.

16   "the Third Rome": Avvakum, *The Life of the Archpriest Avvakum*, p. 8; see also Hosking, *Russia and the Russians*, p. 107.

16   exceeded the size of the surface of the full moon: Pipes, *Russia Under the Old Regime*, p. 84.

CHAPTER 2

17   Vitaly Komar and Alex Melamid: For more on the early work of Komar and Melamid, see Carter Ratcliff, *Komar and Melamid* (New York: Abbeville, 1988).

24   a humor magazine called the *Harvard Lampoon*: Reed was elected to the *Lampoon* in February of his sophomore year. As a Westerner (Portland, Oregon), Reed did not have the social standing required for election to prestigious clubs like the Porcellian, and so the *Lampoon* became an important refuge. He rose to the position of Ibis, the *Lampoon's* second-highest office. Reed also was a cheerleader at Harvard football games and wrote a fight song that defied Yale. See Hicks, *John Reed*, pp. 28–40.

24   following Pancho Villa's armies: See Reed's excellent *Insurgent Mexico*, a book of his Mexican dispatches.

24   banned from the Western front: Hicks mentions this incident (p. 168), as does David C. Duke in *John Reed* (Boston: Twayne, 1987), p. 149. Reed never wrote about it himself, but a reporter named Robert Dunn, who was with him at the time and also took two shots at the French, later wrote up the adventure for the *New York Evening Post*, which ran the account on February 27, 1915, p. 1.

24   "Russia's is an original civilization": Reed, *War in Eastern Europe*, p. 210.

24   "The whole beautiful land is even more glorious": Freeman, *American Testament*, p. 270.

24   two months in a rented room: Hicks, *John Reed*, pp. 170, 325; also Duke, *John Reed*, pp. 41, 114.

25   Lenin himself admired it: See Gardner, *"Friend and Lover,"* p. 187. After the book's publication, Reed wrote Bryant, "The big chief [Lenin] thinks my book the best." Lenin later contributed a one-paragraph "introduction" praising the book. Today this paragraph would be called a blurb.

25   not quite thirty-three: Reed died three days before his thirty-third birthday. See Reed, *Education of John Reed*, p. 38.

25   in the Kremlin Wall: Reed is buried next to Inessa Armand, girlfriend of Lenin, who died the same year; see the photo of the site in Gardner, *"Friend and Lover."* The other American buried in the wall is "Big Bill" Haywood, a union organizer.

27   Farley Mowat, the Canadian author: Mowat, *The Siberians*, p. 14.

27   Valentin Rasputin, the Siberian short-story writer: Rasputin, *Essays*, pp. 94, 72.

27   Among scholars who have studied the question: Baikalov, *Notes on the Origin of the Name Siberia*, pp. 287–89. See also Bretschneider, *Mediaeval Researches*, 2:37.

27   Etymologists say: Baikalov, *Notes on the Origin of the Name Siberia*; see also the entry for *Sibir'* in Vasmer, *Etimologicheskii Slovar' Russkogo Yazyka*, vol. 3. This is the authoritative etymological dictionary Russians use.

27   The first appearance of the word *Sibir'*: Pritsak, *The Origin of the Name* Sibir', pp. 271–72.

28   "After Joci had subjugated the People of the Forest": Rachewiltz, *Secret History of the Mongols*, pp. 164–65. (I have not reproduced certain orthographic symbols in the translation.)

28   in the reign of his son Batu: Florinsky, *Russia*, 1:56.

28   Jochi's line, by the way: Izhboldin, *Essays on Tatar History*, p. 31.

28   the Persian traveler and historian Rashid ad-Din: Bretschneider, *Mediaeval Researches*, 2:37; also Howorth, *History of the Mongols*, p. xxi, and Quatremère, *Histoire des Mongols de la Perse*, p. 413.

28   in the Russian chronicles of 1406: Baikalov, *Notes on the Origin of the Name Siberia*, p. 288.

28   The first known reference: Ibid.

28   Schiltberger led a tumultuous life: Schiltberger, *Bondage and Travels*.

29   King Sigismund of Hungary: Schiltberger spells the name "Sigmund"; elsewhere it is more usually spelled "Sigismund." See an account of this crusade in Norwich, *A Short History of Byzantium*, pp. 359–60.

29   This former Turkic tribal chief: For more on Tamerlane, see Grousset, *The Empire of the Steppes*, pp. 406ff.

30   reciting the Ave Maria: Schiltberger, *Bondage and Travels*, p. xxviii.

CHAPTER 3

37 Barguzin is more than 350 years old: See map in Grousset, *The Empire of the Steppes*, pp. 534–35, which gives 1648 as the date of Barguzin's founding.

37 Katarina Breshkovskaya: This well-known revolutionary appears often in the accounts of the time. Both John Reed and Louise Bryant met and admired her—see his *Ten Days That Shook the World*, p. xxii, and Gardner, "*Friend and Lover*," p. 90. George Kennan regarded her as a hero—see his *Siberia and the Exile System*, 1:12–22.

37 "Barguzin Wind": Rytkheu, *Stories from Chukotka*, p. 18.

37 traded furs and gold by caravan: Barguzin is older than Irkutsk (founded 1661), historically the main city of that part of Siberia. Barguzin was an important entrepôt on an early route of caravans to China. Even today, the fanciest sable fur sold in America is called Barguzin sable. See Lantzeff and Pierce, *Eastward to Empire*, p. 151.

38 Wilhelm Küchelbecker: On Wilhelm Küchelbecker and his duel with Pushkin, see Vitale, *Pushkin's Button*, pp. 266–67.

38 Barguzin's Küchelbecker: Sutherland, *Princess of Siberia*, p. 255. For more on Mikhail Karlovich Küchelbecker, see Barratt, *Voices in Exile*, p. 257.

38 highly fashionable accessories: Sutherland, *Princess of Siberia*, p. 214. When the craze for Decembrist shackle rings and bracelets took off, ironsmiths in Siberia soon began to turn out counterfeits (Barratt, *Voices in Exile*, p. 260).

44 Russians can really dance: This trait must go back a long way. The Marquis de Custine, in *Empire of the Czar*, about the journey he made in 1839, called Russia "this nation of dancers" (p. 181).

45 even for someone who knows how: See *Collected Works of Velimir Khlebnikov*, vol. 3, *Selected Poems*, translated by Paul Schmidt (Cambridge, MA: Harvard University Press, 1997).

CHAPTER 4

47 George Kennan: Basic biographical details of George Kennan's life are from Travis, *George Kennan and the American-Russian Relationship*.

47 A relative named Sam Wildman: He was the brother of Emily Jane Wildman Wickham (1838–1919), my two-greats grandmother.

47 My three-greats grandfather: Frederick Christian Wickham (1812–1901), editor of the *Norwalk Reflector*, published George Kennan's letter from Petropavlovsk, Kamchatka, on January 30, 1866. At the time, Kennan was twenty years old.

47 piano lessons from George Kennan's sister: Henry Timman, esteemed historian of Norwalk, Ohio, doubts that George Kennan's sister could have taught Winthrop Wickham piano, due to the difference in their ages and the fact that their life spans had not many years of overlap. But Cousin Winthrop (or "Wumpy," as the family called him), who is now dead, did tell me he had studied with her.

49 an underwater cable from Newfoundland to Ireland: The Atlantic Telegraph Company, organized in 1856, laid a transatlantic cable in July 1858. Queen Victoria sent President Buchanan a congratulatory telegram over it, but the connection went dead when the cable broke three weeks later. The company, reorganized as the Anglo-American Telegraph Company, finally laid a working cable in July 1866. See Strouse, *Morgan*, pp. 64–65.

49 Perry McDonough Collins: Bobrick, *East of the Sun*, pp. 351–52. The spirit of Collins's enterprise may be found in Collins's *A Voyage Down the Amoor*, in which he says, "Russia, descending from the heights of the Altai to the great Eastern Ocean by way of the mighty Amoor, and the United States, descending to its opposite shore from the heights of the Sierra Nevada, will shake the friendly hand in commercial intercourse upon that mighty sea, and here two great nations will only vie with each other in developing the resources of their respective countries" (p. 78).

51 "in a state of boyish wonder": Travis, *George Kennan*, p. 28.

51 In a letter from St. Petersburg: Ibid.

51 He gave his first Siberia lecture: Ibid., p. 38. Of the lecture Kennan gave in Norwalk soon after, the *Reflector* (December 6, 1869) said, "The large audience who filled Whittlesey Hall on that occasion, will bear witness that it was one of the most interesting ever delivered in Norwalk, the merits of which would not deteriorate in comparison with the best."

52 On a grand tour he made as tsarevitch: Wortman, *Rule by Sentiment*, pp. 745–51.

52 where no member of the Imperial family had ever been: The significant fact that no tsar, tsarina, or tsarevitch until Alexander II had ever crossed the Urals appears in ibid., p. 747; see also Florinsky, *Russia*, 2:879. (There was a rumor, however, that Alexander I, who died in the Crimea in 1825, had actually faked his death and gone to Siberia to spend the rest of his life in the guise of a holy hermit named Fyodor Kuzmich. If so, Alexander I would own the distinction of being the first Siberian-traveler tsar.)

52 forty-eight million serfs: Randall, *N. G. Chernyshevskii*, preface.

52 a young man named D. V. Karakozov: Florinsky, *Russia*, 2:974.

52 a bomb in the Winter Palace: Bely, *Petersburg*, p. 309n; see also Florinsky, *Russia*, 2:1080ff.

53 blew the tsar apart: Bobrick, *East of the Sun*, p. 299; Hosking, *Russia and the Russians*, p. 317. The day was snowy, and the bombs were painted white, to resemble snowballs (Warner, *Tide at Sunrise*, pp. 59–60).

53 His successor, Alexander III: Hosking, *Russia and the Russians*, p. 318; also Florinsky, *Russia*, 2:1139–40.

54 a ship called the *Jeannette*: Mowat, *The Siberians*, p. 157; also Bobrick, *East of the Sun*, p. 357.

54 "the hardest journey and the most trying experience": Kennan, *Siberia and the Exile System*, 1:x. There are more recent editions of this book, but I found the original 1891 edition the most useful, and it is the one I refer to throughout.

55 ashamed to go on the street: Ibid., 2:73–74.

55 he found himself weeping: Ibid., p. 28.

55 "the flower of Russian young manhood": Ibid., p. 451.

55 the outlandish colors the people loved: Ibid., 1:23; also 1:353.

57 "thank God for dynamite!": Travis, *George Kennan*, p. 178.

57 when they were smuggled into Russia: *Siberia and the Exile System* was banned when it came out in 1891. The ban was lifted after the 1905 revolution. See Stephan, *Russian Far East*, p. 68.

58 George Frost Kennan: For details of Kennan's life, see his *Memoirs*, 2 vols. (Boston: Little, Brown, 1967–72).

59 He and the original George Kennan: John Lewis Gaddis, biographer of George Frost Kennan, told me the story of the two George Kennans' meeting. George F.

had told it to him. In his memoirs, George F. does not mention ever meeting his namesake. I thank Professor Gaddis for his generosity in sharing his research with me.

59 "the relationship of Kennan's work": Kennan, *Siberia and the Exile System*, abridged edition, p. xvi.

60 "had no personal interest in the crime": Hosking, *Russia and the Russians*, p. 312.

60 upward of four thousand local and national officials: Ibid., p. 360.

61 Breshkovskaya had also smuggled bombs: She joked with Louise Bryant about it; see Gardner, *"Friend and Lover,"* p. 90.

61 Alexander Ulyanov: Bobrick, *East of the Sun*, pp. 299–300. See also Warner, *Tide at Sunrise*, pp. 62–63.

61 "hypocritical": My source is the novelist D. M. Thomas, who told me this in Gaines-ville, Florida, in 1995.

62 "deeply interested in the country": Travis, *George Kennan*, p. 140.

62 In 1901, he went back to Russia: The *Reflector* article about Kennan's trip appeared on July 21, 1901.

63 At his return to Norwalk for his sister's funeral: *Norwalk Reflector-Herald*, April 4, 1923.

CHAPTER 5

65 Fred Brodin: Dr. Brodin later changed his name to Suuqiina Iglahlig. He has moved to Southern California.

66 Robert Sheldon: Reverend Sheldon is now (2010) chaplain at the Red Dog Mine, north of Kotzebue.

69 I mainly read about the Bering expedition: The book I spent the most time with was Len'kov, Silant'sev, and Staniukovich's *The Komandorskii Camp of the Bering Expedition*.

69 Bering merely shrugged: Bancroft, *History of Alaska*, p. 80.

69 Commander Island: All details about the archaeology are from Len'kov, Silant'sev, and Staniukovich, *The Komandorskii Camp*.

70 the skeleton retraced its route to Commander Island: Bering was reburied on Sep-tember 14, 1992; see "18th Century Explorer Vitus Bering to Be Buried in Russia," Associated Press, July 30, 1992.

72 Vic Goldsberry: Chukotka-Alaska is still (January, 2010) doing business in Nome under the same ownership.

73 an anthology of short works: Otto F. Bond and George V. Bobrinskoy, eds., *Graded Russian Readers: Books One to Five* (Boston: Heath, 1961).

77 Lynne Cox swam the Bering Strait: "Cox Swims Strait," *The Nome Nugget*, August 13, 1987.

77 At Gorbachev's historic meeting: Gorbachev's comments were made at a state din-ner during the third summit between Reagan and Gorbachev in Washington, D.C., in December 1987. The text of the participants' remarks may be found in the online archives of the Ronald Reagan Presidential Library and Museum.

77 a Mexican illegal alien: "Gateway to Siberia: Nome, Alaska, Feels It Has a Certain Ring," *The Wall Street Journal*, September 28, 1987, p. 1.

77 a joint U.S.-Soviet expedition: *The Nome Nugget*, January 5, 1989.

77 two Soviet journalists: Ibid., April 27, 1989.

77   a doctor from Austin, Texas: Dr. Walter Meyer; *The Nome Nugget*, August 13, 1992.
77   Sir Ranulph Twisleton-Wykeham-Fiennes: Ibid., March 14, 1996.
77   Dmitri Shparo: Ibid., March 28, 1996. For more on Shparo's Bering Strait adventures, see *Anchorage Daily News*, April 27 and June 2, 1988, September 26, 1989.
78   a sculptor named David Barr: *The Nome Nugget*, July 21, 1988.
78   a delegation of Alaskans journeyed to Provideniya: "Flight Across Bering Sea Symbolically Breaks Ice in Superpowers' Relations," *The Washington Post*, June 15, 1988, p. B5.
78   Bering Air, a small Nome airline: *The Nome Nugget*, July 13, 1989.
78   Trans-strait telephone connections: Ibid., August 31, 1989.
78   Soviet Young Pioneers: Ibid., month and day missing, 1989.
78   A burn victim: Ibid., October 4, 1990.
79   A story from *The Washington Post*: "There's No Place Like Nome for the Cold War Meltdown," July 1, 1990, p. B5.

CHAPTER 6
84   "I visualize . . . ," Solzhenitsyn wrote: *The Gulag Archipelago*, 1:550*n*.
87   a party of thirty-seven Yupiks: See "Bering Claims Boaters: 2 Russians Die in Native Skiffs," *Anchorage Daily News*, August 5, 1999, p. 1.
88   swamped in a storm and drowned: This drowning occurred on September 7, 1995, in the course of a research project on social change in Bering Strait villages funded by the National Science Foundation. On the way to Provideniya from a village, the skin boat in which the scientists were riding overturned, and they and five villagers drowned. See "Hard Times," *Anchorage Daily News*, June 23, 1996, p. C1.
91   Heidi Bradner: Many details of Heidi Bradner's story are in the *Anchorage Daily News* report of August 5, 1999. See also "Search Still on for Russian Boaters" (ibid., August 6, 1999, p. 1) and "Coast Guard Abandons Search for Russian Boaters" (ibid., August 7, 1999, p. B1).
91   Russian bureaucracy makes it hard for Yupiks: Heidi Bradner was telling me what the Yupiks had told her. Other Siberians confirmed this fact to me and said all natives in Chukotka had this problem.
92   shot through the lung: "Witness to a Bloody Rebellion," *Anchorage Daily News*, October 24, 1993, p. A1.
94   no sign of boats or men had been found: See *Anchorage Daily News* stories cited above.

CHAPTER 7
96   Chukchis: The Chukchi are one of the Siberian peoples who have been found to be close, genetically, to Native Americans. GM°A G, an immunoglobulin haplotype found in 86 percent of the Chukchi, is also found in 98 percent of Canada's Northern Cree. See Crawford, *Origins of Native Americans*, p. 6.
101   *"Pushkin lyubil kidat'sya kamnyami"*: from *"Anegdoti iz Zhiznii Pushkina"* [Anegdotes from the Life of Pushkin], in Kharms's collection of absurdist pieces, *Starukha: Rasskazy, Stseny, Povest'* [Old Woman: Stories, Scenes, Novella], p. 42.
103   the Russian Imperial double-headed eagle: Forsyth, *A History of the Peoples of Siberia*, p. 150; also Lantzeff and Pierce, *Eastward to Empire*, p. 219.

105 found among his papers after his death: The title of the poem is "Unto Myself I Reared a Monument." It was published posthumously in 1841.

105 *I Fin, i nyne díki Tungús*: This and other essential Russian poems can be found in a little volume called *Three Russian Poets*, translated by Vladimir Nabokov, which is interesting not only for the poems but for Nabokov's commentary. Of Pushkin, Nabokov says, "His life was as glamorous as a good grammarian's life ought to be." Describing Georges-Charles d'Anthès, the "blond, fatuous adventurer" who killed Pushkin in a duel, Nabokov notes, "after shooting Pushkin through the liver [d'Anthès] returned to France, had a glorious time under Napoleon III, was mentioned by Victor Hugo in one of his poetical diatribes and lived to the incredible and unnecessary age of 90."

107 The missing Yupiks had been found: "4 Russians Rescued in Bering Sea," *Anchorage Daily News*, August 8, 1999, p. A1, and "Last of Six Lost Boaters Found, Safe," ibid., August 9, 1999, p. A1.

113 bribes: Evidence shows that when America bought Alaska from Russia for $7.2 million, the Russians spent $200,000 on kickbacks to persuade American officials to pass the unpopular measure; see Florinsky, *Russia*, 2:976.

CHAPTER 8

117 a Taoist monk named Ch'ang ch'un: The story of Ch'ang ch'un and his travels is in Bretschneider, *Mediaeval Researches*, pp. 37ff.

118 John of Plano Carpini: "The Voyage of Johannes de Plano Carpini into the Northeast Parts of the World, in the Yeere of Our Lord, 1246," in Hakluyt, *The Principal Navigations, Voyages, Traffiques and Discoveries*, 1:134.

118 another Franciscan, William de Rubruquis: "The Journal of Frier William Rubruquis a French Man of the Order of Minorite Friers, unto the East Parts of the Worlde. An. Dom. 1253," ibid., p. 229. See also Bretschneider, *Mediaeval Researches*, pp. 204–205.

119 enough order so that people could travel there: Howorth, *History of the Mongols*, p. 111; also Grousset, *The Empire of the Steppes*, pp. 312–13.

119 The Mongols: Important sources on the fascinating topic of the Mongols are "The Voyage of Johannes de Plano Carpini"; Florinsky, *Russia*; Grousset, *The Empire of the Steppes*; Gryaznov, *The Ancient Civilization of Southern Siberia*; Hosking, *Russia and the Russians*; Howorth, *History of the Mongols*; and Sinor, *The Cambridge History of Early Inner Asia*.

119 invention of the bronze bit: Sinor, *The Cambridge History of Early Inner Asia*, p. 94; the invention of the stirrup several centuries earlier freed the horseman's hands, making him more able to use his weapons; see Hosking, *Russia and the Russians*, p. 2.

119 his mobility let him find new pastures: Gryaznov, *The Ancient Civilization of Southern Siberia*, p. 131.

119 Herodotus said they descended from Hercules' son: Strahlenberg, *Russia, Siberia, and the Great Tartary*, p. 21.

119 Sarmatians: Custine, *Empire of the Czar*, p. 499.

119 "When the fierce strength of the mighty Boreas": Quoted in Gryaznov, *The Ancient Civilizations of Southern Siberia*, p. 132.

120 mocked the Islamic cry *"la ilaha illa allah"*: The historian Ibn al-Athir, quoted in Grousset, *The Empire of the Steppes*, p. 262.

120 he was their punishment: After a massacre, Genghis Khan told survivors in a mosque, "If you had not committed great sins, God would not have sent a punishment like me upon you." Kennedy, *Mongols, Huns and Vikings*, p. 138.

121 "sing and make merry": Carpini, in Hakluyt, *The Principal Navigations*, p. 138.

121 "made the fullest use of the terror": Grousset, *The Empire of the Steppes*, p. 225.

121 the Mongols had subdued northern China: Graves of the subject peoples during the Mongol era were so poor in treasure that even grave robbers knew not to bother with them. Mongol graves, however, had leather garments, mirrors, Chinese lacquer, and other pillage; see Okladnikov, *Ancient Population of Siberia*, p. 65.

121 "not one in a thousand of the inhabitants survived": The historian al Juwani, quoted in Nicolle, *The Mongol Warlords*, p. 46.

121 "to cut my enemies in pieces": Vernadsky, *The Mongols of Russia*, p. 43; also Nicolle, *The Mongol Warlords*, p. 9.

122 Whenever women were captured: Howorth, *History of the Mongols*, p. 107.

122 geneticists from Oxford University: "A Prolific Genghis Khan, It Seems, Helped People the World," *The New York Times*, February 11, 2003, p. F3.

122 bring Mongol rule to the Russian principalities: For details of Batu's campaigns, see Howorth, *History of the Mongols*, and Vernadsky, *Mongols of Russia*. See also Curtin, *Mongols*; Fennell, *Crisis of Medieval Russia*; Hartog, *Russia and the Mongol Yoke*; and Saunders, *History of the Mongol Conquests*.

123 The Mongols—or Tatars: The word "Tatar" can cause some confusion. It resembles the word "Tartar," which is sometimes used in similar contexts. Originally, the Tatars were a Turkic people known as fierce horseback warriors. They and the Mongols were hereditary enemies. After the Mongol invasion of Russia, "Tatar" came to be applied to all non-Russian tribal horsemen who raided Russian lands, such as the Crimean Tatars and the horsemen of the Golden Horde. "Tartar" has a different derivation. It is said to come from "Tartarus," i.e., hell, the Tartars' supposed place of origin (Vernadsky, *The Mongols of Russia*, p. 12). Russians seldom or never use "Tartar," generally preferring "Tatar" as the word for these peoples.

123 "Like dense clouds the tatars pushed themselves": Bretschneider, *Mediaeval Researches*, 1:318.

123 "an innumerable multitude of dead men's skulls": Carpini, in Hakluyt, *The Principal Navigations*, p. 152.

123 nothing significant left to destroy: Curtin, *The Mongols*, p. 240.

123 did not particularly cover themselves with glory: Florinsky, *Russia*, 1:56.

124 sacked and burned many times: One historian counts forty-eight Tatar invasions of Russia between 1236 and 1462 (ibid., 1:61). In August 1382, Khan Tokhtamysh destroyed Moscow and burned books gathered from all around. When Grand Duke Dmitri returned, he paid one ruble for every eighty corpses buried. He ended up paying for the burial of twenty-four thousand (Vernadsky, *Mongols of Russia*, pp. 266–67).

124 the institutions of the Orthodox church: Mongol largess to the church was not without its price—the clergy were obliged, in return, to pray for the khan. And they had to do it sincerely: "Mongol edict reminded them that to pray 'with mental reservations' was a sin" (Vernadsky, *Mongols of Russia*, p. 166).

125 as the church chronicles had prophesied: Fennell and Stokes, *Early Russian Literature*, p. 82.

127 "introduced into the Russian soul": The historian P. N. Savitsky, quoted in Izhbol-
     din, *Essays on Tatar History*, p. 20.
127 words like *yamshchik*: Ibid., p. 9.
127 continued to serve the Siberian part of the Russian empire: Hartog, *Russia and the
     Mongol Yoke*, pp. 164–65.
127 behaving carelessly at the threshold of their dwellings: See Figes, *Natasha's Dance*,
     p. 371: "The archaeologist Veselovsky traced the Russian folk taboos connected
     with the threshold (such as not to step on it or not to greet a person across it) to the
     customs of the Golden Horde." Friar Carpini, on his way to visit the Great Khan in
     Mongolia in 1245–46, was taken to a "Tartar" duke who cautioned him not to step
     on the threshold (Carpini, in Hakluyt, *The Principal Navigations*, p. 162).
127 as the poet Anna Gorenko did: Akhmatova's mother was said to be descended from
     Khan Akhmat, assassinated in 1481; he is known as the last khan to receive tribute
     from Russian rulers. Another reason for Akhmatova's change of name was her fa-
     ther's fear that her poetry would disgrace her family. See Reeder, *Anna Akhmatova*,
     pp. 4, 17.
127 Even Vladimir Nabokov: Nabokov, *Strong Opinions*, p. 119.

CHAPTER 9
130 completely surrounded by a brick wall: Baddeley, *Russia, Mongolia, China*, 2.68.
130 accomplished little besides annoying the Chinese emperor: After much waiting for
     an audience with the emperor, Spathary would not kowtow to him, and he gave
     rude answers back. A subsequent unsatisfactory meeting ended with the emperor
     (called the khan) ordering Spathary to leave Peking that day (ibid., 2:387ff).
130 "Soops and pottages": Ides, *Three Years' Travels*, p. 62.
131 "the best model perhaps": Bell, *Journey from St. Petersburg*, p. v.
132 K'ang-hsi: See Baddeley, *Russia, Mongolia, China*, pp. xciii, 218. Of K'ang-hsi's per-
     sonal qualities, an observer reported that the emperor had "great Strength, of Body
     as well as Mind. He abstained from Wine, Women and Sloth, and though according
     to the national Custom he took many Wives, yet he was hardly ever observed to go
     among them in the Day time" (quoted in Mancall, *Russia and China*, p. 203).
132 the first-ever treaty between China and a European power: Bobrick, *East of the
     Sun*, p. 93.
132 "Office for the Regulation of the Barbarians": Bell, *Journey from St. Petersburg*,
     p. 15.
132 "It seemed somewhat strange to a Briton": Ibid, p. 161.
132 "From what I have said concerning it": Ibid., p. 209.
133 Avvakum Petrovich: For more on him, see Fennell and Stokes, *Early Russian Lit-
     erature*, pp. 231ff.
135 In 1978, a team of Soviet geologists: Peskov, *Lost in the Taiga*.
135 crossed themselves defiantly with two fingers: In the Old Believer way of cross-
     ing oneself, the thumb and ring finger were joined, with the little finger beside them,
     and the first and the middle fingers were held straight. The thumb, ring finger,
     and little finger represented the Holy Trinity; the first two fingers signified Christ's
     double nature as God and Man (Strahlenberg, *Russia, Siberia, and Great Tartary*,
     p. 284).

135 George Steller: See Müller, *Bering's Voyages*, pp. 174ff.; also Bobrick, *East of the Sun*, pp. 207–208.

135 Sven Waxell: Waxell, *The American Expedition*.

136 Müller published this scoop: Müller's description of his remarkable find is quoted in Fisher, *The Voyage of Semen Dezhnev*, p. 32. For Müller to come upon this information in an archive in Yakutsk is as if the Lewis and Clark expedition had discovered, in an archive in Spokane, that the nonexistence of the Northwest Passage had already been confirmed by an earlier expedition they'd never heard of.

136 Benyowsky: See Bancroft, *History of Alaska*, pp. 179ff. The unreliable account is *Memoirs and Travels of Mauritius Augustus Count de Benyowsky*.

136 "their eyes were the color of sharks": Müller, *Bering's Voyages*, p. 172.

136 In 1789, Japanese sailors: *Imago Mundi*, v. 9 (1952), pp. 103–105.

136 the famous John Ledyard: See Ian Frazier, *Great Plains* (New York: Farrar, Straus and Giroux, 1989), pp. 185ff.

137 a young sea captain named John D'Wolf: D'Wolf, *A Voyage to the North Pacific*.

138 Captain John Smith: A comprehensive bibliography of Russian travel narratives is Nerhood, *To Russia and Return*. See also Babey, *Americans in Russia*.

138 Buchanan was shocked: "Although I am far from believing that a puritanical observation of Sunday is required of us; yet I confess I have been shocked with its profanation in this Country. The Emperor & Empress who are models of correct moral deportment in other respects give their balls & grand fetes on Sunday evening; & I am confident it has never entered their thoughts that in this respect they were acting incorrectly." *The Works of James Buchanan*, 2:218.

138 Alexander Herzen: Herzen, *My Past and Thoughts*, p. 480.

139 Cochrane tied the waistcoat around his middle: Cochrane, *Narrative of a Pedestrian Journey*, p. 71.

140 German-speaking scientists in Siberia: Besides Humboldt, the list includes Müller, Steller, and Daniel Gottlieb Messerschmidt, of the Bering expedition; also, Strahlenberg, Adolph Erman, and Peter Simon Pallas; Pallas wrote the classic study of Siberian rodents.

140 American aggressiveness in trade: John Foster Fraser, an Englishman who traveled Siberia in 1901, expressed his displeasure at the great number of American products sold there in comparison to the scarcity of English ones: "That my country should purvey to Siberia little else but sauce—I felt like smashing the bottle!" (*The Real Siberia*, p. 127).

140 the long ride of Captain Fukushima Yasumasa: Stephan, *The Russian Far East*, p. 78.

140 Another timely idea of Count Muraviev's: Lengyel, *Siberia*, p. 117.

141 pushed a wheelbarrow of dirt: Bobrick, *East of the Sun*, p. 353.

141 "intelligently comments": Nerhood, *To Russia and Return*, p. 105.

141 "extremely superficial": Babey, *Americans in Russia*, p. 164.

142 "*Tovarish soldiers*": Williams, *Through the Russian Revolution*, p. 67.

142 whom the low ceilings had knocked off: Lengyel, *Siberia*, p. 208.

142 were held in Tobolsk: Florinsky, *Russia*, 2:1436.

143 including a Colt .45: Alekseev, *The Last Act of a Tragedy*, p. 152.

143 about fifty thousand Czech soldiers: Many histories of the period talk about the Czech Legion and its adventures. See Stephan, *The Russian Far East*, pp. 122ff.; Bobrick, *East of the Sun*, pp. 393ff.; Figes, *Natasha's Dance*, pp. 530–31.

143 unless he had killed someone that day: Graves, *America's Siberian Adventure*, p. 241.

143 playing the "Internationale": Stephan, *The Russian Far East*, p. 137.

144 referring to the Russian peasants as "swine": Graves, *America's Siberian Adventure*, p. 19.

144 through a hole in the ice: Bobrick, *East of the Sun*, p. 411.

145 poured molten lead down his throat: Mayakovsky, *Vladimir Ilyich Lenin: A Poem*.

145 friendship mission to Siberia: Wallace, *Soviet Asia Mission*.

146 "Where I Was Wrong": Culver and Hyde, *American Dreamer*, pp. 339, 474.

146 Ivan Fedorovich Nikishov: Ivan Nikishov is mentioned, for example, in Ginzburg's memoir, *Within the Whirlwind*, where a boy in the camp says, "When I grow up I'm going to be Nikishov. And everyone will be afraid of me" (p. 225). Solzhenitsyn, in *The Gulag Archipelago*, tells of a performance in Magadan when Nikishov interrupted Vadim Kozin, a widely known singer of that time: "All right, Kozin, stop the bowing and get out!" Kozin subsequently tried to hang himself but was taken down from the noose (2:498).

146 "The larch were just putting out their first leaves": Wallace, *Soviet Asia Mission*, p. 35.

146 "drenched with the blood of Russian 'common men'": Dallin and Nicolaevsky, *Forced Labor in Soviet Russia*, pp. xiii, xiv.

146 "We visited gold mines": Owen Lattimore, "New Road to Asia," *National Geographic*, December 1944, p. 64.

147 Lattimore later conceded: Stephan, *The Russian Far East*, p. 232.

CHAPTER 10

160 Morskoi Kabinet: In *The Empire of the Czar* (pp. 255ff.), Custine describes a tour of the Cottage Palace in which his guide was the Grand Duke (the future Alexander II): "I had earnestly begged Madame — – to procure for me admission to the English cottage of the emperor and empress. It is a small house which they have built in the midst of the noble park of Peterhof, in the new Gothic style so much in vogue in England."

Custine found the Cottage Palace to be much like the houses of the English rich but without any outstanding pictures or sculpture to indicate a love of the arts, and "too servile" in its following of English fashion in its furnishings. On the stairs, partway into the tour, the Grand Duke excused himself and left, but in such a manner that Custine was charmed: "To know how to leave a guest without wounding his feelings is the height of urbanity."

Custine proceeded upstairs to the Morskoi Kabinet, which he said was "a tolerably large and very simply ornamented library, opening on a balcony which overlooks the sea. Without leaving this watch-tower, the emperor can give his orders to his fleet. For this purpose he has a spy-glass, a speaking-trumpet, and a little telegraph which he can work himself."

160 "Depending on the wind": Brodsky, *On Grief and Reason*, p. 59.

162 Cape Smythe Air: This company name no longer exists; Cape Smythe Air merged with Frontier Flying Service in 2005.

162 Eric Penttila: Eric is now the manager of Evergreen Helicopter in Nome. He is no longer the pilot.

163 a tale of heroism: The rescue took place on Friday, August 13, 1993. A number of news stories and articles told of Eric Penttila's heroism; for example, "Plane Down in the Bering Sea," *Today's Christian*, September–October 1996, p. 28.

165 "The weather becoming clear": Bobrick, *East of the Sun*, p. 223. This quote appears to be a revision of the entry of July 6, 1779, in the journal kept by Captain Charles Clerke, who took command after Cook was killed in the Hawaiian Islands in February of the same year. The quote in Clerke's journal is: "At 10 the Weather becoming somewhat clearer we saw the peak'd Hill upon the American Shore bearing s 64 e, this is the only remarkable Hill about this part of the Country and is therefore an excellent Landmark, its Lat[itude] is 65 33 n & its Longitude 191 34 e. The East Cape of Asia at the same time bore s 40 w distant 5 Leagues, there is a great deal of Ice adhering to the shores of this part of Asia we are running by and the Hills are totally immers'd in Snow. The Weather continued throughout Mod: & hazy, we pass'd in the Night many small pieces of Ice . . ." Cook, *Journals*, vol. 3, part 1, pp. 688–89. The revised version of the quote does give the gist of the original accurately; the sailors did see both continents at the same time, and from their position they would also have seen the Diomedes, which the journal notes elsewhere.

167 absolute quiet in your soul: Rytkheu, *Stories from Chukotka*, p. 118.

CHAPTER 11

175 sixty-six satellites in low-earth orbit: For details of the Iridium system, I thank Liz DeCastro, public information officer at Iridium headquarters in Bethesda, Maryland.

179 driving too fast: Russians have always had a love for driving fast. The Russian nobility of the eighteenth century called it *"le vertige de la vitesse"* (the vertigo of speed). Countess Maria Volkonsky, hurrying across Siberia to join her husband in exile, sped along in "the 'bird troika,' as Gogol was to call it, driven by Russian horses 'with the whirlwind sitting upon their manes'" (Sutherland, *The Princess of Siberia*, p. 136). Rattled by the fast driving of Russian coachmen, Custine learned to say *"Tikho!"* (Take it easy! or, Calm yourself!) (*Empire of the Czar*, pp. 362–63). That's still what you say today.

CHAPTER 12

192 from Vologda to Velikii Ustyug by sled: Ides, *Three Years' Travels*, pp. 1–2.

193 a village on the Pinega River: Fisher, *Voyage of Semen Dezhnev*, p. 120.

CHAPTER 13

202 the blankness of the place: Since I visited, a church has been built on the site of the Ipatiev House.

203 In the early 1970s: Information about the discovery, analysis, and reburial of the bodies can be found in the *Los Angeles Times*, March 11, 2004, p. A22, and *The New York Times*, July 18, 1998, p. A1.

204 "When we passed through the gate of Ekaterinburg": Kennan, *Siberia and the Exile System*, 1:49.

204 1,445 freight wagons: Ibid.

204 tea caravans: On the subject of what a nuisance the tea caravans were, see Gowing, *Five Thousand Miles in a Sledge*, pp. 195–96.

204 Tea that came overland: Custine mentioned "this famous tea of the caravans, so delicate, as is said, because it comes overland" (*Empire of the Czar*, p. 518). About sixty years later, John Foster Fraser wrote, "There are old-fashioned Russians who declare that tea loses its flavour if it gets within breath of sea air." The better, non-sea-air-contaminated tea was called "overland tea" (*The Real Siberia*, p. 84).

205 "No other spot": Kennan, *Siberia and the Exile System*, 2:52.

CHAPTER 14

208 In a document dated 1592: Müller, *Istoriia Sibiri*, 1:343. The author is the scientist of the Bering expedition.

208 sent the bell to Siberia, too: Kennan, *Siberia and the Exile System*, 1:421.

208 may have melted there in a fire: Rasputin, *Siberia, Siberia*, p. 86.

209 the Code of Laws of 1648: Solzhenitsyn, *The Gulag Archipelago*, 3:355–56.

209 seven thousand four hundred exiles in Siberia: Wood, *The History of Siberia*, pp. 117–18.

209 removing the disfigured from public view: Kennan, *Siberia and the Exile System*, 1:75.

209 Empress Elizabeth: Wood, *The History of Siberia*, p. 7.

209 four classes of exiles: Kennan, *Siberia and the Exile System*, 1:79–80.

209 "The memory of this torture": Dostoyevsky, *The House of the Dead*, p. 126.

210 Pokoinik: Kennan, *Siberia and the Exile System*, 1:143.

210 Fourierist discussion group: Florinsky, *Russia*, 2:812; also Wood, *The History of Siberia*, p. 12.

210 a letter by Vissarion Belinsky: Berlin, *Russian Thinkers*, p. 173. Belinsky's arguments so moved reform-minded young Russians that many had the letter committed to memory; it was not permitted to be printed in full until 1905. See Florinsky, *Russia*, 2:820.

210 Prince Dolgoruky: Strahlenberg, *Russia, Siberia, and Great Tartary*, p. 253.

210 Abram Petrovich Gannibal: Rasputin, *Siberia, Siberia*, p. 394.

210 Alexander Menshikov: Solzhenitsyn, *The Gulag Archipelago*, 3:339.

211 Natalie Lopukhin: Fries, *A Siberian Journey*, p. 161.

211 Serfdom, as an institution: Hill and Gaddy, *The Siberian Curse*, p. 76. Historically, a serf who ran away was regarded as free if he wasn't caught within six years (Rasputin, *Siberia, Siberia*, pp. 80–81).

213 I have seen one of those: On the title page, it says, "*Puteshestvie, iz' Peterburga v' Moskvu* [no author listed], *1790. V' Sanktpeterburg.*" There is also an epigraph: "'*Chudishche oblo, ozorno, ogromno, stoz'vno, i layai*'—Tikhlemakhida, Tomb II, Kn: xviii, sti: 514." The *Tikhlemakhida* is a translation of Fénelon's *Adventures of Telemachus*, done by the Russian poet V. K. Trediakovskii; the epigraph means "A monster ugly, repulsive, huge, hundred jawed, and barking." Very likely it is intended to refer to serfdom. After all the hard knocks the author and his book went through, the sight of the Houghton Library's ex libris on his book's endpaper, with the school's motto, "Veritas," gladdens the heart.

214 Herzen and his friend Nikolai Ogarev: Masters, *Bakunin*, p. 46.

214 "I am certain that three-quarters of the people": Herzen, *My Past and Thoughts*, p. 271. Herzen published the chapters having to do with his exile in a separate volume, titled *My Exile in Siberia*. Sticklers for geographic accuracy might point out that Viatka, Herzen's place of exile, was not technically in Siberia, being west of the Urals. Today Viatka is the city of Kirov. We passed through it on our way to Perm and Ekaterinburg.

214 refusing to say where he got it: Kennan, *Siberia and the Exile System*, 1:326. All the exile stories in this paragraph are from Kennan's book.

215 a prisoner named Tumanov: Wood, *The History of Siberia*, p. 122.

215 Mikhail Bakunin: Details of Bakunin's biography are from Masters, *Bakunin*. A close study of his escape from exile is Carr, "Bakunin's Escape from Siberia," pp. 377–88.

216 by leaving her behind: In fairness to Bakunin, he did later send for her. She met him in Stockholm, and their odd marriage continued, although in 1868 she had a child whose father was rumored to be Bakunin's associate Carlo Gambruzzi. She was not with Bakunin when he died, in July 1876.

217 "'Can one get oysters here?'": Edmond de Goncourt, quoted in Herzen, *My Past and Thoughts*, p. xxxiv.

217 a revolutionary named Leib Bronshtein: Stephan, *The Russian Far East*, p. 69.

218 267 times as much: Shalamov, *Graphite*, p. 272. Shalamov expresses the weights in *puds*, a unit of measurement used in former times; one *pud* equaled about 36 pounds. The Decembrist prisoners (according, he says, to the memoirs of Maria Volkonsky) had a quota of 3 *puds* of earth a day. Miners in the Kolyma mines had a quota equal to about 800 *puds* a day. Three into 800 is about 267.

218 "I read memoirs": Shalamov, *Kolyma Tales*, p. 344.

218 used fake ration cards: Some of these offenses are listed in Solzhenitsyn, *The Gulag Archipelago*, 3:255–56. Others are in Dallin and Nicolaevsky, *Forced Labor in Soviet Russia*, p. 175, and Diment and Slezkine, *Between Heaven and Hell*, p. 236.

218 "Don't feed us Soviet straw": Dallin and Nikolaevsky, *Forced Labor in Soviet Russia*, p. 22.

218 A woman got ten years: Conquest, *The Great Terror*, p. 284.

219 "Let's remember his soul": Asher, *Letters from the Gulag*, p. 54.

219 the Tibetan Buddhist High Lama: Forsyth, *A History of the Peoples of Siberia*, p. 330.

219 "Oh, it's boring": Solzhenitsyn, *The Gulag Archipelago*, 3:576.

219 Vyacheslav Molotov ambassador to Mongolia: Hosking, *Russia and the Russians*, pp. 531–32.

219 Penal Colony Number 10: David Remnick, "The Tsar's Opponent," *The New Yorker*, October 1, 2007, p. 66.

CHAPTER 15

222 Members of a tribe called the Tungus: Ides, *Three Years' Travels*, p. 31.

222 retreated into smoke-filled huts: Erman, *Travels in Siberia*, 1:201.

222–23 "delicate portion of my privy parts": Fries, *A Siberian Journey*, p. 137.

223 "It seemed as though the walls and ceiling": Chekhov, *The Island*, p. 121.

223 they put out his campfire: Arsenyev, *Dersu Uzala*, p. 90.

223 Dostoyevsky waxed lyrical: Dostoyevsky, *The House of the Dead*, p. 283.

223 "much pestered by gnats": Bell, *Journey from St. Petersburg*, p. 86.

223 descending on young foals: Fries, *Siberian Journey*, p. 137.

223 suffocating reindeer: Stephan, *The Russian Far East*, p. 11.

224 paint them all over with tar: Erman, *Travels in Siberia*, 2:95.

224 The Lonely Planet guidebook: Vic Hawthorn, *Russia, Ukraine & Belarus*, 2d ed. (Oakland, CA: Lonely Planet, 2000), p. 569.

229 "sailed on the 8th day of June": Armstrong, *Yermak's Campaign*, p. 131.

229 *Remezov Chronicle*: Ibid., pp. 27–28.

229 "then all the infidels": Ibid., p. 140.

229 "a vision of a shining Christian city": Ibid., p. 112.

231 Shaybani, a brother of Batu: Groussett, *The Empire of the Steppes*, pp. 393–94.

231 Shaybanids often fought with the Taibugids: Ibid., pp. 489–90; also Armstrong, *Yermak's Campaign*, p. 2.

231 Hanefite teachings: *Oxford Dictionary of World Religions* (New York: Oxford University Press, 1997), pp. 86–87.

232 a lenient, even generous attitude: Izhboldin, *Essays on Tatar History*, pp. 105ff. See also Armstrong, *Yermak's Campaign*, p. 61.

232 the founders of Russian noble families: "According to the avowedly approximate computations of [the historian V. O.] Kliuchevsky, at the end of the seventeenth century about 17 percent of the Moscow upper class was of Tatar or eastern origin" (Florinsky, *Russia*, 1:63).

232 convert to Christianity: Oliver Roy, *The New Central Asia: The Creation of Nations*, pp. 28–29.

CHAPTER 16

237 spent time in an ancient prison in Omsk: Solzhenitsyn, *The Gulag Archipelago*, 3:50.

247 "Em Che Ess": Men of this organization are seen all over Russia; it also makes public-service safety announcements on TV.

CHAPTER 17

252 the most beautiful city in Siberia: Chekhov, *"The Crooked Mirror" and Other Stories*, p. 200.

254 goes back to John Quincy Adams: See Adams, *John Quincy Adams in Russia*. The ladies of Russia get no mercy from J.Q. For example, "After dinner came some additional company; among whom Princess Woldemar Galitzin, venerable by the length and thickness of her beard. This is no uncommon thing among the ladies of this Slavonian breed. There is at the Academy of Sciences a portrait of a woman now dead, but with a beard equal to that of Plato" (p. 141); also, "Count St. Julien was looking through his glass at the dancers and lamenting that the sex in Russia was not handsome . . . Oh, at Vienna not a guingette of chambermaids but would show more handsome women than all Petersburg could produce" (p. 343). (A guingette is a suburban tavern.)

254 too manlike, rough, and otherwise unattractive: Babey, *Americans in Russia*, pp. 81, 85.

254 "all the vague and shadowy delicacy": Custine, *Empire of the Czar*, p. 498.

255 personally had won that war: Clay, *Life of Cassius Marcellus Clay*, p. 462: "I did more than any man to overthrow slavery. I carried Russia with us, and thus prevented what would have been the strong alliance of France, England and Spain against us; and thus was saved the Union!"

255 married Russian women: Stephan, *The Russian Far East*, p. 134.

255 as many as thirty couples at a time: Ibid., p. 140.

255 "Entirely too many of these women": Graves, *America's Siberian Adventure*, pp. 309–10.

256 turn on her heel and walk away: Blakely, *Siberia Bound*, pp. 130–32.

256 One article I read: Caroline Moorehead, "Women and Children for Sale," *The New York Review of Books*, October 11, 2007.

259 Second River transit prison: Mandelstam died in the Vtoraya Rechka (Second River) transit camp on December 27, 1938. See Bobrick, *East of the Sun*, p. 450.

259 "people who believed in only one thing": Kennan, *Siberia and the Exile System*, 2:361ff.

CHAPTER 18

263 the country's interim dictator: Mazour, *The First Russian Revolution*, p. 162.

263 His wife, Ekaterina: Mazour, *Women in Exile*, pp. 44ff.

264 later a saint of the Orthodox church: Figes, *Natasha's Dance*, pp. 72–73.

264 Pushkin rhapsodized: Mazour, *Women in Exile*, p. 61.

264 Prince Andrei Bolkonsky in *War and Peace*: This is from the guides at the Volkonsky house-museum.

264 Tolstoy planned to write a book about the Decembrists: Vladimir Fyodorov, ed., *The First Breath of Freedom*, trans. Synthia Carlile (Moscow: Progress Publishers, 1988), p. 312.

265 only three were over forty years old: Mazour, *The First Russian Revolution*, p. 221.

265 "a perfect galaxy of brilliant talent": Sutherland, *The Princess of Siberia*, p. 3.

265 They began their young manhood: Information about the origins and development of the Decembrist movement may be found in Barratt, *Voices in Exile*; Barratt, *The Rebel on the Bridge*; Zetlin, *The Decembrists*; and the books by Christina Sutherland and Anatole G. Mazour cited above.

266 Ivan Dmitrievich Yakushkin: The source on Yakushkin I used is *Zapiski I. D. Yakushkina* [Memoirs of I. D. Yakushkin] (*redactor: Evgenii Yakushkin; 1905*), which includes his memoir and selected letters. I do not believe an English translation of this book exists; it's a charming and interesting book and would be well worth a translator's time. The editor, Evgenii Yakushkin, was the author's son.

266 "[We] were standing not far from the golden carriage": Ibid., pp. 8–9. The translation is mine, with the assistance of Boris Zeldin.

267 An Arakcheev story: Herzen, *My Past and Thoughts*, pp. 40–41.

268 One day a small group of intimates: Yakushkin, *Zapiski*, pp. 11ff. Yakushkin devotes much of his memoir to the secret society's beginnings and early years. He describes how he and some of the other founding members were careful to keep Pushkin, who was somewhat younger than them, in the dark about the society's existence, and how it pained the future great poet of Russia to be left out. Pushkin was thought to be too talkative and emotionally volatile to make a reliable member. As Yakushkin describes his own encounters with the poet, the judgment seems to be justified.

268 Destutt de Tracy: His *Commentaire* was published in Paris in 1819. It was a translation of an English version published in 1811 in Philadelphia. Montesquieu had

argued in favor of constitutional monarchy, and Jefferson and Destutt de Tracy wrote their book in rebuttal; they did not want monarchy of any kind. See Dvoichenko-Markov, "Jefferson and the Russian Decembrists."

269 "Of all of us he alone": Yakushkin, *Zapiski*, p. 23.

269 Novosiltsov-Chernov duel: Mazour, *The First Russian Revolution*, p. 130; see also the account of Prince Y. P. Obolensky in Barratt, *Voices in Exile*, pp. 24–26.

270 "her affections . . . fixed on another world": Buchanan, *The Works of James Buchanan*, 2:351.

270 "exorcist-like oaths": Yakushkin, *Zapiski*, p. 24.

271 dampened his enthusiasm for the honor: Konstantin had also disqualified himself from being the next in line by divorcing his first wife and marrying a Polish countess. See Florinsky, *Russia*, 2:745–48.

271 "You can't have a rehearsal": Barratt, *The Rebel on the Bridge*, p. 64.

271 "We shall die": Mazour, *The First Russian Revolution*, p. 164.

272 "pools of blood on the snow": Sutherland, *The Princess of Siberia*, p. 103.

272 killed another high-ranking officer: Colonel Sturler, who was also trying to negotiate; see Mazour, *The First Russian Revolution*, p. 177.

272 "Voilà un joli commencement": Ibid., p. 178.

272 Sergei Volkonsky: Sutherland, *The Princess of Siberia*, pp. 104ff.

273 by starting to laugh: Zetlin, *The Decembrists*, p. 269.

273 Yevgenii Obolensky went through a religious epiphany: Barratt, *Voices in Exile*, p. 19.

273 threw himself at the tsar's feet: Zetlin, *The Decembrists*, p. 334; also Mazour, *The First Russian Revolution*, p. 207

273 "After about ten minutes": Yakushkin, *Zapiski*, pp. 64–65.

274 turning the pages of his French-Russian dictionary: Barratt, *The Rebel on the Bridge*, p. 125.

274 dancing with the tsar: Sutherland, *The Princess of Siberia*, pp. 118–19.

275 "I wept like a child": Yakushkin, *Zapiski*, p. 96.

275 Nicholas brought out his seven-year-old son: Korff, *Accession of Nicholas I*, p. 267. This long-after-the-fact account, compiled by Alexander II's secretary of state (Alexander II, of course, was the seven-year-old referred to), is naturally pro-Nicholas. There is no question, though, that Nicholas's bravery on December 14 saved his reign, and possibly the monarchy.

276 a dreaded part of his job: Jeanne Haskett, "Decembrist N. A. Bestuzhev in Siberian Exile, 1826–1855," *Studies in Romanticism* 4, no. 4 (Summer 1965): 185ff.

276 "Though many of us had made careless statements": Barratt, *Voices in Exile*, p. 264.

277 attend a public concert: After years of prison and exile, when the Volkonskys were living in Irkutsk, Maria went to the theater with her daughter and was informed that "wives of state criminals were barred from attending public entertainment places" (Mazour, *Women in Exile*, pp. 50–51).

277 "We [Decembrists] were the first to appear": Mazour, *The First Russian Revolution*, p. 256.

277 The Volkonskys had a healthy son: Volkonsky raised Mikhail as his son. Gossip suggested the actual father might be a family friend to whom Maria become very close as her husband receded into eccentricity. See *The Princess of Siberia*, passim.

278 "Pestel and Bestuzhev": Ibid., p. 263.

278 with tear-filled eyes: Barratt, *The Rebel on the Bridge*, p. 166.
278 Moscow to Irkutsk in fifteen days: Sutherland, *The Princess of Siberia*, p. 312.

CHAPTER 19

280 its church dedicated to St. Nicholas: Ides, Bell, and Fries all went there—the first in 1693, the second in 1720, and the third in 1776.
284 sawed houses in half: Rasputin, *Siberia, Siberia*, p. 188; his source is *The Notes of an Irkutsk Resident*, by Ivan Kalashnikov (1905).
285 the corpse of the unlucky admiral: Bobrick, *East of the Sun*, p. 411. Peter Fleming says that the bodies of Kolchak and his prime minister were pushed through a hole in the ice not on the Angara but on a tributary called the Ushakovka, just outside the city (*The Fate of Admiral Kolchak*, pp. 212ff.).
293 to replenish his supply of paper: Strahlenberg, *Russia, Siberia, and the Great Tartary*, p. 24; also Bobrick, *East of the Sun*, p. 179.
293 another fifteen hundred miles to Peking: Cochrane, *Narrative of a Pedestrian Journey*, 2:168.
293 bathed in the Ingoda: Sutherland, *The Princess of Siberia*, p. 194.

CHAPTER 20

298 his (or his ghost writer's) romantic novel: *Fencing Master* (*Maître d'armes*) came out in 1859. When Dumas was on a subsequent trip to Russia, he actually met the Annenkovs at the house of the governor of Nizhnii Novgorod. Dumas's account of his conversation with them at this meeting is suspiciously brief; maybe the prolific novelist did not recall exactly what he had said about them in the book he supposedly wrote. See Dumas, *Adventures in Czarist Russia*, p. 159.
303 Next to the Bible, *Shto Delat'?*: Randall, *N. G. Chernyshevskii*, p. 142.
303 "You haven't heard?": Chernyshevsky, *What Is to Be Done?*, pp. 413–14.
303 "[Chernyshevsky] plowed me up more profoundly": Ibid., p. 32.
304 "grotesque as a work of art": Berlin, *Russian Thinkers*, p. 228.
304 a student named Hypolite Myshkin: Kennan, *Siberia and the Exile System*, 2:251–52.
304 Boleslav Shostakovich: Volkov, *Shostakovich and Stalin*, p. 45.
305 "He had some grasp on many things": Randall, *N. G. Chernyshevskii*, p. 159.

CHAPTER 21

314 suspends certain visa and customs regulations: Kotkin and Wolff, *Rediscovering Russia in Asia*, p. 279.
318 Volochaevka: Stephan, *The Russian Far East*, pp. 152ff., 213.
319 thirty-one years old: For a detailed account of Blyukher's career during the Terror, see Conquest, *The Great Terror*, pp. 200–202, 428–31. It is important to note that Blyukher participated in show trials before his own downfall.
319 even the cooks were delighted: Zhukov, *Reminiscences and Reflections*, 2:105.
319 Molchanov died in San Francisco: Stephan, *The Russian Far East*, p. 154. See also Molchanov's obituary in *Pervopokhodnik* (First Campaigner) 22 (December 1974): 46–50.

320 begins in 1902: The first sentence of the book is, "In 1902 I led a crew of six Siberian riflemen and four pack-horses up the Tsimuho, which drains into Ussuri Bay near the village of Shkotovo."

320 kill and carry off dogs: Gowing, *Five Thousand Miles in a Sledge*, p. 48.

320 trailed off into a purr: Arsenyev, *Dersu Uzala*, p. 152.

325 Unluckily for the Bikin mechanic: Stephan, *The Russian Far East*, p. 242.

326 N. M. Przhevalskii: The rumor that Przhevalskii was Stalin's father is mentioned in Robert Conquest's *The Great Terror* (p. 55). Conquest discounts it. Przhevalskii was a hero of Chekhov's (Figes, *Natasha's Dance*, p. 401); maybe that contributed to Chekhov's decision to make a Siberian journey himself.

CHAPTER 23

348 besides slaves and furs: Fisher, *The Russian Fur Trade*.

348 Kiev: Ibid.

348 and then to Ustyug: Martin, *Treasure of the Land of Darkness*, pp. 88ff.

349 the captured supply of sable furs: Ivan offered amnesty to Yermak and his men after Yermak sent him a caravan of furs; see Lengyel, *Siberia*, p. 51.

349 the wounds that had been inflicted: Fisher, *Voyage of Semen Dezhnev*, pp. 103–106.

349 a certain quota of sable skins: Wood, *The History of Siberia*, p. 31. Occasionally *yasak* could be replaced by *yasyr*, or "woman tribute," in which women were substituted for furs (Stephan, *The Russian Far East*, pp. 22–23).

350 remains of a three-hundred-year old settlement: Gibson, *Feeding the Russian Fur Trade*, p. 24n.

350 did silver begin to replace furs: Fisher, *Voyage of Semen Dezhnev*, p. 9.

350 two hundred thousand Siberian sables: Lengyel, *Siberia*, p. 56.

350 a third of the state's total revenues: Stephan, *The Russian Far East*, p. 20. Fisher puts the figure lower, at about 10 percent (*The Russian Fur Trade*, p. 119).

350 A hundred rubles was a fortune then: Fisher, *The Russian Fur Trade*, p. 29.

351 pestering the young Queen Elizabeth: Ivan had a fixation on the English and wished to form an alliance with them. Not only did he look into marrying an English noblewoman (Florinsky, *Russia*, 1:187–88), he also offered Elizabeth asylum in his country, should she ever need it, and he requested the same from her. She replied that she did not need the right of asylum for herself but would grant it to him (Izhboldin, *Essays on Tatar History*, p. 109).

351 sent her a present of sable furs: Martin, *Treasure of the Land of Darkness*, p. 107.

351 for one unicorn horn: Baddeley, *Russia, Mongolia, and China*, 1:xcvii.

351 eight hundred ordinary people for life: This estimate may be high. Fisher estimates the value of a sable fur at ten to twenty rubles (*The Russian Fur Trade*, p. 29). But a record of customs transactions in Velikii Ustyug (and other fur trade cities) details purchases of sable furs in quanities of forty and up for prices averaging about a ruble each. A. I. Yakovlev, ed., *Tamozhennye Knigi Moscovskovo Gosudarstva XVII Veka* [Customs Records of the State of Moscow of the Seventeenth Century] (1951), pp. 22–23. Eight hundred rubles for a (fake) unicorn horn was still a lot of money.

351 traded the finest silks for them: Fur for cloth was the basic transaction of the Moscow–Peking caravan trade. China sent not only silk but also damask, nankeen, satin, and other fabrics (Mancall, *Russia and China*, pp. 185–86). Other items of

this transcontinental trade included (from China) jasper, porcelain, cardamom, saffron, fireworks, erotic artwork, rhubarb, dried fruits, and of course tea; from Russia came reindeer horns, reindeer-horn jelly, dogs, mammoth ivory, carved bowstring-finger guards of walrus ivory, clocks, mirrors, telescopes, samovars, brandy . . .

351 prisoner ransoms: Fisher, *The Russian Fur Trade*, p. 135.
351 Greek Orthodox bishop of Gaza: Ibid., p. 134.
351 Representatives of the tsar paid sables to the Cossacks: Ibid., p. 131.
351 bribed the Tatar khan of Crimea: Ibid., p. 138.
351 1,003 *soroks* of sables: Baddeley, *Russia, Mongolia, and China*, 1:xcvi.
351 the actual Golden Fleece: Ibid., 2:xii.
351 used the cloak as a gift: Saunders, *History of the Mongol Conquests*, p. 48.
351 audience tent lined with sable pelts: Baddeley, *Russia, Mongolia, and China*, 1:xcvi.
351 Vladimir Monomakh: Krasheninnikov, *Explorations of Kamchatka*, p. v.
351 The Caliph of Baghdad: Clot, *Haroun al-Rashid*, p. 189.
352 vowed not to wear their sables: Martin, *Treasure of the Land of Darkness*, p. 52.
352 no one below the rank of lord: Baddeley, *Russia, Mongolia, and China*, 1:xcvi.
352 King Henry VIII: Martin, *Treasure of the Land of Darkness*, p. 104.
352 a "short loose coat of sable": Bell, *Journey from St. Petersburg*, p. 135.
352 a seven-foot-high throne: Milescu (Spathary), who saw Kang H'si on his throne in 1676, said the throne was seven feet high; he also observed Kang H'si to be wearing "a sable robe with a lining of watered silk and gold" (Baddeley, *Russia, Mongolia, and China*, 2:360). Ides, who saw the throne in 1694, reported that it was covered in black sables (*Three Years' Travels*, p. 72).
352 a photographic history: Moynahan, *The Russian Century*, p. 244.

CHAPTER 24

362 Vtoraya Rechka (Second River) transit camp: See Taplin, *Open Lands*, pp. 295–96. In his visit to Vladivostok, Taplin went to the site of the camp and found most of it covered by a housing project. The building that was the camp's infirmary still remained, and there were traces of the stone quarry where the prisoners had labored. Mandelstam was probably buried in a mass grave near the old camp's perimeter.
362 luckily died of heart failure: The unhappy later fates of Arsenyev and his family are in Stephan, *The Russian Far East*, passim.

CHAPTER 25

373 slid into fissures and drowned: Ides, *Three Years' Travels*, p. 37.
375 The idea of building a second railroad: Information about the construction of BAM may be found in Malashenko, *The Great Baikal–Amur Railway*, and in contemporary coverage in *The New York Times* ("Soviet Building Port in Far East," November 11, 1975, p. 47; also articles of January 30, 1977, p. IES25; August 31, 1977, p. 21; March 24, 1991, p. E2; August 15, 1994, p. A7; and July 11, 2004, p. TR3.) "A Siberian Railroad, from 'Hero' to Disaster" is the title of one of the more recent articles. Malashenko's book makes no mention of the hundreds of thousands of prison laborers who worked on BAM.
380 Dervla Murphy: Her book about this journey is *Through Siberia by Accident*.

CHAPTER 26

389 Wendell Willkie: Wendell L. Willkie, "One World," in *Prefaces to Peace: A Symposium* (New York: Columbia University Press, 1943), pp. 71–72. See also Herman O. Makey, *Wendell Willkie of Elwood* (Elwood, IN: National Book Co., 1940), and Neal, *Dark Horse.*

389 hogs running loose in the villages: Kennan, *Siberia and the Exile System*, 1:68.

389 smallpox epidemics: Smallpox ravaged the Tungus, the Samoyeds, and other Siberian tribes in the 1600s, as it was also doing at that time to native peoples in the Americas; see Forsyth, *A History of the Peoples of Siberia*, p. 58.

390 tribes descended from the ancient Hebrews: Chekhov reported that the Ainu, a tribe on Sakhalin Island, were said to be descended from the ancient Hebrews (*The Island*, p. 195). Similar stories were among the most persistent myths of the American frontier.

390 overplowing and dust storms: Lincoln, *The Conquest of a Continent*, p. 374.

390 no bridge: As near as I can determine, no bridge crosses the Lena upstream of Yakutsk until Ust-Kut, where it meets the Baikal–Amur Mainline, about 750 miles from Yakutsk. Downstream to the Arctic Ocean, no major year-round thoroughfares intersect the Lena.

CHAPTER 27

403 the Even were called the Lamuts and the Evenk the Tungus: Forsyth, *A History of the Peoples of Siberia.*

404 perhaps 50 percent of all the gold: Dallin and Nicolaevsky, *Forced Labor in Soviet Russia*, p. 148.

404 about one life for every two pounds of gold: Ibid.

405 This air-transfer arrangement: See Hays, *The Alaska-Siberia Connection*; Jones, *Road to Russia*; and Chandonnet, *Alaska at War.*

405 73 went down: See Tat'iana Kosheleva, "The Construction and Use of the Fairbanks–Krasnoiarsk Air Route," in Chandonnet, *Alaska at War*, p. 332.

406 yellow boots those pilots wore: Yevtushenko, *Divided Twins*, p. 35. See also Kosheleva, "Construction and Use."

CHAPTER 28

410 at least one other Siberian north–south route: Conquest, *The Great Terror*, p. 332, gives details of an attempted railroad line along the Ob River to the Arctic Ocean with *lagers* every nine miles along the route; it also was abandoned after Stalin's death.

412 sables had the reputation of being merry creatures: "Now the sable is a beast full marvelous and prolific, and it is found nowhere else in the world but in Northern Siberia . . . a merry little beast it is, and beautiful: and its beauty comes with the snow, and with the snow it disappears." This quotation of Nicolae Milescu is part of the epigraph to his book of travels (included in Baddeley, *Russia, Mongolia, China*, 2:xiiff.). The reference to the sable's beauty disappearing comes from the fact that the sable's fur deteriorates in the warmer months, when, it is thought, the sables eat a kind of berry that makes them itch their fur off.

CHAPTER 29

422 fifteen to eighteen feet: This and many other details of prison camp life are from
    Dallin and Nicolaevsky, *Forced Labor in Soviet Russia*, pp. 9ff.
423 characteristic sounds of the camps: Conquest, *The Great Terror*, p. 318.
423 barrel of machine grease: Shalamov, *Kolyma Tales*, p. 175.
423 ate them on the spot: Solzhenitsyn, *The Gulag Archipelago*, 1:ix.
424 boundary indicated by pieces of red cloth: Shifrin, *Guidebook to Prisons*, pp. 169–70.
424 get a day or two off: Ibid.
424 More than a million died: Bobrick, *East of the Sun*, p. 422.
425 pray for atomic war: Solzhenitsyn, *The Gulag Archipelago*, 3:395.
425 the criminals in the camps were more dangerous: Varlam Shalamov, an inspiringly
    good writer who deserves to be more widely known, wrote many stories about the
    criminals of the camps and the dangers they posed. Shalamov's first book published in
    the United States, *Kolyma Tales*, won praise from Saul Bellow and was nominated for
    a National Book Award. On the dust jacket of Shalamov's second book, *Graphite*, his
    name was misspelled. Solzhenitsyn considered Shalamov's own life a refutation of
    Shalamov's claim that no one in the camps escaped corruption. Solzhenitsyn regretted
    that Shalamov renounced his own stories in 1972 (*The Gulag Archipelago*, 2:623).
425 named one puppy Ladle and the other Pail: Ginzburg, *Within the Whirlwind*, p. 7.
426 a prisoner named Krivoshei: Shalamov, *Kolyma Tales*, pp. 351ff.
427 some of the barbed wire: Jones, *Roads to Russia*, p. x.
427 9.2 million tons: Ibid., pp. 84–85.
427 sold handcuffs to the NKVD: Stephan, *The Russian Far East*, p. 236.
427 "On the mirror-like blade": Shalamov, *Kolyma Tales*, p. 180.
427 a large Marion excavator: Conquest, *Kolyma*, p. 117.
427 very few prisoners sent to them survived: Lincoln, *The Conquest of a Continent*,
    p. 346.
428 the *Dzhurma*: A number of books tell the story of this ship. I have relied on Dallin
    and Nicolaevsky, *Forced Labor in Soviet Russia*, pp. 128ff. The triumphant rescue
    of the crew of the *Chelyuskin* is explained in abundant detail (with no mention of
    the *Dzhurma*) in an exhibit at the Museum of the Arctic and the Antarctic (see
    p. 177 in the above).
431 "It's not the people who vote that count": The original source of this quotation is
    Vospominaniya Byvshego Sekretarya Stalina, by Boris Bazhanov. The relevant pas-
    sage (pp. 79–80) I translate as: "While the conversation proceeds at these heights,
    Stalin is silent and sucks on his pipe. Properly speaking, his opinion is of no interest
    to Zinoviev and Kamenev—they are convinced that in questions of political strat-
    egy, the opinion of Stalin generally has little of interest to offer. But Kamenev is a
    very polite and tactful man. Therefore he says, 'And you, comrade Stalin, what do
    you think about this question?' 'Ah,' says comrade Stalin, 'about which question,
    exactly?' (In fact, many questions had been brought up.) Kamenev, trying to get
    down to Stalin's level, says, 'On this question of how to win a majority in the party.'
    'You know, comrade,' says Stalin, 'what I think concerning this question is: I regard
    as completely unimportant who will vote in the party, and how; but what is ex-
    tremely important is who will count the votes, and how.' Even Kamenev, who must
    know Stalin already, clears his throat significantly."
431 on the cover of *Time* magazine eleven times: He was on the cover of the issues of
    June 9, 1930; February 24, 1936; December 20, 1937; January 1, 1940; October 27,

1941; January 4, 1943; February 5, 1945; July 17, 1950; October 6, 1952; March 16, 1953; and November 10, 1967. On three of the covers he appeared in a group with other world leaders. By comparison, Franklin D. Roosevelt was on the cover fourteen times, Churchill seven times, and Hitler five times. Stalin's son, Lieutenant General Vasily Stalin, was on the cover once.

437 "You must ask Ivan Borisovich": Herzen, *My Past and Thoughts*, p. 187.

438 than had been shot in the event: Figes, *Natasha's Dance*, p. 460.

438 "The Holy Family," by Domenico: The Hermitage website's Digital Collection lists a painting called "The Holy Family with St. John the Baptist and St. Catherine," by Domenico Beccafumi (Domenico di Giovanni di Pace), painted 1530–35. It is a good candidate for the painting Yakushkin admired. The provenance of this painting presents a slight hitch, however; the museum lists its source as unknown but adds that it was in the collection of V. D. Nabokov of Petrograd, and that the museum acquired it in 1919. V. D. Nabokov and his family, including his son, Vladimir, left Russia permanently in 1919. Whether this painting went from the tsar's collection to the Nabokovs and then back to the Hermitage, and if so, how, are questions unanswered. Still, it is possible that the painting Yakushkin admired while under interrogation later hung on the Nabokovs' wall.

438 Yakushkin had the cool-headedness: Iakushkin, *Zapiski*, p. 64.

CHAPTER 30

446 The first three letters of Lukoil's name: Goldman, *Petrostate*, p. 61. This is an excellent overview of the oil and natural gas industry in Russia, and of the recent oil boom.

447 the third-largest company: Ibid., p. 2.

447 Gazprom became the chief supplier: Figures on Russia's natural gas exports to Europe are from *The New York Times*, October 5, 2004, p. W1.

447 "Russia is in a stronger position": Goldman, *Petrostate*, p. 178.

448 "like a Holy Bible": Ibid., p. 163.

448 In rural America: The improving fortunes of fur trappers in the United States during the years of the Russian oil boom can be followed in the pages of *Fur-Fish-Game* magazine. See, e.g., references to the Russian fur market in the magazine's "Fur Market Report," September 2009, p. 50.

448 His focus on Siberia: The most famous recent photo of Putin in Siberia is of him riding bare-chested on horseback in the Altai. This photo and similar ones, like the photo of him wearing khaki pants, a T-shirt, and a canvas bush hat while sitting in a tree in Tuva, were meant to evoke tales of Russian folk heroes, observers said.

449 "It was minus 45 degrees": ITAR-TASS *Weekly News*, January 1, 2006.

449 the Environmental Protection Agency: *The New York Times*, October 15, 2009, p. A1.

449 "like cities on fire": Ibid., March 28, 2006, p. C1.

450 a British public relations firm: The company's name is Identica Branding and Design. See *The Washington Post*, May 11, 2003, p. A20.

454 the exact middle of Russia: *Moscow News*, December 5, 2008.

456 an Iridium satellite crashed: This event received extensive coverage at the time. The most detailed report about it appeared in *The Washington Post*, February 14, 2009, p. A3.

456 over the Taimyr Peninsula: For details of the collision, I am grateful to Paul "Mack" Insch (Capt. USN, ret.), and to Col. Richard W. Boltz, commander of the Joint Space Operations Center of Stratcom at Vandenberg Air Force Base, whose helpful e-mail Captain Insch forwarded to me.

459 "Siberia, where Russians waited": *The New York Times*, May 17, 2008, p. C4.

463 What to make of this: Statistics and other gloomy information about Russia today are from assorted news sources described above. A concentration of bad news may be found in a *Washington Post* story, "Behind the Bluster, Russia Is Collapsing," by Murray Feshbach, October 5, 2008, p. B3.

463 dying in car wrecks: The Russian accident figures are for 2008, the German figures are for 2007. See *The New York Times*, August 9, 2009, p. A8.

464 The government men confiscated: For information on the Memorial raid, see the letter from Orlando Figes to *The New York Review of Books*, January 15, 2009, p. 61.

464 a Russian television station conducted a poll: The station was Telekanal "Rossiya," and the poll was called Imya Rossiya: Istoricheskii Vybor 2008.

467 MOGUCHESTVO ROSSII PRIRASTAT' BUDET SIBIR'IO: Mikhail Lomonosov (1711–65) was also a poet and historian, and the founder of the first university in Russia.

468 they forgot the Russian language: Rasputin, *Siberia, Siberia*, p. 303: "Maydell recounts how in one large Russian village in the Olekminsk Region, where he had traveled, not a single person understood Russian." Olekminsk, founded 1635, is a city on the Lena River southwest of Yakutsk.

469 German cargo ships: "Arctic Shortcut, Long a Dream, Beckons Shippers as Ice Thaws," *The New York Times*, September 11, 2009, p. A1.

469 scientists from the University of Alaska: *Natural History*, March, 2009, p. 12.

469 that kept the lake from freezing: *The New York Times*, October 25, 2005, p. F1.

470 The Decembrists: Information about the last years of Prince Sergei Volkonsky and other Decembrists may be found in Mazour, *Women in Exile*, p. 77; Sutherland, *The Princess of Siberia*, pp. 313ff; Barratt, *Voices in Exile*, pp. 19ff; and Haskett, "Decembrist N. A. Bestuzhev in Siberian Exile, 1826–1855."

Selected Bibliography

Adams, Charles Francis. *John Quincy Adams in Russia: Comprising Portions of the Diary of John Quincy Adams from 1809 to 1814*. Edited by Charles Francis Adams. New York: Praeger, 1970 [1874].

Alekseev, V. V. *The Last Act of a Tragedy: New Documents About the Execution of the Last Russian Emperor Nicholas II*. Translated by B. Ye. Yarubin, Ye. V. Alekseyeva, and W. H. Schettler. Ekaterinburg: Urals Branch of the Russian Academy of Sciences, 1996.

Armstrong, Terence, ed. *Yermak's Campaign in Siberia: A Selection of Documents*. Translated by Tatiana Minorsky and David Wileman. London: Hakluyt Society, 1975.

Arsenyev, Vladimir. *Dersu Uzala*. Translated by Victor Shneerson. Moscow: Raduga, 1990 [1934].

Asher, Oksana Dray-Khmara. *Letters from the Gulag: The Life, Letters, and Poetry of Michael Dray-Khmara*. New York: R. Speller, 1983.

Avvakum. *The Life of the Archpriest Avvakum by Himself*. Translated by Jane Harrison and Hope Mirrlees; preface by Prince D. S. Mirsky. London: Hogarth, 1924.

Babey, Anna M. *Americans in Russia 1776–1917: A study of the American Travelers in Russia from the American Revolution to the Russian Revolution*. New York: Comet Press, 1938.

Baddeley, John F. *Russia, Mongolia, China: Being Some Record of the Relations Between Them . . .* 2 vols. Mansfield Center, CT: Martino, 2007 [1919].

Baikalov, Anatole V. "Notes on the Origin of the Name Siberia." *The Slavonic and East European Review* 29 (December 1950): 287–89.

Bancroft, Hubert Howe. *History of Alaska, 1730–1885*. San Francisco: A. L. Bancroft & Co., 1886.

Barratt, Glynn R. V. *The Rebel on the Bridge: A Life of the Decembrist Baron Andrey Rozen, 1800–84*. Athens: Ohio University Press, 1975.

———. *Voices in Exile: The Decembrist Memoirs*. Montreal: McGill-Queen's University Press, 1974.

Bazhanov, Boris. *Vospominaniya Byvshego Sekretarya Stalina* [Memoirs of Stalin's Former Secretary]. Paris: Tretyaya Volna, 1980.

Bell, John. *A Journey from St. Petersburg to Pekin: 1719–22*. Edited by J. L. Stevenson. Edinburgh: Edinburgh University Press, 1966 [1763].

Bely, Andrey. *Petersburg*. Translated by Robert A. Maguire and John E. Malmstad. Bloomington: Indiana University Press, 1978 [1922].

Benyowsky, Mauritius August, Count de. *Memoirs and Travels*. Translated by William Nicholson. London: G.G.J.&G. Robinson, 1790.

Berlin, Isaiah. *Russian Thinkers*. New York: Penguin, 1979.

Beveridge, Albert. *The Russian Advance*. New York: Praeger, 1970 [1903].

Blakely, Alexander. *Siberia Bound: Chasing the American Dream on Russia's Wild Frontier*. Naperville, IL: Sourcebooks, 2002.

Bobrick, Benson. *East of the Sun: The Epic Conquest and Tragic History of Siberia*. New York: Henry Holt, 1992.

Bookwalter, John Wesley. *Siberia and Central Asia*. New York: J. J. Little, 1899.

Bretschneider, E. *Mediaeval Researches from Eastern Asiatic Sources*. 2 vols. London: Kegan Paul, Trench, Trubner, 1910.

Brodsky, Joseph. *On Grief and Reason: Essays*. New York: Farrar, Straus and Giroux, 1995.

Buchanan, James. *The Works of James Buchanan*. 12 vols. Vol. 2 (1830–36). Collected and edited by John Bassett Moore. Philadelphia: Lippincott, 1908–11.

Carr, E. H. "Bakunin's Escape from Siberia." *The Slavonic and East European Review* 15, no. 44 (January 1937): 377–88.

Chandonnet, Fern, ed. *Alaska at War*. Fairbanks: University of Alaska Press, 2008.

Chappe d'Auteroche, Jean. *A Journey into Siberia, Made by Order of the King of France*. London: T. Jefferys, 1770.

Chekhov, Anton. *"The Crooked Mirror" and Other Stories*. Translated by Arnold Hinchcliffe. New York: Kensington Publishing Corp., 1992.

———. *The Island: A Journey to Sakhalin*. Translated by Luba and Michael Terpak. New York: Washington Square Press, 1967.

Chernyshevsky, Nikolai. *What Is to Be Done?* Translated by Michael Katz. Ithaca, NY: Cornell University Press, 1989 [1863].

Clay, Cassius Marcellus. *The Life of Cassius Marcellus Clay: Memoirs, Writings and Speeches*. New York: Negro Universities Press, 1969.

Clot, André. *Haroun al-Rashid and the World of the Thousand and One Nights*. Translated by John Howe. New York: New Amsterdam, 1989.

Cochrane, John Dundas. *Narrative of a Pedestrian Journey Through Russia and Siberian Tartary, from the Frontiers of China to the Frozen Sea and Kamchatka*. 2 vols. New York: Arno Press, 1970 [1824].

Collins, David N., comp. *Siberia and the Soviet Far East*. World Bibliographic Series. Santa Barbara: Clio Press, 1991.

Collins, Perry McDonough. *A Voyage down the Amoor: With a Land Journey Through Siberia . . .* New York: D. Appleton, 1860.

Conquest, Robert. *The Great Terror: A Reassessment*. New York: Oxford University Press, 1990.

———. *Kolyma: The Arctic Death Camps*. New York: Viking, 1978.

Cook, Capt. James. *The Journals of Captain James Cook on His Voyages of Discovery*. 4 Vols. Edited by J. C. Beaglehole. Cambridge: Cambridge University Press, 1955–74.

Crawford, Michael H. *The Origins of Native Americans: Evidence from Anthropological Genetics*. New York: Cambridge University Press, 1998.

Culver, John C., and John Hyde. *American Dreamer: The Life and Times of Henry A. Wallace.* New York: Norton, 2000.

Curtin, Jeremiah. *The Mongols: A History.* Foreword by Theodore Roosevelt. Boston: Little, Brown, 1908.

Custine, Astolphe, marquis de. *Empire of the Czar: A Journey Through Eternal Russia.* New York: Doubleday, 1989 [1843].

Dallin, David J., and Boris I. Nicolaevsky. *Forced Labor in Soviet Russia.* New Haven: Yale University Press, 1947.

Destutt de Tracy, comte Antoine Louis Claude. *A Commentary and Review of Montesquieu's Spirit of Laws.* Clark, NJ: Lawbook Exchange, 2006 [1811].

Diment, Galya, and Yuri Slezkine, eds. *Between Heaven and Hell: The Myth of Siberia in Russian Culture.* New York: St. Martin's Press, 1993.

Dostoyevsky, Fyodor. *The House of the Dead.* Translated by David McDuff. New York: Penguin, 1985.

Dumas, Alexandre. *Adventures in Czarist Russia.* Translated by Alma Elizabeth Murch. Philadelphia: Chilton, 1961.

———. *Le Maître d'armes* [The Fencing Master]. Paris: Editions des Syrtes, 2002.

Dvoichenko-Markov, Eufrosina. "Jefferson and the Russian Decembrists." *American Slavic and East European Review* 9, no. 3 (October 1950): 162–68.

D'Wolf, John. *A Voyage to the North Pacific and a Journey Through Siberia.* Fairfield, WA: Ye Galleon Press, 1998 [1848].

Erman, Adolph. *Travels in Siberia.* 2 vols. Translated by William Desbrough Cooley. New York: Arno Press, 1970 [1850].

Fasmer: see Vasmer.

Fennell, John. *The Crisis of Medieval Russia, 1200–1304.* New York: Longman, 1983.

Fennell, John, and Antony Stokes. *Early Russian Literature.* London: Faber, 1974.

Figes, Orlando. *Natasha's Dance: A Cultural History of Russia.* New York: Metropolitan Books, 2002.

Fischer, Louis. *The Life of Lenin.* New York: Harper, 1964.

Fisher, Raymond H. *The Russian Fur Trade, 1550–1700.* Berkeley: University of California Press, 1974.

———. *The Voyage of Semen Dezhnev in 1648: Bering's Precursor, with Selected Documents.* London: Hakluyt Society, 1981.

Fleming, Peter. *The Fate of Admiral Kolchak.* New York: Harcourt, 1963.

Florinsky, Michael T. *Russia: A History and an Interpretation.* 2 vols. New York: Macmillan, 1953.

Forsyth, James. *A History of the Peoples of Siberia: Russia's North Asian Colony 1581–1990.* New York: Cambridge University Press, 1992.

Fraser, John Foster. *The Real Siberia, Together with an Account of a Dash Through Manchuria.* New York: Cassell, 1902.

Freeman, Joseph. *An American Testament: A Narrative of Rebels and Romantics.* New York: Farrar and Rinehart, 1936.

Fries, Jakob. *A Siberian Journey: The Journal of Hans Jakob Fries, 1774–1776.* Translated by Walther Kirchner. London: Cass, 1974.

Gallant, Roy A. *The Day the Sky Split Apart: Investigating a Cosmic Mystery.* New York: Atheneum, 1995.

Gardner, Virginia. *"Friend and Lover": The Life of Louise Bryant.* New York: Horizon, 1982.

Gibson, James R. *Feeding the Russian Fur Trade: Provisionment of Okhotsk Seaboard and the Kamchatka Peninsula, 1639–1856*. Madison: University of Wisconsin Press, 1969.

Ginzburg, Eugenia Semyonovna. *Within the Whirlwind*. Translated by Ian Boland. New York: Harcourt, 1967.

Goldman, Marshall I. *Petrostate: Putin, Power, and the New Russia*. New York: Oxford University Press, 2008.

Gowing, Lionel F. *Five Thousand Miles in a Sledge: A Midwinter Journey Across Siberia*. New York: D. Appleton, 1890.

Graves, William S. *America's Siberian Adventure, 1918–1920*. New York: J. Cape & H. Smith, 1931.

Grousset, René. *The Empire of the Steppes: A History of Central Asia*. Translated by Naomi Walford. New Brunswick, NJ: Rutgers University Press, 1970.

Gryaznov, Mikhail P. *The Ancient Civilization of Southern Siberia*. Translated by James Hogarth. New York: Cowles Book Co., 1969.

Hakluyt, Richard. *The Principal Navigations, Voyages, Traffiques and Discoveries of the English Nation Made by Sea or Over-land to the Remote and Farthest Distant Quarters of the Earth at Any Time Within the Compass of These 1600 Yeers*. 12 vols. New York: A. M. Kelley, 1969 [1589].

Hartog, Leo de. *Russia and the Mongol Yoke*. New York: British Academic Press, 1996.

Hays, Otis Jr. *The Alaska-Siberia Connection: The World War II Air Route*. College Station: Texas A&M University Press, 1996.

Herzen, Aleksandr. *My Exile in Siberia*. London: Hurst & Blackett, 1855.

———. *My Past and Thoughts: The Memoirs of Aleksandr Herzen*. 6 vols. Translated by Constance Garnett. London: Chatto, 1924–27.

———. *My Past and Thoughts: The Memoirs of Aleksandr Herzen*. Translated by Constance Garnett; abridged by Dwight Macdonald. New York: Knopf, 1973.

Hicks, Granville. *John Reed: The Making of a Revolutionary*. New York: Macmillan, 1936.

Hill, Fiona, and Clifford G. Gaddy. *The Siberian Curse: How Communist Planners Left Russia out in the Cold*. Washington, D.C.: Brookings Institution Press, 2003.

Hosking, Geoffrey. *Russia and the Russians: A History*. Cambridge, MA: Harvard University Press, 2001.

Howorth, Henry H. *History of the Mongols, from the 9th to the 19th Century*. 4 Vols. London: Longmans, 1876–1927.

Hughes, Langston. *I Wonder as I Wander: An Autobiographical Journey*. New York: Hill and Wang, 1993 [1956].

Iakushkin, Evgenii, ed. *Zapiski I. D. Yakushkina* [Memoirs of I. D. Iakushkin]. Moscow, 1905.

Iakushkin, Ivan D. *Zapiski, Stati, Pis'ma Dekabrista* [Memoirs, Articles, and Letters of the Decembrist]. Moscow, 1951.

Ides, Evert Ysbrantzoon. *Three Years' Travels from Moscow Over-land to China*. London: W. Freeman, 1706.

Izhboldin, Boris S. *Essays on Tatar History*. New Delhi: Book Society of India, 1963.

Jones, Robert H. *The Road to Russia: United States Lend-Lease to the Soviet Union*. Norman: University of Oklahoma Press, 1969.

Kennan, George. *Siberia and the Exile System*. 2 vols. New York: Praeger, 1970 [1891].

————. *Siberia and the Exile System*. Introduction by George Frost Kennan. Abridged from edition of 1891. Chicago: University of Chicago Press, 1958.

————. *Tent Life in Siberia and Adventures Among the Koraks and Other Tribes in Kamchatka and Northern Asia*. New York: Skyhorse, 2007 [1870].

Kennedy, Hugh. *Mongols, Huns and Vikings: Nomads at War*. London: Cassell, 2002.

Kharms, Daniil. *Starukha: Rasskazy, Stseny, Povest'* [Old Woman: Stories, Scenes, Novella]. Moscow: Yunona, 1991.

Korff, Modest M., baron. *The Accession of Nicholas I. Compiled, by Special Command of the Emperor Alexander II, by His Imperial Majesty's Secretary of State, Baron M. Korff*. London: John Murray, 1857.

Kotkin, Stephen, and David Wolff, eds. *Rediscovering Russia in Asia: Siberia and the Russian Far East*. Armonk, NY: M. E. Sharpe, 1995.

Krasheninnikov, Stepan Petrovich. *Explorations of Kamchatka, North Pacific Scimitar: Report of a Journey Made to Explore Eastern Siberia in 1735–1741, by Order of the Russian Imperial Government*. Translated by E.A.P. Crownhart-Vaughan. Portland: Oregon Historical Society, 1972 [1755].

Lantzeff, George V., and Richard A. Pierce. *Eastward to Empire: Exploration and Conquest on the Russian Open Frontier, to 1750*. Montreal: McGill-Queen's University Press, 1973.

Lengyel, Emil. *Siberia*. New York: Random House, 1943.

Len'kov, V. D., G. L. Silant'ev, and A. K. Staniukovich. *The Komandorskii Camp of the Bering Expedition: An Experiment in Complex Study*. Translated by Katherine L. Arndt. Anchorage: Alaska Historical Society, 1992.

Lincoln, W. Bruce. *The Conquest of a Continent: Siberia and the Russians*. New York: Random House, 1994.

Malashenko, V. I. *The Great Baikal–Amur Railway*. Moscow: Progress Publishers, 1977.

Mancall, Mark. *Russia and China: Their Diplomatic Relations to 1728*. Cambridge, MA: Harvard University Press, 1971.

Marsden, Kate. *On Sledge and Horseback to Outcast Siberian Lepers*. London: Phoenix, 2001 [1892].

Martin, Janet. *Treasure of the Land of Darkness: The Fur Trade and Its Significance for Medieval Russia*. New York: Cambridge University Press, 1986.

Masters, Anthony. *Bakunin, the Father of Anarchism*. New York: Saturday Review Press, 1974.

Mayakovsky, V. *Vladimir Ilyich Lenin: A Poem*. Honolulu: University of Hawaii Press, 2003 [1950].

Mazour, Anatole G. *The First Russian Revolution, 1825: The Decembrist Movement, Its Origins, Development, and Significance*. Stanford: Stanford University Press, 1961 [1937].

————. *Women in Exile: Wives of the Decembrists*. Tallahassee: Diplomatic Press, 1975.

Melamid, Alexander, and Vitaly Komar. *Monumental Propaganda*. Edited by Dore Ashton. New York: Independent Curators, 1994.

Mowat, Farley. *The Siberians*. Boston: Little, Brown, 1970.

Moynahan, Brian. *The Russian Century: A Photographic History of Russia's 100 Years*. New York: Random House, 1994.

Müller, Gerhard Friedrich. *Bering's Voyages: The Reports from Russia*. Translated by Carol Urness. Fairbanks: University of Alaska Press, 1987.

————. *Istoriia Sibiri* [A History of Siberia]. Moscow: Vostochnaya Literatura, 1999.

Murphy, Dervla. *Through Siberia by Accident*. London: John Murray, 2005.

Nabokov, Vladimir. *Strong Opinions*. New York: McGraw-Hill, 1973.

————, trans. *Three Russian Poets: Selections from Pushkin, Lermontov and Tyutchev in New Translations*. Norfolk, CT: New Directions, 1944.

Neal, Steve. *Dark Horse: A Biography of Wendell Willkie*. Garden City, NY: Doubleday, 1984.

Nerhood, Harry W., comp. *To Russia and Return: An Annotated Bibliography of Travelers' English-Language Accounts of Russia from the Ninth Century to the Present*. Columbus: Ohio State University Press, 1968.

Nicolle, David. *The Mongol Warlords: Genghis Khan, Kublai Khan, Tamerlane*. Dorset, UK: Firebird Books, 1990.

Norwich, John Julius. *A Short History of Byzantium*. New York: Knopf, 1997.

Okladnikov, Aleksei Pavlovich. *Ancient Population of Siberia and Its Cultures*. Cambridge, MA: Peabody Museum, 1959.

Pallas, Peter Simon. *A Naturalist in Russia: Letters from Peter Simon Pallas to Thomas Pennant*. Minneapolis: University of Minnesota Press, 1967.

Pasternak, Boris. *Safe Conduct: An Early Autobiography, and Other Works*. Translated by Alee Brown. New York: New Directions, 1958.

Peskov, Vassily. *Lost in the Taiga: One Russian Family's Fifty-Year Struggle for Survival and Religious Freedom in the Siberian Wilderness*. New York: Doubleday, 1994.

Pipes, Richard. *Russia Under the Old Regime*. New York: Scribner, 1974.

Pritsak, Omeljan. "The Origin of the Name *Sibir'*," in von Walther Hessig and Klaus Sagaster, eds., *Gedanke und Wirkung: Festschrift zum 90, Geburtstag von Nikolaus Poppe* [Ideas and Impressions: Festschrift on the 90th Birthday of von Nikolaus Poppe]. Wiesbaden: O. Harrassowitz, 1989.

Quatremère, Étienne, ed. and trans. *Histoire des Mongols de la Perse [par] Raschid-Eldin* [History of the Mongols of Persia]. Amsterdam: Oriental Press, 1968 [1836].

Rachewiltz, Igor de, trans. *The Secret History of the Mongols: A Mongolian Epic Chronicle of the Thirteenth Century*. Boston: Brill, 2004.

Radishchev, Aleksandr Nikolaevich. *A Journey from St. Petersburg to Moscow*. Translated by Leo Weiner. Cambridge, MA: Harvard University Press, 1958 [1790].

Randall, Francis B. *N.G. Chernyshevskii*. New York: Twayne, 1967.

Rasputin, Valentin. *Essays*. Translated by Holly Smith. Moscow: Raduga, 1988.

————. *Siberia, Siberia*. Translated by Margaret Winchell and Gerald Mikkelson. Evanston, IL: Northwestern University Press, 1996.

Reed, John. *Ten Days That Shook the World*. Mineola, NY: Dover, 2006 [1919].

————. *The Education of John Reed: Selected Writings*. Edited by John Stuart. New York: International Publishers, 1955.

————. *Insurgent Mexico*. New York: Simon and Schuster, 1969 [1914].

————. *The War in Eastern Europe*. New York: Scribner, 1916.

Reeder, Roberta. *Anna Akhmatova: Poet and Prophet*. New York: St. Martin's Press, 1994.

Remnick, David. *Lenin's Tomb: The Last Days of the Soviet Empire*. New York: Random House, 1993.

Rytkheu, Iurii. *Stories from Chukotka*. Translated by David Fry. London: Lawrence & Wishart, 1956.

Saunders, J. J. *The History of the Mongol Conquests*. London: Routledge, 1971.

Schiltberger, Johannes. *The Bondage and Travels of Johann Schiltberger, a Native of Bavaria, in Europe, Asia, and Africa, 1396–1427*. Translated by J. Buchan Telfer. New York: B. Franklin, 1970 [1879].

Sebag Montefiore, Simon. *Stalin: The Court of the Red Tsar*. New York: Knopf, 2004.

Seyfi, Celebi. *L'Ouvrage de Seyfi Celebi, Historien Ottoman du XVIᵉ Siècle* [The Works of Seyfi Celebi, Ottoman Historian of the 16th Century]. Translated by Joseph Matuz. Paris: Maisonneuve, 1968.

Shalamov, Varlam. *Graphite*. Translated by John Glad. New York: Norton, 1981.

———. *Kolyma Tales*. Translated by John Glad. London: Penguin, 1994.

Shifrin, Avraam. *The First Guidebook to Prisons and Concentration Camps of the Soviet Union*. New York: Bantam, 1982.

Sinor, Denis, ed. *The Cambridge History of Early Inner Asia*. New York: Cambridge University Press, 1990.

Solzhenitsyn, Alexander. *The Gulag Archipelago, 1918–1956: An Experiment in Literary Investigation*. 3 vols. Translated by Thomas P. Whitney. New York: Harper, 1974–78.

Steller, George Wilhelm. *Journal of a Voyage with Bering 1741–1742*. Translated by Margritt A. Engel and O. W. Frost. Stanford: Stanford University Press, 1988.

———. *Steller's History of Kamchatka*. Fairbanks: University of Alaska Press, 2003.

Stephan, John J. *The Russian Far East: A History*. Stanford: Stanford University Press, 1994.

Strahlenberg, Philip Johann von. *Russia, Siberia, and Great Tartary*. New York: Arno Press, 1970 [1738].

Strouse, Jean. *Morgan: American Financier*. New York: Random House, 1999.

Sutherland, Christine. *The Princess of Siberia: The Story of Maria Volkonsky and the Decembrist Exiles*. New York: Farrar, Straus and Giroux, 1984.

Taplin, Mark. *Open Lands: Travels Through Russia's Once Forbidden Places*. South Royalton, VT: Steerforth Press, 1998.

Travis, Frederick F. *George Kennan and the American-Russian Relationship, 1865–1924*. Athens: Ohio University Press, 1990.

Trubetskoy, Nikolai Sergeevich. *The Legacy of Genghis Khan and Other Essays on Russia's Identity*. Translated by Anatoly Liberman. Ann Arbor: Michigan Slavic Publications, 1991.

Vasmer, Max. *Etimologicheskii Slovar' Russkogo Yazyka* [Etymological Dictionary of the Russian Language]. Moscow: Progress, 1987.

Vernadsky, George. *The Mongols of Russia*. New Haven: Yale University Press, 1953.

Vitale, Serena. *Pushkin's Button*. Translated by Ann Goldstein and Jon Rothschild. Chicago: University of Chicago Press, 2000.

Volkov, Solomon. *Shostakovich and Stalin: The Extraordinary Relationship Between the Great Composer and the Brutal Dictator*. Translated by Antonina W. Bouis. New York: Knopf, 2004.

Wallace, Henry A. *Soviet Asia Mission*. New York: Reynal & Hitchcock, 1946.

Warner, Denis, and Peggy Warner. *The Tide at Sunrise: A History of the Russo-Japanese War, 1904–1905*. New York: Charterhouse, 1974.

Waxell, Sven. *The American Expedition*. Translated by M. A. Michael. London: W. Hodge, 1952.

Williams, Albert Rhys. *Through the Russian Revolution*. Westport, CT: Hyperion, 1978
    [1921].
Wood, Alan, ed. *The History of Siberia: From Russian Conquest to Revolution*. New
    York: Routledge, 1991.
Wortman, Richard. "Rule by Sentiment: Alexander II's Journeys Through the Russian
    Empire." *American Historical Review* 95, no. 3 (June 1990): 745–71.
Wright, George Frederick. *Asiatic Russia*. New York: McClure, Phillips, 1902.
Yakushkin: see Iakushkin.
Yevtushenko, Yevgeny. *Divided Twins: Alaska and Siberia*. Translated by Antonina W.
    Bouis. New York: Viking, 1988.
Zetlin, Mikhail. *The Decembrists*. Translated by George Panin. New York: International
    Universities Press, 1958.
Zhukov, G. K. *Reminiscences and Reflections*. 2 vols. Translated by Vic Schneirson. Mos-
    cow: Progress Publishers, 1985.

Acknowledgments

These thank-yous begin, as did this book, with Alex Melamid and Katya Arnold. Twenty-five years ago, when I lived in lower Manhattan and Alex's painting studio was a few blocks away on Canal Street, our conversations about his life in Russia gave me a desire to go there. Katya's insistence that I accompany them on their trip to Moscow and Ulan-Ude in 1993 started me on my Siberia journeys. As I did research, studied Russian, and wrote the manuscript, Katya provided counsel all along the way. Alex's painting of a Siberian scene served as the cover for one of the issues of *The New Yorker* in which an excerpt of the book appeared. I can't thank Alex and Katya enough for their brilliance, and for their generosity in sharing their past with me.

Boris Zeldin helped me greatly with the book's literary, linguistic, and cultural details. Almost any question I asked, Boris knew the answer to. He found references I needed in his own extensive library and read the manuscript for *kliukvi*—the kind of errors travelers in Russia stumble into. Boris's wife, Sophia, also read the manuscript and offered her perspective and suggestions. To my friends the Zeldins, deepest thanks.

Luda Sokolova, the Zeldins' longtime friend in St. Petersburg, rented me her apartment and helped me generally in getting around there. In Moscow, Lyudmila Borisovna Melamida, Mitya and Irena Arnold, and Tatiana (Chuda) Kotreleva and Kolya Kotrelev kindly put me up on several occasions. Tisha Kotrelev, Chuda and Kolya's son, showed me around the city. Thanks and best regards to them all.

I could not have done my longer trips in Siberia without the assistance of Victor Serov and Sergei Lunev. I am grateful for their competence, hard work, and patience. Vladimir Chumak helped the 2001 trip go smoothly and was the best driver I ever saw. To Victor, Sergei, and Volodya—thank you. I hope you always have successful journeys.

Aleksandr (Sasha) Khamarkhanov, now deceased, and his wife, Tania, hosted Alex and Katya and me in Ulan-Ude. Elsewhere I have expressed my admiration and thanks to Sasha, but want to thank him and Tania again here.

Sergei Prigarin and Sveta, his daughter, were of key assistance to me in Novosibirsk and Akademgorodok, as was Ivan Logoshenko. They are chief among the reasons that I rank Novosibirsk as my favorite part of Siberia.

In Alaska and Chukotka, I benefited from the help of Vladimir Bychkov, Eric Penttila, and Jim Stimpfle.

A number of gifted and patient teachers of the Russian language led me through its intricacies and did the best they could inserting them into my resistant brain. Many thanks to Irina Katz, Katya Popova, Lioudmila Tomachevskaya, Dina Kupchenka, and the master, Boris Shekhtman.

The late publisher Roger Straus, of Farrar, Straus and Giroux, took an interest in the idea of a book about Siberia when I first suggested it. He sent me Siberia-related materials he knew would be useful and otherwise encouraged me. Jonathan Galassi, my editor at FSG for the last twenty-two years, has always been completely great. My gratitude and affection go to Roger, Jonathan, Jesse Coleman, Susan Mitchell, Jennifer Carrow (who designed this book's cover), Chris Peterson, and everybody at FSG. Thanks are also due my excellent agents, Jin Auh and Andrew Wylie, of the Wylie Agency. David Remnick, editor of *The New Yorker*, helped me greatly with his expertise on Russia and with financial support so I could travel there, while *The New Yorker*'s Ann Goldstein, assisted by John Bennet, did an outstanding job of turning sections of the book into a three-part magazine article. Mike Peed, of the magazine's fact-checking department, pursued factual accuracy with rigor while never neglecting to listen for the poetical—a rare skill. He also did invaluable checking work on the manuscript as a whole. Katia Bachko, also of *The New Yorker*, made checking calls to Russia in which her language fluency shed light into previously murky areas. I also thank Maddy Elfenbein,

Chris Glazek, Blake Eskin, and everybody else who worked on the excerpts in *The New Yorker*.

John Lewis Gaddis, Lee Clark, Glenn Eichler, Robert Carey, Bill McClelland, Jonathan Alter, David Smith, Sumie Ota, John McPhee, Hedda Sterne, Marie D'Origny, Rich Cohen, José Manuel Prieto, Alec Wilkinson, Luda Stiler, Henry Timman, and Jean Strouse all helped me in one way or another. Many thanks to them all. For support at important moments during the travel, research, and writing, I am grateful to the Lyndhurst Foundation; the Lila Wallace–Readers' Digest Foundation; and the Dorothy and Lewis B. Cullman Center for Scholars and Writers, at the New York Public Library.

When I started working on this book, my daughter, Cora, was four, and my son, Thomas, was seven months. In later years, Cora helped with typing the manuscript and Thomas expertly handled all problems that came up with the computer. My wife, Jacqueline Carey, helped me plan my trips, stayed near the phone while I traveled, read and reread the manuscript, and managed to write books of her own. This book is dedicated to her.

Index

INDEX